Sidonius Apollinaris' Letters, Book 2

Edinburgh Studies in Later Latin Literature

Series Editors
Gavin Kelly and Aaron Pelttari, University of Edinburgh

Ground-breaking scholarship on Latin literature from the later Roman and post-Roman world

Edinburgh Studies in Later Latin Literature offers a forum for new scholarship on important and sometimes neglected works. The later Roman and post-Roman world, between the second and seventh century, saw the creation of major texts and critical developments in writing. Texts of all kinds are treated here with careful attention to their various historical contexts.

Volumes include scholarly monographs and editions with commentaries. Modern critical and theoretical methods together provide new interpretations of the surviving Latin literature; these approaches include textual history, transmission, philology in the broad sense, and reception studies. This series provides access to our best understanding of what survives in the written record and makes modern interpretations of later Latin literature more widely available.

Editorial Advisory Board
Therese Fuhrer, University of Munich
Lucy Grig, University of Edinburgh
Isabella Gualandri, University of Milan
Philip Hardie, University of Cambridge
Calum Maciver, University of Edinburgh
Justin Stover, University of Edinburgh

Books available
Judith Hindermann, *Sidonius Apollinaris' Letters, Book 2: Text, Translation and Commentary*

https://edinburghuniversitypress.com/series-edinburgh-studies-in-later-latin-literature

SIDONIUS APOLLINARIS' LETTERS, BOOK 2

Text, Translation and Commentary

Judith Hindermann

EDINBURGH
University Press

Edinburgh University Press is one of the leading university presses in the UK. We publish academic books and journals in our selected subject areas across the humanities and social sciences, combining cutting-edge scholarship with high editorial and production values to produce academic works of lasting importance. For more information visit our website: edinburghuniversitypress.com

© Judith Hindermann, 2022, 2024

Edinburgh University Press Ltd
The Tun – Holyrood Road
12(2f) Jackson's Entry
Edinburgh EH8 8PJ

First published in hardback by Edinburgh University Press 2022

Typeset in Bembo
by R. J. Footring Ltd, Derby
A CIP record for this book is available from the British Library

ISBN 978 1 3995 0630 4 (hardback)
ISBN 978 1 3995 0631 1 (paperback)
ISBN 978 1 3995 0632 8 (webready PDF)
ISBN 978 1 3995 0633 5 (epub)

The right of Judith Hindermann to be identified as the author of this work has been asserted in accordance with the Copyright, Designs and Patents Act 1988, and the Copyright and Related Rights Regulations 2003 (SI No. 2498).

Contents

Acknowledgements	vii
Introduction	viii
Abbreviations for Books, Series and Reference Works	xxvii

Text and Translation

Epistula 1	2
Epistula 2	6
Epistula 3	16
Epistula 4	18
Epistula 5	20
Epistula 6	22
Epistula 7	24
Epistula 8	26
Epistula 9	30
Epistula 10	36
Epistula 11	42
Epistula 12	44
Epistula 13	46
Epistula 14	52

Commentary

Epistula 1	57
Epistula 2	82
Epistula 3	178
Epistula 4	189
Epistula 5	199
Epistula 6	205
Epistula 7	210
Epistula 8	217
Epistula 9	246
Epistula 10	290
Epistula 11	344

CONTENTS

Epistula 12	350
Epistula 13	362
Epistula 14	390
Bibliography	399
Index Locorum	426
Index of Personal Names (Antiquity)	464

Acknowledgements

My fascination with Sidonius began in 2012 when I applied to be part of the Leverhulme project on Sidonius Apollinaris.[1] The project officially started with a conference about Sidonius in Edinburgh in autumn 2014, where the groundwork was laid for the *Edinburgh Companion to Sidonius Apollinaris*. My thanks therefore go to Gavin Kelly and Joop van Waarden, who invited me into the Sidonius community and accompanied my commentary in the following years with their great knowledge. Thanks to the support of the Leverhulme Trust, Gavin Kelly was able to travel to Basel for the revision of my translation. I would also like to thank Michael Hanaghan, Margot Neger, Roy Gibson, Franca Ela Consolino and Aaron Pelttari, who gave me feedback on the content and language of my drafts. My book also benefited from the conference on leisure and the Muses in Sidonius' poems and letters, which I organised with Henriette Harich-Schwarzbauer in Basel in January 2018 (the proceedings of which were published 2020 as a special edition of the *Journal of Late Antiquity*, 13.1). I thank her for her great support and the many years of fruitful cooperation since I started working with her as a doctoral student in Basel.

Further, I would like to thank my parents, Esther and Christian Hindermann, who have always supported me in various ways, my godfather, Andreas Fischer, who has read many of my publications and enriched this book with his feedback, and above all my partner, Donner Trepp, for his interest in my studies and his love. The book is dedicated to him and our three wonderful children, Gianna, Nora and Ennio.

---

1. See <https://sidonapol.org>.

INTRODUCTION

This commentary on Sidonius' second book of letters is part of a larger international project that gives a comprehensive overview of Sidonius' work and builds upon the preliminary research published in the *Edinburgh Companion to Sidonius Apollinaris*, edited by Gavin Kelly and Joop van Waarden (2020a). As Sidonius' life and many aspects of his work are covered in that volume, I will keep this introduction brief and limit myself to four important themes of the second book of letters: (1) Sidonius' life between *otium* and *negotium* and the position of Book 2 in the collection of letters; (2) the date and order of letters in Book 2; (3) Book 2 as a response to Pliny the Younger's *Letters* and the question of intertextuality; and (4) the epigrams in Sidonius' letters. I shall also (5) discuss the basis of the text and the aims of the translation. Here I will briefly present my theses and the grounds for them; the details will be found in the commentary.

1. Sidonius' life between *otium* and *negotium* and the position of Book 2 in the collection of letters[2]

Sidonius' second book of letters is devoted to the subject of *otium*.[3] The question of how to spend one's leisure time honourably is a literary motif explored by many famous Romans before Sidonius – Cato, Horace, Sallust, Cicero, Seneca and Pliny the Younger among them[4] – and was also addressed

---

2. For the following section, I draw on my article (Hindermann 2020a) on the second book of Sidonius' letters as a book of leisure, which appeared in a special issue of the *Journal of Late Antiquity* devoted to the theme of leisure and the Muses in Sidonius' letters and poems (Harich-Schwarzbauer and Hindermann 2020).
3. This thematic focus has been noticed by many: Harries (1994) 10, Giannotti (2001a) 36, André (2006), van Waarden (2010) 38, Gibson (2012) 69, Prévot (2013) 3, 9, Montone (2017) 26.
4. For *otium* as a literary motif, see Bernert (1949–50), André (1962), Hasebrink and Riedl (2014), Eickhoff et al. (2016), Hindermann (2016) and Wiegandt (2020).

by Christian authors.[5] The authors before Sidonius who devoted themselves to the subject denoted different things by *otium*, depending on the genre of their literary works. The meaning of *otium* ranges from the negatively connoted 'idleness' to the *otium honestum*, 'honourable retirement', after a fulfilled political or military career. *Otium* is also associated with concepts such as 'freedom', 'idyll' and 'happiness'. It is often opposed to *negotium*, that is, occupation and professional commitment.[6]

Sidonius is aware that he is part of a long tradition and demonstrates his knowledge of *otium* as a literary motif through intertextual allusions. Pliny the Younger, in particular, who in his letters extensively dealt with life in the villa, is a central role model for Sidonius' discussion of *otium* in the second book.[7] Sublime literature, according to Pliny, cannot be produced in the hustle and bustle of the city, but only in peace and solitude, the *otium* of the countryside.[8] In his second book, Sidonius adopts this attitude and gives prominence to the duality of city and countryside.[9]

For Sidonius, however, the question of how to deal with free time is more than literary play. *Otium* appears in his second book as the ideal way of life among Roman aristocrats, a lifestyle he wants for himself, despite external adversities. Sidonius experienced multiple upheavals in his eventful life, which led to an alternation between professional commitments and leisure.[10] Born between 429 and 432 in Lyon, between 452 and 455 he married Papianilla, daughter of the future emperor Avitus, and had four children with her.[11] From Avitus (by inheritance or as part of Papianilla's dowry) Sidonius also received the estate of Avitacum, situated on Lake Aydat, which appears prominently as a place of leisure in the second book.[12] Sidonius had achieved great public success when he was invited to recite his panegyric (*Carm.* 7) for his father-in-law in Rome on 1 January

---

5. See Schlapbach (2013) 363–8 for the Christian transformation of *otium* and its adaption to the monastic lifestyle.
6. Bernert (1949–50) and Harter (2016).
7. See section 3 of this Introduction, 'Book 2 as a response to Pliny the Younger's *Letters* and the question of intertextuality'.
8. Hindermann (2016).
9. See the section 'Major themes and further reading' in the commentary on *Ep.* 2.2.
10. For Sidonius' biography, see Stevens (1933), Harries (1994), Hanaghan (2019) 2–8, van Waarden (2020a).
11. See the commentary on *Ep.* 2.12.2, *Severiana, sollicitudo communis....*
12. See the commentary on *Ep.* 2.2.3, *nomen hoc praedio....*

456.[13] Although Avitus' reign was short-lived – he was defeated by Ricimer and Majorian in October 456 and subsequently killed[14] – his son-in-law Sidonius did not suffer any long-term disadvantages in his career. In 458 he recited another panegyric (*Carm.* 5) to the new emperor, Majorian. After Majorian was murdered in 461, Sidonius spent time in Lyon and on his estate Avitacum, and he also visited the estates of his friends[15] in the west of Gaul until he travelled to Rome in 467. This period is important for the second book because the dramatic date of most of the letters falls in this time span.[16] In the letters from the first half of the 460s Sidonius presents himself as being preoccupied with the activities of the traditional Roman *otium*. His involvement with friends, family, literature, sports and entertainments of all kinds appears to be a means of surviving a politically difficult time. In the autumn of 467, Sidonius travelled to Rome as head of an Arvernian delegation to welcome the new emperor, Anthemius, and to draw his attention to the difficult situation in Auvergne caused by the Visigoth king Euric.[17] He also composed a panegyric (*Carm.* 2) for the new emperor, was promoted to the rank of a *patricius* and was nominated prefect of Rome (*praefectus urbi*) in the year 468. As prefect in Rome and subsequently as bishop in Clermont,[18] he led a life full of *negotium* but still enjoyed *otium* in the traditional senatorial manner. However, his career was interrupted once more by political upheaval so that he was forced again into a kind of involuntary *otium*: he suffered greatly from his exile at Livia near Carcasonne in the years 475 and 476.[19] In 476 or 477 he was pardoned and reinstated as bishop; the year of his death is uncertain.

Sidonius' thematic focus on aristocratic leisure in Book 2 has an impact on the arrangement of letters, the choice of topics and the intertextual references. The arrangement of the second book within the letter compilation as a whole is a key indicator of the importance that Sidonius attributes to the subject of leisure. According to the ancient custom of discussing *otium* in the context of its opposite, *negotium*, Sidonius' second book of letters is framed by two books dedicated to Sidonius' career. In the first book, which deals

---

13. Sidon. *Carm.* 8.7–10, *Ep.* 9.16.3 v. 25–8; see Hanaghan (2017b) 273–4 and van Waarden (2020a) 26–7.
14. For Avitus, Ricimer and Majorian, see the commentary on *Ep.* 2.13.3 *Hic si omittamus*....
15. See Sidon. *Carm.* 22 and 23.
16. See section 2, 'The date and order of letters in Book 2'.
17. See van Waarden (2020a) 27.
18. Sidonius became bishop between 469 and 471.
19. For Sidonius' self-presentation in exile, see Hanaghan (2018).

with Sidonius' life before he became bishop,[20] Sidonius records in detail the pinnacle of his career, the journey to Rome and the office of *praefectus urbi* in 468. His professional life thus demonstratively occupies the first place in the collection, followed by his *otium* in the second book.

Sidonius links the second book closely not only to the first,[21] but also to the third, which starts without a pause or a new prologue and consists, like the second, of fourteen letters.[22] Furthermore, Sidonius continues his reverence for Pliny by thematising the assumption of his consulship in Book 3, analogous to Pliny's assumption of the consulship in his Book 3.[23] After the break described in the second book, Sidonius shows himself busy again in the third book.[24] As bishop of Clermont, Sidonius fights for the Auvergne and its inhabitants during the sieges of Clermont by the Visigoths in the years 471–4. The letters of the third book are not only arranged within the book,[25] but also within the corpus of the first three books, suggesting a unity among them: *Ep.* 3.13, with its critical description of the parasite Gnatho, recalls the idealistic description of Theoderic II in *Ep.* 1.2, and the last letter, *Ep.* 3.14, with its reasoning about writers and writing, takes up a theme of the introductory *Ep.* 1.1. The first three books can therefore be read as a triad under the keywords 'career', 'leisure' and 'crisis'. The fourth book is again dedicated to literature and thus is linked to Sidonius' second book, in which his literary predecessors play a significant role.[26]

Sidonius' book of *otium* is carefully embedded in the surrounding books, which show Sidonius active and busy in his offices as prefect and bishop. His letters contain positive representations of *otium* but he nevertheless orders his friends to interrupt their *otium* and turn to *negotium*.[27] Thus the second book, which spans an important part of Sidonius' life, concerns his self-presentation as an aristocrat. However, it represents only one aspect and cannot be fully understood without Books 1 and 3. With the structure of

---

20. See Köhler (1995) 5, 17–18.
21. See section 2, 'The date and order of letters in Book 2'.
22. Giannotti (2016) 37 points to Sidonius' self-portrayal as an important and busy person, the importance of friendship and the same addressees (Ecdicius in *Ep.* 2.1 and 3.3; Felix in *Ep.* 2.3 and 3.7; Donidius, addressee in *Ep.* 2.9 and subject in *Ep.* 3.5) in both books. In addition, in the second and third books Sidonius writes several times about his fellow citizens, the Arverni (Avernians) (*Ep.* 2.1.1, 2.6.2, 3.3.1).
23. See Gibson (2012) 69, and section 2, 'The date and order of letters in Book 2'.
24. See Giannotti (2016) 28–9.
25. See Giannotti (2001a) 30–31.
26. See Giannotti (2016) 28–9.
27. See section 2, 'The date and order of letters in Book 2'.

the books Sidonius presents the idea that *otium* does not stand alone but is part of career and politics and can be enjoyed only in contrast to them.

2. The date and order of letters in Book 2

While four letters of the first book (*Ep.* 1.5, 1.7, 1.9 and 1.10) are clearly anchored in time and place, and a chronology can be inferred from some of the others, in the second book there are fewer references to historical events. Sidonius does not address bishops and only rarely refers to politics, religion or specifically Gallic subjects. Instead, most of the letters depict the traditional Roman lifestyle, show the importance of social obligations and the importance of literature, and reflect on a balanced relationship between *otium* and *negotium*. Only the first and thirteenth letters refer to events that can be clearly located historically.[28] Sidonius' *otium* happens in a somewhat timeless 'classical' Roman world, which makes dating the letters difficult. Hanaghan (2019) 76 compares the setting of Sidonius' second book to the 'timeless quality of Seneca's epistles which facilitates his philosophical contemplation'. For Sidonius, the relative timelessness of the letters has the effect that his reflections on leisure become timelessly valid and fit various phases of his life. The letters of the second book have as their dramatic date the 460s,[29] the time between the assassination of the emperor Majorian in 461, when Sidonius had to spend an extended period in seclusion on his estate Avitacum, and 467, when Sidonius travelled to Rome at the head of an Arvernian delegation to welcome the new emperor, Anthemius. The authors of the *Prosopography of the Later Roman Empire* (*PLRE*) therefore date most of the letters between the years 461 and 467. Loyen (1970a) opts for the year 469 for many of the letters because he sees a gap between Sidonius' prefecture and the episcopate. While Loyen (1970a) looks for signs of Sidonius' increasing Christian faith to date the letters as precisely as possible in his edition, Zelzer (1994/1995) 349 and Kelly (2020a) 185 rightly point out that the dramatic date and date of composition need not coincide. Kelly (2020a) 191 argues that Sidonius mentions his episcopate of 469/470 in *Ep.* 3.1 only for compositional reasons – in analogy to Pliny the Younger's consulate, according to Gibson (2013b) 347–8 – and that this cannot be used as a *terminus ante quem* to date the letters of the first two books. In my

---

28. Montone (2017) 25.
29. Giannotti (2001a) 36, Kelly (2020a) 191.

commentary I discuss the evidence for the dating of the individual letters, but mostly refrain from a further attempt to date outside the approximate range of the 460s.

It has been suggested that Sidonius uses the term *libellus* in announcing the completion of his first and second books because of the close connection between them.[30] The second book was either published in ca. 470, along with or soon after the first book, or it was published within a complete series of Books 1–7 in 477, that is, after Sidonius' return from his exile.[31] The second book is closely connected with the first book through intense intratextuality and the arrangement of letters. While in *Ep.* 1.6.3 the rural *otium* of the addressee, Eutropius, is renounced and an active life at the emperor's court in Rome is preferred, in *Ep.* 2.2 Sidonius tries to attract his friend by depicting his own relaxed lifestyle in a rural villa. And while in the first letter of the second book his brother-in-law Ecdicius is summoned to help with his military forces, he is shown in *Ep.* 2.2.15 peacefully playing ball with Sidonius. Moreover, with *Ep.* 1.11 and 2.2 (the longest letters in the collection after *Ep.* 7.9), Sidonius' first *sphragis* and the first description of his life in the villa are in the first two books. In *Ep.* 1.11.1, Sidonius characterises himself as a private and ageing man (*id iam agens otii*) in voluntary *otium*, immediately before he starts his second book, which is dedicated to leisure. The first letter of the second book, which deals with Sidonius' political enemy Seronatus, a confidant of the Visigoth king Euric, forms a bridge into the world of *otium*. If *Ep.* 1.11 can be read as a Menippean satire in epistolary form, *Ep.* 2.1 is an invective in prose in which Sidonius demonstrates his skills as a satirist in an even more elaborate style.[32] Like Pliny's arch-enemy Regulus, Seronatus is the personified evil who threatens

---

30. *Ep.* 4.10.2: *post terminatum libellum, qui parum cultior est* ('after I finished my little book, which is a little bit more polished').
31. This is suggested for example by Harries (1994) 10 and Mathisen (2013). Stevens (1933) 168–9 advocates the first book as a separate book (with reference to *Ep.* 3.14.1); see *Ep.* 4.22.1 and Amherdt (2001) 27–9, 275–6, 456. Kelly (2020a) 194 expresses scepticism about the thesis of separate publication of individual books before 477 but, if so, believes that it was just first and not the second book that would have appeared. On the general difficulty of dating Sidonius' letters, see Gibson (2013a), Mathisen (2013), Hanaghan (2019) 170–6, Kelly (2020a).
32. Neger (2020) 382. *Ep.* 1.11 is especially rich in literary allusions (to Horace, Martial, Petron, Vergil, Terence, Pliny the Younger and Lucan – see Neger 2020) and anticipates the second book in its intense intertextuality. For satire in Sidonius, see p. xxi, n. 61.

Sidonius' quiet leisure, described in the following letters.[33] Seronatus serves as a negative counter-example to the positively portrayed *nobiles* with whom Sidonius spends his free time in the second book.[34] With the second letter of the second book, which is second longest of all the letters in his collection,[35] Sidonius invites the addressee, Domitius (and thus the implied reader), to flee from the heat and inconvenience of the city into the countryside on his estate Avitacum. In a ring composition, the last two letters of Book 2 are also dedicated to the topics *negotium* and *otium*: letter 2.13 shows the dangers of *negotium*, using the example of the political career of the emperor Petronius Maximus.[36] The last letter, 2.14, reverses letter 2.2: Sidonius is in the city (in winter) and laments the absence of the addressee, Maurusius, whom he is going to visit in the countryside.[37] *Ep.* 2.12, about the illness of Sidonius' daughter, describes how the family flees from the heat of the city to the healthy country estate, thus reversing the theme of letter 2.2. *Ep.* 2.9 is also devoted to the aristocratic life in the villa but focuses on the social aspect. While the second letter presents the architecture of Sidonius' villa, the ninth shows a typical day in his relatives' villas with various activities and pastimes. Another aspect of the discourse around leisure is the role of one's wife in one's study of and production of literature, addressed in *Ep.* 2.10.[38] In between the 'villa letters' are letters showing Sidonius busy as patron and friend: he congratulates, gives recommendations and offers (legal) help to friends and clients in need.[39] Like his predecessor Pliny, Sidonius also inserts a letter (*Ep.* 2.8) about the correct way of mourning and commemorating a friend as a duty of friendship.[40]

With the selection and arrangement of the letters in the second book (summarised in Table 1), Sidonius thus conveys several messages. He shows the connection between *otium* and *negotium*, emphasises the importance of the villa as a place of *otium* and, above all, he reveals himself as socially

---

33. On the Regulus series in Plin. *Ep.* 1.5, 1.20, 2.20, 4.2, 4.7, 6.2, see Ludolph (1997) 142–66, Hoffer (1999) 55–91.
34. See Montone (2017) 37.
35. Sidon. *Ep.* 7.9 is even longer but consists of a letter and an attached speech.
36. See Hanaghan (2019) 114.
37. See Hanaghan (2019) 170.
38. See Hindermann (2022d).
39. See *Ep.* 2.3, a congratulatory letter to Felix; *Ep.* 2.4, a letter of recommendation for Proiectus; *Ep.* 2.5, help for the friend Iohannes in a lawsuit; *Ep.* 2.6, approval of Menstruanus; *Ep.* 2.7, plea for legal help; *Ep.* 2.11, confirmation of his friendship with Rusticus.
40. See Hindermann (2020a).

Table 1. Sidonius' collection of letters, Books 1–3

Book: letter	negotium/otium	Subject
Book 1: *Ep.* 1–10	negotium	Sidonius' career
Book 1: *Ep.* 11	otium	Dinner with the emperor Majorian First inserted epigram
Book 2: *Ep.* 1	negotium	Appeal for help against Seronatus to Ecdicius
Book 2: *Ep.* 2	otium	Invitation to Domitius to travel to the countryside Description of the villa Avitacum (first villa letter)
Book 2: *Ep.* 3–7	otium	Various duties of friendship
Book 2: *Ep.* 8	otium	Ideal wife, daughter and mother Second inserted epigram
Book 2: *Ep.* 9	otium	Description of leisure in the countryside (second villa letter)
Book 2: *Ep.* 10	orium	Ideal marriage Third inserted epigram
Book 2: *Ep.* 11	otium	Duty of friendship
Book 2: *Ep.* 12	otium	Travel to the countryside because of illness
Book 2: *Ep.* 13	negotium	Warning of the dangers of a political career
Book 2: *Ep.* 14	otium	Sidonius invites Maurusius, who is in the countryside, to the city
Book 3: Ep. 1–14	negotium	

connected and engaged. Although he lives in retirement and is not engaged in a professional activity now, he is not idle but active as a friend, patron and writer.

3. Book 2 as a response to Pliny the Younger's Letters and the question of intertextuality

Sidonius' relationship with Pliny, which is especially evident in the second book, has been discussed in many articles.[41] Sidonius' second book of letters is generally characterised by a high degree of structural and textual

---

41. On the structural parallels between Pliny and Sidonius, see Gibson (2011), Gibson (2012) 69, Gibson (2013a), Gibson (2013b), Gibson (2020) 386–92. For parallels in the use of

intertextuality with Pliny's *Epistulae*, which Sidonius announces in his programmatic opening letter, Sidon. *Ep.* 1.1. By taking up and varying Plinian terminology right at the beginning of his letter collection in Sidon. *Ep.* 1.1.1,[42] Sidonius shows that he will follow Pliny structurally, but will also incorporate new emphases in his letters.

In his second book, Sidonius often expands on topics which Pliny only touches on in his letters, such as the baths in the villa descriptions and the importance of the company of friends and relatives during their stay (*Ep.* 2.2 and 2.9) (see Table 2). For example, in *Ep.* 2.2.12, Sidonius includes a lengthy description of the view over the lake, the fishermen at work and different methods of fishing, whereas Pliny merely mentions his villa's vicinity to a body of water and the abundance of fish that it offers.[43] He also combines subjects that Pliny treats separately, like the description of a natural wonder, a lake in his villa description in *Ep.* 2.2; Pliny writes about his villas and about a lake in separate letters.[44]

Sidonius reflects on the classical concept of *otium* in dialogue with Pliny by writing about the semantics of *otium* (*Ep.* 2.10.3 and 2.14.2) and shows himself engaged with networking instead of producing literature in seclusion.[45] Similarly, the themes of death, mourning and consolation, which Pliny treats in an exemplary manner in his letter 1.12 about the friend and politician Corellius Rufus and which he takes up again later in his collection of letters, are innovatively developed further by Sidonius. Sidonius treats the subject in allusion to Plin. *Ep.* 5.16 in his letter about the deceased lady Filimatia in Sidon. *Ep.* 2.8. He not only offers a eulogy in prose like Pliny

---

architectural vocabulary in the villa letters, see Whitton (2013) 35–6, 218–55, Visser (2014), Cam (2003). For Pliny's relevance to Sidonius' *Ep.* 2.2, see Hanaghan (2019) 44–6, 78–9, 176–8; for parallels in the edition and circulation of the work, see Hanaghan (2019) 170–6. Regarding Pliny's influence on Sidonius' second book, see Hindermann (2020a) and on Pliny and Sidonius' depiction of marital relations in Sidon. *Ep.* 2.10, see Hindermann (2022d). On Pliny's *Ep.* 5.16 and Sidon. *Ep.* 2.8, see Hindermann (2022b).

42. On Plin. *Ep.* 1.1.1 and Sidon. *Ep.* 1.1.1, see Köhler (1995) 99–106, Hindermann (2020a) 96, van Waarden (2021). Sidonius alludes to Pliny not only in the first letter but also in many others, either mentioning him directly by name (Sidon. *Ep.* 2.10.5, 4.3.1, 4.22.2, 8.10.3, 9.1.1) or dealing with the same topics. See the commentaries on *Ep.* 2.2, 2.8, 2.9, 2.10 and 2.14.

43. See Hindermann (2020a) 104.

44. For the villa, see Plin. *Ep.* 2.17, 5.6; for the lake, see Plin. *Ep.* 8.20.

45. On *otium* in Sidonius, see André (2006), Hanaghan (2019) 44–6, 78–9, 176–8 and Hindermann (2020a). On the close connection between letters and *otium*, see Eickhoff et al. (2016).

Table 2. Parallels between Sidonius and Pliny the Younger

Sidonius	Content	Parallels in Pliny's *Epistulae*
Ep. 2.1	Negative example/enemy Seronatus	Regulus series: *Ep.* 1.5, 1.20, 2.20, 4.2, 4.7, 6.2
Ep. 2.2	City–countryside; *otium–negotium* Description of his villa Description of his lake/natural wonder	*Ep.* 1.9, 4.23, 7.3 *Ep.* 1.3, 2.17, 5.6, 9.7.2 *Ep.* 4.30, 8.8, 8.20
Ep. 2.3	Congratulations on promotion	*Ep.* 4.8, 5.14
Ep. 2.4	Letter of recommendation Arranging marriage	*Ep.* 1.14
Ep. 2.5-2.6	Letter of recommendation Recommendation as *amicus*	*Ep.* 2.9, 2.13, 3.2, 3.3, 3.8, 4.4, 4.12, 4.15, 6.6, 6.8, 6.9, 6.23, 7.8, 7.16, 7.22, 7.28, 7.31, 9.30
Ep. 2.7	Request for help for a friend in a legal matter	Legal matters: *Ep.* 2.16, 3.4, 3.9, 3.20, 4.9, 4.10, 4.17, 4.22, 4.24, 4.29, 5.1, 5.4, 5.7, 5.9, 5.13, 6.2, 6.5, 6.13, 6.18, 6.19, 6.22, 6.23, 6.29, 6.31, 6.33, 7.6, 7.10, 8.14
Ep. 2.8	Deceased friend Eulogy and epitaph on Filimatia	*Ep.* 1.12, 2.7, 3.21, 4.21, 5.16, 5.21, 6.10, 8.5, 8.23, 9.9, 9.19
Ep. 2.9	Daily routine in the villa	*Ep.* 3.1, 9.36, 9.40
Ep. 2.10	Praise of studies and educated wives	Praise of studies: *Ep.* 1.10, 1.13, 4.3, 5.17, 6.11, 6.21, 6.23 Educated wives: *Ep.* 1.16, 4.19
Ep. 2.11	Lament about the separation from a friend	*Ep.* 6.1
Ep. 2.12	Worries about the sick daughter Severiana	Worries about sick relatives or friends: *Ep.* 1.22, 5.19, 5.21, 6.4, 7.1, 7.19, 7.26, 7.30, 8.1, 8.10, 8.11
Ep. 2.13	Warning against glory	
Ep. 2.14	Letter of friendship, grape harvest	*Ep.* 9.16

but inserts an epitaph to the deceased. Most obviously, in *Ep.* 2.10.5–6 Sidonius develops Pliny's model of the wife as muse by writing about eleven 'power couples'. Presumably Sidonius' wife Papianilla, as the daughter of a well-connected aristocrat and high official who even rose to become emperor, was very important to him both personally and in his career. Sidonius therefore also lends weight to the wives of his literary predecessors in his letter of advice to the newly married Hesperius (*Ep.* 2.10). In this list, Pliny and his wife Calpurnia are positioned in the middle of the first series of writers who are supported by their wives.[46]

Besides the omnipresent Pliny, there are other major intertexts for villa letter *Ep.* 2.2, which sets the tone for the second book: Statius, Martial and Lucan for the villa's luxurious interior design, Martial and Juvenal for the negative description of the city, the classroom, symposiastic scenes and the relaxed way of living in the countryside, Vitruvius for architectural details, Vergil for the description of the summer heat, the scenery and the ship race, and Ausonius for the description of the lake and the fishing scene.[47]

The choice of Pliny as a model can be explained by the fact that the two authors are similar in their aim of portraying themselves positively by means of a collection of letters and in their shared topic of aristocratic *otium*.[48] Sidonius' treatment of Pliny is essentially a matter of developing Pliny's texts: he takes up themes and elaborates on them or reshapes them. Why Pliny is so important for Sidonius is unclear. Is it due to his general preference for the Trajan period, did he see in Pliny a kindred spirit whom he wanted to make better known, or was Pliny also popular with other intellectuals in Sidonius' time?[49]

With an author like Martial, to whose mocking or obscene epigrams Sidonius also alludes within a serious context, the question of how to read intertextual allusions becomes more difficult. There is extensive discussion about whether a specific form of intertextuality existed in Late Antiquity and, if so, what it looked like.[50] For the second book in particular, the

---

46. See Hindermann (2022d).
47. See the commentary on *Ep.* 2.2.
48. See Küppers (2005).
49. On the reception of Pliny in Late Antiquity, see Cameron (1965), Cameron (1967), Cain (2008), Gibson and Rees (2013b).
50. Pelttari (2014) 161–4 writes in general about the figure of the reader in late antique poetry of the fourth century and argues that by juxtaposing allusive fragments of classical poetry the writers open a room for the reader on the level of the text: the reader structures and interprets the different layers of allusions and thus gives the text full meaning.

passages in which Sidonius transposes obscene quotations from Martial into the praise of the deceased Filimatia in *Ep.* 2.8.2–3 and the description of the church of the bishop Patiens in *Ep.* 2.10.4 have provoked discussion among researchers. Does Sidonius want to distance himself from his predecessors with this transfer, does he simply reuse appealing phrases, or does he create a special connection to the learned readers through the seemingly inappropriate reminiscences? I will show in my commentary that there is no universal rule for Sidonius' treatment of his literary predecessors, but that he alludes to a variety of authors and literary genres in different ways in the second book.

There are several lists of literary models in the second book,[51] which contribute to Sidonius' explicit dialogue with classical authors. Sidonius takes up the theme of the literary canon in the second villa letter, *Ep.* 2.9.4, where he lists four authors who represent a certain literary genre: Augustine and Varro stand for Christian and pagan prose, Horace and Prudentius for pagan and Christian poetry. Here, balance is important to Sidonius: each author represents one type of literature and they are equally placed on the same bookshelf for hosts and guests to choose from.[52]

In his letter to Hesperius (*Ep.* 2.10), which functions as a wedding gift and marriage guide in equal measure, the selection of his literary canon appears more personal and inferences can be drawn about Sidonius. He starts the letter with the polyptoton *amo–amas* and a series of pronouns (*in te, nobis, tua, nostra* and later with the first person plural *defleamus*) to underline the similarity and closeness between himself and the addressee, Hesperius, his alter ego. They both love literature and everything connected with it.[53] Stressing the closeness between writer and addressee is a frequent motif in a letter of friendship, and the role of an older friend guiding a younger writer

---

In his analysis of *Carm.* 11, alluding to Claudian and Statius, Rijser (2013) 86 comes to a different conclusion, namely that the comprehensive collection and inclusion of material is Sidonius' main concern and more important to him than sense or grammar. As Fontaine (1977) shows in his study on Ausonius, Ambrose and Ammianus, the mix of genres and tones is typical of late antique aesthetics. According to Kaufmann (2017), the late antique authors add a new variant to the previous form of intertextuality, namely that of alluding to other authors on a purely formal level. Thus, the two poles of intertextuality, the essential part of the content and the formal feature, exist side by side. For a cautious approach towards allusiveness in late antique literature in general, see Kelly (2008) 161–221 on Ammianus Marcellinus.

51. For the importance of lists in Sidonius' letters and poems, see the introduction to *Ep.* 2.10 and Hindermann (forthcoming a).
52. See the introduction to *Ep.* 2.9 as well as the commentary on *Ep.* 2.9.4.
53. In Sidon. *Ep.* 1.1.3 Sidonius expresses the same thought to the addressee, Constantius, whose poetry he also mentions in *Ep.* 2.10.3.

in his endeavours is also found, for example, in Pliny's letters to Caninius.⁵⁴ It is therefore plausible to draw conclusions from Sidonius' lists of authors about his self-image as an author and husband.

To encourage his addressee Hesperius to continue his literary studies even as a (soon-to-be) husband, Sidonius adds two lists of famous author-couples in *Ep.* 2.10.5–6. In section 5 he introduces five married authors with highly supportive wives who spent their nights beside their husbands' writing desks. Sidonius selects both the examples and the object the women hold to illuminate their husbands' nocturnal writing: a *candelabrum*, a candle holder.⁵⁵ While in other literary genres, a scene with a lamp and a couple usually signifies an erotic atmosphere, Sidonius creates a different context by alluding to the topos of *lucubratio*, working by lamplight, as do various Roman authors before him.⁵⁶ In the letter to his literary friend and follower Hesperius, Sidonius also makes programmatic statements about himself and his attitude towards literature and the importance of studies. Sidonius is concerned about the survival of the correct Latin language, and he repeatedly encourages his friends to stand up for it as vigorously as he does. In Sidonius' account, the knowledge of literature is the last remaining token of nobility and a field of activity that enables Gallo-Romans to distinguish themselves from the 'barbarians'.⁵⁷

It is striking that in Book 2 of his letters, on Roman *otium*, Sidonius frequently draws inspiration from earlier authors, whereas in the later books, especially Books 6 and 7, he breaks completely away from the Plinian model and generally alludes to other authors less often.⁵⁸ The second book thus has a special position in the collection of letters, in that it demonstrates the meaning of literature in its own guise through its particularly elaborate intertextuality.

---

54. Plin. *Ep.* 1.3, 2.8, 3.7, 6.21, 7.18, 8.4, 9.33; see Ludolph (1997) 121, Hindermann (2011). The idea of encouraging a friend to write and praising his literary work is also found in others of Pliny's letters, for example Plin. *Ep.* 4.20, 4.27 and 5.17.
55. See Hindermann (2022d) for the meaning of the candelabra and an interpretation of this scene.
56. Cic. *Fam.* 9.2.1, Sen. *Ep.* 8.1, Plin. *Nat. Praef.* 18, Auson. *Praef. Var.* 5 (Green) vv. 7–12, Gell. *Praef.* 4, Quint. 10.3.25–7, Hier. *Ep.* 64, 108.32.
57. See the commentary on *Illud appone...* in *Ep.* 2.10.1.
58. See Gibson (2012) 69.

4. The epigrams in Sidonius' letters[59]

Sidonius' second book of letters is also distinguished by the fact that it contains two longer poems, integrated into letters 2.8 (fifteen verses) and 2.10 (thirty verses). The first book, on the other hand, which is devoted primarily to Sidonius' career (*negotium*),[60] contains only a two-line poem at the very end of the last letter, 1.11. In this first, short poem, Sidonius defends himself to the emperor Majorian against the charge of having written scurrilous verses, which was forbidden by a series of laws in the Theodosian code (9.34.1–10).[61] The poetry in his first book thus serves political-rhetorical purposes – although it is created in the context of *otium*, a dinner in illustrious company. Sidonius presents his poetological programme only in the second book, which is dedicated to studies (*studia*) and the production of literature. It contains the two types of poems that are the most frequent in Sidonius' letter collection, especially in Books 1–7: the funeral epitaph and the inscription on objects or buildings (*titulus*). Sidonius inserts one poem of each of these genres in *Ep.* 2.8 (a funeral poem to the deceased lady Filimatia) and in *Ep.* 2.10 (an inscription in the church of bishop Patiens in Lyon). These two types of poem announce the poems in the following seven letter books, where they appear in alternating order: epitaphs are inserted in *Ep.* 2.8.3, 3.12.5, 4.11.6, 7.17.2 and 8.11.3, inscriptions are inserted in *Ep.* 2.10.4, 4.8.5, 4.18.5 and 5.17.10.[62] Except in the sixth book of letters, addressed to bishops, who do not receive poems from Sidonius, Sidonius includes one or more poems in each book. He thus contradicts his announcement to renounce poetry with his episcopate.[63] In the first seven

---

59. This section draws on my article about the letter as a place for the publication of epigrams (Hindermann 2020b) and my article on grave epitaphs and letters of mourning (Hindermann 2022b).
60. See section 1, 'Sidonius' life between *otium* and *negotium* and the position of Book 2 in the collection of letters'.
61. See Sidon. *Ep.* 1.11.14 *scribere me satyram qui culpat, maxime princeps | hanc rogo decernas aut probet aut timeat.* 'I beg you, supreme emperor, to decide that whoever accuses me of having written a satire proves it or fears it.' The model for letter 1.11 is Plin. *Ep.* 9.13. On the political background of the poem, see Consolino (2020), Köhler (1995) 288–92, Harries (1994) 93–5. Neger (2020) interprets letter *Ep.* 1.11 as Sidonius' first *sphragis* (the second being the last letter, 9.16), referring to his publication of verses and letters and to Horace's second book of satires (Hor. *Sat.* 2.1 and 2.8). Sidonius refers to his satire also in *Carm.* 12.22; see also *Ep.* 4.22.5, 5.8.3, 8.11.6.
62. Hindermann (2020b).
63. Cited p. xxiii, n. 74.

INTRODUCTION

books the poems are shorter; in Books 8 and 9 they are considerably longer and composed in different metres.[64]

While the epigrams included within the letters are oriented towards the addressee and the occasion of the letter, the sender and the structure of the book must also be considered. Previous analyses of the epigrams in Sidonius' letters mostly concerned the genre of the individual poems. There are various studies on individual epigrams or on specific types of epigrams, for example on the funerary epigrams or the inscriptions on objects and buildings.[65] It is only in the more recent research literature that it has been recognised that the poems in Sidonius' letters are a carefully arranged collection.[66]

I interpret Sidonius' inclusion of poems in the letters against the background of Pliny's collection of letters, which is the first epistolary prosimetrum handed down to us. This literary form became popular with Late Antique epistolographers like Symmachus, Ausonius, Paulinus of Nola, Sidonius Apollinaris and Ennodius.[67] Sidonius includes a total of sixteen or seventeen[68] poems within his letters and thus goes beyond Pliny, both in the number of poems and in their thematic range. Pliny includes two of his own poems and two poems by other people about him; they show his light, easy-going side. They also prove that Pliny is a subject worthy of poetic celebration.[69] Sidonius also pursues a biographical purpose with the poems in his letters, but in a different way. He sorts the literary genres according to

---

64. See Neger (2019) 397–8, Mratschek (2017) 314–22.
65. See Condorelli (2013a) on the epitaphs, Wolff (2014c) on *tituli* and epitaphs, and Furbetta (2013), Consolino (2015) and Amherdt (2001) 21 on the epigrams in general. Consolino (2020) analyses the poems inserted in the letters and the separate collection of the *Carmina minora* by type across the letter and collection boundaries.
66. Neger (2019, 2020), in her comments on *Ep.* 1.11 and 5.17, points to the function of the poems for the narrative context of the letter. She also denotes the collection of poems embedded in Sidonius' letters as an anthology, Neger (2020) 383. Hindermann (2020b, 2022b) points to the importance of the two poems in the second book for the whole collection, and to Sidonius' discussion of the materiality of his poems. Stoehr-Monjou (2018) examines the arrangement of the poems in the letters and their relationship with the addressees.
67. See Neger (2018).
68. Depending on whether one counts the palindrome within *Ep.* 9.14.6 as single or double, there are sixteen or seventeen poems (in the text that follows they will be counted as two palindromes). Mascoli (2003) 156 counts only fourteen poems and the epitaph on Filimatia as the first poem: 'L'epitafio è il primo dei quattordici inserti poetici che si trovano nell'epistolario di Sidonio.'
69. Plin. *Ep.* 7.4.6 and 7.9.11 (poems by Pliny) and *Ep.* 3.21.5, 4.27.4 (poems about Pliny). See Hindermann (2022b).

their appropriateness for a particular stage of life:[70] satire suits youth and is consequently embodied in the two-liner at the beginning of the collection in *Ep.* 1.11. In this letter 1.11, which forms the conclusion of the first book, he also shows how he wants to be perceived as a poet.[71] The other end of the poetry collection is constituted by an autobiographical retrospective in the form of a long poem (eighty-four verses) (*Ep.* 9.16.3). Thus, the end of the collection of letters and the end of the embedded collection of poems coincide and thereby reinforce each other.[72] The importance of poetry is also shown by the fact that Sidonius includes six poems (out of seventeen in Books 1–9, or 51.7% of the verses),[73] more than in any other book. Sidonius thus contradicts his 'vow' in *Ep.* 9.12.1 to do without poetry.[74] Book 9 is Sidonius' literary testament to posterity, and poetry has a special importance in it, as Sidonius thereby addresses the younger generation and presents himself successfully as a stylistic model.[75]

Like Pliny's programmatic letters in his first book,[76] Sidonius' second book announces important topics that dominate the letter collection, among them the two types of epigram he most often integrates in his letters, epitaph and inscription. Letters 2.8 and 2.10 are not only linked through their embedded poems, but also through the theme of ideal marriage and the exemplary behaviour of wives, subjects that are also important in Pliny's letters.[77] Both poems also anticipate a theme that reappears in the letters

---

70. Egelhaaf-Gaiser (2010) 275–7.
71. Stoehr-Monjou (2018) 161–4.
72. Sidon. *Ep.* 9.16.3; see Consolino (2020). In addition, there are five epigrams on other topics in Book 9: two poems with reflections on metrics (*Ep.* 9.13.2, 9.15.1), an invitation to a lecture of Petrus' works (*Ep.* 9.13.5), and one or two poems (the palindrome mentioned in the text, which can be viewed as one poem or two) on a river crossing (*Ep.* 9.14.6).
73. See Stoehr-Monjou (2018) 152.
74. Sidon. *Ep.* 9.12.1: *primum ab exordio religiosae professionis huic principaliter exercitio renuntivai, quia nimirum facilitati posset accomodari, si me occupasset levitas versuum, quem respicere coeperat gravitas actionum.* 'But in the first place, I especially renounced this exercise of verse-writing from the very beginning of my religious profession because undoubtedly it might be a concession to weakness if I occupied myself with the levity of verse-writing when seriousness of action had become my duty.' See also *Ep.* 7.18.4.
75. See Stoehr-Monjou (2018) 164: 'Book 9 is built so as to play with effects of opposition and paradoxes. Sidonius wants to quit but he publishes a last book; he has renounced poetry yet he publishes verses; and where he dwells mainly on poetry, he insists on concluding with prose, using a poet as back-up.' See also Stoehr-Monjou (forthcoming).
76. Ludolph (1997) examines the first eight letters of the first book, in which Pliny anticipates all the topics that will be relevant in the following books.
77. See Hindermann (2022d).

with epigrams: the question of materiality and the place of poetry, stone, paper, cloth and silver. Sidonius repeatedly addresses the age-old question of how poetry can be given eternity and which materials are suitable for which type of poem. Since we have received all the poems only on paper and not in the other media Sidonius mentions, his strategy of publishing the poems also in a collection of letters as paratexts proves to be successful.[78]

Authors like Sidonius and his model Pliny who quote their own poems in their letters safeguard their intellectual property. Should the poetry books be lost as a whole, individual poems are nevertheless preserved as samples of the author's skill by the various recipients of the letters. We can therefore assume that the author sends particularly successful poems as a gift for the addressee of the letter. The poems are closely linked to the prose text, as they discuss the same subject. They illustrate a certain theme and embellish it, but the metre and the layout keep them separate from the rest of the letter. The poems should therefore not be separated from their context, as this would result in the loss of important paratextual information for interpretation from the letters and the letter books. Instead, their arrangement should be interpreted in the same way as the arrangement of the letters in a collection.

5. Text and translation

The Latin text of the second book is based on the edition by Lütjohann (1887), which, according to current research on editions, is the one that comes closest to the archetype (see Dolveck 2020). Based on Dolveck (2020), Giulia Marolla (2021) has created a simplified stemma for the letters, which is reproduced in Figure 1. The basic rule implied by Dolveck's stemma is that if the readings of α (the family represented by C in Loyen's stemma) agree with one of the branches of δ (the remaining manuscripts), this represents the reading of the archetype. Since Loyen (1970a, 1970b) was very fond of the readings of L (because of its antiquity) and a number of manuscripts in the same family, this leads to many potential changes across Sidonius' whole oeuvre. In discussing the few text-critical problems of the second book, I follow Loyen's (1970a) designation of *sigla*. *Vat*1661 represents Vaticanus Latinus 1843, and Sch denotes Paris IRHT Collection privée 347 (ex-Schøyen collection).

---

78. See Hindermann (forthcoming b).

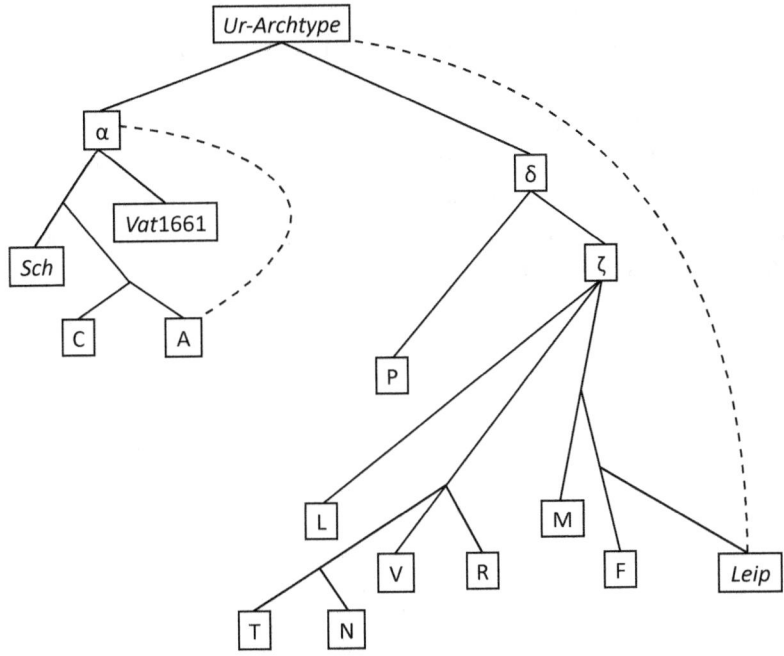

Figure 1. Giulia Marolla's stemma for Sidonius' letters (Marolla 2021)

My departures from Lütjohann's edition, which are all discussed in the commentary, are in the following places:

2.1.1	*quique* instead of *quippe*
2.1.1	*ipse* instead of *iste*
2.1.3	*hospitibus* instead of *hostibus*
2.2.8	*elutis* instead of *elautis*
2.2.10	*monubilibus* instead of *monolithis*
2.2.10	*hypodromus* instead of *hippodromus*
2.2.11	*sensim non breviatis* instead of *sensim breviatis*
2.8.1	*matris amissae <filia>* instead of *matris amissae*
2.8.1	*subolis* instead of *soboles*
2.8.1	*liberum* instead of *liberorum*
2.8.2	*si quis* instead of *si qui*
2.8.3 v. 2	*natis* instead of *gnatis*
2.9.4	*hac ... hac ... hac* instead of *huc ... huc ... huc*
2.10.1	*interitamque* instead of *interemptamque*

In addition, following Lütjohann, at 2.2.5 I omit *ipsa vero convenientibus mensuris exactissima spatiositate quadratur*, while other modern editions include it.

My translation of the second book is intended to make the complex Latin text intelligible while staying as close as possible to the original. The Latin text and the English translation are printed on opposite pages. The quotations of other Sidonian passages are based on Anderson's translation (1936, 1965), modified when it seemed appropriate.

Abbreviations for Books, Series and Reference Works

Blaise	A. Blaise, *Dictionnaire Latin-Français des auteurs chrétiens*, Turnhout, 1954
BNP	H. Cancik et al. (eds), *Brill's New Pauly*. English translation edited by C. F. Salazar and F. G. Gentry <https://referenceworks.brillonline.com/browse/brill-s-new-pauly>
CE	F. Bücheler (ed.), *Carmina latina epigraphica*, 2 vols, Leipzig, 1895–7. *Supplement* edited by E. Lommatzsch, Leipzig, 1926 (reprinted Amsterdam, 1972)
CIL	T. Mommsen et al. (eds), *Corpus inscriptionum latinarum*, Berlin, 1863–
OLD	A. P. Glare et al., *Oxford Latin Dictionary*, Oxford, 1968–82 (2nd edition 2012)
PCBE 4	*Prosopographie chrétienne du Bas-Empire*, vol. 4. See Pietri and Heijmans (2013)
PLRE 1, 2	A. H. M. Jones, J. R. Martindale and J. Morris (eds), *The Prosopography of the Later Roman Empire*, vol. 1, *A.D. 260–395*, Cambridge, 1971; J. R. Martindale (ed.), *The Prosopography of the Later Roman Empire*, vol. 2 *A.D. 395–527*, Cambridge, 1980
RAC	T. Klauser et al. (eds), *Reallexikon für Antike und Christentum*, Leipzig and Stuttgart, 1941–
TLL	F. Vollmer et al. (eds), *Thesaurus Linguae Latinae*, Leipzig and Munich, 1900– <https://www.degruyter.com/view/db/tll?rskey=8yEUr2&result=2>

Text and Translation

Epistula I

Sidonius Ecdicio suo salutem.

1. Duo nunc pariter mala sustinent Arverni tui. 'Quaenam?' inquis. Praesentiam Seronati et absentiam tuam. Seronati, inquam: de cuius ut primum etiam nomine loquar, sic mihi videtur quasi praescia futurorum lusisse Fortuna, sicuti ex adverso maiores nostri proelia, quibus nihil est foedius, bella dixerunt; quique etiam pari contrarietate fata, quia non parcerent, Parcas vocitavere. Rediit ipse Catilina saeculi nostri nuper Aturribus, ut sanguinem fortunasque miserorum, quas ibi ex parte propinaverat, hic ex asse misceret.

2. Scitote in eo per dies spiritum diu dissimulati furoris aperiri: aperte invidet, abiecte fingit, serviliter superbit; indicit ut dominus, exigit ut tyrannus, addicit ut iudex, calumniatur ut barbarus; toto die a metu armatus, ab avaritia ieiunus, a cupiditate terribilis, a vanitate crudelis non cessat simul furta vel punire vel facere; palam et ridentibus convocatis ructat inter cives pugnas, inter barbaros litteras; epistulas, ne primis quidem apicibus sufficienter initiatus, publice a iactantia dictat, ab impudentia emendat. 3. Totum quod concupiscit quasi comparat nec dat pretia contemnens nec accipit instrumenta desperans; in concilio iubet, in consilio tacet, in ecclesia iocatur, in convivio praedicat, in cubiculo damnat, in quaestione dormitat; implet cotidie silvas fugientibus, villas hospitibus, altaria reis, carceres clericis; exultans Gothis insultansque Romanis, inludens praefectis conludensque numerariis, leges Theodosianas calcans Theodoricianasque proponens, veteres culpas nova tributa perquirit.

4. Proinde moras tuas citius explica et quicquid illud est, quod te retentat, incide. Te exspectat palpitantium civium extrema libertas. Quicquid sperandum, quicquid desperandum est, fieri te medio, te praesule placet. Si nullae a republica vires, nulla praesidia, si nullae, quantum rumor est, Anthemii principis

Epistula I

Sidonius greets his dear Ecdicius

1. There are now two evils your fellow Arvernians endure in equal measure. 'What kind of evils?', you ask. 'The presence of Seronatus and your absence. Of Seronatus, I answer. To speak first also about his name: Fortuna seems to me to have played a trick, as if already aware of the future. Just like our ancestors called wars – there is nothing more horrible than these – 'nice' from their opposite. With equal contrariness they also called the fates 'Parcae' because they spare no one. This man, the very Catiline of our time, has recently returned from Aire so he can create utter chaos here with the blood and fortune of the wretched, which he had only a partially taste of there.

2. You should know that the spirit of madness that he has long dissimulated is more and more evident in him from day to day. He is envious openly, he pretends abjectly, and he is proud slavishly; he commands like a master, demands like a tyrant, sentences like a judge and lies like a barbarian. All day long he is armed out of fear, goes hungry from stinginess, is fearsome from greed, cruel from vanity, and he unceasingly both punishes thefts and commits them. In public, while everybody around is laughing, he rants about battles in front of civilians, and about literature in front of barbarians; although he barely knows the alphabet, he dictates letters in public to show off and corrects them out of impertinence. 3. Everything that he covets he procures in some way, but neither does he pay in his disdain nor does he accept any contracts in his suspicion. In the council he commands, in the counsel he is silent, in church he jokes, at the banquet he preaches, he convicts in his bedroom and keeps falling asleep during court examination. Every day he fills the woods with refugees, estates with barbarians, the altars with defendants, the prisons with priests. He exalts the Visigoths and insults the Romans. He mocks the prefects and colludes with the accountants, he tramples on the laws of Theodosius and issues those of Theoderic, he eagerly seeks out old claims and new taxes.

4. You should therefore very quickly sort out your delay and break off whatever is holding you back. The trembling citizens with their endangered liberty await you. Whether there is hope or despair, we want it to be brought

opes, statuit te auctore nobilitas seu patriam dimittere seu capillos. Vale.

about with you amidst us and you as our leader. If there are no troops from the government, no support, if – as rumour says – the emperor Anthemius is indeed penniless, under your leadership our nobility is willing to risk losing home – or hair. Goodbye.

Epistula 2

Sidonius Domitio suo salutem.

1. Ruri me esse causaris, cum mihi potius queri suppetat te nunc urbe retineri. Iam ver decedit aestati et per lineas sol altatus extremas in axem Scythicum radio peregrinante porrigitur. Hic quid de regionis nostrae climate loquar? Cuius spatia divinum sic tetendit opificium, ut magis vaporibus orbis occidui subiceremur. Quid plura? Mundus incanduit: glacies Alpina deletur et hiulcis arentium rimarum flexibus terra perscribitur; squalet glarea in vadis, limus in ripis, pulvis in campis; aqua ipsa quaecumque perpetuo labens tractu cunctante languescit; iam non solum calet unda sed coquitur. 2. Et nunc, dum in carbaso sudat unus, alter in bombyce, tu endromidatus exterius, intrinsecus fasceatus, insuper et concava municipis Amerini sede compressus discipulis non aestu minus quam timore pallentibus exponere oscitabundus ordiris: 'Samia mihi mater fuit.' Quin tu mage, si quid tibi salubre cordi, raptim subduceris anhelantibus angustiis civitatis et contubernio nostro aventer insertus fallis clementissimo recessu inclementiam canicularem? 3. Sane si placet, quis sit agri, in quem vocaris, situs accipe. Avitaci sumus: nomen hoc praedio, quod, quia uxorium, patrio mihi dulcius. Haec mihi cum meis praesule deo, nisi quid tu fascinum verere, concordia. Mons ab occasu, quamquam terrenus, arduus tamen inferiores sibi colles tamquam gemino fomite effundit, quattuor a se circiter iugerum latitudine abductos. Sed donec domicilio competens vestibuli campus aperitur, mediam vallem rectis tractibus prosequuntur latera clivorum usque in marginem villae, quae in Borean Austrumque conversis frontibus tenditur.

4. Balneum ab Africo radicibus nemorosae rupis adhaerescit et si caedua per iugum silva truncetur, in ora fornacis lapsu velut spontaneo deciduis struibus impingitur. Hinc aquarum surgit

Epistula 2

Sidonius greets his dear Domitius

1. You complain of my being in the countryside, though if anything I could complain that you are now held back in the city. Already spring gives way to summer and the sun, at the highest point of its course, stretches out with wandering ray to the distant Scythian pole. What shall I say here about the climate of our region? Divine workmanship arranged our area so that we are more exposed to the warmth of the western world. What more to say? The world has heated up, the ice in the Alps is disappearing and the earth is inscribed with gaping and curving dry furrows. The gravel is parched in the fords, the mud on the banks, the dust in the fields. All the waters that normally flow continuously now dribble weakly and the liquid is not just hot, but boiling. 2. And now, while one man sweats in linen and another in silk, you are wearing a woollen cloak on the outside and underneath you are wrapped with bands. Moreover, cramped in a curved chair of wicker from Ameria and yawning, you start commenting on the verse 'A Samian was my mother' to students who are pale from the heat no less than from fear. Why not rather, if you care for your health, save yourself quickly from the suffocating constrictions of the city and eagerly join my company, defying the Dog Star's inclemency in the most clement of retreats? 3. Anyway, if you'd like to know the situation of the estate to which you are invited, listen. We are at Avitacum: this is the name of the estate, which, because it is my wife's, is dearer to me than my father's. Under God's protection – unless you suspect it to be witchcraft – I live there with my family in harmony. A steep mountain, though covered in earth, lies in the west. It rolls out into smaller hills, as though in two branches, which extend away from it to a breadth of about four *iugera*. But up to the point where there is a wide space big enough for an entrance-court for my domicile, the hillsides follow the valley in the middle in straight lines until they come to the border of my villa. Its fronts face north and south.

4. The bath clings in the south-west to the bottom of a wooded rock, so when the wood which is ready for felling is cut on the ridge above, it is cast down into the mouth of the oven in tumbling heaps as if it had itself decided

cella coctilium, quae consequenti unguentariae spatii parilitate conquadrat excepto solii capacis hemicyclo, ubi et vis undae ferventis per parietem foraminatum flexilis plumbi meatibus implicita singultat. Intra conclave succensum solidus dies et haec abundantia lucis inclusae, ut verecundos quosque compellat aliquid se plus putare quam nudos.

5. Hinc frigidaria dilatatur, quae piscinas publicis operibus extructas non impudenter aemularetur. Primum tecti apice in conum cacuminato, cum ab angulis quadrifariam concurrentia dorsa cristarum tegulis interiacentibus imbricarentur, ita ut ministeriorum sese non impediente famulatu tot possit recipere sellas, quot solet sigma personas, fenestras e regione conditor binas confinio camerae pendentis admovit, ut suspicientum visui fabrefactum lacunar aperiret. Interior parietum facies solo levigati caementi candore contenta est. 6. Non hic per nudam pictorum corporum pulchritudinem turpis prostat historia, quae sicut ornat artem, sic devenustat artificem. Absunt ridiculi vestitu et vultibus histriones pigmentis multicoloribus Philistionis supellectilem mentientes. Absunt lubrici tortuosique pugilatu et nexibus palaestritae, quorum etiam viventum luctas, si involvantur obscenius, casta confestim gymnasiarchorum virga dissolvit. 7. Quid plura? Nihil illis paginis impressum reperietur, quod non vidisse sit sanctius. Pauci tamen versiculi lectorem adventicium remorabuntur minime improbo temperamento, quia eos nec relegisse desiderio est nec perlegisse fastidio. Iam, si marmora inquiras, non illic quidem Paros, Carystos, Proconnesos, Phryges, Numidae, Spartiatae rupium variatarum posuere crustas; neque per scopulos Aethiopicos et abrupta purpurea genuino fucata conchylio sparsum mihi saxa furfurem mentiuntur. Sed etsi nullo peregrinarum cautium rigore ditamur, habent tamen tuguria seu mapalia mea civicum frigus. Quin potius quid habeamus quam quid non habeamus ausculta. 8. Huic basilicae appendix piscina forinsecus seu, si graecari mavis, baptisterium ab oriente conectitur, quod viginti circiter modiorum milia capit. Huc elutis e calore venientibus triplex medii parietis aditus per arcuata intervalla reseratur. Nec pilae sunt mediae sed columnae, quas architecti peritiores 'aedificiorum purpuras' nuncupavere. In hanc ergo piscinam fluvium de supercilio montis elicitum canalibusque circumactis

to fall. Here rises the room with hot water, which is the same size as the following anointing room except for a spacious tub shaped in a semicircle, where a powerful hot stream enclosed by the bends of the pliant lead-piping gurgles through the pierced wall. Inside the room, which is heated from below, there is full daylight and, indeed, so much light that it forces modest people to think that they are more than naked.

5. Next the cool room stretches out, which without boasting can bear comparison with the pools built in public baths. First, the rooftop is pointed into a cone while the ridges, converging from the four corners, are covered with ridge-tiles and flat roof-tiles lie in between, so that there can be put as many seats as the couch has places and the slaves are not disturbing each other while they are working. The builder put two windows facing each other where roof and wall meet, so that a skilfully formed ceiling would present itself to the gaze of those looking up. The interior surface of the wall is simply covered with the plain white colour of the smoothed stone. 6. Here no shameful story is exposed through painted bodies in their naked beauty, which displays artfulness as it discredits the artist. There are no actors, ridiculous with their costumes and faces, who imitate Philistio's outfit with multicoloured paints. There are no slippery wrestlers, twisted around boxing and gripping, whose entangling the chaste rod of the master of the gym pulls apart even in real life, should they clasp each other too obscenely. 7. What more? You will not find anything impressed on this surface that would have been more virtuous not to have seen. A few little verses will delay the newly arrived reader with their far from naughty nature because you neither wish to reread them nor feel repugnance in reading them through. Now, if you were to ask about the marble: neither Paros, Carystos, Proconnesos, the Phrygians, Numidians nor Spartans have placed here their slabs of multicoloured stone; nor are there stones from the Ethiopian cliffs and slopes coloured purple by the native shell-fish, simulating for me the scattered bran. But although we are not rich with the chilliness of foreign stone, my huts and cottages have their local coolness. However, you should rather hear about what we have than about what we do not have. 8. Adjoining this hall on the eastern side is an open-air swimming pool, or, if you prefer speaking Greek, a *baptisterium*, which contains about twenty thousand *modii*. After having been washed really clean one comes from the heat hither through a triple passage in the middle of the wall whose intervals are arched. There are no pillars in between, but instead columns, which experienced architects have called 'the purple of buildings'. Into this pool a stream pours down from the ridge of the mountain and it flows around in

per exteriora natatoriae latera curvatum sex fistulae prominentes leonum simulatis capitibus effundunt, quae temere ingressis veras dentium crates, meros oculorum furores, certas cervicum iubas imaginabuntur.

9. Hic si dominum seu domestica seu hospitalis turba circumstet, quia prae strepitu caduci fluminis mutuae vocum vices minus intelleguntur, in aurem sibi populus confabulatur; ita sonitu pressus alieno ridiculum affectat publicus sermo secretum. Hinc egressis frons triclinii matronalis offertur, cui continuatur vicinante textrino cella penaria discriminata tantum pariete castrensi. 10. Ab ortu lacum porticus intuetur, magis rotundatis fulta collyriis quam columnis invidiosa monubilibus. A parte vestibuli longitudo tecta intrinsecus patet mediis non interpellata parietibus, quae, quia nihil ipsa prospectat, etsi non 'hypodromus', saltim 'cryptoporticus' meo mihi iure vocitabitur. Haec tamen aliquid spatio suo in extimo deambulacri capite defrudans efficit membrum bene frigidum, ubi publico lectisternio exstructo clientularum sive nutricum loquacissimus chorus receptui canit, cum ego meique dormitorium cubiculum petierimus. 11. A cryptoporticu in hiemale triclinium venitur, quod arcuatili camino saepe ignis animatus pulla fuligine infecit. Sed quid haec tibi, quem nunc ad focum minime invito? Quin potius ad te tempusque pertinentia loquar. Ex hoc triclinio fit in diaetam sive cenatiunculam transitus, cui fere totus lacus quaeque tota lacui patet. In hac stibadium et nitens abacus, in quorum aream sive suggestum a subiecta porticu sensim non breviatis angustatisque gradibus ascenditur. Quo loci recumbens, si quid inter edendum vacas, prospiciendi voluptatibus occuparis. 12. Iam si tibi ex illo conclamatissimo fontium decocta referatur, videbis in calicibus repente perfusis nivalium maculas et frusta nebularum et illam lucem lubricam poculorum quadam quasi pinguedine subiti algoris hebetatam. Tum respondentes poculis potiones, quarum rigentes cyathi siticuloso cuique, ne dicam tibi granditer abstemio, metuerentur. Hinc iam spectabis, ut promoveat alnum piscator in pelagus, ut stataria retia suberinis corticibus extendat aut signis per certa intervalla dispositis tractus funium librentur hamati, scilicet ut nocturnis per lacum excursibus rapacissimi

curved canals at the side of the pool through six protruding pipes that end in lion heads, which are so similar to nature that for someone who enters casually there seems to be a real row of teeth, pure fury in the eyes and a proper mane on the neck.

9. Here, when the crowd of one's own people or of guests stands around the master of the house because the noise of the falling stream makes them less able to understand the words exchanged, the crowd speaks into each other's ears. So public conversation, harassed by the sound from outside, adopts an air of ridiculous secrecy. Once you leave this place you can see the front end of the ladies' dining room, to which a room for weaving is attached that is separated only by a partition from a storeroom. 10. On the east side there is a portico which overlooks the lake, and it is supported by rounded pillars rather than by monumental columns, which cause envy. At the side of the entrance-court there is a long covered hallway which is not divided by walls in between. Because there is no view, I will not call it a *hypodromus* but, to speak for myself, at least with some justice, a *cryptoporticus*. This passage, though, cuts a bit off at the far end and thereby builds a nicely cooled room, which the talkative choir of poor wards and nurses use to retreat into and enjoy a common dinner, while I go with my family to the bedchamber. 11. From the *cryptoporticus* one comes into the winter dining room, which is dark with soot from the fire that is often lit in the bow-formed furnace. But why do I tell you this, as it is really not the hearth I am inviting you to? I should rather talk about things that suit you and the season. From this dining room there is a passage into a parlour or little dining room, from which the whole lake opens out and which is completely open toward the lake. In this room is a couch and a splendid table. You walk in this area or rather platform from the portico that lies below it by steps which are not made either short or narrow. Reclined here, if you have some time during the meal, you will be occupied by the pleasure of looking out. 12. When a cold drink is brought to you from this very famous fountain, you will find in the suddenly filled goblets pieces of snow and bits of mist, and how the slippery lustre of the cups is dulled by some sort of film from the sudden cold. And then there are drinks that match the cups, of whose cold ladles every drinker is wary of, but I do not need to tell you this as you are very sober. From here you will also watch how a fisherman steers his boat onto the lake and puts out gill nets with pieces of the cork-tree or how lengths of rope with hooks are balanced by floats set out at fixed intervals. For the purpose, of course, that the predatory trout on their nightly forays through the lake are lured by bait

salares in consanguineas agantur insidias: quid enim hinc congruentius dixerim, cum piscis pisce decipitur?

13. Edulibus terminatis excipiet te deversorium, quia minime aestuosum, maxime aestivum. Nam per hoc, quod in Aquilonem solum patescit, habet diem, non habet solem, interiecto consistorio perangusto, ubi somnulentiae cubiculariorum dormitandi potius quam dormiendi locus est. 14. Hic iam quam volupe auribus insonare cicadas meridie concrepantes, ranas crepusculo incumbente blaterantes, cygnos atque anseres concubia nocte clangentes, intempesta gallos gallinacios concinentes, oscines corvos voce triplicata puniceam surgentis Aurorae facem consalutantes, diluculo autem Philomelam inter frutices sibilantem, Prognen inter asseres minurientem! Cui concentui licebit adiungas fistulae septiforis armentalem Camenam, quam saepe nocturnis carminum certaminibus insomnes nostrorum montium Tityri exercent, inter greges tinnibulatos per depasta buceta reboantes. Quae tamen varia vocum cantuumque modulamina profundius confovendo sopori tuo lenocinabuntur. 15. Porticibus egresso, si portum litoris petas, in area virenti vulgare, quamquam non procul nemus: ingentes tiliae duae conexis frondibus, fomitibus abiunctis unam umbram non una radice conficiunt. In cuius opacitate, cum me meus Ecdicius inlustrat, pilae vacamus, sed hoc eo usque, donec arborum imago contractior intra spatium ramorum recussa cohibeatur atque illic aleatorium lassis consumpto sphaeristerio faciat.

16. Sed quia tibi, sicut aedificium solvi, sic lacum debeo, quod restat agnosce. Lacus in Eurum defluus meat, eiusque harenis fundamenta impressa domicilii ventis motantibus aestuans umectat alluvio. Is quidem sane circa principia sui solo palustri voraginosus et vestigio inspectoris inadibilis: ita limi bibuli pinguedo coalescit ambientibus sese fontibus algidis, litoribus algosis. Attamen pelagi mobilis campus cumbulis late secatur pervagabilibus, si flabra posuere; si turbo austrinus insorduit, immane turgescit, ita ut arborum comis, quae margini insistunt, superiectae asperginis fragor impluat.

17. Ipse autem secundum mensuras quas ferunt nauticas in decem et septem stadia procedit, fluvio intratus, qui salebratim saxorum obicibus affractus spumoso canescit impulsu et nec longum scopulis praecipitibus exemptus lacu

consisting of their relatives. How could I express it more fittingly, when one fish is literally caught by another?

13. After you have finished your meal, a lodging place expects you, which is not hot and therefore perfect for summer. Because it opens only to the north, it admits daylight, but not sunshine. In between lies a very narrow room for the slaves, rather a place to keep falling asleep than to sleep for the drowsy chamber-slaves. 14. Now, what a pleasure we have here for the ears, when the chirring cicadas are resounding at noon, the croaking frogs as dusk falls, the honking swans and geese when everybody is sleeping and the crowing cocks in the middle of the night, the prophetic ravens greeting with their triple caw the purple torch of the rising dawn, at dawn the whistling nightingale between the bushes and the chirping swallow on the posts. You can add to this concert the shepherd's song on the seven-holed pipe, which the sleepless Tityruses of our mountains play in nightly song contest amid their jingling flocks which re-echo over the grazed pasture. Yet all these different sounds of voices and songs will allure and foster your sleep. 15. If you leave the portico, and make for the port at the shore, you come into an open green space with a grove nearby. Two huge lime trees with their entwined leaves and separated branches give one shared shade, even though they do not have the same root. In its shadow, if my Ecdicius brightens my life by visiting, we spend our leisure time playing ball, but only until the shadow of the trees is cast in a narrower space between the branches and is so confined that it gives just enough room there for the tired players to have a game of dice after the space for ball play is used up.

16. But while I have described the building to you, I still owe you a description of the lake. So hear what remains. The lake flows towards the east, and a raging inundation, if it is moved by strong winds, moistens the foundations of my house, which are pressed into its sand. At its beginnings it is full of eddies because of the muddy soil and inaccessible to the step of an observer: in such a way does the fat, dank mud come together in a competition of frigid streams and algae-covered shores. However, the moving surface of the lake gets carved by boats sweeping across it far and wide, but only if the blasts of the wind have decreased. If a southern whirlwind darkens, it keeps swelling so fiercely that a crash of falling spray rains down on the leaves of the trees that stand at the edge.

17. The lake itself extends over seventeen *stades* according to the measure they call nautical. It is entered by a river, which is roughly blocked by scattered rocks and shines white with foam from the impact and after a short run is released from the steep crags and hidden in the lake. If it

conditur; quem fors fuat an incurrat an faciat, praeterit certe, coactus per cola subterranea deliquari, non ut fluctibus, sed ut piscibus pauperaretur; qui repulsi in gurgitem pigriorem carnes rubras albis abdominibus extendunt: ita illis nec redire valentibus nec exire permissis quendam vivum et circumlaticium carcerem corpulentia facit. 18. Lacus ipse, qua dexter, incisus flexuosus nemorosusque, qua laevus, patens herbosus aequalis. Aequor ab Africo viride per litus, quia in undam fronde porrecta ut glareas aqua, sic aquas umbra perfundit. Huiusmodi colorem ab oriente par silvarum corona continuat. Per Arctoum latus ut pelago natura, sic species. A Zephyro plebeius et tumultuarius frutex frequenterque lemborum superlabentum ponderibus inflexus; hunc circa lubrici scirporum cirri plicantur simulque pingues ulvarum paginae natant salicumque glaucarum fota semper dulcibus aquis amaritudo. 19. In medio profundi brevis insula, ubi supra molares naturaliter aggeratos per impactorum puncta remorum navalibus trita gyris meta protuberat, ad quam se iucunda ludentum naufragia collidunt. Nam moris istic fuit senioribus nostris agonem Drepanitanum Troianae superstitionis imitari. Iam vero ager ipse, quamquam hoc supra debitum, diffusus in silvis, pictus in pratis, pecorosus in pascuis, in pastoribus peculiosus.

20. Sed non amplius moror, ne, si longior stilo terminus, relegentem te autumnus inveniat. Proinde mihi tribue veniendi celeritatem (nam redeundi moram tibi ipse praestabis), daturus hinc veniam, quod brevitatem sibi debitam paulo scrupulosior epistula excessit, dum totum ruris situm sollicita rimatur; quae tamen summovendi fastidii studio nec cuncta perstrinxit. Quapropter bonus arbiter et artifex lector non paginam, quae spatia describit, sed villam, quae spatiosa describitur, grandem pronuntiabunt. Vale.

happens to end in the lake or create it, I do not know, but the river certainly flows through the lake. Its water is forced to flow through some kind of underground fish traps, so it is not deprived of its waters, but of its fish. The fishes are driven into calmer water and there enlarge their red flesh by filling their white bellies. Thus they cannot swim back nor leave, and their corpulence turns into a living prison they are carrying around with them. 18. The lake's right bank is indented, bayed and wooded; on the left bank it is open, grassy and uniform. Its surface is green on the south-west side near the shore because the leaves hang over the water and, as the waters cover the gravel, so the shade covers the waters. A similar crowd of trees makes the colour continuous on the eastern side. On the northern side, the lake is like the sea in its nature and appearance. In the west there is low scrub that grows uncontrolled, often pressed down by the weight of the vessels that glide over it. Around it the soft tufts of bulrushes are folded, the thick sheets of the swamp-grass float and the bitter grey willows are ever nourished by the sweet water. 19. In the middle of the lake, where the water is deep, there is also a small island, where above large blocks of stone, piled up by nature, a post sticks out, marked by the indentations of the oars that hit it during the naval races. At this place the players collide in mock shipwrecks. Here it was the custom for our forebears to imitate the contest of Drepana according to the Trojan religious rite. Now I want to describe the land, even though this is more than I promised to tell. It is overspread with woods, coloured with meadows, rich in cattle on its pastures and remunerative for its herdsmen.

20. But I will not delay any longer, so that autumn does not find you still reading if my pen is given a later deadline. Grant me the speed of your arrival (for you will grant yourself a longer period for your return home) and you will forgive me from here for the fact that my somewhat too detailed letter has exceeded the brevity befitting it while it has examined my whole estate carefully, but to avoid boredom, has not touched on everything after all. Accordingly, a just judge and a skilful reader will not give the letter, which describes the space, but the estate, which is spaciously described, the designation 'grandiose'. Goodbye.

Epistula 3

Sidonius Felici suo salutem.

1. Gaudeo te, domine maior, amplissimae dignitatis infulas consecutum. Sed id mihi ob hoc solum destinato tabellario nuntiatum non minus gaudeo. Nam licet in praesentiarum sis potissimus magistratus et in lares Philagrianos patricius apex tantis post saeculis tua tantum felicitate remeaverit, invenis tamen, vir amicitiarum servantissime, qualiter honorum tuorum crescat communione fastigium, raroque genere exempli altitudinem tuam humilitate sublimas.

2. Sic quondam Quintum Fabium magistrum equitum dictatorio rigori et Papirianae superbiae favor publicus praetulit; sic et Gnaeum Pompeium super aemulos extulit numquam fastidita popularitas; sic invidiam Tiberianam pressit universitatis amore Germanicus. Quocirca nolo sibi de successibus tuis principalia beneficia plurimum blandiantur, quae nihil tibi amplius conferre potuerunt, quam ut si id noluissemus, transiremus inviti. Illud peculiare tuum est, illud gratiae singularis, quod tam qui te aemulentur non habes quam non invenis qui sequantur. Vale.

Epistula 3

Sidonius greets his dear Felix

1. I am pleased, noble sir, that you received the insignia of highest rank. But I am no less pleased that you have sent me a messenger to pass on the news for that reason alone. Even though you are in the current state of affairs the most influential of all magistrates and the honorary title of *patricius* has returned to the home of the Philagrii after such long ages because of your felicity alone, still, as a man so dedicated to your friendships, you find how the pinnacle of your honours grows through sharing them, and in a rare type of example you elevate your dignity through your humility.

2. In this way public opinion preferred Quintus Fabius, the master of the horse, over Papirius' dictatorial rigour and arrogance. So too Gnaeus Pompeius' efforts to please the people, which he never stopped, lifted him above his rivals. And in this way Germanicus held the envious Tiberius at bay, supported by the love of one and all. Therefore, I do not want the imperial grace to flatter itself with the greatest part of your success: it could not have given you more than the fact that we would be being overruled unwillingly if we had not wanted this. This is your characteristic feature, this is the reason for your extraordinary popularity; neither do you have anybody to rival you nor can you find those who are able to follow you. Goodbye.

Epistula 4

Sidonius Sagittario suo salutem.

1. Vir clarissimus Proiectus, domi nobilis et patre patruoque spectabilibus, avo etiam praestantissimo sacerdote conspicuus, amicitiarum tuarum, nisi respuis, avidissime sinibus infertur, et cum illi familiae splendor, probitas morum, patrimonii facultas, iuventutis alacritas in omne decus pari lance conquadrent, ita demum sibi tamen videbitur ad arcem fastigatissimae felicitatis evectus, si gratiae tuae sodalitate potiatur. 2. Optantii clarissimi viri nuper vita functi filiam, quod Deo prosperante succedat, licet a matre pupillae in coniugium petierit obtinueritque, parum tamen votorum suorum promotum censet effectum, nisi assensum tuum super his omnibus seu sedulitate sua seu precatu nostrae intercessionis adipiscatur. Namque ipse, quantum ad institutionem spectat puellae, in locum mortui patris curarum participatione succedis, conferendo virgini parentis affectum, patroni auctoritatem, tutoris officium. 3. Quocirca, quia dignus es, ut domus tuae celeberrimam disciplinam etiam procul positorum petat ambitus, sicut decet bonarum partium viros, benignitate responsi proci supplicis verecundiam munerare et, qui ita expetitus deberes illi expetere pollicendam, securus permitte promissam; quia sic te condicioni huic meritorum ratio praefecit, ut nec superstiti Optantio in liberos suos decuerit plus licere. Vale.

Epistula 4

Sidonius greets his dear Sagittarius

1. The *vir clarissimus* Proiectus, a noble in his locality, his father and a paternal uncle being bestowed with the title *spectabilis*, and also notable because of his grandfather, a famous priest, is eager to enter the embrace of your friendship, if you are not averse. And though his family's splendour, the probity of his character, the amplitude of his inheritance, and the alacrity of his youth agree in like manner to perfect glory, he will see himself as having finally be raised to the pinnacles of loftiest fortune, if he should obtain your companionable favour. 2. Even though he asked for, and received, permission to marry the daughter of the recently deceased *vir clarissimus* Optantius from her mother as guardian – which I hope will turn out well with the help of God – he is nevertheless of the opinion that the fulfilment of his wishes is not promoted enough if he does not obtain your consent for this whole matter, either through his own assiduity or through the medium of my pleas. For it is you, as far as the girl's upbringing is concerned, who takes the place of her deceased father and shares his concern for her, offering the young woman the love of a parent, the authority of a patron and the sense of duty of a guardian. 3. So, because you deserve the solicitude even of people from far away who seek out the well-known order of your house – this befits men who belong to the side of the good – please present the modest and suppliant suitor with a kind answer. If you had been requested you would have needed to ask the girl, yet to be promised, on his behalf; as it is you can without concern hand over the girl already promised. This is because the extent of your merits puts you in such a key position in the matter of this marriage, that not even Optantius, if he were still alive, could have a better right to decide about his children. Goodbye.

Epistula 5

Sidonius Petronio suo salutem.

1. Iohannes familiaris meus inextricabilem labyrinthum negotii multiplicis incurrit et donec suarum merita chartarum vel vestra scientia vel si qua est vestrae (si tamen est ulla) similis inspexerit, quid respuat, quid optet ignorat. Ita se quodammodo bipertitae litis forma confundit, ut propositio sua quem actionis ordinem propugnatura, quem sit impugnatura non noverit. 2. Pro quo precem sedulam fundo, ut perspectis chartulis suis, si quid iure competit, instruatis, quae qualiterve sint obicienda, quae refellenda monstrantes. Non enim verebimur, quod causae istius cursus, si de vestri manaverit fonte consilii, ulla contrastantum derivatione tenuetur. Vale.

Epistula 5

Sidonius greets his dear Petronius

1. Iohannes, a close friend of mine, is lost in an inextricable labyrinth of a complicated affair, and until you with your expertise or someone that has similar expertise (if that even exists) examines the merits of his papers, he does not know what he should reject and what he should choose. The nature of this bipartite legal dispute is so mixed up that in the statement of the facts he does not know at all which line of argumentation to support and which to oppose. 2. On his behalf I eagerly beg you to check his documents and to instruct him, if he demands rightfully, what he can obstruct in his defence and in what manner, and what he must refute. For I will not have to fear that the course of the process, if it has sprung from the source of your advice, has a chance of drying up through some diversionary manoeuvre of his opponents. Goodbye.

Epistula 6

Sidonius Pegasio suo salutem.

1. Proverbialiter celebre est saepe moram esse meliorem, sicuti et nunc experti sumus. Menstruanus amicus tuus longo istic tempore inspectus meruit inter personas nobis quoque caras devinctasque censeri, opportunus elegans, verecundus sobrius, parcus religiosus et his morum dotibus praeditus, ut, quotiens in boni cuiusque adscitur amicitias, non amplius consequatur beneficii ipse quam tribuat. 2. Haec tibi non ut ignoranti, sed ut iudicio meo satisfacerem, scripsi. Quam ob rem triplex causa laetandi: tibi prima, cui amicos sic aut instituere aut eligere contingit; Arvernis secunda, quibus hoc in eo placuisse confirmo, quod te probasse non ambigo; illi tertia, de quo boni quique bona quaeque iudicaverunt. Vale.

Epistula 6

Sidonius greets his dear Pegasius

1. It is a famous saying that good things take time; this is what I too experienced recently. Your friend Menstruanus, whom I have watched here for a long time, has proved worthy to be counted among the persons who are dear to us and completely devoted. He is helpful and elegant, modest and sober, frugal and pious and endowed with such gifts of character that, if he obtains the friendship of some excellent man, he does not acquire more benefit than he can himself offer. 2. I did not write you this because you do not know it, but to justify my opinion. That is why there are three reasons to be happy: first for you, because you manage to either train up or choose good friends in this way; secondly for the Arvernians, whom I can confirm were pleased by this quality of his, which I am not unaware that you approved of; and thirdly for him: all good men think only good things of him. Goodbye.

Epistula 7

Sidonius Explicio suo salutem.

1. Quia iustitia vestra iure fit universitati per conplura recti experimenta venerabilis, idcirco singulas quasque personas id ipsum efflagitantes in examen vestrum libens et avidus emitto, quam primum ambiens me discussionis, illos simultatis onere laxari; quod demum ita sequetur, si non ex solido querimonias partium verecundus censor excludas: quamquam et hoc ipsum, quod copiam tui iurgantibus difficile concedis, indicium sit bene iudicaturi. Quis enim se non ambiat arbitrum legi aut pretio aliquid indulturus aut gratiae? 2. Igitur ignosce ad tam sanctae conscientiae praerogativam raptim perniciterque properantibus, quandoquidem sententiam tuam nec victus ut stolidus accusat nec victor ut argutus inridet, veritatisque respectu dependunt tibi addicti reverentiam, gratiam liberati. Proinde inpense obsecro, ut inter Alethium et Paulum quae veniunt in disceptationem, mox ut utrimque fuerint opposita, discingas. Namque, ni fallor, supra decemvirales pontificalesque sententias, aegritudini huius prope interminabilis iurgii sola morum tuorum temperantia solita iudicandi salubritate medicabitur. Vale.

Epistula 7

Sidonius greets his dear Explicius

1. Since your justice has rightly become admirable to all through multiple experiences of your righteous behaviour, I therefore gladly and eagerly send any individual persons to your arbitration, when they demand this urgently themselves. I ask that as soon as possible you release me from the examination of their case and them from that of their enmity. And it will happen in this way, if as a modest censor you do not completely deny both parties' complaints; though also the very fact that you do not want to offer your help easily for the disputants is a sign of your good judgement. After all, who would not seek to be elected arbitrator if he was willing to be compliant in exchange for money or other gratitude? 2. Therefore forgive those who are running hastily to the privilege of your sacred conscience, since neither do losers lament your verdict as if they have been foolish, nor do victors smile as if they have been clever. Because they respect truthfulness, the convicted have reverence for you and the exonerated express their gratitude. That is why I beg you urgently to settle the dispute coming to judgement between Alethius and Paulus, as soon as both plead their cases. I think I am right to believe that the moderation of your character will heal the sickness of this virtually interminable dispute better than the decisions of the *decemviri* and pontiffs, thanks to the habitual good sense of your judgement. Goodbye.

Epistula 8

Sidonius Desiderato suo salutem.

1. Maestissimus haec tibi nuntio. Decessit nudius tertius non absque iustitio matrona Filimatia, morigera coniunx, domina clemens, utilis mater, pia filia, cui debuerit domi forisque persona minor obsequium, maior officium, aequalis affectum. Haec cum esset unica iam diu matris amissae, facile diversis blandimentorum generibus effecerat, ne patri adhuc iuveni subolis sexus alterius desideraretur. Nunc autem per subita suprema virum caelibatu, patrem orbitate confodit. His additur, quod quinque liberum parens immaturo exitu reddidit infortunatam fecunditatem. Qui parvuli si matre sospite perdidissent iam diu debilem patrem, minus pupilli existimarentur. 2. Hanc tamen, si quis haud incassum honor cadaveribus impenditur, non vispillonum sandapilariorumque ministeria ominosa tumulavere; sed cum libitinam ipsam flentes omnes, externi quoque, prensitarent remorarentur exoscularentur, sacerdotum propinquorumque manibus excepta perpetuis sedibus dormienti similior inlata est. Post quae precatu parentis orbati neniam funebrem non per elegos sed per hendecasyllabos marmori incisam planctu prope calente dictavi. Quam si non satis improbas, ceteris epigrammatum meorum voluminibus applicandam mercennarius bybliopola suscipiet; si quid secus, sufficit saxo carmen saxeum contineri. 3. Hoc enim epitaphion est:

> Occasu celeri feroque raptam
> natis quinque patrique coniugique
> hoc flentis patriae manus locarunt
> matronam Filimatiam sepulchro.
> O splendor generis, decus mariti, 5
> prudens, casta, decens, severa, dulcis
> atque ipsis senioribus sequenda,

Epistula 8

Sidonius greets his dear Desideratus

1. It is with the greatest sadness that I inform you of the following. Three days ago the lady Filimatia died and all business was suspended in mourning for her. She was an accommodating wife, a merciful mistress, a helpful mother, a dutiful daughter, who was due the obedience of younger persons inside the house and outside, the respect of her seniors and love of her peers. Even though she was the only child of a mother long gone, with her various forms of kindness she easily ensured that her father, still young, did not feel the lack of a child of the other sex. With her sudden death, though, she gave her husband the pain of singleness and her father of childlessness. In addition, the mother of five children turned her fertility into misfortune through her early death. If these young children had lost their already feeble father while their mother had been unharmed, they would seem less orphaned. 2. But at least – if we do not honour the bodies of dead in vain – she was not buried by the portentous services of undertakers and corpse-bearers. Instead, while everyone, even outsiders, were crying and trying to touch the bier, to hold it back and even to kiss it, she was carried by the hands of the priests and her relatives and, looking more as if she were asleep, was laid to rest in her last bed. After this I wrote a funerary dirge at her bereaved father's request, not in elegiac distiches, but in verses of eleven syllables, which was engraved on marble while grief was still raw. If you do not wholly disapprove, the hired scribe will take it to add to the other volumes of my poems; if you think otherwise, it is enough that the stony poem is set in stone. 3. This is my epitaph:

> She was seized by a sudden cruel death
> from her five children, her father and husband
> and the hands of her weeping homeland put
> the matron Filimatia in this grave.
> O you, glory of your whole family, your husband's ornament,   5
> prudent, chaste, decent, severe, sweet
> and a model even for elders,

discordantia quae solent putari
morum commoditate copulasti:
nam vitae comites bonae fuerunt 10
libertas gravis et pudor facetus.
Hinc est quod decimam tuae saluti
vix actam trieteridem dolemus
atque in temporibus vigentis aevi
iniuste tibi iusta persoluta. 15

Placeat tibi carmen necne: tu propera civitatemque festinus invise. Debes enim consolationis officium duorum civium domibus afflictis. Quod ita solvas deum quaeso, ne umquam tibi redhibeatur. Vale.

characteristics generally thought contradictory
you combined through your amiability of character.
For accompanying you in your good life   10
were dignified freedom of speech and eloquent modesty.
That is why we grieve for your life
after you barely completed your tenth triad of years,
and in the prime of your life
the deserved honours are undeservedly performed for you.   15

Whether you like the poem or not: please hurry and visit our city quickly. You need to render the service of consolation to the families of two citizens severely hit. I pray to God that you do this without anybody doing you the same favour. Goodbye.

Epistula 9

Sidonius Donidio suo salutem.

1. Quaeris, cur ipse iam pridem Nemausum profectus vestra serum ob adventum desideria producam. Reddo causas reditus tardioris nec moras meas prodere moror, quia quae mihi dulcia sunt tibi quoque. Inter agros amoenissimos, humanissimos dominos, Ferreolum et Apollinarem, tempus voluptuosissimum exegi. Praediorum his iura contermina, domicilia vicina, quibus interiecta gestatio peditem lassat neque sufficit equitaturo. Colles aedibus superiores exercentur vinitori et olivitori: Aracynthum et Nysam, celebrata poetarum carminibus iuga, censeas. Uni domui in plana patentiaque, alteri in nemora prospectus, sed nihilominus dissimilis situs similiter oblectat.

2. Quamquam de praediorum quid nunc amplius positione, cum restet hospitalitatis ordo reserandus? Iam primum sagacissimis in hoc exploratoribus destinatis, qui reditus nostri iter aucuparentur, domus utraque non solum tramites aggerum publicorum verum etiam calles compendiis tortuosos atque pastoria diverticula insedit, ne quo casu dispositis officiorum insidiis elaberemur. Quas incidimus, fateor, sed minime invite, iusque iurandum confestim praebere compulsi, ne, priusquam septem dies evolverentur, quicquam de itineris nostri continuatione meditaremur. 3. Igitur mane cotidiano partibus super hospite prima et grata contentio, quaenam potissimum anterius edulibus nostris culina fumaret; nec sane poterat ex aequo divisioni lancem ponere vicissitudo, licet uni domui mecum, alteri cum meis vinculum foret propinquitatis, quia Ferreolo praefectorio viro praeter necessitudinem sibi debitam dabat aetas et dignitas primi invitatoris praerogativam.

4. Ilicet a deliciis in delicias rapiebamur. Vix quodcumque vestibulum intratum, et ecce huc sphaeristarum contrastantium paria inter rotatiles catastropharum gyros duplicabantur, huc inter aleatoriarum vocum competitiones frequens crepitantium

Epistula 9

Sidonius greets his dear Donidius

1. You ask why, even though I already set off for Nîmes a long time ago, I prolong your desire to see me with my tardiness in arriving. I will tell you the reasons for my late return and I do not hesitate to explain my hesitation, because everything I like, you like too. Amid the most wonderful estates, among their most hospitable owners, Ferreolus and Apollinaris, I have spent a most pleasurable period. Their estates have a common border, their houses are close, the walk between them tires the walker, but is not worth riding a horse for. The hills above the houses are cultivated by vine-dressers and olive-dressers. You would think they were Aracynthus and Nysa, mountains praised by poets in their poems. One house has a prospect on to open plains, the other into the woods, but nonetheless the dissimilar sites are similarly delightful.

2. But why in fact should I talk more about the site of the estates, if there is still to tell about the sequence of the hospitality? First of all, the most shrewd scouts were sent out to watch for the route of our return; both households not only waited on the public roads, but also the footpaths, full of turns and short-cuts, and the shepherds' by-ways, so there was not the slightest chance we could escape the meticulous ambush of hospitality. I fell into this trap, I must admit, but not at all against my will, and we immediately had to swear that we would not even think about continuing our journey until seven days had passed. 3. Therefore there was every morning an early but agreeable contest between the two parties over their guest, in particular whose kitchen could first emit smoke for our meals. Nor for sure could a rotation have fairly shared this right, even though the one house had close ties with me, the other with my relatives, because Ferreolus had, as a former prefect as well as being next of kin, the prerogative of inviting first because of his age and dignity.

4. Instantly, we were rushed from delight to delight. I had hardly entered one or the other entrance court, and there on one side were pairs of opposing ball players, who were bent double as they ran in circles throwing the ball. On the other side one could hear the noise of clattering dice and dice cups

fritillorum tesserarumque strepitus audiebatur; huc libri affatim in promptu (videre te crederes aut grammaticales pluteos aut Athenaei cuneos aut armaria extructa bybliopolarum); sic tamen quod, qui inter matronarum cathedras codices erant, stilus his religiosus inveniebatur, qui vero per subsellia patrumfamilias, hi coturno Latiaris eloquii nobilitabantur; licet quaepiam volumina quorumpiam auctorum servarent in causis disparibus dicendi parilitatem: nam similis scientiae viri, hinc Augustinus hinc Varro, hinc Horatius hinc Prudentius lectitabantur.

5. Quos inter Adamantius Origenes Turranio Rufino interpretatus sedulo fidei nostrae lectoribus inspiciebatur; pariter et, prout singulis cordi, diversa censentes sermocinabamur, cur a quibusdam protomystarum tamquam scaevus cavendusque tractator improbaretur, quamquam sic esset ad verbum sententiamque translatus, ut nec Apuleius Phaedonem sic Platonis neque Tullius Ctesiphontem sic Demosthenis in usum regulamque Romani sermonis exscripserint.

6. Studiis hisce dum nostrum singuli quique, prout libuerat, occupabantur, ecce et ab archimagiro adventans, qui tempus instare curandi corpora moneret, quem quidem nuntium per spatia clepsydrae horarum incrementa servantem probabat competenter ingressum quinta digrediens. Prandebamus breviter copiose, senatorium ad morem, quo insitum institutumque multas epulas paucis paropsidibus apponi, quamvis convivium per edulia nunc assa, nunc iurulenta varietur. Inter bibendum narratiunculae, quarum cognitu hilararemur, institueremur, quia eas bifariam orditas laetitia peritiaque comitabantur. Quid multa? Sancte pulchre abundanter accipiebamur.

7. Inde surgentes, si Vorocingi eramus (hoc uni praedio nomen), ad sarcinas et deversorium pedem referebamus; si Prusiani (sic fundus alter nuncupabatur), Tonantium cum fratribus, lectissimos aequaevorum nobilium principes, stratis suis eiciebamus, quia nec facile crebro cubilium nostrorum instrumenta circumferebantur. Excusso torpore meridiano paulisper equitabamus, quo facilius pectora marcida cibis cenatoriae fami exacueremus.

amid the competing shouting of the dice players. Elsewhere books were abundantly to hand (one could believe one was seeing the bookshelves of a grammar-school teacher, the wedge-shaped tiers of the Athenaeum or the filled chests of a bookseller). The books were arranged in such a way that around the armchairs of the ladies were the volumes of religious literature, while those near the benches of the heads of the family were distinguished by the high style of Latin eloquence; nevertheless, any book by any author had the same literary quality despite different content. Thus men of similar skills, for example Augustine here and Varro there, or Horace here and Prudentius there were frequently read.

5. Among these Adamantius Origen in the translation of Tyrannius Rufinus was diligently consulted by readers of our faith; and together we gave our different opinions according to our individual feelings, and we discussed why Origen was criticised by certain priests of the mystic rites as a misguided exegete that one should avoid, even though his works had been translated so accurately in word and sense that neither Apuleius' translation of Plato's *Phaedo* nor Tullius' translation of Demosthenes' *Ctesiphon* can match them in respect of the usage and rules of the Roman language.

6. While everyone was occupied with these activities according to individual preferences, there came a messenger from the head chef, who admonished us that it was time to care about our physical well-being. The fifth hour was just over and agreed with the messenger, who had observed the passing of time with the help of the water clock and thus came in at the right time. We had a short but abundant lunch in the way senators have, whereby it is ingrained and traditional to bring in many courses on a few platters. Nonetheless, the meal is varied with grilled and boiled food. While we were drinking, stories were told which were entertaining and instructive at the same time, because they were created from two places, wit and wisdom. What more can I say? We were entertained with style, taste and abundance.

7. After we left the table, and when we were at Vorocingus (this was the name of one of the estates), we went to our own luggage at the apartment for guests; when we were at Prusianum (that was the name of the other estate), we had to dislodge Tonantius and his brothers, the first and best of the nobles of their age, from their beds, because it would not have been easy to transport our bedclothes around often. After we shook off the midday tiredness we went out for a little ride, so that we could more easily stimulate our stomachs, which were sluggish from the food, to be hungry for dinner.

8. Balneas habebat in opere uterque hospes, in usu neuter; sed cum vel pauxillulum bibere desisset assecularum meorum famulorumque turba conpotrix, quorum cerebris hospitales craterae nimium immersae dominabantur, vicina fonti aut fluvio raptim scrobis fodiebatur, in quam forte cum lapidum cumulus ambustus demitteretur, antro in hemisphaerii formam corylis flexilibus intexto fossa inardescens operiebatur, sic tamen, ut superiectis Cilicum velis patentia intervalla virgarum lumine excluso tenebrarentur, vaporem repulsura salientem, qui undae ferventis aspergine flammatis silicibus excuditur. 9. Hic nobis trahebantur horae non absque sermonibus salsis iocularibusque; quos inter halitu nebulae stridentis oppletis involutisque saluberrimus sudor eliciebatur; quo, prout libuisset, effuso coctilibus aquis ingerebamur harumque fotu cruditatem nostram tergente resoluti aut fontano deinceps frigore putealique aut fluviali copia solidabamur: siquidem domibus medius it Vardo fluvius, nisi cum deflua nive pastus inpalluit, flavis ruber glareis et per alveum perspicuus quietus calculosusque neque ob hoc minus piscium ferax delicatorum.

10. Dicerem et cenas et quidem unctissimas, nisi terminum nostrae loquacitati, quem verecundia non adhibet, charta posuisset; quarum quoque replicatio fieret amoena narratu, nisi epistulae tergum madidis sordidare calamis erubesceremus. Sed quia et ipsi in procinctu sumus teque sub ope Christi actutum nobis invisere placet, expeditius tibi cenae amicorum in mea cena tuaque commemorabuntur, modo nos quam primum hebdomadis exactae spatia completa votivae restituant esuritioni, quia disruptum ganea stomachum nulla sarcire res melius quam parsimonia solet. Vale.

8. Both of my hosts had a bathhouse under construction, neither of them in use. But as the drinking crowd of my entourage and the local slaves stopped their drinking for a moment – their brains were ruled by the hospitable bowls which were filled all too often – then a pit was hastily dug near a spring or river; into it a heap of stones heated all around was thrown haphazardly, and then the pit as it heated up was covered by a cave woven from flexible branches into the shape of a hemisphere; so that, when a covering of goat skin was thrown over it, the still open gaps between the branches were closed and daylight excluded in order to keep in the rising steam, which is generated from the spray of the water, seething from the inflamed stones. 9. Here we used to spend hours not without witty and jocular chat, and meanwhile we were covered by and wrapped in the hissing steam and mist, and a healthy sweat was drawn out of us. When we had poured out as much as we liked, we dived into the hot water and, as soon as its warmth had cleansed our indigestion and made us all soft, we made ourselves firm again in the cold of a spring, a well or the river's flow: since halfway between the two estates passes the River Vardo, which, except when white because fed on melting snow, is reddish from its golden gravel and runs clear, peaceful and pebbly over its bed and is nevertheless rich with delicious fish.

10. I would love to write about the dinners – and very sumptuous they were too – if the writing paper did not stop my loquacity, which my modesty fails to do. Telling about these dinners and thereby repeating them would be a nice subject, if I were not embarrassed to dirty the reverse of the letter with my drunk reed-pen. But because I am ready to travel and I am looking forward to seeing you soon with Christ's help, my dinners with my friends will be more conveniently remembered when you and I have dinner together. I just hope the interval of a full week puts me back into the desired hungry state as soon as possible, since nothing is better than fasting to restore a stomach that has almost burst from gluttony. Goodbye.

Epistula 10

Sidonius Hesperio suo salutem.

1. Amo in te quod litteras amas et usquequaque praeconiis cumulatissimis excolere contendo tantae diligentiae generositatem, per quam nobis non solum initia tua verum etiam studia nostra commendas. Nam cum videmus in huiusmodi disciplinam iuniorum ingenia succrescere, propter quam nos quoque subduximus ferulae manum, copiosissimum fructum nostri laboris adipiscimur. Illud appone, quod tantum increbruit multitudo desidiosorum, ut, nisi vel paucissimi quique meram linguae Latiaris proprietatem de trivialium barbarismorum robigine vindicaveritis, eam brevi abolitam defleamus interitamque; sic omnes nobilium sermonum purpurae per incuriam vulgi decolorabuntur. 2. Sed istinc alias: interea tu quod petis accipe. Petis autem, ut si qui versiculi mihi fluxerint, postquam ab alterutro discessimus, hos tibi pro quadam morarum mercede pernumerem. Dicto pareo; nam praeditus es quamquam iuvenis hac animi maturitate, ut tibi etiam natu priores gerere morem concupiscamus. Ecclesia nuper exstructa Lugduni est, quae studio papae Patientis summum coepti operis accessit, viri sancti strenui, severi misericordis, quique per uberem munificentiam in pauperes humanitatemque non minora bonae conscientiae culmina levet. 3. Huius igitur aedis extimis rogatu praefati antistitis tumultuarium carmen inscripsi trochaeis triplicibus adhuc mihi iamque tibi perfamiliaribus. Namque ab hexametris eminentium poetarum Constantii et Secundini vicinantia altari basilicae latera clarescunt, quos in hanc paginam admitti nostra quam maxume verecundia vetat, quam suas otiositates trepidanter edentem meliorum carminum comparatio premit. 4. Nam sicuti novam nuptam nihil minus quam pulchrior pronuba decet, sicuti, si vestiatur albo, fuscus quisque fit nigrior, sic nostra, quantula est cumque, tubis circumfusa potioribus stipula vilescit, quam

Epistula 10

Sidonius greets his dear Hesperius

1. I love it about you that you love literature, and I strive on every occasion to praise with the highest commendation the nobility of your great dedication, with which you not only recommend to us your own first attempts, but also my efforts. When I see the talents of the young prospering in fields of this sort, on account of which I too 'have pulled my hand away from the rod'; then I receive the richest reward for my work. Consider too that the multitude of idle people has so increased that, if there were not at least a very few people like you defending the pure and correct Latin language from the rust of everyday barbarisms, we would soon have to bewail its destruction and death. Thus all the purple of this noble language will lose its colour because of the people's negligence. 2. But let us talk another time about this. Meanwhile, you should get what you ask for. You ask that if some verses have flowed out of me since we last parted from each other, I should account them to you as payment for my tardiness. I obey your command: because even though you are still a young man, your mind is endowed with such maturity that even those of us who are older than you want to oblige you. Not long ago a church was built in Lyon, and the work begun came to the point of completion through the efforts of bishop Patiens, a man pious but active, stern but compassionate, who also, with his abundant generosity towards the poor and with his kindly nature, builds the not less lofty edifice of a good conscience. 3. In the most remote part of this building I had this hasty poem inscribed, which I composed at the request of the aforementioned bishop in the triple trochees that have been familiar to me up to now and soon will be to you too. For the walls of the basilica near the altar are already distinguished with the hexameters of the illustrious poets Constantius and Secundinus – my modesty vehemently forbids me to include them in this letter, because the comparison with better poems puts my modesty under pressure, as I only nervously publish the products of my leisure time. 4. Because just as a new bride needs nothing less than a matron of honour more beautiful than her, and just as every dark-skinned person seems even darker when dressed in white clothes, so my own pipe, whatever

mediam loco, infimam merito despicabiliorem pronuntiari non imperitia modo sed et arrogantia facit. Quapropter illorum iustius epigrammata micant quam istaec, quae imaginarie tantum et quodammodo umbratiliter effingimus. Sed quorsum ista? Quin potius paupertinus flagitatae cantilenae culmus immurmuret.

 Quisquis pontificis patrisque nostri
 conlaudas Patientis hic laborem,
 voti compote supplicatione
 concessum experiare quod rogabis.
 Aedes celsa nitet nec in sinistrum   5
 aut dextrum trahitur, sed arce frontis
 ortum prospicit aequinoctialem.
 Intus lux micat atque bratteatum
 sol sic sollicitatur ad lacunar,
 fulvo ut concolor erret in metallo.   10
 Distinctum vario nitore marmor
 percurrit cameram solum fenestras,
 ac sub versicoloribus figuris
 vernans herbida crusta sapphiratos
 flectit per prasinum vitrum lapillos.   15
 Huic est porticus applicata triplex
 fulmentis Aquitanicis superba,
 ad cuius specimen remotiora
 claudunt atria porticus secundae,
 et campum medium procul locatas   20
 vestit saxea silva per columnas.
 Hinc agger sonat, hinc Arar resultat.
 Hinc sese pedes atque eques reflectit
 stridentum et moderator essedorum,
 curvorum hinc chorus helciariorum   25
 responsantibus alleluia ripis
 ad Christum levat amnicum celeuma.
 Sic, sic psallite, nauta vel viator;
 namque iste est locus omnibus petendus,
 omnes quo via ducit ad salutem.   30

its meagre worth, sounds worthless if surrounded by loud trumpets. Being middle in position but lowest in merit, my poem is declared contemptible not only by my inexperience but also by my presumptuousness. That is why their inscriptions shine with greater justice than these lines, which I have shaped just in draft and as it were in shadowy fashion. But what is the point? Instead, let my poor reed whisper the song you asked for:

> You who fervently praise the work
> of our father and bishop Patiens here,
> may you find what you ask for
> with religious solemnity granted.
> The temple shines loftily and does not spread to the left 5
> or to the right, but with its fortified front looks
> out to the equinoctial sunrise.
> Inside, the light sparkles
> and the sun is attracted to the gilded ceiling
> so that it moves, the same in colour over the tawny metal. 10
> Marble marked with various hues
> covers the arched roof, the floor, the windows;
> and under figures of changeable colours
> the grassy green mosaic
> angles the sapphire-coloured stones amid the green glass. 15
> There is an adjoining threefold portico,
> haughty with its Aquitanian pillars,
> and in its likeness other porticos
> close the forecourt on the further side,
> and the plain in between 20
> is surrounded by a forest of stone, made of columns set wide apart.
> Here the street sounds, here the River Saône resounds.
> From the first side walkers and riders take a turn,
> and the drivers of creaking chariots,
> and from the other the choir of the bent-down hauliers 25
> direct their river shanty to Christ
> while the banks echo the hallelujah.
> Exult therefore, sailor and traveller,
> here is the place where everybody should come,
> where the road leads all to salvation. 30

5. Ecce parui tamquam iunior imperatis. Tu modo fac memineris multiplicato me faenore remunerandum, quoque id facilius possis voluptuosiusque, opus est ut sine dissimulatione lectites, sine fine lecturias; neque patiaris, ut te ab hoc proposito propediem coniunx domum feliciter ducenda deflectat, sisque oppido meminens, quod olim Marcia Hortensio, Terentia Tullio, Calpurnia Plinio, Pudentilla Apuleio, Rusticiana Symmacho legentibus meditantibusque candelas et candelabra tenuerunt.
6. Certe si praeter oratoriam contubernio feminarum poeticum ingenium et oris tui limam frequentium studiorum cotibus expolitam quereris obtundi, reminiscere, quod saepe versum Corinna cum suo Nasone complevit, Lesbia cum Catullo, Cesennia cum Gaetulico, Argentaria cum Lucano, Cynthia cum Propertio, Delia cum Tibullo. Proinde liquido claret studentibus discendi per nuptias occasionem tribui, desidibus excusationem. Igitur incumbe, neque apud te litterariam curam turba depretiet imperitorum, quia natura comparatum est, ut in omnibus artibus hoc sit scientiae pretiosior pompa, quo rarior. Vale.

5. You see I have obeyed your orders as if I were the younger one. Remember, however, that I am to be repaid with compound interest, and so that you can achieve this more easily and with more pleasure, you must read often without carelessness and you must desire to read without end. And you should not let your wife, whom you are soon happily going to bring to your home, distract you from this purpose. On the contrary, please remember well that in the past Marcia held the candelabra with its candles for Hortensius, Terentia for Tullius, Calpurnia for Pliny, Pudentilla for Apuleius, Rusticiana for Symmachus, while they were reading and reflecting. 6. But if you complain that through living with women not only the oratorical art, but also poetic talent and the file of your eloquence, sharpened on the grindstone of your constant studies, is becoming blunted, remember that often Corinna finished a line in collaboration with her Naso, Lesbia with Catullus, Caesennia with Gaetulicus, Argentaria with Lucan, Cynthia with Propertius, Delia with Tibullus. So it is clear that, for those who want to study, marriage gives an opportunity, for the idle, an excuse. That is why you should continue, and the crowd of the uncultivated should not depreciate your effort for literature, because it is a law of nature that in every art the splendour of skill is the more valuable, the rarer it is. Goodbye.

Epistula II

Sidonius Rustico suo salutem.

1. Si nobis pro situ spatiisque regionum vicinaremur nec a se praesentia mutua vasti itineris longinquitate discriminaretur, nihil apicum raritati licere in coeptae familiaritatis officia permitterem neque iam semel missa fundamenta certantis amicitiae diversis honorum generibus exstruere cessarem. Sed animorum coniunctioni separata utrimque porrectioribus terminis obsistit habitatio, equidem semel devinctis parum nocitura pectoribus. 2. Sed tamen ex ipsa communium municipiorum discretione procedit quod, cum amicissimi simus, raritatem colloquii de prolixa terrarum interiectione venientem in reatum volumus transferre communem, cum de naturalium rerum difficultate nec culpa nos debeat manere nec venia. Domine inlustris, gerulos litterarum de disciplinae tuae institutione formatos et morum erilium verecundiam praeferentes opportune admisi, patienter audivi, competenter explicui. Vale.

Epistula 11

Sidonius greets his dear Rusticus

1. If we were neighbours as regards the location and distance of our regions, and if we were not kept apart from each other's presence by the length of a vast journey, I would not permit the rarity of letters fulfilling the duties of our newly started acquaintance to be possible, nor would I cease in strengthening the foundations now already established on one occasion of our competing affection with various kinds of honours. But against the union of our minds stands the fact that our habitations are far apart, with a lot of land in between – though this will do little harm to our hearts, which were once bound together. 2. But still it results from the very separation of our respective towns that, even though we are very friendly we tend to convert the rarity of our exchange, arising from the extensive interposition of territory between us, into a mutual accusation, even though because of the difficulty of the natural circumstances there is no need for blame nor forgiveness. Noble sir, I welcomed suitably the carriers of your letter, who have been educated by the teaching of your discipline and exhibit modesty in accord with the manners of their master; I listened to them patiently; and I gave them a proper explanation. Goodbye.

Epistula 12

Sidonius Agricolae suo salutem.

1. Misisti tu quidem lembum mobilem, solidum, lecti capacem iamque cum piscibus; tum praeterea gubernatorem longe peritum, remiges etiam robustos expeditosque, qui scilicet ea rapiditate praetervolant amnis adversi terga qua deflui. Sed dabis veniam, quod invitanti tibi in piscationem comes venire dissimulo; namque me multo decumbentibus nostris validiora maeroris retia tenent, quae sunt amicis quoque et externis indolescenda. Unde te quoque puto, si rite germano moveris affectu, quo temporis puncto paginam hanc sumpseris, de reditu potius cogitaturum.

2. Severiana, sollicitudo communis, inquietata primum lentae tussis impulsu febribus quoque iam fatigatur, hisque per noctes ingravescentibus; propter quod optat exire in suburbanum; litteras tuas denique cum sumeremus, egredi ad villulam iam parabamus. Quocirca tu seu venias seu moreris, preces nostras orationibus iuva, ut ruris auram desideranti salubriter cedat ipsa vegetatio. Certe ego vel tua soror inter spem metumque suspensi credidimus eius taedium augendum, si voluntati iacentis obstitissemus. 3. Igitur ardori civitatis atque torpori tam nos quam domum totam praevio Christo pariter eximimus simulque medicorum consilia vitamus assidentum dissidentumque, qui parum docti et satis seduli languidos multos officiosissime occidunt. Sane contubernio nostro iure amicitiae Iustus adhibebitur, quem, si iocari liberet in tristibus, facile convincerem Chironica magis institutum arte quam Machaonica. Quo diligentius postulandus est Christus obsecrandusque, ut valetudini, cuius curationem cura nostra non invenit, potentia superna medeatur. Vale.

Epistula 12

Sidonius greets his dear Agricola

1. You have sent me a swift and solid boat, which has also room for a couch next to the catch of fishes; besides, an experienced steersman, and strong and expedient oarsmen, who certainly fly over the surface of the river going upstream with the same rapidity as downstream. But you will pardon me for refusing your invitation to accompany you on a fishing expedition, because I am held back by much stronger nets of sadness about sick family members, which causes pain to friends as well as to outsiders. That is why I think that you too, if you properly feel brotherly love, will rather think about turning back the minute you get this letter.

2. Severiana, our common cause of anxiety, was first disturbed by a tenacious fit of coughing, and now she also is exhausted by a fever, which gets worse night by night. That is why she wants to move out to our suburban place; when we got your letter we were preparing to leave for our little estate. So whether you come or stay, help our wishes with your prayers that this move will heal her, keen as she is for the country air. Certainly your sister and I are in suspense between hope and fear, and we thought her indisposition could increase if we opposed the patient's wishes. 3. I am therefore removing myself and my whole household together from the heat and torpor of the city with the help of Christ and thus I am escaping at the same time from the advice of the doctors who sit by and disagree, and who, little taught but eager enough, kill many sick people very dutifully. Iustus of course will be received in our home by right of friendship, and if it were allowed to make a joke in sad circumstances, I could easily prove him to be trained rather in the art of Chiron than of Machaon. So we must pray to Christ all the more diligently and beg him that heavenly power heals the illness, for which our concern does not find a cure. Goodbye.

Epistula 13

Sidonius Serrano suo salutem.

1. Epistulam tuam nobis Marcellinus togatus exhibuit, homo peritus virque amicorum. Quae primoribus verbis salutatione libata reliquo sui tractu, qui quidem grandis est, patroni tui Petronii Maximi imperatoris laudes habebat; quem tamen tu pertinacius aut amabilius quam rectius veriusque felicissimum appellas, propter hoc quippe, cur per amplissimos fascium titulos fuerit evectus usque ad imperium. Sed sententiae tali numquam ego assentior, ut fortunatos putem qui rei publicae praecipitibus ac lubricis culminibus insistunt.

2. Nam dici nequit, quantum per horas fert in hac vita miseriarum vita felicium istorum, si tamen sic sunt pronuntiandi qui sibi hoc nomen ut Sulla praesumunt, nimirum qui supergressi ius fasque commune summam beatitudinem existimant summam potestatem, hoc ipso satis miseriores, quod parum intellegunt inquietissimo se subiacere famulatui. Nam sicut hominibus reges, ita regibus dominandi desideria dominantur. 3. Hic si omittamus antecedentium principum casus vel subsecutorum, solus iste peculiaris tuus Maximus maximo nobis documento poterit esse, qui quamquam in arcem praefectoriam patriciam consularemque intrepidus ascenderat eosque quos gesserat magistratus ceu recurrentibus orbitis inexpletus iteraverat, cum tamen venit omnibus viribus ad principalis apicis abruptum, quandam potestatis inmensae vertiginem sub corona patiebatur nec sustinebat dominus esse, qui non sustinuerat esse sub domino. 4. Denique require in supradicto vitae prioris gratiam potentiam diuturnitatem eque diverso principatus paulo amplius quam bimenstris originem turbinem finem: profecto invenies hominem beatiorem prius fuisse quam beatissimus nominaretur. Igitur ille, cuius anterius epulae mores, pecuniae pompae,

Epistula 13

Sidonius greets his dear Serranus

1. Your letter was shown to me by the advocate Marcellinus, an experienced person and a man with friends. After offering a greeting with its preliminary words, in the rest of its course, which is certainly considerable, it contained the praise of your patron the emperor Petronius Maximus. You call him most lucky – with more determination or friendship than accuracy or truth – because he was elevated through the most important offices up to imperial power. But I can never consent to such an opinion of thinking that those who set foot upon the steep and slippery heights of our state are fortunate.

2. For there is no telling how much misery in earthly life hourly the lives of these fortunate ones entail, if one nevertheless wants to call them that, because they arrogate the name to themselves like Sulla – of course because they go beyond what is lawful and right and think the highest power to be the highest happiness, and they are all the more unhappy precisely because they understand too little that they are subject to a most restless servitude. For just as kings have mastery over men, the wish for mastery masters kings. 3. If we omit at this point the cases of the preceding and following emperors, by himself this Maximus, who is special to you, can provide us with maximum proof; though he ascended fearlessly to the height of the prefecture, the patriciate and the consulate, and though he insatiably repeated the offices that he had held for a second time as if following in his own tracks, still, when he came after mobilising all his forces to the cliff-edge of imperial honour, under the crown he suffered a sort of vertigo at his measureless rank and he could no longer bear to be the master, just as he had not endured being under a master. 4. And as for the aforementioned man, look next at the favour, the power and the durability of his earlier life; and on the contrary the beginning, the storminess and the end of his principate, which lasted not much longer than two months. Certainly, you will find out that the man was happier before he was called the happiest. This man, whose banquets and habits, fortune and pomp, education and magistracies, patrimony and patronage were previously prosperous, the very patterns of

litterae fasces, patrimonia patrocinia florebant, cuius ipsa
sic denique spatia vitae custodiebantur, ut per horarum
disposita clepsydras explicarentur, is nuncupatus Augustus ac
sub hac specie Palatinis liminibus inclusus ante crepusculum
ingemuit, quod ad vota pervenerat. Cumque mole curarum
pristinae quietis tenere dimensum prohiberetur, veteris
actutum regulae legibus renuntiavit atque perspexit pariter
ire non posse negotium principis et otium senatoris.

5. Nec fefellerunt futura maerentem; namque cum
ceteros aulicos honores tranquillissime percurrisset,
ipsam aulam turbulentissime rexit inter tumultus militum
popularium foederatorum; quod et exitus prodidit novus
celer acerbus, quem cruentavit Fortunae diu lenocinantis
perfidus finis, quae virum ut scorpius ultima sui parte
percussit. Dicere solebat vir litteratus atque ob ingenii
merita quaestorius, partium certe bonarum pars magna,
Fulgentius ore se ex eius frequenter audisse, cum perosus
pondus imperii veterem securitatem desideraret: 'felicem te,
Damocles, qui non uno longius prandio regni necessitatem
toleravisti.'

6. Iste enim, ut legimus, Damocles provincia Siculus,
urbe Syracusanus, familiaris tyranno Dionysio fuit.
Qui cum nimiis laudibus bona patroni ut cetera scilicet
inexpertus efferret: 'vis', inquit Dionysius, 'hodie saltim
in hac mensa bonis meis pariter ac malis uti?'—'libenter',
inquit. Tunc ille confestim laetum clientem quamquam
et attonitum plebeio tegmine erepto muricis Tyrii seu
Tarentini conchyliato ditat indutu et renidentem gemmis
margaritisque aureo lecto sericatoque toreumati imponit.
7. Cumque pransuro Sardanapallicum in morem panis
daretur e Leontina segete confectus, insuper dapes cultae
ferculis cultioribus apponerentur, spumarent Falerno
gemmae capaces inque crystallis calerent unguenta
glacialibus, hinc suffita cinnamo ac ture cenatio spargeret
peregrinos naribus odores et madescentes nardo capillos
circumfusa florum serta siccarent, coepit supra tergum
sic recumbentis repente vibrari mucro districtus e
lacunaribus, qui videbatur in iugulum purpurati iam
iamque ruiturus; nam filo equinae saetae ligatus et ita

whose life were so well organised that his appointments were measured with a water clock indicating the hours, when he was named Augustus and was shut up under this pretext within the thresholds of the Palace, groaned even before dusk because he had achieved his desires. And since he was prevented from retaining his former quiet lifestyle to the same extent because of the weight of his duties, he had to renounce immediately the rhythm of his old life and he realised that the business of a ruler could not be transacted in the same way as the leisure of a senator.

5. And the future did not deceive him in his distress; for though he had passed most peacefully through the other offices of court, he governed his own court chaotically amid the uproar of the military, the people, the federates. This is also shown by his death, which was novel, swift and terrible. He was bloodied by the treacherous end of his Fortune, who had long favoured him; she struck the man like a scorpion with its tail. An educated man who because of the merits of his mind was a quaestor, certainly an important member of the party of good men, Fulgentius, said that he had frequently heard the words from his mouth, when, hating the burden of imperial command, he longed for his old security: 'lucky you, Damocles, who did not have to bear longer than one meal the necessities of government'.

6. This Damocles was, as we read, from the province of Sicily, from the city of Syracuse, and a confidant of the tyrant Dionysius. When he once extolled with excessive praises the fortune of his patron which, like everything else, he had not experienced, Dionysius said: 'would you like just for today to experience at my table the good and bad sides of my position in equal measure?' – 'with pleasure', he said. Then without delay Dionysius took the plebeian clothes away from his delighted but also astonished client and enriched him with a garment coloured with the purple fish from Tyre or Tarentum, and he sat him gleaming with jewels and pearls on a golden bed with covers made of silk. 7. And expecting to dine in the style of Sardanapallus, he was given bread made of corn from Leontini; moreover, precious repasts were served to him on even more precious plates; capacious jewelled cups were foaming with Falernian wine; in icy crystal cups unguents were warm; from one side of the dining room, fumigated with cinnamon and incense, spread foreign smells around his nostrils; wreaths of flowers which were put around his head dried his hair wet with nard. But behind his back as he reclined a drawn sword-blade began suddenly to shudder from the ceiling which seemed on the very point of crashing down into the neck of the man in purple: it was tied by a thread of horsehair and was menacing

pondere minax ut acumine gulam formidolosi Tantaleo frenabat exemplo, ne cibi ingressi per ora per vulnera exirent.

8. Unde post mixtas fletibus preces atque multimoda suspiria vix absolutus emicatimque prosiliens illa refugit celeritate divitias deliciasque regales, qua solent appeti, reductus ad desideria mediocrium timore summorum et satis cavens, ne beatum ultra diceret duceretque qui saeptus armis ac satellitibus et per hoc raptis incubans opibus ferro pressus premeret aurum. Quapropter ad statum huiusmodi, domine frater, nescio an constet tendere beatos, patet certe miseros pervenire. Vale.

with its weight and its sharpness, and thus it curbed the gluttony of the guest, terrified in the manner of Tantalus, that the food would come in through his mouth and go out through his wounds.

8. Hence, after pleas mixed with tears and manifold sighs, he was at last released and jumping up in a flash he fled those royal riches and delicacies in the same haste with which they are normally sought after; he was led back to aspiring for middling things out of fear for the highest, and took good care not to not to say or think a man happy who was surrounded by arms and attendants and thus sitting on stolen riches, pressed down by steel as he himself pressed down on gold. That is why, my lord brother, I do not know whether it can be agreed that happy men aim for such a state, but it is certainly clear that only wretched ones get there. Goodbye.

Epistula 14

Sidonius Maurusio suo salutem.

1. Audio industriae tuae votisque communibus uberiore proventu, quam minabatur sterilis annus, respondere vindemiam. Unde et in pago Vialoscensi, qui Martialis aetate citeriore vocitatus est propter hiberna legionum Iulianarum, suspicor diuturnius te moraturum; quo loci tibi cum ferax vinea est, tum praeter ipsam praedium magno non minus domino, quod te tuosque plurifaria frugum mansionumque dote remoretur. 2. Ilicet si horreis apothecisque seu penu impleta destinas illic usque ad adventum hirundineum vel ciconinum Iani Numaeque ninguidos menses in otio fuliginoso sive tunicata quiete transmittere, nobis quoque parum in oppido fructuosae protinus amputabuntur causae morarum, ut, dum ipse nimirum frueris rure, nos te fruamur, quibus, ut recognoscis, non magis cordi est aut voluptati ager cum reditibus amplis, quam vicinus aequalis cum bonis moribus. Vale.

Epistula 14

Sidonius greets his dear Maurusius

1. I hear that the vintage responds to your diligence and our wishes with greater abundance than this dry year threatened. Therefore, I also suspect that you will stay for a longer time in the district of Vialoscensis which was named 'Martial' in recent times because of the winter-quarters of the Julian legions; you own there a fertile vineyard and also an estate, not inferior to its important master, which holds you and your family back with its manifold endowment of crops and dwellings. 2. And if you spontaneously decide, when granaries and wine cellars and the larder are filled, to stay there till the swallows and storks come back to spend the snowy months of Ianus and Numa in a smoky calm and in tunic-clad ease, then my few and unprofitable reasons for staying in town will immediately be cut off, in order that, while you of course enjoy living in the countryside, I can enjoy you. For me, as you know, an estate with big revenues is not closer to my heart and does not bring more pleasure than a neighbour of the same age with a good character. Goodbye.

COMMENTARY

Epistula 1

Introduction

Summary

Sidonius describes how his fellow citizens in the Auvergne regret the absence of Ecdicius, Sidonius' brother-in-law. They hope for his help against Seronatus, a Gallic official and confidant of the Visigothic *rex* ('king') Euric. To describe his bad character, Sidonius employs etymological explanations and a comparison with the famous conspirator Catiline. Sidonius gives many examples to illustrate Seronatus' tyrannical nature and shows how Seronatus does not behave in a manner suitable to the occasion and place. The letter ends with an urgent plea: Ecdicius should hasten his return and decide what to do next about Seronatus.

Addressee

Ecdicius, brother of Sidonius' wife Papianilla (see the commentary on *Ep.* 2.2.3 *nomen hoc praedio…* and *Ep.* 2.12) and son of the late emperor Avitus, is the recipient of the prestigious first letter of the second book. He is not only a close relative, but also an important military ally, as described in this letter. In 471 Ecdicius raised an army of cavalry to drive Visigothic raiders away from Clermont; in *Ep.* 3.3.7 Sidonius panegyrically praises Ecdicius' deeds. In 474 Ecdicius became commander in Gaul (*magister militum*) and was given the honorary title *patricius* by the emperor Iulius Nepos (see *Ep.* 5.16.1). In 475 he was summoned to Italy and replaced as head of the army (see Jord. *Get.* 240–1). Ecdicius is also the addressee of *Ep.* 3.3, in which Sidonius begs him to return to the Auvergne. As Giannotti (2016) 37 shows, the second and third books have several common addressees (including Felix in *Ep.* 2.3 and Donidius in *Ep.* 2.9). Ecdicius is mentioned in a private setting in *Ep.* 2.2.15 (Sidonius plays ball with his brother-in-law at his estate Avitacum, which he got from his wife's family – see the commentary on *Ep.* 2.2.3 *Avitaci sumus*) and in 5.16.1 (to Papianilla about Ecdicius' honorary title). He counts among the individuals who are mentioned most often in Sidonius' texts (five times); Mathisen (2020a) 41. According to Greg. Tur. *Hist. Franc.* 2.24, during a famine Ecdicius provided relief for 4,000 destitute people at his own expense. Gregory is very positive about Sidonius, and by extension Ecdicius, as he positions Sidonius as his own literary and historical exemplum of an ideal *Arvernus*.

For Ecdicius' life, see *PLRE* 2, 383–5, *PCBE* 4, 607–9; see also Banniard (1992) 418–20, Mathisen (1993) 53, 64, 237–8, Harries (1994), Kaufmann (1995) 176–7, 213, 297–9, Prévot (1999) 72, Giannotti (2002), Mratschek (2008) 365, 378, Drinkwater (2013) 64–5, Giannotti (2016) 133–4, Fascione (2019) 87–8, Kulikowski (2020) 212, Mathisen (2020a) 91, Mratschek (2020a) 230.

Date

The letter must have been written during the reign of the emperor Anthemius (467–72), who is mentioned in the last sentence of the letter (see the commentary below on 2.1.4). It has been dated to 469 or 470, before Sidonius' ordination as bishop and Ecdicius' defence of Clermont from the attacks of the Visigoths. Hanaghan (2017c) shows that Sidonius did publish letters critical of Anthemius during Anthemius' reign, including *Ep.* 1.5. An argument for a later date, namely 472, is the fact that there is no help to be expected from the emperor Anthemius: Sidonius links Rome's lack of power specifically to Anthemius' rule – see the commentary on *Ep.* 2.1.4 *Si nullae ... Anthemii principis opes*. Furthermore, Sidonius depicts Ecdicius as some sort of local leader in the resistance against the Visigoths, which he would actually become in 471 or 472.

The date of the letter is discussed in Loyen (1970a) 43, 216 n. 1, 246 n. 1, Harries (1994) 229, Kaufmann (1995) 176–7, 213, 297–9, Gillett (1999) 28 n. 98, Sivonen (2006) 153–4, Delaplace (2015) 248 n. 71, Hanaghan (2017c) 645, Hanaghan (2019) 94, 106. On the general difficulty of dating Sidonius' letters, see the Introduction, '2. The date and order of letters in Book 2'.

Major themes and further reading

Structure

Whereas *Ep.* 1.1 served as a prologue to the whole letter collection, 2.1 shows Sidonius in the midst of policital activities and close to persons of the highest rank. The reproachful letter 2.1 (as well as 3.13, where Gnatho is similarly criticised; Hanaghan 2019, 93–5) acts as counterpart to the laudatory letters, 1.2 (the Gothic king Theoderic II as a civil, cultured ruler) and 8.11 (the rhetor Lampridius), as well as to all Sidonius' interactions with noblemen; van Waarden (2010) 440, Montone (2017) 31, 37. Within Book 2, the negative portrait of Seronatus contrasts with the descriptions of Sidonius' friends, for example Menstruanus in *Ep.* 2.6. Cain (2009) 207–19 suggests in his analysis of Jerome's letters a new taxonomy of ancient letters which is based on the two most comprehensive letter-writing handbooks to survive from the Greco-Roman world, pseudo-Demetrius' *Typoi epistolikoi* and pseudo-Libanius' *Epistolimaioi characteres*; see also Fögen (2018) 49–55. *Ep.* 2.1 is a mixture of the reproaching (directed at Seronatus) and the exhorting (directed to Ecdicius) types of letter.

Seronatus and his literary models
Seronatus is a Gallic official and confidant of the Visigothic *rex* ('king') Euric (466–84), the ruler of the kingdom of Toulouse, who in Sidonius' interpretation, and that of many modern scholars, aggressively fought against Rome and thus tried to overcome his status as a federate; Gillett (1999), Maier (2005) 240–45, Gualandri (2000) 118–29. Delaplace (2015) 247–53 instead deconstructs Sidonius' anti-Gothic statements as resulting from his collusion with the Burgundians and shows the Goths and Euric to be loyal Roman allies. For Sidonius' critical attitude towards and his (ironic and secretive) strategies against the Goths in general, see Overwien (2009a, 2009b), Mratschek (2020a) 231–2. Sidonius describes Seronatus here and elsewhere as a Gallo-Roman collaborator with the Visigoths and accuses him of offering provinces to the barbarians (*Ep.* 7.7.2). Sidonius thus places the theme of foreign rule at the beginning of the second book, as he does in other epistolary books (*Ep.* 1.2, 3.1, 3.2, 3.3, 6.1); see Fascione (2019) 11–12. Sidonius condemns Seronatus also in *Ep.* 5.13.1–3, as *belua* (monster) and *bestia* (beast), and describes his execution in *Ep.* 7.7.2; see Postel (2011) 173–5, Fascione (2016) 455–7. The parallel with the Gallic prefect Arvandus, who also was accused of seeking rapprochement with Euric and the Visigoths in 468/9, is interesting (Teitler 1992). While Sidonius fiercely condemns Seronatus' deeds, he keeps Arvandus' case vague in *Ep.* 1.7. Apparently, Seronatus did not have the aristocratic support that saved Sidonius' friend Arvandus from execution; see Mathisen (1998), van Waarden (2020a) 22, Hess (2021) 179–82. Arvandus also appears as a background theme in letters 2.3, 2.5 and 2.13.

Seronatus' exact official function is disputed; suggestions are that he was praetorian prefect of Gaul (this is unlikely, as we have many identified prefects in the period), *vicarius* of the Seven Provinces (most probably) or governor of the province of Aquitanica Prima; see the discussions in Anderson (1936) 412–13 n. 1, *PLRE* 2, 995–6, Heather (1992) 92, Teitler (1992), Kaufmann (1995) 176–7, Percival (1997) 289, Prévot (1999) 69, van Waarden (2010) 355–6, Delaplace (2014) 24–5, Delaplace (2015) 247–8. For Seronatus' political aims, see Maier (2005) 119, 243–4, 277.

In Sidonius' description of Seronatus, several literary intertexts can be identified. Seronatus' traits are found in the description of historical tyrants (see Hdt. 3.80) and hypocrites (Sen. *De ira* 2.28.7–8) before him. There are also parallels with the invective against Pliny's arch-enemy Regulus (cf. the Introduction, pp. xiii–xiv, and the commentary on *Ep.* 2.1.2 *aperte invidet* ...), who is also a model for Sidon. *Ep.* 1.11.16; see Plin. *Ep.* 1.5.8, 9.13.21, Neger (2020) 381. Gibson (2013b) 347 argues for an allusion through reversal to Plin. *Ep.* 2.1, which records the public funeral honouring Verginius Rufus, a loyal and modest man. For the comparison of Seronatus to Catiline see Fascione (2016). Blänsdorf (1993) 129–30 reads *Ep.* 2.1 as an invective, influenced by Claudian. Interestingly, Sidonius' Seronatus appears in a sermon against corruption and slavery in Lisbon in 1655 by the Jesuit court preacher Padre Antônio Vieira.

Commentary

Section 1

Sidonius Ecdicio suo salutem: On the addressee, Ecdicius, see the introduction to this letter. Sidonius uses here, and in fact throughout the second book of letters, the simple formula of salutation (the addressee's name in the dative accompanied by the possessive pronoun *suo*), following the examples of Seneca, Pliny and Symmachus rather than of Christian letter-writers such as Augustine and Jerome; Zelzer (1994/1995) 543, Gibson (2020) 376. As Mratschek (2017) 311 shows, Sidonius' distinction between personal (as in Book 2) and official letters to high-ranking clergy or others becomes apparent from the opening and closing saluations of any letter. At the beginning of *Carm.* 9, Sidonius writes his name in full, Sollius Apollinaris Sidonius. For Sidonius' greeting formula *domino papae* in Book 7, see Zelzer and Zelzer (2002) 404, van Waarden (2010) 44–5, van Waarden (2016) 40–1.

Duo nunc pariter mala sustinent: Book 2 starts with the word *duo*, 'two', probably not incidentally, as Sidonius is highly aware of the number and position of his letters and books; Gibson (2013a), Gibson (2013b) 346. The opening sentence states the subject directly (see van Waarden 2010, 47 on type 1a) and takes the reader *in medias res*: Sidonius' and Ecdicius' countrymen have to endure two evils in equal measures (*pariter ... sustinere*). For *pariter*, 'in like manner', 'equally', 'in equal measure' (*TLL* 10.1, 278.52–85.69), a frequently used adverb in Sidonius and elsewhere, see van Waarden (2016) 188, on *Ep.* 7.16.1. In Book 2 it is used again in *Ep.* 2.9.5, 2.12.3, 2.13.4, 2.13.6. Sidonius generally favours adverbs ending in *-(i)ter*, which are a feature of later Latin; Amherdt (2001) 120, van Waarden (2010) 344. In Book 2 they are: *Ep.* 2.1.2 *serviliter*, 2.2.12 *granditer*, 2.2.19 *naturaliter*, 2.6.1 *proverbialiter*, 2.7.2 *perniciterque*, 2.9.1 *similiter*, 2.9.6 *breviter*, 2.10.4 *umbratiliter*, 2.10.5 *feliciter*, 2.12.2 *salubriter*. Other instances of *sustinere*, 'to suffer', 'to endure', with an accusative object (*mala*) to express endurance, appear in *Ep.* 1.7.13, 7.7.1, 9.3.2; see van Waarden (2010) 344.

Arverni tui: The subject of the first sentence follows demonstratively at the end, *Arverni tui* ('your fellow Arvernians'). Sidonius uses the possessive pronoun *tui* emphatically to make his addressee Ecdicius deal with Seronatus and assume his responsibility towards his Arvernians. Sidonius esteems his fellow countrymen and talks about his new *patria* on several occasions, though himself was born and educated in Lyon. See *Ep.* 3.2.1 *populus Arvernus* ('the community of the Arverni'), 3.3.1 *Arvernis meis* ('by my Avernians'), 4.21.3 *Arverni ... tui* ('your Avernians'), 7.1.2 *populus Arvernus* ('the community of the Arverni'); Stevens (1933) 63–5, Bonjour (1980), Kaufmann (1995) 105, Köhler (1995) 273, Prévot (1999), Amherdt (2001) 435. The Arvernians are also mentioned in *Ep.* 2.6.2. In his panegyric on Avitus, Sidonius praises the emperor's (and his own) homeland, the Auvergne, in a lengthy description (*Carm.* 7.139–52); Henning (1999) 125–6, Sivonen (2006) 74–6. For the importance of *patria* for Sidonius and for the Auvergne, a region in south-central France, as his place of belonging, see the commentary on 2.1.4 *statuit te auctore nobilitas....* The Arverni were originally a mighty Celtic tribe in the Auvergne. In 122/121 BC they were defeated by the Romans, and in 52 BC the Arvernian king Vercingetorix led all of Gaul to revolt (see Caes. *Bell. Gall.* 1.31, 1.45, 7.7). Like other late Roman Gauls, however, Sidonius focuses in his letters on the noble Trojan ancestry of his people; see the commentary on *Ep.* 2.2.19 *nam moris istic fuit senioribus nostris agonem Drepanitanum Troianae superstitionis imitari*.

'Quaenam?' inquis: Sidonius assumes a colloquial tone and imagines the recipient asking questions as in a conversation. In ancient epistolary theory, a letter is imagined as 'half of a dialogue' (Demetr. *Eloc.* 223) and as an instrument to overcome the separation between writer and recipient. The topos is frequent already from Cicero on, for example Cic. *Ad Q. fr.* 1.1.45; see Thraede (1970) 27–47, 162–5, Cugusi (1983) 32–3, 43–4, 73–4, Malherbe (1988), Poster (2007), Ebbeler (2007), Ebbeler (2009), van Waarden (2010) 538–9. As Hanaghan (2019) 159–60 shows, many of Sidonius' epistles begin by responding to a request from the addressee (for specific information, for the inclusion of a poem, or for a letter) and some of them are in direct speech. The letters thus assume a communicative rather than a narrative function, and these functions sometimes change within a letter. Examples of similar questions with *inquis* at the beginning of a letter include Sidon. *Ep.* 5.11.1 *quaenam, inquis, in me tibi probanda placuere?* ('what are my merits that you like?') and 6.12.1 *quorsum istaec?, inquis* ('to what purpose?, you ask me'), and also Plin. *Ep.* 1.6.1 *'ipse?' inquis* ('you yourself?, you ask'), 6.23.1, 6.24.2, 9.6.1. See the commentary on Sidon. *Ep.* 2.9.6 *Quid multa?...* and van Waarden (2010) 174 on 7.2.6 *quid morer multis* ('to cut a long story short') and van Waarden (2010) 538 on 7.10.1 *sed quid ... loquar* ('but why speak?'). For elements of the *sermo cotidianus* in letters in general see Cugusi (1983) 36, 78–83.

Praesentiam Seronati et absentiam tuam: To lament the addressee's absence and to utter the wish to see the other person is a common motif in letter writing; see Thraede (1970) 165–8, Cugusi (1983) 77, and the commentaries on *Ep.* 2.9.1 *Quaeris, cur ... desideria producam* and on *Ep.* 2.11.1 *Si nobis pro situ*. Sidonius uses here the term *absentia*, 'absence'. It also appears several times in Pliny, for example Plin. *Ep.* 6.7.1 *scribis te absentia mea non mediocriter affici* ('you write that you are affected by my absence in no small way'), 6.4.4, 7.3.1. In the following text of *Ep.* 2.1, the traditional theme is intermingled with praise of the addressee, Ecdicius, as saviour, as well as the plea for his return. As a new twist within the old topos, not only the absence (*absentia*) of the recipient of the letter is lamented, but also the presence (*praesentia*) of another person, namely Seronatus. On Seronatus, see the commentary on *Seronati, inquam...*, immediately below, and the section 'Major themes and further reading' in the introduction to this letter.

Seronati, inquam: de cuius ut primum etiam nomine loquar: According to ancient rhetoric, one can deduce a person's or thing's nature from its name;

see Cic. *Topic.* 35, *De Inv.* 1.34, Varro *Ling.*, Curtius (1948) 488–92. Roman poets like Vergil or Ovid reflected on names (e.g. Verg. *Aen.* 1.267–8, Ov. *Fast.* 1.317–34), as did Christian writers, especially Jerome and Augustine; see Mohrmann (1935/1936), Gualandri (2017) and the commentary below on *sicuti ex adverso*. Seronatus' name is derived from *sero natus*, 'born too late'; in Sidonius opinion, however, it is antiphrastic. He thinks that Seronatus is not born too late but too early, and his name is thus a euphemism, like the well known rhetorical examples *bellum* or *Parcae*; see Hanaghan (2019) 93–5 and the commentary below on *sicuti ex adverso … Parcas vocitavere*. Similarly, Rutilius Namatianus reflects on the name Lepidus, 'pleasant', 'agreeable', which does not fit with the clan's baleful deeds (Rut. Nam. 1.309–12), and Jerome plays on the name of Vigilantius, who deserves to be called Dormitantius (Hier. *C. Vigil.* 1.6). Sidonius often makes puns on names or uses them to establish a connection or a deeper meaning. Demonstratively he begins his collection with a letter to Constantius (*Ep.* 1.1) and ends with one to Firminus (*Ep.* 9.16), moving from constancy to firmness and thus responding to Pliny's evolution from light to dark (Plin. *Ep.* 1.1 to Clarus, *Ep.* 9.40 to Fuscus). Sidonius also plays with the names of his friends Domitius and Felix; see the commentaries below on *Ep.* 2.2 and 2.3. Other examples of Sidonius' reflection on and play with names are *Ep.* 4.3.1, 4.18.5 v. 20, 4.24.1, *Carm.* 16.127–8; Mathisen (1991) 29–44, Amherdt (2001) 123, 416, Gibson (2011), Gibson (2013b) 349, Wolff (2020) 412. Hanaghan (2019) explores multiple name puns: see p. 42 on *Ep.* 1.8, p. 112 on *Ep.* 2.13, p. 128 on *Ep.* 6.2, pp. 156–7 on *Ep.* 4.12, p. 161 on *Ep.* 9.9, p. 167 on *Ep.* 6.4, p. 174 on *Ep.* 8.1. Sidonius also plays with his own name in *Carm.* 13.25–6. The name Citonatus is attested elsewhere as a proper name, for example of a deacon under bishop Symmachus of Rome in 499; Rüpke and Glock (2005) 873. With *inquam* and *loquar* Sidonius continues his mimesis of speech he started with '*Quaenam?*' *inquis* (see the commentary above, p. 62).

sic mihi videtur quasi praescia futurorum lusisse Fortuna: The adjective *praescius*, 'foreknowing', 'prescient' (*TLL* 10.2, 822.21–59), is often applied to Greco-Roman gods and later also to the Christian God. Here it is reinforced with the genitive *futurorum*, a combination which frequently appears in late antique authors, especially in Augustine (e.g. Aug. *Civ.* 5.10, 8.23). *Fortuna* appears like the *Parcae* personified as the Roman goddess of fate; see the commentary on *Ep.* 2.13.5 *quod et exitus prodidit … quem cruentavit Fortunae*.…

sicuti ex adverso maiores nostri proelia, quibus nihil est foedius, bella dixerunt; quique etiam pari contrarietate fata, quia non parcerent, Parcas vocitavere: The etymologies of *bellum* and *Parcae* are two examples of *antiphrasis*, a rhetorical device which expresses the opposite of what is meant. Sidonius announces this topos first with *ex adverso*, 'in a position opposite', or 'from the opposite side' (*TLL* 1, 868.83–9.11) (see Quint. 4.2.22). In the second part of the sentence he repeats the notion with *pari contrarietate*, 'opposition', 'contrariety', 'contrariness', a Late Latin term, also used in Sidon. *Ep.* 4.11.3, 4.12.3, 8.5.2; Amherdt (2001) 290, 316. The two etymologies are *bella*, n. pl. of *bellum*, 'war', or of *bellus*, 'pretty', 'handsome', 'neat' and *Parcae*, 'the Fates', three goddesses, who decide over men's lifespan and do not spare (*parcere*) anybody. These examples of antiphrasis are well known and used in late antique texts. Examples include: Donat. *Ars maior* 3.6 *Antiphrasis est unius verbi ironia, ut bellum, lucus et Parcae: bellum, hoc est minime bellum, et lucus eo quod non luceat, et Parcae eo quod nulli parcant* ('an antiphrasis is irony within a single word, like for example *bellum*, *lucus* and *Parcae*: *bellum*, that is not at all pleasant, and *lucus* because it does not shine and *Parcae* because they do not spare anyone'); Hier. *Ep.* 78.35 *quomodo Parcae dicuntur ab eo quod minime parcant, et bellum, quod nequaquam bellum sit, et lucus, quod minime luceat* ('That is how the *Parcae* got their name because they spare very little and *bellum*, because it is not pleasant at all, and *lucus*, because it shines very little'); Aug. *Dialect.* 6 *Nam lucus eo dictus putatur quod minime luceat et bellum quod res bella non sit et foederis nomen quod res foeda non sit* ('because *lucus* seems to have its name because it shines very little, and *bellum* because it is not a pleasant thing, and *foedus* has its name because it is not a horrible thing'). With *bellum* and *Parcae* Sidonius uses two fitting examples to explain Seronatus' name, as he not only brings war to the Arverni, but also ends their lives. This is why Seronatus – in Sidonius' opinion – was born too early and not too late, as his name suggests; see the commentary on *Ep.* 2.1.1 *Seronati, inquam....* Lütjohann (1887) 21 emends *quique* to *quippe*, unnecessarily according to Dolveck (2020) 484 n. 20. I agree, since *quique etiam* appears several times in Sidonius' *Carmen* 16 (16.18, 16.35, 16.40, 16.47, 16.64), but *quippe etiam* does not appear at all.

Rediit ipse Catilina saeculi nostri nuper Aturribus: Sidonius explicitly compares Seronatus with L. Sergius Catiline (106–62 BC), a Roman politician who was notorious for attempting insurrection against the Roman republic in 63 BC. Marcus Tullius Cicero (106–43 BC) was consul then and delivered speeches against the rebel (*Orationes in Catilinam*), which finally persuaded the Senate to vote for the death penalty for Catiline's co-conspirators. The summary execution of Roman citizens was not universally welcomed and led to Cicero's banishment from Rome in 58 BC; Odahl (2010), Berry (2020). Thanks to Cicero's speeches and the historical work *De coniuratione Catilinae* written by the historian Sallust (86–35 BC) Catiline became synonymous with a dangerous conspirator. Sallust's portrait of Catiline was especially influential as a literary paradigm of villainy and a ravaged mind, passing from historical writing into poetry; see for example Verg. *Aen*. 8.668–9, where Catiline represents the forces of anarchy, Val. Max. 5.8.5, Oros. *Hist*. 6.3.1, 6.6.5–7, and, famously, the portrayal of the heretic Priscillian in Sulpic. Sev. *Chron*. 2.46–51; Levick (2015) 109–19. Sidonius uses the Sallustian model for his villain Seronatus; see Gualandri (1979) 122, Fascione (2016), Montone (2017) 25, and the commentaries below on *ut sanguinem fortunasque miserorum ...* and on *Ep*. 2.1.2 *Scitote in eo per dies....* For Seronatus' ignorance, which is modelled on Sallust's depiction of Catiline (Sall. *Catil*. 5), see the commentary below on *Ep*. 2.1.2 *epistulas, ne primis quidem ....* With the pronoun *noster* Sidonius signals the rhetorical figure antonomasia (an attribute which stands for a person or a person who stands for an attribute), here Catiline to denote the negative character of Seronatus; see Köhler (1995) 307 about a similar passage in *Ep*. 1.11.5 *splendidam ... dotem Chremes noster Pamphilo suo dixerat* ('our Chremes promised his Pamphilus a generous dowry'). Sallust was part of the curriculum in Late Antique schooling; Stevens (1933) 4, Harries (1994) 39. The Sallustian intertext is also important elsewhere in Sidonius' books of letters, and he cites *De coniuratione Catilinae* or alludes to it several times (see the commentary on *Ep*. 2.13.2 *nam sicut hominibus reges...*). In *Ep*. 7.7.2 and 5 Sidonius presents himself as a new Cicero and, like him, assumes the role of a *pater patriae* ('father of the fatherland'), defending his country against usurpers like Catiline; Mratschek (2013) 266. In *Ep*. 8.1 and 8.8 Sidonius also identifies with Cicero and in 8.8.1 he even cites the first words of Cicero's speech against Catiline: *dic, Gallicanae flos iuventutis, quousque tandem ruralium operum negotiosus urbana fastidis?* ('Tell me, flower of the Gallo-Roman youth, how long are you going to be busy with rustic activities and despise those of the town?'); Overwien (2009a) 106–7, Fascione (2019) 96–7. For Cicero's impact on Sidonius' letters apart from Catiline's conspiracy, see the commentaries on *Ep*. 2.9.5 *ut nec Apuleius Phaedonem ...* and on 2.10.5 *quod olim Marcia Hortensio ....* The city Atura or *civitas Aturensium* was part of the Visigothic kingdom and also a royal residence alongside Toulouse and Bordeaux. The name of the city – present-day Aire-sur-L'Adour – derives from *Atur(r)us*, a river in Gascony, present-day Adour;

Kaufmann (1995) 178, Anderson (1936) 414 n. 1. Lütjohann (1887) 21 unnecessarily emends *ipse* to *iste* against all manuscripts. The focus here is not on the negative or possessive ('of yours', 'of ours') meaning of the pronoun *iste* (*Catilina* is enough of a negative marker and *saeculi nostri* refers to the affiliation of the new Catiline to Sidonius' time), but it is emphasised that Seronatus himself (*ipse*) comes to the city.

ut sanguinem fortunasque miserorum, quas ibi ex parte propinaverat, hic ex asse misceret: This sentence is hard to translate, as Sidonius combines two metaphors. He uses the images of drinking (*sanguinem ... propinare, miscere*) and fortune (*fortunas, ex asse*) to describe how Seronatus in Aire-sur-L'Adour only started to destroy the inhabitants' lives and finished in Clermont what he started there. The verb *propinare* means 'to drink (to a person, in practice by proposing a toast)' (*OLD* 1492, 1a) and is in a zeugmatic construction with the accusative objects *sanguinem* and *fortunas*. With this phrase Sidonius hints at the idea of drinking blood, a powerful picture to describe an especially cruel and ruthless enemy; see Hdt. 1.212, 1.214. A prominent intertext is again Sallust: Sall. *Catil.* 22.1 *humani corporis sanguinem vino permixtum in pateris circumtulisse* ('they are said to have passed around blood of the human body mixed with wine in cups'), on the Catilinarian conspirers, already mentioned in the sentence before, who allegedly confirmed their oaths by drinking human blood together; see the commentary above on *Ep.* 2.1.1 *Rediit ipse Catilina*.... For a different meaning of *propinare* see Sidon. *Ep.* 7.7.2 ('making a complimentary present of') and van Waarden (2010) 355–6. Fascione (2016) 454 refers to another intertext, Silius Italicus' *Punica* 11.51–4, about the corruption of Capua. *Ex asse*, 'in all', 'entirely', 'completely', 'down to the last penny', is one of Sidonius' favourite expressions, but attested only once elsewhere (*Conc. Turon.* a. 567). It is used here in opposition to *ex parte*; see also Sidon. *Ep.* 1.11.7, 3.3.9, 3.14.2, 4.18.1, 6.11.1, 6.12.8, 7.2.9, 8.6.9, 9.2.1, 9.3.7, 9.14.2; Amherdt (2001) 403, van Waarden (2010) 190, Giannotti (2016) 156. With *misceret*, 'to stir up', 'embroil', 'disturb', 'mix', 'prepare (a drink)' Sidonius continues the image of drinking blood he began with *propinare*.

Section 2

Scitote in eo per dies spiritum diu dissimulati furoris aperiri: Ecdicius has been referred to in the singular up until this point, but now Sidonius, with the imperative *scitote*, 'you should know', 'know', changes to the plural and thus includes a wider readership. The subject of the letter is of interest not only to its recipient, but to everybody who is reading it and especially all the Arvernians. For Sidonius' complex game with 'you' and 'I' in general, see van Waarden (2010) 49–52, van Waarden (2016) 45–8, van Waarden (2020b) and the commentary on *Ep.* 2.1.1 *Arverni tui*. For a change from singular to plural similar to that with *scitote* here see *Ep.* 7.8.3; van Waarden (2010) 396. *Scito* is an expression typical of the colloquial tone of a letter; Cugusi (1983) 79–80. Sidonius thus refers back to the initial question – see the commentary on *Ep.* 2.1.1 *'Quaenam?' inquis*. The expression *dissimulati furoris aperiri* recalls Sallust's description of Catiline as *simulator ac dissimulator* ('a man who pretends and deceives') (Sall. *Catil.* 5.4) and 'Catiline's rage' (*Catilinae furor*) (Sall. *Catil.* 24.2). For further parallels in the characteristics of Seronatus and Catiline, see Fascione (2016) 455 and the commentary above, pp. 64–5, on *Ep.* 2.1.1 *Rediit ipse Catilina* …. Seronatus appears not only as a traitor to his homeland, but as a barbarian, a Visigoth; Fascione (2016) 454. Clearly, then, Gothi and Romani are accentuated here as two opposing groups, and Seronatus is scorned for his behaviour as a treacherous border crosser; Hess (2019) 85. To lay open Seronatus' *spiritum furoris*, his 'spirit of madness', Sidonius enumerates his vices in a series of rhetorically stylised expressions (tricolon, parallelism, alliteration, comparison).

aperte invidet, abiecte fingit, serviliter superbit: Characteristic of Sidonius' descriptions, which were very influential among medieval writers, are long series of parallel expressions, with or without assonance and chiasmus; Faral (1946). The description is stylistically similar to the negative characterisation of Gnatho in *Ep.* 3.13.2–4. Here Sidonius starts with a clause consisting of three phrases (adverb + verb) to illustrate Seronatus' behaviour. As these stylistic means influence grammar and content and follow their internal aesthetic logic of a person's description, not every part of the enunciation should be taken literally, according to van Waarden (2010) 55–9, 576–84. With the moral charges against Seronatus, Sidonius takes up the rhetoric of decay in Cicero's first speech against Catiline (Cic. *Catil.* 1.1). Furthermore, Seronatus' behaviour is part of the topos of the *verkehrte Welt* ('topsy-turvy world'); Curtius (1948) 102–6, Blänsdorf (1993) 130. Similarly, Pliny describes in Plin. *Ep.* 4.2.5 his enemy Regulus, who behaves inappropriately: *est in summa avaritia sumptuosus, in summa infamia gloriosus* ('he is wasteful in his extensive greed, and bragging in his deepest ill fame'). See also Sidon. *Ep.* 7.9.12, where in a very similar series he criticises wrong behaviour in an anonymous group of persons, and *Ep.* 1.8.2 about the city of Ravenna: *indesinenter rerum omium lege perversa* ('the laws of nature are continually turned upside down'). With the adverb *serviliter*, 'like a slave', 'slavishly', Sidonius shows a negative attitude towards slaves, as he does elsewhere (e.g. *Ep.* 1.6.2, 1.11.9). There are other instances, though, where Sidonius focuses on the good relationship between master and slave, such as *Ep.* 7.14.11. On the subject of slavery in Sidonius, see Samson (1992), Kaufmann (1995) 248, Näf (1995) 138, Amherdt (2001) 256–7.

indicit ut dominus, exigit ut tyrannus, addicit ut iudex, calumniatur ut barbarus: The next clause consists of four comparisons in the same construction (verb + *ut* + noun). In *Ep.* 4.3.6–7 Sidonius uses the same structure to praise the style of Claudianus Mamertus in a much longer list, of twenty-eight comparisons (*sentit ut Pythagoras, dividit ut Socrates ...* – 'he makes judgements like Pythagoras, distinguishes like Socrates ...'). In Sidonius' description of Seronatus, typical activities are associated with certain roles, which Seronatus combines in his person. The first verb, *indico*, 'to order (someone to do something)', 'command', is used by Sidonius in an absolute sense only in this instance (*TLL* 7.1, 1157.49–51). Similarly, the third verb, *addico* (*aliquem/aliquid alicui*), 'to sentence', a juridical *terminus technicus* often combined with *iudex* (*TLL* 1, 574.45–5.32), is usually constructed with an object. For the participle *addictus*, see the commentary on *Ep.* 2.7.2 *quandoquidem sententiam ... veritatisque respectu dependunt tibi addicti reverentiam ....* The second and the fourth verbs (*exigo* and *calumnior*) are used with an object and in an absolute sense. *Calumnior*, 'to lie', 'accuse falsely', 'scheme' (*TLL* 3, 191.12–2.36) is classical, for instance Cic. *Verr.* 2.3.15. The verb is found several times in Augustine (e.g. Aug. *Civ.* 15.27) and also again in Sidon. *Ep.* 7.14.2. The term *barbarus*, 'barbarian', conjures up several images, often conveying 'us versus them' in antique texts; Mathisen (1993) 1. For educated Romans, it was not the geographical origin but the non-conforming habits that made a person a barbarian; Mathisen (1993) 43. Sidonius uses the term to criticise unaristocratic behaviour, denoting an 'uncultivated person', in Sidon. *Ep.* 1.7.6; Egetenmeyr (2021) 157–9. He recommends avoiding the barbarians in *Ep.* 7.14.10 *barbaros vitas, quia mali putentur; ego, etiamsi boni* ('you avoid the barbarians because they have a bad reputation; I avoid them even if they are good') and complains about their smell, appearance (*Carm.* 12) and excessive drinking (*Ep.* 8.3.2). There are only two letters in the collection (*Ep.* 4.17, 7.16) addressed to a recipient known to be of barbarian ancestry; Everschor (2007) 209–20. More often than the term *barbarus*, Sidonius uses the nationality designations of the barbarian peoples; Egetenmeyr (2021) 152. For Sidonius' attitude towards barbarians see the commentary below, p. 70, on *palam et ridentibus ... inter barbaros litteras* and also *Ep.* 1.6.2, 3.3.3, 3.5.2, 3.7.3–4, 4.17.1, 5.5.3, 5.7.1, 5.7.4, 6.12.4, 7.7.2, 8.11.3. There is an abundance of secondary literature on 'barbarians' in Sidonius: Stevens (1933) 48–9, Harries (1992), Luiselli (1992) 396–7, Mathisen (1993) 42–3, Kaufmann (1995) 168–70, 271–3, Näf (1995) 138, Amherdt (2001) 40–43, Gualandri (2000), Gerth (2013) 211–9, Fascione (2018), Fascione (2019), Hess (2019) 78–99, Raga (2019), Egetenmeyr (2021). For the always-shifting appreciation of the role of 'barbarians' in Late Antiquity (and for the concept of identity in general) see Mathisen (1993) 39–49, Heather (1999), Gillett (2009). The discussion is nowadays shifting towards 'otherness', from objective to subjective; see Maas (2012) 68 for the new categories of 'heretic' and 'pagan' which displaced *barbarus* as the most significant category of otherness. For the term *barbarismus*, 'an impropriety of speech', and Sidonius' concern for the purity of the Latin language, see the commentary on *Ep.* 2.10.1 *Illud appone ... meram linguae Latiaris*.

toto die a metu armatus, ab avaritia ieiunus, a cupiditate terribilis, a vanitate crudelis non cessat simul furta vel punire vel facere: To characterise Seronatus, Sidonius adds another clause consisting of four parallel elements (a + noun in ablative + adjective). Seronatus' behaviour is explained by a certain (wrong) reason; for example, he is armed because he is afraid and he fasts because he is stingy; Raga (2009) 182. Fasting for the wrong reason is also part of the description of the parasite Gnatho in *Ep.* 3.13.3: *ieiunat, quotiens non vocatur* ('he fasts when he has received no invitation'). The priest Himerius (*Ep.* 7.13.3), as well as Eutropia (*Ep.* 6.2.1), Vettius (*Ep.* 4.9.3) and bishop Patiens (*Ep.* 6.12.3), instead fast moderately and for religious reasons; Shanzer (2001) 221. *Cupiditas*, 'greed', probably recalls (like *concupiscit* in Sall. *Catil.* 3.1) Sallust's description of Catiline in Sall. *Catil.* 5.4 as *alieni appetens, sui profusus, ardens in cupiditatibus* ('he strives for the goods of other people, is wasteful with his own things and burns in his desires'); Montone (2017) 25. There is also a parallel to Verres, the greedy governor of Sicily, against whom Cicero also made speeches. For the expression *furta vel punire vel facere*, see: Sen. *De ira* 2.28.8 *punit furta sacrilegus* ('one who steals from a temple punishes thefts'); and Plin. *Ep.* 8.22.1 *et gravissime puniunt, quos maxime imitantur?* ('and they most severely punish those whom they imitate the most').

palam et ridentibus convocatis ructat inter cives pugnas, inter barbaros litteras: The next clause consists of two examples of inappropriate behaviour in front of the wrong audience. To civilians Seronatus talks about war, to barbarians about literature. Sidonius plays with the classical stereotype that barbarians are uneducated and associates the Gallo-Roman collaborator Seronatus with the barbarians. A similar antithesis between the inappropriate occupation with war or studies is found in *Ep.* 1.8.2 *student … armis eunuchi litteris foederati* ('eunuchs are keen on war, our allies on literature'). The verb *ructo*, 'to belch', 'to disgorge with belches' (of food, drink or natural forces) (OLD 1664) is used with an accusative object similarly in Fronto *Ad. Anton. De eloqu.* 2.4 *sapientiam ructarit* ('he utters wisdom'). Here the verb has a pejorative meaning, 'to belch words', 'to rant', 'to burst out'. For Christian writers *ructo* often has the meaning of 'to talk' (*loquendo proferre*); Gualandri (1979) 131, Amherdt (2001) 220, 385–6, 512–13. As Fascione (2019) 23–4 shows, Sidonius establishes a connection between the element of water and the barbarian population, among other things by often using the verb *ructo*. It also appears in Sidon. *Carm.* 2.337, 12.15, 23.253, and *Ep.* 4.7.2, 4.17.1, 4.25.2, 5.14.1. See also Ruric. *Ep.* 1.3.2 *verba ructuamus* ('we belch words'); Neri (2009) 180. For Sidonius' concept of barbarians and the term *barbarus*, see the commentary above, pp. 68–9, on *Ep.* 2.1.2 *indicit ut dominus, … calumniatur ut barbarus*.

epistulas, ne primis quidem apicibus sufficienter initiatus, publice a iactantia dictat, ab impudentia emendat: Sidonius hyperbolically describes how Seronatus barely knows the alphabet and yet dictates texts publicly. The model for Seronatus' lack of wisdom is again Sallust's description of Catiline; see Montone (2017) 25 and the commentary above, pp. 64–6, on *Ep.* 2.1.1 *Rediit ipse Catilina*…. In *Ep.* 9.9.2 Sidonius quotes verbatim Sallust's statement *Catilinam culpat habuisse 'satis eloquentiae sapientiae parum'* ('he blamed Catiline for having had "plenty of eloquence but not enough wisdom"') (Sall. *Catil.* 5.4). For the importance of education and the knowledge of classical authors as a sign of moral integrity, or its absence, in the characterisation of Seronatus, see Schwitter (2015) 83. Sidonius uses the noun *apex*, here 'letter of the alphabet', very often in its various meanings (*TLL* 2, 226.47–8.41). For the meaning of 'letter', see the commentary on *Ep.* 2.11.1 *nihil apicum raritati licere*…; for 'the highest ornament or honour', see the commentary on *Ep.* 2.3.1 *et in lares Philagrianos*…; for 'top of', 'summit', see *Ep.* 1.2.2 and 2.2.5. In *Ep.* 1.11.3, *apex* denotes 'letters, types'. Sidonius uses the term *iactantia*, 'boasting', 'bragging', 'showing-off' (*TLL*

7.1, 43.13–4.66) several times, also humorously in relation to himself in connection with the publication of his literary work; see Sidon. *Ep.* 1.9.8, 1.11.15, 4.3.17, 7.8.1, 7.13.3, 8.6.3, 8.13.1, 9.9.14; see also Plin. *Ep.* 1.8.13. The last part of the sentence is difficult to understand. Out of *impudentia*, 'shamelessness', 'impudence', 'impertinence' (*TLL* 7.1, 709.23–10.46), Seronatus corrects his texts. Sidonius probably means that Seronatus does not understand what the scribe wrote, but still changes it just to make a point. Sidonius also uses the term *impudentia* playfully about himself, in *Ep.* 3.11.2, 7.3.1, 9.15.1 v. 52. See also *Ep.* 1.7.9 (about Arvandus), 5.20.3, 7.5.1. *Emendo*, 'to correct', 'to emend' (*TLL* 5.2, 462.11–3.26) is the technical term to denote the revision of a literary work and is used in Cicero (Cic. *Att.* 2.16.4) and very frequently in Pliny's letters, for example Plin. *Ep.* 1.2.1, 2.5.10, 5.12.2, 7.17.2, 7.17.7. Interestingly, despite the Plinian model, in Sidonius the term appears only once again, in *Ep.* 5.19.2, where it means 'to compensate' (for a wrongdoing).

Section 3

Totum quod concupiscit quasi comparat nec dat pretia contemnens nec accipit instrumenta desperans: Seronatus illegally gets everything he desires, the typical behaviour of a tyrant. The verb *concupiscit*, 'to covet', 'to desire eagerly' probably recalls Sallust's description of Catiline (Sall. *Catil.* 5.4), cited in the commentary above on *Ep.* 2.1.2 *toto die a metu armatus*. The term *instrumenta* refers to the *instrumenta emptionis*, 'written contracts between vendor and intending purchaser' (*TLL* 7.1, 2014.4–13); see Iustin. *Inst.* 3.23.1, Anderson (1936) 414 n. 2. The second part of this sentence is later cited – different only in verb tenses – along with five other letters of Sidonius by Greg. Tur. *Hist. Franc.* 4.12, when he discusses bishop Cautinus of Clermont: *quibus et a quibus, ut Sollius noster ait, nec dabat pretia contemnens nec accipiebat instrumenta desperans* ('to those and of those, as our Sollius says, he neither pays in his disdain nor accepts any contracts in his suspicion'); Mathisen (2020b) 634.

in concilio iubet, in consilio tacet, in ecclesia iocatur, in convivio praedicat, in cubiculo damnat, in quaestione dormitat: Sidonius starts a new series of Seronatus' wrongdoings, consisting of six phrases that can be grouped into three pairs according to content. In these three pairs the verbs and nouns are inverted and fit the other half of the pair. Inappropriate behaviour is similarly described by Sidonius in *Ep.* 5.7.4 in his criticism of informants who betrayed the brother of Thaumastus: *in foro Scythae, in cubiculo viperae, in convivio scurrae, in exactionibus Harpyiae, in conlocutionibus statuae, in quaestionibus bestiae, in tractatibus cocleae, in contractibus trapezitae* ('In the forum they are Scythians, in a room they are vipers, at a dinner party they are buffoons, in their exactions harpies, in conversations statues, in investigations brute beasts, in discussions snails, in contracts usurers'). Furthermore, the passage at hand recalls the negative description of Arvandus in *Ep.* 1.7.3 *omnium colloquia ridere, consilia mirari, officia contemnere, pati de occurrentum raritate suspicionem, de assiduitate fastidium* ('he mocked every one of them when they conversed with him, professed astonishment at their suggestions, and ignored their services; if only few sought to accost him he nursed suspicion, if many, contempt'). For a similar sequence with paired members, see the positive description of Theoderic II in *Ep.* 1.2.7 and the praise of Potentinus in *Ep.* 5.11.2.

Concilium and *consilium* are the first of the three pairs and the closest. Whereas a *concilium* is an assembly for consultation (*in concreto*), *consilium* signifies the counsel (*in abstracto*) that is employed in such an assembly. The meanings, however, are often mixed up (see *TLL* 4, 44.14–38). Here the two terms refer to two different types of assembly, a public meeting (*concilium*) and a private assembly (*consilium*). The opposition between *iubere*, 'to command', and *tacere*, 'to be silent', shows the right behaviour in both of the bodies, which Seronatus fails to do: restraint in the public meeting and authority in a private assembly. Instead, he orders around his peers or superiors and fails to guide his inferiors. The appropriate behaviour in a *consilium*, 'council', 'board', was to participate in the discussion by making suggestions and proposals, as in *Ep.* 7.9.22 *in consilio praecellens* ('distinguished in the council') and 7.13.2 *si quid vel deliberet forte vel suadeat* ('whether he discusses something or advises'); van Waarden (2010) 520, van Waarden (2016) 90. What kind of public assembly Sidonius means by *concilium* is not clear from the text. Loyen (1970a) 44 identifies *concilium* with 'the Council of the Seven Provinces'. The *Concilium septem provinciarum* consisted of Gallo-Roman aristocrats (*iudices, honorati, possessores/curiales*) from the Diocese of the Seven Provinces or *Diocesis Viennensis*, which comprised the provinces Aquitania I and II, Novempopulana, Narbonensis I and II, Viennensis and Alpes Maritimae. The governing body met from 418 on (see the *constitutio Honorii*) annually in Arles between 13 August and 13 September. The length of the session depended on the matters which the Council had to discuss, one function being the control of officials; Zeller (1905) 15–17. On the Council of the Seven Provinces in general, see Zeller (1905), Mathisen (1989) 19, 42, Mathisen (1993) 19, Heather (1992) 91. Sidonius uses the non-specific word *concilium* for different kinds of meetings also in *Ep.* 1.3.3, 1.6.4, 4.25.1, 5.20.1, 7.7.4; Köhler (1995) 174, 226–7, van Waarden (2010) 368. For the opposition of *concilium* and *consilium*, see also *Ep.* 7.7.4–5. See also *Ep.* 8.11.4 *praeterea etsi consilio fragilis, fide firmissimus erat* ('moreover, although weak in counsel, he was completely steadfast in fidelity').

The opposition in the second pair, *in ecclesia iocatur, in convivio praedicat*, is not stressed by alliteration or assonance. *Convivium*, 'a social feast', 'banquet' (*TLL* 4, 881.25–5.80), however, recalls the first pair, *concilium* and *consilium*. See Sidon. *Ep.* 8.5.2 *consilio gravius convivio laetius colloquio iucundius* ('more weighty than your counsel, more cheerful than your company, more delightful than your conversation'). Sidonius uses the term frequently, for example also in *Ep.* 1.2.6, 2.9.6, 5.7.4, 7.13.4, 8.12.8, 9.4.2, 9.13.4, *Carm.* 22.5, 23.439. *Convivium* is often used in opposition to or connection with *cubiculum*, as in Sidon. *Ep.* 5.7.4 *in cubiculo viperae, in convivio scurrae* ('in the bedroom they are vipers, at dinner they are buffoons'), and also in Sen. *Ep.* 47.7 *in cubiculo vir, in convivio puer est* ('in the bedroom he is a man, during dinner he is a boy'); there are further examples in *TLL* 4, 1267.48–68. Here, however, Sidonius combines the bedroom not with the banquet, but with the courthouse in the third pair. The term *cubiculum*, 'bedroom' (*TLL* 4, 1266.30–9.50), does not have a well defined single function, but is a space of the Roman house with many strong associations, among them rest, sex, adultery, controlled display of art, murder and suicide, and reception; Riggsby (1997) 37–43. When describing his villa in *Ep.* 2.2.10 Sidonius writes *dormitorium cubiculum* to denote the bedchamber. It is a place where at least some of the rules of public behaviour are relaxed and it is closely linked to the ancient discourse on public and private spheres. Many of the references to business meetings in *cubicula* suggest that those meetings were inappropriate; for example those arranged by Verres, who, along with Catiline, is a role model for Seronatus' inappropriate behaviour. These include meetings leading to judicial decisions and the awarding of tax-collection rights; see Cic. *Verr.* 2.2.53, 2.3.23, 2.3.34, 2.5.11. See also Cic. *Phil.* 8.29, Riggsby (1997) 47. Convicting someone privately for crimes (*in cubiculo damnat*) is a topos associated with bad rulers. Cicero was accused thereof after the Catilinarian conspiracy; see Sall. *In Tull.* 3. The emperor Claudius was infamous for his private interest in judicial causes and unjust indictments; see Suet. *Claud.* 14.1–15.4. Pliny conversely praises the emperor Trajan for conducting his business in public, where it could be judged by the people, in Plin. *Pan.* 51.5, 83.1; Riggsby (1997) 48. *Quaestio*, 'a judicial investigation, inquiry' (*OLD* 1534, 3; *Blaise* 688, 2), is a juridical *terminus technicus* which here refers to the proceedings in court attended by Seronatus. With the frequentative verb *dormito*, 'to keep falling asleep', 'to drowse' (*TLL* 5.1, 2034.83–5.41) Sidonius expresses Seronatus' neglect of his duty as a judge. Its alternative meaning of 'to be negligent, careless' (*TLL* 5.1, 2035.83–6.9) probably also comes into effect here. *Dormito* is used in Sidon. *Ep.* 2.2.13 in opposition to *dormio* (see the commentary on *Ep.* 2.2.13 *interiecto consistorio … dormitandi potius quam dormiendi locus est*); see also 7.6.3 *dormitantum … pastorum* ('of the dozing shepherds'), van Waarden (2010) 292, Montone (2017) 25, Fasione (2019) 39, and Sidon. *Carm.* 5.201, 23.512, where the verb means 'to have leisure', 'to be lazy'.

implet cotidie silvas fugientibus, villas hospitibus, altaria reis, carceres clericis: To complain about Seronatus, Sidonius adds another clause consisting of four parallel elements (accusative + instrumental ablative), all structured by the initial verb *implet*. As regards their content, the four elements can be divided into two pairs. The second element (*villas hospitibus*) of the first pair of contradicting places/persons causes some textual difficulties. The manuscripts LCT² – followed by Lütjohann (1887) 21 and Dolveck (2020) 488 – have *hostibus*, while the manuscripts NVMT – followed by Loyen (1970a) 44 and Anderson (1936) 414 – have *hospitibus*. Stevens (1933) 113 n. 2 also prefers *hospitibus*, as the *lectio difficilior*, 'the technical term for barbarians … billeted on Roman estates'. The connection with *villa* is the clue for my decision for *hospitibus* instead of *hostibus*. *Hospes* alludes to the practice of *hospitalitas*, that is, the settlement of barbarians on rural estates (see *TLL* 6.3, 3036.39–43). This method was applied by the Roman government to the Visigoths in Aquitania in 418 and subsequently to other groups. The conditions of these settlements – whether they happened to be on public or on private grounds or whether the barbarians just received tax revenues from the estates instead of the land itself – are much debated. For *hospitalitas* in general, see Lot (1928), Thompson (1963) 118–22, Barnish (1986), Krieger (1991) 30–75, Mathisen (1993) 30, Liebeschütz (2006), Halsall (2007) 422–47, esp. 434, Goffart (2013), Delaplace (2015) 29–31. For *hospitalitas* in the sense of 'hospitality', 'welcoming friends', see *Ep.* 2.9.2. The manuscripts show the same confusion between *hostis* and *hospes* in Sidon. *Carm.* 5.563. In *Ep.* 7.7.2 the Visigoths are described as *hostes publici*; van Waarden (2010) 352. In *Ep.* 8.4.1 Sidonius talks about *hospites* on Consentius' estate Octavianum, near Narbonne. Here, in *Ep.* 2.1.3, the barbarians could have been simply guests or (more probably) those resident in areas where they had been officially permitted to settle – see Overwien (2009a) 101.

The second pair, *altaria reis, carceres clericis*, suggests that villains are preaching at the altar while priests are in prison. The combination of *reus*, 'accused', 'defendant', and *altarium*, 'altar', is also suggestive of the sacred asylum at the altars in antiquity and the asylum granted by the church; Traulsen (2004). The term *altarium* is used for the altars of Roman gods and of the Christian and Jewish god (*TLL* 1, 1727.64–9.81). It is also used in Sidon. *Ep.* 2.10.3, 4.11.6 v. 14, 4.15.2, 4.25.4, 7.6.8. *Clericus* is ecclesiastical Latin and denotes 'a Catholic priest', 'clergyman' (*TLL* 3, 1339.48–40.71); see also Sidon. *Ep.* 1.8.2, 4.11.4.

exultans Gothis insultansque Romanis, inludens praefectis conludensque numerariis: To express that Seronatus prefers the Visigoths over the Romans and conspires with subordinate ranks against their superiors Sidonius joins two pairs of similar-sounding participial constructions. The first pair is *ex(s)ulto*, 'to exult', 'praise', 'exalt' (constructed with ablative) (*TLL* 5.2, 1946.66–53.31), and *insulto* 'to insult' (with dative) (*TLL* 7.1, 2042.63–5.51). The same combination is found in Sidon. *Ep.* 9.9.3 *exulto tantum, verum insulto* ('I not only exult but insult you'). For examples of the use of *insulto* see also 7.6.3, 7.14.7, 8.12.7; for *exulto* see 3.13.3, 4.25.5. The second pair is *illudo*, 'to make sport of', 'speak mockingly of', 'mock' (*TLL* 7.1, 389.14–25; *OLD* 829–30, 1a), and the quite rare verb *colludo*, 'to act in collusion', 'collude' (*TLL* 3, 1658.30–50; *OLD* 354, 2). Both verbs are constructed with the dative, which is common for *illudo* but rare for *colludo*. A *praefectus*, 'superior', 'head' (*TLL* 10.2, 623.9–31.47), is a Roman functionary with comprehensive responsibilities for a certain task, for example a commander of the imperial body or governor of a province of the Roman Empire. In the later Roman Empire the title is restricted to the praetorian prefects (*praefectus praetorio*), an office descended from the commander of the Praetorian Guard, but predominantly civilian since Constantine and with regional responsibility (either of the Gallic provinces or of Italy in Sidonius' period), and to the prefects of the city of Rome (and the equivalent in Constantinople), that is, the office of *praefectus urbi*, who was directly responsible to the emperor; Gutsfeld (2001a), Gutsfeld (2001b), Maier (2005) 274–9. Sidonius mentions the office of a *praefectus* in the second book also in *Ep.* 2.9.3 and 2.13.3. Sidonius became *praefectus urbi*, governor of the city of Rome, in 468 (see the Introduction to this book, p. x). A *numerarius* was an 'accountant in all civilian and military authorities'. As this function was generally considered suspect, there were preventive regulations and harsh sanctions against profiteering in accounting; Gizewski (2000). On the office of a *numerarius*, see also Sidon. *Ep.* 1.11.6, 5.7.3, Köhler (1995) 312.

leges Theodosianas calcans Theodoricianasque proponens, veteres culpas nova tributa perquirit: In principle, Sidonius contrasts the Gothic law with the Roman law in this clause. The *Codex Theodosianus* contained the laws of the Roman Empire since 312 and was published in 438 during the reign of Theodosius II, emperor of the Eastern Roman Empire from 408 to 450. It was still used in Sidonius' time; Liebs (2002) 97–9. The second part of the clause, which refers to Gothic law, causes more problems: there is no consensus as to which of the Theoderics is meant with *Theodoricianas*. For chronological reasons, it cannot be the most famous king of this name, the Ostrogothic king Theoderic the Great (reigned 493–526). The association would probably have been with the Visigothic king Theoderic I (reigned 418–52) or Theoderic II (reigned 453–66). Sidonius praises the latter in a lengthy description in Sidon. *Ep.* 1.2 and *Carm.* 7.495–6 (where he asserts that Theoderic studied Roman law), 23.69–74; Sivan (1989), Kaufmann (1995) 106–39, Köhler (1995) 119–24, Mathisen (2020a) 123. *Leges Theodoricianas* could hint at the so-called *edictum Theodorici*, a collection of laws that dates from the fifth or sixth century, mostly taken from Roman law and attributed to various authors, among them the Ostrogothic king Theoderic the Great or the Visigothic king Theoderic II; on the *edictum Theodorici*, see Liebs (1987) 191–4, Amory (1993) 78–9 n. 187, Collins (1998) 10–11. Theoderic I probably issued individual laws on demarcation, attested in the *Codex Euricianus*, section 227 *pater noster in alia lege praecepit* ('our father ordered in another law'); Liebs (2002) 157–8. Visigothic law codes (based on Roman law) were issued by the king Euric (466–84) in 476 (*Codex Euricianus*) and by king Alaric II (484–507) in 506 (*Breviarium Alaricianum*) to maintain certain Roman legal structures (property and testamentary rights); see Sidon. *Ep.* 8.3.3, Barnwell (1992) 74–6, Heather (1999) 248–53, Liebs (2002) 157–63. It may be that the 'laws of Theoderic' thus just demonstrate Sidonius' love of assonance and symbolise a concept of Gothic law in general in a witty antithesis to Roman law; Harries (1994) 126–7, Delaplace (2014) 31 n. 14, Mratschek (2020a) 231. An overview of the various Germanic laws in contrast to the *Codex Theodosianus* is given by MacDonald (2000) 242–4. Written law also figures centrally in other sources when barbarian and Roman societies are compared. Orosius (*Hist.* 7.43.6) reports that Athaulf, king of the Visigoths (411–15), supported

Roman law instead of replacing it with Gothic law because his men were unable to obey written law. Heather (1999) 237–8 gives further examples. For an overview of the extensive juridical discussion of the Sidonian passage at hand, see Mathisen (1993) 133–4, Kaufmann (1995) 127–8, 131, Halsall (2007) 462–6, Herrero de Jáuregui (2017) 137–41. Sidonius broaches the subject of the loss of Roman law in *Ep.* 4.17.2 *etsi apud limitem ipsum Latina iura ceciderunt* ('even though Roman law went down at our border'). The manuscripts contain different spellings: Lütjohann (1887) 22 emends to *Theodoricianasque*, LM and Loyen (1970a) 44 have *Theudoricianasque*, P *Teudoricianasque*, C *Theudericianasque*, T *Theodicianasque*, F *Theodotianasque*. The Sangallensis manuscript has *Theodoricianas*; Mathisen (2020b) 641. Even if something beginning with *Theud-* may well be an authentic spelling, I opt for *Theodoricianasque* for the sake of the play on words.

Section 4

Proinde moras tuas citius explica et quicquid illud est, quod te retentat, incide: With *mora*, 'delay' (*TLL* 8, 1466.82–68.13), and the plea to Ecdicius to hasten his return, Sidonius ends his letter. As van Waarden (2020d) 159 shows, the word *mora* frames the entirety of Book 2, in 2.1 signifying the delayed assistance in war, in 2.14.2 in a ring composition *nobis ... in oppido ... amputabuntur causae morarum* ('then my reasons for staying in town will be cut off') the delay in yielding to a vacation. Sidonius thus starts the second book with war and ends it with a description of peaceful life in the countryside. See also *Ep.* 1.5.2 *ubi sane vianti moram non veredorum paucitas sed amicorum multitudo faciebat* ('delays on my journey were due not to scarcity of post-horses but to multiplicity of friends') and *Ep.* 4.8.1 for the same motif of being held back from travelling. The collocation *moras ... explicare* is also attested in *Pass. Paul.* 13 *tu explica moras, quibus iussionem differs* ('you, however, explain the delays by which you are deferring this order'); Eastman (2015) 163. While the combination of *mora* with verbs like *rumpere* (Verg. *Aen.* 4.569), *pellere* (Ov. *Met.* 10.659), *corripere* (Ov. *Met.* 9.282) or *removere* (Plaut. *Stich.* 309) focuses on the forceful ending of a delay, *explico*, 'disentangle', 'solve', 'settle' (*TLL* 5.2, 1729.24–30.8), hints at problems which hold Ecdicius back and which he has to deal with first. For *explico* in other meanings, see Sidon. *Ep.* 2.11.2, 'send away', and 2.13.4, 'to unfold', 'spread out'. In *Ep.* 2.9.1 Sidonius adds the wordplay *nec moras meas prodere moror* ('I do not hesitate to explain my hesitation'). *Citus*, 'moving or acting quickly' (*TLL* 3, 1209.47–75; *OLD* 329, 1a) is generally used in an adverbial way; see also *Ep.* 4.24.2. It is attested in all the manuscripts except in the *Codex Sangallensis* (190), the earliest extant manuscript testimony, which has the comparative adverb *citius*, 'quicker', 'earlier', 'quite quickly', 'rather quickly' (*TLL* 3, 1210.79–12.80), and probably is right, as the more intensive comparative adverb is typical of late Latin; Dolveck (2020) 484 n. 20, Mathisen (2020b) 641. For *incidere* 'to cut short', 'break off', 'put an end to', see *TLL* 7.1, 909.53–74. The model for this exact expression is Sen. *Ep.* 17.1 *si quid est quo teneris, aut expedi aut incide* ('if there is something that holds you back either free yourself or cut it loose'). Sidonius uses it similarly also in *Ep.* 7.7.5, 7.16.1; van Waarden (2010) 373. For the idea of being held back in a different place, see Plin. *Ep.* 6.6.9 *abrumpe si qua te retinent* ('free yourself if something holds you back'). The humanist Rodolphus Agricola (1444–85) cites Sidonius in his letter 2.2 *rumpe, queso, moras omnes … vel explica vel incide*; van der Laan and Akkerman (2002) 64, 271.

Te exspectat palpitantium civium extrema libertas: To give greater emphasis to his request, Sidonius makes the threatened *libertas* ('freedom', 'liberty') the subject of the sentence, thereby personifying her and recalling her role in Roman mythology. The goddess Libertas had a temple on the Aventine from 283 BC; Stoffel (1999). For the fear of liberty at stake, see Sidon. *Ep.* 5.12.2, 7.7.6 *quorum est moritura libertas* ('whose freedom will disappear'), van Waarden (2010) 377, Fascione (2019) 89. In her study, Postel (2011) 173–9 shows that Sidonius uses the term *libertas* in his letters to refer above all to the striving to preserve the political independence of the Auvergne from Burgundian and Visigothic power and to consolidate the consensus of the educated *cives* against the brute *barbari*. For Sidonius, freedom, birth and education are the hallmarks of the ruling class (see *Ep.* 5.8.2) and *libertas* is also a quality he attributes to a noblewoman, Filimatia (2.8.3 v. 11). *Libertas* is also used about Rome (*patriam libertatis*, 'the hometown of freedom') in *Ep.* 1.6.2; Egetenmeyr (2021) 152. The verb *palpito*, 'to tremble', 'to quiver', is attested from Cicero onwards and appears several times in Seneca and then is frequently used by Christian writers. Other examples of *palpito* meaning as here 'trembling with fear' (*TLL* 10.1, 165.26–36) include Petron. 100.4 and Hier. *Ep.* 14.11; Montone (2017) 25.

Quicquid sperandum, quicquid desperandum est, fieri te medio, te praesule placet: The proximity between hope and despair is expressed by the parallel construction of *sperandum* and *desperandum* in the first part of the sentence. Sidonius pins all his hope on Ecdicius and lets him decide what to do. Pliny shows a similar attitude in a political crisis in Plin. *Ep.* 1.5.10 *exspecto Mauricum (nondum ab exilio venerat)* ('I am waiting for Mauricus (he had not returned from exile))' and Plin. *Ep.* 1.5.16 *mihi et temptandi aliquid et quiescendi illo auctore ratio constabit* ('whether I will do something or let the matter rest will depend on his decision'). With *te medio*, 'you amidst us', Sidonius expresses the unity of all citizens regarding Ecdicius' leading role. On *te praesule*, 'you as our leader', 'under your leadership', see the commentary on *Ep.* 2.2.3 *Haec mihi cum meis praesule deo*. Sidonius hints that Ecdicius might become some sort of local leader in the resistance against the Visigoths, as he would actually be in the year 471 or 472, when he breaks the Visigothic sieges of Clermont; see the introduction to *Ep.* 2.1, Wood (2000) 507, Ward-Perkins (2005) 48–9 on *Ep.* 3.3.7, Sivonen (2006) 154, Drinkwater (2013) 65. See also the commentary below, p. 80, on *Ep.* 2.1.4 *statuit te auctore nobilitas....*

Si nullae a republica vires, nulla praesidia, si nullae, quantum rumor est, Anthemii principis opes: At the end of the letter, Sidonius names the higher authority which, along with Seronatus, is responsible for the desperate situation. Anthemius was the Western Roman Emperor from 467 to 472. In Gaul, he had to face the ambitious Visigothic king Euric (466–84). Anthemius' attempts to recover any part of Gaul with his military offensives in 469 and 471 failed and the Visigoths even expanded their kingdom (see the introduction on the date of this letter). Only small imperial pockets remained, including in the Auvergne; Mathisen (1998), *PLRE* 2, 96–8. The land of the Arverni was formally handed over to the Visigothic king Euric by the Roman emperor Julius Nepos in 475. The relationship between Sidonius and Anthemius was complex. Initially, it appears to have been strong; Sidonius delivered a panegyric for Anthemius, after which the emperor appointed Sidonius as *praefectus urbi* for the year 468, see *Carm.* 2 and *Ep.* 1.9.5–6, Henning (1999) 155. The reason for this position of honour was probably that Sidonius belonged to the ruling class in Gaul, whose support Anthemius needed in order to be able to maintain his authority in the west outside Italy. Good relationships between the parts of the Roman state (*concordia imperii*) was a major goal of Anthemius' reign. At some point during or after 468, their relationship soured; Stevens (1933) 101, Harries (1994) 147–8, Mathisen (1998), Henning (1999) 42–6, 199–202. On Sidonius' *panegyricus* on Anthemius, its composition and reception, see Günther (1982), Sivan (1989), Watson (1998), Henning

(1999) 154–69, Bruzzone (2013) 356–7, 371–3, Harries (forthcoming). In his letters, however, Sidonius depicts Anthemius several times in a negative light and links Rome's lack of power to Anthemius' rule; see *Ep.* 1.5 about the nuptial celebrations of the emperor Anthemius' daughter Alypia and the barbarian potentate Ricimer, and *Ep.* 1.7, 1.9.1; Hanaghan (2017c), Hanaghan (2019) 104–8. In *Ep.* 2.3 Sidonius refers to Anthemius without explicitly naming him (see the introduction to *Ep.* 2.3). In the first two books of letters, Anthemius thus appears, according to Hanaghan (2019) 104, as an 'inept, haughty spendthrift' and through these negative portraits Sidonius distances himself from this unloved ruler who was still in power. Sidonius uses *rumor*, 'hearsay', 'rumour' (*OLD* 1667, 2), instead of *fama*, also in *Ep.* 7.1.1, where he starts the letter with *rumor est Gothos in Romanum solum castra movisse* ('there is a rumour that the Goths have moved their camp onto Roman soil'); van Waarden (2010) 84.

statuit te auctore nobilitas seu patriam dimittere seu capillos: In the last sentence of his letter Sidonius appeals again to Ecdicius to take the lead, *te auctore* (*TLL* 2, 1197.39–98.37); see the commentary above, pp. 78–9, on *Ep.* 2.1.4 *Quicquid sperandum ... te praesule placet*. Ecdicius' leadership brings two possible losses: the first is to lose the homeland. For the importance of *patria* for Sidonius and the Auvergne as his place of belonging (*patria naturae*) as opposed to Lyon, his place of birth, see *Ep.* 4.21, *Carm.* 17.19–20, Bonjour (1980), Amherdt (2001) 236–7, 435, 444–6, and the commentary on 2.1.1 *Arverni tui*. What Sidonius means by the second possible loss is disputed. The most popular solution is to interpret *dimittere capillos* as 'tonsure', 'cutting hair as a sign of religious devotion'; see the translation by Dalton (1915) 35, 'our nobility is determined to follow your lead, and give up their country or the hair of their heads'; similarly Stevens (1933) 113, Anderson (1936) 416–17, Loyen (1970a) 44, Köhler (2014) 42; see also the discussion in Sirmond (1614) 42, Mathisen (1984) 168, Mathisen (1993) 89–104, Harries (1994) 39–40, Näf (1995) 137, Condorelli (2008) 190 n. 18, Mratschek (2020a) 226. See also *Ep.* 4.24.3 *tum coma brevis barba prolixa* ('moreover, his hair was short and the beard long'), where short hair is a sign of a monk, a clergyman or a penitent. As long hair is a sign of nobility and liberty, losing one's hair also could hint at slavery; see Frye (1994), who translates 'risking their country or their freedom', and similarly Delaplace (2014) 24. Another possible interpretation is to take *capilli* as part of the head (*caput*), that is, a person and the safety of a person, and translate as 'losing one's life' or 'die'. Momigliano (1973) 406 explains Sidonius' expression as an allusion to *Gallia comata* ('the long-haired Gaul'), which is replaced with the *Gallia tonsurata* ('the shaved Gaul'). *Comata Gallia* was the Roman name for the part of Gaul subjugated by Caesar (*Tres Galliae*), in contrast to the 'Gauls in the toga' (*Gallia togata* = *Cisalpina*) and the 'trouser Gauls' of southern Gaul (*bracata*); see Cic. *Phil.* 8.27, Plin. *Nat.* 4.105 and Suet. *Caes.* 22; Ihm (1900).

Vale: Sidonius ends his letter with a simple *Vale*. In accordance with the practice of Pliny and Symmachus, the endings of most of Sidonius' letters (and all of those in the second book) are as simple as their beginnings; Zelzer and Zelzer (2002) 404, Mratschek (2017) 311, Gibson (2020) 376. Based on comparison with contemporary letters (by Faustus of Riez and Ruricius of Limoges) Mathisen (2013) 240–2 suggests that Sidonius implemented these standardised formulas only when revising the letters, to replace longer and more elaborate greetings in the original letters.

Epistula 2

Introduction

Summary

While Sidonius is in the countryside, the addressee, Domitius, is still in the city. Sidonius describes the hot climate that prevails in the area at the moment. Sidonius taunts Domitius by imagining his tiring life as a teacher in the heat of the city. After praising the climate in the countryside and inviting Domitius to join him, Sidonius describes his estate, Avitacum, beginning with the baths, that is, the hot room, the room for applying oil and the cool room. Sidonius praises the lack of immoral pictures on its walls. A description of the swimming pool and its water supply follows. The stream that pours into the pool is so noisy that you cannot understand a word if you talk nearby. Next, Sidonius describes his wife's dining room, a weaving room, a store room, a portico with a wonderful view over the lake. He praises the quality of the cool drinks one can enjoy there while watching the fishermen on the lake. There follows a description of the guest room and the pleasant animal sounds that will be heard there. Sidonius describes a shady place where he plays ball and dice with his brother-in-law Ecdicius, and the nearby lake, its dimensions, tributary river, fish population, banks, colour, and surroundings. There is even an island in the middle of the lake where boat races are held in imitation of Vergil's *Aeneid*. Finally, Sidonius again asks the addressee Domitius to hurry and visit him and he apologises for the undue length of the letter.

Addressee

The addressee, Domitius, is a teacher (probably located in Clermont) whom Sidonius also mentions in *Carm.* 24.10–15 as a severe critic, whose judgement he values. Based on Domitius' association with the Muses (*Carm.* 24.10) Mathisen (2020a) 90 thinks that Domitius is a teacher of rhetoric for older students (*rhetor*) rather than for basic studies (*grammaticus*), as he appears to be in this letter. Domitius, with his interest in literature, is a fitting addressee for one of Sidonius' most elaborate letters, full of literary allusions. Sidonius certainly also chooses him because he reminds him of Pliny's friend Domitius Apollinaris, the addressee of one of Pliny's famous villa letters (Plin. *Ep.* 5.6); Harries (1994) 10, Mratschek (2008) 373–4, Gibson (2013b) 345–6, Mratschek (2017) 311–13. Sidonius likes puns on names and alludes to Pliny's addressees also in *Ep.* 9.16; see Gibson (2011) 657–9, Gibson (2013b) 345–6, and above on *Ep.* 2.1.1 *Seronati, inquam*....

For Domitius' life, see Mathisen (2020a) 90, *PLRE* 2, 371 n. 2, *PCBE* 4, 584, Loyen (1943) 64–5, Kaster (1988) 209, 274, Kaufmann (1995) 295, Gemeinhardt (2007) 372–3, Visser (2014) 28–9. Sidonius also addresses a teacher, the *grammaticus* Iohannes, whose learning he praises, in *Ep.* 8.2.1; Mratschek (2008) 367, 377. On the role of teachers in the context of the late Roman Empire, and in Sidon. *Ep.* 4.11, see John (2021b).

Date

Since the letter is set in a somewhat timeless period of leisure that recalls the classical Rome *otium*, there is no evidence for an exact date of this letter; see the Introduction, '2. The date and order of letters in Book 2'.

Major themes and further reading

Structure

Formally, letter 2.2 is a letter of invitation: it starts with the *salutatio* ('greeting') and *captatio benevolentiae* ('winning of goodwill') in sections 1 and 2, followed by the lengthy *narratio* ('narration') in sections 3–19; see Cugusi (1983) 222, but see also Gibson (2020) 383–5 about the problem of categorising ancient letters in general. The thematic sequence of *Ep.* 2.1 and 2.2 reflects the content of Book 1, about business (*negotium*), and Book 2, about leisure (*otium*): the first letter thus is political, serious and has a tone of invective, while the second letter is private and relaxed; see Hindermann (2020a) 96–9 and Introduction to this book. The same order is found in Plin. *Ep.* 1.5 and 1.6. Sidonius is generally very interested in the topic of the villa and its lifestyle – see the next section: 'Life in the villa: cultural identity and intertextuality'. Whereas in *Ep.* 2.2 he focuses on architectural details and the landscape, *Ep.* 2.9 is dedicated to the daily routine in the villa; see the introduction to *Ep.* 2.9 and the commentary on 2.9.8 *Balneas habebat* …. There is also a parallel to *Ep.* 2.12, where Sidonius describes a flight from the city, but in a serious context: Sidonius' daughter Severiana is ill and therefore in need of the healthy suburban villa. Another parallel within the second book is to the last letter, *Ep.* 2.14, where Sidonius is in the city (in winter) and laments the absence of the addressee, Maurusius, whom he is going to visit, while in *Ep.* 2.2 Sidonius is the host (in summer) and the addressee, Domitius, complains about his absence from the city; Hindermann (2020a) 109–11 Hanaghan (2019) 73, 170 focuses on the important structural role of seasons in Sidonius' letters: in Book 2 a clear sense of the progression of time is conveyed from early summer in *Ep.* 2.2 – a letter which would not work in a winter setting – to late autumn in *Ep.* 2.14. This seasonal progression continues into Book 3 (winter in *Ep.* 3.2, and then summer in *Ep.* 3.3) and thus connects the two books.

Life in the villa: cultural identity and intertextuality
Ep. 2.2 was the first part of Sidonius' work to be translated in 1589 by the poet Pascal Robin du Faut; Green (2020) 618. It deals with the major social obligations of a Roman aristocrat in residence at his villa, that is, to entertain family members and friends who have come to the villa in order to share with him the pleasures of country; see Rossiter (1991) 202. Like his predecessors, Sidonius uses his villa, Avitacum, to express his cultural identity and to display his social status – see for example Mart. 3.58, 4.64, 10.30, Stat. *Silv.* 1 *praef.* 29–31, 1.5, Hor. *Carm.* 1.17, 3.16; Myers (2005), Newlands (2013) 68–9, Bergmann (2016) 205, Hanaghan (2019) 27–8, 42–9, Hanaghan (2020) 131–3, Mratschek (2020b) 248–53. In *Ep.* 4.9.1, Sidonius explicitly draws conclusions from the house of Vettius about his character; see Symm. *Ep.* 1.1 for the importance of a villa in one's self-characterisation. Writing about villas always has a competitive element in Sidonius' work. Sidonius mentions his villa and especially its bath also in *Carm.* 18 and 19 and compares his bath to the baths of his uncles Apollinaris and Ferreolus in *Ep.* 2.9; see Hanaghan (2020) 125–31. The similarities between Sidonius' description of his villa and that of Pontius Leontius' estate Burgus (*Carm.* 22) connect the two texts and buildings in favour of Sidonius; see Hanaghan (2020) 123–5. Other letters and poems where withdrawal into the country and villa life are described are *Ep.* 1.6.3, 3.1, 3.3.5, 4.15, 4.18.3, 4.21.6, 5.17.1, 8.4.1–2, 8.8, *Carm.* 22, 24; the related literature is discussed in the 'Further reading' section below. In *Ep.* 8.8 Sidonius

reproaches his correspondent for spending too much time in the countryside and not fulfilling his duties in the city (and also in *Ep.* 1.6.3, 5.14.1, 5.14.3, 7.15) while Sidonius' own dutiful service looms in the background; see Frye (2003) 193–6. His own villa, though, is of existential importance to him and he mourns its loss caused by his banishment in *Ep.* 8.9; Henke (2008) 166–9, Overwien (2009a) 108–11. Sidonius' villa has various rooms, including seasonal dining rooms, which were a status symbol of country villas (the rooms included the *matronale triclinium, textrinum, cella penaria, porticus, vestibulum, cryptoporticus, membrum frigidum, dormitorium cubiculum, hiemale triclinium, diaeta/cenatiuncula, deversorium, consistorium*); Hanaghan (2019) 27. There is also the bath, with its different rooms (*cella aquarum coctilium, cella unguentaria, frigidaria, piscina*), and places in the garden (*area virenti, nemus, aleatorium*), where Sidonius and his guests like to spend time.

Sidonius describes his life in the countryside with a mosaic of literary allusions, which the skilled reader (*artifex lector*) has to decipher. In his most artful and highly intertextual letter Sidonius cites and alludes to several authors: for the overall structure of a villa letter and the description of a lake as a natural wonder, Pliny the Younger is his major source of inspiration – see Plin. *Ep.* 1.9, 2.17, 4.30, 5.6, 8.8, 8.20, 9.7.2; Sherwin-White (1966) 186–9. Like Pliny, Sidonius describes his estate in the second book of his letter collection; Gibson (2013b) 345. He adds different features, though, which Pliny treats only briefly, omits or treats in a separate letter, naemly the climate, the bath and the geographical description of the site and the lake nearby; Hindermann (2020a) 99–108. Like Pliny, Sidonius devotes himself not only to the architecture of the villa, but also to the activities and timetable of an ideal day in the country, which, however, he describes in another villa letter, *Ep.* 2.9, concerning the villas of his relatives Tonantius Ferreolus and Apollinaris; see Riggsby (2003) on the treatment of space and time in Pliny's villa descriptions and Riggsby (1997) 48–54 on the role of 'public' and 'private' rooms in the villa, both of which articles are relevant to Sidonius' villa descriptions.

While Pliny largely omits the staff and family in his descriptions of villas and presents himself as a lonely poet, Sidonius repeatedly refers to his or his friends' slaves, as with 2.2.5 *ita ut ministeriorum...*, 2.2.10 *ubi publico lectisternio...*, 2.2.13 *interiecto consistorio perangusto...*, 2.9.6 *studiis hisce dum nostrum...* and 2.9.8 *sed cum vel pauxillulum...*; Du Prey (1994) 14, Myers (2005) 119, Bergmann (2016) 205, Hindermann (2020a) 106. In *Ep.* 4.9.1 Sidonius mentions that his friend Vettius has different staff in his country villa and in his city villa; Frye (2003) 191–2. For the depiction of the lower-ranking, unprivileged persons in Sidonius' world in general, see Mielsch (1987) 133–46, Amherdt (2004), Mathisen (2020a) 64.

Besides Pliny, there are other major intertexts. For the luxurious interior design of a villa, Statius (especially Stat. *Silv.* 1.2, 1.5, 2.2) is a major model for Sidon. *Carm.* 22, the description of the estate (Burgus) of Pontius Leontius. For the description of the city, the classroom, symposiastic scenes and a relaxed way of living in the countryside, see Martial (e.g. Mart. 3.58, 6.42, 10.62, 14.116) and Juvenal (e.g. Iuv. 5.50, 6.259–60). Vitruvius is a model for architectural details, Vergil for the scenery and the ship race, and Ausonius for the description of the lake and the fishing scene. The allusions are analysed in detail in the commentary below. For Sidonius' intertextual techniques in general, see Schwitter (2015) 205–9, Gualandri (2020), Di Stefano and Onorato (2020). In addition to being richly intertextual, the letter is also highly adorned with metrical clausulae; van Waarden and Kelly (2020).

Sidonius' bath

A striking and innovative element of Sidonius' villa letter is his detailed description of the bath, in sections 4–8, where Sidonius combines elements of modesty and the presentation of luxury in an innovative way; Fagan (1999) 176 n. 2, Hanaghan (2019) 25. Sidonius' bath consists of three rooms and an open-air swimming pool (*piscina*): a hot room, a room for applying oil and a cool room, which Sidonius is especially proud of. Hanaghan (2019) 25 points out that Sidonius' description of his baths might be incomplete, as they lack other rooms (e.g. the *tepidarium*, 'warm room') while he writes in detail about his pool; Balmelle (2001) 178, Thébert (2003) 108 n. 100. The prominence of the bath in Sidonius' villa description is striking. He probably starts with the place of refreshment and recovery from the heat to entice his addressee. Pliny describes his baths in less detail (Plin. *Ep.* 2.17.11, 5.6.25–6) and they are located in the main building of his villa, whereas Sidonius' baths are separate. Sidonius therefore adds a new feature to the villa letter. He uses his bath to represent himself, and to associate his person with Roman elite lifestyle; Percival (1997) 286–7, Cam (2003) 148, 155, Dark (2005) 337, Visser (2014) 35. Sidonius not only talks about his bath again in *Carm.* 18 and 19 (probably the verses on the wall of the baths), but also about the villa and baths of Pontius Leontius in *Carm.* 22.4 vv. 134–41, 179–86, and the baths under construction in the villas of Apollinaris and Ferreolus near Nîmes in *Ep.* 2.9.8–9. Baths are also mentioned in *Carm.* 23.495–9 and *Ep.* 8.4.1 and a vacation at hot springs in 5.14.1.

Further reading

There is abundant literature concerning Sidonius' estate. On parallels to Plin. *Ep.* 2.17 on his estate, Laurentum, see Whitton (2013) 35–6, 218–55. There are many allusions to Pliny's villa letters, including the artificiality of nature, the subject of climate and different rooms for each season. For Sidonius' use of literary (and especially Plinian) motifs in the description of his and others' estates, see Pavlovskis (1973) 48–51, Mratschek (2008) 373–4, Dewar (2014) 92–105, Visser (2014), Mratschek (2020b) 250. The strong literary parallels to Pliny's villas, which Sidonius combines into one villa in his description of Avitacum, even led Harries (1994) 10, 131–2 to doubt the reality of Sidonius' villa, *contra* Dark (2005) 335. See also Robert (2011) on the reality of Sidonius' description of Pontius Leontius' Burgus. There are also studies that investigate the metaphorical function of the villa. For the ancient villa as *locus amoenus* and the relation between architecture and nature, see Schneider (1995) 45–6, Colombi (1996), Mathisen (2003/2004), Hindermann (2009), Lucht (2011) 32–3, Morvillez (2017), Mratschek (2020b), Hindermann (2021). For the discourse on the preference of town or country in Sidonius and in Ausonius' *De Herediolo*, see Frye (2003), Sowers (2016). For Sidonius' leisure (*otium*) in the countryside versus business (*negotium*) in the city, see André (2006). Egelhaaf-Gaiser (2018) 270–4. On the parallels between Sidon. *Ep.* 8.12 and Plin. *Ep.* 5.6 and 7.3, see Hindermann (2020a). See also Dell'Anno (2020) on *Carm.* 22 as an ecphrasis of *otium* and Guipponi-Gineste (2017) on the relation of poetry (especially the poems in *Ep.* 5.17 and 9.13) to *otium* in Sidonius. For Sidonius' second book of letters as a book of *otium*, see the Introduction to the present volume.

On the other hand, there are scholars who focus on the archaeological background: Stevens (1933) 185–95 points out the geographical details in Sidonius' description, which show precise knowledge of the area. Percival (1992), Ellis (1995) and Balmelle (2001) discuss the Roman villa in Late Antiquity with Sidonius' Avitacum as an example. Fages (2015) shows the difference between Sidonius' descriptions of villas in Late Antique Gaul in *Ep.* 2.2 and 2.9 and the actual excavations in the villa of Séviac near present-day Montréal-Du-Gers in Occitania. Bergmann (2000) refers to Sidonius in her study of the villa of Chiragan (near present-day Toulouse, by the River Garonne). Fernández López (1994) 204–29 treats *Ep.* 2.2 and 2.9 together under 'cartas descriptivas de lugares y personas: descripción amplia'. For Enoch d'Ascoli's reception of Sidonius' villa letter in 1451, see Mastrorosa (2002).

Sections 4–8 of *Ep.* 2.2 are frequently used as a source for the bath culture of Late Antique Gaul. For the interpretation of Sidon. *Carm.* 18 and 19, see Furbetta (2013) 245–53, Hanaghan (2020). For the literary models of Roman bath descriptions, see Busch (1999) 66–83. For the baths in the villa of Pontius Leontius, see Delhey (1993) 130–8, 162–4. For the construction and use of baths in antiquity in general, see Brödner (1983), Nielsen (1990), Yegül (1992), Maréchal (2020). On the moral implications (pleasures and dangers) of the bath, see Dunbabin (1989). Studies of archaeological excavations of baths in Late Antique Gaul are Bouet (1997–1998) on the villa of Montmaurin (Haute-Garonne), Bouet (2003) on the *thermae* of Barzan (Charente-Maritime) and Fages (2015) 144–5 on the villa of Séviac (near present-day Montréal-Du-Gers in Occitania). For the motif of water in Sidonius, see Squillante (2014).

Commentary

Section 1

Sidonius Domitio suo salutem: For the simple greeting formula, see the commentary on *Ep.* 2.1.1 *Sidonius Ecdicio suo salutem*. For the addressee Domitius, see the introduction to this letter.

Ruri me esse causaris, cum mihi potius queri suppetat te nunc urbe retineri: These initial keywords (*ruri–causaris–urbe*) mark Sidonius' dialogue with Pliny's villa letters, where rural leisure (*otium*) in a pleasant spot (*locus amoenus*) is set in opposition to life in the bustling city (see the introduction to this letter). The city that Sidonius means is most probably Clermont, which is about 20 km from Lake Aydat, where Sidonius' villa was probably located; Loyen (1970a) 217 n. 8, Kaster (1988) 274. Sidonius talks about the subject of *rusticitas* and *urbanitas* in a figurative sense in *Ep.* 4.3.1; Amherdt (2001) 123–4. For the opposition of *otium* in the countryside and *negotium* in the city see also *Ep.* 2.13.4, 4.18.3, 5.14.1. Sidonius starts his letter with *causari*, 'to complain', 'to lament' (*TLL* 3, 706.35–6), pretending to answer a previous complaint and thus approaches the subject indirectly. For Sidonius' opening sentences in general, see van Waarden (2010) 46–8, Appendix D. With his first sentence, Sidonius imitates Pliny and Symmachus, who similarly begin their letters with a defence of why they are in the country: Plin. *Ep.* 2.17.1 *miraris cur me Laurentinum … tanto opere delectet* ('you wonder why my Laurentinum delights me so much'), Symm. *Ep.* 8.18 *in agro me esse* *miraris* ('you wonder why I am in the fields'). See also Sidon. *Ep.* 1.8.1 *morari me Romae congratularis* ('you congratulate me for staying in Rome') and *Ep.* 1.6.3, where Sidonius criticises his friend Eutropius for indulging too much in his living in the countryside.

Iam ver decedit aestati et per lineas sol altatus extremas in axem Scythicum radio peregrinante porrigitur: Writing about weather and season is an important element of a villa letter, for example Plin. *Ep.* 2.17.3, where spring is the 'default season' according to Whitton (2013) 241. In Pliny's Etruscan villa (*Ep.* 5.6), though, summer predominates, as in Sidonius' description here; Whitton (2013) 227. For the seasonal norms, see Plin. *Ep.* 9.36 (Tusci in summer) and 9.40 (Laurentinum in winter). For *decedere*, 'give way to', in a figurative sense about seasons or day and night-time, see *TLL* 5.1, 121.3–9. Particularly close are Sidon. *Ep.* 5.6.1 *cum primum aestas decessit autumno* ('when first summer gave way to autumn') and Symm. *Ep.* 2.6.2 *aestas prope decessit autumn* ('summer nearly gave way to autumn'). For *decedere*, see also van Waarden (2010) 163 on *Ep.* 7.2.4. *Linea* is used to denote the course of the sun or stars elsewhere (*TLL* 7.2, 1435.7–31), for example Manil. 3.314 *una quod aequali lustratur linea Phoebo* ('there is one course that is traversed by an equal sun'), Eusthatius *In Hexameron Basilii* 6.8.5 *inde se sol mox ad aestivam lineam deflectendo per confinia arctoa transit* ('from there the sun passes over to the northern border by turning aside to its summer course'). The sun is so high that its rays reach the north, which Sidonius describes with the expression *in axem Scythicum*. The Scythians were nomadic tribes in the north, beyond the Black Sea, and therefore lived on the periphery of the Roman Empire. They are probably mentioned here as inhabitants of a remote place because of Mart. 10.62.8, an intertext for the school scene in *Ep.* 2.2.2 (see the commentary on *Ep.* 2.2.2 *discipulis non aestu* ...). Scythian, a term already used by Herodotus to describe steppe nomads in the fifth century BC, is a millennium later used more generally to denote people from north of the Black Sea, that is, the Goths or the Huns, for example in Amm. 20.8.1; Maas (2012) 62. Sidonius thus might allude to the danger of a Gothic invasion described in *Ep.* 2.1. The verb *peregrinor*, 'to sojourn in a strange land', 'be an alien', 'travel', 'wander' (*TLL* 10.1, 1304.17–7.26), appears several times in Sidonius' letters, but not in the poems: Sidon. *Ep.* 1.5.10, 1.6.2, 7.14.2, 8.3.4, 8.12.2, 9.3.4. The participle also appears in *Ep.* 5.9.2, 6.5.1, 7.7.6, 8.6.17 (used as an adjective or as a noun). As the frequent appearance of related words like *peregrinus* or *peregrinatio* shows, the subject was important for Sidonius.

Hic quid de regionis nostrae climate loquar?: With this question Sidonius continues the colloquial beginning of the letter (see the commentaries on *Ep.* 2.2.1 *Ruri me esse causaris...* and on *Ep.* 2.1.1 *'Quaenam?' inquis*). Sidonius adds a detailed description of the weather, with melting ice and dried-up rivers, thus adding new colour to the traditional topos of the contrast between countryside and city; see Gualandri (1979) 94–6 and the introduction to this letter. The following section is full of poetic allusions, recalling especially Vergil's *Georgics* (see the commentary below on *Ep.* 2.2.1 *Quid plura? Mundus incanduit incanduit: glacies Alpina deletur et hiulcis* ...). The subject is not new in a letter though; already Cicero had complained about the heat in Rome and longed to go to his estate, where the climate was milder: Cic. *Ad Q. fr.* 3.1.1 *ex magnis caloribus* ('away from the great heat'), *Tusc.* 5.26.74 *cum vim caloris non facile patiatur* ('if one does not easily tolerate the great heat'). Horace also describes the summer's heat to highlight the advantages of the country over town: Hor. *Ep.* 1.10.13–7, *Carm.* 3.29.17–24; similarly Symm. *Ep.* 3.50 and Ruric. *Ep.* 1.11.2 *siquidem inibi torridae fervor aestatis tam umbrarum quam undarum rigore depellitur* ('since there the boiling heat of torrid summer is driven away by the coolness of the shadows as much as the waves'). Related to the topic of weather is its influence on health; see the commentary below on *Ep.* 2.2.2 *quin tu mage, si quid tibi salubre cordi*. In his villa letter *Ep.* 5.6.3–6, Pliny writes about the climate at his estate, Tusci, and its impact on plants and people.

Cuius spatia divinum sic tetendit opificium, ut magis vaporibus orbis occidui subiceremur: For the first time in Book 2, Sidonius mentions God. *Opificium*, 'a working', 'the doing of a work', appears often in combination with the pagan gods or the Christian God, especially in Lactantius (*TLL* 9.2, 706.38–73). Instead of *opificium Dei* Sidonius choses a paraphrase with the adjective *divinum*. God's influence on the climate thus appears less prominent. On Sidonius' mentions of God, see the commentary below on *Ep.* 2.2.3 *Haec mihi cum meis praesule deo....* For the expression *orbis occidui*, 'the western world', also used in Sidon. *Ep.* 7.1.7, see van Waarden (2010) 121.

Quid plura? Mundus incanduit: glacies Alpina deletur et hiulcis arentium rimarum flexibus terra perscribitur: With the rhetorical question *Quid plura?* Sidonius continues the colloquial beginning of the letter; see the commentaries on *Ep.* 2.2.1 *Ruri me esse causaris...* and on *Ep.* 2.1.1 *'Quaenam?' inquis*. In the following sentences, Sidonius describes a terrible heat wave. Sidonius uses the verb *incandesco*, 'become warm or hot', 'flare up' (*TLL* 7.1, 844.68–5.21) once more, but in a figurative sense related to a person; see also *Ep.* 7.14.1, van Waarden (2016) 125. By describing the heat, Sidonius is probably alluding to Vergil, Verg. *Georg.* 3.479 *tempestas totoque autumni incanduit aestu* ('and the weather became hot because of the heat of fall'). See also Solin. *Mirab.* 29.4 <*mundus*> *incanduerit* ('The world has become warmer') and similarly *Anth. Lat.* 236.5 *incanduit aestas* ('the summer became hot'). The expression *glacies Alpina*, 'the ice in the Alps', is also found in Claud. *Carm. min.* 35.1, *Rapt. Pros.* 2.176; see also the description of the snowy Alps in Sidon. *Ep.* 4.15.3 and Amherdt (2001) 366 on Sidonius' literary models in describing the Alps. The adjective *hiulcus*, 'gaping', 'split', 'cleft' (*TLL* 6.3, 2847.14–8.37), is used in connection with heat already in the intertext of this passage, in Verg. *Georg.* 2.353 *ubi hiulca siti findit Canis aestifer arva* ('where the dog star splits the cleft fields'), and also in Stat. *Theb.* 4.708. In *Carm.* 16.79–80, a thanksgiving to bishop Faustus, Sidonius creates a similar image of dry land: *cum solis torridus ignis | flexilibus rimis sitientes scriberet agros* ('when the torrid fire of the sun inscribed the thirsty fields with curved cracks'); Santelia (2012) 123–4. In *Ep.* 6.7.1 Sidonius uses the adjective *hiulcus* again in a figurative sense: *ulcerosae conscientiae nimis hiulca vulnera* ('the widely gaping wounds of my conscience'). In *Ep.* 2.2 Sidonius wants to save Domitius from the heat, and in *Carm.* 16.82 Sidonius is accepted as a guest by Faustus and rewarded with *pax, domus, umbra, latex, benedictio, mensa, cubile* ('peace, home, shade, water, blessing, food and bed'). In *Ep.* 1.8.2 Sidonius describes the city of Caesena as *furnus*, 'oven'. The verb *perscribo*, 'to inscribe', is transferred here to the soil; see *TLL* 10.1, 1673.22–6. The formulation *terra perscribitur* is interesting, because the verb also means 'describe' or 'finish a written work', and this is what Sidonius does in his letter. Perhaps Sidonius is alluding to the written form inherent in Pliny's country estate, in Plin. *Ep.* 5.6.35, where letters of boxwood form the names of Pliny and his garden designer. In both Sidonius and Pliny, the landscape is described in such a way that it resembles a papyrus (thanks to Margot Neger for this idea).

squalet glarea in vadis, limus in ripis, pulvis in campis: To describe the heat, Sidonius inserts a tricolon with the verb *squalere*, 'to be caked or crusted with dirt' (of things) (*OLD* 1811, 2a), or 'to lay waste' (*OLD* 1811, 4a); see also Sil. 14.591 *squalebat tellus* ('the earth was parched'). To make it fit all three objects, I translate it here as 'to be parched'. *Glarea*, 'gravel' (*TLL* 6.2, 2034.34–5.53), is also mentioned in the description of Sidonius' lake in *Ep.* 2.2.18 and of the River Vardo in *Ep.* 2.9.9, where, unlike here, the stream is not dried up. See also *Ep.* 1.5.7, where Sidonius explains that the River Rubico takes its name from the reddish pebbles (*de glarearum colore puniceo*); Hanaghan (2017c) 642. See also Ausonius in his description of the River Moselle, in Auson. *Mos.* 67. For *limus*, 'slime', 'mud', 'mire', see the various examples in *TLL* 7.2, 1429.61–30.10, especially Verg. *Georg.* 1.116 and 2.188 about rivers which overflow or transport mud. See also Sidon. *Ep.* 2.2.16 for the muddy shore of a lake and *Carm.* 24.46. A very similar remark appears in *Carm.* 7.407–10, where Sidonius also describes an unpleasant heat: *pax elementorum fureret vel sicca propinquus | saeviret per stagna vapor limusque sitiret | pulvereo ponti fundo, tunc unica Phoebi | insuetum Clemens exstinxit flamma calorem* ('when the harmony of the elements was stirred to fury, when the hot breath came close and ranged madly over the drying pools, and the parched mud thirsted on the dusty bottom of the sea, then Phoebus' gentle fire alone quenched that unwonted heat').

aqua ipsa quaecumque perpetuo labens tractu cunctante languescit: Every body of water which normally flows constantly now dribbles weakly. The contrast between the normal situation and the current weather is expressed by the alliteration *labens* and *languescit*. *Tractus* denotes 'the action of causing things to move in a particular course, direction, etc.' (*OLD* 1955, 2). The combination of *labor*, 'to slide, glide' (*TLL* 7.2, 779.73–89.25), and *tractus* is found elsewhere of rivers and stars, for example Curt. 3.4.8 *Cydnus … leni tractu e fontibus labens* ('Cydnus glides with gentle course from its springs'). The combination of *perpetuus*, 'continuous', 'perpetual', and *tractus* is also found in Lucr. 5.1216 *perpetuo possint aevi labentia tractu* ('or whether they can move in the constant flow of time') in relation to celestial bodies. The verb *languesco*, 'to become faint, weak, languid' (*TLL* 7.2, 922.77–4.5), is also used of water elsewhere, for example in Ov. *Fast.* 2.775 *fluctus* ('floods'); Curt. 4.7.22 *fons* ('fountain'). See also Plin. *Paneg.* 30.2 *quia piger Nilus cunctanter alveo sese ac languide extulerat* ('because the lazy Nile only hesitantly and languidly exceeded its channel').

iam non solum calet unda sed coquitur: The image of the boiling hot flood is probably again an allusion to Vergil, Verg. *Georg.* 4.427–8 *flumina | … radii tepefacta coquebant* ('the rays of the sun heated the tepid rivers'). The combination of *calere*, 'to be hot', and *coquere*, 'to burn', is also found in Mart. 10.62.6–7, which is the intertext for the school scene in 2.2.2; see the commentary on *Ep.* 2.2.2 *discipulis non aestu*….

Section 2

Et nunc, dum in carbaso sudat unus, alter in bombyce: After the hot climate in the first section, Sidonius devotes himself to a closely related topic in the second. He shows the addressee, Domitius, suffering from the heat in a comic scene with allusions to Juvenal, Martial and Terence. Domitius appears as a sweating schoolmaster in front of tired pupils. See Hanaghan (2019) 91: 'Domitius is stuck in the city during summer, wrapped up in women's clothes, reading the part of the courtesan in Terence's *Eunuchus*. One can hardly envisage that this is how Domitius hoped to be depicted and, for that matter, memorialised in Sidonius' collection.' In the sweltering weather one sweats even in light clothes. The passage is reminiscent of Mart. 12.18, where Martial is on his estate in Spain and writes to Juvenal, who is sweating and busy in the heat of Rome (5: *sudatrix toga*, 'the sweaty toga'). Sidonius names two pieces of clothing: *carbasus*, a 'very fine Spanish flax', 'fine linen' (*TLL* 3, 428.66–9.74), also mentioned in a figurative sense in Sidon. *Carm*. 2.537, 22.4, v. 8; and *bombyx*, 'a silken garment', 'silk' (*TLL* 2, 2070.10–40), which probably is an allusion to Iuv. 6.259–60, which is about demanding women – *tenui sudant in cyclade, quarum | delicias et panniculus bombycinus urit* ('they sweat in their thin robe and the light garments of silk irritates their delicate skin'). They, like Domitius, complain constantly; Hanaghan (2019) 79. In addition, Juvenal also uses the terms *endromidas* and *fascia* in the same context; Colton (1982) 63–4 and the commentary immediately below. In a ring composition at the end of Book 2, Sidonius refers back to the theme of proper dress in leisure with the expression *tunicata quiete* – see the commentary on *Ep*. 2.14.2 *in otio fuliginoso*.... Sidonius also mentions clothing that is too warm in *Ep*. 7.16.2, when he sends a cowl to his friend, Abbot Chariobaudus, even though summer is approaching.

tu endromidatus exterius, intrinsecus fasceatus: Sidonius distinguishes his addressee by using Greek technical terms to describe his clothes and thus connects him with his villa, which he also describes in Greek terms; see the commentary on *Ep*. 2.2.8 *si graecari*.... At the same time, Domitius' attire seems to be ridiculous in the heat, like his decision to stay in the city. His clothing (cloak and undergarment) is arranged in a chiastic phrase; Hanaghan (2019) 79. The adjective *endromidatus*, 'wearing an *endromis*, cloak' (*TLL* 5.2, 561.56–9), derives from the coarse cloth athletes wore after exercise and is a Sidonian hapax. This garment is also mentioned in epigram and satire, for example in Mart. 4.19, 14.126, Iuv. 3.103, 6.246, Tert. *Pall*.

4.4. With *exterius*, 'on the outside', 'outward', and *intrinsecus*, 'on the inside, inwardly', Sidonius brings together an opposing pair, one of his favourite stylistic means, for example in *Ep.* 6.9.2 *intrinsecus ... extrinsecus* ('within ... without'), 7.14.9 *intrinsecus ... forinsecus* ('inwardly ... outwardly'); van Waarden (2016) 157. On Sidonius' bipolar style, see van Waarden (2010) 55–6. The common form is *fascio*, 'to bind', 'envelop with bands, swaths', but Sidonius has *fasceo*. The participle *fasceatus* – like *endromidatus* – is very rarely used (*TLL* 6.1, 301.55–9). It is though used in Sidon. *Ep.* 8.11.3 v. 13 to denote the bands by means of which sandals are strapped to the feet: v. 12–14 *perges sic melius volante saltu, | si vestigia fasceata nudi | per summum digiti regant* ('you will advance more easily with flying leaps if naked toes guide your sandalled feet'). See also Sidon. *Carm.* 2.400; Anderson (1936) 42–3 n. 1. The phrase is reminiscent of Iuv. 6.263 *poplitibus sedeat quam denso fascia libro* ('how the bandages sit tightly rolled around her knees').

insuper et concava municipis Amerini sede compressus: This clause contains a text-critical problem. There are different variants of the text in the manuscripts: *municipi samerini* L, *municipii amerini* C, *municipii camerini* MFP. Sirmond (1614) 42 explains Camerini or Amerini as a misspelled gloss for (*municipii*) *Arverni*. Housman (1900) and Loyen (1970a) 217 see an allusion to the town of Ameria, fifty-six miles from Rome, present-day Umbrian Amelia (Terni), which was known for its basketwork; see Verg. *Georg.* 1.265 *atque Amerina parant lentae retinacula viti* ('and prepare bands of Amerian willow for the pliable vine'), Plin. *Nat.* 16.177. *Amerinus* (*TLL* 1, 1886.19–45) is an adjective derived from the town America, whose *municeps*, 'citizen', is the *salix*, 'willow', 'osier'. Anderson (1936) 419 provides the translation 'squeezed into a deep chair made of Ameria's population'. Visser (2014) 29–30 claims a literary allusion to Plin. *Ep.* 8.20.3, where Ameria is mentioned in connection with Lake Vadimo, which Pliny describes as a natural wonder. She also sees an allusion to Cicero's defence of Sextus Roscius (Cic. *Rosc.* 15), described as *municeps Amerinus*, and thus translates the expression with 'sitting in a hollow chair of a citizen of Ameria'. Visser interprets the allusion to Cicero as a statement about what Domitius teaches his pupils (prose in addition to poetry, which is included with the citing of Terence; see the commentary below on *Ep.* 2.2.2 '*Samia mihi mater fuit*'). In my opinion, though, Sidonius focuses on the fact that Domitius is not only constrained by his clothes but also by the chair and exposed to the heat (*endromidatus ... fasciatus ... compressus*). The invitation to the cool and shady villa with its bath thereby becomes more enticing.

discipulis non aestu minus quam timore pallentibus exponere oscitabundus ordiris: Next, Sidonius adds a comical scene in a classroom, where the students are not only full of fear of their master but also half asleep because of the heat, while their teacher is declaiming verses from comedy. A probable intertext is Mart. 10.62.6–12, where Martial begs the teacher to close the school for summer. Because of the heat of summer the pupils will not learn anything. As in Sidonius, the fear of punishment is mentioned: *albae leone flammeo calent luces | tostamque ferens Iulius coquit messem. | cirrata loris horridis Scythae pellis, | qua vapulavit Marsyas Celaenaeus, | ferulaeque tristes, sceptra paedagogorum, | cessent et Idus dormiant in Octobres: | aestate pueri si valent, satis discunt* ('Pale dawns are hot under blazing Leo and torrid July bakes the toasted harvest. The fringed skin of the Scythian with rough lashes which Marsyas from Celaenae was flogged with, and the sad rods, the sceptres of the teachers, shall pause and be quiet till the ides of October. If the kids are healthy during the summer, they learn enough'). There is a similar violent scene from the classroom in Sidon. *Ep.* 2.10.1 – see the commentary on *Ep.* 2.10.1 *Nam cum videmus in huiusmodi disciplinam*.... Comedy was an important subject in late antique schooling; see the commentary immediately below on *Ep.* 2.2.2 '*Samia mihi mater fuit*'; Nathan (2000) 140–2. Martial was an especially important author at the school in Lyon where Sidonius got his basic education; Horváth (2000) 153, Styka (2008) 169. For Sidonius' use of Martial in detail, see the commentary below on *Ep.* 2.2.6 *Absunt ridiculi vestitu* .... Teachers, schooling and the value of education are frequent themes in Sidonius' as well as in Pliny's letters, for example Sidon. *Ep.* 5.5.2 and Plin. *Ep.* 2.18, 4.13; Horváth (2000), Bernstein (2008), Overwien (2009a) 96–7, Squillante (2009) 141, Gerth (2013). *Oscitabundus* is an adjective derived from *oscito*, 'to open the mouth wide', 'yawn', and refers to the teacher; see the translations in Loyen (1970a) 45, Anderson (1936) 419 and Hanaghan (2019) 79. Yawning while teaching does not quite fit with Domitius' description of a severe schoolmaster. Visser (2014) 28 thus transfers the verb grammatically incorrectly to the pupils ('you begin to explain ... to your yawning pupils') whereas Köhler (2014) 42 translates the expression referring to Domitius 'mit bedeutend geöffnetem Mund', that is, 'to recite'. In the two other instances (*Ep.* 1.3.2, 5.14.2), however, Sidonius uses the verb in the common sense of 'to yawn', so I think it is the right choice here as well. Adjectives ending in *-bundus* are frequently used and often newly coined by Sidonius; Gualandri (1979) 179, Amherdt (2001) 406–7 with several examples. The school scene described by Sidonius is also reminiscent of an epigram of Kallimachos, *AP* 6, 310: there a tragic mask of Dionysos hangs in a classroom, yawning at the children's recitations of drama; in this case the children are reciting from Euripides' *Bacchae* (thanks to Margot Neger for this idea). For Sidonius' knowledge of Greek, see the commentary on *Ep.* 2.2.8 *si graecari mavis*....

'Samia mihi mater fuit': With this quotation from Ter. *Eun.* 107 Sidonius even tells the reader which text Domitius teaches to his uninterested pupils. There, the courtesan Lais directs the sentence at the slave Parmeno as an example of a true statement. Terence is one of the classical authors most esteemed by Sidonius; for example, in *Ep.* 4.12.1–2 he describes how he enjoyed reading the play *Hecyra* with his son. Sidonius quotes or mentions Terence by name several times on other occasions: *Ep.* 1.9.8, 1.11.5, 3.13.1, 7.9.19, *Carm.* 13.36, 23.147; Horváth (2000) 154, Amherdt (2001) 311–12, Castagna (2004), Styka (2008) 162–3, van Waarden (2010) 506, Cain (2013b) 384, 388. That Sidonius lets his friend quote one of his favourite authors could be a sign of special appreciation. On the other hand, he lets him play the role of the courtesan and sweat in his clothes – see the commentary above on *Ep.* 2.2.2 *Et nunc*.... Hanaghan (2019) 79–80 n. 61 suggests that Sidonius and Domitius may have read this text together or shared some other personal experience. In Roman schools it was customary for young children to memorise and copy well-known moral precepts from authors like Terence, not only to improve their linguistic skills but also to build their character and memory. In a later stage of their education they studied the plays word by word under an expert in Latin language and literature (*grammaticus*); Cain (2013b) 383–4.

Quin tu mage, si quid tibi salubre cordi: To convince a friend to accept an invitation, usually the writer describes at length the food and entertainment one can expect, as in Hor. *Ep.* 1.5 and Plin. *Ep.* 1.15, and see also Mart. 1.43, 3.60. Instead, Sidonius starts with the climate and health as reasons for the invitation. Health issues are frequently mentioned as a reason to travel or flee to the countryside: Sidon. *Ep.* 2.12.2, Sen. *Ep.* 104.1 and 6 on his flight from the polluted air in Rome (*gravitatem urbis excessi*), Catull. 44, Cic. *Leg.* 2.3, Hor. *Sat.* 2.6.16–9, Mart. 10.12, Plin. *Ep.* 5.6.1–2 and 45, 5.19.7, 6.4.1, 8.1.1 and 3; Schneider (1995) 22–3. The good climate and the healthy atmosphere of the suburban villa are also praised in various texts, including Sen. *Ben.* 4.12.3, Cic. *Rep.* 1.1, Symm. *Ep.* 2.22.1, 3.50; Mayer (2005) 152–4. For the climate as a subject in a letter, see the commentary on *Ep.* 2.2.1 *Hic quid de regionis nostrae climate loquar?*

raptim subduceris anhelantibus angustiis civitatis et contubernio nostro aventer insertus: In *Ep.* 2.12 Sidonius describes a similar hurried flight from the heat of the city. The context there is more serious, however, as Sidonius' daughter Severiana is seriously ill; see the commentary on *Ep.* 2.12.3 *Igitur ardori civitatis....* Sidonius often uses the rhetorical device of enallage (exchange of attributes) and thus personifies inanimate things, here the city that pants because of the heat; for further examples see Gualandri (1979) 139. The metaphor *contubernio nostro*, which in military language originally denoted a 'tent companionship', 'a dwelling together in a tent' (*TLL* 4, 791.57–2.11), was early transferred from the military sphere to the general meaning 'a living together', 'fellowship', 'company' (*TLL* 4, 792.12–3.46), and is used in *Ep.* 2.12.3 in a similar context to describe the reception of a friend by his family. Sidonius uses *contubernium* often in various meanings, as in *Ep.* 2.10.6 'marriage', 9.6.1 'concubinage between master and slave', 'affair', 3.9.2 'comradeship', 'companionhip'. The word is also used in *Ep.* 3.13.1, 4.6.1, 4.15.1, 4.21.6, 5.9.2, 5.14.3, 5.17.2, 6.1.3, 7.5.2, 7.9.22, 7.14.10, 9.14.3; Amherdt (2001) 197, 361, van Waarden (2010) 261. The rarely used adverb *aventer* derives from *aveo*, 'willingly', 'eagerly', 'earnestly' (*TLL* 2, 1314.49–51). It is also used in Amm. 18.5.6, 19.9.7, 29.2.10.

fallis clementissimo recessu inclementiam canicularem?: Sidonius describes the climate with the wordplay of the assonant adjective *clementissimus*, 'very quiet', 'mild', 'placid', 'clement', which is often used about natural phenomena (*TLL* 3, 1332.68–3.22) and its opposite, *inclementia*, 'harshness', 'unkindness', 'inclemency', used of places, the sea or the weather (*TLL* 7.1, 938.29–35). With the adjective *clemens*, Sidonius again evokes the villa as *locus amoenus*. See also Plin. *Ep.* 5.6.4 *aestatis mira clementia* ('the summer is remarkably mild'); Mratschek (2020b) 251. See also the introduction to this letter. Sidonius recommends avoiding the mercilessness of Sirius, a bright star in the constellation Canis Major, indicated by the circumlocution *canicularis*, 'of or pertaining to the dog star'. For the expression see Hor. *Carm.* 1.17.17–18, where Horace invites his mistress Tyndaris to his Sabine estate: *hic in reducta valle caniculae | vitabis aestus* ('here in the secluded valley you will avoid the heat of the dog star'). Similarly also Sidon. *Ep.* 8.12.5 *sereni brumalis infida vitabis* ('you will avoid the treachery of the clear winter'), where Sidonius explains to his friend Trygetius how he will avoid the cold; Stoehr-Monjou (2013) 156–7. For the description of the climate, see the commentary above on *Ep.* 2.2.1 *Hic quid de regionis nostrae climate loquar?*

Section 3

Sane si placet, quis sit agri, in quem vocaris, situs accipe: In section 3, Sidonius starts to describe his estate, Avitacum (*narratio*: sections 3–19). The description of the estate and the lake nearby comprises most of the letter, and has spatial and temporal aspects. The reader is shown through the estate as if he or she were a guest who has just arrived and thereby experiences the bath, lunch, siesta and afternoon at the lakeside; Visser (2014) 31–2. Pliny instead treats his daily schedule in separate letters, in Plin. *Ep.* 9.36, 9.40; see the commentary above on 2.2.1 *Ruri me esse causaris*.... The first sentence of section 3 echoes Plin. *Ep.* 5.6.3 *accipe temperiem caeli, regionis situm, villae amoenitatem* ('hear about the climate, the landscape and the pleasantness of my estate'); Gibson (2013b) 345. Similarly, Pliny uses the imperative *accipe* in several other instances for 'hear', but Sidonius again only in *Ep.* 2.10.2 and 9.9.9. As Hanaghan (2020) 128 shows, Sidonius' description of Avitacum is hodotic. There are fifteen demonstratives as Sidonius guides the reader through the villa (section 4 *hinc*; 5 *hinc*; 6 *hic*; 8 *huic, huc, hanc*; 9 *hic, hinc*; 10 *haec*; 11 *haec, hoc, hac*; 13 *hoc*; 14 *hic*; 18 *hunc*). According to Hanaghan (2020) 128, this approach 'adds to the feeling of permanency that Sidonius conveys throughout the epistle, which acts as a guidebook that seems to advertise and highlight what will always be there'. The manuscripts VMC and Lütjohann (1887) 22 exhibit the archetypal reading *placet*, whereas LNT and Loyen (1970a) 46 have *placitum*. With the expression *sane si placet* Sidonius continues the colloquial beginning of the letter; see the commentaries on *Ep.* 2.2.1 *Ruri me esse causaris*... and on *Ep.* 2.1.1 *'Quaenam?' inquis*.

Avitaci sumus: Sidonius' villa is still unexplored archaeologically. It is probably situated in or near present-day Aydat in the Auvergne, 23 km south-west of Clermont-Ferrand; Stevens (1933) 185–95, Kaufmann (1995) 49, Cam (2003) 140. The estate Avitacum ('of Avitus') takes its name from the family of Sidonius' wife, that is, from her father, the emperor Avitus (for Avitus see the commentary on *Ep.* 2.13.3 *Hic si omittamus...*). It had come to Sidonius through his marriage as part of her dowry or of her inheritance after the death of her father. See also Sidon. *Ep.* 3.1.1, *Carm.* 18.1 *si quis Avitacum dignaris visere nostram* ('if someone thinks my Avitacum to be worth a visit') and the commentary immediately below, p. 99. In describing his estate, Sidonius combines two of Pliny's villa letters, *Ep.* 2.17 and 5.6; see the commentary on *Ep.* 2.2.1 *Ruri me esse causaris*.... Like Pliny's villa, Laurentinum, Avitacum is situated next to water and like the villa in

Tuscany it is described as a summer residence in the countryside. Elsewhere, Sidonius talks about estates in female terms (*Carm.* 18.1 *Avitacum ... nostram* 'my Avitacum', 22.3 *Burgum tuam ... meam feci* 'I turned your Burgus into mine') as the gender of *villa* is feminine. Presumably as an indication of the estate's large size, Sidonius treats his estate here grammatically as town (*municipium*) and uses the locative case; Anderson (1936) 418 n. 3. See also Plin. *Ep.* 5.6.35 *in opere urbanissimo* ('in the midst of urban refinement').

nomen hoc praedio, quod, quia uxorium, patrio mihi dulcius: Sidonius uses the term *praedium* several times in his letters to designate a privately owned property: *Ep.* 2.9.1–2 and 7, 2.14.1, 3.1.2, 3.5.2, 4.11.5, 4.18.1–2, 4.24.1, 5.7.3, but never in his poems. In *Ep.* 4.25.2 Sidonius writes about the *ecclesiastica ... praedia* ('the estates of the church'). Pliny also writes about his paternal or maternal estates in his letters: Plin. *Ep.* 2.15.2 *me praedia materna parum commode tractant, delectant tamen ut materna, et alioqui longa patientia occallui* ('my maternal estates do not treat me in a very friendly way; nonetheless they delight me as they were my mother's and besides I have developed a thick skin from long suffering'), 7.11.5 *ego illi ex praediis meis, quod vellet et quanti vellet, obtuli exceptis maternis paternisque; his enim cedere ne Corelliae quidem possum* ('I offered her whichever of my estates she wanted for whatever price, except for my maternal and paternal estates, which I cannot give away not even to Corellia'); Gibson and Morello (2012) 202–3, 223–4, Quint. 6.3.44. On the emotional significance of estates and villas that were owned by aristocratic families for generations see Page (2015) 322–5, with further literature.

Between 452 and 455 Sidonius married Papianilla, daughter of the later emperor Avitus, former owner of the estate Avitacum; Kaufmann (1995) 328–9, Mascoli (2010) 35–45, Mascoli (2014) 35–7, MacDonald (2000) 61–5, van Waarden (2020a) 27, and see the Introduction, pp. ix–x. Sidonius claims to prefer the estate his wife brought into marriage (see the commentary above, p. 98, on *Ep.* 2.2.3 *Avitaci sumus*) over the one he got from his father. Sidonius emphasises the good relationship with his wife (*concordia*) and thereby also aligns himself with Pliny, who represents himself as devoted to Calpurnia, recalling elegiac motifs (e.g. Plin. *Ep.* 4.19.5, 7.5.1) as well as to Statius (e.g. Stat. *Silv.* 3.5.26, 5.1.43–4); see Hindermann (2010) and the commentary on *Ep.* 2.10.5 *quod olim Marcia Hortensio....* Another intertext may be Symmachus' programmatic letter 1.1, about the estate his wife inherited; Salzman and Roberts (2011) 5–11. Papianilla and her family are also mentioned in *Carm.* 23.430, *Ep.* 2.9.3,

2.12.1–2, 7.12.1, and 5.16, where she is the addressee of the only letter to a woman that Sidonius includes in his collection. For the subject of marriage and the ideal wife in Sidonius, see Santelia (2002) 90–4. For literature about women in Sidonius' letters, see the introduction to *Ep.* 2.8. The statement, unusual for ancient readers, that the beloved is worth more than father and mother (*dulcius*, transferred here to the estate; see the commentary below on *Ep.* 2.8.3 v. 6 *prudens, casta, decens, severa, dulcis*), is also found in Roman elegy, for instance Prop. 1.11.23. The term *uxorius*, 'belonging or relating to a wife', does not indicate whether the estate was part of Papianilla's dowry or a heritage; Arjava (1996) 153 n. 110, MacDonald (2000) 94–6. The term is also used in Sidon. *Ep.* 1.4.1, 9.6.4. For the term *uxor*, 'wife', see the commentary on *Ep.* 2.8.1 *morigera coniunx*…. Stevens (1933) 20 n. 2 wonders why Papianilla should get the ancestral estate, as she had two living brothers. Sidonius keeps a striking distance from his family of origin. He never even alludes to his father's estate (Sidon. *Ep.* 3.12 comes closest). Sidonius does not mention his father's name, whereas he does name his grandfather Apollinaris; Mathisen (1981) 97, Harries (1994) 27–9. Despite his pride in his father's prefecture (e.g. *Ep.* 5.9.2, 8.6.5), silence reigns, while Sidonius' relations with his wife and her father Avitus are emphasised, probably because he owed his political and episcopal offices to the family connections of his wife and mother; see Harries (1994) 31, 'more truly a member of his mother's and wife's family', MacDonald (2000) 62–3, Hanaghan (2020) 132–3. As Mathisen (1979) 166 notes, Sidonius does not mention Avitus by name, however.

Haec mihi cum meis praesule deo, nisi quid tu fascinum verere, concordia: Sidonius denies that his peaceful family life is caused by a magic spell (*fascinum*), but he attributes this to God's work (*praesule deo*). This is a strange remark – probably Sidonius wants to avert the evil eye and envy that are caused by the description of his splendid mansion; Rakoczy (1996). Originally *praesul* meant 'a leader in a dance, leader of a procession', in Christian use 'patron', 'advocate'. As an ablative absolute in combination with *deus* it is also attested in Sidon. *Ep.* 3.1.5, 9.9.5 and Christian writers like Ambrose and Jerome; *TLL* 10.2, 948.60–4, *Blaise* 656, 4, Delhey (1993) 71–2. For similar pious interjections to ensure God's help, see Cugusi (1983) 82, Köhler (1995) 217, Amherdt (2001) 79, van Waarden (2010) 88, and the commentaries on *Ep.* 2.4.2 *quod Deo prosperante succedat*, 2.9.10 *sed quia et ipsi … sub ope Christi…* and 2.12.3 *igitur ardori … praevio Christo….* Sidonius usually does not emphasise religion in his self-representation; Bailey (2020)

361. Sidonius invokes God mainly for help with illnesses, but not with legal disputes or deaths; Hess (2021) 169–70. *Fascinum* is 'a bewitching, witchcraft' or the '*membrum virile* as a preventive against witchcraft' (*TLL* 6.1, 301.28, *Blaise* 345, 1); see also Gell. 16.12.4. The term frequently appears in Symmachus' letters, which commentators have noted as early as Savaron (1599) 103; see for example Symm. *Ep.* 1.13.4, 3.25.2, 3.86.2; Furbetta (2020) 554. The expression *haec mihi cum meis ... concordia* is reminiscent of tomb inscriptions, where the harmony between married couples is often remembered; see for example *CIL* 2.3596 *iucundam vitam aequabili concordia vicisset* ('she had lived a joyous life in equal harmony'), Lattimore (1962) 279–80, von Hesberg-Tonn (1983) 122–6, and the epitaph for the *matrona Filimatia* in Sidon. *Ep.* 2.8.3. The term *concordia*, 'harmony', 'peace', 'amity' (*TLL* 4, 83.22–7.46) also appears in literary descriptions of the relation between husband and wife; see for example the commentary above on *Ep.* 2.2.3 *nomen hoc praedio....* See also *Ep.* 5.16.4, addressed to Sidonius' wife Papianilla: *quantum concordia fruor* ('as much as I enjoy this harmony'). At the same time, the ideal harmony between the *pater familias* and his *familia* – including the slaves – is implied; Kaufmann (1995) 245, Amherdt (2001) 256, van Waarden (2016) 165. There are other examples of lenient masters in Sidonius' letters, as in *Ep.* 2.8.1 about Filimatia, 4.9.1 about Vettius, 7.14.11 about Philagrius. On *concordia* as a Roman virtue and its representation on sarcophagi, see Muth (2005) 268–72.

Mons ab occasu, quamquam terrenus, arduus tamen inferiores sibi colles tamquam gemino fomite effundit: Sidonius' villa lies at the foot of a steep mountain covered in earth, rather than having bare rock. Visser (2014) 32 identifies the *mons terrenus* as the Puy de la Rodde, a volcanic mountain 1127 metres high near Aydat. In the following description, Sidonius emphasises the power of nature. By indicating cardinal points he gives the reader orientation and, to a certain extent, a map. For *terrenus*, 'consisting of soil', 'earthy' (*OLD* 1928, 3), see Plin. *Ep.* 5.6.8 *terrenique colles* ('hills made of earth'). *Colles*, 'hills', are also part of the description of Sidonius' description of the villa in *Ep.* 8.4.1. *Fomes*, 'kindling wood', 'tinder', is here used in the sense of 'branch' (*TLL* 6.1, 1021.78–22.6); see also Sidon. *Ep.* 2.2.15, 3.13.9, 8.11.12, *Carm.* 2.402. The term is used to refer to the two ranges of hills into which the mountain divides. Embedded between them is Sidonius' villa.

quattuor a se circiter iugerum latitudine abductos: An *iugerum* is a Roman unit of land, a rectangle measuring about five-eighths of an acre;

Anderson (1936) 419 n. 5, Schulzki (1998). Four *iugera* therefore are 2.48 acres or 10,120 m². For the dimension of the lake near Sidonius' estate, see Sidon. *Ep.* 2.2.17.

Sed donec domicilio competens vestibuli campus aperitur: The temporal conjunction *donec*, 'as long as', 'while', here has a local meaning 'up to the point where' (*TLL* 5.1, 2001.11–62). Here as well as in *Ep.* 2.2.16 Sidonius uses the term *domicilium*, 'domicile', 'abode' (*TLL* 5.1, 1873.71–5.58), to denote his house, whereas *praedium* describes the whole estate; see the commentary above on *Ep.* 2.2.3 *nomen hoc praedio*.... The term is similarly used in Sidon. *Ep.* 1.5.2, 1.8.2, 2.9.1, 3.2.1, 3.3.8, 4.7.2, 8.4.1. For *domicilium* in a transferred sense as 'home', see *Ep.* 1.6.2 (of the laws), 4.6.2 (of piety). Sidonius does not use this word in his poems. *Competens*, 'corresponding to', 'appropriate' with dative (*TLL* 3, 2068.262–9.3), is Late Latin, used from Apuleius on and also found in Sidon. *Ep.* 4.11.4, 7.9.15, 8.2.3, 8.14.2; Amherdt (2001) 291. Here it refers to an open space which has to be 'big enough' for Sidonius' entrance court. A *vestibulum* is 'an enclosed space before a house', 'a forecourt', 'an entrance court' (*OLD* 2048, 1a); Gell. 16.5.3, Vitr. 6.5.1–2, Förtsch (1993) 127–34. It is also part of the description of Consentius' estate, Octavianum, in Sidon. *Ep.* 8.4.1 *vestibulo campo colle amoenissimus* ('its entrance court, its park, its hill present a most lovely view'). For *campus*, here an 'open space', 'wide space', as part of a building, see the commentary on *Ep.* 2.10.4 vv. 20–1 *et campum medium*....

mediam vallem rectis tractibus prosequuntur latera clivorum usque in marginem villae, quae in Borean Austrumque conversis frontibus tenditur: After descriptions of the western part and the mountain, Sidonius adds descriptions of the other sides of his estate. Boreas is 'the north wind', Auster 'the south wind'; they are used here to indicate the cardinal points north and south. In his work *De architectura* Vitruvius discusses climate and orientation in building and recommends that buildings should be closed towards the north and open towards the warmer side: Vitr. 6.1.2 *conclusa et non patentia, sed conversa ad calidas partes oportere fieri videntur* ('they should be shut and not open, but facing the warm part'). Buildings in the south should be open and facing north or north-east: *patentiora conversaque ad septentrionem et aquilonem sunt faciunda* ('they should be built in an open way and facing north or north-east'). Sidonius' estate has sides facing north and south.

Section 4

Balneum ab Africo radicibus nemorosae rupis adhaerescit: In sections 4–8 Sidonius describes in detail his bath, the pride of his estate; see the introduction to this letter for the role of the bath in Sidonius' villa letters and poems. The term *balneum* or *balineum*, 'a bath', 'a place for bathing' (*TLL* 2, 1704.38–8.67), derives from Greek βαλανεῖον. Sidonius uses both forms, but he uses *balneum* more often than *balineum*. Here the manuscripts LN have *balineum*, MCPF have *balneum*. In *Ep.* 2.9.8 all the manuscripts have *balneas* (plural). The term also appears in *Ep.* 1.8.2, 5.8.2, 5.17.10 v. 1, *Carm.* 19.1, 22.4 v. 135, 22.6, 23.495. *Africus* is 'the south-west wind'; *ab Africo* therefore means 'in the south-west'. Vitruvius (Vitr. 1.2.7, 1.6.5, 5.10.1, 6.4.1) recommends building the winter apartments and the baths oriented towards south-east and Sidonius follows this advice; Cam (2003) 150. See also Sidon. *Ep.* 2.2.18. *Radix*, 'the lower part', 'foot', 'base' (*OLD* 1571, 4b), is commonly used to indicate the bottom of a hill or mountain, for example in Caes. *Bell. Gall.* 7.69.2, Ov. *Met.* 15.548. *Nemorosus*, 'covered with woods or forest', 'wooded' (*OLD* 1170), is poetic and also used in post-Augustan prose, for example Verg. *Aen.* 3.270, Plin. *Nat.* 4.30. It is used by Sidonius in two other instances: *Ep.* 4.8.2 and 2.2.18; Amherdt (2001) 233–4. Woody hills are also mentioned in Iuv. 3.191 *positis nemorosa inter iuga Volsiniis* ('amid the woody hills in Volsinii'); Plin. *Ep.* 8.8.2 *collis ... nemorosus et opacus* ('a hill ... full of woods and shady'). For adjectives ending in *-osus*, see the commentary on *Ep.* 2.2.18 *Lacus ipse ... flexuosus nemorosusque....* The verb *adhaeresco*, 'to stick to', 'adhere', 'cling' (*TLL* 1, 636.62–7.65), is used here in its proper meaning. In a figurative sense it also appears in *Ep.* 4.6.2. In *Ep.* 3.3.6 it means 'to remain still', 'not move'; Giannotti (2016) 147.

et si caedua per iugum silva truncetur, in ora fornacis lapsu velut spontaneo deciduis struibus impingitur: Sidonius stresses the practical sides of his bath, starting with the important topic of heating; see the commentary below on *Ep.* 2.2.4 *Intra conclave succensum....* While Vitr. 5.10, in his section about building a bath, deals at length with the heating system, Vitruvius omits the point how to get wood for the furnace (*fornax*). Sidonius on the other hand shows where the wood for heating the water comes from and coins a precise term (*ora fornacis*); Thébert (2003) 76 n. 4, 475 n. 97. The combination of *caeduus*, 'that can be cut without injury', 'ready for felling', 'fit for cutting' (*TLL* 3, 64.1–14), and *silva*, 'wood', is frequent, especially in agrarian writers, for example Cato *Agr.* 1.7, Varro *Rust.* 1.7.9, Colum.

3.3.1, Plin. *Nat.* 17.141. In his villa letter Pliny uses the same expression: Plin. *Ep.* 5.6.8 *inde caeduae silvae cum ipso monte descendunt* ('and then the woods, fit for cutting, descend with the mountain itself'). *Caeduus* is used in a metaphorical sense in Sidon. *Carm.* 7.277. For the idea of a land of milk and honey, where the wood cuts itself, see Mart. 1.49.27 *vicina in ipsum silva descendet focum* ('the nearby wood will descend by itself into the oven') and 12.18.19–20 about wood for heating from one's own forest.

Hinc aquarum surgit cella coctilium: First, Sidonius describes the hot water room. With *hinc* and the following demonstratives Sidonius guides his readers through his estate; see the commentary above on *Ep.* 2.2.3 *Sane si placet....* The rarely used adjective *coctilis* means 'burnt', 'cooked' (*TLL* 3, 1401.54–66). With *aquarum cella coctilium* Sidonius coins a unique term for a 'hot room'. Usually the principal bath chamber for a hot-water bath is called the *caldarium*. Hot rooms existed in different forms, the most common of which in later times were the round and semicircular forms; Vitr. 5.10.1 and 4, 8.2.4, Plin. *Ep.* 5.6.26; Nielsen (1990) 156–7.

quae consequenti unguentariae spatii parilitate conquadrat excepto solii capacis hemicyclio: The hot room is as big as the 'anointing room' (*unctorium*), which is usually situated next to the cool room with pool(s) of cold water (*frigidarium*). The adjective *unguentarius*, 'belonging to ointments', must be thought of here as a complement to another *cella*. Nielsen (1990) 161 suggests that the *unctorium* here is also used as a *tepidarium* ('warm room'), which is missing in Sidonius' description of his bath; see Plin. *Ep.* 2.17.11 on his *unctorium*. The noun *parilitas*, 'equality', appears from the second century onwards, for the combination with quantities or measures (*TLL* 10.1, 397.59–73). Here it is combined with *spatium*, 'room', 'space', in the genitive. *Parilitas* is also used in Sidon. *Ep.* 2.9.4, 3.1.1, 3.6.3, 4.4.1; Amherdt (2001) 72, Giannotti (2016) 112–13, Fascione (2019) 100–101. *Conquadro*, 'to agree with', 'to be portioned to', 'to build a square' (*TLL* 4, 350.9–22), is a rarely used verb (attested from Varro *Sat. Men.* 96 and Colum. 8.3.7 on) and appears also in Sidon. *Ep.* 2.4.1, 3.7.4, and in four instances in different texts by Augustine, such as Aug. *C. Parm.* 2.10.20; Giannotti (2016) 187. A *solium* is a 'tub', 'pool'. In Late Antiquity the term is used for a communal pool in the *caldarium* ('hot bath'). Sidonius frequently uses the adjective *capax*, 'spacious', 'roomy' (*TLL* 3, 300.54–304.39), either as an absolute, as here and in *Ep.* 2.13.7, 3.3.5, 4.8.4, 4.15.1, 4.18.4, 5.17.3, 9.13.5 v. 39, *Carm.* 5.14, 22.5, or with an object, as in *Ep.* 2.12.1, 5.9.1, 9.14.3. The pool in

Sidonius' villa is shaped as a *hemicyclium,* 'a half-circle' or 'semicircle'. The term derives from Greek ἡμικύκλιον, one of the Grecisms Sidonius announces in *Ep.* 2.2.8; Nielsen (1990) 157. See also Cic. *Lael.* 1.2 *tum memini domi in hemicyclio sedentem* ('I remember him sitting at home on his semicircular garden bench') and Plin. *Ep.* 5.6.33 *rectus hic hippodromi limes in extrema parte hemicyclio frangitur mutatque faciem* ('this straight path of the hippodrome turns at its end into a semicircle and changes its appearance'). The term *hemicyclium* also appears several times in Vitruvius in an architectural context, for instance Vitr. 5.1.8; for further examples see *TLL* 6.3, 2601.72–2.27.

ubi et vis undae ferventis per parietem foraminatum flexilis plumbi meatibus implicita singultat: Next, Sidonius describes the technique by which the water is heated. We find a similar description of the heating of the bath with hot air in Pliny's description of his villa, in Plin. *Ep.* 2.17.9 *qui suspensus et tubulatus conceptum vaporem salubri temperamento huc illuc digerit et ministrat* ('this passage has a basement and a heating system that brings from there the warm air in agreeable temperature here and there and directs it further'); see also Auson. *Mos.* 338–40. The participle *foraminatus,* here used as an adjective meaning 'bored or pierced through, having holes' (*TLL* 6.1, 1034.56–9), is only found in Sidonius, also in *Ep.* 1.5.6, 3.3.5; Gualandri (1979) 180, Giannotti (2016) 145–6. The adjective *flexilis,* 'pliant', 'pliable', 'flexible' (*TLL* 6.1, 906.39–47), is used in poetry and in post-Augustan prose instead of *flexus,* for example in Apul. *Met.* 6.1.3. It is also used in Sidon. *Ep.* 2.9.8, 3.3.5, *Carm.* 16.80, 23.327; Santelia (2012) 123, Giannotti (2016) 145. *Plumbi* is poetical for 'leaden pipes' (*TLL* 10.1, 2455.34–44); see also Hor. *Ep.* 1.10.20, Vitr. 8.6.10, Stat. *Silv.* 1.3.67. The general term *meatus,* 'going', 'passing', is also a technical agricultural term meaning a 'water channel' (*TLL* 8, 514.4–14), as in Colum. 8.17.3, Ruric. *Ep.* 1.5.2; Neri (2009) 189. *Singulto,* 'to catch the breath', 'gasp' (*OLD* 1769, 1), is here used to mean 'gurgle' water. Sidonius does not go into the details of the functioning of a *hypocaustum* and just mentions the warmth. See also Sidon. *Carm.* 22.4 v. 190; Nielsen (1990) 161, Delhey (1993) 173, Busch (1999) 445–7. For the heating system in the villa and its baths, see Plin. *Ep.* 2.17.9, 2.17.23, 5.6.24–5, Stat. *Silv.* 1.5.57–9, Vitr. 5.10.2.

Intra conclave succensum solidus dies et haec abundantia lucis inclusae: After the heating, Sidonius goes on to describe the interior design and begins with the lighting conditions. The manuscripts LNVM have *intra,* TCF *inter.* The *conclave succensum* is 'a bathing-room heated from below', 'a sweating-chamber'. For Sidonius' use of *solidus* in the meaning of *integer*, 'entire', 'complete', 'full', see van Waarden (2010) 124, who refers to Hor. *Carm.* 1.1.20. The lighting conditions are an important criterion for the quality of a bath. Whereas a bright bath is praised, darkness (*tenebrae*) is condemned, for example in Mart. 6.42.8–10, Sen. *Ep.* 86.4–12, Plin. *Ep.* 1.3.1; Dunbabin (1989) 8–9. The image of 'enclosed light' is frequently used by Late Antique authors also in a metapoetical sense, for example Alc. Avit. *Ep.* 50, 78.18–19, *Hom.* 29, p.150.11–13, Ven. Fort. *Carm.* 1.15.55–8; see Schwitter (2015) 173–87 on the importance of light and radiance in Late Antique literature and Fowden (2004) 42–3 on the *caldarium* of the bath in Quṣayr 'Amra, which also shows this feature. The same praise of light (*lux micat*) in a building is also found in Sidonius' description of the church of bishop Patiens in *Ep.* 2.10.4 v. 8 (see the commentary there). Herbert de la Portbarré-Viard (2014), Hernández Lobato (2010) 303. Mratschek (2020b) 252 suggests Plin. *Ep.* 2.17.7 as intertext as he describes a similar lighting effect in his living room.

ut verecundos quosque compellat aliquid se plus putare quam nudos: Because Sidonius' bath is full of light, 'modest' (*verecundos*) visitors feel more than naked, that is, ashamed. Sidonius uses the term *verecundia*, 'an attitude of restraint', 'modesty', several times to denote appropriate behaviour; see the commentary on *Ep.* 2.4.3 *benignitate responsi ... verecundiam munerare*. Bathing naked was the habit until the end of antiquity. Under Christian influence the attitude towards nudity and bathing changed, however. On nakedness in the public Roman baths, see Nielsen (1990) 140–1, Busch (1999) 463–512, 535–6, Henriksén (2012) 148; on Christian attitudes towards bathing in Late Antiquity, see Yegül (1992) 314–21, Maréchal (2020) 69. For the formulation see Sidon. *Ep.* 1.7.13 *aliquid nunc amplius quam vivere* ('there is anything he now dreads more than life'). In *Carm.* 23.498–9 Sidonius writes to Consentius that the private bath ensures shamelessness: *ad thermas tamen ire sed libebat | privato bene praebitas pudori* ('but we decided to go to the baths fittingly provided for privacy and modesty'); Thébert (2003) 482 n. 120.

Section 5

Hinc frigidaria dilatatur, quae piscinas publicis operibus extructas non impudenter aemularetur: In section 5 Sidonius describes the large impressive room containing the bath with cold water. The *frigidarium* (from *frigeo*, 'to be cold') is the cool room, with pool(s) of cold water, one enters after the *caldarium* ('hot bath') and the *tepidarium* ('tepid bath'). When describing his cold bath, Sidonius alludes to Vitruvius and uses his vocabulary several times; see Vitr. 5.10.1, 5.11.2 and the commentary, p. 109, on *ipsa vero convenientibus mensuris ... exactissima ...* and that (p. 111) on *Ep.* 2.2.5 *Interior parietum facies solo levigati caementi candore levigati caementi candore contenta est*; see also Plin. *Ep.* 2.17.11, 5.6.25–6; Guérin-Beauvois (1997) 706–7, Cam (2003) 148. Sidonius holds Vitruvius in high esteem and mentions him by name in *Ep.* 4.3.5, 8.6.10; Amherdt (2001) 137. The *frigidarium* was often the largest room in the baths and contained one or more cold-water pools, called *piscina*. The pools could have different shapes, but mostly they were rectangular. The term *piscina* denotes either a small pool with cool water, designed to sit in after the hot bath, or, as here and in *Ep.* 2.2.8, a proper swimming pool (also called *natatio*), which is either inside the *frigidarium* or in the open; see Plin. *Ep.* 5.6.25 *si natare latius aut tepidus velis, in area piscina est* ('if you want to swim longer distances or warmer, there is a pool in the court'), Sen. *Ep.* 56.2, Mart. 3.44.13, Auson. *Mos.* 342; Nielsen (1990) 153–4. In section 5, Sidonius also compares his private bath with public baths. The Roman baths varied in terms of their owners and size, and were designated correspondingly as *thermae* (large, state-owned baths) or *balnea* (smaller, privately owned establishments); Nielsen (1990) 119–24, Yegül (1992) 43. Sidonius is proud of the size of his cold baths (*frigidaria*), which are as large as those in public baths; see Fages (2015) 144–5 for the enormous dimensions of the bath complex (around 1500 m^2) in the villa of Séviac (from the end of the fourth century), near present-day Montréal-Du-Gers in Occitania, and Bouet (1997–1998) 218–25 on the villa of Montmaurin (Haute-Garonne), thoroughly renovated between 325 and 330. Sidonius often uses the verb *aemulor*, 'to rival', 'to emulate', in a positive or a negative sense (e.g. *Ep.* 1.1.2, 1.4.1, 1.7.3, 2.3.2, 7.4.3). For the related nouns *aemulus, aemulator* and *aemulationem*, see the commentary below on *Ep.* 2.3.2 *sic et Gnaeum Pompeium super aemulos*. Here one thing rivals another, a use also attested in Plin. *Nat.*, for example in 14.30 (about two different kinds of grapes); see also *TLL* 1, 975.26–44. For the comparison of private with public buildings (*quae piscinas publicis operibus extructas ... aemularetur*), see the similar wording in Plin. *Ep.* 2.17.16 *hinc cryptoporticus prope publici operis extenditur* ('from there a covered passage extends which has nearly the size of a public building'); Sherwin-White (1966) 196. See also Sidon. *Carm.* 18.3 (cited in the commentary below, p. 108, on *Primum tecti apice in conum cacuminato*), Mart. 4.25.1 *aemula Baianis Altini litora villis* ('the beach of Altinum which can compete with the estates in Baiae'). See also Mart. 10.79.3–4 on the *vici magister* Otacilius, who seeks to imitate the *thermae* of the consul Torquatus. In *Carm.* 23.495–9 Sidonius also compares private to public baths. Consentius' private bath is much smaller and not so luxurious, but it offers privacy and guarantees personal modesty instead: *hinc ad balnea, non Neroniana | nec quae Agrippa dedit vel ille cuius | bustum Dalmaticae vident Salonae, | ad thermas tamen ire sed libebat | private bene praebitas pudori* ('Hence to the baths; they were not those of Nero or those given by Agrippa or by him whose tomb Damatian Salonae views, but we decided to go to baths fittingly provided for privacy and modesty').

Primum tecti apice in conum cacuminato: Sidonius highlights the shape and height of his bath-house's roof by using vocabulary from a military context; Guérin-Beauvois (1997) 700–9. *Apex* here means 'top of', 'summit'; see the commentary on *Ep.* 2.1.2 *epistulas, ne primis quidem apicibus sufficienter initiatus*.... The adjective *conus* means 'cone-shaped' as well as 'apex of a helmet', and is not usually used to describe a roof. In *Carm.* 18.3–4 Sidonius uses it again when he compares the roof of his bath-house with one of the famous domed bath complexes at the well-known seaside resort Baiae: *aemula Baiano tolluntur culmina cono | parque cothurnato vertice fulget apex* ('the roof-top is exalted rivalling the cone-shaped roofs of Baiae and the pinnacle gleams as much with its peaked top'); Busch (1999) 69–70, Furbetta (2013) 247–9. *Cacuminato* is the participle of the rarely used verb *cacumino*, 'to make pointed', 'sharpen' (*TLL* 3, 12.20–25), which appears first in Ov. *Met.* 3.195 (about ears) and four times in Sidonius – here and Sidon. *Ep.* 7.12.2 (of Ferreolus' merits), *Carm.* 5.91 (of teeth), 7.412 (of a sword); van Waarden (2016) 67.

cum ab angulis quadrifariam concurrentia dorsa cristarum tegulis interiacentibus imbricarentur: Next, Sidonius describes the different tiles and patterns with which the roof is covered. The translation of this clause causes some difficulties and accordingly the suggestions differ. Dalton (1915) 37 ('the spaces between the converging ridges are covered with imbricated tiles') and Visser (2014) ('while the ridges are covered from the four corners with imbricated rain-tiles') abbreviate the Latin text. Köhler (2014) 43 and Anderson (1936) 421 ('the four faces of this erection are covered at the corners where they join by hollow tiles, between which rows of flat tiles are set') differentiate between two kinds of tiles. According to Guérin-Beauvois (1997) 703, the nature of the roof is not exceptional, but with the mixture of technical and metaphorical vocabulary Sidonius makes it difficult to understand. The *cristae* mentioned are the 'round ridge tiles which cover the tops of the roofs' (*TLL* 4, 1210.62–68); see Sidon. *Ep.* 7.1.3 *culminum cristas* ('the tiles of the roof tops'); van Waarden (2010) 99. Guérin-Beauvois (1997) 704–5 suggests a military aspect of the whole passage, as *cristae* also means 'crest of a helmet' and *conus* 'apex of a helmet'. The verb *imbrico*, 'to cover with gutter tiles' (*TLL* 7.1, 426.46–9), is a hapax; Gualandri (1979) 180. But why does Sidonius care so much about an architectural detail that has nothing to do with bathing as such? The roof of the bath-house is important as a landmark, as a distinctive sign of Sidonius' villa for travellers. Accordingly, Sidonius describes his roof with particular stylistic adornment; Stevens (1933) 177.

[ipsa vero convenientibus mensuris exactissima spatiositate quadratur ('the room is spaciously built with perfect measurement into a square')]: I have not included this phrase, which is placed either after *imbricarentur* or after *personas*, a little later. It is included in a group of manuscripts (*Berl*1, *Berl*2, *Mtp*4, *Thott*, *Par*2171, *Reg*216) with the same innovative characteristics. The sentence is lacking in the main manuscripts L, N, V, M, C, T cited by Loyen (1970a) 47 and the manuscripts at the top of the stemma. Loyen (1970a) 47 and Anderson (1936) 42 include it in their editions, while Lütjohann (1887) 23 omits it. The phrase is missing in the *editio princeps* of Nicolaes Ketelaer and Geraert van Leempt (1473/4), but included in the editions of Woweren (1598) and Savaron (1599); see Furbetta (2020) 544, 550 n. 34, 554 n. 46, 556 n. 52. According to Dolveck (2020) 492 n. 39 it is a gloss. It is strange, however, that it is the only gloss in Sidonius that gets into the text in this way. In this clause there are various allusions to concepts from Vitruvius' *De architectura*. On *convenientibus mensuris*, see the Vitruvian notion of order and symmetry (*quantitas*) in Vitr. 1.2.2–4; Cam (2003) 148. The superlative *exactissima*, 'faultless', 'supremely excellent', is also used in Sidon. *Ep.* 3.11.1, 5.11.2, 7.8.3, and recalls the Vitruvian notion of *exactio*, 'the exact proportion of parts', Vitr. 3.1.4, 4.1.12; Cam (2003) 148, van Waarden (2010) 401, Giannotti (2016) 209. *Spatiositate*, 'wideness', 'spaciousness', is a very rarely used word, a hapax according to Gualandri (1979) 180, but it also appears in a translation of Philo *De statu Essaeorum*, from the fourth century.

ita ut ministeriorum sese non impediente famulatu tot possit recipere sellas, quot solet sigma personas: Sidonius stresses the fact that there is enough space in his bath-house. He compares it to a dining room where the slaves are able to fulfil their duties without disturbing the guests; Petron. 34.5. The abstract noun *ministerium* stands for the person, that is, the slaves, who are working in the bath-house; see also Sidon. *Ep.* 1.11.14 *celerantia ministeria* ('the hurrying slaves'). *Famulatus* here denotes 'the duty or task of a slave' (*TLL* 6.1, 261.13–23); see the commentary on *Ep.* 2.13.2 *hoc ipso satis miseriores ... se subiacere famulatui*. Slaves as necessary means of the household also appear in the description of the daily life in the villa of Apollinaris and Ferreolus – see *Ep.* 2.9. *Sigma* denotes the letter Σ in its later lunate form C, and by extension the shape of a 'semi-circular couch for reclining at table' (*OLD*, 1757). This sort of couch replaced the rectangular dining couch by the fourth to fifth century; see Sidon. *Carm.* 17.6, 22.4 v. 212, Mart. 10.48.6, 14.87. *Sigma* is used elsewhere as a synonym for a *stibadium* 'semicircular dining couch'; see the commentary below on *Ep.* 2.2.11 *In hac stibadium*.... Here *sigma* refers to a bathing tub of the same semicircular shape. How many persons could find place in it is hard to tell, though. *Sigmae* and *stibadia* varied in size, usually offering room for five to eight guests, but sometimes there was also room for more; Rodenwaldt (1923) 2324. *Persona* here denotes neutrally the 'individual person' who sits on the dining couch. Sidonius uses the term *persona* (*TLL* 10.1, 1715.29–29.34) in various ways. In classical literature, the term most often denotes a 'mask', 'role' (in theatre) or a 'official role' or 'habit', for example in Cic. *Phil.* 8.29, *Planc.* 100, *Pis.* 24, 71; Fuhrmann (1979) 85–91 provides further examples. In Late Antique texts, *persona* can be used with an adjective denoting social rank, a usage that goes back at least to Cicero; see Sidon. *Ep.* 2.8.1, Amm. 28.1.15, 18.1.2, 30.4.16. Sidonius uses the term also in the neutral meaning of 'person', 'man', as here, or of those who are close to him and connected with personal ties, that is, meaning 'friend', 'acquaintance', 'client'; see also Sidon. *Ep.* 2.6.1, 2.7.1; Fuhrmann (1979) 92.

fenestras e regione conditor binas confinio camerae pendentis admovit: Next, Sidonius refers to the anonymous builder of his bath-house and its windows. Here *conditor* means 'architect', 'builder'. In the sense of 'founder' it is used in Sidon. *Ep.* 4.18.5 v. 12, *Carm.* 22.4 v. 142; Delhey (1993) 138. The term *camera* denotes an 'arched roof' but also 'any kind of roof' (*TLL* 3, 203.25–4.11). The term is also used of a building in Sidon. *Ep.* 2.10.4 v. 12 (as here in combination with *lacunar* – the commentary, p. 111, on *ut suspicientum visui fabrefactum lacunar aperiret*) and *Ep.* 9.13.5 v. 49; Di Salvo

(2005) 140. *Pendentis* is found in the manuscripts LNMC, *pendentes* in VT. The prose rhythm (cretic spondee) and the stemma support *pendentis*.

ut suspicientum visui fabrefactum lacunar aperiret: Instead of the sky, an artistic ceiling opens up to the visitor of the bath-house, which is illuminated by the two windows. *Fabrefactum* is the perfect passive participle of *fabrefacio*, 'to make, frame, fashion, or do skilfully' (*TLL* 6.1, 12.31–68). A *lacunar* is a 'wainscoted and gilded ceiling, panel-ceiling, ceiled roof' (*TLL* 7.2, 858.78–9.76); see Vitr. 7.2, Hor. *Carm.* 2.18.2 (cited in the commentary on *Ep.* 2.13.6 *et renidentem gemmis margaritisque...*); Höcker (1999). Sidonius mentions it also in *Ep.* 2.10.4 v. 9 (of a church – see the commentary there), 2.13.7 (of a palace); see Delhey (1993) 140–1, Di Salvo (2005) 139–40.

Interior parietum facies solo levigati caementi candore contenta est: The inner walls of the bath-house, however, are unadorned. *Parietum facies* denotes a 'surface', 'outer layer' (*TLL* 6.1, 51.38–9); see Sidon. *Ep.* 7.1.2 *ambustam murorum faciem* ('the burnt surface of the walls'); van Waarden (2010) 90–1. Sidonius probably again alludes to Vitruvius by using the architectural terms *levigatus* ('smoothed') and *candor* ('whiteness'); Cam (2003) 153. *Caementum* most often denotes a 'rough, unhewn stone' (as it comes from the quarry) (*TLL* 3, 95.57–6.65), seldom 'mortar', 'plaster' (*TLL* 3, 96.66–70). Here it refers to 'marble' that is ground into powder and applied smoothly as the top layer on the wall.

Section 6

Non hic per nudam pictorum corporum pulchritudinem turpis prostat historia: The baths in private villas were usually richly decorated with wall paintings, mosaics and statues; Dunbabin (1989) 12–32, Nielsen (1990) 42–3, 145, Stirling (2012), Maréchal (2020) 196–8. Sidonius describes his baths' interior with a list of points in the negative, reminiscent of a *recusatio*. First, he lists common motifs with which baths are usually decorated, namely scenes from mythology, theatre or wrestling, but rejects them in favour of the ornaments on his walls (*illis paginis*). The walls of his bath-house instead are plain white, apart from written verses; see Yegül (1992) 322, Balmelle (2001) 200–1, Cam (2003) 252–5 and the commentary on *Ep.* 2.2.7. Percival (1992) 158 and Harries (1994) 132 perceive the missing pictures as a decline in standards in villas in fifth-century Gaul and Dewar (2014) 97 suggests that not even wealthy men like Sidonius could affort to hire artists to decorate their villas. With *nudam ... pulchritudinem* Sidonius hints at a mythical scene. A popular motif of decoration, suitable for a bath, was the naked Aphrodite (Anadyomene), for example in *Anth. Pal.* 9.606, 9.619, 9.633, Stat. *Silv.* 1.5; Dunbabin (1989) 12–13, 23–4, Busch (1999) 282–9, 98–9, Mielsch (2001) 161. On the moral problems caused by naked statues in baths for Late Antique viewers, see Stirling (2012) 77–9. According to Fowden (2004) 59–60, the absence of nudes was relatively unusual for a Late Antique bath; see also Dunbabin (1989) 9, Hanaghan (2020) 129. *Prostat*, 'to set out', 'display', is used to describe the presentation of a work of art; see *TLL* 10.2, 2239.3–8, and also Tert. *Apol.* 16.6. Perhaps the meaning of the verb as 'to prostitute onself' (*TLL* 10.2, 2239.16–47) also resonates here.

quae sicut ornat artem, sic devenustat artificem: Although the depictions are artistic, they discredit the artist according to Sidonius. For examples of the rarely used verb *devenusto*, 'to disfigure', 'deform' (*TLL* 5.1, 850.82–1.6), see Sidon. *Ep.* 1.7.12, 7.9.8, 9.2.3; Köhler (1995) 254, van Waarden (2010) 463, Wolff (2020) 401. The verb is first attested in Gell 12.1.8 and also sometimes in Symmachus, for example Symm. *Ep.* 1.79, 1.94, but its use is rare. *Artifex*, 'artist' (*TLL* 2, 696.42–702.82, *OLD* 176–7) is a term frequently used in Seneca's philosophical works, Pliny's *Natural History* and in Ennodius. Sidonius uses it as a noun in *Ep.* 4.3.5, 5.10.4, 9.9.12, 9.12.2 as well as an adjective in *Ep.* 2.2.20, 4.1.3, 7.14.8, 8.1.2, 8.11.5, 9.11.9, but not in his poems.

Absunt ridiculi vestitu et vultibus histriones pigmentis multicoloribus Philistionis supellectilem mentientes: Not only naked mythological figures, but also comic scenes from mime are missing on Sidonius' walls. Philistion was a Greek mime actor and mime writer in Augustan Rome; Garton (1982) 204 n. 42. By mentioning this famous figure of folk culture, Sidonius alludes to a mime scene in general; Benz (2000). With the specific combination of *ridiculus* and the name Philistio, Sidonius refers to Mart. 2.41.15 *mimos ridiculi Philistionis* ('the mimes of the amusing Philistio'). On Sidonius' use of Martial's vocabulary and ideas in general, see Gualandri (1979) 86–7, Franzoi (2008), Canobbio (2013), Wolff (2014b) 96. Colton (1976, 1985a, 1985b) only lists the passages, but offers no interpretation. *Supellex*, 'outfit', 'paraphernalia' (*OLD* 1872, 1b), here denotes the set of articles necessary for an actor. For the costume of a mime artist, that is, simple dress mostly without a mask, but with a phallus, see Benz (2000) 205. The term also appears in Sidonius' villa letter *Ep.* 8.4.1 denoting household effects, in 8.12.7 in the context of cooking and in Sidon. *Carm.* 10.3 in relation to gods.

Absunt lubrici tortuosique pugilatu et nexibus palaestritae: In antiquity, public and private baths often included rooms for exercise, such as boxing, wrestling, weight-lifting, walking and ball games; Nielsen (1990) 144. Scenes of a wrestling match are therefore a suitable decoration for the walls of a bath, but are also missing, as are the motifs from myth and mime in Sidonius' villa. Sidonius again alludes to Martial, who describes in his epigram Mart. 3.58 two kinds of villas, one a place for idle luxury (including a wrestling room), the other a place of agricultural productivity; see the commentary above, p. 112, on *Absunt ridiculi vestitu*.... A *palaestrita*, 'wrestler' (*TLL* 10.1, 101.18–49), is *lubricus*, 'slippery' (*TLL* 7.2, 1688.19–26), because of the oil he rubs himself with; see Mart. 3.58.25 *nec perdit oleum lubricus palaestrita* ('and no oily wrestler wastes his oil') and Auson. *Grat.* 14.64 *quis palaestram tam lubricus expedivit?* ('who so slippery completed the exercise of wrestling?'). At the same time, *lubricus* hints at the dubious morals of these professionals and is frequently used by Christian authors to denote shamelessness and adultery (*TLL* 7.2, 1690.45–84). Martial and Apuleius use the adjective to describe young (and therefore hairless) boys in an erotic context, for example Mart. 9.56.11, Apul. *Met.* 9.22.6. In *Ep.* 8.7.2, Sidonius uses the image of the wrestler oiling himself as a metaphor. He uses *lubricus* in the meaning of 'soft', 'flexible', 'smooth', also applied to things and plants – see *Ep.* 2.2.12, 2.2.18, 2.13.1, 3.2.3, 8.11.5, 9.7.3. The adjective *tortuosus*, 'characterized by curves or bends', 'winding', 'sinuous' (*OLD* 1952, 1), otherwise used for roads or rivers (see the commentary on *Ep.* 2.9.2), means here the intertwined limbs of the wrestlers.

quorum etiam viventum luctas, si involvantur obscenius, casta confestim gymnasiarchorum virga dissolvit: Sidonius explicitly addresses the erotic aspect of wrestling in this phrase. *Lucta* denotes 'a wrestling', 'wrestling-match' (*TLL* 7.2, 1725.37–80), and the plural is very rarely used, but see also Sidon. *Carm.* 9.187 *unctas ... luctas* ('oily wrestling'), 11.87 *luctaque Achelous* ('Achelous by wrestling'). *Involvo*, 'to roll one's self around', 'to wind around' (*TLL* 7.2, 265.40–59), is often used of snakes that wrap themselves around people, but here it refers to wrestling. The entangling of the fighters is described as *obscenius*, 'in a too obscene way' (*TLL* 9.2, 161.58–75); see also Sidon. *Ep.* 3.13.11 *vivat obscene* ('who lives immorally'). The adverb appears several times in Cicero, in the context of oratory which can relate immoral things without being indecent itself, for example Cic. *Off.* 1.128, *Orat.* 154. *Gymnasiarchus*, 'master of a gymnasium' (*TLL* 6.2, 2378.71–81), is a rarely used word, first attested in Cic. *Verr.* 2.4.42. The *gymnasiarchus* was responsible for all the matters of a gymnasium, in Sidonius' description also for the moral standards imposed there, and therefore his stick is described in an enallage as 'chaste'. The adjective *castus*, 'morally pure', is used metonymically of things (*de rebus corporeis*) (*TLL* 3, 567.76–8.11), here of *virga* 'stick', 'rod', 'switch'. The need for good morals in teachers and pedagogues (*castus, sanctus*) is mentioned by Pliny and Quintilian and attested in inscriptions, such as Plin. *Ep.* 3.3.3; *CIL* 6.8012; see Bonner (1977) 105–6. See also the commentary on *Ep.* 2.8.3 v. 6 *prudens, casta*.... Similarly, Servius comments on Mercury's stick in Verg. *Aen.* 4.242 *et hodieque tam athletarum quam gladiatorum certamina virga dirimuntur* ('and also today the competitions of both athletes and gladiators are broken up by a rod').

Section 7

Quid plura? Nihil illis paginis impressum reperietur, quod non vidisse sit sanctius: After enumerating what cannot be found on his walls for moral reasons, Sidonius describes the decoration of his bath. Instead of immoral pictures or costly marble (see the commentary below on *Ep.* 2.2.7 *Iam si marmora inquiras...*), there is a verse inscription on the wall, 'a kind of "anti-ekphrasis" of missing pictures within the ekphrasis' Mratschek (2020b) 252. In an architectural context *pagina* means 'leaf', 'slab' (*TLL* 10.1, 91.1–12); see Plin. *Nat.* 16.225, Paul. Nol. *Carm.* 21.588, Pallad. 6.11.3, Sidon. *Ep.* 3.12.4 *levigata pagina* ('a smooth slab of stone') and 8.14.4 *paginam altaris* ('the altar slab'). Van Waarden (2016) 221 translates *pagina* here as 'panel'. The common meaning which predominates also in Sidonius is 'a leaf of paper', 'sheet', 'page', 'letter', for example in Sidon. *Ep.* 2.2.20, 2.10.3, 2.12.1, 5.6.2, 5.12.1–2, 6.9.1, 7.2.2, 8.5.1, 8.9.4, 8.11.3, 8.11.14, 8.14.7, 9.1.3, 9.3.6, 9.9.2, 9.11.5, 9.12.1, 9.15.1, 9.16.2. By using *pagina* in the description of his villa, Sidonius probably alludes to his writing and the following passage can be read in a metapoetical way. In Sidonius' work there is, as in his bath-house, no immorality; Hanaghan (2020) 129: 'The writing of poetry onto the walls of the baths turns the baths into a learned space'. The atmosphere of Sidonius' uncles' baths in *Ep.* 2.9.9, where drinking and jokes dominate, is very different. For the content of the verses, see the commentary immediately below on *Ep.* 2.2.7 *Pauci tamen versiculi*.... It is not certain whether the verses are painted or engraved on the wall; van Waarden (2016) 221. *Imprimere* is regularly used in the meaning of 'to write' (*TLL* 7.1, 682.30–55). For *impressum*, 'impressed', see also Sidon. *Ep.* 7.17.2, where he uses the rarely seen noun *impressus*, 'impress', for verses which will be inscribed by his *stilus*, 'pen', on the tomb of the deceased Saint Abraham; van Waarden (2016) 221. In *Ep.* 2.8.2 Sidonius uses *incisus*, 'engraved', for a poem which was engraved in a marble plate on a tomb; in *Ep.* 2.10.3 Sidonius uses *inscribere*, 'inscribe for placing on'; see the commentary there. According to Dark (2005) 334, no inscriptions are found in villas that are historically and geographically comparable to Avitacum. He explains the poems on the wall simply in terms of Sidonius' interest in literature. Scheibelreiter-Gail (2012) 151–4 instead shows that inscriptions in Late Antique houses were common; painted wall inscriptions, engraved inscriptions and graffiti are attested. There are several extant epigrams in which baths or fountains are praised; Lausberg (1982) 180–5. Rut. Nam. 1.269–70, for example, similarly mentions verses inscribed on the walls of a bath: *intrantemque capit discedentemque moratur | postibus adfixum dulce poema sacris* ('a sweet poem attached to the holy threshold catches one's attention on arriving and holds one back at departure'); see also Ven. Fort. *Carm.* 1.18, 1.20. There are also some bath poems included in the *Anthologia Latina* from Vandal Africa, presumably roughly contemporary; Busch (1999) 240–65. Several of the bath poems in the *Anthologia Latina* may have been inscribed on the walls of public baths; Miles (2005) 311. Sidonius emphasises his statement of moral purity with the double cretic *vidisse sit sanctius*. For the formulation, see also Plin. *Ep.* 3.3.6 *nihil discet, quod nescisse rectius fuerit* ('he will not learn anything that would have been better not to know'). In this letter Pliny recommends Iulius Genitor to Corellia as a morally apt teacher for her son.

Pauci tamen versiculi lectorem adventicium remorabuntur minime improbo temperamento, quia eos nec relegisse desiderio est nec perlegisse fastidio: The verses Sidonius alludes to are probably his own, Sidon. *Carm.* 18 *De balneis villae suae* and *Carm.* 19 *De piscina sua*, which describes a swimming pool and addresses the bathers directly in the second person plural: *intrate algentes post balnea torrida fluctus | ut solidet calidam frigore lympha cutem; | et licet hoc solo mergatis membra liquore, | per stagnum nostrum lumina vestra natant* ('enter the cold floods after the steaming hot bath, so that the water by its coldness makes the heated skin firm; and though you dip your limbs only in this liquid, your eyes swim through our pool'); Busch (1999) 75–6, Mondin (2008) 399, Furbetta (2013) 251–3. As *Carm.* 18 describes the baths in the estate Avitacum, the plural *versiculi* probably thus refers back to both poems; Consolino (2020) 355. Hernández Lobato (2015) 608–9 suggests that they were inscribed on the walls of the *frigidarium* and at the entrance to the pool. To describe his poem, Sidonius, in a gesture of modesty, uses the diminutive *versiculus*, 'a brief line of verse' (*OLD* 2040, 2), as he does in *Ep.* 2.10.2 in referring to his poem for the church of bishop Patiens in Lyon. The term is attested in Catull. 50.4 denoting easy (*levis*) and elegant poetry, but can also have a pejorative meaning, as in Mart. 3.9.1. Like Sidonius, Pliny (e.g. Plin. *Ep.* 9.16.2; see also Plin. *Ep.* 3.21.2–5 for Martial's verses about Pliny) and Cicero use the diminutive in their letters to refer to their own poetry, for example Cic. *Att.* 5.1.3, *Ad Brut.* 1.14.1; Condorelli (2008) 196. With the combination of *versiculi* and *fastidium*, Sidonius probably alludes to Ausonius, who writes in the preface to his collection of funerary epigrams, Auson. *Parent. Praef.* A: *scio versiculis meis evenire ut fastidiose legantur* ('I am aware that my little verses happen to be read with disgust'); Squillante (2018) 373–4, Hindermann (2020a) 103. Both Ausonius and Sidonius frequently introduce their poetry with witty and ironic prefaces and thus distance themselves from their classical predecessors; Elsner and Hernández Lobato (2017b) 16. For a further example of the fear of causing repulsion (*fastidium*) through one's writing, see also Ruric. *Ep.* 1.3.2. For Sidonius' demonstrative modesty, see also the commentary on *Ep.* 2.9.10 *Dicerem et cenas ... nisi terminum nostrae loquacitati ...* and Consolino (2020) 357 n. 74 on Sidon. *Carm.* 29. Sidonius describes his poems as not bad enough to not be read till the end (*perlegere*), but as not good enough to be reread (*relegere*). Convincingly, Kelly (2020b) 154 identifies Rutilius Namatianus' reference to a poem by Messala, which is inscribed above the gate of the Thermae Tuarinae (near Centumcellae, present-day Civitavecchia), as a model for Sidonius; see Rut. Nam. 1.269–70 *intrantemque capit discedentemque moratur | postibus adfixum dulce poema sacris* ('the sweet poem attached to the hallowed doorposts grabs one on entering and delays one on leaving'). In contrast to Sidonius, Messala, the poet and former praetorian prefect of Italy (also mentioned in Sidon. *Carm.* 9.305), regards his poems as good enough to be read twice. The adjective *adventicius* 'coming from abroad', 'from the outside' (*TLL* 1, 834.22–5.32), in local use is found in Varro *Rust.* 1.8.4 and several times in Cicero, for example Cic. *Div.* 2.120. For *fastidium*, 'aversion', see also Sidon. *Ep.* 1.7.3 and 5.4.2 on account of attention felt too much, or *Ep.* 2.2.20 in relation to an overly long letter; van Waarden (2010) 547.

iam, si marmora inquiras, non illic quidem: Marble was very often used in Roman architecture, in both public and private buildings; Drerup (1981) 8–15, Dodge and Ward-Perkins (1992), Förtsch (1993) 86, Bedon (2004) 371–5, Borghini (2004), Greenhalgh (2009), Pullen (2015). For a discussion of the hierarchy of marble, see Gauly (2006) 464–5. The use of precious materials was criticised as a sign of luxury and often set in opposition to the simple life and the beauty of nature, for example in Sen. *Ep.* 86.6 (about the extensive use of costly stone in baths), Hor. *Ep.* 2.2.180–2, *Carm.* 2.18.17, Iuv. 11.175, Mart. 1.55.5–8, 12.50.4, Auson. *Mos.* 48–52, Luc. 10.111–17. However, writing about marble was, at the same time, a favourite subject in Roman poetry; Bedon (2004) 282–5. While Pliny highlights the parts of his villa which are made of marble (e.g. *Ep.* 5.6.20, 22, 24, 36, 38, 40), Sidonius claims to renounce precious foreign stones in favour of simple domestic embellishment. With his second *recusatio* (after the list of negatives in relation to immoral wall paintings in *Ep.* 2.2.6) Sidonius nonetheless includes the precious stones from various regions and alludes to previous literary catalogues such as those of Martial, Statius or Lucan – Mart. 6.42.11–15, 9.75.7–9, Stat. *Silv.* 1.2.148–53, 1.5.34–41, 2.2.85–93, 4.2.26–9, Luc. 10.110–22; Bedon (2004) 374–6, Gauly (2006), Henriksén (2012) 307–11, Consolino (2013). See also Maugan-Chemin (2006), especially 124–5, with a overwiew of the different marbles mentioned in Pliny the Elder, Statius and Martial. For a catalogue of marbles in a bath, see Lucian. *Hipp.* 5–8; Dunbabin (1989) 8–9. By rejecting and at the same time quoting his literary models, Sidonius emphasises the moral value of his *otium* as he does not need a luxurious environment to enjoy his leisure; Hindermann (2020a) 103–4. Marble is a subject Sidonius also writes about in his poems, for example in Sidon. *Carm.* 5.34–9 (about the throne of the goddess Roma), 11.17–26 (about the temple of Venus), 22.4 vv. 136–41 (about the marbles in the bath of Pontius Leontius); Delhey (1993) 134–8, Busch (1999) 80, Bedon (2004) 375, Robert (2011) 388, Brolli (2013) 100–102, Kaufmann (2015) 489–90, Onorato (2016) 94–9, Kaufmann (2017) 153–5. Fages (2015) 148–50 compares the decline in valuable ornaments in the bath of the villa of Séviac (where in renovations during the fifth century the marbles were replaced with plaster and bricks) with Sidonius' description of the Burgus of Pontius Leontius in *Carm.* 22. For the importance of marble in Late Antique texts about Christian buildings, see Herbert de la Portbarré-Viard

(2016). While Sidonius in *Ep.* 2.10.4 v. 11–12 unrestrainedly describes the splendour of the marble used for a church (though without great detail), in the context of his villa he feels able to do so only in the form of a list of negatives. The reason for this could be that luxury in private buildings was frowned upon, but accepted in public buildings; see for example Cic. *Mur.* 76, *Flacc.* 28, Suet. *Cal.* 37.1; Gauly (2006) 461–2. We find a similar albeit much shorter *recusatio* of statues made of marble and bronzes or pictures also in Sidon. *Carm.* 23.500–6 *post quas nos tua pocula et tuarum | Musarum medius torus tenebat, | quales nec statuas imaginesque | aere aut marmoribus coloribusque | Mentor, Praxiteles, Scopas dederunt, | quantas nec Polycletus ipse finxit | nec fit Phidiaco figura caelo* ('After the bath your cups and a couch in the midst of your Muses would claim us: no statues or likenesses to compare with these were ever fashioned in bronze or marble or colours by Mentor, Praxiteles, or Scopas: Polycletus himself did not mould any so great, nor did Phidias with his chisel'). For the literary motif of the list, an important feature of ancient and Late Antique literature, see also the commentary on *Ep.* 2.10.5 *quod olim Marcia Hortensio....*

Paros, Carystos, Proconnesos, Phryges, Numidae, Spartiatae rupium variatarum posuere crustas: The island of Paros, one of the Cyclades, was famous for its gleaming white, translucent marble, often used for statues; see also Sidon. *Carm.* 11.18, 22.4 v. 140, Plin. *Nat.* 4.67, 36.14 (denoted *lychnites*), Verg. *Georg.* 3.34, *Aen.* 1.593, 6.471, Ov. *Pont.* 4.8.31–2, *Met.* 7.465, Mart. 1.88.2–3, 6.13.3 (denoted *lygdos*), 6.42.21, Hor. *Carm.* 1.19.5–6, Prud. *Perist.* 12.51; Dodge and Ward-Perkins (1992) 154, Gnoli et al. (2004) 250, Pullen (2015) 88.

Carystos, present-day Karysto, was an ancient town on the south coast of Euboea. Its marble is watery green, striated with dark-green or light-grey micaceous bands, today called 'cipollino verde ondato'. It was mainly used for columns, veneer, paving and floor inlay; see Sidon. *Carm.* 22.4 v. 140, Plin. *Ep.* 5.6.36, 36.48, Stat. *Silv.* 1.2.149–50, 1.5.34, 4.2.28, *Theb.* 7.370, Mart. 9.75.7, Plin. *Nat.* 4.64, Tib. 3.3.14, Sen. *Tro.* 836, Luc. 5.232; Dodge and Ward-Perkins (1992) 156, Gnoli et al. (2004) 202–3, Pullen (2015) 101.

Proconnesos is present-day Marmara in Turkey, an island in the Propontis (Sea of Marmara), famous for its white marble, which was used throughout the Mediterranean. There are several varieties; the most commonly used for architecture is white or grey, with parallel bands of dark blue and light grey; see also Plin. *Nat.* 5.151; Dodge and Ward-Perkins (1992) 154, Gnoli et al. (2004) 252.

All three kinds of marble Sidonius mentions next (*Phryges, Numidae, Spartiatae*) are also part of Martial's and (the first two) of Statius' description of Claudius Etruscus' bath, in Mart. 6.42, Stat. *Silv.* 1.5.36–8; Kaufmann (2017) 153–5. Phrygia is a region in the western part of Asia Minor in present-day Turkey. Here Sidonius uses its people (*Phryges*) to denote the region. Phrygian marble (today called 'pavonazzetto') is white and characterised by its very irregular veins of dark red with bluish and yellowish tints; Gnoli et al. (2004) 264–5, Pullen (2015) 107–8. With his wording Sidonius suggests that Phrygian slaves carry the marble and thus recalls Mart. 6.42.12–13. In *Carm.* 11.17–18 Sidonius calls the stone *lapis … Phrygius* ('Phrygian stone'); see also Hor. *Carm.* 3.1.41, Auson. *Mos.* 48 (cited in the commentary below on *Ep.* 2.10.4 vv. 11–12), Iuv. 14.306–7, Stat. *Silv.* 1.2.148, 1.5.37–8, 2.2.87–9, 4.2.27, Tib. 3.3.13. More often, the Romans referred to the marble of Phrygia by the name of the city of Sinnas; see for example Mart. 9.75.8, Stat. *Silv.* 1.5.37–41, 2.2.87–9, Sidon. *Carm.* 5.37, 22.4 v. 138.

The *Numidae* are a people of northern Africa. Numidian marble (today called 'giallo antico') was of yellow colour, crossed by purple, sometimes with brown veins. It was quarried in Simitthus, present-day Chemtou in Tunisia, and one of the most favoured marbles in antiquity; see Iuv. 7.182, 9.75.8, Mart. 6.42.12–13, 8.53.8, 9.75.8, Stat. *Silv.* 1.2.148, 1.5.36, 2.2.92, 4.2.27, Sidon. *Carm.* 5.37, 11.18, 22.4 v. 138; Delhey (1993) 136, Bedon (2004) 377, Gnoli et al. (2004) 214–15, Pullen (2015) 96–8. Its use was associated with the expansion of the Roman Empire; Gauly (2006) 465.

The *Spartiatae* are the inhabitants of Sparta, the capital of Laconia, near present-day Mistra. Laconian marble (today called 'porfido serpentine verde') was green with large, lighter watery-green inclusions; see Sidon. *Carm.* 5.38–9, 11.18, Plin. *Nat.* 36.55, Mart. 1.55.5, 6.42.11, 9.75.9, Stat. *Silv.* 1.2.148, 1.5.40, 2.2.90–1, Tib. 3.3.14, Iuv. 11.175; Dodge and Ward-Perkins (1992) 158, Bedon (2004) 377, Gnoli et al. (2004) 277, Pullen (2015) 162.

Rupes, a general term for 'rock', is used here and by other authors to denote marble specifically (along with similar terms such as *saxum* and *lapis*, for example in Sidon. *Carm.* 11.17), often combined with a place name to indicate where the valuable stone comes from, as in Sidon. *Carm.* 5.35–6, Stat. *Silv.* 1.5.39; Bedon (2004) 370, Herbert de la Portbarré-Viard (2016) 283. *Crusta* generally means 'a hard surface', 'crust', 'shell', here a 'marble plate' (*TLL* 4, 1253.55–82); see also Sen. *Ep.* 86.6 *Numidicis crustis* ('with Numidian marble'), Auson. *Mos.* 48 (cited in the commentary below on *Ep.* 2.10.4 vv. 11–12), Paul. Nol. *Ep.* 32.17 v. 22, Symm. *Ep.* 1.12.1;

Herbert de la Portbarré-Viard (2016) 285–9. In Sen. *Ben.* 4.6.2 and Luc. 10.114 *crusta* or the participle *crustata* stands for 'veneer' in opposition to the whole slab of marble. For *crusta* as 'veneer', see also Plin. *Nat.* 35.154, Luc. 10.114–15, Hier. *Ep.* 130.14. In Sidon. *Ep.* 2.10.4 v. 14 the word appears as a *terminus technicus* to denote a 'mosaic work'; see also Ennod. *Carm.* 2.10.2, cited below in the commentary on *Ep.* 2.10.4 vv. 5–7. With the meaning 'ice', the word appears in Sidon. *Carm.* 11.96 and *Ep.* 4.6.4. In *Ep.* 9.7.3 it is used for a surface made of crystal or onyx, in *Carm.* 17.10 for the decoration of a cup made of gold. See also the description of Aurora's palace in Sidon. *Carm.* 2.418–19 with the participles *crustante* and 22.4 v. 146 *crustatus*.

neque per scopulos Aethiopicos et abrupta purpurea genuino fucata conchylio sparsum mihi saxa furfurem mentiuntur: There is no consensus as to which stone is meant with *scopulos Aethiopicos … purpurea … fucata*. According to Loyen (1970a) 218 and Anderson (1936) 422 n. 2 it is *lapis Syenites*, a pink-red granite quarried near present-day Aswan in southern Egypt and well known because of its widespread use; today it is called 'granito rosso'. See also Plin. *Nat.* 36.63 and 157; Bedon (2004) 377, Dodge and Ward-Perkins (1992) 158–9, Gnoli et al. (2004) 225–6, Pullen (2015) 163. Delhey (1991), however, claims that red porphyry (*porphyrites*) is meant here, as it is in *Carm.* 5.34–6, where Sidonius also uses the terms *purpura* and *Aethiopum de monte*. See also Sidon. *Carm.* 11.17–19 *lapis … Aethiops … purpureus* ('the Aethiopian stone is purple'). For the use of red porphyry, a very precious and symbolical stone associated with imperial power, see Raff (1994) 88–93, Gnoli et al. (2004) 274, Pullen (2015) 159–61 and, for example, Stat. *Silv.* 1.2.150–1.

Purpurea, 'purple', 'red' (of stones, cf. *TLL* 10.2, 2711.72–12.13) refers to *saxa*, together with *fucata*, the participle of *fuco*, 'to colour', 'paint', 'dye'. See also Sidon. *Carm.* 5.50–51 *scopulos iaculabile fulgur | fucat* ('the lightning that may be hurled stains the rocks'), 15.127–8, *Ep.* 7.5.1, 9.13.5 v. 17. For the noun *purpura*, see the commentary on *Ep.* 2.2.8; for the participle *purpuratus*, see the commentary on *Ep.* 2.13.7 *coepit supra tergum … in iugulum purpurati*. *Conchylium*, 'purple color', 'purple' (*TLL* 4, 30.45–73), is already used by Cicero (Cic. *Verr.* 2.4.26) as a sign of debauchery, and appears in Pliny's *Natural History*, for example Plin. *Nat.* 9.127. See also Sidon. *Carm.* 15.129 *ebria nec solum spirat conchylia sandix* ('and the sated vermilion showed not only purple colour'), and the commentary on *Ep.* 2.13.6 *Tunc ille confestim … conchyliato ditat indutu*. *Mihi* is a dative of disadvantage, a regular construction with *mentiri* (*TLL* 8, 777.57–70). *Mentiri* here means 'to fake', 'imitate' (*TLL* 8, 780.20–81.74); see also Sidon. *Carm.* 5.37–8 *Nomadum lapis … antiquum mentitus ebur* ('Numidian marble which imitates old ivory'); Bedon (2004) 378–9. The main meaning of *furfur*, 'bran', is here transferred to the dappled look of the coloured stone. See also Plin. *Nat.* 36.57 *rubet porphyrites in eadem Aegypto; ex eodem candidis intervenientibus punctis leptopsephos vocatur* ('and in the same Egypt the red porphyry appears; because there are little white dots in it, it is called leptopsephos'). On the characteristic mottle of the stone, see Delhey (1991). *Furfurem mentiuntur* is a Cretic ditrochee.

Sed etsi nullo peregrinarum cautium rigore ditamur, habent tamen tuguria seu mapalia mea civicum frigus: Sidonius stresses that his bathhouse is cool even without foreign stones. There is an opposition between foreign and domestic stone (*peregrinarum* versus *civicum*). Their cool effect (*rigor* versus *frigus*) is difficult to differentiate. Implied is the quality of the stone for the building as well as its aesthetic effect, and therefore the overall impact on the visitor's opinion. Accordingly the translations vary: Anderson (1936) 423 has 'but although I am not enriched by the chill starkness of foreign rocks, still my buildings … have their native coolness'; Loyen (1970a) 48 'la solidité d'aucune pierre étrangère … fraîcheur du pays'; Köhler (2014) 44 'Steifheit auswärtiger Klippen … einheimische Vornehmheit'; Visser (2014) 34 'by rigour of foreign stone … civic coldness'. Sidonius expresses the difference between an intimidating chilliness of foreign precious stones and an agreeable coolness of domestic marble; see also Vitruvius, Vitr. 1.2.8, who recommends using local materials. See for a similar expression Sidon. *Ep.* 6.9.2 *frigoribus fontium civicorum* ('the chilly waters of his native springs'). The coolness (*frigus*) of marble (*marmor*, see *TLL* 8, 411.14–15) is mentioned elsewhere. See also Mart. 1.55.5 *quisquam picta colit Spartani frigora saxi* ('he reveres someone with colourful coldness of the Spartan stone'), 12.60.12, Ov. *Met.* 2.338–9; Busch (1999) 76; see also Bedon (2004) 381 for further examples. See also Sidon. *Carm.* 24.55 *frigore marmorum* ('with the cold of marble'), where marble in the house of Apollinaris is praised as a remedy for the summer heat. Cam (2003) 153 identifies *civicum frigus* as 'sans doute le marbre des Pyrénées' ('certainly the marble of the Pyrenees'). Mining of marble took place in Gaul not only in the Pyrenees but also in the valley of the Garonne and present-day Philippeville in Belgium; Hanaghan (2019) 46–7, Pensabene (2004) 49. The Younger Pliny also praises the coolness (*frigus*) of his estates, for example in Plin. *Ep.* 2.17.17, 5.6.30. Plin. *Nat.* 1.36.3 uses the adjective *peregrinus* in connection with marble *peregrino* *marmore columnas* ('columns made from foreign marble'); see also *Nat.* 36.7. *Rigor* (OLD 1655, 2a and 2c) denotes 'the state of being stiff with snow or ice, frozen condition (of the ground, water, etc.)', and in general the 'ice-cold quality (of water and other things)'. Using the topos of modesty, Sidonius describes his villa as a hut (*tuguria seu mapalia mea*). Pliny also stresses the simplicity of his villa; see Plin. *Ep.* 2.17.4 *atrium frugi* ('a simple hall'), 2.17.11 *duae cellae magis elegantes quam sumptuosae* ('two rooms that are more elegant than sumptuous'). For *tugurium*, 'hut', 'cottage of shepherds, peasants', see Verg. *Eclog.* 1.68 *tuguri ... culmen* ('the roof of the hut'). For *mapalia*, 'huts', 'cottages of the Africans', 'useless things', 'follies', see Sidon. *Carm.* 5.591, Sall. *Iug.* 18.8, Sen. *Apoc.* 9.1, Verg. *Georg.* 3.340. The closest parallel is Mart. 10.20.7–8, about a close friendship that is independent of place and luxury. Martial also mentions different humble dwellings: *tecum ego vel sicci Gaetula mapalia Poeni | et poteram Scythicas hospes amare casas* ('with you I could learn to love the Gaetulian huts of the thirsty Carthaginians and as a guest the Scythian sheds'); Mastrorosa (2002) 204.

Quin potius quid habeamus quam quid non habeamus ausculta: Sidonius ends the section with the decision to describe his swimming pool, which, unlike his uncles' baths (*Ep.* 2.9), still functions and is in use; see Hanaghan (2020). With the transitional formula *quin potius*, '(but) rather', 'in fact', Sidonius continues the colloquial beginning of the letter – see the commentaries on *Ep.* 2.2.1 *Ruri me esse causaris...* and on *Ep.* 2.1.1 *'Quaenam?' inquis*. It is also used in *Ep.* 1.6.3, 4.16.2, 4.18.1, 6.1.2, 7.6.4, 7.8.1, 8.10.4, 9.3.4, 9.9.15; Köhler (1995) 223. For *quin potius* after a rhetorical question, see the commentary on *Ep.* 2.2.11 *Quin potius.... Ausculto*, 'to hear with attention', 'to listen to' (*TLL* 2, 1534.27–6.16) is frequently found in comedy (e.g. Plaut. *Ps.* 427, 453, *Truc.* 95, 400) and Apuleius, but rarely in works by classical authors.

Section 8

Huic basilicae appendix piscina forinsecus seu: In section 8 Sidonius describes his impressive swimming pool. *Basilica* is used here in the meaning of 'a hall in a private house' (*TLL* 2, 1763.84–4.14). In all other instances Sidonius uses the word to refer to a church, as in *Ep.* 2.10.3, 4.18.4, 5.17.3, 6.12.4, 7.6.8; Amherdt (2001) 409, van Waarden (2010) 230–1. According to Cam (2003) 153 Sidonius here alludes to Vitr. 6.5.2 *praeterea bybliothecas,* *basilicas non dissimili modo quam publicorum operum magnificentia comparatas* ('in addition libraries and basilicas built in a similar fashion with the magnificence of public structures'). The noun *appendix*, 'addition', 'continuation', only here denotes a part of a building (*TLL* 2, 277.31). Sidonius uses the word also in *Ep.* 9.14.5 *pluviis appendicibus intumescentem* ('swollen by the additional rain') to indicate the increase of water in a river. For *piscina*, here a 'swimming pool', see the commentary above on *Ep.* 2.2.5.

si graecari mavis, baptisterium ab oriente conectitur: The verb *graecari*, 'to imitate the Greeks', 'live in the Greek manner', is first attested in Hor. *Sat.* 2.2.11. On Sidonius' attitude toward the Greek language and literature and the discussions about his (limited) knowledge of Greek, see Loyen (1943) 26–30, Gualandri (1979) 156 n. 44, Näf (1995) 137, Prévot (1995) 221, Styka (2008) 174–6, Cameron (2011) 547–54, Consolino (2020) 355 n. 61, Gualandri (2020) 285 n. 35, John (2021a) 862–4. Sidonius seems to allude to Varro, who complains about the practice of naming one's villa with Greek terms – Varro *Rust.* 2 praef 2 *nec putant se habere villam, si non multis vocabulis retinniat Graecis, quom vocent particulatim loca, procoetona, palaestram, apodyterion, peristylon, ornithona, peripteron, oporothecen* ('and they do not think they have a villa if it does not resound with many Greek words, as they particularly name the places, for example as an antechamber, a place of exercise, a room for disrobing, a peristyle, a birdhouse, a building surrounded with a row of columns on the outside and a fruit room'). See also Varro *Rust.* 3.10.1 *vos philograeci* ('you, lovers of Greek'). Sidonius thus wittily introduces the following term *baptisterium*, a Latinised form of Greek βαπτιστήριον, from βαπτίζω, 'to dip', 'drown'. Here it stands for a 'bath-tub', 'pool', an obvious allusion to Plin. *Ep.* 2.17.11 and 5.6.25, as in Sidonius' time the word usually denotes a baptismal font; see *TLL* 2, 1719.83–20.23 and Sidon. *Ep.* 4.15.1; Nielsen (1990) 155, Amherdt (2001) 361–2. According to Shanzer and Wood (2002) 62 'almost all of Sidonius' Greek words come from Pliny'. Further Grecisms in *Ep.* 2.2. are from the field of architecture (*hemicyclio* 2.2.4, *baptisterium* 2.2.8, *architectus* 2.2.8, *hypodromus* 2.2.10, *cryptoporticus* 2.2.10–11, *diaetam* 2.2.11, *sphaeristerio* 2.2.15) as well as the description of a (fictional) wall painting (2.2.6 *palaestritae, gymnasiarchorum*). In the second villa letter, *Ep.* 2.9, Sidonius also uses many Grecisms; see especially *Ep.* 2.9.6 describing the lunch Sidonius and his hosts enjoyed together.

quod viginti circiter modiorum milia capit: A *modius* is 'a corn-measure', 'peck' (*TLL* 8, 1242.57–9), but also used of liquids, for example in Plin.

Nat. 23.88, Marcell. *Med.* 36.57. A *modius* is 8.7 litres or two gallons, and so 'twenty thousand' *modii* would be some 175 m^3; that is, Sidonius' pool is quite large, covering around 100 m^2 (for a depth of 1.75 m); Busch (1999) 75, Balmelle (2001) 178–9, Maréchal (2020) 51.

Huc elutis e calore venientibus: All the manuscripts have *elutis*, the participle of *eluo*, 'to wash out', 'rinse out'. Lütjohann's (1887) 24 emendation to *elautis*, the participle of *lavo*, 'to wash', 'bathe', is not necessary, the verb *eluo* fits the context of the letter, namely Domitius' sweating in the city. The translations vary: Anderson (1936) 423 has 'those who come out of the heat after the bath'; Loyen (1970a) 48 'Pour ceux qui y viennent au sortir de la chaleur du bain'; Köhler (2014) 45 'Kommt man ermattet aus der Hitze'. See also Sidon. *Ep.* 3.3.8 on washing bodies: *quibus nec elutis vestimenta nec vestitis sepulchra tribuebant* ('nor did they wash the bodies and then clothe them and consign them thus clothed to tombs'). The transition from hot to cold is also mentioned in Sidon. *Carm.* 19.1–2 (cited in the commentary on *Ep.* 2.2.7 *Pauci tamen versiculi* …).

triplex medii parietis aditus per arcuata intervalla reseratur: Next, Sidonius describes how one comes from the heat of the hot bath to the swimming pool through an opening in the wall that consists of three arches. Sidonius uses the adjective *triplex*, 'triple', 'threefold' (*OLD*, 1976) several times, which is not surprising for a writer who appreciates stylistic means like *tricola*. It appears in *Ep.* 2.6.2, 2.10.3, 2.10.4 v. 16, 4.11.6 v. 4, 5.8.1, 7.12.1, 9.1.2. For a villa's symmetrical walls, see *Ep.* 8.4.1 on Consentius' estate Octavianum: *quod domicilium parietibus attollitur ad concinentiam scilicet architectonicam fabre locatis* ('that the house rises high, with walls skilfully arranged so as to produce an undoubted architectural symmetry'). *Arcuatus*, 'bow-shaped', 'arched' (*TLL* 2, 473.75–4.42, *OLD* 164, a), derives from *arcus*. It is also used in Plin. *Ep.* 10.37.2. Sidonius uses *intervallum*, originally the term for the open space within the mound or breastwork of a camp to denote the 'extent of space between two things, distance', 'interval' (*TLL* 7.1, 2296.21–31, *OLD* 950, 1a). The term also appears in a spatial sense in Sidon. *Ep.* 2.2.12 (for the placement of fishing hooks), 2.9.8 (for a cave woven from flexible branches), *Carm.* 15.70 (stars), 23.411 (horses) and in a temporal sense in *Ep.* 4.12.4. *Resero* here means 'to open (a place) to access or passage, make accessible' (*OLD* 1628, 2). In *Ep.* 2.9.2 the verb is used metaphorically in the meaning of 'to make known', 'disclose'.

Nec pilae sunt mediae sed columnae, quas architecti peritiores 'aedificiorum purpuras' nuncupavere: Sidonius differentiates between two types of columns, *pilae* and *columnae*; both terms are also combined in Sen. *Nat.* 6.20.6, Petron. 79.4. According to Anderson (1936) 424 n. 1 *pilae* (*TLL* 10.1, 2135.14–54) may be angular pilasters or half-cylindrical pillars (see Cato *Agr.* 14.1), while *columnae* (*TLL* 3, 1737.72–9.43) are cylindrical columns; see Sidon. *Ep.* 1.11.7, 2.2.10, Plin. *Ep.* 8.8.7, 9.39.4; Höcker (2001) 1214. With *mediae*, according to Anderson (1936) 424 n. 1, Sidonius expresses that only the middle of the three entrances had purple pillars. *Architectus*, 'architect' (*TLL* 2, 465.6–6.40), is another Grecism which Sidonius announces in his initial remark to the section – see the commentary above on *Ep.* 2.2.8 *si graecari mavis*.... The term *architectus* is also used in Sidon. *Ep.* 8.6.10, the abstract *architectonica* ('architecture') in *Ep.* 5.2.1, the adjective *concinentiam ... architectonicam* ('architectural symmetry') in 8.4.1. *Purpura* here means 'ornate', 'ornament' (*TLL* 10.2, 2705.20), here related to the house, that is, columns of porphyry. See also Luc. 10.115–16 *stabatque sibi non segnis achates | purpureusque lapis* ('agate and porphyry were found there not only as ornaments'). At the same time, *purpura* hints at the colour and material of the columns, probably red porphyry; see also Sidon. *Carm.* 22.4 v. 141; Anderson (1936) 424 n. 1, Loyen (1970a) 48, Delhey (1993) 137–8, Busch (1999) 79–81. The purplish decorative stone was admired in Late Antiquity and usually the prerogative of emperors. Mratschek (2020b) 252 therefore suggests that Sidonius thus reminds his readers of the status of Avitus, and in particular the villa's previous owner; see the commentary on *Ep.* 2.2.3 *nomen hoc praedi*.... Sidonius uses the adjective *purpureus* elsewhere: see the commentary on *Ep.* 2.2.7 *neque per scopulos Aethiopicos et abrupta purpurea*... and in 2.13.7 the participle *purpurati*. In *Ep.* 2.10.1 Sidonius uses the term *purpura* also to describe an elaborate speech.

In hanc ergo piscinam fluvium de supercilio montis elicitum: A swimming pool was usually supplied directly from a conduit (*canalibus circumactis* – see the commentary on p. 126) and had a drain; Nielsen (1990) 23–4, 154–5, Maréchal (2020) 200–201. Sidonius' pool, however, does not seem to be filled by a cistern or a spring, as was common in Late Antique Roman baths, but by a nearby river that flowed down the mountain. This may also explain why Sidonius' swimming pool is quite large. The sentence is an allusion to Verg. *Georg.* 1.108–10, where Vergil describes the artificial irrigation of fields: *ecce supercilio clivosi tramitis undam | elicit? Illa cadens raucum per levia murmur | saxa ciet, scatebrisque arentia temperat arva* ('just look, from the summit of the steep course he elicits the wave? It falls over smooth stones and creates a hoarse murmuring and with its bubbling water it calms the fields'). There are two bodies of water (*fluvium* in Sidonius, *undam* in Vergil); *elicitum* echoes *elicit* and the noun *supercilio* appears in both texts; see Colton (2000) 40 and for Sidonius' allusions to Vergil in general Gualandri (1979) 88–104. Similarly, Sidonius describes his bath in Sidon. *Carm.* 18.5–6 *garrula Gauranis plus murmurat unda fluentis | contigui collis lapsa supercilio* ('the babbling water that falls from the top of the adjoining hill murmurs more loudly than the flood that streams of the Gaurus'). For a similar water supply in the bath of Pontius Leontius, see Sidon. *Carm.* 22.4 vv. 184–6; Delhey (1993) 167–9, Furbetta (2013) 249.

canalibusque circumactis per exteriora natatoriae latera curvatum sex fistulae prominentes leonum simulatis capitibus effundunt: With *canales* Sidonius denotes the 'conduits' that transport water to the pool; see also Sidon. *Carm.* 22.4 v. 185; Delhey (1993) 168–9. They are not only functional, but at their end adorned with lionheads which spit the water into the pool. Waterspouts in the form of animal heads (here six lions) have been found in other rural settlements; Dark (2005) 334. They are mentioned in a papyrus from the seventh century; Maréchal (2020) 89. Waterspouts with lion heads may be found also on the estate of Pontius Leontius, in Sidon. *Carm.* 22.4 vv. 179–83; Hanaghan (2020) 124–5. Hanaghan (2020) 130 shows that Sidonius gives importance to his fountains, as lion heads were used to represent power and often appeared on thrones. Sidonius thus links the water-dispensing function of the lion heads to the potential for intrigue; see the commentary on *Ep.* 2.2.9 *quia prae strepitu ... mutuae vocum vices minus intelleguntur....* The adjective *natatorius*, 'of or belonging to a swimmer', is used here as a female substantive, *natatoria*, 'a bath', 'a pool' (*TLL* 9.1, 130.11–44). The word is mostly used referring to the pool of Bethesda, where Christ miraculously healed a paralysed man, and the pool of Siloam; see Vet. Lat. *Ioh.* 5.2, 9.7. The usual term for a swimming pool is *piscina* (see the commentary on *Ep.* 2.2.5); seldom used is *natatio*; Nielsen (1990) 153–5. A *fistula* is a 'pipe', used here for a water pipe (*TLL* 6.1, 829.5–38), but more often for a reed pipe or shepherd's pipe; see the commentary on *Ep.* 2.2.14 *Cui concentui licebit adiungas fistulae septiforis armentalem Camenam.*

quae temere ingressis veras dentium crates, meros oculorum furores, certas cervicum iubas imaginabuntur: For other examples of the combination of the two adjectives *veras ... meros*, see Plin. *Ep.* 8.24.2 *illam veram et* *meram Graeciam* ('that true and pure Greece'), Hor. *Ep.* 1.18.8 *mera veraque virtus* ('true and pure virtue'). The expression *dentium crates* ('row of teeth') seems to be Sidonian and is unattested elsewhere; it recalls the famous Homerian ἕρκος ὀδόντων ('the enclosure of your teeth'), for example in Hom. *Od.* 1.64.

Section 9

Hic si dominum seu domestica seu hospitalis turba circumstet: For the difference between members of the *familia* and foreigners (*domestica seu hospitalis turba*), see Sidon. *Ep.* 1.9.3. Sidonius uses *domesticus* also in the sense of 'personal', for example in Sidon. *Ep.* 8.3.3 or in *Ep.* 6.10.2 as 'a brother in faith'. For *hospitalis* instead of the genitive of *hospes*, see Plaut. *Poen.* 75, Liv. 25.18.7, Sen. *Herc. Fur.* 483. Sidonius frequently uses the adjective instead of a noun in the genitive; see for example the commentaries on *Ep.* 2.9.4 *huc libri affatim ... videre te crederes aut grammaticales pluteus ...* and 2.9.9 *aut fontano deinceps frigore puteálique aut fluviali copia solidabamur*.

quia prae strepitu caduci fluminis mutuae vocum vices minus intelleguntur, in aurem sibi populus confabulatur; ita sonitu pressus alieno ridiculum affectat publicus sermo secretum: The noise of the falling water drowns out conversation. In the *locus amoenus* setting of a rural villa, the sound of water is normally discreet; see Plin. *Ep.* 5.6.23 *fonticulus in hoc, in fonte crater, circa sipunculi plures miscent iucundissimum murmur* ('in this room there is a little fountain, in the fountain a basin, and several little water pipes mix together a pleasant murmuring'). And in the same section (Plin. *Ep.* 5.6.23) *sed ante piscinam ... strepitu visuque iucundam; nam ex edito desiliens aqua suscepta marmore albescit* ('but first you see a pool ... which is pleasant regarding sound and sight, because the water falls down from above and is caught in a basin of marble and foams white'). With his scene Sidonius outdoes Plin. *Ep.* 2.17.25 *haec utilitas, haec amoenitas deficitur aqua salienti* ('there is only a fountain missing in all this usefulness and pleasantness'). The subject of noise also reappears in section 10 with the talking crowd of slaves (*nutricum loquacissimus chorus*) and in section 14 with the description of the sounds of various animals. Hanaghan (2020) 130–1 convincingly interprets the passage against its political background – the rise and fall of his father-in-law Avitus and the attempt by his successor Majorian to calm the situation in Gaul through a personal visit: 'Sidonius' lions are a subtle reminder of his political importance as a Gallo-Roman aristocrat, who is well connected, surrounded by a crowd of guests, each of whom is afforded the privacy to whisper in secret in his baths, safe from being overhead by the deafening roar of the pipes. The idea that guests could conspire in Sidonius' baths is nowhere near as ridiculous as Sidonius pretends' (131). Mratschek (2020b) 251 refers to Sidon. *Carm.* 18.5 as an onomatopoetic parallel for the noise of the stream: *garrula Gauranis plus murmurat unda fluentis* ('the chattering water babbles more busily than the streams that flow from Gaurus'). *Caducus*, 'falling', 'fallen' (*TLL* 3, 33.72–6.84) is regularly used with water, for example in Varro *Rust.* 3.5.2 *et ex eis caduca quae abundat per fistulam exire* ('and the excess water overflowing from <the canals> must exit through a pipe'), Ov. *Am.* 3.6.91 *nomen habes nullum, rivis collecte caducis* ('you do not have a name, you reservoir of decrepit trickle'). Sidonius uses the adjective also in *Ep.* 5.13.1, 7.1.3. *Confabulor*, 'to converse together', 'discuss something with one' (*TLL* 4. 169.74–70.15), is rarely used – by Plautus, Terence and later again by Fronto. The paeon spondee clausula *pressus alieno* suggests a break after *alieno*, putting emphasis onto *ridiculum*. Also note Sidonius' play on the opposites *publicus* and *secretum*. For the ancient discourse on proper behaviour in public and in private, see Riggsby (1997) 48–53.

Hinc egressis frons triclinii matronalis offertur: Sidonius continues the description of his villa with the dining room for the ladies, which is right next to the room used for weaving, an activity reserved to women; see Dark (2005) 339 and the commentary immediately below. In addition to this dining room, there is also a dining room for winter, mentioned in section 11. Having several dining rooms for different seasons and occasions is a typical element of noble country villas, for example in Plin. *Ep.* 2.17.5, 2.17.7, 2.17.13, 5.6.19, 5.6.23, 5.6.29–31, Paul. Pel. *Euch.* 205–6; Dark (2005) 334. On the lack of information about women's accommodation and tasks in Late Antiquity, see Clark (1993) 94–101. Sidonius also mentions a reading corner for the ladies in *Ep.* 2.9.4. *Frons*, 'front', 'main part', is used here as an architectural *terminus technicus* (*TLL* 6.1, 1361.50–2.59). *Triclinium*, from Greek τρικλίνιον, is the term for a couch running around three sides of a table for reclining on at meals and a room for eating in, that is, a dining room; Förtsch (1993) 100–4. Sidonius uses the adjective *matronalis*, 'belonging to a married woman or matron', 'matronly' (*TLL* 8, 489.28–90.13), here and in *Ep.* 4.6.2, 4.18.2. It also appears in Plin. *Ep.* 5.16.2, 7.24.1. For the term *matrona*, see the commentary on *Ep.* 2.8.1 *Decessit nudius tertius non absque iustitio matrona Filimatia*.

cui continuatur vicinante textrino cella penaria discriminata tantum pariete castrensi: Next, Sidonius mentions his *textrinum*, 'weaving chamber'. For a similar passage, including the verb *continuare*, 'to connect', 'continue uninterruptedly', see the description of the estate of Pontius Leontius in Sidon. *Carm.* 22.4 vv. 192–3 *continuata dehinc videas quae conditor ausus | aemula Palladiis textrina educere templis* ('adjoining that you may see the weaving chamber that the builder dared to build similar to the temples of Pallas'); Delhey (1993) 174, Kaufmann (1995) 242. In *Carm.* 15.126 Sidonius mentions Minerva's weaving chamber. In the verses *Carm.* 22.4 vv. 197–9, Sidonius praises Leontius' wife for dutifully performing her task of spinning. In Sidonius' estate, the weaving chamber is located right next to the ladies' dining room; see the commentary above on *Ep.* 2.2.9 *hinc egressis frons triclinii matronalis offertur*. In this way Sidonius takes up the ancient tradition of listing female virtues (*casta fuit, domum servavit, lanam fecit*); see the commentary below on *Ep.* 2.8 about the death of the lady Filimatia; Bonjour (1988) 46. The rarely used verb *vicinor*, 'to be neighboring', 'near' (*Blaise* 846), is Late Latin; see for example Mart. Cap. 6.608. It also appears in Sidon. *Ep.* 2.10.3, 2.11.1, 6.9.1, 7.2.6, 7.14.1, 8.3.2; van Waarden (2010) 171, Montone (2017) 27. The *cella penaria* is 'a storeroom', 'storehouse'; the expression is also found in classical times, for instance Cic. *Verr.* 2.2.2, *Cato* 56, Suet. *Aug.* 6. *Pariete castrensi* is a combination used only here. While the overall sense is clear from its context – it is just a makeshift wall, not a proper wall – it is not clear what it looked like. The translations differ accordingly: Grégoire and Collombet (1836) 201 have 'des murs avec de la terre et du gazon', Dalton (1915) 39 'separated only by a movable partition', Anderson (1936) 425 'with only a barrack partition', Loyen (1970a) 48 'cloison', Köhler (2014) 45 'Wand'. According to Dark (2005) 335 this kind of division is widely attested in Roman rural sites. Sidonius uses the adjective *castrensis*, 'of/in the camp' (*TLL* 3, 544.51–5.48), also in *Ep.* 8.6.1, *Carm.* 23.223. The verb *discrimino* in the meaning 'to divide', 'part', 'separate' (*TLL* 5.1, 1362.73–3.14) is also used in *Ep.* 1.2.3, 2.11.1, 9.4.1.

Section 10

Ab ortu lacum porticus intuetur: Offering different, framed views was a key function of the Roman villa. The villa owners enjoyed the surroundings through carefully positioned windows and doors, and praised the views (*prospectus*) of their mansions. Statius, a major inspiration not only for Sidonius' poems (Goldlust 2013, 201–11, Kaufmann 2015) but also for letter 2.2, begins his first villa poem, *Silv.* 1.3, with *cernere* ('to look'). In another villa poem he describes in detail Pollius Felix' *speculatrix villa profundi* ('a villa that looks towards the sea') at Surrentum. Its windows look at the Bay of Naples from different angles (Stat. *Silv.* 2.2.73–85); Gauly (2006) 463, Newlands (2013) 69–70. A *porticus* is a 'covered walk between columns', 'colonnade', 'arcade', 'portico', one of the most important elements in a luxury villa; see Sidon. *Ep.* 8.4.1, Plin. *Ep.* 2.17.4–5, 5.6.15–23, Stat. *Silv.* 2.2.30, Cic. *Ad Q. fr.* 3.1.1; Förtsch (1993) 58–62, 85–90, Zarmakoupi (2011). For *porticus* as part of a church see the commentary on *Ep.* 2.10.4 vv. 16–21. For the construction of an inanimate subject with *intueri*, 'to look over' things, see *TLL* 7.2, 90.57–64. The same use is found in Plin. *Ep.* 5.6.28 *cubiculum ... hippodromum, vineas, montes intuetur* ('the room ... looks onto the hippodrome, the vineyards and the mountains'); see also Plin. *Ep.* 2.17.6 *hac et subiacens mare longius quidem, sed securius intuetur* ('from here one looks to the sea in front, from a longer distance, though, but undisturbed'). By choosing verbs like *videt, fruitur, prospicit, despicit* and others, the villa or parts of the villa are personified, as in Plin. *Ep.* 2.17.13, 2.17.15, 2.17.20, 5.6.23; Drerup (1959), Drerup (1990) 130–2, Schneider (1995) 76–7, 84–93, Bergmann (2016) 211–12, Morvillez (2017) 15–17, and see the commentary on *Ep.* 2.2.10 *quae, quia nihil ipsa prospectat*....

magis rotundatis fulta collyriis quam columnis invidiosa monubilibus: This passage contains various text-critical problems. The general sense is a comparison between simple columns, which Sidonius ostensibly prefers and are part of the *porticus* at hand, and more luxurious ones in other buildings. Here Sidonius again takes up the theme of rejecting luxury, after his negative lists of wall paintings and expensive marble in his bath-house in sections 6 and 7. Sidonius' colonnade consists of columns which are 'rounded', *rotundatis*, the participle of *rotundo*, 'to make round', 'to round off' (*OLD* 1663). In the sense of 'to elaborate', 'to smooth', 'to finish', *rotundo* also appears in Sidon. *Ep.* 8.4.2, 9.7.3. Sidonius uses the related noun *rotunditas*, 'well-roundedness', to describe Symmachus' letters in Sidon. *Ep.* 1.1.1. The word used for the columns is *collyriis* in the manuscripts LM, *colliriis* in TCFP. Sirmond (1614) 45, Anderson (1936) 424, and Loyen (1970a) 48 emend it to *coluriis*; Löfstedt (1985) 207. Whereas *colurium*, 'a kind of a simple column' (*TLL* 3, 1743.4–9), is attested only here and in one other instance (*Pass. coron.* 4 *coeperunt artifices quadratarii incidere lapidem ad colurium columnae* – 'the skilled stone-cutters began to cut the stone in the form of a column'), *collyrium* is more frequent. It derives from Greek κολλύρα, 'a kind of pastry of a round, elongated form'. Κολλύριον is a mass looking similar to the *collyra* dough, hence it signifies 'suppository' in a medical context, and Sidonius here uses it metonymically for his rounded simple pillars. The text describing the second pillar is also uncertain. The manuscripts FP and the editio princeps have *monubilibus*, 'reminding, admonishing', followed by Loyen (1970a) 48. L has *monobilibus*, C^2 *munibilibus* corrected from *munubilibus*, T *volubilibus*, Vaticanus Latinus 1661 has *mobilibus*, A *munubilibus* corrected by hand two to *monubilibus*. Given that A is corrected against a highly positioned member of its family, I opt for this reading. Lütjohann (1887) 24 emends it to *monolithis*, 'consisting of a single stone', because of the phrase in Laber. *Mim.* 38 *columnas monolithas*, 'monolitic pillars'; see Panayotakis (2010) 232–3 and *TLL* 8, 1426.3–12 on *monolithus,-a,-um*. For *invidiosa*, 'exciting envy', see for example Sen. *Ep.* 87.7 *quia tantum suburbani agri possidet, quantum invidiose in desertis Apuliae possideret* ('because he owns estates near the city so great that men would grudge his holding them in the waste lands of Apulia').

A parte vestibuli longitudo tecta intrinsecus patet mediis non interpellata parietibus: For *vestibulum*, 'an entrance court', see the commentary on *Ep.* 2.2.3. *Patere* means 'to stretch out', 'extend'; see also Sidon. *Carm.* 22.4 v. 179; Delhey (1993) 163. *Non interpellata parietibus*, 'not divided by walls', is a rare use of *interpello* (*TLL* 7.1, 2241.72–9), with other examples of *vi locali* including Vitr. 4.5.2, 5.3.6, 8.6.5.

quae, quia nihil ipsa prospectat, etsi non 'hypodromus', saltim 'cryptoporticus' meo mihi iure vocitabitur: *Prospecto* means 'to look towards', 'to lie or be situated towards' (of localities). The same wording is found in Plin. *Ep.* 2.17.5 *a fronte quasi tria maria prospectat* ('in front one looks as if on three seas'), *Ep.* 5.6.19 *hac adiacentis hippodromi nemus comasque prospectat* ('and here it looks towards the trees of the hippodrome nearby'), similarly also Plin. *Ep.* 2.17.20 *prospicit*, 5.6.15 *spectat* and 5.6.23 *despicit*. For the importance of the view on a landscape from a point of rest in a villa, see the commentaries on Sidon. *Ep.* 2.2.10 *Ab ortu lacum porticus intuetur*, *Ep.* 2.2.11 *Quo loci recumbens ... prospiciendi voluptatibus occuparis* and *Ep.* 2.9.1 *Uni domui ... in nemora prospectus*.... In *Ep.* 2.10.4 v. 7 Sidonius uses *prospicit* of a church. Sidonius ponders what technical term he should use to describe his covered hallway. Because there is no view, 'hypodromus' is unsuitable, but 'cryptoporticus' will do nicely. There is confusion in the manuscripts between *hippodromus*, 'a race course for horses', 'a promenade', and *hypodromus*, 'an underpass', 'an underground passage', from Greek ὑπόδρομος (*TLL* 6.3, 3157.5–13). The manuscript T, Sirmond (1614) 46, Anderson (1936) 424 and Loyen (1970a) 49 have *hypodromus*, L and Lütjohann (1887) 24 *hippodromus*, VMC *hipodromus*, F *ypodromus*. Whereas *hippodromus* is attested in Plaut. *Bacch.* 431, *Cist.* 549, Mart. 12.50.5, and in Plin. *Ep.* 5.6.19, 28, 32–3, 40 (Förtsch 1993, 67–8, 78–80), *hypodromus* is attested only here, as part of Sidonius' announcement that he will use Greek terms (*graecari*, see the commentary above on *Ep.* 2.2.8 *si graecari mavis*...). A *cryptoporticus* is 'a walled and roofed arcade', 'a vault' (*TLL* 4, 1261.55–66), a bilingual compound of κρυπτός, 'hidden', 'secret', and *porticus*, 'covered walk between columns', 'colonnade', 'arcade', 'portico'; Bergmann (2016) 210–11. The word was probably invented by Pliny to denote an architectural structure generally known before as *crypta*, and no other author used *cryptoporticus* until Sidonius Apollinaris. Pliny defines it as a covered and enclosed walkway (above ground as well as semi-subterranean), an alternative to open-air walkways (*porticus*) or open-air walkways lined with trees (*xystus*); Zarmakoupi (2011) 50, 54. In Sidonius' letter the *cryptoporticus* is part of his announced series of Grecisms; see the commentary on *Ep.* 2.2.8 *si graecari mavis* .... He uses it again in *Ep.* 5.17.3 *quem capacissima basilica non caperet quamlibet cincta diffusis cryptoporticibus* ('too great for the very spacious church to contain, even with the expanse of covered porticoes which surrounded it'). See also Sidon. *Carm.* 24.67 for a natural *porticus* formed by trees. With the emphasis *meo mihi iure* Sidonius probably distances himself from Pliny, who uses the term several times in his villa descriptions in Plin. *Ep.* 2.17.16–20, 5.6.27–31, 7.21.2, 9.36.3; Sherwin-White (1966) 195, Förtsch (1993) 41–8, Whitton (2013) 242. *Porticus* and *cryptoporticus* counted among the most characteristic architectural element of a Roman luxury villa; Zarmakoupi (2011) 50. The same metrical pattern (paeon I + cretic) as *iure vocitabitur* is found in Sidon. *Ep.* 4.3.10 *iure venerabitur* and 7.11.1 *iure retinebitur*; van Waarden (2010) 554.

Haec tamen aliquid spatio suo in extimo deambulacri capite defrudans efficit membrum bene frigidum: At the end of the covered hallway there is a room that the slaves use. For a similar room which is 'cut out' at the end of a *cryptoporticus*, see Plin. *Ep.* 5.6.28 *in summa cryptoporticu cubiculum ex ipsa cryptoporticu excisum* ('at the end of this foyer is a chamber cut out of it'). A *deambulacrum* is 'a place to walk in', 'a promenade' (*TLL* 5.1, 81.49–58), a rare Late Latin word also found three times in Jerome: Hier. *Interpret Iob* 41.23, *In Ezech.* 40.44, 42.12. Instead of Pliny's *excisum*, Sidonius uses the participle *defrudans*. The verb appears in Roman comedy and also in classical authors like Cicero with the meaning 'to defraud', 'cheat' (*TLL* 5.1, 372.55–3.31). The meaning to 'diminish', 'lessen' (*TLL* 5.1, 373.32–47) of inanimate things is Late Antique, for example in Auson. *Mos.* 109 (in connection with the tributary of the River Moselle). Sidonius uses it again in *Ep.* 1.2.1; Köhler (1995) 129. The term *membrum* for 'room' is already found in Cic. *Ad Q. fr.* 3.1.2, Vitr. 5.11.2; see also Plin. *Ep.* 2.17.9. *adhaeret dormitorium membrum* ('there is an adjacent bedroom'), 5.6.15 *multa in hac membra* ('there are many rooms in it').

ubi publico lectisternio exstructo clientularum sive nutricum loquacissimus chorus receptui canit: With the description of his slaves' lunch as an abundant display by their master, Sidonius playfully evokes the status-negotiating element of a banquet; van Waarden (2016) 79. For Sidonius' depiction of the slaves in his villa, see the introduction to *Ep.* 2.2. The expression *lectisternium publicum*, 'a feast of the gods', 'an offering of food for the images of the gods' (*TLL* 7.2, 1089.40–5), denotes a sacred feast to appease the gods. It was customary to place images of the gods on couches and to offer them food; Anderson (1936) 426 n. 1. The term is rarely used in a secular context as here and means 'spreading of a (dining) couch', 'a bed to put the food on'; see Sidon. *Ep.* 4.15.1; Amherdt (2001) 360–1. Conspicuously, Sidonius only writes about his female slaves, *clientulae* and *nutrices*. The manuscripts TCV¹M¹ have *clientularum*, LNVM *clientiarum*. *Clienta* is attested a few times in Roman comedy in the meaning of 'servant', 'slave' (*TLL* 3, 1346.72–83), for example Plaut *Mil.* 789, and also Hor. *Carm.* 2.18.8, but then not until Fronto. Another, rare meaning of *clienta* is 'a female client' (*TLL* 3, 1346.83–7); see Auson. *Parent.* 24.11–12 *Tarraco Hibera ... affectans esse clienta tibi* ('the Iberian Tarraco wanted to be your client'). The diminutive *clientula* is only attested here (*TLL* 3, 1348.2–5) and its meaning is unclear. Kaufmann (1995) 242 suggests that the term refers to wives and daughters of poor men who subjected themselves to *patrocinium* (a system of feudal tenure which was common in Late Antiquity) or the wives and daughters of *coloni* or other labourers in the villa. On the representation of (slave) women in Sidonius, see Bonjour (1988). On slavery in fifth- and sixth-century Gaul, see Samson (1992). The 'nurses', *nutrices*, were among the many slaves who worked in the villa. 'Nurse' is a well attested profession of a female slave, especially in Roman comedy; Mielsch (1987) 133–4, Kaufmann (1995) 241–2. Sidon. *Ep.* 5.19 is about how the daughter of Sidonius' nurse runs off with the son of the neighbour's nurse; Grey (2008).

Both groups of women are described as *loquacissimus chorus*, 'a very talkative' choir. Garrulity is a negative behaviour frequently attributed to women in ancient literature and a topos of satirical texts about women, for example Mart. 9.29, Iuv. 6.190, 438–40; Hobert (1967) 159–65, Watson and Watson (2014) 135, 219; see also the noisy Gothic women in Sidon. *Ep.* 8.3.2. For the subject of environmental noise in *Ep.* 2.2, see the commentary on *Ep.* 2.2.9 *quia prae strepitu … mutuae vocum vices minus intelleguntur*…. The adjective *loquax*, 'talkative', 'chattering' (*TLL* 7.2, 1653.55–5.67) is also used in a derogatory context about people and especially writings and letters; see for example *Ep.* 1.8.2 *municipalium ranarum loquax turba* ('the garrulous crowd of frogs, the fellow citizens'), 1.9.7 *charta* ('papyrus'), 3.13.2 and 11 Gnatho, 5.17.2 *praefatio* ('preface'), 7.2.10 *epistulae* ('letters'), 8.6.9 Sidonius, 9.11.5 *paginae* ('pages'), 9.11.9 *litterae* ('letter'), *Carm.* 13.35 *Musa* ('Muse'), 23.208 *unda* ('wave'); Amherdt (2001) 277. In *Ep.* 2.9.10 Sidonius playfully mocks his own 'talkativeness'; see the commentary on *Ep.* 2.9.10 *loquacitas*, which also appears several times in the letters. *Chorus* is regularly used in the meaning of 'group', 'crowd', 'assembly' (*TLL* 3, 1025.31–6.26). *Receptui canit* is a military expression, 'a drawing or falling back', 'a retiring', 'retreat', for example in Liv. 34.39.13, Caes. *Bell. Gall.* 7.47. Pliny uses the expression in *Ep.* 3.1.11 (about old age). Sidonius uses the phrase again in *Ep.* 3.3.9, 3.7.4, 6.1.4 in a military sense; Giannotti (2016) 157. Here it denotes that Sidonius and his family retire to their room, *dormitorium cubiculum*, for a siesta after lunch; see the commentary immediately below.

cum ego meique dormitorium cubiculum petierimus: The slaves did not sleep in their master's bedroom; see the commentary on *Ep.* 2.2.13 *interiecto consistorio perangusto, ubi somnulentiae cubiculariorum dormitandi potius quam dormiendi locus est* and Riggsby (1997) 45–6. The local separation between master and *familia* is documented in Plin. *Ep.* 2.17.24. The expression *dormitorium cubiculum*, 'bedroom', is also found in Plin. *Nat.* 30.52 *ante cubiculum dormitorium* ('in front of the bedroom'), Plin. *Ep.* 2.17.9 *dormitorium membrum* ('bedroom'), 2.17.22 *cubiculum noctis et somni* ('a room for the night and sleep'), 5.6.21 *dormitorium cubiculum* ('bedroom'). For the various notions of the term *cubiculum*, see the commentary above on *Ep.* 2.1.3 *in concilio iubet … in cubiculo damnat*…. The *cubiculum dormitorium*, where the family sleeps, is different from the *deversorium*, 'private guestroom', 'lodging place', where the visitors are accommodated; see the commentary on *Ep.* 2.2.13 *Edulibus terminatis excipiet te deversorium*…. In *Ep.* 2.9.7 Sidonius uses the term *cubile* to denote the bedroom, in *Ep.* 7.8.3 *cubiculum* without an adjective but it is clear from the context (he cannot find sleep because of the noisy Gothic women) that it is the room where he sleeps.

Section 11

A cryptoporticu in hiemale triclinium venitur: For *cryptoporticus*, see the commentary on *Ep.* 2.2.10 *quae, quia nihil* ... '*cryptoporticus*' .... With the rhetorical form of a *praeteritio*, the announcement not to mention something, Sidonius describes his *hiemale triclinium*, 'winter dining room'; for *triclinium*, see the commentary on *Ep.* 2.2.9 *Hinc egressis frons triclinii matronalis offertur.* Rooms for different seasons are important for the convenience of a villa; already Varro *Rust.* 1.13.7 complained about this unnecessary new luxury. Pliny often mentions different rooms that were used in different seasons: Plin. *Ep.* 2.17.7 *hoc hibernaculum* ('this is the winter apartment'), 2.17.10 *cubiculum ... altitudine aestivum, munimentis hibernum* ('a room that is ideal for the summer due to its height and for the winter due to its protection'), 5.6.24 *cubiculum hieme tepidissimum* ('this room is nice and warm in winter'), 5.6.29 *aestiva cryptoporticus* ('a hall for summer'), 5.6.31 *porticus ante medium diem hiberna, inclinato die aestiva* ('a portico that is cold like winter in the morning and warm like summer in the evening'); Delhey (1993) 189, Förtsch (1993) 26, 108. The villa of Pontius Leontius also has a winter dining room; see Sidon. *Carm.* 22.4 v. 212 *mos erit hic dominis hibernum sigma locare* ('here the masters of the house used to place their dining couch in winter').

quod arcuatili camino saepe ignis animatus pulla fuligine infecit: The winter dining room even has an oven. For *caminus*, 'oven', 'furnace' (*TLL* 3, 205.59–7.8), see also Sidon. *Carm.* 22.4 vv. 189–90, 5.303; Delhey (1993) 171–3. The very rarely used adjective *arcuatilis* means 'bow-formed' (*TLL* 2, 473.54–7) and is attested only here and in Alc. Avit. *Hom.* 1, 137.16.

Sed quid haec tibi, quem nunc ad focum minime invito: According to Whitton (2013) 237 Sidonius here pokes fun at Pliny, who alternates between the seasons when describing his villa Laurentinum; see Plin. *Ep.* 2.17.12 describing his place for ball games (*sphaeristerium*).

Quin potius ad te tempusque pertinentia loquar: Sidonius corrects himself with *quin potius*, '(but) rather', 'in fact', after a rhetorical question also in *Ep.* 2.10.4, 7.7.6, 7.8.4, and see also Plin. *Ep.* 3.13.5, 6.8.9; van

Waarden (2010) 375 and see the commentary on *Ep.* 2.2.7 *Quin potius* ....
The participle neuter plural *pertinentia*, 'things that belong to', is here used
as a substantive (*TLL* 10.1, 1797.39–43).

Ex hoc triclinio fit in diaetam sive cenatiunculam transitus, cui fere totus lacus quaeque tota lacui patet: Sidonius leads over to another room (*diaeta* or *cenatiuncula*), from which there is a wonderful view over the lake. This room seems to be the highlight of the villa and Sidonius' second favourite place, after his baths. Similarly, Statius praises his favourite room with a spectacular view and combines it with a catalogue of marbles, in Stat. *Silv.* 2.2.83–96; Gauly (2006) 463. For *triclinium*, see the commentary on *Ep.* 2.2.9 *Hinc egressis frons triclinii matronalis offertur. Diaeta*, from Greek δίαιτα, means 'room', 'suite' (*TLL* 5.1, 947.46–8.4), and thus is one of Sidonius' Grecisms, signposted in section 8; see the commentary on *Ep.* 2.2.8 *si graecari mavis* .... The precise architectural meaning of the word is not clear: it denotes single rooms as well as whole parts of a house; Förtsch (1993) 50–1. Pliny describes his favourite place in the villa in *Ep.* 2.17.20 similarly as *diaeta est, amores mei, re vera amores* ('this room is my love, really my love') and uses the term frequently elsewhere in his villa letters: *Ep.* 2.17.12, 15, 24, 5.6.20–21, 27–8, 31, 6.16.14, 7.5.1; Förtsch (1993) 48–57, Whitton (2013) 238, 246; see also Stat. *Silv.* 2.2.83 *una tamen cunctis, procul eminet una diaetis* ('but one room from all the rest stands far out'). With *sive*, 'or', Sidonius reflects on the uncertainty of definition and the difference to *cenatiuncula*, 'a small dining room' (*TLL* 3, 782.44–7), a very rarely used word, which is attested here and in Plin. *Ep.* 4.30.2 in a different context: *fons oritur in monte, per saxa decurrit, excipitur cenatiuncula manu facta* ('the fountain originates in the mountains, flows through the rocks and is held back in an artificial dining room'). For the overall construction of the sentence see Plin. *Ep.* 2.17.12 *cenatio quae latissimum mare longissimum litus ... possidet* ('a dining room which gives view to the very wide sea and the long beach'), and especially Plin. *Ep.* 2.17.10 *deinde vel cubiculum grande vel modica cenatio, quae plurimo sole, plurimo mare lucet* ('then either a big room or a modest dining room, which is radiant from the light of the sun and the sea'); Gibson (2013b) 345. Whitton (2013) 235 comments on this passage: 'Sidon. *Ep.* 2.2.11 follows P. closely here, with room-names, watery view, mannered bicolon and (a different) syllepsis'. In this figure of speech a word is applied to two others, of which it grammatically suits only one. Here *patere*, 'to stand open' (*TLL* 10.1, 657.64–67.68), is combined with *lacus* and *cenatiuncula*: 'a room or little dining room that looks over the whole lake and is completely open toward the lake'. For the verb *patere*, see the commentary on *Ep.* 2.2.10 *tecta intrinsecus patet*. The lake is completely visible from the dining room and the dining room has an open front towards the lake. Sidonius underlines his uninterrupted axis of vision with the repetition of *totus*. Pliny and Statius, on the other hand, describe views framed by windows dividing the sea: Plin. *Ep.* 2.17.5 *quasi tria maria prospectat* ('in front one looks as if on three seas'), Stat. *Silv.* 2.2.73–4 *sua cuique voluptas | atque omni proprium thalamo mare* ('every room has its delight and each its own sea'); Schneider (1995) 92.

In hac stibadium et nitens abacus: A *stibadium* is a 'semicircular dining couch', synonymous with *sigma* in Mart. 14.87 (see the commentary on *Ep.* 2.2.5 *ita ut ministeriorum ... sigma personas*). The Greek term στιβάδιον is the diminutive of στιβάς, 'bed', 'mattress'. Lütjohann (1887) 25, Anderson (1936) 426, Loyen (1970a) 49 choose the spelling *stibadium* while the manuscripts LMTCFP have *stipatium*. Isidore of Seville (Isid. *Orig.* 20.1.2) explains this spelling with the Latin verb *stipare*, 'to surround', 'crowd upon'; see Köhler (1995) 327 on Sidon. *Ep.* 1.11.14. A *stibadium* is already mentioned in the late first and early second century in Martial and Pliny the Younger, but came into fashion and was used instead of the rectangular triclinium in the third century. Serv. *Aen.* 1.698 explains the difference between the curved *stibadium* and the traditional, rectangular *triclinium*. By the fourth century, formal dining was associated with this kind of curved couch, set around a small D-shaped or round table called *orbis* or *mensa*. Dunbabin (1991) 132–3 suggests that the *stibadium* form may have been intended primarily for outdoor banquets. The *stibadia* varied in size, offering room for five to twelve guests, with seven perhaps the norm. For larger parties, rooms with three apses were built, each containing a *stibadium*; Rossiter (1991) 202–5, Dunbabin (1991) with archaeological examples. In Plin. *Ep.* 5.6.36, the *stibadium* is an outdoor dining pavilion with a curved marble couch under a vine pergola and a basin in front, in which dishes floated with food. Similarly, in Sidonius' villa, the *stibadium* is a couch in an open dining room with a wonderful view over the lake; Dunbabin (2003) 172, 192. For the *stibadium* as an element of the Roman villa and its garden in general, see Zanker (1979) 481–92, Rossiter (1991), Förtsch (1993) 93–100, Ellis (1995) 169–73, Stein-Hölkeskamp (2005) 34–7, 131–3. In Sidonius' dining room, the curved couch is paired with an *abacus*, a 'precious table, the top of which was made of marble, sometimes silver, gold, or other precious materials' (*TLL* 1, 42.25–60), mentioned for example in Cic. *Verr.* 2.4.16, 2.4.25, *Tusc.*

5.61, as a piece of furniture to put vases on. The participle *nitens* refers to the splendour of the table, an important element in Late Antique aesthetics; see the commentary on *Ep.* 2.10.4 v. 5 *Aedes celsa nitet nec in sinistrum*. On precious tables in the Roman dining rooms, see Stein-Hölkeskamp (2005) 136–9; see also Sidon. *Ep.* 9.13.5 v. 41 *abacum torosque pingant* ('and colour the sideboard and couches'), *Carm.* 17.7–8 *nec per multiplices abaco splendente cavernas | argenti nigri pondera defodiam* ('I will not bury masses of dark silver in the manifold recesses of a shiny sideboard'). Köhler (1995) 147 refers for the combination of *nitor* and *silver* to Hor. *Sat.* 2.2.4; Auson. *Prof.* 1.33; Paul. Pel. *Euch.* 207.

in quorum aream sive suggestum a subiecta porticu sensim non breviatis angustatisque gradibus ascenditur: Again, Sidonius uses *sive* to express his doubts about the right choice of words; see the commentary on *Ep.* 2.2.11 *Ex hoc triclinio fit in diaetam sive cenatiunculam*.... Both terms, *area* and *suggestus*, refer to a kind of open-air platform with seats and a table instead of a closed dining room. *Suggestus* or *suggestum* denotes a 'raised surface', 'platform', 'stage or tribune for a speaker' (*OLD* 1863), and appear in the latter sense in Sidon. *Ep.* 8.10.3 *de centumvirali suggestu* ('from the centumviral tribunal'). For *porticus*, see the commentary on *Ep.* 2.2.10 *Ab ortu lacum porticus intuetur*. The phrase *sensim non breviatis angustatisque gradibus ascenditur* raises some questions due to the transmission of the text. The manuscripts LVM, Lütjohann (1887) 25, and Loyen (1970a) 49 have *sensim breviatis*, the manuscripts NTCFP and Anderson (1936) 426 have *sensim non breviatis*, which is the stemmatically justified reading. It is also more logical for Sidonius to praise a gentle ascent instead of a steep and narrow staircase. *Breviatis* is the participle of *brevio*, 'to shorten', 'abbreviate'; for its local use see *TLL* 2, 2171.59–75, Ps. Matth. *Evang.* 22.1 *Ego viam vobis breviabo, ut quod spatio triginta dierum ituri eratis, in hac una die perficiatis* ('I will shorten the distance for you so that the distance you would walk in thirty days is done in one day'). See also Sidon. *Ep.* 4.15.3 *autumnus iam diem breviat* ('autumn is already shortening the day'), 7.18.1 *si numerus breviaretur* ('if the number is shortened'); van Waarden (2016) 262. *Angustatis* is the participle of *angusto*, 'to make narrow' (*TLL* 2, 61.70–2.37), and is also used in Sidon. *Ep.* 3.13.6, *Carm.* 10.3, 22.4 v. 170. The manuscripts NMCT and Lütjohann (1887) 25, and Anderson (1936) 426 have *ascenditur*, L and Loyen (1970a) 49 *escenditur*, while T[1] has *scanditur*. Both verbs, *escendere* (*TLL* 5.2, 856.53–8.25) and *ascendere* (*TLL* 2, 754.3–9.4), mean 'mount', 'ascend', 'board', but the latter is more common. As here, the manuscripts have both variants in *Ep.* 1.5.3,

1.11.6, 4.15.3, 4.25.5. In *Ep.* 7.14.7 only *ascenditur* is attested. Although the stemma suggests *ascenditur*, Engelbrecht (1898) 296 argues for *escenditur* because in his opinion Sidonius prefers the rarely used *escendere* to the simple *ascendere*; see also the discussions in Mossberg (1934) 14, Köhler (1995) 193, Amherdt (2001) 367. Van Waarden (2016) 150 claims that Sidonius differentiates between *ascendere* for the figurative meaning of building a career (as in *Ep.* 2.13.3, 3.6.1, 7.14.7; see also Plin. *Paneg.* 58.3, 61.2, *Ep.* 3.2.4) and *escendere* for the literal meaning of climbing steps (as here). Depending on whether one omits the *non*, the translations differ: either there seems to be a kind of steep staircase that leads to the plattform – Loyen (1970a) 49 'par un escalier qui raccourcit et réduit le trajet', Visser (2014) 36 'gradually through short and narrow steps' – or, on the contrary, a ramp which avoids the steep ascent – Anderson (1936) 427 'there is a gentle ascent from the portico by steps which are not made either short or narrow', Köhler (2014) 46 'ohne seine Schritte kürzer oder enger setzen zu müssen'.

Quo loci recumbens, si quid inter edendum vacas, prospiciendi voluptatibus occuparis: Elsewhere, Sidonius uses the common *vacare* with dative, 'have leisure for an activity, pursuit, etc.' (*OLD* 2001, 7); see also *Ep.* 1.2.4 *aut thesauris inspiciendis vacaturus aut stabulis* ('and spends time inspecting his treasures or his stables'), 2.2.15 *pilae vacamus* ('we spend our leisure time playing ball'), 4.3.10, 8.3.4, 8.4.3, 9.13.3. With an accusative the verb is used as here also in Sidon. *Ep.* 5.14.1 *quicquid illud est, quod vel otio vel negotio vacas* ('whatever you have time for in leisure or at work'); see also *Ep.* 8.9.5 v. 19. With the expression *prospiciendi voluptatibus* Sidonius hints at the most esteemed traits of a Roman villa: to offer different spectacular views; see the commentary on *Ep.* 2.2.10 *quae, quia nihil ipsa prospectat.... Recumbo*, 'to lie down', 'to recline at table' (*OLD* 1587, 3a), is the usual verb to describe the participation in a meal, for example in Plin. *Ep.* 9.23.4, Iuv. 3.82; it is also used in Sidon. *Ep.* 1.11.10, 2.13.7.

Section 12

Iam si tibi ex illo conclamatissimo fontium decocta referatur: In section 12, Sidonius describes the drinks that his guest will get. The drinks are just as refreshing as Sidonius' baths and should therefore also lure the addressee, Domitius, out of the hot city. In a natural *locus amoenus*, the drinks are taken directly from a well (for this topos see Christian 2015, 302, 320).

In Sidonius' artificial pleasure garden, however, the drinks are brought in a valuable cup. The source (*fons*) from which the drinks come is called *conclamatus*, 'known', 'celebrated' (*TLL* 4, 71.46–7), participle of *conclamo*. The superlative is attested only here and in Sidon. *Ep.* 6.1.3 *conclamatissimum primipilarem* ('the most famous captain'), 8.3.3 *conclamatissimas declamationes* ('most famous speeches'). *Decocta* is a drink made of boiled water, which is cooled down with snow, allegedly a Neronian invention; see Suet. *Nero* 48. Plin. *Nat.* 31.40 describes how Nero cooled down the water by placing the cup in the snow. Sidonius, on the other hand, has the ice put into his cups. Later, Sidonius emphasises the coldness of the drink; see also Mart. 14.116 *quo tibi decoctae nobile frigus aquae* ('why do you need the noble coldness of cooked water'), Iuv. 5.50 *frigidior Geticis petitur decocta pruinis* ('a drink is demanded colder than the Getan hoar-frost'). Having ice on a property in the south is a sign of great prosperity, as the ice had to be transported from the mountains and stored in a suitable room; see Mart. 5.64.2, 6.86, 9.22.8, 12.17.6, 14.117–118; Weeber (2015) 26.

videbis in calicibus repente perfusis: With the second-person indicative future (*videbis*) Sidonius continues the hodotic mode of the villa description; see the commentary on *Ep.* 2.2.3 *Sane si placet*.... Elsewhere, he uses this verbal form to express that his wish will be fulfilled; van Waarden (2010) 209; see also Sidon. *Ep.* 2.2.20 *praestabis* ('you will choose'), 2.12.1 *dabis* ('you will give'). Sidonius evokes the image of an opulent feast with overflowing cups. The word *calix*, 'cup', 'goblet' (*TLL* 3, 161.71–5.37), is frequently used in satire (Mart. 2.1.10, 4.43.6, 4.85.2, 9.87.1, 14.109, Iuv. 1.57), in Roman elegy (Tib. 2.5.98, Prop. 2.33.40) and in the Roman novel (Apul. *Met.* 2.11.3, 2.15.6, 2.19.1, 2.24.5, 4.7.4, 8.11.3). The adverb *repente* means 'without warning', 'suddenly' or 'in an instant', 'all at once' (*OLD* 1617); here it is probably used to indicate the quick service as a sign of hospitality as well as the fleeting nature of snow. Here and in the following Sidonius enjoys the idea of entertaining guests; see also Sidon. *Ep.* 8.4.1 and Mratschek (2008) 373 on the importance of the villa in establishing and maintaining friendship (*amicitia*).

nivalium maculas et frusta nebularum: To emphasise the coldness of his drink, Sidonius uses an unusual formulation. Whereas *aqua nivalis*, 'snow water', is attested elsewhere (e.g. Mart. 14.118.1), *nivalium macula*, 'spot', 'blot', 'stain of snow' (*TLL* 8, 25.38–43), is a Sidonian expression. *Frustum*, 'a piece', 'a bit' (*TLL* 6.1, 1440.74–41.13), with genitive, is more often used of solid food, but also of frozen wine in Ov. *Trist.* 3.10.24 *vina, nec hausta meri, sed data frusta bibunt* ('they do not drink wine in sips, but in bites'); see also Sidon. *Carm.* 5.210 *Ligerimque ... per frusta bibit* ('he drinks the River Liger piece by piece'). The genitives plural denoting the snow (*nivalium, nebularum*) frame the whole expression and thus create unity.

et illam lucem lubricam poculorum quadam quasi pinguedine subiti algoris hebetatam: The cold drink cools the cup and thus changes its surface. Sidonius describes this phenomenon with alliterations (on l-p-q) and the unusual combination of the words *lucem* and *lubricus* 'smooth', 'slippery' (*TLL* 7.2, 1688.60). In the context of the cocktail party evoked by Sidonius, *lubricus* may have also an ambiguous meaning; see the commentary on *Ep.* 2.2.6 *Absunt lubrici ... palaestritae*. The word *pinguedo*, 'fatness', 'fat' (*TLL* 10.1, 2162.68–70), is frequently used from the fourth century on, especially by Christian writers. Only here is it used in the meaning of 'film'. See also Sidon. *Ep.* 2.2.16 (about mud), 3.13.7 (about the parasite Gnatho). The pronoun *quadam* tones down the metaphor, similarly in Sidon. *Ep.* 6.12.4, 7.5.1; van Waarden (2010) 255. The participle *hebetatus*, 'blunt', 'dull', 'dim' (*TLL* 6.3, 2585.40–56), is also used by other authors about light sources like the sun, moon and stars. For a similar cooled cup, see Sidon. *Ep.* 2.13.7.

Tum respondentes poculis potiones, quarum rigentes cyathi siticuloso cuique, ne dicam tibi granditer abstemio, metuerentur: Another alliteration and wordplay with similar-sounding and etymologically related words (*poculis/potiones*) illustrate Sidonius' promise that the drinks are as delicious as the cups are precious. For *respondere*, 'suit', 'harmonise with', see Sidon. *Ep.* 7.9.16; van Waarden (2010) 493. Sidonius warns the drinkers of the cold of the cups and especially Domitius, who is not used to drink. This is another little jibe at Domitius: see the two commentaries on *Ep.* 2.2.2 *Et nunc, ...* and '*Samia mihi mater fuit*'. A *cyathus* is a 'small ladle for transferring the wine from the mixing-bowl to the drinking-cup' (*TLL* 4, 1581.81–2.15), also used metonymically for the whole cup, frequently in Plautus (e.g. *Pers.* 772, *Poen.* 274) and Martial (e.g. Mart. 1.71.1); see also Sidon. *Carm.* 23.287. The adjective *siticulosus*, 'thirsty', 'dry', 'parched' (*OLD* 1774), here means 'a drinker', 'a drunk', and is set in opposition to *abstemius*, 'temperate', 'sober', 'abstinent' (*TLL* 1, 188.52–9.14), that is the addressee, Domitius ('but I do not need to tell you this as you are very sober'). Sidonius thereby again addresses the stern side of his friend. He uses the term *abstemius* also in *Ep.* 6.1.5, 6.12.3, 7.9.10, 8.3.5, *Carm.* 16.107. *Abstemius* is frequently used in connection with wine, for example in Plin. *Nat.* 22.115, Paul. Nol. *Ep.* 22.2, *Carm.* 6.68. For adjectives ending in *-osus*, see the commentary on 2.2.18 *Lacus ipse ... flexuosus nemorosusque....* The adverb *granditer*, 'very' (*TLL* 6.2, 2187.81–8.36), does not appear until the third century. Sidonius often uses it with verbs or with adjectives, for example in *Ep.* 3.4.1, 3.8.2, 3.13.1, 7.2.3; Amherdt (2001) 120, 293, van Waarden (2010) 160, 344. For the adverbs ending in *-(i)ter*, see the commentary on 2.1.1 *Duo nunc pariter mala sustinent*.

Hinc iam spectabis, ut promoveat alnum piscator in pelagus: With his lengthy description of the view over the lake and the fishermen at work, Sidonius expands a topic which is familiar from Pliny's letters. Particularly close are Plin. *Ep.* 9.7.4 *ex illa possis despicere piscantes, ex hac ipse piscari hamumque de cubiculo ac paene etiam de lectulo ut e naucula iacere* ('from there you can look down and watch the fishermen, from there you could even fish and cast the fishing hook from the room and even the bed as from a ship'), and Plin. *Ep.* 2.17.28 *mare non sane pretiosis piscibus abundat, soleas tamen et squillas optimas egerit* ('The sea does not abound with precious fish, but offers soles and very nice prawns'). In *Ep.* 2.8.1 Pliny describes fishing as a pastime for spending one's leisure in the villa: *studes an piscaris an venaris an simul omnia? possunt enim omnia simul fieri ad Larium nostrum. nam lacus piscem, feras silvae ... adfatim suggerunt* ('Are you studying or fishing or hunting or everything at the same time? All these things can happen together in our Larium. Because the lake offers abundant fish and the woods wild animals'). Fishing as a pastime for the Gallo-Roman elite appears again in Sidon. *Ep.* 2.12, the counterpart to *Ep.* 2.2; see the commentary on *Ep.* 2.12.1 *Misisti tu quidem ... cum piscibus*. Sidonius writes here (as he did with the climate and the baths) again about a subject that Pliny does not deal with in depth in his letters, but only hints at. Sidonius expands on the different methods of fishing, whereas Pliny just mentions his villa's vicinity to a body of water and the abundance of fish that it offers. At the same time, Sidonius avoids Plinian vocabulary and chooses epic expressions. Sidonius thus leaves the comical/satirical drinking scene and sets the poetic/epic tone for the description of the lake that follows. Instead of the Plinian *naucula*, Sidonius uses *alnus*, 'the alder' (*TLL* 1, 1705.22–6.22), a poetic word for anything made of alderwood, especially a ship, which is frequently used by Lucan, Statius, Valerius Flaccus, and Claudian. It is also used in Sidon. *Carm.* 7.325–6. Sidonius also adds a Gallic hue to the scene by alluding to Ausonius; see Hanaghan (2019) 42–4 and the commentary immediately below. For the convenience of fishing out of one's bed, see Mart. 10.30.16–18. The collocation *navem/ratem promovere*, 'to sail' (*TLL* 10.2, 1894.59–61), is attested in Sil. 3.129 *promota ratis* ('and the ship was moving'). The term *piscator*, 'fisherman', 'fisher' (*TLL* 10.1, 2199.15–65), is widely attested since Plautus, as the profession of a free man or the task of a slave; see for example Plaut. *Mil.* 1182 *erus habet piscatores* ('the master has fishermen'). For the unfree or dependent workers on Sidonius' estate, see Samson (1992) 220–2, Kaufmann (1995) 242, Mathisen (2020a) 64–7. *Pelagus*, 'the sea', is frequently used by Vergil, Catullus and Lucan (see also Sidon. *Ep.* 2.2.18); here it denotes hyperbolically Sidonius' 'lake' (*TLL* 10.1, 992.52–8), a rare use, but see Damas. *Carm.* 12.1 (of the lake of Genezareth). *Pelagus* derives from Greek πέλαγος; see the commentary on *Ep.* 2.2.8 *si graecari mavis*....

ut stataria retia suberinis corticibus extendat aut signis per certa intervalla dispositis tractus funium librentur hamati: In a complicated phrase with elaborate wording Sidonius describes two different fishing techniques: first, fishing with a net which is kept on the surface by pieces of cork and pulled along from the boat, and then fishing with a hooked fishing line. This passage alludes to Auson. *Mos.* 245–6, where Ausonius describes a fisherman on the river: *ast hic, tranquillo qua labitur agmine flumen, | ducit corticeis fluitantia retia signis* ('but this one moves the floating nets with floats made of cork on the tranquil motion as the river glides by'); Roberts (1984) 345–8, Gruber (2013) 194–5. Sidonius repeats Ausonius' *retia*, but changes *fluitantia* to *stataria*, 'standing firm', 'stationary' (*OLD* 1814), only here used of a fishing net. He also replaces Ausonius' *corticeis signis* with the adjective *suberinus*, 'of the cork tree' (also a Sidonian hapax; more common are *subereus* or *subernus*) and *cortex*, 'bark (of the cork tree)', 'cork' (*TLL* 4, 1070.46–56); see Claud. *Carm. min.* 26.46 *et levis exili cortice terra natat* ('and the light earth floats with a thin crust'). For fishing with nets held by cork, see Ov. *Trist.* 3.4.11–12; Hanaghan (2019) 43. The Ausonian *signis* is transferred to the next part of the clause, where Sidonius describes fishing with hooks attached to a fishing line, held up with floats (*signis*). On Sidonius' thorough knowledge of Ausonius' work, see Santelia (2002) 30, Furbetta (2014/2015), Furbetta (2018b), Squillante (2018), Consolino (2020), Wolff (2020) 401. The adjective *hamatus*, 'with fishing hooks' (*TLL* 6.3, 2521.64–70), in its proper sense is attested only here, but metaphorically about syllogisms also in Sidon. *Ep.* 4.3.2 and Plin. *Ep.* 9.30.2; Amherdt (2001) 126. Sidonius treats the subject of fishing also in *Carm.* 21, where he describes that he fished with hooks (*hamis*) during the night and sends two fish to his friend.

In *Ep.* 8.9.2, Sidonius uses fish caught in a net as a metaphor for poets (*ut pisciculi retibus*, 'like little fish in the nets'). In *Ep.* 8.12.7 Sidonius describes different types of fish which are delicious to eat. For fishing with a net, the most important method in Greco-Roman times, see Opp. *Hal.* 3.79–84, Verg. *Georg.* 1.141–2, Aesch. *Cho.* 506–7; for fishing with a fishing line, see Opp. *Hal.* 3.72–8, Ael. *Nat.* 1.5. On antique fishing techniques in general, see Kuhn (1998), Montebelli (2009) 103–16. On fishing as a motif in Gallic arts and literature, see Sivan (1993) 203 n. 82. Later in this letter, in section 16, Sidonius again alludes to Ausonius, in another fishing scene. For *intervallum*, see the commentary on *Ep.* 2.2.8 *triplex medii parietis aditus per arcuata intervalla reseratur*.

scilicet ut nocturnis per lacum excursibus rapacissimi salares in consanguineas agantur insidias: The next part of the sentence is also an allusion to Ausonius: Auson. *Mos.* 88, where the very rarely used word *salar*, 'trout', appears. In Ausonius, the fish is characterised by the red spots on its back: *purpureisque salar stellatus tegora guttis* ('the trout covered with spots on its back'), a description similar to that of a species of lizard (*stellio*) in Ov. *Met.* 5.461; Gualandri (1979) 98, Gruber (2013) 149–50. See also Auson. *Mos.* 129, where the *salar* is mentioned again, and 104, where a similar description of the fishes' bellies is used; see the commentary on *Ep.* 2.2.17 *qui repulsi … carnes rubras albis abdominibus extendunt*. As Hanaghan (2019) 43 shows, Symmachus highly praises Ausonius' fish catalogue (*Mos.* 75–149) in Symm. *Ep.* 1.14 and compares Ausonius to Vergil. The word *salar* has a Gallic ring according to Adams (2007) 304–5. It was either a local variant, that is, a fourth-century Gallic regionalism for *tructa*, 'trout', or a more specialised term. It is also mentioned in Polemius Silvius' list of fish (p. 544.18). Which fish is meant is disputed: see the discussion in Adams (2007) 304–5 n. 130. For the brown trout, which could be meant here, see Hünemörder (1999). The trout are attracted by other fish as bait. With the adjective *consanguineus*, 'related by blood' (*TLL* 4, 359.59–74), Sidonius humanises the fish. He mentions the two characteristics (red colour and spikes) also in *Carm.* 18.7–10: *Lucrinum stagnum dives Campania nollet, | aequora si nostri cerneret illa lacus. | Illud puniceis ornatur litus echinis: | piscibus in nostris, hospes, utrumque vides* ('rich Campania would not want the Lucrine pond if she saw the surface of our lake. That other shore is decorated with red sea urchins, in our fish, o guest, you see both'). This description, which correlates with the actual fish species currently found in Aydat, is discussed by Hanaghan (2019) 43–4 n. 122. The trout Sidonius mentions in his allusion to Ausonius therefore is not just a literary phrase, but based on observation. Today, Lake Aydat is still popular for fishing and various species of fish (pike, perch, carp, tench, eel, trout and whiting) are found in it, among them also the kind of trout Sidonius describes. The notion of the fisherman's ruse to catch the fish (*nocturnis ... excursibus, insidias*) is repeated with the expression *piscis pisce decipitur*; see the next commentary.

quid enim hinc congruentius dixerim, cum piscis pisce decipitur: Sidonius ends the section with one of his many puns; see the commentary on *Ep.* 2.2.13 *Edulibus terminatis ... aestuosum, maxime aestivum*. In Latin literature *decipere* often stands for fishing with lures and hooks, for example in Ov. *Met.* 3.586–7 *pauper et ipse fuit linoque solebat et hamis | decipere et calamo salientis ducere pisces* ('he was poor and used to deceive the leaping fish with thread and a hook and with the rod he pulled them out'), Sen. *Ep.* 8.3 *et fera et piscis spe aliqua oblectante decipitur* ('wild animals and fish are deceived by a delightful hope'), Mart. 5.18.8. In Ausonius, the same idea of deception is found in a fishing scene; see Auson. *Mos.* 244 *nodosis decepta plagis examina verrit* ('he sweeps with knotted nets deceived shoals') and 250 *ignara doli* ('all unsuspecting'); see Roberts (1984) 348, Hanghan (2019) 43. In Sidonius the fish itself, the *salar*, 'trout', literally deceives and then catches another fish by ambushing it. With the literally taken expression *piscis pisce decipitur* and the allusions to Ausonius, Sidonius thus modifies a fixed expression in an original way. Again it becomes clear that the structure of Sidonius' villa letter is generally inspired by Pliny, but is filled with Sidonius' own poetic content.

Section 13

Edulibus terminatis excipiet te deversorium, quia minime aestuosum, maxime aestivum: In section 13 Sidonius describes the guest room in which Domitius can lie down and take a nap after his meal, a practice Sidonius also describes in *Ep.* 2.9.7. Perhaps Sidonius is also referring to Domitius' tiredness; see the commentary on *Ep.* 2.2.2 *discipulis non ... oscitabundus ordiris*. The adjective *edulis* is frequently used as a noun in the neutral plural, *edulia*, 'eatables', 'food', 'eating' (*TLL* 5.2, 124.8–66). It is also used in Sidon. *Ep.* 1.11.11, 2.9.3, 2.9.6, 7.13.3. The *deversorium*, 'private guestroom', 'lodging place' (*TLL* 5.1, 852.66–3.47), here seems to be integrated in Sidonius' villa and to consist only of one room; see the translations of Loyen (1970a) 50 'un salon', Anderson (1936) 429 'drawing-room', Köhler (2014) 'Quartier'. Sidonius uses the term *deversorium* (also spelt *diversorium*) five times in its different meanings. In *Ep.* 2.9.7 it denotes a 'private apartment for guests'; see the commentary on *Ep.* 2.9.7 *Inde surgentes ... ad sarcinas et deversorium pedem referebamus....* In Sidon. *Ep.* 8.3.2 *deversorium* also denotes a private lodging, probably also consisting of more than one room; Carrié (2010) 281. In Sidon. *Ep.* 1.5.9 and 7.2.6 instead the term denotes a 'public guesthouse', 'inn'; Köhler (1995) 209, Symm. *Ep.* 1.1.2. Vitruvius, an intertext for Sidon. *Ep.* 2.2, also gives advice on how to build rooms for guests, but does not use the term *deversorium*; see Vitr. 6.5.1, 6.7.4. For archaeological identification of *deversoria*, guestrooms for aristocratic guests, see Balmelle (2001) 135 and especially Carrié (2010), who describes the *deversorium* as a central element of the prestigious, status-enhancing architecture of a villa in Late Antiquity and distinguishes it from the simple quarters for common visitors (*hospitalia*). Pliny, on the other hand, does not use the term in the description of his estates in *Ep.* 2.17 and 5.6, but uses only the general term *cubiculum*; Carrié (2010) 282–3. The guestroom in Sidonius' estate, Avitacum, is described with two similar-sounding adjectives: *aestuosus*, 'burning hot', 'glowing', and *aestivus*, 'of summer', 'summer-like'. The paronomasia ('play upon words which sound alike') is probably an allusion to Vitruvius: Vitr. 6.4.2 *aestiva ad septentrionem, quod ea regio, non ut reliquae per solstitium propter calorem efficiuntur aestuosae* ('the summer dining rooms should face toward north, for while the other sides, at the solstice, become burning hot because of the heat'). *Aestuosus* is frequently used in connection with places (*TLL* 1, 1115.29–43), for example in Cic. *Att.* 5.14.1 (*via*), of a room (*cubiculum*) also in Cass. Fel. 64. For Sidonius' use of adjectives ending in *-osus* in general, see the commentary on *Ep.* 2.2.18 *Lacus ipse ... flexuosus nemorosusque.... Aestivus* is also frequently applied to places (*TLL* 1, 1109.23–46); see Sidon. *Carm.* 22.4 v. 179 *porticus ... aestiva* ('a summer portico'), Cic. *Ad Q. fr.* 3.1.2 *aestivum locum* ('a summer place'), Mart. 8.61.6 *rus habemus aestivum* ('I have a summer house'), Vitr. 7.3.4. Sidonius likes this kind of wordplay with assonances and uses it often in his letters and poems, for example in *Ep.* 8.8.3 *non tam honorare censor quam censetor onerare* ('that he is not honoured by the censor but burdened by the tax assessor'), *Carm.* 2.529 *a rastris ad rostra roga* ('ask from the rake to the rostra'), 5.453 *et pontum sub ponte daret* ('building a bridge over the breakers'); see the commentaries on 2.2.12 *quid enim hinc ... piscis pisce decipitur* and 2.9.4 *licet quaepiam ... disparibus dicendi parilitatem*, and Loyen (1943) 138–40.

Nam per hoc, quod in Aquilonem solum patescit, habet diem, non habet solem: Because the guest room opens only to the north, there is light, but no sun. *Aquilo* is the 'north wind', 'north' (*TLL* 2, 376.4–7.49); see also Sidon. *Ep.* 9.13.5 v. 119. According to Vitruvius, Vitr. 6.4.2, the rooms or parts of the house which are used in summer time should be oriented towards the north, and winter rooms towards the south. Sidonius refers to this rule also in the description of the estate of Pontius Leontius in *Carm.* 22.4 vv. 179–82 *porticus ad gelidos patet hinc aestiva triones;* | *hinc calor innocuus thermis hiemalibus exit* | *atque locum in tempus mollit; quippe illa rigori* | *pars est apta magis* ('then there is a summer portico open on one side to the cold north; at the other end a harmless warmth comes out from the winter baths and makes the place cozy, when the season requires it; so this part of the building is best suited to the cold'), Cam (2003) 150. For *patesco*, 'to be laid open', 'open' (*TLL* 10.1, 702.27–46), see Sidon. *Ep.* 3.13.6, Plin. *Ep.* 5.6.32 *hippodromus ... medius patescit* ('the hippodrome is open in the middle'), and the commentary on *Ep.* 2.2.10 *tecta intrinsecus patet*.

interiecto consistorio perangusto, ubi somnulentiae cubiculariorum dormitandi potius quam dormiendi locus est: Adjacent to the guest room is a very small room for the slaves. While Sidonius, his family and guests sleep soundly, the slaves have mostly to be on duty and are permitted only short naps. For Sidonius' depiction of the slaves in his villas, see the introduction to *Ep.* 2.2. A *consistorium* is 'a place of assembly' (*TLL* 4, 472.81–3.40), rarely used as here in a general sense of a private house. The adjective *perangustus*, 'very narrow' (applied to various objects) (*TLL* 10.1, 1188.24–33), is rarely used. Plin. *Ep.* 2.17.22 describes a similar passageway: *iunctum est cubiculum noctis et somni. non illud voces servolorum, non maris murmur, non tempestatum motus, non fulgurum lumen ac ne diem quidem sentit nisi fenestris apertis* ('There is an adjacent bedroom for sleeping. There you do not hear the voices of the slaves nor the sound of the sea nor the movements of storms nor the the flash of lightning and you do not even see daylight unless you open the windows'). *Somnulentia*, 'sleepiness', 'drowsiness', is a Sidonian hapax. The personal slave of the master is called *cubicularius*, 'chamber-slave' (*TLL* 4, 1265.40–6.20); Kaufmann (1995) 242, Riggsby (1997) 45–6. Here Sidonius uses the frequentative verb *dormito*, 'to keep falling asleep', 'to drowse', in opposition to *dormio*, 'to sleep'; see the commentary on *Ep.* 2.1.3 *in concilio iubet ... in quaestione dormitat*. For a similar verbal polyptoton (the stylistic scheme in which words derived from the same root are repeated), see Plin.

Ep. 2.17.8 *non legendos libros, sed lectitandos* ('books not for reading once, but for studying intensively').

Section 14

Hic iam quam volupe auribus insonare: Section 14 is dedicated to the sound of the animals that the addressee, Domitius, will hear during his visit to Sidonius. The pleasant singing of birds is a typical trait of the bucolic *locus amoenus* and part of the desciption of one's villa as a *locus amoenus*; see Plin. *Ep.* 5.6.22, 37 (only artificial birds, though), Ruric. *Ep.* 1.11.2 *cantus avium* ('the songs of the birds'); Curtius (1948) 200–5. To emphasise the comfort of the villa, Sidonius adds other animal sounds – many of them with a poetic connotation – that can be heard day and night; Littlewood (1987) 28–9, Mratschek (2020b) 251. Sidonius does not always use the common expressions for the animals' various sounds, but chooses rarely used verbs or verbs belonging to other animals. Oddly enough, the animal sounds are often described by other authors as annoying and not as conducive to sleep. A very similar list with the connection of animal sound and time of day can be found in Apul. *Flor.* 13 *hirundinibus matutinum, cicadis meridianum, noctuis serum, ululis vespertinum, bubonibus nocturnum; gallis antelucanum* ('the morning song to the swallows, noon to the cicadas, dusk to the night owls, the evening to the screech owls, the night to the horned owls, dawn to the roosters'). Lists of times of day are found in Censor, *De die natali* 24, Macrob. *Sat.* 1.3.12–15; see Gualandri (1979) 103. Gualandri (2017) 133–5 also refers to the *Historia Augusta* (*Geta* 5.4–5) as a parallel text, where the emperor Geta is portrayed asking grammarians questions about animal sounds. Aiello (2005) indentifies Sidonius' description of various bird sounds in *Ep.* 2.2.14 as a literary model for the *Carmen de Philomela* (*Anth. Lat.* 762 Riese), a text from the eleventh century. *Volupe*, 'with pleasure', 'pleasurably', is the neuter of the adjective *volupis*. The common form for the adverb is *volup* (*OLD* 2102). It is preclassical and frequently used in comedy, for example Plaut. *Mil.* 277, *Most.* 153, Ter. *Phorm.* 610. The verb *insonare*, 'to sound loudly' (*TLL* 7.1, 1938.83–40.65), is poetic and first documented in Vergil, for example Verg. *Aen.* 2.53, 7.515. Applied to animals as here the verb only appears in Isid. *Orig.* 12.2.25 (of a dog), in Plin. *Ep.* 7.27.9 about a ghost, who is rattling his chains. Sidonius uses the verb also in *Ep.* 1.10.2, 9.15.1 v. 45; Köhler (1995) 286–7.

cicadas meridie concrepantes: Sidonius inserts a list of animal sounds in short phrases, which Gualandri (1979) 102 interprets as a parody of a bucolic scene because of its monotony. Sidonius starts his series of animal noises with the *cicada*, 'cicada', 'tree-cricket' (*TLL* 3, 1045.74–6.38), one of the most characteristic insects of the Mediterranean world, which is loved or hated for its chirping sound, produced by rubbing the ridges of the wings together; see for example Mart. 10.58.3. Often it is the only sound heard on a hot summer day and thus a symbol of summer; see Ov. *Ars* 1.271, Iuv. 9.69. The cicadas are also an attribute of the Muses, a symbol of the poet, often inhabiting a *locus amoenus* and praised for their singing, for example in Plat. *Phdr.* 230c, Theocr. *Idyll.* 1.148, Ach. Tat. 1.15.8; Schönbeck (1962) 59–60, Hünemörder (2002b). Sidonius lets the cicadas sing at 'noon', *meridie*, when everyone takes a siesta and the chirping of the cicadas is the only sound to be heard. The cicadas also appear in Vergil's *Eclogae* and *Georgica*, which are important intertexts for the whole of section 14, though in Vergil's account they sing in the morning: Verg. *Ecl.* 2.13 *resonant arbusta cicadis* ('the trees resound from the cicadas'), *Georg.* 3.327–8 *inde ubi quarta sitim caeli collegerit hora | et cantu querulae rumpent arbusta cicadae* ('when the fourth hour of heaven induced thirst and the wailing cicadas rupture the trees with their song'). Sidonius is the only one who applies the verb *concrepo*, 'to rattle', 'creak', 'sound' (*TLL* 4, 94.22–51), to a cicada. Other authors describe the sound they make with the verbs *resonare* (Verg. *Ecl.* 2.13), *fremere* (App. Verg. *Culex* 153), *stridorem edere* (Plin. *Nat.* 11.107), *fritinnire* (*Anth. Lat.* 762.35); see further examples in *TLL* 3, 1046.15–35.

ranas crepusculo incumbente blaterantes: Next come the frogs, which start croaking at *crepusculum*, 'twilight', 'dusk' (*TLL* 4, 1175.39–66). The combination of *crepusculum* (see also Sidon. *Ep.* 2.13.4) with *incumbere*, 'to lean', 'lay oneself', is unattested elsewhere. In *Ep.* 4.24.2 Sidonius uses the combination *morbo incumbente* ('under the weight of illness'). For *blatero*, 'to talk idly or foolishly', 'to babble', 'to prate', especially of the sound camels, *TLL* 2, 2049.60–5 refers to Paul. Fest. p. 34, and of frogs to *Gloss.* V 171.51; Gualandri (1979) 102 n. 99. The frogs' croaking is a nuisance for men and gods in Aristophan. *Ran.* 226–69 and Hor. *Sat.* 1.5.14–15, and frogs are used as a means of witchcraft. But frogs were also esteemed for their prophetic powers and are thus connected to Apollo; Hünemörder (1998a). Croaking frogs are also mentioned in an important intertext of this section, in Verg. *Georg.* 1.378 *veterem ... ranae cecinere querellam* ('the frogs sang their old lament'), 3.431 *ranisque loquacibus* ('with chattering frogs').

cygnos atque anseres concubia nocte clangentes: Dusk is followed by night, whose animals are swan and goose. The *cygnus* or *cycnus*, 'swan' (*TLL* 4, 1585.16–68), from Greek κύκνος, is a symbol of love, poetry and prophecy and is associated with the gods Apollo and Venus; see Sidon. *Ep.* 9.15.1 vv. 32–4. The swan is legendary for the beautiful song it sings before it dies. Antipatros (*Anth. Pal.* 9.92) compares the singing of the swan with that of the cicada, which he appreciates more; Hünemörder (2001c). The *anser*, 'goose' (*TLL* 2, 124.53–5.20), is also an animal known for its voice. Poets criticise its loud gabbling and garrulity; Hünemörder (1998b). The comparison of the swan's melodious music and the cackling goose is proverbial; see Sidon. *Carm.* 22.3, Verg. *Ecl.* 9.35–6, Prop. 2.34.83–4, Symm. *Ep.* 1.1.4. In *Ep.* 9.2.2 alluding to Apul. *Flor.* 17.17, Sidonius also combines goose and swan (there, however, called *olor*); Condorelli (2017) 64–9. To describe the sound of both animals, Sidonius chooses the verb *clangere*, 'to clang', 'to sound', a verb rarely used to denote animal sounds (*TLL* 3, 1262.2–5), whereas *clangor* is the usual term for a goose's sound, as in Plin. *Nat.* 18.363 (for further examples see *TLL* 3, 1262.40–65). In *Ep.* 8.9.4, Sidonius also uses *clangor* for the sound of the dying swan: *quia cantuum similes fuerint olorinorum, quorum est modulatior clangor in poenis* ('because they were like the songs of swans, whose cry is more tuneful in moments of agony'). The adjective *concubius* 'of lying asleep', 'to the time of sleep' (*TLL* 4, 100.76–1.3), appears only in connection with *nocte*; see also Sidon. *Ep.* 1.2.9; Köhler (1995) 159.

intempesta gallos gallinacios concinentes: *Intempesta nocte*, 'the dead of night' (*TLL* 7.1, 2110.29–84), is a common expression in prose and poetry; see Cic. *Phil.* 1.8; Verg. *Aen.* 3.587. The rooster announces the early morning with its crowing in Plin. *Nat.* 10.46, and it has an apotropaic function, banishing demons; see Ael. *Nat.* 3.31; Hünemörder (1998c) 750. The common form of *gallinacios* is *gallinaceos*, 'of hens, of fowls' (*TLL* 6.2, 1683.83–4.80), the combination with *gallus*, dunghill-cock, or *pullus*, 'a young fowl', is frequent, for example in Plaut. *Aul.* 465, *Capt.* 849. The verb *concinere*, 'to sound in concert', 'to sing harmoniously' (*TLL* 3, 52.48–3.8), is used of a poultry-cock only here, of a swan in Ov. *Her.* 7.2 *ad vada Maeandri concinit albus olor* ('in the shallow water of the River Maeandrus the white swan sings') and of instruments in Sidon. *Ep.* 8.9.5 v. 14. Sidonius uses the noun *concinentia*, 'symmetry', in an architectural context in the description of the estate Octavianum in Sidon. *Ep.* 8.4.1; Cam (2003) 146–7.

oscines corvos voce triplicata puniceam surgentis Aurorae facem consalutantes: The dawn's animal in Sidonius' list is the raven. He thus alludes to Horace, Hor. *Carm.* 3.27.11–12 *oscinem corvum prece suscitabo | solis ab ortu* ('I will stir up the prophetic raven with my prayer when the sun rises'). Both texts contain the sunrise and the combination of *corvus* with *oscen*. While in Horace the prophetic raven appears in a serious context, Sidonius uses it humorously in his list of noises; Stoehr-Monjou (2013) 148. *Oscen* means 'divining bird', 'bird of augury' (*TLL* 9.2, 1101.28–52), and often appears in combination with a certain bird's name. The prophetic *corvus*, 'raven' (*TLL* 4, 1079.31–63), is Apollo's holy bird; it forecasts the weather and is known for its wisdom and helpfulness; Hünemörder (2001a). The participle of *triplico*, 'triple' (*OLD* 1976), is rare, but in combination with *corvus* it also appears in Plin. *Nat.* 7.153 (about the raven's life span, three times longer than the life of a deer according to Hesiod) *attribuit ... id triplicatum corvis* ('he attributed the ravens the triple of this'). *Puniceus*, 'reddish', 'purple' (*TLL* 10.1, 2048.10–17), in combination with Aurora, 'dawn', is a common expression in the epic, for example in Verg. *Aen.* 12.77. Aurora is the goddess of the morning, daughter of Hyperion and wife of Tithonus; the personification of dawn is frequent especially in Ovid and Vergil (see the examples in *TLL* 2, 1523.51–4.62) and also used in Sidon. *Carm.* 2.343, 9.21, 22.4 v. 49.

diluculo autem Philomelam inter frutices sibilantem: Sidonius connects dawn with the nightingale and the swallow, birds with a cruel mythological background. The noun *diluculum*, 'daybreak', 'dawn', is the opposite of *crepusculum*, 'twilight', 'dusk'; see the commentary on *Ep.* 2.2.14 *ranas crepusculo incumbente blaterantes*. The same opposition is found in Ambr. *Hymn.* 1.7.26–8. The ablative singular *diluculo* in place of a local adverb is also used in Sidon. *Ep.* 4.8.2, 8.11.11; see *TLL* 5.1, 1188.2–14. Philomela was the daughter of Pandion, king of Athens, and the sister of Procne. After she was violated by her brother-in-law, Tereus, he cut her tongue out to prevent her from telling what had happened. Philomela still managed to tell her plight by weaving her story into a garment which she sent to her sister. Procne liberated her and in revenge they killed Itys, Tereus and Procne's son, and prepared a meal out of his flesh for his father. To prevent Tereus from taking revenge, Jupiter changed them into birds, a nightingale and a swallow; see Plaut. *Rud.* 604, Hyg. *Fab.* 45, Ov. *Met.* 6.426–674, Mart. 14.75.1–2; Hünemörder (2001b), Waldner (2001a). The connection between the mythical story and the bird is so close that poets called the nightingale simply 'philomela', as here, for example in Maxim. *Eleg.* 2.49. The nightingale is famous for its song; Hünemörder (2000). To describe the birdsong, Sidonius uses the verb *sibilo*, 'to make a hissing sound' (*OLD* 1753), commonly used of snakes, not of birds, for example in Ov. *Met.* 4.589, Luc. 6.690. Whereas the nightingale in Sidonius sings at dawn, in Verg. *Georg.* 4.514–15 it laments during the night: *flet noctem, ramoque sedens miserabile carmen | integrat et maestis late loca questibus implet* ('she cries during the night and sitting on a tree she renews her lamenting song and she fills the place all around with sad laments'); Montone (2017) 30. *Frutex* is one of Sidonius' favourite words. It denotes 'various plants which are taller than herbs and smaller than trees' (*TLL* 6.1, 1443.2–6.39); see also Sidon. *Ep.* 2.2.18, 7.6.8; Gualandri (1979) 100 n. 87, van Waarden (2010) 321. The expression *inter frutices* is used elsewhere, for example in *Priap.* 15.5, Calp. *Ecl.* 6.85.

Prognen inter asseres minurientem: Most manuscripts have *Prognen*; LCF attest *Prognem*. Procne here stands for 'swallow'; for her story, see the commentary, p. 151, on *diluculo autem Philomelam inter frutices sibilantem*. *Asser*, 'a stake', 'a post' (*TLL* 2, 862.29–3.15), is attested since Plaut. *Aul.* 357. Here it appears as a *pars pro toto* (a part for the whole) for the roof of a house, where the swallows build their nests; see also Ov. *Met.* 6.668–9 *quarum petit altera silvas, | altera tecta subit* ('of those one seeks the woods, the other flies under a roof'). To describe its sound, Sidonius uses the onomatopoetical verb *minurrio*, 'to twitter', 'chirp' (*TLL* 8, 1044.51–60), which is very uncommon; Sirmond (1641) 47–8. It is also used in the *Historia Augusta* (*Geta* 5.5) *palumbes minurriunt* ('the pigeons coo'). Its spelling varies; most manuscipts and Lütjohann (1887) 25 have *minurientem*, but L and Loyen (1970a) 50 have *minurrientem*.

Cui concentui licebit adiungas fistulae septiforis armentalem Camenam: After the series of birds and times of day, Sidonius adds a bucolic scenery, strongly reminiscent of Vergil's *Eclogae*; Colton (2000) 9–11. *Concentus*, 'concert', of the singing birds is also used in Sidon. *Ep.* 1.5.4 and attested in other authors (*TLL* 4, 20.17–21). An intertext is probably Verg. *Georg.* 1.422–3 *hinc ille avium concentus in agris | et laetae pecudes et ovantes gutture corvi* ('from there the singing of birds comes to the fields and the joyful cattle and the crows with their rejoicing sound'). A further intertext might be Verg. *Ecl.* 2.36–7, where the shepherd Corydon declares: *est mihi disparibus septem compacta cicutis | fistula* ('I own a flute which is built from seven dissimilar stalks of the hemlock'). Sidonius mentions the 'shepherd's pipe', *fistula*, also in *Ep.* 4.18.5 *pone fistulas ipse pastorias* ('lay down the shepherds' pipes yourself'), 9.13.5 v. 76, *Carm.* 1.16. See the commentary above on *Ep.* 2.2.8 *canalibusque circumactis … sex fistulae …* for *fistula* as 'water pipe'. Similarly, Sidonius describes his own poems in bucolic images in *Ep.* 2.10.3 when he talks about his *stipula* and *culmus*; see the commentary on *Ep.* 2.10.4 *sic nostra … stipula vilescit*. Here *fistula* denotes the syrinx, the shepherd's characteristic flute, which consisted of several pipes (five to nine, but later up to eighteen). They gradually decreased in length and calibre and were bound or glued together; see Waldner (2001b) and for example Verg. *Ecl.* 2.32, Ov. *Met.* 1.689–712. The adjective *septiforis*, 'having seven openings', is very unusual and first attested in Sidonius; it later also appears in Alc. Avit. *Hist.* 1.83 *septiforem vultum* ('the face with seven openings'). It derives from the rarely used verb *forare* ('to bore', 'pierce'), augmented by the prefix *septi*. For the construction of the Sidonian term, see *septipedes*, 'sevenfoot', in Sidon. *Carm.* 12.11, *Ep.* 8.9.5 v. 34. For the combination with *fistula*, 'reed pipe', 'shepherd's pipe' (*TLL* 6.1, 829.70–30.7), see Gualandri (1979) 62–3 on *fistulam biforem* (about the openings of Gnathos' ears) in Sidon. *Ep.* 3.13.6. In *Ep.* 8.9.1 Sidonius uses the Apuleian term *multiforatilis* to describe a pipe; see Wyslucha (2018) on flutes with several holes (*multifora, multiforatilis, multiforabilis*) and the difficult identification with a known specimen of a Greek flute, that is, a polymodal aulos in Ov. *Met.* 12.158, Sen. *Ag.* 348, Apul. *Met.* 10.32.2, *Flor.* 3.1. For the rare adjective *armentalis*, 'of a herd', 'one of a herd' (of cattle, horses) (*TLL* 2, 610.25–36), see Verg. *Aen.* 11.571, Calp. *Ecl.* 1.29, Symm. *Ep.* 6.17. *Camena*, 'muse', is the Latin name of the Greek Μοῦσα, frequent in Horace, for example Hor. *Carm.* 3.4.21, and in Verg. *Ecl.* 3.59. *Camena* is only one of the Muses' names, but according to Sidonius the right one; see *Ep.* 5.2.1 *veriora nomina Camenarum* ('the truer names of the Camenae'). Sidonius calls them by this name also in *Carm.* 9.130, 215, 318. Sidonius invokes the Muse(s) many times in various ways, jesting, asking them for help and inspiration, even rejecting them (*Carm.* 16.1–6), and similarly to Pliny he depicts his estates as temples of the Muses: Sidon. *Carm.* 1.9, 4.6, 5.373, 5.568, 6.30–31, 6.36, 7.14, 7.174, 9.18, 9.261, 9.276, 9.313, 9.341, 10.17, 12.10, 12.20, 13.35, 14.4 v. 6, 22.4 v. 12, 22.4 v. 20, 22.4 v. 214, 23.8, 23.124, 23.205, 23.266, 23.306, 23.435, 23.501, *Ep.* 1.9.6–7, 4.3.9, 5.2.1, 5.17.1, 5.17.9, 5.21.1, 8.9.5 v. 1, 8.11.3 v. 2, 8.16.2, 9.13.5 v. 99; André (2006) 71–3, André (2009), Schmitzer (2015) 87–90, Hernández Lobato (2017), Harich-Schwarzbauer and Hindermann (2020), Mratschek (2020c), Schlapbach (2020). For the importance and changing role of the Muse(s) in Late Antiquity in general, see Walde (2000), Schindler et al. (2013), Schlapbach (2014).

quam saepe nocturnis carminum certaminibus insomnes nostrorum montium Tityri exercent: Sidonius announces that Domitius can fall asleep to the sound of Tityrus' flute. The major intertext for this bucolic passage is again Vergil's *Eclogae*, especially *Ecl.* 7.16, about the singing match between a goatherd and a shepherd: *certamen erat Corydon cum Thyrside magnum* ('there was a big contest, Corydon against Thyrsis'). Expanding Vergil's *certamen*, 'contest', 'struggle', 'strife', Sidonius composes the phrase *nocturnis carminum certaminibus*. Elsewhere, Sidonius uses *certamen* in a military context; see *Carm.* 2.287, 2.294, *Ep.* 3.3.4, 3.3.7, 7.7.2. He changes the names of the shepherds to a generic 'Tityrus' in the plural, which is also the name of a shepherd in Vergil's *Eclogae*, used later on, as here, metonymically for any shepherd; see Verg. *Ecl.* 1.1 *Tityre, tu patulae recubans sub tegmine fagi* ('Tityrus, you recline under the roof of a wide beech tree'), 3.20, 3.96, 5.12, 6.4, 8.55, 9.23–4, *Georg.* 4.566, Sidon. *Ep.* 1.5.5; Coleman (1977) 71, Köhler (1995) 196, Colton (2000) 9–11, Montone (2017) 40 n. 33. Tityrus also appears in Sidon. *Ep.* 8.9.5 v. 12 and 56, where Sidonius writes about the loss of his property, and in *Carm.* 4.1, in which Sidonius refers to Vergil and Horace in order to discuss his own situation, addressing the emperor Majorian; Harries (1994) 87, Gualandri (2000) 122–5, André (2006) 72–3. Here Sidonius describes the rivalling shepherds as being *insomnes* and *nostrorum montium*. He thus adds local flavour and builds an antithesis to the slumbering guest, probably alluding to Verg. *Ecl.* 1.79 *hic tamen hanc mecum poteras requiescere noctem* ('but you could rest here for this night with me'). Another intertext may be Verg. *Georg.* 1.342 *tum somni dulces densaeque in montibus umbrae* ('then the sleep is sweet and the mountains are in deep shadows'); Montone (2017) 29.

inter greges tinnibulatos per depasta buceta reboantes: Again, Sidonius expands Vergil's bucolic scenery; see Verg. *Ecl.* 7.2 *compulerantque greges Corydon et Thyrsis in unum* ('Corydon and Thyrsis have assembled their herds at the same place'). To describe the cattle, Sidonius adds the adjective *tinnibulatus*, 'belled', 'wearing bells', a hapax; Gualandri (1979) 180. The MS T has *tintinnabulatos*; the corresponding noun *tintin(n)abulum*, 'bell' (*OLD* 1943), is also used of the bells animals wear, for example in Phaedr. 2.7.5. Fernández López (1994) 259 suggests that the repetitions of -*t* and -*i* in this passage imitate the shepherd's flutes and the sounds of the bells the animals wear. *Depasta*, 'grazed by animals' (*TLL* 5.1, 561.39–71), probably also echoes Verg. *Ecl.* 1.53–5 *hinc tibi, quae semper, vicino ab limite saepes* | *Hyblaeis apibus florem depasta salicti* | *saepe levi somnum suadebit inire susurro* ('from the nearby border, the hedge, whose flowering willow bushes are grazed by bees from Hybla, will invite you to slumber, often with a gentle buzz'). See the similar passage in Sidon. *Ep.* 7.6.8 *videas armenta ... herbosa viridantium altarium latera depasci* ('you can see the cattle grazing the grassy sides of the green altars'); van Waarden (2010) 322, Montone (2017) 29. The participle *depastus* is also used in Sidon. *Carm.* 22.4 v. 189 (of a fire) *flamma ... depasta trabes* ('the fire devours the logs'). *Bucetum*, 'pasture for cattle', 'cow-pasture' (*TLL* 2, 2231.23–34) is a rarely used word; see Luc. 9.185, Gell. 11.1.1. *Reboare*, 'to re-echo', 'to resound' (*OLD* 1578), in Sidonius' letters is only used here, but it does also appear in *Carm.* 5.495, 8.10, 23.420. Among earlier works that use this poetic verb are Verg. *Georg.* 3.223, Catull. 63.21.

Quae tamen varia vocum cantuumque modulamina profundius confovendo sopori tuo lenocinabuntur: All these animal sounds mix and form a calming background noise for the guest and help him fall asleep. For the idea of a sound sleep in the quiet surroundings of a villa, see Mart. 1.49.35–6, where Martial also writes about an ideal lifestyle. See also Hor. *Carm.* 3.1.20–22, about the sleep of the innocent in the countryside. The expression *varia vocum cantuumque modulamina* echoes Manil. 4.153 *per varios cantus modulataque vocibus ora* ('through various chants and harmonious sounds and mouths that make sounds'); Montone (2017) 29. *Modulamen*, 'melody', 'euphony' (*TLL* 8, 1243.46–4.14), first appears in Gell. 13.21.16; after that it is not used again until the fourth century. It also appears in Sidon. *Carm.* 1.9 *Castalidumque chorus vario modulamine plausit* ('And the choir of the Castalian muses applauded with varied melody'). For *profundius*, 'deeper', of sleep, see the examples in *TLL* 10.2, 1754.1–7, for example Alc. Avit. *Hom.* 6, p. 112.8 *sopitum profundius Dominum nostrum interrita quiete iacuisse* ('and our Lord lay there deeply asleep in undisturbed peace'). *Confoveo*, 'to warm', 'foster' (*TLL* 4, 252.1–71), is postclassical and mostly used by Christian writers. *Lenocinor*, 'to pander', 'flatter' (*TLL* 7.2, 1153.56–4.17), is used with things as subjects, as in Sidon. *Ep.* 2.13.5, Plin. *Ep.* 1.8.6, 2.19.7, and with persons, for example in Sidon. *Ep.* 8.1.1.

Section 15

Porticibus egresso, si portum litoris petas, in area virenti vulgare, quamquam non procul nemus: After the description of the house Sidonius leaves the building and describes the garden and its use. For *porticus*, see the commentary on *Ep.* 2.2.10 *Ab ortu lacum porticus intuetur*. Most modern translators interpret *vulgare* as second-person singular passive of the verb *vulgo*, 'to expose to public view' (*OLD* 2121, 3d), as the ending on *-re* is a variant of the more common ending on *-ris*; see Loyen (1970a) 50 'on se trouve exposé à la vue, sur un espace gazonné', Visser (2014) 37 'you come into a green park', Köhler (2014) 47 'kommst du auf einen offenen, grünen Platz'. In the epic of Lucan to which Sidonius probably alludes, *vulgaris*, however, is an adjective, 'common to or shared by all' (*OLD* 2121, 5a): Luc. 5.219–20 *dumque a luce sacra, qua vidit fata, refertur | ad volgare iubar, mediae venere tenebrae* ('when she returned from the holy light, where she saw the future, to the sunlight, darkness came over her'). Lucan here describes how the Delphic prophetess returns into daylight after her prophecy. Anderson (1936) 430–1 thus emends the text to *vulgare iubar*, 'exposed to the light of common day'. *Nemus* denotes not only a wood or forest, but is also used of groups of trees (*OLD* 1170, 1c). For *nemus* as part of a villa garden, see Ruric. *Ep.* 1.11.1 *quoniam amoenitati nemoris vestri ... voluistis adiungi* ('as you wanted to add to the pleasantness of your forest'); see also Plin. *Nat.* 12.13 *nemora tonsilia* ('trees, cut in shape'). The younger Pliny mentions forests several times in his villa letters, as they contribute to the the pleasure they offer: Plin. *Ep.* 5.6.7, 5.6.19, 5.6.39.

ingentes tiliae duae conexis frondibus, fomitibus abiunctis unam umbram non una radice conficiunt: Using various stylistic devices, Sidonius depicts the connection between the two trees also on a stylistic level. There is a chiasmus (*conexis frondibus, fomitibus abiunctis*), a figura etymologica (words with the same etymological derivation are used in the same passage) (*unam .. una*) and there are alliterations (on *f-* and *u-*). For *fomes*, 'branch', see the commentary on *Ep.* 2.2.3 *Mons ab occasu ... fomite effundit*. The *tilia*, 'lime tree', is used for timber; see Verg. *Georg.* 1.173, 2.449, 4.183. In Ov. *Met.* 8.611–724 the old couple Philemon and Baucis are metamorphosed into two trees, one of them a lime tree.

In cuius opacitate, cum me meus Ecdicius inlustrat: Of his numerous visitors, Sidonius highlights one in particular by calling him by name, his brother-in-law Ecdicius. After the first letter of book two, which is addressed to Ecdicius and shows him as a capable military leader, the second letter focuses on private friendship matching the overriding theme of leisure in the second book. For Ecdicius' biography, see the introduction to *Ep.* 2.1. Though Sidonius and Ecdicius sit in the shadow of the trees (*umbra*, *opacitas*), the guest brings light through his presence; cf. Anderson (1936) 430–31 n. 2. Sidonius is very fond of this kind of subtle wordplay, cf. the commentary on *Ep.* 2.2.13 *Edulibus terminatis … aestuosum, maxime aestivum*. *Opacitas*, 'shadiness', 'shade', is used here in the usual construction with a *genitivus inhaerentiae* (*TLL* 9.2, 655.79–82). The verb *illustro*, 'to light up', 'make light', 'illuminate', is used here simultaneously in the concrete and in the figurative sense ('to visit') (*TLL* 7.1, 399.39–52).

pilae vacamus: Playing with a *pila*, 'ball', was among the very favourite pastimes in Greco-Roman antiquity. One played ball in public baths or places, as well as in private villas, as here. The balls were of different sizes and weights, and made of different materials (filled with feathers, air or hair); see for example Mart. 4.19.6–7, 7.32.7, 14.45–8. Famous men like the emperor Augustus (see Suet. *Aug.* 83) or the younger Cato (see Sen. *Ep.* 104.33) were known to have a predilection for playing ball; Mendner (1956) 118–28, Väterlein (1976) 61–98, Hurschmann (1997), Amherdt (2001) 176–8, Lucht (2011) 87–8. Sidonius writes in *Ep.* 5.17.6 that he himself likes to play ball as much as he likes to read – *sphaerae primus ego signifer fui, quae mihi, ut nosti, non minus libro comes habetur* ('I was the first leader of the ball, which is, as you know, no less than a book my companion') – and often refers to ball games; see Schwitter (2015) 72–7 and for *sphaeristerium* as a place for playing ball see the commentary below on *Ep.* 2.2.15 *atque illic aleatorium … sphaeristerio faciat*. In *Ep.* 2.9.4 playing ball appears as part of the daily routine of aristocrats in the countryside and Sidonius describes a certain kind a ball play in detail; see the commentary on *Ep.* 2.9.4 *Vix quodcumque vestibulum intratum, et ecce huc sphaeristarum….* For *vacare* see the commentary on *Ep.* 2.2.11 *Quo loci recumbens, si quid inter edendum vacas….*

sed hoc eo usque, donec arborum imago contractior intra spatium ramorum recussa cohibeatur: This is the only instance where *imago*, 'image', means 'shadow' (*TLL* 7.1, 408.81–2); Gualandri (1979) 97–8. For the whole image of a shadow that becomes smaller, see Ov. *Met.* 3.144 *iamque dies medius rerum contraxerat umbras* ('and already noon has contracted the shadows'). For *recutere*, 'drive back', see Sidon. *Ep.* 7.1.4, *Carm.* 2.427–8; van Waarden (2010) 107–8.

atque illic aleatorium lassis consumpto sphaeristerio faciat: Sidonius draws a vivid picture to illustrate the reduction of the shadow and the effect on his daily routine. Depending on the size of the trees' shadow the shady place under them serves Sidonius and Ecdicius first as a *sphaeristerium*, 'a place for playing ball', and later as an *aleatorium*, 'a place for games of chance'. Both activities count among the pastimes in the daily routine of a villa; Mielsch (1987) 128. Sidonius mentions them among others like reading, writing, riding a horse, running and swimming also in *Ep.* 2.9.4 (see there for *sphaerista*, 'ball-player'), *Ep.* 3.3.2 (also about Ecdicius playing) *hic primum tibi pila pyrgus ... ludo fuere* ('here you first played with ball and dice-box'), 4.4.1, 5.17.6–7, 8.11.8, 8.12.5, *Carm.* 23.490–94; Carter (1990) 229–30, Kaufmann (1995) 112–13. Games of dice were very popular among members of all classes. One played with different types and numbers of dice (*tesserae*) and a cup (*fritillus*), often as entertainment before a meal; see Sidon. *Ep.* 2.9.4, Macrob. *Sat.* 1.5.11; Rossiter (1991) 201, Köhler (1995) 153–4, Amherdt (2001) 176–8, Hurschmann (2002b), Lucht (2011) 51. Sidonius refers to dice games (without mentioning ball games) also in *Ep.* 1.2.7, 8.8.1, 8.12.5. *Aleatorius*, 'belonging to gamblers or games of chance' (*TLL* 1, 1523.11–17, *OLD* 94), is a very rarely used adjective (see Cic. *Phil.* 2.67, Gell. 18.13.6, Sidon. *Ep.* 2.9.4) and only used here as a substantive. In *Ep.* 5.17.6 Sidonius uses the noun *aleator* instead. *Sphaeristerium*, 'a place for playing ball' or 'a game at ball' (*OLD* 1804), is the last of the Greek *termini technici* announced in section 2.2.8; see the commentary on *Ep.* 2.2.8 *si graecari mavis* .... It is the Latinised form of σφαιριστήριον and derives from σφαῖρα, 'ball' (for *sphaera*, see *Ep.* 5.17.6). A *sphaeristerium* was often an element of a private villa or public baths, but the term *palaestra* is more common (*TLL* 10.1, 98.54–9.8), as in Cic. *Att.* 2.4.7; Yegül (1992) 37, Nielsen (1990) 163–5. The term that actually designates the place is here transferred to the game; Gualandri (1979) 156 n. 44. For a *sphaeristerium* in a shady place, see Plin. *Ep.* 2.17.12, about his villa Laurentinum: *nec procul sphaeristerium quod calidissimo soli inclinato iam die occurrit* ('and not far away is my place for playing ball which only in the evening lies in the hottest sun'). In the villa Tusci, the *sphaeristerium* is on the first floor, above the bath: Plin. *Ep.* 5.6.27 *apodyterio superpositum est sphaeristerium, quod plura genera exercitationis pluresque circulos capit* ('above the undressing room is the place for playing ball, which offers room for various kind of exercises and many groups of players'); see also Stat. *Silv.* 1.5.57–9, Suet. *Vesp.* 20.1. Romans used to do sports before a bath, as a type of preparation for it; see for example Plin. *Ep.* 3.1.8, Mart. 7.32.7–8, 12.82.1–6, 14.163, Sen. *Ep.* 56.1; Busch (1999) 404–7. Here, Sidonius changes the order and starts with the bath, perhaps so as not to deter his addressee, while in *Ep.* 2.9 he maintains the traditional order: sports before bath.

Section 16

Sed quia tibi, sicut aedificium solvi, sic lacum debeo, quod restat agnosce: Following the description of his estate, Sidonius dedicates sections 16–19 to the nearby lake, probably Lake Aydat. He thus changes the topic and adds the description of a natural wonder, whereas Pliny treats villa (*Ep.* 2.17, 5.6) and lake (*Ep.* 4.30.2, 8.20) separately. Again, Sidonius is innovative and does not simply follow his predecessor; Whitton (2013) 235. He adds to his villa a portrait of wild nature and gives his letter a bucolic twist, whereas Pliny represents his villa as a place of manmade culture; Visser (2014) 40. According to Hanaghan (2019) 46, Sidonius presents his lake as a sea to position his villa against Pliny's villas, both of which have sea vistas. Sidonius describes the lake near his estate also in *Carm.* 18.8 *aequora si nostri cerneret illa lacus* ('if she saw the waters of our lake'); Busch (1999) 73. The description of the natural wonder in sections 16–19 is again influenced by Vergil, Pliny the Elder and Ausonius. At the same time, Sidonius coins a new expression, attested only here, in the description of his lake, which is very dear to him. For the size of the lake, see Sidon. *Ep.* 2.2.17. *Solvere* here means 'keeping the promise to do something', also used in Sidon. *Ep.* 9.3.3; see van Waarden (2010) 545 on *Ep.* 7.10.2 *vel verba solventi* ('because I pay at least my due of words').

Lacus in Eurum defluus meat, eiusque harenis fundamenta impressa domicilii ventis motantibus aestuans umectat alluvio: The lake is not a calm body of water but is moved by strong winds, and access to it is difficult because of its muddy shore. Eurus, from Greek εὖρος, 'the south-east wind', is poetic, especially in epic, for 'the east' (*TLL* 5.2, 1080.30–50); see Luc. 8.812, Stat. *Theb.* 2.379, Val. Fl. 1.538. Sidonius uses the word also in *Ep.* 9.13.5 v. 118. The adjective *defluus*, 'flowing down', 'moving downwards' (*TLL* 5.1, 365.50–61), is not widely used, but appears several times in Sidonius: *Ep.* 2.9.9, 2.12.1, *Carm.* 22.4 v. 110. The adjective is first attested in Stat. *Theb.* 9.325 and *Silv.* 1.3.54; Delhey (1993) 122. Symm. *Orat.* 2.23 uses the adjective in connection with the River Rhine. Visser (2014) 40 claims that *eiusque harenis fundamenta impressa* is a reference to Matth. *Evang.* 7.26 *similis erit viro stulto qui aedificavit domum suam supra harenam* ('he will be similar to the stupid man who built his house on sand'). The frequentative *moto*, 'to keep moving', 'stir', 'agitate' (*TLL* 8, 1531.82–2.6), is also attested elsewhere in combination with wind; see Verg. *Ecl.* 5.5, Serv. *Georg.* 2.437. *Aestuo*, 'to rage', 'to burn', is also used in the sense of 'to fluctuate' (of the sea and streams) (*TLL* 1, 1113.43–63), especially in epic; see for example Verg. *Aen.* 6.297, Luc. 10.247. Sidonius uses the verb several times in a transferred sense: Sidon. *Ep.* 4.3.6 *vernat ut Hortensius aestuat ut Cethegus* ('he blooms like Hortensius, he rages like Cethegus'), 8.7.4, 8.11.6, 8.14.5. The manuscripts LNV have *umectat*, while the other manuscripts have *humectat*. *Alluvio*, 'force of water', 'inundation' (*TLL* 1, 1700.69–701.19), is Late Latin, attested since Apul. *Mund.* 23 and used several times in Augustine, for example Aug. *Civ.* 12.12.

Is quidem sane circa principia sui solo palustri voraginosus et vestigio inspectoris inadibilis: The phrase describing the muddy area full of pools at the beginning of the lake is reminiscent of *Bell. Hisp.* 29.2 *rivus ... palustri et voraginoso solo currens erat ad dextrum* ('the small stream runs on the right side through a marshy and swampy ground'). See also Plin. *Nat.* 36.95, on the building of the temple for Artemis in Ephesos: *in solo id palustri fecere* ('they built it on swampy ground'). The adjective *paluster* or *palustris*, 'marshy', 'swampy' (*TLL* 10.1, 179.72–80.18), occurs several times together with place names in various authors. In connection with a lake it is also used in Vitr. 8.3.7 (about lakes in Egypt). *Voraginosus*, 'full of holes or chasms', 'muddy', 'swampy' (*OLD* 2103), is a rarely used adjective, and also appears in Sidon. *Carm.* 23.421–2, about the sea, *voraginoso,* | *quae vallat sale Bosphorum Propontis* ('nor Propontis, which the Bosporus with its voraginous salty waves surrounds with a wall'), and in *Ep.* 5.13.1, about a street. See also Apul. *Met.* 9.9.1 *viam ... lacunosis incilibus voraginosam* ('a street full of potholes and cracks'), Ruric. *Ep.* 1.17.2 *semitam ... caeno voraginosam* ('a path full of potholes because of the mud'). For adjectives ending in -*osus*, see the commentary on *Ep.* 2.2.18 *Lacus ipse ... flexuosus nemorosusque.... Vestigium* denotes 'footprint', 'track' as well as 'a movement of the foot in walking', 'step' (*OLD* 2048, 1a, and 2049, 4a). The noun *inspector*, 'a viewer', 'observer' (*TLL* 7.1, 1946.26–43), is first found in Sen. *Ben.* 1.9.3 and also used in Sidon. *Ep.* 6.12.3. *Inadibilis*, 'unapproachable', 'inaccessible' (*TLL* 7.1, 808.49–64), is a rarely used adjective, but is similarly used in Cassiod. *Hist. Eccl.* 11.18.7 in combination with *terra*. See Amherdt (2001) 199 on *Ep.* 4.6.1 (*culpabiles*) on the preference of Late Antique authors for adjectives ending in -*bilis*. Notice the alliteration on *v*- and *in*- at the end of this clause.

ita limi bibuli pinguedo coalescit ambientibus sese fontibus algidis, litoribus algosis: Sidonius describes the mud in a vivid picture. For *limus*, 'mud', see the commentary on *Ep.* 2.2.1 *squalet glarea in vadis, limus in ripis....*

Bibulus, 'drinking readily', 'thirsty', transferred to inanimate objects 'that suck in or absorb moisture' (*TLL* 2, 1968.71–69.32), is first attested in Lucr. 2.376 *bibulam … harenam* ('the thirsty sand'). See also Sidon. *Ep.* 1.5.4 *soli* ('soil'), 5.17.10 v. 4 and 9.13.5 v. 19 *vellus* ('fleece'), 9.11.9 *atomos* ('particle'); Gualandri (1979) 135 n. 99, Köhler (1995) 196. In Sidon. *Ep.* 8.3.2 we have the pejorative adjective *bibax*, 'drunken'. For *pinguedo*, 'fatness', 'fat', see the commentary above on *Ep.* 2.2.12 *et illam … quadam quasi pinguedine*…. In the expression *fontibus algidis, litoribus algosis* we have a parallel construction and a wordplay with two similar-sounding words. The first one, *algidus*, 'cold' (*TLL* 1, 1544.52–71), is already attested in Naevius and Catullus, but more frequent in Late Latin authors like Martianus Capella and Ennodius. The second one, *algosus*, 'abounding in seaweed' (*TLL* 1, 1545.51–4), is a rarely used adjective, but also used in Ausonius' description of mussels taken from the south of Gaul: Auson. *Ep.* 15.42–3 *set primore vado post refugum mare | algoso legitur litore concolor* ('but after the sea has receded they are picked in the nearest shallows, matching in colour a shore full of seaweed'); see also Sidon. *Ep.* 8.9.5 v. 33, Plin. *Nat.* 32.95. Again (on *salar* see the commentary above on *Ep.* 2.2.12 *scilicet ut nocturnis per lacum excursibus rapacissimi salares*…), Sidonius gives his villa ecphrasis a distinctly Gallic hue; Hanaghan (2019) 44. For adjectives ending in *-osus*, see the commentary on *Ep.* 2.2.18 *Lacus ipse … flexuosus nemorosusque*….

Attamen pelagi mobilis campus cumbulis late secatur pervagabilibus, si flabra posuere: Sidonius' lake is navigable and used by boats when there is no wind. The sentence is full of poetic allusions and unusual words. First, *pelagi mobilis campus* is reminiscent of Sen. *Herc. Fur.* 540 *stat pontus, vicibus mobilis annuis* ('the sea is calm, then again agitated according to the time of the year'); Squillante (2014) 221. The adjective *mobilis*, 'easy to be moved', is frequently used of liquids and especially the sea; see Ov. *Her.* 2.128 (*aequor*) and further examples in *TLL* 8, 1196.45–56. See also the commentary on *Ep.* 2.12.1 *Misisti tu quidem lembum mobile*…. A *cymbula*, 'a small boat', is the diminutive of *cymba*, from Greek κύμβη. The word is very rarely used; see *TLL* 4, 1589.72–9, Montebelli (2009) 140–1. Sidonius thereby probably alludes to Plin. *Ep.* 8.20.7, where it is used in his letter about a lake with floating islands, which are similar to small boats: *saepe minores maioribus velut cumbulae onerariis adhaerescunt* ('frequently the smaller ones adhere to the bigger like small boats to transport ships'). The spelling of *cumbulis* varies in the different manuscripts. The manuscripts MTP have *cymbulis*, F *cimbulis*, C *cimbalis*, while Lütjohann (1887) 26, Anderson (1936) 430 and Loyen

(1970a) 51 emend to *cumbulis*, which I find convincing because of the parallel passage in Pliny. *Pervagabilibus*, 'ranging or sweeping through', is a Sidonian hapax (*TLL* 10.1, 1836.53–5). Similarly, Sidonius creates many other adjectives through suffixation; Wolff (2020) 398. For adjectives ending in -*bilis*, see the commentary on *Ep.* 2.2.16 *Is quidem ... vestigio inspectoris inadibilis.* The verb *pervagor*, from which it derives, is already attested in Cic. *Verr.* 2.5.37, in the context of sailing: *hic te praetore praedonum naviculae pervagatae sunt* ('here, during your praetorship, the boats of the pirates sailed around'). The plural word *flabra*, 'blasts', 'breezes', 'winds' (*TLL* 6.1, 833.5–42), is poetic for wind; for examples see Lucr. 6.428, Verg. *Georg.* 2.293. For an example of winds calming down, see Verg. *Aen.* 7.27–8 *cum venti posuere omnisque repente resedit | flatus et in lento luctantur marmore tonsae* ('when the winds calmed and every blowing suddenly stopped and in the immobile sea the oars were struggling'). For examples of winds stirring up the waves or calming them down, see also Hor. *Carm.* 1.3.16, describing a ship carrying Vergil to Greece: *tollere seu ponere volt freta* ('whether he wants to stir up or to calm down the waves'). Stoehr-Monjou (2013) 148 interprets the allusion to Horace as follows: 'The choice of Horace exalts Sidonius' estate, but the light contextual discrepancy wittily underlines the slippage towards a more prosaic reality'.

si turbo austrinus insorduit, immane turgescit: Next, Sidonius describes how the strong south wind stirs up the waves of the lake; see also Sidon. *Ep.* 9.9.6 in a figurative sense about the storm of angry nations: *cuius immanis hinc et hinc turbo tunc inhorruerat* ('which had surged up in an awful whirlwind on every side'). In this sentence he probably alludes to Rutilius Namatianus, who is the first Latin writer to employ the rarely used verb *insordescere*, 'to become dirty or foul', 'to darken' (*TLL* 7.1, 1942.73–81): Rut. Nam. 1.616–17 *aptabam nitido pendula vela Noto, | cum subitis tectus nimbis insorduit aether* ('I adjusted the hanging sails to the clear south wind when the overcast sky became darkened by rising clouds'). It is also used in Sidon. *Ep.* 4.12.3, 5.13.1; Amherdt (2001) 315, Kelly (2020b) 154–5. The poetic adjective *austrinus*, 'southern', is probably inspired by Rutilius Namatianus' *Noto*, 'the south wind' (*TLL* 2, 1562.25–56), and it is frequently used in Plin. *Nat.*, for example at 2.123, 17.11. *Turgesco*, 'to begin to swell' (*OLD* 1993), is mainly used of plants or in the figurative sense in relation to an inflated or bombastic style, but only here of winds. According to Squillante (2014) 222, another intertext of the passage may be Ov. *Trist.* 1.2.25 *inter utrumque fremunt immani murmure venti* ('inbetween the winds howl with a terrible roaring').

ita ut arborum comis, quae margini insistunt, superiectae asperginis fragor impluat: The waves are so high that a crash of falling spray rains down on the leaves of the trees that stand at the edge. *Coma*, 'the hair of the head', is frequently used in a figurative sense for objects resembling the hair in appearance or in its ornamental effect, especially of grass or leaves. The combination with a 'tree' (*arbor*) is common; there are examples in *TLL* 3, 1752.75–4.37, such as Ov. *Rem.* 196, Gell. 19.12.9, Hier. *Ep.* 60.12. Gualandri compares the expression *superiectae asperginis fragor impluat* to Ov. *Met.* 1.572–3 *summisque adspergine silvis* | *impluit* ('it rains upon the top of the trees with sprinkling') about the River Peneus, which noisily runs through the Tempe valley and Sidon. *Carm.* 22.4 vv. 132–3 *excutitur torrens ipsisque aspergine tectis* | *impluit* ('a torrent leaps forth and rains upon the roofs with its spray') about the confluence of the Rivers Garonne and Dordogne; Gualandri (1979) 87–8 and Gualandri (2020) 287. The use of *superiacere*, 'to cast or throw over or upon' (*OLD* 1875, 1a), is rare in connection with water but see Verg. *Aen.* 11.625–6, Hor. *Carm.* 1.2.11; Gualandri (1979) 88 n. 41. *Aspergo*, 'a sprinkling', 'besprinkling', 'moisture', is first attested in Cato. *Agr.* 128. The meaning of 'spray of the sea' (*TLL* 2, 817.28–18.35), is poetic and first attested in Verg. *Aen.* 3.534 *obiectae salsa spumant aspergine cautes* ('and projecting rocks are foaming with salty sprinkling'). The noun *fragor*, 'a crashing', 'crash', 'noise', is common for natural forces such as the sea or rivers; see the examples in *TLL* 6.1, 1233.64–4.2. Pliny uses *fragor* as well as *aspergo* in his villa letter about the effect of the sea, in Plin. *Ep.* 2.17.13 *quod turbati maris non nisi fragorem et sonum patitur* ('which, when the sea is turbulent, only allows its noisy sound to be heard') and Plin. *Ep.* 2.17.14 *buxus … quamquam longinqua aspergine maris inarescit* ('the boxwood withers when exposed to the sea spray, even from a long distance'). Pliny uses *aspergo* also of the spray of a fountain in Plin. *Ep.* 5.6.20 *aqua exundat circumiectasque platanos et subiecta platanis leni aspergine fovet* ('the water overflows and nourishes the plane trees around and the ground below with a light spray'). Whitton (2013) 240 interprets Sidonius' oxymoron *asperginis fragor impluat* as a reflex of Pliny's letter. Sidonius uses the term similarly in *Carm.* 2.336. More frequently, he uses *fragor* to denote the applause of an audience, or the noise of men in general: *Carm.* 2.146, 5.592, 7.571, 7.586, 23.376, 23.416, *Ep.* 1.9.7, 1.10.2, 1.11.11, 1.11.15, 4.25.2, 7.17.2 v. 15, 8.3.2, 9.13.5 v. 110, 9.14.8. It is also used of a trumpet (*tuba*) in *Carm.* 5.408, and of falling leaves in autumn in *Ep.* 4.15.3.

Section 17

Ipse autem secundum mensuras quas ferunt nauticas in decem et septem stadia procedit: The next section deals with the extent of the lake and its stock of fish. Lake Aydat today extends about 1,100 m north to south and 850 m west to east; the circumference is around 5.5 km, the surface about 0.65 km² (0.25 square miles). According to Sidonius, the lake used to be bigger. The ancient Greek measurement unit *stadium* – used by the Romans for nautical and astronomical measurements – denotes 'a stade' (*OLD* 1813, 2a), which is 625 *pedes*, a distance equal to 606 feet 9 inches or 184.95 m. Seventeen *stadia* are thus equal to 21/8 Roman miles, or two miles or 3.2 km; Stevens (1933) 186, Anderson (1936) 431 n. 4. The adjective *nauticus*, 'belonging to ships or sailors', 'ship-', 'nautical' (*TLL* 9.1, 256.42–8.39), is not combined with *mensura* elsewhere. *Procedere* with accusative is commonly used to indicate a distance (*TLL* 10.2, 1500.11–30).

fluvio intratus, qui salebratim saxorum obicibus affractus spumoso canescit impulsu et nec longum scopulis praecipitibus exemptus lacu conditur: Next, Sidonius describes the foaming river that flows into the lake. Mratschek (2020b) 250 refers to Plin. *Ep.* 4.30.2, on the spring flowing into Lake Como, as a parallel for the rocky stretch of river described here: *fons oritur in monte, per saxa decurrit ... in Larium lacum decidit* ('A spring rises in the mountains, hurries over rocks to the valley and ... pours into lake Larius'). There is also a waterfall with white spray in Pliny's villa; see Plin. *Ep.* 5.6.24 *nam ex edito desiliens aqua suscepta marmore albescit* ('because the water falls down from above and is caught in a basin of marble and foams white'). For *intrare*, 'to flow in' (of a river into a body of water), see the examples in *TLL* 7.2, 61.71–81, such as Val. Fl. 2.11. The adverb *salebratim*, 'ruggedly', 'roughly', is a Sidonian hapax (derived from *salebra*, 'irregularity', 'unevenness'; *OLD* 1680). Sidonius likes adverbs ending on *-tim* because of their archaic ring. Quite a few of them are attested only in Sidonius, for example *Ep.* 5.14.1 *cavernatim* ('through caverns'), 5.17.8 *trochleatim* ('with a block'); Gualandri (1979) 177 n. 111, Amherdt (2001) 130. The verb *adfrangere*, 'to strike upon or against something' (*TLL* 1, 1247.8–13) is attested only here and in Stat. *Theb.* 5.150, 10.47, *Silv.* 5.1.36. *Canescere* means 'to whiten', 'grow white' (*TLL* 3, 249.63–50.23), but Sidonius uses the verb also in the meaning of 'to become hoary' in *Ep.* 3.13.7. Rivers are described as *spumosus* elsewhere, for example Verg. *Aen.* 12.524, Ov. *Met.* 1.570. For the combination of *canescere* and *spumosus*, 'covered with foam', see *OLD*

1811 and, for example, Avien. *Phaen.* 1486 *spumosum late pelagus canescere cernes* ('you will see how the foamy sea turns white everywhere'), Hier. *Ep.* 1.2 *spumei fluctus canescunt* ('the foaming waves turn white'). For adjectives ending in *-osus*, see the commentary on *Ep.* 2.2.18 *Lacus ipse ... flexuosus nemorosusque....* The adjective also appears in Sidon. *Ep.* 7.8.1, with a transferred meaning about actions. *Exemptus* is the participle of *eximo*, 'to take away', 'remove'; it appears elsewhere in connection with natural objects (*TLL* 5.2, 1497.15–21), for example in Stat. *Silv.* 5.3.207, about Mount Vesuvius.

quem fors fuat an incurrat an faciat, praeterit certe, coactus per cola subterranea deliquari, non ut fluctibus, sed ut piscibus pauperaretur: In this clause, Sidonius describes how the current carries the fish into some sort of creek or inlet from which they cannot escape. Sidonius continues his series of fishing techniques (see the commentary on *Ep.* 2.2.12 *ut stataria retia...*) by adding a kind of natural fish trap and thus again alludes to Ausonius. Anderson (1936) 432–3 n. 1 offers a lengthy explanation of this natural phenomenon that keeps the fish back so they cannot struggle back to the lake against the current. The manuscripts LN have *fors fuat*, MC have *forfuat* and T *confluat*. Sidonius uses the expression *fors fuat (an)*, 'it might so happen that', 'perchance', 'perhaps' (*TLL* 6.1, 1129.18–32), also in *Ep.* 8.3.6, 9.7.1. The expression is attested from Plaut. *Ps.* 432 onwards and also used a few times in Symmachus' letters, for example Symm. *Ep.* 1.39.2, 4.28.1. *Colum*, 'bow net', 'a net of wicker-work for catching fish' (*TLL* 3, 1729.79–83), is attested only here and in Auson. *Ep.* 13.56–7 *et iacula et fundas et nomina vilica lini | colaque et [...] hamos* ('and darts and slings and rural names of flax and bow nets and hooks'). Fishing with a bow-net is mentioned for example in Plin. *Nat.* 21.114, Opp. *Hal.* 4.47–64; Kuhn (1998), Montebelli (2009) 120–4. *Deliquare*, 'to clarify', 'to strain' (*TLL* 5.1, 464.29–48), is a rarely used verb and only used here of a river. *Pauperare*, 'to impoverish', 'rob', 'deprive' (*TLL* 10.1, 852.18–46), is attested from Plautus onwards; see Plaut. *Mil.* 729, *Ps.* 1128. Sidonius also uses it in *Ep.* 4.11.4, 6.12.3; Amherdt (2001) 292. All manuscripts and Loyen (1970a) 51, Lütjohann (1887) 26 have *pauperaretur*, but Anderson (1936) 432 emends to *pauperetur*.

qui repulsi in gurgitem pigriorem carnes rubras albis abdominibus extendunt: After discussing fishing techniques, Sidonius alludes to Ausonius again in describing the look of the fish, specifically Auson. *Mos.*

104–5 *praesignis maculis capitis, cui prodiga nutat | alvus opimatoque fluens abdomine venter* ('it is remarkable because of the spots on its head and its lavish stomach and overflowing belly shake because of the fat paunch'). In *Carm.* 18.9–10 (cited in the commentary on *Ep.* 2.2.12 *scilicet ut nocturnis per lacum...*) Sidonius similarly refers to the fish in his lake. The adjective *piger*, 'unwilling', 'backward', 'slow-moving' (*TLL* 10.1, 2109.27–52, *OLD* 1378, 2a), is used elsewhere for streams or bodies of water, for example in Plin. *Ep.* 4.30.9. For *abdomen*, 'lower part of the belly', 'abdomen' (*TLL* 1, 59.39–46), of fish, see Auson. *Mos.* 105, Plin. *Nat.* 9.48. Sidonius uses the term also for a man's (Gnatho's) belly in *Ep.* 3.13.9. Athen. 7.302 d–f, 9.399 c–d writes about the special quality of the belly-cut of fish.

ita illis nec redire valentibus nec exire permissis quendam vivum et circumlaticium carcerem corpulentia facit: Sidonius recapitulates the lake's special quality as a natural fish trap with a triple alliteration on *-c*. *Circumlaticius*, 'that may be carried around', from *circumferre*, is a Sidonian hapax (*TLL* 3, 1153.3–6). *Corpulentia* in the meaning of 'corpulence', 'grossness or fleshiness of the body' (*TLL* 4, 997.11–20), is uncommon, but see Plin. *Nat.* 11.283. Sidonius uses the noun also in *Ep.* 3.13.9 (again of Gnatho), 5.13.1 (a whale), 7.14.3 (men in general).

Section 18

Lacus ipse, qua dexter, incisus flexuosus nemorosusque, qua laevus, patens herbosus aequalis: In this section, Sidonius describes the lake's shores and its characteristic plants from all directions, starting with the south-western part, followed by the eastern, northern and western shores. For the lake's dimensions, see the commentary on *Ep.* 2.2.17 *Ipse autem ... in decem et septem stadia procedit*. The right and the left side of the lake are described with a similar verbal structure. On this less common tripartite clause and its third member connected by *-que*, see van Waarden (2010) 58, 404, Appendix F. *Incisus* is the participle of *incidere*, 'to cut into', 'to cut through', here in the rare use of an adjective meaning 'cleft' (*TLL* 7.1, 910.65–76). The word appears in two other instances in Sidonius' letters in the more common sense of 'engraved (in marble or metal)' (*TLL* 7.1, 907.49–8.27): *Ep.* 2.8.2, 5.3.4, and also for example Hor. *Carm.* 4.8.13. Sidonius frequently uses or coins adjectives ending in *-osus*, expressing abundance, for example in *Ep.* 1.2.6 *suspiriosus* ('breathing deeply'), 1.2.9 *litigiosus* ('quarrelsome'),

1.7.11 *laboriosus* ('laborious'), but he combines three only in this sentence. Adjectives ending in *-osus* are a feature of colloquial diction, appearing often in the comedies of Plautus, Cicero's letters and Petronius' *Satyricon*. But they are also common in Roman poetry, especially in Vergil's *Eclogues* and *Georgics*, and in Ovid's *Metamorphoses*. The adjectives ending in *-osus* therefore create a colloquial and also a poetic impression; Ernout (1949), Knox (1986), Clausen (1994) 37–8. For *flexuosus*, 'full of turns or windings' (*TLL* 6.1, 907.52–62), used of a river bank, see Prob. *Verg. Georg.* 4.371 *Eridani sive Padi ... ripae incisae ut cornua sunt* ('the borders of the Rivers Eridanus or Padus are carved in like horns'). The adjective is also used in Sidon. *Ep.* 5.13.2 *flexuosa calumniarum fraude circumretit* ('he ensnares them in the tortuous deception of false accusations') and 8.11.7 *nunc in alcaico flexuosus* ('now with supple modulation in the Alcaics'). Pliny uses it in his villa letter to describe a plant: Plin. *Ep.* 5.6.36 *acanthus hinc inde lubricus et flexuosus* ('again an acanthus, smooth and full of windings'). For *nemorosus*, see the commentary on *Ep.* 2.2.4 *Balneum ab Africo radicibus nemorosae rupis adhaerescit*. For *herbosus*, 'full of grass or herbs' (*TLL* 6.3, 2625.81–6.27), see Verg. *Georg.* 2.199, Ov. *Met.* 2.689, 15.574, Sidon. *Ep.* 7.6.8; van Waarden (2010) 322. The adjective is used of a river also in Prop. 1.3.6, Auson. *Mos.* 85, Ven. Fort. *Carm.* 7.4.13; Formicola (2009) 101. In the meaning of 'green' (describing marble) it is also used in Sidon. *Carm.* 5.39, 22.4 v. 139; see Delhey (1993) 137 and the commentary on *Ep.* 2.10.4 vv. 14–15 relating to *herbidus*. *Aequalis*, 'smooth', 'even', 'plain' (*TLL* 1, 998.36–64), is used of flat and even surfaces, often the sea. Pliny uses the same adjective in his lake letter: Plin. *Ep.* 8.20.4 *lacus est in similitudinem iacentis rotae circumscriptus et undique aequalis* ('the lake is similar to a lying wheel and is evenly round'). For *aequalis* meaning 'of the same age', see the commentary on *Ep.* 2.8.1 *cui debuerit domi forisque ... aequalis affectum*.

Aequor ab Africo viride per litus, quia in undam fronde porrecta ut glareas aqua, sic aquas umbra perfundit: Trees that are reflected in the water also appear in the other two most important intertexts for Sidonius' lake description: Plin. *Ep.* 8.8.4 and especially Auson. *Mos.* 192–3 *quis color ille vadis, seras cum propulit umbras | Hesperus et viridi perfundit monte Mosellam!* ('what colour is on the water when Hesperus has driven forward the late shadows and overspreads Moselle with the green mountain'); Gualandri (1979) 96–7, Gruber (2013) 179. The water of the lake is as clear as that of the River Vardo, which runs through the estates of Sidonius' relatives Apollinaris and Ferreolus; see *Ep.* 2.9.9. *Aequor*, 'level surface', is very often used of the sea or other bodies of water (*TLL* 1, 1023.71–7.47); it echoes *aequalis* in the previous sentence and connects to the following *ab Africo*. For *ab Africo*, 'in the south-west', see the commentary on *Ep*. 2.2.4 *Balneum ab Africo*.... In *Carm*. 18.7–8 Sidonius uses the same expression about his lake, cited in the commentary on *Ep*. 2.2.12 *scilicet ut nocturnis per lacum*.... For *umbra* meaning 'reflection' (*OLD* 2088, 1c), see Gualandri (1979) 96 n. 77. Statius similarly mentions the reflection of leaves in the water in his description of the villa of Manilius Vopiscus at Tibur: Stat. *Silv*. 1.3.18–19 *fallax responsat imago | frondibus, et longas eadem fugit umbra per undas* ('a deceptive image reflects the leaves and the same shadow flees along the long stream'); see also Stat. *Theb*. 5.52 *Athos nemorumque obscurat imagine pontum* ('Athos darkens the sea with the shadow of its forests'). For *glarea*, 'gravel', see the commentary on *Ep*. 2.2.1 *squalet glarea in vadis*.... The verb *perfundo*, 'to pour over' (*TLL* 10.1, 1422.26–53), is regularly used to describe the spreading of light and colour. Here the shade of the dense foliage covers the lake's surface and causes its green (*viride*) colour.

Huiusmodi colorem ab oriente par silvarum corona continuat: The green row of trees extends from the south-western shore of the lake to its eastern end. The term *corona*, 'a garland', 'chaplet', 'wreath' (*TLL* 4, 987.55–63), is used for mountains and, as here, for trees standing in a circle.

Per Arctoum latus ut pelago natura, sic species: On the northern side, the lake is like the sea in its nature and appearance. The adjective *arctous*, 'pertaining to *arctos*, the Great and the Lesser Bear', hence 'northern' (*TLL* 2, 472.15–69) is attested only from Seneca's tragedies onwards and mostly poetic. It appears also in Sidon. *Carm*. 5.535, 6.26. The word *pelagus* is poetic and is used in post-Augustan prose instead of *mare*, 'the sea'. In *Ep*. 2.2.12 it denotes Sidonius' lake; see the commentary on *Ep*. 2.2.12 *Hinc iam spectabis ... piscator in pelagus*. The sea's agitated, fervent and noisy nature or alternatively its tranquillity are frequently mentioned, especially in Vergil's *Aeneid* (e.g. 1.154, 3.555, 5.870); see *TLL* 10.1, 990.9–49 for further examples. As Hanaghan (2019) 45–6 highlights, Sidonius continually represents his lake as a large body of water similar to the sea and thus competes with Pliny.

A Zephyro plebeius et tumultuarius frutex: Next, Sidonius turns to the *Zephyrus*, 'a gentle west wind', that is, the western part of the lake. This side is covered with 'shrubs' or 'scrub', *frutex* (*TLL* 6.1, 1443.2–6.39), probably a kind of water reed, because the small boats still can go through and over them; see the commentary on *Ep.* 2.2.14 *diluculo autem Philomelam inter frutices sibilantem*. For the collective singular of *frutex*, see Phaedr. 1.11.4. The *frutex* is described as *plebeius*, 'widespread', 'wild' (used of plants also for example in Plin. *Nat.* 13.48, about the date palm; *TLL* 10.1, 2378.25–33), and it is 'casual', *tumultuarius*, 'unplanned' (especially used of fighting and military service; *OLD* 1988, 1c), that is, no gardener plants or weeds them. For *plebeius* (of cloth), see also Sidon. *Ep.* 2.13.6 *plebeio tegmine*. These two attributes are mentioned only here in connection with *frutex*; see *TLL* 6.1, 1446.11–37, Gualandri (1979) 99 n. 84. The adjective *tumultuarius* also appears in connection with a hasty funeral in *Ep.* 3.3.8 (*tumultuarii caespitis mole*) and to describe a poem in *Ep.* 2.10.3; see the commentary on *Ep.* 2.10.3 *Huius igitur … tumultuarium carmen*….

frequenterque lemborum superlabentum ponderibus inflexus: A *lembus* is 'a small fast-sailing vessel with a sharp prow' (*TLL* 7.2, 1136.45–81), attested from Plautus on, for example Plaut. *Bacch.* 279, *Merc.* 193. Sidonius uses the word also in *Ep.* 2.12.1 for a spacious fishing boat and in *Carm.* 7.371 for a pirate ship. The participle *superlabentum* derives from *superlabor*, 'to glide or run over' (*OLD* 1876), and is also used in Sidon. *Ep.* 1.2.5, 3.3.8, but very rarely elsewhere; see Sen. *Ep.* 90.42 of stars (*sidera*).

hunc circa lubrici scirporum cirri plicantur: Sidonius uses the adjective *lubricus* quite often in different contexts; see the commentary above on *Ep.* 2.2.6 *Absunt lubrici … palaestritae*. Here it means 'soft', 'flexible', probably also 'slick', 'slippery' (*TLL* 7.2, 1687.37–42), as the boats can glide over and through the plants. Plin. *Ep.* 5.6.36 similarly denotes a plant: *acanthus hinc inde lubricus et flexuosus* ('again an acanthus, smooth and full of windings'). Gualandri (1979) 100 n. 90 explains *lubricus* as 'not having knots' and refers to the saying *nodum in scirpo quaerere* ('looking for difficulties where there are none'). *Scirpus* denotes 'a marsh plant used for weaving and basket-work' (*OLD* 1706); see Plin. *Nat.* 7.206, 16.178. *Cirrus* appears here in the meaning of 'filaments of plants similar to tufts of hair' (*TLL* 3, 1189.49–53); see Plin. *Nat.* 26.36, 27.25.

simulque pingues ulvarum paginae natant: Here *pinguis*, 'fat', 'thick', 'dense', 'juicy', is applied to (part of) plants; see Plin. *Nat.* 12.42 and further examples in *TLL* 10.1, 2167.9–16). Horace, Hor. *Sat.* 2.4.42, describes a boar (*aper*), which is *ulvis et harundine pinguis* ('fattened by sedges and reed'). *Ulva* is a collective term for aquatic plants, 'swamp-grass', 'sedge' (*OLD*

2087); see Plin. *Nat.* 16.4. *Pagina* is only here used of a plant, meaning 'leaf', 'sheet' (*TLL* 10.1, 91.18–19). The common meaning, which predominates also in Sidonius, is 'a leaf of paper', 'sheet', 'page', 'letter'. As the ancient papyri were made of a similar plant which thrives in marshes and stagnant waters (*Cyperus Papyrus*; see Plin. *Nat.* 13.68–76), Sidonius probably associates it with the plant in his lake and therefore chooses the unusual term *pagina*. Possibly the combination of *pingues* and *paginae* can also be interpreted metapoetically as an allusion to *Ep.* 2.2, which is already quite extensive. See also the commentary above on *Ep.* 2.2.7 *Quid plura? Nihil illis paginis.…*

salicumque glaucarum fota semper dulcibus aquis amaritudo: *Salix* means 'willow', 'osier' (*OLD* 1681); for its very frequent combination with *glaucus*, 'blue-grey', 'grey-green', see the examples noted in *TLL* 6.2, 2039.16–39, *OLD* 766, 1d. An important intertext is Verg. *Georg.* 4.181–2, where the same expression is used in a list of plants the bees feed from: *pascuntur et arbuta passim | et glaucas salices casiamque crocumque rubentem …* ('they feed everywhere from the strawberry tree and the grey willows and the wild cinnamon and the reddish saffron'), and similarly Verg. *Georg.* 2.13 *glauca … salicta* ('the grey willow'). For the bitterness of the willow, which here contrasts with the sweet water, see Verg. *Ecl.* 1.78. Fascione (2019) 27 examines the adjective *glaucus* in Sidonius and shows that it mostly occurs in connection with water, in *Carm.* 5.27, 7.27, 7.371, *Ep.* 8.9.5. v. 31. For *fovere*, 'to nourish' (*TLL* 6.1, 1120.78–21.26), with plants and a body of water, see Sidon. *Ep.* 1.5.4 *quae cuncta virgulta tumultuatim super amnicos margines soli bibuli suco fota fruticaverant* ('for all this undergrowth, nourished on the moisture of the spongy soil, had sprouted confusedly along the river banks') and Plin. *Ep.* 5.6.20 *aqua exundat circumiectasque platanos et subiecta platanis leni aspergine fovet* ('the water overflows and it fosters the plane trees around and the ground below with a light spray'); Gualandri (1979) 99.

Section 19

In medio profundi brevis insula: This and the last sections of Letter 2 go back to the Trojan past and thus once again give greater importance to his estate. This section deals still with the lake. Hanaghan (2019) 46 n. 133 identifies the turning point for the boat races described by Sidonius with the small island in Lake Aydat, called 'île Saint Sidoine' (island of Saint Sidonius). For the use of *in medio* in Sidonius, see Köhler (1995) 201 on Sidon. *Ep.* 1.5.6. The noun *profundum* is derived from the adjective *profundus*, 'deep', and frequently denotes the sea (*TLL* 10.2, 1748.12–9.22), not only in poetry, but also in prose; see Sidon. *Ep.* 8.9.5 v. 33. Less often, it denotes, as here, a 'lake' (or river) (*TLL* 10.2, 1749.23–32); see also Stat. *Silv.* 1.5.54, Mart. 4.30.8.

ubi supra molares naturaliter aggeratos per impactorum puncta remorum navalibus trita gyris meta protuberat: A *molaris* is 'a rock as large as a millstone used as a missile', 'boulder' (*OLD* 1126); see for example Verg. *Aen.* 8.250, Ov. *Met.* 3.59. For adverbs ending in *-(i)ter*, like *naturaliter*, see the commentary on *Ep.* 2.1.1 *Duo nunc pariter mala sustinent*. *Aggeratus* is the participle of *aggero*, 'to heap up', 'to pile up' (*TLL* 1, 1311.27–70), and used in poetic and in post-Augustan prose; see Sidon. *Ep.* 8.12.6. *Gyrus* denotes a circle run by a horse, such as a lap in a race. Sidonius is the only author who uses the word for the course that ships take (*TLL* 6.2, 2386.72–3). For the use of *gyrus*, see also the commentary below on *Ep.* 2.9.4 *inter rotatiles catastropharum gyros* (about the movements of ball players). See also Sidon. *Ep.* 3.12.6 (of years), 4.8.4 (of the bottom of a bowl). *Meta*, 'turning post', 'goal' is also a term from the Roman circus. It denotes the conical colums set in the ground at each end of the circus and thus continues the image, started with *gyrus*. Here *meta* denotes the 'turning-point in the ship-race' (*TLL* 8, 865.12–17), and conveys an epic and above all Vergilian tone; see Verg. *Aen.* 5.129, 5.159, 5.171, and the commentary below on *Ep.* 2.2.19 *Nam moris istic fuit senioribus ... imitari*. Unlike Vergil's turning point, that of Sidonius is a natural phenomenon; Hanaghan (2019) 45–6. The verb *protubero*, 'to swell or bulge out', 'to grow forth' (*TLL* 10.2, 2297.60–72), is rarely used but it is also used in Sidon. *Ep.* 3.13.6 (of warts) and 8.11.12 (of eyes).

ad quam se iucunda ludentum naufragia collidunt: During these boat races there is a shipwreck. Sidonius probably means that the boats capsize and their crew fall into the water. With *iucundus*, 'pleasant', 'agreeable', and *ludere*, 'to play', Sidonius signals that there is no danger – the contestants just playfully hit the mark in the middle of the race circuit. Sidonius uses the term *naufragium*, 'shipwreck' (*TLL* 9.1, 213.39–17.12), also in *Ep.* 8.6.14; elsewhere in his letters it denotes in a transferred meaning a calamity or wreck; see *Ep.* 1.2.8, 8.2.1, 8.12.1, 9.6.2, and the adjective *naufragiosum* in *Ep.* 4.12.1. Sidonius describes a similar scene in *Carm.* 22.4 vv. 133–4 *tollit nautas et saepe iocoso | ludit naufragio* ('it lifts up the sailors and often mocks them with a jesting shipwreck'); Delhey (1993) 134. See also Auson.

Mos. 217–18 *innocuos ratium pulsus pugnasque iocantes | naumachiae* ('or as the harmless collisions of the boats and playful battles of the mock seafight').

Nam moris istic fuit senioribus nostris agonem Drepanitanum Troianae superstitionis imitari: Sidonius' ancestors used to imitate the ship race of Drepana (Sicily). Sidonius focuses on the Arvernians' Trojan ancestry, a subject he also dwells on in *Ep.* 7.7.2 (alluding to Luc. 1.427–8) and *Carm.* 7.139–40. His attempt to join a Trojan line of ancestors and his allusions to Vergil's *Aeneid* are often commented on, for example by Gualandri (1979) 20, Harries (1992) 298, Harries (1994) 187–9, Mratschek (2008) 365, van Waarden (2010) 347–8, Mratschek (2013) 255–7, Hanaghan (2019) 45–6; see the commentary above on 2.2.1 *Arverni tui*. Here Sidonius alludes to Verg. *Aen.* 5.124–286, who describes the ship contest the Trojans held in Sicily after their adventure in Carthage and before they sailed to the Italian mainland. Both regattas have a large stone as a turning point (*meta*); see the commentary above on *Ep.* 2.2.19 *ubi supra ... meta protuberat*. According to Sivonen (2006) 74–6 and Drinkwater (2013) 69–70, the important role models for educated Gauls were great Greeks and Romans, whereas the local Gallic history was nearly forgotten. Hanaghan (2019) 44, on the other hand, focuses not only on the Roman but also on the Gallic elements in Sidonius' villa representation. For the huge power of the Vergilian myth and the *Aeneid*'s impact on Sidonius panegyrics, see Veremans (1991), Bruzzone (2013). Sidonius describes the custom of the Trojans which his ancestors adopted as *superstitio*, 'irrational religious awe or credulity', 'superstition', a term which also was applied without derogatory overtones to foreign or non-orthodox religious practices or doctrines (*OLD* 1878, 1b). Sidonius, though, uses the term pejoratively elsewhere; see *Ep.* 6.12.7 *Eleusinae superstitionis* ('of Eleusinian superstition'), 8.13.1 *sine superstitione religiosum* ('to be religious without superstition') and the adjective *superstitiosus* in 8.6.15 *plus ob hoc tristi quod superstitioso ritu* ('a rite which is all the more tragic for being due to superstition'). For *agon*, again a Greek term meaning 'contest', 'combat in the public games', see *TLL* 1, 1411.39–83. *Drepanitanus* is the adjective 'of Drepanum', a town on the western coast of Sicily, now Trapani (*TLL* 3, 251.60–352.17). *Imitari*, 'to imitate', not only refers to the Avernians imitating the Trojans, but also Sidonius imitating Vergil; Hanaghan (2019) 45.

Iam vero ager ipse, quamquam hoc supra debitum, diffusus in silvis, pictus in pratis, pecorosus in pascuis, in pastoribus peculiosus: The change of theme from the lake back to the natural surroundings of the estate as a whole is rather confusing, as Sidonius has given an overview of the entire complex in section 3, when describing the situation of the villa. According to Hanaghan (2019) 27 it stands out as Sidonius' only statement regarding the productivity of Avitacum, and draws attention to his wealth. Sidonius excuses himself for the length of the letter by explaining that the next sentence about his estate is an addition to the promised description of the villa. This is an announcement of the *brevitas topos* to which section 20 is dedicated; see the commentary on *Ep.* 2.2.20 *daturus hinc veniam, quod brevitatem*.... Sidonius concludes his description of his estate with another example of his stylistic virtuosity. There are alliterations on *-d* and *-p*, parallelisms and, as in section 18, adjectives ending in *-osus*. *Diffusus*, 'extended', 'wide', is frequent with places or buildings (*TLL* 5.1, 1112.29–81). *Pecorosus*, 'rich in cattle', is a rarely used adjective (*TLL* 10.1, 902.14–23), first attested in Prop. 4.9.3, later in Stat. *Theb.* 4.45, 10.229. See also Sidon. *Carm.* 16.18, where it is used about king David: *adsumptum pecorosi de grege Iesse* ('from amid the sheep of Jesse'); Santelia (2012) 95–6. For the profession of *pastor*, 'herdsman', the unfree or dependent workers on Sidonius' estate, see Samson (1992) 220–2, Kaufmann (1995) 242, Mathisen (2020a) 64–7. *Peculiosus*, 'wealthy' (*TLL* 10.1, 928.53–60), is also an unusual adjective, first found in Plaut. *Rud.* 112. For Sidonius' use of adjectives ending in *-osus*, see the commentary on *Ep.* 2.2.18 *Lacus ipse ... flexuosus nemorosusque*....

Section 20

Sed non amplius moror, ne, si longior stilo terminus, relegentem te autumnus inveniat: Sidonius jokingly ends his long letter with another reference to the season, a typical trait of a villa letter. He claims that because of its length it may take Domitius from summer until autumn to read it. The comparative *amplius* is frequently used in the sense of 'longer' (in space or time); see *TLL* 1, 2014.6–38. It counts among Sidonius' favourite words and appears in the second book also in *Ep.* 2.3.2, 2.6.1, 2.9.2, 2.13.4. For the superlative, see the commentary on *Ep.* 2.3.1 *Gaudeo te ... amplissimae dignitatis infulas consecutum*. In Sidonius' work *stilus* can mean 'the use of the stylus' (*OLD* 1820, 3b), that is, the 'action of writing', as well as the instrument, the 'pen' (*OLD* 1820, 4a), for example in *Ep.* 1.9.8, 3.7.2, 4.3.1, 4.17.1. Here one is to imagine that someone should take Sidonius' pen away, because otherwise he will not stop describing his villa; similarly also in *Ep.* 1.2.10 *simul et stilo finem fieri decet* ('it is also fitting that my pen should come to a stop'). More often, though, *stilus* means 'mode of composition', 'style' (*OLD* 1820, 4b); see the commentary below on *Ep.* 2.9.4 *sic tamen quod ... stilus his religiosus inveniebatur*. Pliny also uses the word frequently in both meanings, 'style' (e.g. *Ep.* 1.8.5, 3.18.10, 7.9.7) and 'pen' or 'writing' (e.g. *Ep.* 1.6.1, 4.25.4). *Terminus* means 'the end', 'the point at which an activity stops' (*OLD* 1926, 4). For a similar combination of *stilus* and *terminus*, see Val. Max. 8.7. ext. 9, about Isocrates: *nobilissimum librum ... quartum et nonagesimum annum agens ... conposuit ... neque hoc stilo terminos vitae suae clausit* ('he wrote his very famous book in his ninety-fourth year and he did not close the limits of his life with his pen').

Proinde mihi tribue veniendi celeritatem (nam redeundi moram tibi ipse praestabis): Sidonius adds a very complicated expression for 'come quickly'. Late Antique authors often preferred the *elocutio artifex* over a simple and clear way of expression; Schwitter (2015) 154. At the same time, abstract words such as *celeritas*, 'swiftness', 'quickness', 'speed', are more frequent in Late Latin; Wolff (2020) 404. For the hodotic second singular future *praestabis*, see the commentary on *Ep.* 2.2.12 *videbis in calicibus repente perfusis*.

daturus hinc veniam, quod brevitatem sibi debitam paulo scrupulosior epistula excessit: At the end of the longest letter in the whole collection (*Ep.* 7.9 is even longer, but consists of a letter and an attached speech), Sidonius addresses the need for *brevitas*, one of the most common topoi in epistolography (and other genres); see Demetr. *Eloc.* 228, Iul. Vict. *Rhet.* 27; Curtius (1948) 481–7, Cugusi (1983) 34–5, 69–75, Malherbe (1988), Conring (2001) 7–16, Pausch (2004) 65, Cain (2009) 56 n. 55, Neri (2009) 180, Schwerdtner (2015) 125–33, Fögen (2020). Sidonius also writes about this topic in his other long letters, *Ep.* 1.2.1, 1.2.10 and 7.2.9. In his long letter 1.11, however, he does not apologise, at 1.11.2; Köhler (1995) 276, 288, 296. Sidonius also addresses the topos of *brevitas* and apologises for the undue length at the end of his second villa letter, 2.9; see the commentary on *Ep.* 2.9.10 *Dicerem et cenas ... nostrae loquacitati...*, and in his *Carmina*, see the witty remark in *Carm.* 22.6 *haec me ad defensionis exemplum posuisse sufficiat, ne hace ipsa longitudinis deprecatio longa videatur* ('let this suffice as a specimen of my self-defence, lest this justification of length should itself seem too long'); Consolino (2020) 365–7. An apology for exceeding the customary length is part of the topos as well; van Waarden (2010) 187. To conclude his letter, Sidonius again alludes to Pliny, who also adds apologies for being too long in his villa letter (Plin. *Ep.* 5.6.41, 44) and elsewhere (Plin. *Ep.* 2.5.13, 3.5.20, 7.9.16, 9.13.26); Fögen (2020). As Hanaghan (2020) 122 observes, Sidonius' letter 2.2 is approximately half the length of Pliny's villa letter 5.6, and so he has again outdone Pliny, as he conforms to the conventions of brevity, while Pliny's villa letter appears overly long. The expression *hinc ... quod* to indicate a cause is used elsewhere in Sidonius' letters: *Ep.* 2.8.3 v. 13, 4.11.3, 4.24.5; Amherdt (2001) 290. *Scrupulosus*, 'minutely careful or thorough' (*OLD* 1712, 2), is also used by Pliny for the style or content of one's writings: Plin. *Ep.* 3.5.7 *miraris, quod tot volumina multaque in his tam scrupulosa* ('you wonder that he wrote so many volumes and in them such tricky things') (of his uncle's work); see also Gell. *Praef.* 13 *in his commentariis pauca quaedam scrupulosa et anxia* ('among these notes there are a few careful and solicitous comments'). For adjectives ending in *-osus*, see the commentary on *Ep.* 2.2.18 *Lacus ipse ... flexuosus nemorosusque....* For *epistula* as subject of the letter, see the commentary immediately below on *dum totum ruris situm sollicita rimatur*.

dum totum ruris situm sollicita rimatur: Pliny ends his villa letter with a similar summary, Plin. *Ep.* 5.6.40 *vitassem iam dudum ne viderer argutior, nisi proposuissem omnes angulos tecum epistula circumire* ('I would have avoided appearing too wordy for a long time if I had not promised to go around to all the corners with you in this letter'), and 5.6.44 *cum totam villam oculis tuis subicere conamur* ('when I tried to show you the whole villa'). With *sollicita*, 'anxiously or painstakingly careful, attentive, etc.' (*OLD* 1786, 4a), referring to the subject *epistula*, Sidonius personifies his letter in the manner of Horace, Ovid or Martial, who personify their books; see Hor. *Ep.* 1.20.1–8, Ov. *Trist.* 1.1, 3.1, Mart. 1.3. The verb *rimor*, 'to examine carefully', 'scrutinize', 'explore' (*OLD* 1655, 2 and 3), is also used in Sidon. *Ep.* 1.7.8, 4.2.3, 7.2.8, 8.11.13.

quae tamen summovendi fastidii studio nec cuncta perstrinxit: Sidonius utters his concern that he might be boring (*summovendi fastidii*) on other occasions and combines *fastidium* with various verbs; see *Ep.* 5.2.2, 5.4.2, 5.10.4, 7.10.2, 7.18.4, 8.16.3; van Waarden (2016) 270, Hanaghan (2020) 122. In *Ep.* 5.2.2 Sidonius asks Nymphidius to return a book that he lent him: *si displicuit, debuit movere fastidium* ('if it displeased you, it should have prompted boredom by now'). *Perstringo*, 'to pass over cursorily', 'touch on' (*TLL* 10.1, 1757.17–58), is quite common; it is also used several times in Cicero and Pliny, for example in Cic. *Verr.* 2.4.47, Plin. *Paneg.* 25.1. Sidonius uses it one more time with the same meaning in *Ep.* 7.2.2; van Waarden (2010) 148–9.

Quapropter bonus arbiter et artifex lector: In his final sentence of letter 2.2, Sidonius flatters his reader, who is described as *artifex*. Domitius and, beyond him, the imagined wider audience are assumed to recognise and appreciate the numerous intertextual allusions, thus proving worthy of the author's efforts. According to Gualandri (2020) 313–14, *artifex* implies that the reader is the author's collaborator, as creativity is needed to interpret Sidonius' text. For the adjective and noun *artifex* in Sidonius, see the commentary above on *Ep.* 2.2.6 *quae sicut … devenustat artificem*. The reader is also called an *arbiter*, '(transf.) a judge, umpire', that is, he can distinguish good from bad style (*TLL* 2, 406.1–69, *OLD* 159, 3b). Sidonius likes the term *arbiter*; see *Ep.* 1.2.1, 2.7.1, 4.3.9, 5.5.3, 5.7.2, 5.17.9, 9.1.2, 9.3.7, 9.6.1, 9.16.3, *Carm.* 23.156, 461. Mratschek (2020b) 258–9 suggests an echo of Plin. *Ep.* 5.6.36 and 44, and describes Sidonius as an artful reader of Pliny and as a similar arbiter of good taste for his own epoch. Sidonius' contemporary Claud. Mam. *Anim. praef.* endorsed Sidonius' self-perception by calling him an *arbiter*.

non paginam, quae spatia describit, sed villam, quae spatiosa describitur, grandem pronuntiabunt. Vale: To conclude his villa letter, Sidonius again uses a sentence similar in content to Pliny: Plin. *Ep.* 5.6.44 *similiter nos ut parva magnis … non epistula quae describit, sed villa quae describitur magna est* ('similarly I will, as I compare small things to big ones … not the epistle which describes, but the villa which is described, is big'); Schwerdtner (2015) 245–9. See also Plin. *Ep.* 3.9.27 for a similar play with short and long: *quid enim mihi cum tam longa epistula? … et tamen memento non esse epistulam longam, quae tot dies, tot cognitiones, tot denique reos causasque complexa sit. quae omnia videor mihi non minus breviter quam diligenter persecutus* ('why would I want such a long letter? … remember, however, that a letter is not long when it contains so many days, so many investigations, so many defendants and trials! I think I have explained all this as briefly as I have explained it precisely'). Sidonius finally judges his art and that of Pliny as great; Mratschek (2020) 259. Instead of Pliny's well known opposition *parva magnis* (see Verg. *Georg.* 4.176, Cic. *Orat.* 4.14, *Brut.* 213) Sidonius chooses a new wording. With the polyptota *spatia–spatiosa* and *describit–describitur* he emphasises again the connection between the large villa and his long letter. For the wording see *Paneg. Lat.* 4(9).20.2 *omnium cum nominibus suis locorum situs spatia intervalla descripta sunt* ('the sites of all locations with their names, their extent and the distances between them are described'). For the various meanings of *pagina*, 'a leaf of paper', 'sheet', 'page', 'letter', see the commentary on *Ep.* 2.2.7 *Quid plura? Nihil illis paginis....* For *spatiosus*, 'extensive', 'ample', see *OLD* 1798, 1a. Pliny also uses this adjective in his letters to describe (parts of) a house; see Plin. *Ep.* 7.27.5, 9.7.4 and see also his friend Maximus' writings, Plin. *Ep.* 4.20.2. For Sidonius' extensive use of adjectives ending in *-osus*, see the commentary on *Ep.* 2.2.18 *Lacus ipse ... flexuosus nemorosusque....* For the letter's simple ending with *vale*, see the commentary on *Ep.* 2.1.4 *Vale.*

Epistula 3

Introduction

Summary

Sidonius congratulates his friend Magnus Felix, who was awarded the title of *patricius*, and who despite this great honour still acts as a loyal friend. In the second part of the letter, Sidonius adds three famous historical examples of men who were also promoted or otherwise successful yet still acted humbly and were therefore loved and esteemed (Quintus Fabius Maximus, Pompeius and Germanicus). Whereas the republican dictator Papirius and the emperor Tiberius were envious of the success of their rivals Quintus Fabius Maximus and Germanicus, Sidonius claims to be happy about his friend's luck.

Addressee

The addressee, Felix, is the son of Magnus, who was consul in 460. Felix was made praetorian prefect of Gaul (*praefectus praetorio Galliarum*) and became a *patricius* (the title of a person in a high office at court or in an important military function) around 469 by the emperor Anthemius. He was a friend of Sidonius from their school days (*Carm.* 9.330). Like Sidonius, he is a relative of the emperor Avitus; see *Carm.* 7.156, Anderson (1936) 130 n. 2 and the commentary on *Ep.* 2.2.3 *nomen hoc praedio....* Felix is also the addressee of *Ep.* 3.4, 3.7, 4.5, 4.10 and *Carm.* 9, and is mentioned in *Carm.* 24.91. For the programmatic *Carm.* 9, see Condorelli (2008) 81–116. Felix is one of four addressees who receive as many as four letters (two addressees even get five letters each), and he is among the indivdiuals metioned most in Sidonius' texts (six times); Mathisen (2020a) 41. Like Ecdicius, he is an addressee in Book 2 and Book 3; Giannotti (2016) 37. In *Ep.* 4.5 and 4.10.1 Sidonius complains about Felix' long silence and attempts to resume contact with his old friend in *Ep.* 4.10.2. Harries (1994) 15–16, Delaplace (2014)

23–4 and Delaplace (2015) 236, 241–6 suggest that Sidonius fell out with Magnus' family because of the Arvandus affair (see the introductions to *Ep.* 2.1 and 2.5) as they did not react to his pleas for help as bishop of the Auvergne later on, in 471; Mathisen (2020a) 82, Mratschek (2020a) 230, van Waarden (2020a) 22–4. Felix probably succeeded Arvandus in office as praetorian prefect in 469; Stevens (1933) App. D (196–7), *PLRE* 2, 463–4, Harries (1994) 15, Kelly (2020a) 173–4. In the present letter, there is no sign of this discord; Sidonius praises his friend for his success and is pleased for him. Also, the chosen examples in the second paragraph do not suggest that there are problems between the friends. Sidonius distances himself from the emperor Anthemius in *Ep.* 2.1, but not from Felix.

For Felix' biography, see Loyen (1960) 187 n. 1, Loyen (1970a) 218 n. 23, *PLRE* 2, 463–4, *PCBE* 4, 749–51, Kaufmann (1995) 306–8, Mathisen (1998), Henning (1999) 89–92, 165, 307–8, Amherdt (2001) 185, Santelia (2002) 120–1, Giannotti (2016) 158–9, Mathisen (2020a) 95.

Date

Loyen (1970a) 54, 246 n. 3 dates the letter to around 469, when Felix became a *patricius*; that is, the letter is written immediately after the Arvandus affair in 468/9 (see the introductions to *Ep.* 2.1 and 2.5) and thus challenges the thesis of a rift over this matter between Sidonius and Felix. On the general difficulty of dating Sidonius' letters, see the Introduction, '2. The date and order of letters in Book 2'.

Major themes and further reading

This letter belongs to the congratulatory type of letter and confirms the friendship (*amicitia*) with the addressee; Cain (2009) 213. Both are important topics in ancient letter collections in general and in Sidonius' letters, but not to the extent that they are in other authors, such as Symmachus. Sidonius often encourages his friends to pursue a career (e.g. Sidon. *Ep.* 1.3, 1.6, 8.8) and congratulates them on important achievements (e.g. Sidon. *Ep.* 1.4, 3.6, 5.16, 5.18, 7.6.1, 7.17.1, 8.7, 9.4.1). For Sidonius' letters of friendship, see Cugusi (1983) 107, Fernández López (1994) 103–34, Näf (1995) 154–5, Köhler (1995) 175, Amherdt (2001) 44–5, Schröder (2007) 265–73, Hutchings (2009) 68–9, Overwien (2009a) 105–6, van Waarden

(2010) 279–80, van Waarden (2016) 212, Giannotti (2016) 171–2, Hess (2019) 59–63, Mratschek (2020a) 229, Schwitter (2020). For the meaning and importance of friendship in antiquity in general, see Badian (1996), Konstan (1997), Peachin (2001), Williams (2012); for *amicitia* in Late Antiquity and in the early Middle Ages, see Epp (1999), Müller (2013), Sowers (2016). Congratulations on an honorary office also occur in Pliny's letters, *Ep.* 4.8, 5.14.

In the second part of the letter Sidonius, following the tradition of Livy and Tacitus, uses historical examples (Quintus Fabius Maximus and Papirius; Tiberius and Germanicus) to illustrate envy and resentment of popularity (*invidia*). Sidonius thus varies the usual *exempla* of outstanding friendships, such as Orestes and Pylades or Theseus and Pirithous, whom he mentions in his *Carm.* 5.287–9, 24.26–30; see Stat. *Theb.* 1.473–7, Mart. 7.24.3–4, Val. Max. 4.7, Ruric. *Ep.* 1.10.2; Neri (2009) 208–9, Williams (2012) 7–13. Whereas Papirius and Tiberius are envious and do not like the success of Quintus Fabius and Germanicus, Sidonius claims to be happy about his friend's fortunes. Even though Felix is promoted by the emperor Anthemius, Sidonius does not mention the emperor and echoes his earlier negative portrayal of him in *Ep.* 2.1. Credit for Felix' rise to the patriciate is due to him alone; see Hanaghan (2019) 107–8 and the commentary on 2.1.4 on *Si nullae a republica vires … Anthemii principis opes*. For Sidonius' knowledge of Livy, see Mratschek (2013) 259–60.

Commentary

Section 1

Sidonius Felici suo salutem: For the simple greeting formula, see the commentary on *Ep.* 2.1.1 *Sidonius Ecdicio suo salutem*. For the addressee, Felix, see the introduction to this letter.

Gaudeo te, domine maior, amplissimae dignitatis infulas consecutum: The verb *gaudere*, 'to be pleased, to be glad', appears prominently at the beginning of the first and at the end of the second sentence and thus sets the tone of this congratulatory letter. While the first sentence describes Felix's success, the second deals with the consequence of his promotion for Sidonius. The repeated verb *gaudeo* thus unites writer and addressee. The honorary salutation *domine maior* is only attested in Sidonius; Köhler (1995)

102, Amherdt (2001) 117, 272, van Waarden (2016) 211, Giannotti (2016) 179. With this title Sidonius addresses seven noble men and thus expresses his respect for them: Constantius in *Ep.* 1.1.1, Montius in 1.11.17, Felix in *Ep.* 2.3, Eutropius in 3.6.3, Claudianus Mamertus in 4.3.1, Arbogastes in 4.17.1, and Consentius in 8.4.1. In *Ep.* 4.10.1 Sidonius calls Felix *domine meus*. For other expressions containing *domine* (*domine frater, domine fili*) in Sidonius, see Mathisen (2020a) 35. See also the commentary on *Ep.* 2.13.8 *Quapropter ad statum huiusmodi, domine frater....* The combination of *amplus* and *dignitas* is frequently used from Cicero onward, for example Cic. *Leg. agr.* 2.49 and there are further examples in *TLL* 1, 2010.74–7. The title *amplissimus* is given to the highest offices such as consul, pretorian prefect (*praefectus praetorio*) and prefect of Rome (*praefectus urbi*); van Waarden (2016) 215–16. Sidonius uses the term several times in his letters: *Ep.* 1.4.1, 1.9.2, 1.9.5, 2.13.1, 7.17.1. An *infula* originally was a 'woollen band, worn by priests upon the forehead as a sign of religious consecration and inviolability'. Late Antique authors often use it in a figurative sense for the insignia of a public office, as here; see also Sidon. *Ep.* 7.12.1 *patricias ... infulas* ('patrician insignia') and the examples in *TLL* 7.1, 1499.69–500.20. The combination with *dignitas* also appears in other Late Antique authors; see *TLL* 7.1, 1500.11–14.

Sed id mihi ob hoc solum destinato tabellario nuntiatum non minus gaudeo: An important topic in a congratulatory letter is that the honour the addressee has received through his promotion is shared with his friends. In *Ep.* 4.14.2 Sidonius complains to his old friend Polemius that he has not been informed about his promotion; Näf (1995) 154. Here, on the other hand, Sidonius praises Felix for having sent him a letter just to inform him about his new title. A *tabellarius* is a 'letter carrier', 'courier'. According to Kaufmann (1995) 244 n. 747 the anonymous messenger could be Gozolas, a client of Magnus Felix who appears in this function also in *Ep.* 3.4.1, 4.5.1; see also Amherdt (2001) 186–7. Slaves, friends and acquaintances are often mentioned as letter carriers because the arrival of the letters depended on them and because they often had to deliver oral messages in addition to written ones; see for example Sidon. *Ep.* 2.11.2, 4.12.4, Plin. *Ep.* 2.12.6, 8.3.1, Cic. *Fam.* 9.15.1, 10.31.4; Nikitinski (2001). Sidonius mentions messengers in 20% of his letters, 27 persons in total, that is, 6.1% of the total number of individuals mentioned in Sidonius' letters, ranging from senator to slave; Kaufmann (1995) 244 n. 747, Amherdt (2001) 32, 188, 206, 229, Mathisen (2020a) 67–8, Mratschek (2020a) 226–9. On letter carriers in Late

Antiquity, see Chadwick (1955) 314–15, McGuire (1960) 150, Conring (2001) 118–20 about Jerome, Mratschek (2002) 302–24 about Paulinus of Nola, Schröder (2018) about Cicero. Sometimes it was difficult to find a messenger at all or one had to entrust the letter to an unsuitable person; see *Ep.* 4.7. Trustworthiness is very important with letter carriers and also discussed in *Ep.* 7.2; Amherdt (2001) 210, van Waarden (2016) 191. In the letter at hand, Sidonius feels honoured that Felix sends him a messenger solely to inform him about his new title. Similarly in *Ep.* 6.6.1 he writes *unde misso in hoc solum negotii gerulo litterarum* ('accordingly, I have sent the bearer of my letter with this task alone'). Sidonius uses various terms to denote the messengers; Wolff (2020) 404, Amherdt (2001) 188, 206. The term *tabellarius* is also used in *Ep.* 4.8.1, 7.2.2, 8.9.1, 9.3.2, 9.4.1; in *Ep.* 2.11.2 he calls the messengers *geruli litterarum*. For *gaudeo*, see the commentary immediately above on *Ep.* 2.3.1 *Gaudeo te....*

Nam licet in praesentiarum sis potissimus magistratus: The contracted adverb *in praesentiarum* derives from *in praesentia rerum*; it is more often written in one word, *inp-* or *impraesentiarum*, meaning 'at the present moment', 'now' (*OLD* 851). It is attested first in Cato, but frequently used only from Apuleius on (but not in the *Metamorphoses*); see Sidon. *Ep.* 3.6.1, 4.3.1, 5.9.1, 7.9.15, 8.9.3, 9.9.6, in Claudianus Mamertus (seven times) and Jerome (more than thirty times); see *TLL* 7.1, 673.72–4.41, Giannotti (2016) 173. The adjective *potissimus* is used in the superlative 'most powerful', 'chief' (*TLL* 10.2, 353.36–62, *OLD* 1419, 1) to indicate the power of a person from *Plaut. Men.* 359 on. In combination with an official magistrate it is also used in Symm. *Ep.* 4.28.1 *a qua et optimus princeps et magistratus potissimus abest* ('where the best emperor and the most powerful magistrates are away from'), 2.64.1 *quidquid potissimi magistratus functio quaerit* ('whatever requires executing the most powerful office').

et in lares Philagrianos patricius apex tantis post saeculis tua tantum felicitate remeaverit: The *patricius* Philagrius, one of Felix's ancestors, is only attested here and in Sidon. *Carm.* 7.156, 24.93. He is not identical with the addressee of the same name in *Ep.* 7.14; *PLRE* 2, 463, Anderson (1965) 372–3, Loyen (1970b) 194 n. 78, Harries (1994) 33, Kaufmann (1995) 234 n. 701, van Waarden (2016) 118–19. From the time of the emperor Constantine on, *patricius*, 'patrician', 'noble' (*TLL* 10.1, 747.7–9.30), was the title of a person in a high office at court or in an important military function like *magister militum*. Sidonius himself was given the title for being *praefectus* *urbi* in 468; see Sidon. *Ep.* 5.16.4. For the title *patricius*, see also Sidon. *Carm.* 2.90, 2.207, 11.53, *Ep.* 1.5.10, 1.9.1, 3.5.2, 5.10.2, 5.16.1, 5.16.4, 7.12.1, 8.8.1. Sidonius combines *patricius* with *apex*, 'summit', 'top', also in *Carm.* 7.157 *patricius resplendet apex* ('the patrician dignity is resplendent'), and similarly in *Ep.* 1.3.2 *vicariano apice* ('by the rank of a *vicarius*'), 1.4.1 *titulis apicibusque potiare* ('to win the titles and dignities'), and 2.13.3 *in arcem ... patriciam* ('to the height of the patriciate'). Montone (2017) 36 refers to *Cod. Theod.* 6.28.7 *proconsu(la)ris apicis dignitatis* ('the top of proconsular dignity') for a similar Late Antique use of *apex*; see also *TLL* 2, 228.29–40 for a list of further examples. For other meanings of *apex* in Sidonius, see the commentary on *Ep.* 2.1.2 *epistulas, ne primis quidem apicibus sufficienter initiatus....* With *felicitas*, 'happiness', 'felicity', 'luckiness', 'success' (similarly used for example in *Ep.* 1.9.3, 2.4.1, 2.13.1 and 2.13.2 in connection with a successful career), Sidonius alludes to his addressee's name. Being lucky and successful, thus, is part of Felix' character; see also *Ep.* 1.2.1 on Theoderic II, whose personality is also formed by *felicitas*: *ita personam suam deus arbiter et ratio naturae consummatae felicitatis dote sociata cumulaverunt* ('in his person the governing god and the plan of nature have joined together to endow him with a supreme perfection'). Felix' promotion was not pure luck, though: he earned it with his work. At the beginning of *Carm.* 9 Sidonius plays extensively with his friend's name; see *Carm.* 9.5 *Felix nomine, mente, honore, forma* ('felicitous in your name, intellect, esteem, appearance'). Statius similarly plays with the meaning of the name of his addressee Pollius Felix: Stat. *Silv.* 2.2.23, 107, 122, 151; Gauly (2006) 467–8. For a pun on *felix* and *infelix*, see Sidon. *Carm.* 5.57; for an ironic praise of the eyes, ears and nose of the addressee Catullinus as *felix*, see *Carm.* 12.12–13. The verb *remeo*, 'to go or come back' (*OLD* 1610, 1), is not frequent until after the Augustan period. The combination with the accusative is poetic and characteristic of Late Latin; see Verg. *Aen.* 11.793, Amm. 17.13.33.

invenis tamen, vir amicitiarum servantissime: This clause with its polite compliments has a Symmachan ring. On Symmachus' polite attention to his friends, his systematic restraint in political matters and his allusive, artfully wrought language, see Matthews (1974) 60–5, 81–3, 87–8, 91, Schröder (2007) 158–60, 212–7, Salzman and Roberts (2011) lxvi–lxviii. See also the commentary on *Ep.* 2.10.5 *quod olim ... Rusticiana Symmacho....* The Sidonian wording *vir amicitiarum servantissime* is attested in Symm. *Ep.* 2.68 *a viro amicitiae servantissimo* ('from a most loyal friend'). See also Sidon. *Ep.* 7.9.22 *amicitias ... perenniter servat* ('he kept friendships forever'). Sidonius uses the plural *amicitiae* also where one would expect the singular; see Amherdt (2001) 213 and the commentary below on *Ep.* 2.6.1 *in boni cuiusque adscitur amicitias*. See also *Ep.* 3.13.10 *amicitiarum culmen aedificat* ('he builds the lofty eminences of his friendships'). The subject of friendship, *amicitia*, is common in ancient letters; see the introduction to this letter.

qualiter honorum tuorum crescat communione fastigium: For the meaning of *honor*, 'office', 'post', 'honour', in Sidonius' letters, see van Waarden (2010) 266. Sidonius uses the word *communio*, 'ease of associating with people', 'pleasant manner', benevolence', 'approachability' (*TLL* 3, 1966.53–63), several times for persons in authority who handle their power well; see for example Sidon. *Ep.* 1.11.12, 9.11.10, and especially 7.4.1, which is a letter about *communio*; van Waarden (2010) 217–19, 222–3. Felix' promotion is the right moment to remind him of this important quality. The term *fastigium* means 'summit', 'highest part', 'dignity' of a public office (*TLL* 6.1, 323.61–4.7); see also Sidon. *Ep.* 7.4.2 *sacerdotii fastigium* ('your priestly eminence'). Sidonius often uses words from this semantic field; see the commentary of van Waarden (2010) 486 on the verb *fastigare* and the adjective *fastigatissimus* and my commentary on *Ep.* 2.4.1 *ita demum sibi ... ad arcem fastigatissimae felicitatis evectus*....

raroque genere exempli altitudinem tuam humilitate sublimas: Sidonius praises Felix for his reaction. He does not become proud of his new office, but remains modest; see also Symm. *Ep.* 8.1. For the opposite reaction see Sidon. *Ep.* 4.14.2; Amherdt (2001) 346. Sidonius expresses this notion with the paradoxon *altitudinem–humilitate*. *Altitudo*, 'greatness', 'nobleness', is used elsewhere in a figurative sense of a personal quality (*TLL* 1, 1767.63–8 and 1769.30–50), for example Tac. *Ann.* 3.44.4 *altitudine animi* ('through the nobleness of his mind'), but also in a negative way Sall. *Iug.* 95.3 *ad simulanda negotia altitudo ingenii incredibilis* ('an incredible inscrutability in feigning his business'); Montone (2017) 36. Sidonius adds the antonym *humilitas*, which in ecclesiastical Latin has a positive sense, 'humility' (*TLL* 6.3, 3118.48–19.21). The verb *sublimo*, 'to place in an elevated position', 'raise', 'rise', 'soar' (*OLD* 1843, 1a), appears several times in Apuleius, but is rare elsewhere. Montone (2017) 36 suggests an allusion to Apul. *Socr.* 16 *humilia sublimare* ('to elevate low things'), a passage about the souls of the deceased.

Section 2

Sic quondam Quintum Fabium magistrum equitum dictatorio rigori et Papirianae superbiae favor publicus praetulit: In the second section Sidonius gives historical examples to illustrate the topics of envy and resentment because of professional success. His personal experience, the frictions between himself and Magnus Felix (i.e. Auvergne versus Provence) concerning the Arvandus affair and his request for help in 471 probably form the political background for the *exempla* (*sic quondam...*); see the introduction to this letter. The first example, Quintus Fabius Maximus Rullianus, was *magister equitum* under the dictator L. Papirius Cursor in the war against the Samnites (325 BC), an Italic tribe which lived in Campania. According to Livy, Fabius Maximus won the battle, but was nonetheless sentenced because he went against the orders of Papirius. Thanks to the intervention of the Roman people and members of the Senate he was pardoned; see Liv. 8.30.1–35.9, Val. Max. 2.7.8, 3.2.9, Eutrop. 2.8; Elvers (1998). Papirius was the most famous member of his *gens*, with five consulates in 326, 320, 319, 315 and 313 BC. In 310, during his second dictatorship, he won and triumphed over the Samnites; see Liv. 9.40.1–14. In the historical tradition Papirius is also praised for his physical strength (hence his cognomen *cursor*, 'runner') and esteemed among Rome's best commanders, as famous as Alexander the Great (see Liv. 9.16.11–19); Müller (2000). Sidonius, though, describes him only with negative attributes, like tyrannical behaviour and pride, probably to show Fabius Maximus in a more positive light as an example of popularity. Hanaghan (2019) 107 maintains that by comparing Felix to Fabius, Sidonius implies a comparison between Anthemius and Papirius, both of whom are stern but not very competent rulers who abuse their power. This is a plausible assumption, as Sidonius does not mention Anthemius by name despite his close connection to Felix and thus continues his *damnatio memoriae* of the emperor. The adjective *dictatorius*, 'of a dictator', 'dictatorial' (*TLL* 5.1, 1004.13–25), is first attested in Cic. *Cluent*. 123 (*dictatorium gaudium*, 'dictatorial pleasure') and used several times in Livy, for example Liv. 4.14.2 and 8.30.11 (*dictatoriam maiestatem*, 'dictatorial majesty'), which is also the source for the story at hand. For the combination of *favor* and *publicus* ('public opinion preferred'), see *TLL* 6.1, 385.83–4, and for examples Ov. *Pont*. 4.14.56, Vell. 2.92.4.

sic et Gnaeum Pompeium super aemulos extulit numquam fastidita popularitas: The second example is Gnaeus Pompeius Magnus (106–48

BC), a famous commander and member of the first triumvirate formed with Marcus Licinius Crassus and Gaius Iulius Caesar (60 BC). Sidonius mentions Pompey because of his popularity, which he nevertheless did not enjoy with everyone. While his soldiers gave him the title *Magnus* (linking him thus with Alexander the Great), he was not very popular with his contemporaries; Will (2001) 105–6. After the deaths of Julia (Caesar's daughter and wife of Pompey) in 54 BC and of Crassus in 53 BC, the alliance broke down. Pompey allied himself with the party of the *optimates* and became Caesar's enemy, probably the most important of the rivals (*aemulos*) whose names Sidonius does not mention here. Pompey was defeated in the battle of Pharsalus and killed in Egypt in August 48 BC. Pompey's seeking of *popularitas* was notorious; see for example Cic. *Att.* 1.20.2 *nihil non submissum atque populare* ('everything is submissive and concerned with popularity'), Cic. *Att.* 2.1.6 and Stat. *Silv.* 2.7.69 *et gratum popularitate Magnum* ('and Magnus, pleasing because of his popularity'). Sidonius mentions Pompey also in *Carm.* 7.80 in a list of rulers; Montone (2017) 36. For *aemulus*, which can mean 'rival', 'imitator' and 'enemy', 'hostile opponent' (*TLL* 1, 976.42–80.53, *OLD* 64) in Sidonius' letters, see *Ep.* 3.4.1, 4.3.10, 7.8.3, 7.9.22, 8.8.2; van Waarden (2010) 398; see also the commentary on 2.2.5 *Hinc frigidaria dilatatur ... publicis operibus ... aemularetur*. With the litotes *numquam fastidita* Sidonius accentuates Pompey's effort to be popular. For *fastidio*, 'to feel disgust', 'despise', 'scorn' (*TLL* 6.1, 310.4–58), constructed with abstract words, see for example Claud. *Stil.* 3.28 *strepitus fastidit inanes* ('he renounces this vain noise'). The expression (*numquam*) *fastidita popularitas* is unattested elsewhere. The term *popularitas*, 'the effort to please the people', 'popular bearing', 'populism' (*TLL* 10.1, 2705.29–53), also appears in Sidon. *Ep.* 1.7.3, 5.20.2, 7.9.22, 8.13.1; Köhler (1995) 235–6, van Waarden (2010) 518. In *Carm.* 9.300, 23.141, and 23.400 it has a positive sense 'esteem', 'regard', 'popularity'.

sic invidiam Tiberianam pressit universitatis amore Germanicus: As his third example of a popular man, Sidonius adds Germanicus in opposition to the envious emperor Tiberius (14–37). Whereas Germanicus was a young and heroic commander who was held in high esteem by the people of Rome as well as by his family, Tiberius was never fully accepted by his stepfather and father-in-law Augustus, who preferred other members of the family as his successors; Eck (2002). Germanicus was very popular because of his charisma and his victories over Germanic tribes (*Cherusci*, *Chatti*) which he celebrated with a triumph in Rome in AD 17. He died in Antioch – allegedly poisoned – in AD 19 and was entombed in the mausoleum of

Augustus in Rome. The people in Rome reacted with great distress and honoured him after his death; Eck (1998). Tiberius, on the other hand, was never popular; he had been forced by the emperor Augustus (27 BC – AD 14) to adopt Germanicus in AD 4 for dynastic reasons, even though he had a son of his own. The probable source for Tiberius' *invidia* ('envy') is Tacitus, for example Tac. *Ann.* 2.26.5, 2.71.1–2; Hausmann (2009) 112–41. Hanaghan (2019) 108 interprets Tiberius' unpopularity with the people and his jealousy as a hint to the ruler Anthemius, while the popular Germanicus stands for Felix. For *universitas*, 'a corporate body of persons', 'community' (*OLD* 2094, 2b), see Sidon. *Ep.* 2.7.1, 3.3.3, 3.6.3; see also van Waarden (2016) 150 on *Ep.* 7.14.7 *iudicio universali* ('in the judgement of the whole world').

Quocirca nolo sibi de successibus tuis principalia beneficia plurimum blandiantur: The title *patricius* (see the commentary on *Ep.* 2.3.1 *et in lares Philagrianos patricius…*) was bestowed by the emperor. Here the *princeps* Anthemius is meant (see the introduction to this letter and the commentary on *Ep.* 2.1.4 *Si nullae … Anthemii principis opes*). *Beneficium* here denotes an emperor's 'permission', 'favour', 'support', '(military) promotion' (*TLL* 2, 1886.66–7.55). With the legally correct formulation *principalia beneficia* ('imperial grace, 'imperial benefaction') Sidonius avoids calling the emperor Anthemius by name. For the expression in a legal context, see Iulian. *Dig.* 2.1.5, Paul. *Dig.* 28.6.43 *beneficia quidem principalia ipsi principes solent interpretari* ('only the emperors can interpret imperial benefactions'). For the exchange of *beneficia* in a friendship, see Sidon. *Ep.* 2.6.1. For *blandiri sibi*, 'to flatter oneself with something', 'delude oneself' (*TLL* 2, 2033.1–65), see Sidon. *Ep.* 8.6.11 *ceterum, ut tibi de venatoris officio quam minimum blandiaris, maxume iniungo* ('but I strongly urge you to flatter yourself with the hunter's business only a little bit').

quae nihil tibi amplius conferre potuerunt, quam ut si id noluissemus, transiremus inviti: The contorted expression with the litotes *quam ut si id noluissemus, transiremus inviti* finally highlights the necessity of Felix' promotion. For *amplius*, see the commentary above on *Ep.* 2.2.20 *Sed non amplius moror.*… The verb *noluissemus* repeats *nolo* from the first part of the sentence. By using the first-person plural, Sidonius expresses that he is not alone with his opinion of the friend's legitimate promotion. Sidonius addresses his dear friend Felix in this letter with *tu* but in other letters (*Ep.* 3.7, 4.10) in the plural *vos*, signaling thus an emotional restraint. On the complex play with the forms of address in Sidonius' letters, see van Waarden (2010) 49–52, van Waarden (2016) 45–8, van Waarden (2020b) 427.

Illud peculiare tuum est, illud gratiae singularis, quod tam qui te aemulentur non habes quam non invenis qui sequantur. Vale: In the last sentence of the letter Sidonius stresses that, unlike the historical figures he has mentioned, Felix has no rivals, since no one is equal to him. *Peculiaris* is here used in the wider sense of 'proper', 'special', 'peculiar' (*TLL* 10.1, 924.20–53 and 925.34–56, *OLD* 1316, 2b); see Sidon. *Ep.* 4.3.8 *idque tuum in illo peculiare* ('and there is something special for you therein'). For *aemulentur*, see the commentary on *Ep.* 2.2.5 *Hinc frigidaria dilatatur ... publicis operibus ... aemularetur.* The letter ends with a chiasmus (*aemulentur–non habes–invenis–sequantur*) and alliteration on -*q* and -*t*. For the simple ending with *vale*, see the commentary on 2.1.4 *Vale*.

Epistula 4

Introduction

Summary

In this letter to Sagittarius (or Syagrius) Sidonius recommends Proiectus as a friend. Proiectus is engaged to be married to the daughter of the late Optantius and therefore asks for the consent of Sagittarius (or Syagrius), who is the girl's guardian.

Addressee

The addressee, Sagittarius (or Syagrius), is otherwise unknown; see *PLRE* 2, 971, *PCBE* 4, 1680, Kaufmann (1995) 345, Mathisen (2020a) 120. In Sidon. *Ep.* 2.3.2 he is said to be the guardian (*parens*) of the daughter of the late *vir clarissimus* Optantius, so he is probably her uncle. There are two possible addressees for this letter: most manuscripts (P, L, T, N, V, R, and M) used by Lüthojann (1887) and Loyen (1970a) have *Sagittario* or *Sagitario*, while C has *siagrio* and F *siargio*. The older editions up to Lütjohann (1887) had the letter addressed to Syagrius. Kelly (2021) shows that the manuscripts are evenly divided in terms of stemmatic weight and the variant 'Syagrius' needs to be taken seriously. Syagrius is also a correspondent of Sidonius (*Ep.* 5.5 and 8.8) and the name of a consul, his friend's distinguished great-grandfather (*Ep.* 1.7.4, 5.17.4, 7.12.1). The name Sagittarius is only attested once again after Sidonius; Kelly (2021).

Date

There is no evidence for the date of this letter; see the Introduction, '2. The date and order of letters in Book 2'.

Major themes and further reading

Letters 2.4 and 2.5, like *Ep.* 3.9 and 3.10 and 6.10 and 6.11, are paired letters of recommendation (*litterae commendaticiae*). As many as four successive letters of recommendation are found in *Ep.* 6.2–6.5. For Sidonius' letters of recommendation, see Amherdt (2001) 196 on *Ep.* 4.6 and Furbetta (2015a) 349–53 on *Ep.* 1.10, 2.4, 3.5 and 6.4. Sidonius' letter of recommendation also contains the theme of arranging marriages, which also occurs in Pliny *Ep.* 1.14. For the general structure and characteristic features of ancient letters of recommendation, which survive in considerable number: for example most of the letters in Cic. *Fam.* 13, over twenty in Pliny's epistles, including Plin. *Ep.* 2.9, 2.13, 3.2, 3.3 (see the Introduction, p. xvii), sixteen letters of Fronto, including Front. *Ep.* 1.3, 1.9, and a considerable number in Book 9 of Symmachus' letters; see Cugusi (1983) 111–14, Cotton (1985), Fernández López (1994) 135–48, Rees (2007), Frass (2008), Cain (2009) 211, Furbetta (2015a), Germerodt (2015) 119–26. In the letter at hand, Sidonius recommends Proiectus, a man outside his inner circle of acquaintances. For Sidonius acting as a *patronus*, see Näf (1995) 145, and for the duties of a *patronus*, see Wallace-Hadrill (1989). On Sidonius helping the poor or others in need (of legal advice), see Stevens (1933) 119–20, Kaufmann (1995) 208 n. 634, and the commentary below on *Ep.* 2.7.

Commentary

Section 1

Sidonius Sagittario suo salutem: For the simple greeting formula, see the commentary on *Ep.* 2.1.1 *Sidonius Ecdicio suo salutem*. For the addressee Sagittarius (or Syagrius), see the introduction to this letter.

Vir clarissimus Proiectus, domi nobilis et patre patruoque spectabilibus, avo etiam praestantissimo sacerdote conspicuus: Sidonius begins the letter with a typical element of the letter of recommendation, the positive description of the protégé; Furbetta (2015a) 347–8. However, unlike in letter 2.5, another typical element is missing, namely the relationship between Sidonius and Proiectus. Instead, Sidonius begins the letter with the title of his protégé: *vir clarissimus*. As a consequence of the expansion of the senatorial class, there were different grades of rank within the senatorial order. In ascending order these titles are *clarissimus* ('most distinguished'), *spectabilis* ('respectable') and *illustris* or *illustrissimus* ('most illustrious'). The *viri clarissimi* were thus the lowest rank and were excluded from Senate sessions in the fifth century. *Spectabiles* enjoyed more privileges than *clarissimi*, but fewer than *illustres*. Many civil servants earned the title *spectabilis*, among them the *proconsules* and the *vicarii*, who got the title first and were held in the highest rank; Löhken (1982) 27–8, 122–4, 131–4, 138–9, 153, Mathisen (1993) 10, Schlinkert (1996) 73, 99 n. 32, 166, Gizewski (1998), Groß-Albenhausen (2001, 2002). Proiectus is a *vir clarissimus* and, as Sidonius next notes in the same sentence, had a father and uncle with the title *spectabilis*. In addition, Sidonius describes Proiectus as *domi nobilis* ('a noble in his locality'). The phrase is a late republican one probably picked up from Cicero; see for example Cic. *Verr.* 2.3.87, 2.4.18, *Cluent.* 23. For Proiectus, see Mathisen (2020a) 116, *PLRE* 2, 925, *PCBE* 4, 1548. One's family background was of central importance for the projected image of aristocrats and Sidonius repeatedly describes senators as being of noble origin: *Ep.* 1.3.1, 3.10.1, 4.4.1, 4.21.6, 7.13.5; van Waarden (2016) 104, Mathisen (2020a) 34. For the connection between a recommendation and a young man's pedigree, see also Plin. *Ep.* 1.14.5–6, 6.26.1. Like Proiectus himself, his ancestors are unknown; see *PLRE* 2, 1230 n. 69, 1233 n. 96, Mathisen (2020a) 135–6. The superlative *praestantissimus*, 'outstanding', 'excellent' (*OLD* 1442, 1a), is not a specific title like *clarissimus* and *spectabilis*, and was often used to describe outstanding persons; see for example Cic. *Fam.* 5.8.2; van Waarden (2010) 495. Sidonius thus inserts three titles in his introductory sentence, but the highest, *illustris*, is missing; see the commentary on *Ep.* 2.11.2 *Domine inlustris*. For the overall construction of the sentence, see also Sidon. *Ep.* 8.6.2 *Flavius Nicetius, vir ortu clarissimus, privilegio spectabilis, merito inlustris* ('Flavius Nicetius, a man very distinguished in birth, eminent in privilege, illustrious in merit'), Plin. *Ep.* 3.3.1 *quamquam illi paternus etiam clarus spectatusque contigerit, pater quoque et patruus inlustri laude conspicui* ('even though he had a paternal grandfather who was famous and esteemed, and also his father and uncle were distinguished and outstanding in their reputation'). Other instances of the title *vir spectabilis* appear in Sidon. *Ep.* 3.5.1, 4.13.1, 7.8.2; *vir clarissimus* appears in *Ep.* 3.10.1.

amicitiarum tuarum, nisi respuis, avidissime sinibus infertur: Friendship, *amicitia*, is a frequent subject in ancient letters; see the introduction to *Ep.* 2.3. Like Symmachus, Sidonius uses the plural of *amicitia* where one would expect the singular (for example in *Ep.* 2.6.1); see Amherdt (2001)

213 on 4.7.1. The adverb *avidissime*, 'very longingly', 'very eagerly' (*TLL* 2, 1429.36–43, *OLD* 214, 2), also appears in a letter of recommendation in Plin. *Ep.* 2.13.1 and 8, 3.1.11; see also Cic. *Phil.* 14.1. The superlative is rare elsewhere; see Whitton (2013) 198. The adjective *avidus* appears in a similar context in Sidon. *Ep.* 2.7.1; see the commentary below on *Ep.* 2.7.1 *idcirco singulas ... libens et avidus emitto*. With the expression *sinibus inferre*, 'giving someone hugs', 'pressing someone to one's bosom' (*OLD* 1771, 2b), Sidonius illustrates his close friendship with Sagittarius. This image of comfort and protection is widespread, for example Plin. *Ep.* 2.1.10, 8.16.5 *si in amici sinu defleas* ('if you cry at your friend's bosom'), 9.25.3, Cic. *Tusc.* 5.5; van Waarden (2010) 231. Similarly, hugs and embraces also are a sign of friendship in Sidon. *Ep.* 4.4.2 *complectendis pectoribus* ('by clasping you to my heart') and 7.4.2 *pectus ... fovere complexibus* ('clasp in a close embrace').

et cum illi familiae splendor, probitas morum, patrimonii facultas, iuventutis alacritas in omne decus pari lance conquadrent: Sidonius uses rhetorical flair by mentioning four positive characteristics of Proiectus (*splendor, probitas, facultas, alacritas*), combining each with a genitive attribute and arranging the first as a chiasmus, followed by two parallel elements, which together form a square (*conquadrent*). Origin, character, means and looks are the essential conditions for a marriage; see Sidon. *Ep.* 7.2.7, 9.6.2; van Waarden (2010) 176. For a list of positive traits in the description of a protégé, see Sidon. *Ep.* 2.6.1. Similarly, Pliny also recommends a young man with the same qualities as a worthy suitor in Plin. *Ep.* 1.14; see also Plin. *Ep.* 6.26.1, where Pliny praises a marriage candidate as follows: *puer simplicitate, comitate iuvenis, senex gravitate* ('a boy in his candour, a young man in his kindness, an old man in his dignity'). *Splendor* means 'splendour', 'brilliance', 'glory' (*OLD* 1808, 5a); see Suet. *Vesp.* 1.3 *splendoris familiae* ('the splendour of the family'). The term *splendor* in connection with the renown of a person (in a funerary context) is also used in Sidon. *Ep.* 2.8.3 v. 5, *O splendor generis, decus mariti* (see the commentary). Three of the four nouns describing Proiectus are abstracta with the ending *-tas*. For Sidonius' fondness for nouns ending in *-tas*, see the commentary on *Ep.* 2.2.4 on *parilitas*. The term *patrimonium* denotes 'an estate inherited from a father', 'a paternal estate', 'inheritance' (*TLL* 10.1, 753.52–68); see Sidon. *Ep.* 2.13.4, 8.11.1, Plin. *Ep.* 6.19.4. In combination with *facultas* it is also used in Ulp. *Dig.* 36.1.17 pr. *si patrimonium fuerit rogatus, et si facultates* ('if he is asked about the paternal estate and fortune'). Sidonius uses the noun *alacritas*, 'energy', 'liveliness', 'alacrity' (*TLL* 1, 1475.66–7.2) only here, and the adjective *alacer* in *Ep.* 1.4.1, 1.6.2, 7.6.6; see van Waarden (2010) 313. For the combination with 'youth', 'youthful', see Sulpic. Sev. *Chron.* 2.1.5 *iuvenili alacritate* ('with juvenile liveliness') as a parallel text. *Lanx* is a 'plate', 'platter', 'scale (of a balance)', and the expression *pari lance* or (more frequent) *aequa lance* means 'in equal measure', 'likewise' (*TLL* 7.2, 939.23–54, *OLD* 1000–2). It is similarly used in Sidon. *Ep.* 2.9.3 *ex aequo divisioni lancem ponere* and *Ep.* 6.3.1 *aequali officiorum lance certandum* ('an equally balanced competition in fulfilling one's duties'); Symm. *Ep.* 8.74 has *quod si pari lance reddideris* ('if you give it back to me in equal measure'). Sidonius uses the term *lanx* also in *Ep.* 5.16.1 *non solvit in lance sed in acie* ('he did not pay with the scale but in battle'). For the rarely used verb *conquadro*, see the commentary on *Ep.* 2.2.4 *quae consequenti unguentariae spatii parilitate conquadrat*....

ita demum sibi tamen videbitur ad arcem fastigatissimae felicitatis evectus, si gratiae tuae sodalitate potiatur: After praising Proiectus, Sidonius mentions the happiness that Proiectus could achieve by a favour from Sagittarius. With the theme of happiness, he simultaneously refers back to letter 2.3, which was dedicated to Felix's career. *Arx*, 'top of', 'pinnacle' (*TLL* 2, 742.32–67), is used here (as in Sidon. *Ep.* 2.13.3, 8.6.1, *Carm.* 23.142) in a metaphorical way to denote the excellence of a career; see also Sidon. *Carm.* 2.173. For the meaning 'top of a building', see the commentary on *Ep.* 2.10.4 vv. 5–7. Sidonius uses the participle *fastigatus* from *fastigo*, 'to make pointed', 'to raise or bring to a point' (*TLL* 6.1, 325.40–46), as an adjective in the superlative, which is unattested in other authors; see also Sidon. *Ep.* 1.9.2 *duo fastigatissimi consulares* ('two consulars of the highest rank') and 8.13.2 *gratias fastigatissimae caritatis arce transcendere* ('that you can surpass all these graces by the towering eminence of your charity'). The verb *fastigo* is used in *Ep.* 3.6.3; Giannotti (2016) 178. For *fastigium*, see the commentary on *Ep.* 2.3.1 *qualiter honorum tuorum crescat communione fastigium*. For *felicitas*, 'happiness', 'felicity', 'luckiness', 'success', see the commentary on *Ep.* 2.3.1 *et in lares Philagrianos ... tua tantum felicitate remeaverit*.

Section 2

Optantii clarissimi viri nuper vita functi filiam: Optantius, whose daughter Proiectus wants to marry, is otherwise unknown; *PLRE* 2, 809, *PCBE* 4, 1389, Mathisen (2020a) 110. For his rank of a *clarissimus*, see the commentary on *Ep.* 2.4.1 *Vir clarissimus Proiectus*.... He probably died a natural death; see Faure and Jacquemard (2014) 61, who refer to Sidon. *Ep.* 2.8, 3.5, 4.11, 6.2. The loss or fear of losing a family member also appears in *Ep.* 2.8 and 2.12. The daughter and the wife (see the commentary below on *Ep.* 2.4.2 *licet a matre pupillae* ...) of the late Optantius are not mentioned by name but just in their roles within the family; *PLRE* 2, 1239 n. 15 and 16, Mathisen (2020a) 129. The reduction of female figures to their function as a link between families is often found in Sidonius as well as in other ancient authors; see for example Sidon. *Ep.* 1.11.5 *namque ut familiae superiori per filiam saltim quamquam honestissimam iungeretur* ('he desired to gain anyhow a connection with a family of higher rank through his most honourable daughter'); Bonjour (1988) 46. Anonymous women can be found elsewhere in Sidonius' writings; Mathisen (2020a) 127–33, 145–6 counts forty-three individuals and five groups of anonymous women.

quod Deo prosperante succedat: Sidonius hopes that God will support the project and that Proiectus may marry the girl. The expression *Deo prosperante* is unique in Sidonius, but there are several similar formulaic interjections; see the commentaries on *Ep.* 2.2.3 *Haec mihi cum meis praesule deo...*, on *Ep.* 2.9.10 *sed quia et ipsi ... sub ope Christi ...*, and on *Ep.* 2.12.3 *igitur ardori ... praevio Christo....*

licet a matre pupillae in coniugium petierit obtinueritque: A *pupilla* is an 'orphan girl', 'female ward' (*TLL* 10.2, 2665.39–61); see for example Cic. *Verr.* 2.1.41. According to ancient legal opinion, a fatherless child is an orphan; a *pupilla* with a living mother is therefore not a contradiction in terms; see the commentary on *Ep.* 2.8.1 *Qui parvuli ... minus pupilli existimarentur.* For a couple to become engaged, both *patresfamilias*, the heads of the families, had to consent in addition to the agreement of the partners involved. Usually the mother also was asked for her advice, but her consent was not legally necessary; Treggiari (1997) 897. As the father of the young girl in the present letter has died, the mother is responsible for her marriage; in such cases this was usually with the help of relatives and/or the girl's guardian; Krause (1991) 552–3, Krause (1995) 146–58, Krause (2002), MacDonald (2000) 96–7. Proiectus already has the mother's permission, but as a gesture of courtesy he now also asks the girl's guardian, Sagittarius, who is responsible for her financial situation and her dowry; see the commentary below on *Ep.* 2.4.2 *conferendo ... tutoris officium.* We have a similar (fictive) case in Sidon. *Ep.* 4.24.8, where a brother has to take care of his underaged siblings, by finding a husband for his younger sister and a guardian for his brother; Amherdt (2001) 502. In *Ep.* 7.2.7–9 Sidonius writes about the mother of a young girl who had made a disastrous match for her daughter; Nathan (2000) 146, van Waarden (2010) 174–90.

parum tamen votorum suorum promotum censet effectum, nisi assensum tuum super his omnibus seu sedulitate sua seu precatu nostrae intercessionis adipiscatur: Sagittarius is approached from two sides. On the one hand, Proiectus is trying to further his own cause; on the other hand, Sidonius is writing his letter to support Proiectus. *Sedulitas*, 'painstaking attention', 'application', 'assiduity' (*OLD* 1726), is a positive quality attributed by Sidonius to various persons, for example in Sidon. *Ep.* 1.2.4, 1.4.1, 7.2.5; see also Plin. *Ep.* 3.18.6. See also the commentary on *Ep.* 2.5.2 *Pro quo precem sedulam fundo....* *Precatus*, 'prayer', 'request' (*TLL* 10.2, 1152.15–50), appears first in Stat. *Theb.* 8.332, then again after the fourth century AD. In Sidonius' epistles it appears six times; see *Ep.* 2.8.2 and Amherdt (2001) 103–4 on *Ep.* 4.2.3. While the manuscripts TC and other members of α, Lütjohann (1887) 27, Anderson (1936) 438 and Loyen (1970a) 55 have *adipiscatur*, LMNPF have *adipiscitur*.

Namque ipse, quantum ad institutionem spectat puellae, in locum mortui patris curarum participatione succedis: After Optantius' death Sagittarius is responsible for the education of the girl. Sidonius uses the expression *quantum ad ... spectat*, 'when it comes to ...', in other instances, for example in *Ep.* 4.1.5, 4.6.4, 7.5.4; alternatively he writes *quod ad ... spectat*; see for example *Ep.* 4.3.1, 6.2.1. He uses the term *institutio*, 'upbringing', 'education' (*TLL* 7.1, 1997.36–8.10), in *Ep.* 2.11.2 referring to Rusticus' relation to his letter carriers, probably slaves. For the term *puella*, 'girl', 'young woman' (*TLL* 10.2, 2504.58–9.72), see Plin. *Ep.* 1.14.8, 5.16.1, 6.32.2. Pliny also uses it in the meaning of 'wife', in Plin. *Ep.* 4.21.2; Watson (1983), Hindermann (2010), Hindermann (2013) 153, 158.

conferendo virgini parentis affectum, patroni auctoritatem, tutoris officium: To flatter his addressee, Sidonius describes the function of a guardian in a tricolon which combines parental love and the providence of a patron with a tutor's care for the child's financial interests. The Roman institution of *tutela* prescribed a *tutor* for minors and women who were not under *patria potestas* (paternal power in the form of absolute authority). Either the father appointed a guardian in his will (*tutor testamentarius*) or, failing that, the male next of kin was automatically assigned the office (*tutor legitimus*). Sagittarius' relationship to Optantius thus cannot be known definitively. Officially, women were not allowed to make decisions over someone else's property, not even as widows over their children's property. A law in the *Codex Theodosianus* (3.17.4) finally allowed maternal guardianship in 390, but only if there were no agnatic relatives: *tum demum petendae tutelae ius habebat, cum tutor legitimus defuerit* ('there was then the right to assume guardianship in the absence of a legal guardian'); Arjava (1996) 89–94, Krause (1995) 97–119, 123–9, MacDonald (2000) 96–7, Schiemann (2002). The *tutela* over women was loosened in Late Antiquity, but Optantius' daughter seems to be underaged and therefore in need of a tutor anyway; see the commentary above on *Ep.* 2.4.2 *licet a matre pupillae in coniugium petierit obtinueritque*. In other instances Sidonius plays with the idea of different social roles combined in one person: *Ep.* 3.5.3, 4.11.5, 7.17.1; van Waarden (2016) 216–17. For the term *virgo*, 'a girl of marriageable age' (*OLD* 2071, 1), see Hindermann (2013) 152–3, 156–9, Watson (1983), Plin. *Ep.* 1.16.6, 8.23.7.

Section 3

Quocirca, quia dignus es, ut domus tuae celeberrimam disciplinam etiam procul positorum petat ambitus: In the last section Sidonius adds further flattery. Sagittarius rightly deserves the attention given to him by many clients. Sagittarius appears as an ideal *patronus* who has a widespread network of acquaintances – a motif Sidonius uses elsewhere; see *Ep.* 6.12.1, 7.4.3, 7.5.5, 7.14.1; van Waarden (2010) 236. *Quocirca*, 'in consequence of which', 'so', is a frequent beginning of a sentence in Sidonius; van Waarden (2010) 525 on *Ep.* 7.9.23 counts nineteen instances. *Disciplina*, 'learning', 'knowledge', 'discipline' (*TLL* 5.1, 1318.62–84), is a trait Sidonius often praises in men, see *Ep.* 2.10.1, 2.11.2, 4.25.1, van Waarden (2016) 150 on *Ep.* 7.14.7. The participle *positus* in the meaning of 'living in', 'resident', is rare and only found in Late Latin (also in Symmachus). Sidonius uses it a few times; see for example *Ep.* 1.5.1 and Köhler (1995) 185, *Ep.* 4.17.3 and Amherdt (2001) 394, *Ep.* 6.12.2, 7.4.3. *Ambitus* means the 'corrupt practices in electioneering', 'undue influence, bribery' (*OLD* 115, 6). In the fourth and fifth centuries, *ambitus* is still potentially negative, but it has changed its meaning; the term is less specific and in Sidonius' letters usually used for 'desire for advancement', 'ambition' (*TLL* 1, 1860.80–2.44, *OLD*

115, 9), a meaning also attested in earlier literature, see for example Sen. *Ep.* 84.11, Plin. *Ep.* 3.2.4. The exception is Sidon. *Ep.* 1.3.1, where *ambitus* has a republican ring; Köhler (1995) 167. For *ambire*, see the commentary on *Ep.* 2.7.1 *quam primum ambiens....*

sicut decet bonarum partium viros: Praising the good and criticising the bad is a frequent combination in Sidonius letters; see for example *Ep.* 2.6.1–2, 2.13.5, 3.2.4, 3.6.2, 3.11.1, 4.5.2, 4.15.1, 4.21.6, 7.9.11. The *boni* are different from common people; see *Ep.* 1.11.7 *multorum plus quam bonorum odia admovit* ('he stirred up hate against me among the many rather than among the good') and a minority; see also *Ep.* 7.9.8 *bonorum raritas* ('the rarity of the good'). In Sidonius' letters *boni* is often synonymous with 'the ruling class' or 'the elite', and the *boni* are contrasted with 'the others', *mali*, who have the wrong values and the wrong associates. The *boni* excel in education and champion literature; see the commentary on *Ep.* 2.10.1 *Illud appone....* For the *boni* in Sidonius, see Mathisen (1993) 10–11, Kaufmann (1995) 148 n. 394, Amherdt (2001) 191 on *Ep.* 4.5.2 and Amherdt (2004), van Waarden (2010) 170 on *Ep.* 7.2.5 and 453 on 7.9.6, Giannotti (2016) 132 on *Ep.* 3.2.4, van Waarden (2016) 123, Mathisen (2020a) 49. For the expression *bonarum partium*, see Symm. *Ep.* 9.84 *bonarum partium* ('part of the good ones'), 9.112.1 *summatem civilium partium virum* ('an eminent man of the citizens'), Plin. *Ep.* 1.5.9 *ut decebat optimum virum* ('like it is proper for a noble man'), Cic. *Pro Cael.* 77 *civem bonarum artium, bonarum partium, bonorum virorum* ('a citizen of good skills, belonging to the good party and to good men'). In late republican terms, the *boni* were the conservative faction that Cicero loosely adhered to.

benignitate responsi proci supplicis verecundiam munerare: Sagittarius is shown once again in the position of the powerful one who gives to the petitioner. The gift, *benignitate responsi*, 'with the kindness of your answer', an expression which is unattested elsewhere, is in the ablative; for the construction with the verb *muneror*, see *TLL* 8, 1642.20–73. *Responsi* and *proci supplicis* are two genitives of identity, depending from *benignitate*. The noun *procus*, a 'suitor', 'wooer' (*TLL* 10.2, 1592.70–3.70), is primarily used in poetry from Vergil on; see for example Verg. *Aen.* 4.534. Sidonius uses it in *Carm.* 14.4 v. 11 *mortibus ... procorum* ('through the death of suitors'). In prose it is less common, but Apuleius uses it nine times. The imperative of the deponent *muneror*, 'give', 'present', is constructed here with the accusative *verecundiam*, 'an attitude of restraint', 'modesty' (*OLD* 2035, 1a).

Sidonius uses this term very often in his letters to denote his or others' polite restraint for example in *Ep.* 1.2.3, 1.7.5, 2.9.10, 2.10.3, 2.11.2, 3.5.2, 3.9.1, 4.5.1, 5.3.1, 7.6.3, 7.13.4, 8.6.2, 8.6.6, 9.2.3, 9.10.1, 9.12.2, 9.13.5, 9.14.3; Fascione (2019) 104–5. In his poems it appears only in *Carm.* 22.5.

et, qui ita expetitus deberes illi expetere pollicendam, securus permitte promissam; quia sic te condicioni huic meritorum ratio praefecit, ut nec superstiti Optantio in liberos suos decuerit plus licere. Vale: With the figura etymologica *expetitus–expetere* and the alliteration (on *p-*) and homoioteleuton (the same ending in *-am*) *pollicendam–promissam* Sidonius highlights the fact that the affair is already settled and Sagittarius only has to confirm his ward's engagement. For *licere alicui in aliquem*, 'to have power over someone else' (*TLL* 7.2, 1359.77–83, *OLD* 1028, 3b), see Sidon. *Ep.* 2.11.1, 8.6.16, *Carm.* 2.25–6, Plin. *Ep.* 7.1.1 *vereor tamen, ne quid illi etiam in mores tuos liceat* ('I fear that it also affects your behaviour'), Symm. *Ep.* 9.108 *in sacrae virginis famam nihil patior licere sermonibus* ('but according to me no rumours are allowed against the reputation of a sacred virgin'), *Rel.* 12.4. For the letter's simple ending with *vale*, see the commentary on *Ep.* 2.1.4 *Vale*.

Epistula 5

Introduction

Summary

Iohannes, a friend of Sidonius, needs Petronius' help in a complicated lawsuit. Sidonius asks the lawyer Petronius to help Iohannes find a good strategy.

Addressee

Petronius is a noble lawyer and *vir illustris* (for this title see the commentary on *Ep.* 2.4.1 *Vir clarissimus Proiectus...*) from Arles. He is one of two addressees who received three letters (2.5, 5.1, 8.1); Mathisen (2020a) 41. Petronius, moreover, is a central figure for Sidonius' letter collection, for it was at his suggestion that Sidonius compiled and published his eighth letter book; see *Ep.* 8.1.1 *scrinia Arverna petis eventilari* ('you want to shake my Avernian book cases'). He is also mentioned in *Ep.* 1.7.4, 8.16.1, 8.16.3. In *Ep.* 2.5 and 5.1 Sidonius asks him for legal advice. Together with Tonantius Ferreolus and Thaumastus, Petronius was one of the three Romans from Gaul who were sent to Rome in 468/9 to charge Arvandus for treasonous collusion with the Visigothic court; see *Ep.* 1.7.4–5. As *praefectus urbi* Sidonius was responsible for the judicial process, but he disappeared from Rome before the trial. Sidonius' sympathy for Arvandus made him unpopular among his fellows, including Magnus Felix (see *Ep.* 2.3); Stevens (1933) 103–7, Köhler (1995) 229–32, Mathisen (1998), Delaplace (2015) 241–6, Kelly (2020a) 179–80, 192, Mathisen (2020a) 53, 82, 95–6, 113, 123, van Waarden (2020a) 27.

For Petronius' biography, see *PLRE* 2, 863–64, *PCBE* 4, 1475–6, Kaufmann (1995) 333–4, Köhler (1995) 240, Liebs (2002) 50–2, Overwien (2009a) 94–6, Mathisen (2020a) 113.

Date

Loyen (1970a) 57, 247 n. 5 suggests the year 69, which I find unlikely in view of the Arvandus case, which led to a rift between Sidonius and his friends; see immediately above, on the addressee, Petronius. A date before 468/9, specifically between the years 461 and 467 (*PLRE* 2, 863), seems more likely. On the general difficulty of dating Sidonius' letters, see the Introduction, '2. The date and order of letters in Book 2'.

Major themes and further reading

Like the previous letter (2.4), this one belongs to the many letters of recommendation in Sidonius' collection; see the introduction to *Ep.* 2.4. Whereas in *Ep.* 2.4 the occasion for the letter is a matchmaking, here it is the plea for help in a lawsuit. There is also a parallel between *Ep.* 2.5 and *Ep.* 2.7: in both letters Sidonius asks a lawyer for help in a complicated legal case of a friend. For legal advice as one of the tasks of a *patronus*, see Näf (1995) 145–6, Lintott (2000).

Commentary

Section 1

Sidonius Petronio suo salutem: For the simple greeting formula, see the commentary on *Ep.* 2.1.1 *Sidonius Ecdicio suo salutem*. For the addressee, Petronius, see the introduction to this letter.

Iohannes familiaris meus inextricabilem labyrinthum negotii multiplicis incurrit: Sidonius begins his second letter of recommendation with an element which is typical of the genre: the name of and the relationship between him and his protégé; Furbetta (2015a) 347–8. Unlike in *Ep.* 2.4, there is no praise of Iohannes; instead, Sidonius focuses on the legal case in which Petronius is supposed to help him. There is nothing else known about Sidonius' friend (*familiaris meus*) Iohannes and his lawsuit; Mathisen (2020a) 102. Iohannes' labyrinthine case is called *inextricabilis*, 'impossible to disentangle or sort out', an adjective frequently used of labyrinths (*TLL* 7.1, 1334.83–5.10, *OLD* 893, 1a). The phrase may be an allusion to Verg.

Aen. 6.27, where he describes the Minotaur's labyrinth: *hic labor ille domus et inextricabilis error* ('here the plight of this house, the inextricable maze'). The beginning of the sixth book of the *Aeneid*, where Aeneas invokes Apollo's and the Sibyl's help, is an intertext for the whole letter: see the commentary on *Ep.* 2.5.2 *Pro quo precem sedulam fundo....* The expression is also used in Plin. *Nat.* 36.91 *labyrinthum inextricabilem* ('a labyrinth, impossible to find out') and Hyg. *Fab.* 40.3 *Daedalus Minotauro labyrinthum inextricabili exitu fecit* ('Daedalus made for the Minotaur a labyrinth from which it was impossible to find a way out'). In the letter at hand, *inextricabilis* probably also has the meaning of 'insoluble' (of problems) (*OLD* 893, 1c). See also *Ep.* 2.7.2, where a legal case is described as *interminabilis iurgii*. For adjectives ending in -*bilis* in general, see the commentary on *Ep.* 2.2.16 *Is quidem ... vestigio inspectoris inadibilis*. In ancient literature, *labyrinthus*, 'labyrinth' (*TLL* 7.2, 814.37–81), is used in its literal meaning, but often also as a metaphor for art, a difficult process or, as here, for inexplicability or impenetrability; Doob (1990) 64–91, Amherdt (2001) 287–8. Specifically in Late Antique literature, the term also describes philosophical questions and complex discussions; see for example Macrob. *Sat.* 7.5.2; Schwitter (2015) 196. Sidonius uses 'labyrinth' in its various meanings: as an image for an intellectual problem in *Ep.* 4.11.2 *si forte oborta quarumpiam quaestionum insolubilitate labyrinthica* ('if some questions presented a labyrinthine intricacy'), to praise Petrus' book in *Ep.* 9.13.5 vv. 88–91 *opus editum tenemus,* | *bimetra quod arte texens* | *iter asperum viasque* | *labyrinthicas cucurrit* ('we hold the edited work, which he has artfully combined in both metres, and he has traversed the steep path on labyrinthine paths'), and for the labyrinth of the Minotaur in *Carm.* 11.66. For *negotium* in the meaning of 'legal matter' as here, see for example *Ep.* 1.2.8, 1.7.7, 3.10.1; elsewhere it denotes in general a 'business', 'important matter', for example in *Ep.* 1.5.10, 4.22.3, 5.1.3, 7.8.2, or 'field of work', 'duty' (in opposition to *otium*) for example in *Ep.* 2.13.4, 5.14.1; André (2006) 63–86.

et donec suarum merita chartarum vel vestra scientia vel si qua est vestrae (si tamen est ulla) similis inspexerit: Sidonius starts the letter with a compliment to the addressee: Petronius, or someone else with the same skills – though there is of course no one else with the same skills – should sift through the papers and find the decisive arguments for Iohannes' case. *Meritum* here is used in the sense of 'worth', 'value', 'excellence', 'merit' (*TLL* 8, 821.52–2.72), which is a common use by Late Antique authors; see Sidon. *Ep.* 2.13.5, 4.17.3, *Carm.* 15.37; see van Waarden (2010) 309 on

Sidon. *Ep.* 7.6.6 *ob virium merita terribilis* ('feared for his military strength'). *Chartae* are 'pages or rolls containing literary or other works'; here the term is used meaning 'files', 'papers', 'paperwork' (*TLL* 3, 998.46–9.54, *OLD* 309, 3a); Schipke (2001) 125–32. Plin. *Ep.* 5.14.8 also establishes an opposition between paperwork and literary work: *aliis enim chartis, aliis sum litteris initiatus* ('I am privy to different kinds of papers, in different kinds of books'). In Sidon. *Ep.* 2.9.10, *charta* means 'papyrus (to write a letter on)', 'letter', see the commentary there on *Dicerem et cenas ... charta posuisset*. The subject of the sentence is the abstract *scientia*, which underlines the importance of Petronius' expertise. *Scientia*, 'knowledge', 'learning', 'erudition' (*OLD* 1703, 3), is a trait that Sidonius mentions several times in people he praises; see in the second book *Ep.* 2.9.4, 2.10.6. In *Ep.* 3.14.2, a reply to critics of his literary work, he defines his own style with a series of cultural values, among them *scientia*; Denecker (2015) 412. For further examples, see van Waarden (2010) 449 on *Ep.* 7.9.5, van Waarden (2016) 150 on *Ep.* 7.14.7. For the meaning 'skills', 'artistic mastery', see the commentary on *Ep.* 2.9.4 *nam similis scientiae viri*....

quid respuat, quid optet ignorat. ita se quodammodo bipertitae litis forma confundit, ut propositio sua quem actionis ordinem propugnatura, quem sit impugnatura non noverit: The case is so complicated that it is difficult to find the right strategy, that is, to decide in which area to be defensive and in which to be aggressive. *Bipertitus*, 'that is divided into two parts', 'bipartite' (*TLL* 2, 2002.33–3.7), is also used in Sidon. *Ep.* 5.1.3, 5.17.6, 7.14.8, 7.18.3, 9.9.10, 9.16.3 v. 3. Similarly, Cic. *Inv.* 1.67 mentions different lines of argument (*argumentatio*), one of them also *bipertita*. The *propositio*, 'statement of the facts or substance of a case' (*TLL* 10.2, 2080.29–40, *OLD* 1495, 3b), is the subject of the following clause. It is not Iohannes who does not know how to handle his case, but the case itself that does not know which strategy to choose in the lawsuit at hand (*actionis ordinem*). With this personification the whole affair gets even more confusing and urgent at the same time. For *propositio*, see also Sidon. *Ep.* 1.7.9 *offertur praefectoriis ante propositionis exordium ius sedendi* ('those of prefectorian rank are offered, before the statement of facts begins, the privilege of being seated'). For *actio*, 'suit', 'process' (*TLL* 1, 441.48–4.40, *OLD* 30, 6a) as a juridical *terminus technicus*, see Sidon. *Ep.* 1.7.7; Köhler (1995) 245. Petronius must help to develop a plan for how best to sort the arguments, that is, when to *propugnare*, 'to act as a defence for', 'protect', 'defend' (*TLL* 10.2, 2141.29–34, *OLD* 1497, 2); see Tac. *Ann.* 13.31.3, Gell. 14.5.4. The opposed activity is *impugnare*, 'to oppose by word or action', 'attack', 'impugn' (*TLL* 7.1, 715.2–12, *OLD* 854, 2a), a term used elsewhere in a legal context; see Quint. 2.17.40 *quod saepe, quae in aliis litibus impugnarunt actores causarum, eadem in aliis defendant* ('the same things that advocates have attacked in one case, they often defend in another'). Sidonius also uses this pair of terms in *Ep.* 3.4.1 *nec impugnantum ira nec propugnantum caremus invidia* ('we are spared neither the fury of our invaders nor the malignity of our protectors') and in 6.11.2 *tu quoque potes huius laboriosi, etsi impugnas perfidiam, propugnare personam* ('so even you may well defend this unfortunate man's person while attacking his persuasion').

Section 2

Pro quo precem sedulam fundo, ut perspectis chartulis suis, si quid iure competit, instruatis: At the beginning of the second section Sidonius repeats the request for help. The phrase *precem sedulam* (also in *Ep.* 7.7.6, 9.6.4) is very rarely used either before or after Sidonius. In classical Latin, *sedulus*, 'attentive', 'painstaking', 'sedulous' (*OLD* 1726), is used of persons; with abstract nouns it is combined only from the first century AD on; see van Waarden (2010) 377. See also the commentary on *Ep.* 2.4.2 *seu sedulitate sua seu precatu*. The expression *precem fundere*, 'to beg', 'to plea' (*TLL* 6.1, 1569.25–42), is found elsewhere, but usually with the pleas in plural in both poetry and prose. An important intertext is Verg. *Aen.* 6.55 *funditque preces rex pectore ab imo* ('and the king begged from the bottom of his heart'), where Aeneas invokes Apollo and the Sibyl for help like Sidonius invokes Petronius; see the commentary on *Ep.* 2.5.1 *Iohannes familiaris meus inextricabilem labyrinthum…*, which also is an allusion to the beginning of the sixth book of the *Aeneid*. The expression is also used elsewhere: see Hor. *Epod.* 17.53 *quid … fundis preces* ('why do you beg'), Apul. *Met.* 11.3.1 *fusis precibus* ('with begging'). The diminutive *chartulis*, 'a scrap or piece of papyrus' (*TLL* 3, 1001.67–2.40, *OLD* 309), repeats *charta* from *Ep.* 2.5.1 and adds to the pleading, intimate tone of the letter; see also *Ep.* 8.5.2. The noun is already used in Cic. *Fam.* 7.18.2.

quae qualiterve sint obicienda, quae refellenda monstrantes: After the opposition *propugnare–impugnare* in *Ep.* 2.5.1, Sidonius adds another pair of verbs to propose different strategies. *Obicere*, 'to throw or put before' (*TLL* 9.2, 53.79–60.28), has a specific juridical meaning, 'to raise a plea' (see *TLL*

9.2, 58.68–9.2). It is also used in a broader sense 'to reproach (as a crime)' (*TLL* 9.2, 56.26–7.21), see Plaut. *Mil.* 618–23, Cic. *De orat.* 2.107, Cic. *Att.* 1.16.10, Verg. *Ecl.* 3.7. The verb *refellere*, 'to refute', 'rebut' (an assertion, charge etc.) (*OLD* 1539, 1a), is similarly used as a gerundive to denote two opposite ways of acting in Cic. *De orat.* 2.163 *omne, quod sumatur in oratione aut ad probandum aut ad refellendum* ('everything that can be used in a speech either to prove or to refute something'), Quint. 10.2.27 *quae vis probandi ac refellendi* ('the power to prove or reject').

Non enim verebimur, quod causae istius cursus, si de vestri manaverit fonte consilii, ulla contrastantum derivatione tenuetur. Vale: To conclude his letter, Sidonius uses the flattering metaphor of a stream to describe Petronius as a source of wisdom and help (*cursus, manaverit, fonte, derivatione*). See the similar expression in Sidon. *Ep.* 7.8.1 *veluti ex saluberrimo fonte manaret* ('it would flow like from a very healing spring'). In various other instances Sidonius uses *fons*, 'spring', 'source', in a figurative sense in the meaning of 'a source of wisdom' or 'knowledge'; see Sidon. *Ep.* 3.10.1, 4.17.1, 5.17.9, 6.8.2; Montone (2017) 26–7, 40 n. 20. See also *Paneg. Lat.* 2(12).1.3 *facundiam, quam de eorum fonte manantem* ('the eloquence that flows from their source'). See also Ruric. *Ep.* 1.1.1. In *Ep.* 2.7.2, Sidonius uses the metaphor of the doctor who heals to describe legal advice; see the commentary there on *aegritudini huius prope … solita iudicandi salubritate medicabitur*. For the letter's simple ending with *vale*, see the commentary on *Ep.* 2.1.4 *Vale*.

Epistula 6

Introduction

Summary

Sidonius expresses his approval of Menstruanus, who was recommended to him as a friend by Pegasius, the recipient of this letter. In addition to Sidonius, there are many other people among the Avernians who are pleased with Menstruanus' behaviour.

Addressee

Pegasius, probably a Gallic noble, is otherwise unknown; *PLRE* 2, 856, *PCBE* 4, 1459, Kaufmann (1995) 331, Mathisen (2020a) 113.

Date

There is no evidence for the date of this letter; see the Introduction, '2. The date and order of letters in Book 2'.

Major themes and further reading

Like *Ep.* 2.3 and 2.11, this letter belongs to the category of letters of friendship; see the introduction to *Ep.* 2.3. Fernández López (1994) 191–204 treats *Ep.* 2.6 and 2.12 together under 'cartas descriptivas de lugares y personas: descripción breve' ('descriptive letters of places and persons: brief description'). In his overall positive behaviour, Menstruanus is an antithesis to Seronatus; see the introduction to *Ep.* 2.1.

Commentary

Section 1

Sidonius Pegasio suo salutem: For the simple greeting formula, see the commentary on *Ep.* 2.1.1 *Sidonius Ecdicio suo salutem*. For the addressee, Pegasius, see the introduction to this letter.

Proverbialiter celebre est saepe moram esse meliorem, sicuti et nunc experti sumus: The initial proverb ('good things take time') does not fit properly. It suggests that it took Menstruanus a long time to become the excellent friend he is now. But presumably Sidonius wants to emphasise that he has been observing Menstruanus for a long time; see the commentary immediately below on *Ep.* 2.6.1 *Menstruanus amicus tuus longo istic tempore....* The adverb *proverbialiter*, 'proverbially', also appears in *Ep.* 7.9.19; van Waarden (2010) 505–6. For adverbs ending in *-(i)ter* in general, see the commentary on *Ep.* 2.1.1 *Duo nunc pariter mala sustinent*. The proverb *saepe mora melior* is preserved in Lactantius Placidus' commentary on Statius' epic *Thebaid* 3.719 as an epigram of Lucan (*Epigrammata* frg. 10); Courtney (2003) 355. Its meaning is also attested in different forms in Stat. *Theb.* 10.704 *da spatium tenuemque moram* ('delay a little while'), Ov. *Fast.* 3.394 *habent parvae commoda magna morae* ('short delays have great advantages'), Sen. *Ag.* 130 *quod ratio non quit saepe sanavit mora* ('what reason cannot cure often has been cured by time'); Montone (2017) 41 n. 41. For the use of proverbs in letters in general, see Cugusi (1983) 96–8.

Menstruanus amicus tuus longo istic tempore inspectus meruit inter personas nobis quoque caras devinctasque censeri: Like the addressee, Pegasius, Menstruanus, is probably also a Gallic noble, and otherwise unknown; *PLRE* 2, 756, *PCBE* 4, 1323, Kaufmann (1995) 331, Mathisen (2020a) 108. Perhaps it is another play on the name ('monthly') of the addressee, since the letter mentions the length of time Menstruanus proved himself a friend. For Sidonius' fondness of puns with names, see the commentary on *Ep.* 2.1.1 *Seronati, inquam: de cuius ut primum etiam nomine loquar*. For the subject of friendship (*amicitia*) in Sidonius and ancient letters in general, see the introduction to *Ep.* 2.3. The meaning of *inspicere* (*TLL* 7.1, 1951.9–8.12) here is somewhere between 'get to know' and 'observe'. For *inspicere*, 'to meet', 'get to know', 'learn to know', see *Ep.* 7.13.1 *raptim ac breviter inspectus* ('I met him hastily and briefly'); van Waarden (2016) 88;

see also Plin. *Ep.* 1.10.2 (about the philosopher Euphrates). For *inspicere*, 'to scrutinise', 'inspect', examine', see for example Sidon. *Ep.* 1.2.4, 1.2.7, 1.4.1, 1.7.8, 5.20.4, 6.12.1, 7.2.7, 7.14.9. For the meaning of 'to contemplate', 'look at closely', see for example *Ep.* 3.9.1, 4.20.1, 7.6.9, 7.11.1, 8.16.1, and see the commentary below on 2.9.5 *Quos inter ... lectoribus inspiciebatur.* In Sidonius' *Carmina* the verb appears only twice, in *Carm.* 22.4 v. 10 *inspicis, inspiceris* ('view, you are put on view'). *Persona* here has the meaning of 'friend'; see the commentary on *Ep.* 2.2.5 *ita ut ministeriorum ... quot solet sigma personas.* Sidonius uses *devincere*, 'to bind together', 'to unite closely', in a transferred sense. For examples of the use of the participle *devinctus*, 'obligated', 'devoted' (*TLL* 5.1, 861.4–23), see *Ep.* 2.11.1, 4.6.1, 5.11.1.

opportunus elegans, verecundus sobrius, parcus religiosus et his morum dotibus praeditus: Next, Sidonius adds a list of Menstruanus' positive characteristics. On this asyndetic sequence of adjectives as a stylistic means (*trigeminatio*), see van Waarden (2010) 58. In *Ep.* 2.4.1 we have also a list of positive attributes in the description of a friend: *familiae splendor, probitas morum, patrimonii facultas, iuventutis alacritas*; see the commentary there on *et cum illi familiae splendor....* The praise of Filimatia is also similar, but takes place in a different context, that is, at a funeral; see *Ep.* 2.8.1, 2.8.3 vv. 5–6. For *verecundus*, 'modest', see the commentary on *Ep.* 2.4.3 *benignitate responsi ... verecundiam munerare. Religiosus*, 'devout', 'scrupulous' (*OLD* 1606, 7 and 8), is used in Sidonius mostly in relation to Christian religion or piety; Ernout (1949) 68, 105, and see van Waarden (2016) 102 on Sidon. *Ep.* 7.13.5. For adjectives ending in *-osus* in general, see the commentary on *Ep.* 2.2.18 *Lacus ipse ... flexuosus nemorosusque....* The expression *morum dotibus* is also used in Sidon. *Ep.* 4.25.2, *Carm.* 24.82, but is unattested in other authors; see Santelia (2002) 118. Sidonius uses several similar expressions with *dos*, 'talent', 'virtue', 'quality' (*TLL* 5.1, 2046.56–7.41), to describe the character of persons; see Sidon. *Ep.* 1.2.1, 1.4.1, 9.9.12, 9.16.1; see also Ov. *Ars* 2.112, where Ovid recommends his students of love *ingenii dotes corporis adde bonis* ('add qualities of mind to the benefits of the body'), Sulpic. Sev. *Dial.* 1.8.3 *dotem virtutum* ('the gift of virtues'); Montone (2017) 31. For *dos* in connection with an estate, see the commentary on *Ep.* 2.14.1 *quod te tuosque plurifaria frugum mansionumque dote remoretur.*

ut, quotiens in boni cuiusque adscitur amicitias, non amplius consequatur beneficii ipse quam tribuat: Sidonius' friendship with Menstruanus is valuable, as he returns the favour. Friendships exist among the good men, a group that includes Menstruanus. For the alliance of the elite class of the *boni*, see the commentary on *Ep.* 2.4.3 *sicut decet bonarum partium viros*. The manuscripts offer different variants: *adscitur* LNT, followed by Lütjohann (1887) 28, Anderson (1936) 442, Loyen (1970a) 58, *ascitur* M, *adsciscitur* C. For (*non*) *amplius* with the genitive partitivus, see *Ep.* 1.2.10 *quia et tu cognoscere viri non amplius quam studia personamque voluisti* ('because you did not want to hear more about the man than his interests and personality'). For *amplius* in general, see the commentary on *Ep.* 2.2.20 *Sed non amplius moror*.... The plural of *amicitia* is justified here because Menstruanus cultivates different friendships. For the use of *amicitias* (in plural instead of singular), see the commentary on *Ep.* 2.3.1 *invenis tamen, vir amicitiarum servantissime*. For the topic of friendship in Sidonius' letters, see the introduction to letter 2.3. The exchange of gifts and services (*beneficia*) was a much-discussed philosophical subject, as favours were crucial to the working of ancient society; see Seneca's *De Beneficiis*, Sen. *Ep.* 73.9, and Cicero's *De Officiis*. Both Cicero and Seneca describe the exchange of benefits as a chief bond of society and as an essential means of creating social cohesion; Griffin (2003), Griffin and Inwood (2011) 1–4. In his letters, Pliny the Younger also very often describes the practice of doing and receiving gifts and favours, both between friends of equal rank and in patronage relationships, especially in the tenth book, addressed to the emperor Trajan; see for example Plin. *Ep.* 1.19.4, 2.13.1, 3.4.6, 4.4.3, 10.5.1, 10.6.3, 10.26.1. See also the commentary on *Ep.* 2.3.2 *Quocirca nolo sibi ... principalia beneficia*....

Section 2

Haec tibi non ut ignoranti, sed ut iudicio meo satisfacerem, scripsi. Quam ob rem triplex causa laetandi: In his conclusion, Sidonius points out three groups of people who, besides himself, are satisfied with Menstruanus. The addressee, Pegasius, naturally shares Sidonius' opinion, since he recommended Menstruanus to Sidonius. *Satisfacere*, 'to give satisfaction', 'to satisfy' (*OLD* 1694, 1), is usually constructed with the dative. Here the verb is used in the meaning of 'to justify', 'explain'. For Sidonius' use of *triplex*, see the commentary on *Ep.* 2.2.8 *triplex medii parietis aditus*....

tibi prima, cui amicos sic aut instituere aut eligere contingit: Sidonius extends his praise of Pegasius. Menstruanus is only one positive example of friendship – Sidonius has other such friends. *Amicum* or *amicitiam instituere*, 'make friends', is a common combination (*TLL* 7.1, 1987.68–9, 1988.18 and 23). Both forms of friendship (creating friends or choosing friends who already have the necessary qualities) are described before Sidonius. Cicero, in his theoretical work on friendship, turns to the question of the criteria by which one should choose friends in Cic. *Lael.* 50, 62, 65–6, and see Cic. *Fin.* 1.65–70 on the pleasure that friendship gives. Sen. *Ep.* 3 and *Ep.* 6 deal with the question of how friends influence and teach each other.

Arvernis secunda, quibus hoc in eo placuisse confirmo, quod te probasse non ambigo: Sidonius unexpectedly mentions the Arverni, the inhabitants of the Auvergne, in second place. It is not clear why and to what extent Menstruanus was a positive force for them (*hoc in eo*). Sidonius holds his adopted homeland, the Auvergne, in high esteem and mentions it and its inhabitants several times: see the commentary on *Ep.* 2.1.1 *Arverni tui*. The verb *ambigo*, 'to waver', 'hesitate', 'doubt' (*TLL* 1, 1838.23–9.83), appears several times in Sidonius' letters, but not in his *Carmina*; see Sidon. *Ep.* 1.5.5, 3.10.1, 3.11.2, 3.13.4, 4.11.1, 7.6.6, 7.9.19, 8.4.2, 8.6.16, 8.14.5, and also Plin. *Ep.* 9.26.8.

illi tertia, de quo boni quique bona quaeque iudicaverunt. Vale: Finally, Sidonius mentions Menstruanus as a person who belongs to the group of the good men, which he already mentioned in the first section of the letter. For the role of the *boni*, 'the elite', see the commentary on *Ep.* 2.4.3 *sicut decet bonarum partium viros*. We have a similar wordplay with *bonus* in *Ep.* 7.8.3 *de quo tamen Simplicio scitote narrari plurima bona, atque ea quidem a plurimis bonis* ('you should know that about this Simplicius many good things are related and by many good men') and 7.14.1 *omnes de te boni in commune senserunt omnia bona* ('all the best people unanimously expressed a positive opinion of you'); van Waarden (2010) 57, van Waarden (2016) 123. For the letter's simple ending with *vale*, see the commentary on *Ep.* 2.1.4 *Vale*.

Epistula 7

Introduction

Summary

Sidonius begs Explicius to decide the case of Alethius and Paulus, because his verdicts are accepted by winners and losers. To flatter Explicius, Sidonius compares his work with three venerable offices of the Roman Republic (*censor, decemviri, pontifices*).

Addressee

Explicius is described in Sidon. *Ep.* 2.7 as a highly sought after arbitrator with great legal experience; Loyen (1970a) 219 n. 28, *PLRE* 2, 447, *PCBE* 4, 726, Mathisen (2020a) 94. *PLRE* 2, 447 suggests that Explicius is a bishop, whereas Kaufmann (1995) 304 convincingly notes that both Sidonius' typical formulaic address for bishops (*domino papae*) as well as the closure (*memor nostri esse dignare, domine papa*) are missing; see also Liebs (2002) 46–7.

Date

There is no evidence for the date of this letter; see the Introduction, '2. The date and order of letters in Book 2'.

Major themes and further reading

Sidonius frequently intercedes for his friends and acquaintances. Like *Ep.* 2.4, *Ep.* 2.7 is also about legal advice; see the introduction to *Ep.* 2.4. Other letters in which Sidonius tries to settle (legal) conflicts are *Ep.* 4.6, 4.23,

4.24, 6.2; Amherdt (2001) 196. Various legal matters are also often the subject of Pliny's letters; see the Introduction, p. xvii.

Commentary

Section 1

Sidonius Explicio suo salutem: For the simple greeting formula, see the commentary on *Ep.* 2.1.1 *Sidonius Ecdicio suo salutem.* For the addressee, Explicius, see the introduction to this letter.

Quia iustitia vestra iure fit universitati per conplura recti experimenta venerabilis: Sidonius emphasises the legal subject matter of the letter, referring to the justice (*iustitia*) of the addressee, and adds as a pun that this is rightly (*iure*) appreciated by all. For *universitas*, see the commentary on *Ep.* 2.3.2 *sic invidiam … universitatis amore Germanicus.* For an instance of *experimentum*, 'proof', 'test', 'trial' (*TLL* 5.2, 1656.69–7.7), with the genitive objectivus referring to a state of mind, see Sidon. *Ep.* 1.11.6 *propter experimenta felicis audaciae* ('thanks to the experienced lucky audacity'). The adjective *venerabilis*, 'venerable', 'august' (*OLD* 2027, 1a), is regularly used of persons. Here it is applied to Explicius' justice. For adjectives ending in *-bilis*, see the commentary on *Ep.* 2.2.16 *Is quidem … vestigio inspectoris inadibilis.*

idcirco singulas quasque personas id ipsum efflagitantes in examen vestrum libens et avidus emitto: Sidonius underlines his request for legal help by writing that he is not the only one asking, but that Explicius will be also approached by other persons seeking help. *Persona* is used here in the meaning of 'acquaintance', 'client'; see the commentary on *Ep.* 2.2.5 *ita ut ministeriorum … quot solet sigma personas.* The verb *efflagito*, 'to demand urgently', 'solicit' (with acc. of a person) (*TLL* 5.2, 187.48–82), is also used in *Ep.* 5.17.6 *efflagitata profertur his pila, his tabula* ('it was demanded and brought for these balls, for those dice'). For *examen*, 'examination', 'consideration' (*TLL* 5.2, 1164.56–5.26), see *Ep.* 4.3.1 *in examen aurium tuarum quippe scriptus adducitur* ('he is submitted and even in written form to the judgement of your ears'), 1.9.7, 7.3.2, 8.16.5; van Waarden (2010) 210–11. For the superlative of *avidus*, see the commentary on *Ep.* 2.4.1 *amicitiarum tuarum … avidissime sinibus infertur.* The positive form of *avidus*, 'longing eagerly', 'desirous', also appears in *Ep.* 1.10.1, 3.13.4, 5.16.2, 6.6.2; the adverb *avide* appears in 4.10.2.

quam primum ambiens me discussionis, illos simultatis onere laxari: Explicius' help will be a relief for Sidonius and his clients Alethius and Paulus. *Ambire*, 'to strive for', 'seek to obtain' (*TLL* 1, 1850.74–51.2, *OLD* 113, 3b), is here constructed with the infinitive, as in Sidon. *Ep.* 3.7.3 *ambiunt a barbaris bene agi* ('who seek to secure from the barbarians favourable treatment') and 9.14.2 *audire plus ambiens* ('I would like to hear more'). It is also used in other constructions and meanings in Sidonius' poems and letters: *Ep.* 1.9.3, 3.2.1, 7.9.22, 8.3.5, *Carm.* 22.4 v. 117; see Giannotti (2016) 125–6. The verb is repeated in the last sentence of this section (*ambiat*). For the meaning of *ambitus*, 'ambition', in Sidonius' letters see the commentary on *Ep.* 2.4.3 *Quocirca ... petat ambitus*. *Discussio* means 'an examination', 'discussion', and in the later period of the empire 'a revision', 'control' (*TLL* 5.1, 1371.24–80). For examples of the expression *discussionis ... onere*, see Symm. *Ep.* 5.76.1 *in societatem discussionis admissus* ('he was accepted to take part in the examination'), *Rel.* 26.2 *investigatio discussionis inquireret* ('the investigation of the control requires'). *Laxo*, 'to slacken', 'undo', 'lighten' (*TLL* 7.2, 1071.27–5.22), is regularly used in the sense 'to free oneself from a burden' (*TLL* 7.2, 1074.8–22); see for example Cic. *Tusc.* 1.44, *Fam.* 5.14.3.

quod demum ita sequetur, si non ex solido querimonias partium verecundus censor excludas: With *sequetur* Sidonius denotes the solution he has in mind: Explicius should listen to both parties. For examples of the expression *ex solido*, 'entirely', 'completely' see Sidon. *Ep.* 6.10.1, 9.11.3, *Carm.* 22.3; Delhey (1993) 61. *Censor* was originally a prestigious office of the Roman republic. The tasks of the two elected censors included the selection of senators (*lectio senatus*), review of the management of public assets and moral jurisdiction (*regimen morum*). During the imperial period, these duties of the censors were transferred to the emperor and his officials. In the second century AD censors were appointed less and less and the office eventually disappeared; Gizewski (1997a). The term is used here in the transferred meaning of 'a censurer', 'severe critic' (*TLL* 3, 801.24–71); see also Sidon. *Ep.* 8.6.9, 8.8.3, 8.15.2, 9.11.4, 9.13.5, *Carm.* 3.10, 8.5. In the second section of this letter, Sidonius takes up again the motif of venerable Roman offices, which he transfers to Explicius; see the commentary below on *Ep.* 2.7.2 *Namque, ni fallor, supra decemvirales pontificalesque sententias*. The censor is described as *verecundus*, 'modest'. Sidonius uses the term *verecundia*, 'an attitude of restraint', 'modesty', several times to denote appropriate behaviour; see the commentary on *Ep*. 2.4.3 *benignitate responsi ... verecundiam munerare*.

quamquam et hoc ipsum, quod copiam tui iurgantibus difficile concedis, indicium sit bene iudicaturi. Quis enim se non ambiat arbitrum legi aut pretio aliquid indulturus aut gratiae?: Sidonius even interprets Explicius' reluctance to help as a positive sign and as proof of the quality of his legal decisions. For a man of less integrity, the office of arbitrator would be ideal for personal enrichment or influence. The idea is repeated at the end of the letter; see the commentary on *Ep*. 2.7.2 *aegritudini huius prope ....* Iurgo, 'to quarrel', 'brawl', 'dispute' (*TLL* 7.2, 668.30–58), is here used intransitively as a juridical *terminus technicus*; see Plin. *Ep*. 6.5.7 *homines iurgaturi* ('the men, ready to fight'), *Cod. Theod*. 9.19.4 pr. *damus copiam iurgantibus* ('we give the plaintiffs the possibility'). For *ambiat*, see the commentary on *Ep*. 2.7.1 *quam primum ambiens....* For *arbiter*, see the commentary on *Ep*. 2.2.20 *Quapropter bonus arbiter....*

Section 2

Igitur ignosce ad tam sanctae conscientiae praerogativam raptim perniciterque properantibus: Sidonius begins the second section of his letter with a plea to be forgiven for turning to Explicius at all. *Conscientia* here denotes 'a consciousness of right or wrong', 'the moral sense' (*TLL* 4, 364.61–6.2); see for example Sidon. *Ep*. 1.9.1, Cic. *Mil*. 23.61, *Nat. Deor*. 3.85, Sen. *Ep*. 43.5. For the combination with *sanctus*, see *Paneg. Lat*. 3(11).3.2 *testor ad vicem numinis mihi sanctam conscientiam meam* ('I summon as a witness instead of a divinity my own conscience'). Sidonius here uses *praerogativa*, 'superiority', 'excellence' (*TLL* 10.2, 798.21–38), to formulate a honorific address. The term often appears in Sidonius' letters both absolutely and with a genitive, for example *Ep*. 1.1.2, 1.3.3, 1.9.2, 2.9.3, 4.3.1, 7.5.4, 7.14.7, but not in the poems; Köhler (1995) 112, Amherdt (2001) 121, van Waarden (2010) 266, van Waarden (2016) 150. The adverb *perniciter*, 'nimbly', 'speedily' (*TLL* 10.1, 1596.40–56), also appears in Sidon. *Ep*. 1.3.3, 3.7.4; Köhler (1995) 174. For the adverbs ending in *-(i)ter* in general, see the commentary on *Ep*. 2.1.1 *Duo nunc pariter mala sustinent*.

quandoquidem sententiam tuam nec victus ut stolidus accusat nec victor ut argutus inridet, veritatisque respectu dependunt tibi addicti reverentiam, gratiam liberati: Explicius' decisions are so honourable that they are accepted by the losers as well as the winners. In a parallel construction with the figura etymologica *victus–victor* and with the chiasmus *addicti–liberati* Sidonius establishes linguistic unity between the two parties of a court case. With *ut stolidus* and *ut argutus* Sidonius very briefly gives reasons why losers and winners usually behave unfairly. Anderson (1936) 444 therefore translates the passage elaborately: 'for when you give the verdict the defeated party never impugns it with the idea that he has been outwitted, nor does the successful party sneer at it with the idea that he has played a clever trick'. The verb *dependere*, 'to pay', is used here in a figurative sense (see *TLL* 5.1, 570.1); in combination with *reverentiam* it is also found in Ennod. *Ep.* 2.26.3 *salutationis reverentiam pleno dependens obsequio* ('pay their respects with full attendance'). The use of the participle *addictus* as a noun meaning 'condemned person', 'sentenced' (*TLL* 1, 574.81–5.15), is already attested in comedy, for example Plaut. *Bacch.* 1205. See also Sidon. *Ep.* 1.7.11 *cum duceretur addictus* ('after he was led away condemned'). For the juridical verb *addicere*, 'to sentence', see the commentary on *Ep.* 2.1.2 *indicit ut dominus ... addicit ut iudex*....

Proinde inpense obsecro, ut inter Alethium et Paulum quae veniunt in disceptationem, mox ut utrimque fuerint opposita, discingas: After the introductory phrases Sidonius comes to his actual request for Alethius and Paulus. With the adverb *inpense*, 'greatly', 'eagerly', 'urgently', 'very much' (*TLL* 7.1, 549.10–75), Sidonius probably alludes to Plin. *Ep.* 6.23.1, who writes in a similar legal context: *impense petis, ut agam causam pertinentem ad curam tuam* ('you eagerly ask me to plead in a cause that concerns you'); see also Plin. *Ep.* 7.14.1 *tam impense et rogas et exigis* ('you are asking and demanding so eagerly'), 9.13.1 *tanto impensius postulas* ('you require more eagerly'). Loyen (1970a) 60 and *PLRE* 2, 55 n. 2 identify Alethius with the *vir clarissimus* Alethius, who is honoured with a verse inscription (*CIL* 12.2660) by his anonymous daughter and son-in-law. Mathisen (2020a) 78, on the other hand, identifies Alethius and Paul as decurions, as they appear to have no honorary titles. Paulus is otherwise unknown; *PLRE* 2, 851 n. 19, *PCBE* 4, 1457, Mathisen (2020a) 112–13. *Disceptatio*, 'dispute', 'debate' (*TLL* 5.1, 1290.35–91.56), is a juridical term, but also used of discussions about non-juridical subjects. The combination of *disceptatio* and *venire* is also found in Liv. 39.36.12 *quonam modo ea, quae belli iure acta sunt, in* *disceptationem veniunt?* ('why do these matters, which were negotiated under martial law, go to court?'). *Discingo*, 'to ungird, deprive of the girdle', means in a juridical context in Late Antique texts 'to decide', 'to settle' (*TLL* 5.1, 1316.25–37). It is similarly also used in Sidon. *Ep.* 3.9.2 *sed si inter coram positos aequanimiter obiecta discingitis* ('but if you bring the opponents face to face and decide their accusations with equanimity') – Giannotti (2016) 199–200 – and in *Ep.* 9.3.7 *in quibus tu merus arbiter, si rem ex asse discingas ridebis plurima, plura culpabis* ('in these matters you will be a fair judge; if you look at the case thoroughly, then you will find a great deal to laugh about, and more matters to fault'); see also Symm. *Rel.* 19.10 *discingenda cuncta servavi* ('I took care to settle everything').

Namque, ni fallor, supra decemvirales pontificalesque sententias: To praise Explicius, Sidonius ranks his decision above those of two different judicial committees; see the commentary on *Ep.* 2.7.1 on *quod demum ... censor excludas*. With this learned allusion to ancient offices Sidonius puts Explicius' ruling above juridical decisions of the past. There are several historical events in which the *decemviri* ('ten-man committee') played a part. The first and most famous committee, the *decemviri legibus scribundis*, recorded the entire common and statute law valid in Rome from 451 to 450 BC (*tabulae duodecim*); Gizewski (1997b). Sidonius mentions the *decemviri* also in *Ep.* 1.7.9, in the court case against Arvandus. Their exact juridical function within lawsuits in Sidonius' time remains unclear, though; see Köhler (1995) 248 and Sidon. *Ep.* 8.6.7 *ut decemviraliter loquar* ('to speak in the manner of a decemvir'). The adjective *decemviralis*, 'of or belonging to a *decemvir*', is attested several times in Cicero *Leg. agr.*, but not frequently elsewhere (*TLL* 5.1, 129.53–70). As a second office Sidonius names the *pontifices*, the most eminent college of priests in Rome. They supervised ritual acts and advised the Senate and officials. The basis for their authority was a large written collection of originally spoken formulas and prescriptions; Gordon (2001). For the adjective *pontificalis*, 'of a high priest', 'pontifical', here used of a thing (*sententiae*), see *TLL* 10.1, 2681.59–2.10. Sidonius uses the adjective in the sense of 'belonging to a bishop', 'high-priestly' (compared with *sacerdos*, a priest of lower status) in *Ep.* 4.25.1 *pontificale concilium* ('the episcopal council'), as well as in 6.2.4, 7.4.2; van Waarden (2010) 228.

aegritudini huius prope interminabilis iurgii sola morum tuorum temperantia solita iudicandi salubritate medicabitur. Vale: Finally, Sidonius once again mentions the great conciliatory power of Explicius' moderate character and complains about the *aegritudini ... iurgii*, 'the sickness of the dispute', he has to deal with. *Aegritudo*, 'illness', 'sickness' (*TLL* 1, 951.65–3.57), is used to describe physical and mental pain or sorrow; here it appears as a metaphor. In *Ep.* 6.4.3 Sidonius also uses a medical metaphor for the treatment of a legal dispute (*medicina ... temperamento ... iurgii status*). *Aegritudo* with a *genitivus explicativus* is also attested in a letter of Sidonius' acquaintance, bishop Faustus of Riez (410–95), to their mutual friend Ruricius, bishop of Limoges (485–510); see *Epistolae ad Ruricium aliosque*, 265.9; 1 *et omnia quibus aegritudo deceptae spei et anxietas cumulatur* ('and all this by which the sorrow of deceived hope and anxiety was accumulated'). See also Ruric. *Ep.* 1.1.3; Neri (2009) 167. *Iurgii* and *iudicandi* echo *iudicaturi* and *iurgantibus* from *Ep.* 2.7.1, thus reinforcing the impression of Explicius' cool judgement on the dispute between the two parties. The adjective *interminabilis*, 'endless', 'interminable', is used only by Late Latin authors and refers to trials or quarrels elsewhere, for example Hier. *In Ezech.* 28.45 *interminabiles quaestiones* ('endless inquiries'), Aug. *Ep.* 36.22 *interminabilis ... contentio* ('endless controversy'); for further examples see *TLL* 7.1, 2223.34–44. Sidonius similarly describes another legal case in *Ep.* 2.5.1 as *inextricabilem labyrinthum negotii*; see the commentary there on *Iohannes familiaris meus....* For adjectives ending in *-bilis*, see the commentary on *Ep.* 2.2.16 *Is quidem ... solo palustri voraginosus et vestigio inspectoris inadibilis.* Sidonius uses the term *temperantia*, 'self-control', 'composure', 'stability', 'balance' (*OLD* 1913), one of the four Platonic cardinal virtues, also in *Ep.* 4.9.5, 7.13.5; van Waarden (2016) 102. Pliny also uses the term in his letters and panegyric: Plin. *Ep.* 1.12.9, 5.16.3, 7.1.7, *Paneg.* 2.7, 82.8. *Salubritas*, 'health', 'healthfulness', is frequently used as a metaphor in Sidonius (*Ep.* 3.10.2, 4.1.3, 5.13.4, 6.4.3, 6.6.2, 7.12.3), and also in a spiritual way to describe Christ healing men, as in *Ep.* 4.14.3; Gualandri (1979) 116, Amherdt (2001) 84, van Waarden (2010) 281–2. *Medicari*, 'to help', 'save' (*TLL* 8, 544.71–83), is constructed here with the dative (*aegritudini*) as in *Ep.* 3.3.9 (*exspectationi aegrescenti*); van Waarden (2010) 376. In the parallel letter *Ep.* 2.5.2 Sidonius uses the metaphor of a river to describe juridical advice; see the commentary on *Ep.* 2.5.2 *Non enim verebimur ... si de vestri manaverit fonte consilii....* For the letter's simple ending with *Vale*, see the commentary on *Ep.* 2.1.4 *Vale*.

Epistula 8

Introduction

Summary

With letter 2.8 Sidonius informs his friend Desideratus that the lady Filimatia died three days ago. Sidonius praises Filimatia's qualities as a wife, mother of five children and daughter of a father who, for love of her, did not remarry after his wife died. At Filimatia's funeral, relatives, friends and strangers mourn greatly and Sidonius expresses his grief with a funeral poem which he wrote at the request of Filimatia's father, Filimatius. Sidonius asks Desideratus to evaluate the poem, which he inserts in section 3 of the letter, and he considers including it in a collection of poems. At the end of the letter he begs the addressee, Desideratus, to join the mourning family members of the late Filimatia to console them.

Addressee

Desideratus is otherwise unknown; see Kaufmann (1995) 295, *PLRE* 2, 355, *PCBE* 4, 556, Mathisen (2020a) 90.

Date

Indications for the dating are given by the mention of Filimatia's father, Filimatius, who is also mentioned in two other letters, *Ep.* 1.3 and 5.17. There is a general forward movement in the letters but *Ep.* 5.17 is surely before Sidonius' ordination to bishop. Loyen (1970a) 61, 247 n. 8, dates *Ep.* 2.8 to the end of the year 469 and justifies this with Sidonius' reference to his existing collection of epigrams (see the commentary below on *Ep.* 2.8.2), to which his bookseller can add new poems. Kelly (2020a) 175 n. 50 rejects Loyen's dating of *Ep.* 1.3 to the year 467 and instead dates *Ep.*

1.3 in 455 and *Ep.* 2.8 and 5.17 in the early 460s. Because Eriphius is presented in 5.17 as the son-in-law, Kelly (2020a) 178 also dates the epitaph of Filimatia inserted in *Ep.* 2.8.3 after the elegiacs on Filimatius' face towel in *Ep.* 5.17.10. Eriphius could still be called the son-in-law, although his wife was dead, but it seems more natural to assume that Filimatia is still alive. On the general difficulty of dating Sidonius' letters, see the Introduction, '2. The date and order of letters in Book 2'.

Major themes and further reading

Structure

After a series of short letters (2.3 to 2.7) Sidonius adds a longer text combined with an inserted epigram, the first of Book 2. Like the letters before, *Ep.* 2.8 is also dedicated to the duty of friendship. While in the previous letters Sidonius has provided legal assistance and made recommendations, here he consoles the bereaved about a death. *Ep.* 2.8 thus belongs to the letters of consolation; see Cugusi (1983) 108–9, on 'lettera consolatoria', Fernández López (1994) 48–51, Cain (2009) 211–12. In content and form, the letter is closely related to *Ep.* 2.10, which is also dedicated to female virtue and Sidonius' ideal of marriage, and which contains the second epigram in the Book 2; see the introduction to *Ep.* 2.10. Since Sidonius also asks the addressee to judge the quality of the epitaph he encloses with the letter in section 3, he invokes another function of the friendship letter, literary criticism; Sowers (2016) 523–7. The epitaph on Filimatia, which is entirely devoted to the character of the deceased, is at the same time a counterpart to the epigram about the Visigothic queen Ragnahilda, in which Sidonius praises only her radiant appearance; see *Ep.* 4.8.5 and the commentary below on *Ep.* 2.8.1 *morigera coniunx*…. Other *epitaphia* of Sidonius are inserted in *Ep.* 3.12.5 for his grandfather Apollinaris, in 4.11.6 for Claudianus Mamertus, and in 7.17.2 for Saint Abraham. Related in content is also *Ep.* 8.11.3, which deals with the death of the rhetor and poet Lampridius and also includes a poem, which, however, is not an epitaph, but a playful allocution of the muse Thalia by the god Apollo. Hanaghan (2019) 129 refers to the parallel *Ep.* 6.2, about the lady Eutropia and her recently widowed daughter-in-law, where Sidonius also merges a letter of praise into a narrative of suffering which focuses on the consequences of bereavement. For Sidonius' approach to death in his letters in general, see Hess (2021).

Intertextuality

In *Ep.* 2.8 Sidonius refers to the literary traditions of Pliny's letters of mourning and the literary epitaph to deceased family members, which is handed down in Ausonius' *Parentalia*. In this way he also makes clear his innovation, which consists in a combination of the two genres of the letter of mourning and the epitaph.

The major intertext for letter 2.8 is Pliny's letter 5.16, signalled by the beginning of the letter; see the commentaries on *Ep.* 2.8.1 *Maestissimus haec tibi nuntio* and on *morigera coniunx*.... Both authors praise a woman, Minicia Marcella and Filimatia, respectively, who died young, by emphasising traditional Roman values regarding female behaviour and the ideal of marriage. Both Minicia Marcella and Filimatia are close to the authors because they are daughters of friends, Minicius Fundanus and Filimatius; both letters focus on the close relationship between the widowed fathers and their daughters. At the same time they present what they perceive as the appropriate way of grieving and dealing with loss. Pliny insists that the best way of overcoming grief is to devote time to studies. By writing about his sorrow, he copes with his emotions and rationalises them; Gnilka (1973), Bonjour (1988) 48–9, Tzounakas (2011), Hindermann (2014). Sidonius even surpasses Pliny: he does not just write about the value of one's studies in coping with grief as Pliny does, but includes an epitaph in which he praises Filimatia's character in the tradition of Greek and Roman funerary inscriptions. Sidonius also alludes to other funeral letters of Pliny, namely Plin. *Ep.* 8.5 and 9.9.2; see the Introduction, p. xvii. Gibson (2013b) 347 hints at numerous thematic reminiscences of Pliny's second book: Sidonius *Ep.* 2.8 and Pliny *Ep.* 2.7 commemorate the death of a young person. Pliny also inserts an epitaph (for Verginius Rufus) in his letter collection, although much shorter and not written by himself; see Plin. *Ep.* 6.10.4 and 9.19.1 *hic situs est Rufus, pulso qui Vindice quondam | imperium adseruit non sibi, sed patriae* ('Here lies Rufus, who once, after driving out Vindex, won command not for himself but for his fatherland'). Pliny laments that his friend and role model Verginius Rufus did not receive the posthumous tribute he is entitled to; Klodt (2015), Neger (2021) 255–67. In Plin. *Ep.* 7.29.2, however, Pliny is critical of the undeserved praise in the epitaph for Pallas; see Plin. *Ep.* 8.6.13–15. In Plin. *Ep.* 3.21 Pliny writes an epilogue about the late poet Martial to which Sidonius alludes in Sidon. *Ep.* 8.11.

Another important intertext is Ausonius' *Parentalia*, a collection of thirty epitaphs (mostly in elegiac distichs) to commemorate deceased family members, among them his wife. Sidonius alludes to Ausonius not only in this epitaph but also in his other funeral poems, see Amherdt (2001) 283–4 on Ausonius and the epitaph in *Ep.* 4.11.6 for Claudianus Mamertus; and see van Waarden (2016) 222–43 on the epitaph in *Ep.* 7.17.2 for the saintly abbot Abraham. For Sidonius' thorough knowledge of Ausonius' work, see Santelia (2002) 30, Furbetta (2014/2015), Furbetta (2018b), Squillante (2018), Consolino (2020), Hindermann (2022b). Poetic funerary inscriptions can also be found in the consolatory poems and the epicedia of Statius and Horace; see Stat. *Silv.* 2.1, 2.6, 3.3, 5.1, 5.3, 5.5, Hor. *Carm.* 1.24, 2.17. In addition, Sidonius alludes to Martial's epigrams, both his funerary epigrams and others whose obscene content serves as a counterfoil to Sidonius' letters and epigrams; see the commentaries below on 2.8.2 *non vispillonum sandapilariorumque ministeria ominosa tumulavere*, and on 2.10.4 vv. 22–30.

For Sidonius' letter 2.8, the important question is how to interpret the 'inappropriate' allusions to Martial's obscene epigrams in the serious context in which they occur, the funeral letter and funeral epigram. There is a great deal of discussion about the specific forms of intertextuality in Late Antiquity; see the Introduction to this volume, pp. xv–xx. Egelhaaf-Gaiser (2014) 383–4 interprets the seemingly inappropriate allusions as a means of creating unity between the author and the educated readership. In his comment on *Ep.* 7.16.2 van Waarden (2016) 192–3 argues similarly that Sidonius uses the moral and logical gap with his intertexts to reinforce the relationship with the addressee. Gerbrandy (2013) 76 even identifies the inappropriate adaption of classical texts as Sidonius' hallmark. In a similar case (the reuse in the religious context of *Carm.* 16.45 of *mortua membra*, 'dead bodies', which in Mart. 13.34 indicated the sexual organ) Gualandri (2020) 281–2 hypothesises that Sidonius had memory of the expression, but not of its original context.

For the interpretation of the letter at hand, I am most convinced by the approach of Pelttari (2016) 329–33, who shows that the idea of allusion and intertextuality in Sidonius (and Ausonius) must be rethought. For Sidonius it is no longer a matter of explicitly distancing himself from the ancient authors, but rather of integrating them into his work and claiming that they say the same thing, even if they do not; see the commentary below on *Ep.* 2.10.1 *eam brevi … sermonum purpurae.…* Sidonius leaves the old and the new intact. Thereby, Martial's originally offensive passages in a pious letter were not probably as irritating for contemporary readers as they are for us; see the commentaries below on *Ep.* 2.8.2 *non vispillonum sandapilariorumque…* and on 2.8.3 v. 2 *natis quinque patrique coniugique*.

Further reading

The epigram on Filimatia has been interpreted both in the context of letter 2.8 and in connection with Sidonius' other epitaphs; see Mascoli (2003) for the interpretation of Sidon. *Ep.* 2.8; Bernt (1968) 89–95, Amherdt (2001) 283–4, Giannotti (2001b) 107–10, Condorelli (2013a), Wolff (2014c) 208–9 for Sidonius' epitaphs; Hindermann (2022b) and Hindermann (2020b) for the connection between the poems in Book 2 (inserted in *Ep.* 2.8 and 2.10); and Condorelli (2008) and Consolino (2020) for Sidonius' *Carmina* in general. It is disputed which of Sidonius' inscriptions were written with the intention of actually being engraved in stone, see Wolff (2014c) 216–17, Consolino (2020) 361–2, Hindermann (2022b) and Hindermann (2020b). Sidonius mentions that his poem in *Ep.* 2.8 will also be published in a collection of poems; see the commentary below on *Ep.* 2.8.2 *Quam si non satis improbas, ceteris epigrammatum meorum voluminibus applicandam*. For the metrical analysis of the inserted poem, see Onorato (2016) 410, 417.

The epitaph is one of the oldest and most common subcategories of the literary genus 'epigram'. Its purpose is to secure the memory and immortalisation of the dead person or persons; it differs from other forms of lamentation for the dead by its brevity and concentration on the praise of the deceased. At the same time, Sidonius sets the values of his society in stone; see Wolff (2014c) 212. For the epigraphy of death and the stereotypical attributes of deceased women in funerary inscriptions, see Lattimore (1962), Kierdorf (1980) 33–48, 112–16, Lausberg (1982) 102–70, von Hesberg-Tonn (1983) 106–237, Galsterer (1998), Oliver (2000), Wolff (2000), Kolb and Fugmann (2008), Ronning (2011). For Sidonius' own epitaph, see Prévot (1993), Furbetta (2015b), van Waarden (2020a) 14–15.

Ep. 2.8 is also used as a source for studies about women in Sidonius' letters and poems: Bonjour (1988), MacDonald (2000) 77–8, Mascoli (2000), Santelia (2002) 90–4, Mascoli (2003, 2014), Hindermann (2020b, 2022b). Mathisen (2020a) 44–5 counts 88% male individuals in his database versus 12% female: 'Whereas 292 of the 386 men (76% of the individual men and 66% of all individuals) are named, only a pathetic 16 of the 59 women (27% of the individual women, 5.5% of the named men, and 3.6% of all individuals) are given names.' The epitaph in Sidonius' *Ep.* 2.8 on the deceased Filimatia is thus highlighted by its position as the first poem in the series of epitaphs and by the fact that it is Sidonius' only epitaph dedicated to a woman.

Commentary

Section 1

Sidonius Desiderato suo salutem: For the simple greeting formula, see the commentary on *Ep.* 2.1.1 *Sidonius Ecdicio suo salutem*. For the addressee, Desideratus, see the introduction to this letter.

Maestissimus haec tibi nuntio: In his first sentence Sidonius alludes to Pliny, who begins his letter about the loss of Minicia Marcella, the daughter of Fundanus, with similar words: see Plin. *Ep.* 5.16.1 *tristissimus haec tibi scribo, Fundani nostri filia minore defuncta* ('I write to you in deep sadness as the youngest daughter of our Fundanus is dead'); Bonjour (1988) 48–9, Mascoli (2003) 157, Hindermann (2013) 157–8, Hindermann (2020b, 2022b). Sidonius uses the adjective *tristis* more often in his letters than *maestus* (twelve instances of *tristis* versus one instance of *maestus* in the positive, in *Ep.* 8.9.5 v. 50, and three times in the poems, *Carm.* 7.520, 7.579, 9.110), so his choice of *maestissimus* at the beginning of this letter echoes Pliny by retaining the structure while choosing different words. Because of the rarity of the superlative *maestissimus*, Montone (2017) 34 refers to Verg. *Aen.* 2.270, where the adjective describes Hector, who appears in Aeneas' dream. The superlative of *maestus* is similarly used in Sidon. *Ep.* 5.6.1, about a widower: *Thaumastum ... maestissimum inveni. qui quamquam recenti caelibatu granditer afficiebatur ...* ('I found Thaumastus plunged in grief. Although he was greatly distressed by the recent loss of his wife ...'). For the predicative use of *maestus* with *dicere* or similar verbs, see *TLL* 8, 46.82–7.3.

Decessit nudius tertius non absque iustitio matrona Filimatia: *Nudius*, 'it is now the ... day since' is always connected with ordinal numbers; *nudius tertius* (which is attested since Plautus, for example *Most.* 956) therefore means 'three days ago', important information for the recipient of the letter. In the next section, 2.8.2, Sidonius repeats that his loss was recent and that he is still in fresh mourning (*planctu prope calente*). With the litotes *non absque iustitio* Sidonius stresses the huge impact of Filimatia's death, which has caused great public grief. *Absque*, 'without' (*TLL* 1, 186.10–7.74), is used as a preposition from the second century AD on. In Sidonius it appears also in *Ep.* 2.9.9, 4.16.1, 5.17.9, 6.4.1, 7.1.4, 7.12.4, 8.15.1, 9.11.6, 9.15.1 v. 30, *Carm.* 22.3; Amherdt (2001) 374. The noun *iustitium*, 'a cessation of jurisdiction, public business', 'a public mourning' (*TLL* 7.2, 717.71–18.35), is attested from Cicero (for example Cic. *Har. resp.* 55) onwards and appears frequently in Livy (for example Liv. 3.27.2) and also in Sueton (for example Suet. *Tib.* 52.1); Vidman (1971), Mascoli (2003) 157. The term is also used by other Late Antique authors, see for example Amm. 28.1.15, 29.2.15, Symm. *Orat.* 1.8, Greg. Tur. *Hist. Franc.* 6.30. The use of this term to describe the burial of a woman underlines her importance.

The subject of the letter is the late *matrona* spelled *Filimatia* in all the manuscripts, which is maintained by Lütjohann (1887) 29. Loyen (1970a) 61, Anderson (1936) 446–9 and others changed it to *Philomathia* (referring to a conjecture of Wilamowitz). The spelling was early discussed by Sirmond (1614) 48–9, who argues that the version with *Ph-* is the older one and goes back to the Greek word φίλημα ('kiss'); Köhler (1995) 166. Mascoli (2003) 154 n. 5 traces the Late Antique form *Philomathia* back to the older *Philematium*, similar to other female names ending in *-um*, for example Glycerium. Moreover, it is also a referred back to φιλομάθεια ('eagerness to learn', 'inquisitiveness') by Neger (2019) 411 or to φιλέω + ἱμάτιον ('to love a cloak') by Kelly (2021). The editors of the *Companion to Sidonius* have opted for the standardised form Philomathia found in the reference works (the same applies to her father, Philomathius); see Kelly and van Waarden (2020a) xiii. I prefer the spelling in the manuscripts. For Filimatia, see *PLRE* 2, 877, *PCBE* 4, 1484, Mathisen (2020a) 114 and the literature mentioned in the introduction to this section under 'Further reading'. She is the wife of the *vir clarissimus* Eriphius, the recipient of *Ep.* 5.17 – see Kaufmann (1995) 300, *PLRE* 2, 400, *PCBE* 4, 642, Mathisen (2020a) 92 – and probably the daughter of Filimatius, whom Sidonius encourages in *Ep.* 1.3 to continue his career. Filimatius is also mentioned as a *vir illustris* in *Ep.* 5.17.7; for this title see the commentary on *Ep.* 2.4.1 *Vir clarissimus Proiectus.*... Sidonius writes that Filimatius performed a ceremony for Saint Justus (*Ep.* 5.17.3–7), the former bishop of Lyon who died around 390. For Filimatius, see *PLRE* 2, 877–8, *PCBE* 4, 1485, Loyen (1970a) 219, Kaufmann (1995) 335, Liebs (2002) 49–50, Neger (2019), Mathisen (2020a) 114. Filimatia comes from Lyon, like her father and husband; see Sidon. *Ep.* 1.3.2; Bonjour (1988) 49. Twice (here and in *Ep.* 2.8.3 v. 4) Sidonius bestows on her the respectful epithet *matrona*, which means 'married woman', 'lady' (*TLL* 8, 483.66–9.27), and has the notion of 'estimable', 'virtuous', 'chaste'; Hindermann (2013) 148–9. The combination of a proper name and the term *matrona* is reminiscent of epitaphs; Mascoli (2003) 158. Sidonius regularly uses *matrona* to describe aristocratic women, in Book 2 also in *Ep.* 2.9.4, where the term appears in combination with *patrumfamilias*. For other instances, see Mathisen (2020a) 37–8 on Sidon. *Ep.* 4.6.2, 4.18.2, 6.2.1–4, 7.9.24.

morigera coniunx, domina clemens, utilis mater, pia filia: Filimatia's remarkable feature is that she combines several female roles and shows perfect behaviour in each of them. The first two elements are structured in a chiastic way, while the second pair is arranged in parallel. The short and concise description anticipates the epitaph that Sidonius inserts in section 2.8.3. Here and in the actual epitaph (cited in the commentary on *Ep.* 2.8.3 below) Sidonius focuses on Filimatia's role within the family and household. Sidonius (like his model Pliny with Minicia Marcella) praises Filimatia's character, but is silent about her appearance. In the epigram on the Visigothic queen Ragnahilda (*Ep.* 4.8.5) Sidonius also describes her familial ties (vv. 7–8 *sic tibi, cui rex est genitor, socer atque maritus, | gnatus rex quoque sit cum patre postque patrem* – 'so may you, with father and husband and husband's father all kings, have likewise a son as king with his father and after him'), but also the radiant appearance of the barbarian, who rivals the goddess Venus and the splendour of the silver basin she gets as a gift. Sidonius does not mention her character, though, and at the end of the letter the illiteracy of the Visigoth king's family becomes clear; Becht-Jördens (2017) 133–4, Hanaghan (2019) 99, Neger (2019) 408–10. With his silence about Filimatia's appearance Sidonius follows Pliny and the classical Roman ideal of women; Hindermann (2020b, 2022b). Filimatia fulfils the roles of *matrona, coniunx, domina, mater* and *filia* and receives social recognition for it. She incorporates all the traditional values a woman of her status is expected to represent; see the similar description of Tonantius Ferreolus' wife Papianilla in Sidon. *Carm.* 24.37–43; Santelia (2002) 90–94, Wolff (2014c) 209. MacDonald (2000) 77–8 points to Livy's Lucretia for Sidonius' description of Filimatia as a paragon of ancient Roman virtues. For female virtues in Roman funerary inscriptions in general, see Riess (2012) and the literature mentioned in the introduction to this letter. There is a similar mixture of four female roles in Plin. *Ep.* 5.16.2, about the young girl Minicia Marcella: *et iam illi anilis prudentia, matronalis gravitas erat et tamen suavitas puellaris cum virginali verecundia* ('and she already has the prudence of an old woman, the dignity of a matron, and yet the sweetness of a girl and the modesty of a virgin'); Hindermann (2013) 157–9, Hindermann (2020b, 2022b). For the mixture of female roles, see also Plin. *Ep.* 8.5.1 *amisit uxorem singularis exempli, etiam si olim fuisset ... quot quantasque virtutes ex diversis aetatibus sumptas collegit et miscuit* ('he has lost a wife of singular exemplarity, even if she lived in the past ... how many and how noble virtues, taken from different ages, she combined and unified in herself'), and Plin. *Ep.* 6.26.1, about male roles: *puer simplicitate, comitate iuvenis, senex gravitate* ('he is straightforward like a boy, friendly like a young man, dignified like an old man'). The fulfilling of different roles is also attested as a laudatory element in inscriptions; see *CIL* 8.11294 *incomparabilis coniux, mater bona, avia piissima* ('an incomparable wife, a good mother, a very pious grandmother'). On the combination of the various roles and the topos of the early completion of life as consolation, see Carlon (2009) 152–4, Klodt (2012) 32, 55–6.

The first attribute of the late Filimatia is *morigera*, 'accommodating', 'compliant' (of a person) (*TLL* 8, 1490.56–91.3), which is used by Plautus, Terence and Lucretius, and then starting with Apuleius from the second century AD on; Lolli (1997) 69. It is also attributed to wives in Firm. *Math.* 3.6.9 *morigeras (...) uxores* ('the accommodating wives'), 3.6.12, Paul. Nol. *Carm.* 4.17 *morigera et coniux* ('and the wife is accommodating'), Auson. *Parent.* 2.3 about his mother *morigerae uxoris virtus qui contigit omnis* ('you had every virtue of an obedient wife'), and Auson. *Parent.* 16.4, about his nephew's wife. The only other instance where Sidonius uses the adjective is *Ep.* 4.9.1 *rustici morigeri* ('the slaves in the countryside are obedient'). For the use of *coniunx*, 'wife', which is common in poetry and less frequent than the synonymous *uxor*, see Adams (1972) 252. Pliny, who writes a great deal about wives in his letters, does not use *coniunx*, but *uxor* in all thirty-eight instances. In Cicero's letters *coniunx* is used to emphasise a special bond between partners in times of crisis and it appears less frequently than *uxor*; Hindermann (2013) 151–6. In Sidonius' letters, the term *coniunx* appears only here and in *Ep.* 2.10.5, but several times in his poems: *Carm.* 2.515, 5.28, 5.126, 20.3, 22.4 v. 47, 22.4 v. 98 (of a husband), 22.4 v. 194, 24.37. The term *uxor* instead is only used once in the poems, in *Carm.* 7.383, but appears several times in the letters, for example *Ep.* 4.1.1, 4.9.4, 5.16.3. For the adjective *uxorius*, 'belonging or relating to a wife', see the commentary on *Ep.* 2.2.3 *nomen hoc praedio*....

Clemens, 'quiet', 'mild', 'gentle', is a frequent epithet for rulers (*TLL* 3, 1332.48–65). In combination with *dominus* it appears for example in Suet. *Aug.* 67; see also Sidon. *Ep.* 1.11.13, about the emperor Majorian: *indultu clementiae tuae* ('by the indulgence of your gracious clemency'). By extension, it is also used with imperial women and the title *domina*, for example *CIL* 10.1483 *clementissimae Dominae nostrae Augustae Helenae* ('for our very mild sovereign the Augusta Helena'). Writing about Philagrius, Sidonius also uses *clementia* for indulgence towards slaves in *Ep.* 7.14.11 *summa clementia tibi in famulos esse perhibetur* ('you are credited with the utmost forbearance towards your slaves'); see van Waarden (2016) 165 and the commentary on *Ep.* 2.2.3 *Haec mihi cum meis ... concordia*. For Sidonius' depiction of the slaves in his villa, see the introduction to *Ep.* 2.2. In contrast to Mascoli (2003) 158 I therefore do not think that *domina clemens* is an oxymoron. For the adjective *utilis*, of persons, meaning 'of such a character as to confer advantage or benefit', 'useful', 'helpful' (*OLD* 2118, 4), see Sidon. *Ep.* 4.9.1 *servi utiles* ('useful slaves'); van Waarden (2010) 479. Sidonius values mothers also in *Ep.* 3.1.1 and 4.21.1 *multum est, quod debemus et matribus* ('there is a great deal we owe to our mothers'); Amherdt (2001) 437. The adjective *pius*, 'respectful', 'loyal', 'affectionate', is frequently applied to the relations between parents and children (*TLL* 10.1, 2232.20–57); the expression *pia filia* is common in other forms of literature and also in epitaphs, for example Ov. *Ib.* 613, *CIL* 8.12952; Mascoli (2003) 158, Riess (2012) 492–3.

cui debuerit domi forisque persona minor obsequium, maior officium, aequalis affectum: Relationships with family and friends as part of the eulogy of deceased women replace the usual description of the career of a deceased man. Like Minicia Marcella in Plin. *Ep.* 5.16, Filimatia knows how to deal with other people according to their status and age, and thereby acquires prestige in all age groups (*minor, maior, aequalis*). For *persona*, here used to denote a social rank, see the commentary on *Ep.* 2.2.5 *ita ut ministeriorum ... quot solet sigma personas*. For the difference between *obsequium* (respect) and *officium* (service), see also Sidon. *Ep.* 7.2.4 *grandaevos obsequiis, aequaevos officiis obligare* ('he obliged the older people with his compliance, and his equals with his services'); van Waarden (2010) 165. Sidonius uses *aequalis*, 'of the same age', 'of the same juridical status', 'of the same authority' (*TLL* 1, 997.4–34), several times to denote the equality of persons; see Sidon. *Ep.* 2.14.2, 4.3.10, 5.17.2, 8.3.6, 9.9.16. For *aequalis* meaning 'smooth', see the commentary on *Ep.* 2.2.18 *Lacus ipse ... qua laevus, patens herbosus aequalis*.

Haec cum esset unica iam diu matris amissae, facile diversis blandimentorum generibus effecerat, ne patri adhuc iuveni subolis sexus alterius desideraretur: The fathers play a special role for both women. Both Minicia Marcella and Filimatia have an extraordinarily close relationship with their fathers and take on the role of the lady of the house at an early age; see Plin. *Ep.* 5.16.9; Hindermann (2020b, 2022b). After the death of her mother, Filimatia grows up alone with her father, who has not remarried and has not fathered a son. It was very unusual for widowers (especially with small children) to refrain from remarrying and thus from receiving educational support from their new wives; Krause (1991) 545–6. Ascetic tendencies are given as the reason for such behaviour in Sidon. *Ep.* 4.9.3–5 about Vettius, who is also a widower with a small daughter. In Filimatius' case, however, Sidonius gives as a reason the outstanding character of the daughter, which led her father to renounce remarriage and an heir. Later in the text Sidonius evokes a second time the 'masculinity' of Filimatia; see the commentary below on *Ep.* 2.8.1 *Qui parvuli si matre sospite*.... For Filimatia's father, Filimatius, who is not mentioned by name here, see the commentary above on *Ep.* 2.8.1 *Decessit nudius tertius non absque iustitio matrona Filimatia*. The manuscripts N²MCT have *matri* instead of *matris* in LN. Lütjohann (1887) 29 adds *filia* after *amissae*. Sidonius' favourite cretic spondee clausula supports the reading *matris amissae* chosen by Anderson (1936) 446 and Loyen (1970a) 61. *Blandimentum* denotes 'flattering words', 'blandishment', 'flattery', uttered by persons (*TLL* 2, 2028.63–9.39). Here the term is used in a positive sense; see also Sidon. *Ep.* 9.11.8 *blandimentorum mella* ('the honeyed charm'). It also appears in a negative context in Sidon. *Ep.* 9.6.2 *meretricii blandimenta naufragii* ('the enticements of moral shipwreck with a mistress'), of a young man's inappropriate relationship with a female slave. *Subolis*, 'offspring', 'scion', 'child' (*OLD* 1846, 2a), is transmitted in different spellings in the manuscripts: *soboles* in CT and Lütjohann (1887) 29, *subolis* in L, Loyen (1970a) 61 and Anderson (1936) 446, *sobolis* in N, *suboles* in MN². Cicero uses the word as an archaism in Cic. *De orat.* 3.153. Sidonius thus probably uses it to provide a solemn tone to the passage; see Hier. *Ep.* 108.33 v. 2; Cain (2013a) 476. It also appears in Martial (Mart. 6.25.1, 6.38.7), an important intertext for the whole passage; see the commentary on *Ep.* 2.8.2 *non vispillonum sandapilariorumque*....

Nunc autem per subita suprema virum caelibatu, patrem orbitate confodit: For Eriphius, Filimatia's husband and now a widower, see the commentary on *Ep.* 2.8.1 *Decessit nudius tertius non absque iustitio matrona Filimatia*. For *suprema, -orum* 'the closing moments or end of an existence' (*OLD* 1886, 4c), see for example Plin. *Nat.* 34.93, 16.236. The noun *caelibatus*, 'celibacy', 'single life' (*TLL* 3, 73.11–38), first appears in Sen. *Ben.* 1.9.4. In the sense of 'widower', 'widow', 'widowhood', it is also used in Sidon. *Ep.* 4.9.4, 5.6.1; Amherdt (2001) 264. The verb *confodere*, 'to pierce', 'stab' (*TLL* 4, 245.82–6.32), is used in a figurative sense ('to cause pain'), like here, mostly by Christian writers; similarly also in Sidon. *Ep.* 7.6.2 *quo* *tu spiritualium testimoniorum mucrone confoderis* ('you stabbed him with the sword of spiritual testimony'); van Waarden (2010) 285–6.

His additur, quod quinque liberum parens immaturo exitu reddidit infortunatam fecunditatem: The mother of Filimatia dies before her time, while her five children are still young. *Immaturus* is frequently combined with *mors*, for example in Plin. *Ep.* 2.1.10; further examples are in *TLL* 7.1, 445.68–6.4. We learn the exact age at which she dies only in the following epitaph: see the commentary below on *Ep.* 2.8.3 vv. 12–13. In his *Parentalia*, Ausonius separates the epitaphs for relatives who die at an advanced age (Auson. *Parent.* 1–8) from those who die prematurely (Auson. *Parent.* 9–30). The first epitaph in the second series is the epitaph for his deceased wife (Auson. *Parent.* 9). *Fecunditas*, 'fertility' (*TLL* 6.1, 415.15–51), is a quality usually praised in women. Sidonius, however, plays with the notion that the gift of many children is turned into a misfortune (*infortunatam fecunditatem*) when their mother dies; see also Cic. *Phil.* 2.58. Sidonius' wording suggests that Filomatia died during or after the birth of her fifth child. As Mathisen (2020a) 45 shows, children are nearly absent in Sidonius' work, even in domestic scenes, and he only gives the names of his own children. The manuscripts NMCT, Loyen (1970a) 61 and Anderson (1936) 446 have *liberum*, while LM² and Lütjohann (1887) 29 have *liberorum*. Sidonius uses archaic forms like *liberum* (instead of *liberorum*) elsewhere; Wolff (2020) 402. For Sidonius' archaising tendencies in general, see Gualandri (1979) 163–73, Monni (1999). The term *fecunditas* is regularly used to denote the 'fertility' of women (*TLL* 6.1, 415.15–51); see for example Tac. *Ann.* 2.75 *infelici fecunditate* ('o unfortunate fertility'), Cic. *Phil.* 2.58 *o miserae mulieris fecunditatem calamitosam* ('o ruinous fertility of this wretched woman'); Mascoli (2003) 160. Pliny the Younger compliments women on their numerous offspring using the same term in Plin. *Ep.* 4.15.3, 4.21.2, 8.10.2. Too many children could ruin a family's wealth; medical textbooks therefore offered remedies not only for infertility, but also for over-fertility; Clark (1993) 82.

qui parvuli si matre sospite perdidissent iam diu debilem patrem, minus pupilli existimarentur: Sidonius again evokes the 'masculinity' of Filimatia at the very end of the first section, when he writes that her children would seem less orphaned if their father had died. Filimatia is thus attributed a position of strength. She not only takes on the role of a son for her father, but is also the head of the family, while Eriphius, the father of the children, is already weak and old. In *Ep.* 5.17.3 Sidonius also refers to Eriphius' illness which prevents him from attending a ceremony for Saint Justus: *sed tibi infirmitas impedimento, ne tunc adesses* ('but your weakness prevented you from being present'). In epitaphs the educational achievements of mothers are sometimes mentioned; see Krause (1991) 545 n. 44 and Hier. *Ep.* 117.4. For the blurring of gender-typical roles after the death of the spouse, see also Sidon. *Ep.* 4.9.4, about Vettius: *filiam unicam parvam post obitum uxoris relictam solacio caelibatus alit avita teneritudine, materna diligentia, paterna benignitate* ('for his small only daughter who is left him as comfort after the death of his wife the widower cares with the tenderness of a grandmother, the diligence of a mother and the benevolence of a father'). The adjective *parvulus* or *parvula*, 'very small' (*TLL* 10.1, 548.78–50.21), is frequently used as a noun from Terence on for a 'child' (boy or girl/son or daughter). The diminutive here stresses the vulnerability of the orphans, enhancing the pathos; see Sidon. *Ep.* 7.9.21 *vel tenacitas senum vel intuitus parvulorum* ('the parsimony of the elder and the consideration of the children'), *Carm.* 15.136, van Waarden (2010) 517. In *Ep.* 8.3.2 Sidonius uses the adjective *parvulus* to denote a short amount of time. Legally, children who lose their father are 'orphans', *pupilli*, whereas the death of the mother does not change their legal status; see the commentary on *Ep.* 2.4.2 *licet a matre pupillae*....

Section 2

Hanc tamen, si quis haud incassum honor cadaveribus impenditur: Before Sidonius describes the honours that Filimatia receives from relatives, friends and priests, he turns to the question, discussed by ancient pagan authors, of whether there is life after death and therefore the dead even care about the honours they receive at their funeral; see Plin. *Nat.* 7.188–90; Wolff (2000) 76, Kolb and Fugmann (2008) 10–12. The idea of honouring the dead in vain is uttered elsewhere in similar words, for example Verg. *Aen.* 11.52 *vano maesti comitamur honore* ('sadly we accompany with vain honours'), Verg. *Aen.* 6.885–6, Hor. *Carm.* 2.20.23–4 *sepulcri | mitte supervacuos honores* ('give up the superfluous honours of my grave'). The manuscripts NMCT and Anderson (1936) 446 have *si quis*, whereas *si qui* is attested in L, Loyen (1970a) 61 and Lütjohann (1887) 30. *Quis* is implied by the stemmatics. Together with the preposition *in*, the neuter singular of *cassus*, 'empty', 'void', forms the adverb *incassum*, 'in vain', 'in deception' (*TLL* 3, 522.26–3.24). Sidonius uses the expression in *Ep.* 9.11.6, *Carm.* 5.273, 7.14, 7.331, 9.233; see also *Ep.* 6.4.1. *Cadaver* used of a 'dead human body' (*TLL* 3, 12.68–13.21) is common and has no negative connotations; see Mart. 6.62.4, Iuv. 8.252, Sen. *Ep.* 95.43, Sidon. *Ep.* 1.5.7, 3.3.7, 3.12.1, 8.11.11, 9.16.3 v. 74, *Carm.* 2.365, 2.513, 15.24. The term appears in a negative context in the invective against Gnatho in Sidon. *Ep.* 3.13.5 and in *Carm.* 16.123.

non vispillonum sandapilariorumque ministeria ominosa tumulavere: Sidonius uses terms for undertakers known from epigram and satire – Martial and Juvenal – in the funeral scene; see the discussion of intertextuality in the introduction to this letter. They serve as a counterfoil, because the lady Filimatia is not buried by such shady figures, but by her relatives and priests. Martial also included several funerary epigrams in his collection: Mart. 5.34, 6.28, 6.52, 7.96, 10.53, 10.61, 10.63, 11.13, 11.69; Grewing (1997) 163, 211–12, Wolff (2000) 133–6, Damschen and Heil (2004) 236–7. On Sidonius' predilection for Martial's vocabulary, see the commentary on *Ep.* 2.2.6 *Absunt ridiculi vestitu.... Vispillo*, 'one employed to bury those too poor to afford a funeral' (*OLD* 2077), is mostly known from Mart. 1.30.1–2 and 1.47.1–2, texts about Diaulus, a dubious doctor/undertaker. In Mart. 2.61.3 undertakers are mentioned as men whose occupation is degrading; see also Apul. *Flor.* 19.8 *vispillonum manibus extortum* ('wrested from the hands of the undertakers'). Sidonius also uses *vispillo/vespillo* in *Ep.* 1.11.9 to describe chair-bearing slaves (*cathedrarios servos*) as 'uglier than undertakers' (*vispillonibus taetriores*); Colton (1976) 15, Gualandri (1979) 61, Köhler (1995) 318. Sidonius reinforces *vispillones* with *sandapilarius*, 'a corpse-bearer', a Sidonian hapax and coinage from *sandapila*, 'a pauper's bier' (*OLD* 1687). For other examples of the combination, see Suet. *Dom.* 17.3 *cadaver eius populari sandapila per vispillones exportatum* ('his body was carried out on a public stretcher by porters'). *Sandapila* has a satirical ring in Mart. 8.75.14, 9.2.12, Iuv. 8.175 and is also used in Sidon. *Carm.* 16.46. On the low social status of persons working in the funeral sector, see Kaufmann (1995) 251–2. *Ominosa*, 'portentous', 'ominous' (used about things and rarely people) (*TLL* 9.2, 580.32–56), is not a very frequently used adjective, but see Plin. *Ep.* 3.14.6, Gell. 13.14.16. The classical verb *tumulo* means 'to cover with a burial-mound' (*OLD* 1988) and is also attested in Mart. 11.91.1 and Stat. *Silv.* 4.7.37.

sed cum libitinam ipsam flentes omnes, externi quoque, prensitarent remorarentur exoscularentur: The mourning spectators of the procession try to touch Filimatia, who is carried away in a stretcher (*libitina*). This noun denotes the Roman goddess of corpses, and in a transferred sense the 'requisites for burial', here 'a bier'; see Plin. *Nat.* 37.45; Prescendi (1999), Giannotti (2016) 244. In Mart. 10.97.1 the noun has the meaning of 'a funeral pile'. Sidonius inserts many polysyllabic words here and throughout the section, which adds to the grave tone of the letter and imitates the sounds of the mourners (*prensitarent remorarentur exoscularentur*). As Wolff (2020) 408 shows, Sidonius is fond of the ascending tricolon, where each element is longer than the preceding one; see also Sidon. *Ep.* 4.1.4, 6.12.6. The verb *prensito*, 'to take or catch frequently hold of', is the frequentative form of *prenso*, and only occurs in Sidonius (*TLL* 10.2, 1185.59–62). The verb *exosculor*, 'to kiss eagerly', is most often used of parts of the body, only seldom, as here, of things (*TLL* 5.2, 1593.48–52); see also Prud. *Perist.* 5.556 *exosculamur lectulum* ('we venerate your grave'). The manuscripts LM omit *exoscularentur*, but it should be included in the text because of Sidonius' predilection for *tricola*. Anderson (1936) 446, Loyen (1970a) 61 and Lütjohann (1887) 29 do include it.

sacerdotum propinquorumque manibus excepta perpetuis sedibus dormienti similior inlata est: *Sacerdos* denotes a priest in general (*OLD* 1674, 1a), but here specifically a Christian priest (*Blaise* 729, 6). *Sedes* (*OLD* 1725, 6a) here means 'the resting place of the dead', 'grave'; it is attested in this meaning in funerary inscriptions; see for example *CE* 675.1 *perpetuam sedem ... possides* ('you now own an eternal resting place') and *CIL* 10.1804 *sedem aeternam* ('eternal resting place'). For *perpetuus*, 'permanent', 'forever', in combination with a grave, see *TLL* 10.1, 1645.53–9, Mascoli (2003) 160–61. See also Sidon. *Ep.* 4.18.5 v. 20. The plural of *sedes* for 'grave' is also attested in Verg. *Aen.* 6.328. The idea that death and sleep are closely related is frequently attested in classical Greek and Latin literature, for example Hom. *Il.* 16.672, Hes. *Theog.* 758–9, Verg. *Aen.* 6.278; Cain (2013a) 318–19 provides further examples. Sleep is also a frequent euphemism for death in ancient epitaphs, especially Christian ones, for example Hier. *Ep.* 108.34; Lattimore (1962) 306–7, Wolff (2000) 74, Cain (2013a) 484–5. That a dead person looks like a sleeping person is also found in Pliny; see Plin. *Ep.* 6.16.20 on Pliny the Elder, who died during the eruption of mount Vesuvius: *habitus corporis quiescenti quam defuncto similior* ('the position of the body was more similar to a sleeping person than a dead person'). *Inferre* is regularly used for 'to bring to a place for burial', 'to bury' (*TLL* 7.1, 1379.13–67); see for example Cic. *Leg.* 2.55.

Post quae precatu parentis orbati neniam funebrem non per elegos sed per hendecasyllabos: After the burial, Sidonius writes a funerary poem at the bereaved father's request. For *precatu*, see the commentary on *Ep.* 2.4.2 *parum tamen votorum ... seu sedulitate sua seu precatu....* In classical times, a *nenia* denotes a 'funeral song', 'dirge'. It was sung to the flute in praise of a dead person at the funeral procession; Kierdorf (1980) 96–9, Kierdorf (2000). Here, and in *Ep.* 4.11.6 and 7.17.1, Sidonius uses *nenia* to denote a 'funerary poem', 'epitaph', whereas in *Ep.* 1.9.7, 5.1.2 and 7.18.4, he uses it to self-deprecate his literary production; Amherdt (2001) 283–4, van Waarden (2016) 214. Sidonius is probably inspired by Ausonius, who also uses the term several times in referring to his written epitaphs for relatives and combines it with laments at the funeral (*querellae funereae*; *carmen funereum*), see for example Auson. *Parent. Praef.* B v. 5, *Parent.* 9.2, 15.2, 17.2, 28.7; Lolli (1997) 53. Ausonius also often uses disparaging words about his own poetry; Sowers (2016). Sidonius describes his *nenia* with the adjective *funebris*, 'belonging to a funeral', a term he uses a second time in *Ep.* 3.12.1 *rastris funebribus* ('grave-diggers' tools'); Giannotti (2016) 216–17. Because the usual metre for funerary poetry was the elegiac distich (*per elegos*, see *TLL* 5.2, 339.29–63), the metre for sad topics, Sidonius explicitly mentions that the epitaph (which he adds in the third section of this letter) is written in the hendecasyllable, associated with light poetry (see Sidon. *Ep.* 9.15.1, 9.16.3 vv. 37–8) and popular with Martial and Pliny, who inspired Sidonius. Sidonius uses hendecasyllables in distinctly serious poems, for example in *Ep.* 2.10.4 (*titulus* for the cathedral of Lyon; see the commentary on *Ep.* 2.10.3 *Huius igitur aedis ... trochaeis triplicibus...*), 3.12.5 (epitaph for Sidonius' grandfather), 4.11.6 (epitaph for Claudianus Mamertus), 8.9.5 (about the court of Euric), 8.11.3 (poem for Lampridius), *Carm.* 9, 12, 13.21–40, 14, 23, 24, and mentioned in *Ep.* 5.8.1, 8.4.2, 8.11.5, 9.13.2 v. 1, 9.15.1, 9.16.3 vv. 37–8; Santelia (2002) 43 n. 51, Condorelli (2008) 10, 194, Condorelli (2013a) 276 n. 57, Wolff (2014c) 208–9, Condorelli (2020) 453–5, Consolino (2020) 342, 348. Except in grammatical treatises, the noun *hendecasyllabus* is rarely used (*TLL* 6.3, 2608.13–42), though Pliny mentions his poems written in this metre several times: Plin. *Ep.* 4.14.2 and 8–9, 5.10.1–2, 7.4.1, 3 and 8. The only epitaph Sidonius writes in elegiac couplets is the epitaph for the saintly abbot Abraham (*Carm.* 33 contained in *Ep.* 7.17.2).

marmori incisam planctu prope calente dictavi: The epigram at hand is already engraved in stone (*neniam funebrem ... incisam*) and will also be published later, if the addressee consents; see the commentary below, p. 234, on *Ep.* 2.8.2 *Quam si non satis improbas, ceteris epigrammatum meorum voluminibus applicandam*. The verb *incidere* (see *TLL* 7.1, 907.49–8.27) means 'to inscribe' or 'to have inscribed by a professional engraver', frequently on tombs or monuments; see Hier. *Ep.* 108.33 *incidi elogium sepulchro tuo* ('I have had inscribed a praising inscription on your tomb'), Plin. *Ep.* 8.6.14 *incisa et insculpta sunt publicis aeternisque monumentis* ('they are engraved and carved on eternal, public monuments'), Hor. *Sat.* 2.3.84 *summam incidere sepulcro* ('they wrote the sum on his gravestone'), Cic. *Pis.* 29; Handley (2003) 37–9, Cain (2013a) 473–4. For the participle *incisus* in Sidonius, see also the commentary on *Ep.* 2.2.18 *Lacus ipse ... incisus flexuosus nemorosusque....* For the act of setting a poem in stone, see Sidon. *Ep.* 7.17.2 *exaraturi stili scalpentis impressu* ('by the impress of my scratching stylus'); van Waarden (2016) 221. See also *Ep.* 3.12.5, where Sidonius recommends that the poem should be carved quickly and with care into stone: *tabulae ... celeriter indatur* ('it should be applied promptly to the slab'); Mascoli (2003) 162, Wolff (2014c) 216–17, van Waarden (2016) 215.

Sidonius ends the sentence with the expression *planctu prope calente* and thus repeats that his loss is new; see the commentary on *Ep.* 2.8.1 *Decessit nudius tertius....* For the expression, see Symm. *Ep.* 1.15.1 *iudicio calente dictavi* ('I dictated while my impression was fresh'). Sidonius uses the first-person singular *dictavi* two other times, both in the seventh book: *Ep.* 7.3.1 and *Ep.* 7.18.2, in his concluding survey of his works. For the idea of writing while still in mourning, see Plin. *Ep.* 1.12.12 *quod recenti dolore ... dixi* ('what I said in my fresh pain'). In addition, Montone (2017) 34 refers to Tib. 2.5.77 *lacrimas fudisse tepentes* ('to have shed warm tears') and Prop. 4.7.28 *lacrimis incaluisse* ('to have warmed with tears'). For the theme of one's homage to the deceased written quickly and in pain, see Hier. *Ep.* 108.32 *hunc tibi librum ad duas lucubratiunculas eodem quem tu sustines dolore dictavi* ('I dictated this book in two short nights, affected by the same pain as you'). With its combination of prose letter and an epitaph for Paula, Jerome's *Ep.* 108 is similar to Sidonius' letter for Filimatia; Hindermann (2022b). Despite his pain, Sidonius is nevertheless able to write an epigram, which he integrates into his letter. Sidonius similarly describes hurriedly writing a poem on the grave of his friend, Claudianus Mamertus, see Sidon. *Ep.* 4.11.7 *ecce quod carmen ... conscripsi* ('here you have the poem, which I inscribed') and after his grandfather's grave had been destroyed, see Sidon. *Ep.* 3.12.4 *carmen hoc sane, quod consequetur, nocte proxima feci, non expolitum, credo, quod viae non parum intentus* ('the poem of course, which follows, I wrote last night and it is not refined, I think, because I was concerned about my journey'). In another context Sidonius also emphasises how quickly he can write poetry; see the commentary on 2.10.2 *Petis autem, ut si qui versiculi mihi fluxerint....*

Quam si non satis improbas, ceteris epigrammatum meorum voluminibus applicandam: Sidonius suggests that the epigram he wrote for Filimatia's tombstone, which is already engraved, should also be published additionally in his collection of poems. He therefore asks Desideratus what he thinks about the quality of his poem; Wolff (2014c) 209. Asking a friend to judge the literary quality of a work is a topos of ancient epistolary literature and appears particularly frequently in the letters of Pliny the Younger (Plin. *Ep.* 3.15.1, 4.14, 5.3, 7.20.3, 8.21), but also in other generic traditions, for example in the work of Pliny the Elder and Ausonius; Starr (1987) 213, Sowers (2016) 523–7. Condorelli (2013a) 261 understands the passage differently: if the family of the deceased likes the poem it will be set in stone; if not, it will be included in Sidonius' collection of poems. According to Mascoli (2003) 162–3 the verbal forms *marmori incisam … dictavi* (see the commentary above, pp. 232–3) do not help to decide whether the poem is already set in stone or will only be engraved after Desideratus decides whether it should be done. Which of the (extant or lost) poems are exactly meant with *ceteris epigrammatum meorum voluminibus* is not certain and is frequently discussed in secondary literature. The poem at hand is not in fact included in Sidonius' extant collection of *Carmina*, which consists of three panegyrics and five poems associated with them, along with sixteen occasional poems, called here and in *Ep.* 9.12.3 *epigrammata* or *nugae*, 'trifles'; see *Ep.* 3.14.1, 9.13.6, *Carm.* 8.3, 14.1. They are usually held to have been published around 469, though parts of the collection may have appeared separately before that, especially the imperial panegyrics; Amherdt (2001) 22–3. Sidonius also includes poems in his letters, altogether sixteen (or seventeen, depending on whether one counts the palindrome in *Ep.* 9.14.6 as one or two poems), two of them in Book 2 (*Ep.* 2.8.3 and 2.10.4); see Amherdt (2001) 21 and Consolino (2020) 342–3 with a short overview over all the inserted poems, and Condorelli (2013a) and Wolff (2014c) about the epitaphs and *tituli*. As these poems might not fill whole books, *ceteris voluminibus* therefore possibly refers to other collections of occasional poems which are lost; see the discussion in Stevens (1933) 108–9, Bernt (1968) 89, Santelia (2000) 221–2, Condorelli (2008) 193–4, van Waarden (2010) 9 n. 14, Furbetta (2013), Consolino (2015) 81–3, Furbetta (2017) 255–9, Kelly (2020a) 175–7. Consolino (2020) 360 n. 95 thinks that the *epigrammatum volumina* refer to a compilation of epigrams or an anthology of light poetry. Van Waarden (2020a) 18 n. 35 takes the view that Sidonius' poems were created in a loose, growing collection, so that the publication of a new and the addition of a previous collection of poems merge into one. In my opinion, it is no coincidence that none of the poems in the letters is preserved in the *Carmina*'s collection and I therefore argue that the poems in the letters should be interpreted as a separate collection, in which the genre of the epitaph plays a special role: see Hindermann (2020b, 2022b), and the Introduction to the present volume. The term *epigramma* appears thirteen times in Sidonius, mostly in the meaning of 'a poem' (of various metres, lengths and tones) (*TLL* 5.2, 666.48–84); see Sidon. *Ep.* 8.9.3, 8.11.7, 9.12.3, 9.13.2 v. 16, 9.13.5, 9.14.6, 9.16.3 v. 57, *Carm.* 22.6. Sidonius uses the term also in the meaning of *titulus*, 'metrical inscription' (on things and buildings) (*TLL* 5.2, 666.27–47), in *Ep.* 2.10.4 (poems on the wall of a *basilica*), 4.8.4 (a poem to inscribe in a basin), 4.18.4–5 (a poem on the wall of a *basilica*) and *Ep.* 5.17.10 (a poem to inscribe on a towel). For Sidonius' understanding of the term *epigramma* and its various meanings, see Gualandri (1993) 213, Mondin (2008) 467–74 (in relation to other Late Antique authors), Consolino (2015) (in relation to Pliny's, Ausonius' and Martial's notion of *epigramma* and Statius' *Silvae*), Furbetta (2017) 252–9 and Consolino (2020) 360. For *volumen*, here in the general meaning of 'book', see the commentary below on *Ep.* 2.9.4 *licet quaepiam volumina...*, where the term denotes 'a roll of papyrus forming a book or part of a book'. The verb *improbo*, 'to disapprove', 'blame', 'condemn' (of things) is frequently used (*TLL* 7.1, 687.17–74). It is similarly used of a written work in Quint. 3.5.15, Plin. *Ep.* 5.3.1, 7.12.6. *Applico*, in the figurative sense of 'to add' (*TLL* 1, 298.83–9.15), is used several times in Sidonius, for example *Ep.* 3.10.1, 8.10.1; Santelia (2000) 221 n. 26.

mercennarius bybliopola suscipiet: Sidonius will give the epigram to his bookseller, whom he describes as *mercennarius*, 'hired', 'slave' (*TLL* 8, 792.6–20), an adjective Sidonius also uses relating to the services of a free person in *Ep.* 6.8.1 *hoc ipsum, quod mercennariis prosecutionibus et locaticia fatigatione cognoscitur* ('he is only known for his paid attendances and hired exertions'). The legal status of a *bybliopola*, 'bookseller', 'copyist', 'transcriber of books', 'scribe' (*TLL* 2, 1955.32–51), and thus the correct translation of the term in Sidonius' letters, is controversial. The Grecism *bybliopola* is a rarely used term but is attested in Sidonius' favourite intertexts for this letter, Martial, who writes about his bookseller Tryphon in Mart. 4.72.2 and 13.3.4, and see 14.194.2. The term also appears in Pliny's letters: Plin. *Ep.* 1.2.6, 9.11.2 *bibliopolas Lugduni esse non putabam* ('I did not think that there were booksellers in Lyon'); Sherwin-White (1966) 91, 490, Mathisen (2013) 224–5 n. 12, Santelia (2000) 226–35. Sidonius uses the term *bybliopola* also in *Ep.* 2.9.4, 5.15.1, 9.7.1. According to Kaufmann (1995) 222, 243 there was no book trade in Gaul in Sidonius' time, just private copying of books by slaves. He therefore thinks that the *bybliopola* mentioned in 2.8.2 is a slave (like the one in 5.15.1 because of the added *famulus*), whereas the *bybliopolae* in 2.9.4 are free merchants. Similarly Santelia (2000) 222, 225 thinks that the *bybliopola* is one of Sidonius' slaves who has specific scribal duties. Harries (1994) 4, Kleberg (1967) 55, 96 and Mratschek (2020a) 227, on the other hand, consider the *bybliopola* mentioned here to be a free trader who is paid by Sidonius for his services. In Santelia's (2000) view, Sidonius deliberately uses a special expression with literary connotation instead of the normal expression *librarius* or *scriba*. Similarly, Kelly and van Waarden (2020b) 3 suggest that Sidonius calls his personal secretary a 'bookseller' to conjure up an economic activity that belongs to the Roman past. In my opinion, Sidonius' *bybliopola* is very probably his slave with the added function of a secretary who deals with his publishing; see Schipke (2013) 54, 108–9, 177. Sidonius mentions scribes (*scriba*) also in *Ep.* 1.7.5, 5.17.10, 9.9.8; Mathisen (2020a) 64. For the production and selling of books in Pliny's time, see Page (2015) 273–93. For the development of the book trade in general, with its peak in the first to second century AD, see Starr (1987) 219–23, Cavallo (1997b) and the commentary below on *Ep.* 2.9.4 *huc libri affatim … videre te crederes … bybliopolarum*.

si quid secus, sufficit saxo carmen saxeum contineri: Lütjohann (1887) 30 has *si quid*, Loyen (1970a) 62 and Anderson (1936) 448 have *si quod*. The beginning of the sentence is similar to *Ep.* 7.8.4 *si quid sequius* ('if not so'); van Waarden (2010) 406. Wolff (2020) 397 analyses the expression *si quod secus* in his chapter on the Sidonian syntax and interprets *quod* as a postponed connecting relative. With the figura etymologica *saxo … saxeum* Sidonius playfully hints at the quality of his poem, as *saxeus* means 'consisting or made of stones or rock' (*OLD* 1696, 1; see Sidon. *Ep.* 2.10.4 v. 21) and in a transferred sense 'like rocks in size or hardness', 'unfeeling' (*OLD* 1696, 4–5); see Plin. *Ep.* 2.3.7, Vitr. 8.3.22. The idea is: if Desideratus does not think that the poem is heart-warming, it remains a poem set in stone and does not get published within the collection; Mascoli (2003) 163. A similar play with the inscription on a grave can be found in *CE* 52 *heic est sepulcrum haud pulcrum pulcrai feminae* ('this is the ugly grave of a beautiful woman'). The adjective *saxeus* also appears in inscriptions on tombs; see *CIL* 13.2104.7, where the grave is called a *domus saxea* ('house made of stone'). Montone (2017) 34 suggests that Sidonius with *carmen saxeum* refers to the eternity of his work by alluding to Horace' famous verse *exegi monumentum aere perennius* ('I have constructed a monument more lasting than bronze') (Hor. *Carm.* 3.30.1). Another possible intertext is Mart. 1 *Praef.*, who similarly plays with the notion of *Hispaniensis* and *Hispanus*: *ne Romam, si ita decreveris, non Hispaniensem librum mittamus, sed Hispanum* ('so that, if you decide to do so, I will send to Rome not only a book written in Spain, but a Spanish book'). The *liber Hispaniensis* is a book written in Spain, whereas a *liber Hispanus* is probably a book of poor quality; Neger (2022) 40–1.

Section 3

Hoc enim epitaphion est: After Sidonius first described his poem as *epigramma*, he now uses the term *epitaphion*; see the commentary on *Ep.* 2.8.2 *Quam si non satis improbas, ceteris epigrammatum meorum voluminibus applicandam*. The term *epitaphion* or *epitaphium* (in this spelling in Sidon. *Ep.* 4.11.7) is used by Late Antique authors as a *terminus technicus* only for an inscription on a grave; see for example Ennod. *Carm.* 2.1, 2.2, 2.5, 2.6, Ven. Fort. *Carm.* 4.1–4.28, and further examples in *TLL* 5.2, 687.9–60. This is Sidonius' only known epitaph for a woman; see the introduction to this letter. With his poem, which is set in stone, Sidonius repeats Filimatia's merits already described in prose in *Ep.* 2.8.1–2 and thus reinforces her praise. The epitaph for Filimatia mostly consists of a *laudatio* of the deceased; see the commentary below. At the same time, Sidonius praises himself: he appears in the letter at hand as a respected writer who composes the poem at the request of Filimatia's relatives, and as a self-controlled person capable of writing while experiencing loss; see *Ep.* 2.8.2. For the metre of the epitaph see the commentary above on *Ep.* 2.8.2 *Post quae precatu parentis....* Intertexts for the epitaph at hand probably are Auson. *Parent.* 2, about his mother Aemilia Aeonia, and to Mart. 10.63, about a virtuous wife. There are allusions to other epigrams by Martial; see the section on intertextuality in the Introduction, pp. xv–xx, and the detailed commentary on the epigram.

vv. 1–4 General remarks
The first four verses of the epigram, the description of Filimatia's death (*descriptio mortis*), do not give us more biographical information than Sidonius

already provided in prose in the first two sections of the letter. Filimatia died quickly and unexpectedly and left behind her husband, five children and her now childless father. The reader can thus relate how Filimatia's biography is transformed into a poem and his attention is drawn to Sidonius' artful condensation of facts. Sidonius pursues the same strategy in *Ep.* 4.11.6 in his epitaph for Claudianus Mamertus, where he adapts the first part of the letter for the structure and content of the epitaph, as well as in epitaph 3.12.5, for his grandfather; Amherdt (2001) 282–3, Wolff (2014c) 211–12.

v. 1 Occasu celeri feroque raptam: Sidonius begins the poem with the metaphor of life as light (see Catull. 5.5–6 and the commentary below on *splendor* at v. 5), calling Filimatia's death *occasus*, 'going down', 'falling' (*TLL* 9.2, 340.80–41.28), a term frequently used in Christian poetry for 'death', for example in Prud. *Cath.* 9.103, Paul. Nol. *Carm.* 27.2; Condorelli (2013a) 265–6 gives further examples. In the work of classical authors, *occasus* not only refers to the death of persons, but also to the ruin of peoples and states, for example in Cic. *Pis.* 8, 18, Verg. *Aen.* 2.432; Mascoli (2003) 164. Sidonius describes the death as quick (*celeri ... raptam*) and cruel (*feroque*), a notion which is also attested elsewhere, for example Ov. *Ib.* 396 *quosque ferae morti Lemnia turba dedit* ('to whom the Lemnian crowd gave a cruel death'), Stat. *Theb.* 10.317 *mortisque ferae* ('of the cruel death'), Liv. 27.49.2 *ea celerrima via mortis* ('this very fast way of death'); see also Auson. *Parent.* 9.4, about the death of his wife Attusia Lucana Sabina: *coniugis ereptae mors* ('the death of my wife, who was taken from me').

v. 2 natis quinque patrique coniugique: The expression *natis quinque* varies the prosaic *quinque liberum parens* from *Ep.* 2.8.1. Instead of the poetical form *gnatis* in LNV, the manuscripts MCT have *natis*, favoured by stemmatics. Lütjohann (1887) 30, Anderson (1936) 448 and Loyen (1970a) 62 choose *gnatis*. The motif of numerous children left behind is known from other honorific epigrams for *matronae*, both inscriptions and poems, for example *Anth. Pal.* 7.224.1–2, 7.331.5. A probable intertext is Mart. 10.65.5–8, because it also mentions (twice) five children and their hands burying the dead, despite the unexpectedly unabashed ending of Martial's poem: *quinque dedit pueros, totidem mihi Iuno puellas | cluserunt omnes lumina nostra manus. | contigit et thalami mihi gloria rara fuitque | una pudicitiae mentula nota meae* ('Iuno gave me five boys and as many girls they all closed my eyes with their hands. I was also given a rare glory of the marriage bed: only one cock was known to my modesty'); see the introduction to this letter.

vv. 3–4 hoc flentis patriae manus locarunt | matronam Filimatiam sepulchro: Filimatia is buried with public honours and with great public sympathy. The personified homeland itself buries her with its own hands (*flentis patriae manus locarunt*). For a similar personification of *patria*, see Luc. 1.186–7 *ingens visa duci patriae trepidantis imago | ... voltu maestissima* ('a giant apparition of the trembling fatherland with a very sad face appeared to the commander'). Sidonius also uses a similar image in the epitaph for his deceased grandfather in *Ep.* 3.12.5 v. 8 *maerentis patriae sinu receptus* ('received into the bosom of his mourning country'). These honours are unusual for the funeral of a woman; Mascoli (2003) 164. The wide-spaced hyperbaton *hoc* and *sepulchro* (start and end vv. 3–4) encloses Filimatia. The same hyperbaton is found in Mart. 11.13.7, but within a single verse: *hoc sunt condita, quo Paris, sepulchro* ('they are buried in the same grave as Paris'); Sidonius thus surpasses his model with his ornate epitaph. Martial's epigram Mart. 11.13.5 is also a pre-text for Sidonius' epitaph on Claudianus Mamertus, *Ep.* 4.11.6, v. 1 (*decus et dolor*). This 'shared intertextuality' could provide another link between *Ep.* 2.8 and 4.11 (thanks to Margot Neger for this idea). A similar strategy can also be observed in Pliny, as Marchesi (2008) showed. For *patria*, see the commentary on *Ep.* 2.1.4 *statuit te auctor ... seu patriam dimittere....* Filimatia's home was Lyon; see the commentary on *Ep.* 2.8.1 *Decessit nudius tertius non absque iustitio matrona Filimatia* also for the spelling of her name and her description as *matrona*.

vv. 5–11 General remarks
The next seven verses contain a laudatory description of Filimatia's character (*laudatio*), which varies the characteristics already described by Sidonius in *Ep.* 2.8.1; see the commentary on *Ep.* 2.8.1 *morigera coniunx....* For this repetition of Filimatia's biography, see vv. 1–4 General remarks. The addition of positive attributes in v. 6 is reminiscent of archaeologically attested grave inscriptions, for example *CE* 237 *optima et pulcherrima, lanifica, pia, pudica, frugi, casta, domiseda* ('the best and most beautiful, wool-spinning, pious, modest, frugal, chaste, domestic'), *CE* 1136 *docta, opulenta, pia, casta, pudica, proba* ('learned, respectable, pious, chaste, decent, good'), *CIL* 11.298 *pudica, religiosa, laboriosa, frugi, efficax, vigilans, sollicita, univira, unicuba, [t]otius industriae et fidei matrona* ('modest, religious, laborious, frugal, efficient, vigilant, busy, a woman who has been married and lain with but one husband, a matron of industry and faith'); Mascoli (2003) 164. See also Auson. *Parent.* 19.3, about Namia Pudentilla, Ausonius' sister-in-law: *nobilis haec, frugi proba laeta pudica decora* ('she is noble, frugal, good, cheerful, modest, beautiful').

v. 5 O splendor generis, decus mariti: First, Sidonius praises Filimatia as *splendor generis* and as *decus mariti*. As in section 2.8.1, her value as a person depends on the value she has for her family of origin and her husband. In the poem for the queen Ragnahilda, too, family relations are in the foreground, in *Ep.* 4.8.5 vv. 7–8. With her *splendor*, 'splendour', 'brilliance', 'glory' (see OLD 1808, 5a), she even brings light into the grave (see the commentary above on v. 1 *occasu*), a notion known from epitaphs; see CE 1431 *o lux clara tuo … marito* ('o brilliant light for your husband'), CE 1311 *lux alma parentum* ('kind light of your parents'), Ven. Fort. *Carm.* 3.5.5, addressed to bishop Felix, *lumen generis* ('light of the family'); Sanders (1965) 86. The term *splendor* in connection with the renown of a family is attested in Sidon. *Ep.* 2.4.1 *familiae splendor* ('his family's splendour'); see the commentary there on *et cum illi…*. The term *decus*, 'ornament', is also used elsewhere in a funerary context. Sidonius also uses the term in the epitaph on his late grandfather in *Ep.* 3.12.5 v. 17 *hoc primum est decus, haec superba virtus* ('This is the first glory, a proud merit'). In his epitaph Mart. 11.13.5 Martial calls the pantomimus Paris *Romani decus et dolor theatri* ('the ornament and pain of the Roman theatre'); see also CE 1311 *conubii decus egregium* ('eminent ornament of marriage') and Ruric. *Ep.* 2.4.2, about his deceased daughter-in-law: *decus familiae* ('the ornament of the family'). For the motif of dedication to the husband in epitaphs for women, see for example CE 52, 492, 959 B, and Auson. *Parent.* 2.5 *coniugiique fides et natos cura regendi* ('fidelity to your marriage and care to guide your children'). On the importance of marital harmony, see also Lattimore (1962) 275–80, Lolli (1997) 70 and the commentary on *Ep.* 2.2.3 *Haec mihi cum meis … concordia*. Furthermore, many inscriptions stress that the deceased woman was *univira*, 'married to only one man', which is missing here, however. The term *maritus*, 'husband', appears frequently in Pliny's letters (twenty-two times, for example Plin. *Ep.* 1.14.1, 2.20.2) as well as in Roman epigram or satire (for example Mart. 2.47, 7.71, Iuv. 6.211, 6.432); Hindermann (2013) 153–6, Häger (2019) 63–7.

v. 6 prudens, casta, decens, severa, dulcis: Sidonius uses five adjectives to describe Filimatia's personality: she is *prudens, casta, decens, severa, dulcis* ('prudent, chaste, decent, severe, sweet'). There is a choice of traditional values one can use to describe a *matrona*, and the grave inscriptions therefore often sound similar; see the examples cited above in the commentary on vv. 5–11 General remarks, and Ronning (2011) 89, 98, Riess (2012). It is revealing to see which characteristics Sidonius selects and which he leaves out. Instead of the traditional *pia* or *pudica* Sidonius starts with *prudens*, 'prudent', 'knowing', 'skilled', 'wise' (*TLL* 10.2, 2371.30–5.69), here in absolute use and not with the genitive as is usually the case; see Mascoli (2003) 164. Bonjour (1988) 49 compares this passage to Sidon. *Carm.* 24.96–8, where Sidonius praises his cousin Eulalia for her intelligence. As Sidonius ends the description of Filimatia with *dulcis*, 'sweet', he stresses the emotional qualities of Filimatia. Other typical characteristics like *domiseda*, 'staying at home', 'domestic', which is not compatible with the metre of the epitaph, and *lanifica*, 'spinning wool', are missing. To describe Filimatia's exemplary morality, Sidonius chooses for the second adjective *casta*, which is often used to describe women as 'faithful' (*TLL* 3, 566.53–7.68). Pliny writes about the *castitas* of his ideal Fannia, that is, her marital fidelity, in Plin. *Ep.* 7.19.4 *doleo enim feminam maximam eripi oculis civitatis nescio an aliquid simile visuris. Quae castitas illi, quae sanctitas, quanta gravitas quanta constantia!* ('I suffer from the fact that this most distinguished woman is supposed to be taken away from the eyes of the public and I do not know whether we will ever see something similar. What purity, what sanctity she had, how deep was her dignity and her constancy!'), see Plin. *Ep.* 1.14.8, 4.19.2. *Castitas* or *casta* is also used of to denote the chastity and purity of famous women, for example Lucretia (see Liv. 1.57.6–58.7) and Verginia (see Liv. 3.44–8, Cic. *Rep.* 2.63, *Fin.* 2.66, 5.64); Riess (2012) 492. In Sidon. *Ep.* 3.13.1 Sidonius praises his own son's love of purity (*castitatis adfectu*). The combination of *casta*, 'chaste', and *decens*, 'decent', the third adjective in Sidonius' enumeration, is attested in epitaphs; see for example *CE* 843 *casta pudica decens sapiens generosa probat(a)* ('chaste, modest, decent, knowing, generous, experienced'), *CE* 1140 *casta decens sapiens humilis iucunda* ('chaste, decent, knowing, humble, pleasant'). For *decens*, 'decent' (*TLL* 5.1, 136.29–52), as attribute of a person, see Sidon. *Carm.* 14.4 v. 21 *decensque virgo* ('a decent girl'); Mascoli (2003) 164. The fourth adjective, *severus*, 'not lax or frivolous', 'austere', 'severe', 'strict' (*OLD* 1750, 2), denotes the strictness in one's personal behaviour and morals, used, as here, of a matron in, for example, Ov. *Trist.* 2.309 *supercilii ... matrona severi* ('the matron with severe eyebrow'). For the oxymoron *severa dulcis*, see *CE* 656, Condorelli (2013a) 267. Wolff (2014c) 209 therefore even calls Filimatia an 'oxymore vivant'; see also the commentary below on *libertas grauis et pudor facetus* in v. 11. The series of adjectives describing Filimatia ends with *dulcis*, 'sweet', 'charming', 'agreable' (*TLL* 5.1, 2194.34–5.21), a quality also attested several times (mostly of women) in other epitaphs for example *CE* 1551 D, *CE* 1307, and also in poems, see Catull. 66.33 *pro dulci coniuge* ('for your beloved husband'), 67.1

dulci ... viro ('to my beloved husband'). Riess (2012) 493 counts *dulcissima* among the top five qualities of women praised in funerary inscriptions. In *Ep.* 2.2.3 Sidonius describes his relation to the estate Avitacum which his wife brought into their marriage also as *dulcis*; see above on *Ep.* 2.2.3 *nomen hoc praedio ... patrio mihi dulcius*, and emphasises the harmony (*concordia*) he lives in with his family. Similarly, in Plin. *Ep.* 7.19.7 Pliny praises the terminally ill Fannia as *non minus amabilis quam veneranda* ('not less lovely than admirable'). In Sidon. *Ep.* 2.10.2, the description of the bishop Patiens contains a similarly varied description of a character; see the commentary on *Ep.* 2.10.2 *viri sancti strenui, severi misericordis....*

vv. 7–9 atque ipsis senioribus sequenda, | discordantia quae solent putari | morum commoditate copulasti: For the mixture of roles and qualities of different ages (*atque ipsis senioribus sequenda*), see the commentary above on *Ep.* 2.8.1 *morigera coniunx....* Because of her outstanding character, Filimatia is a role model even for older women; see also *CIL* 8.8854 *quae exemplo esses feminarum* ('who is an example of other women'). The participle *discordantia*, used as a noun in v. 8, is very rare (*TLL* 5.1, 1343.42–51, but see for example Colum. 2.2.3). It is quite astonishing in an epitaph, where usually a life without quarrel (*sine discordia*) is praised, for example in *CIL* 5.2095; Lattimore (1962) 279, von Hesberg-Tonn (1983) 174, Riess (2012) 494. Filimatia overcomes this divide because of her *commoditas*, 'amiability', 'adaptability', 'helpfulness' (*TLL* 1917.55–6), a noun frequently used by Cicero, but by Sidonius only in the transferred sense of integrity (*integritas*); Mascoli (2003) 165. The verb *copulo* is used elsewhere (especially in Cicero, for example Cic. *Fin.* 5.67) to denote the combination of virtues in one's character (*TLL* 4, 921.57–73).

vv. 10–11 nam vitae comites bonae fuerunt | libertas gravis et pudor facetus: The oxymorons *libertas gravis et pudor* resume the opposition *severa, dulcis* of v. 6. The combination *libertas gravis* also recalls Stat. *Silv.* 2.7.68 with its description of Cato's republican values: *libertate gravem pia Catonem* ('harsh Cato with his pious assertion of freedom'). For *libertas* as a quality of the elite, see the commentary on *Ep.* 2.1.4 *Te exspectat palpitantium civium extrema libertas*. Plin. *Ep.* 7.19.4 also praises the *gravitas* of a noble woman, the terminally ill Fannia (cited in the commentary, p. 241, on v. 6). Because of her outstanding character Filimatia manages to unite the different types of behaviour; see above on v. 6 *severa, dulcis*. For a similar oxymoron in a character, see Auson. *Parent.* 2.6, about his mother, Aemilia Aeonia: *et* *gravitas comis laetaque serietas* ('and a friendly dignity and a cheerful seriousness'); Lolli (1997) 71, Dräger (2012) 442, Green (1991) 303–4 with further parallel passages, for example Nep. *Att.* 15.1. In *Parent.* 9.23, Ausonius describes his late wife, the first in a series of early deceased relatives to receive an epitaph, as *laeta pudica gravis* ('cheerful, chaste, worthy'); see also Auson. *Parent.* 7.11. Another intertext might be Plin. *Ep.* 9.9.2 *quam pari libra gravitas comitasque* ('how balanced are dignity and friendliness'), about the deceased Pompeius Quintianus; Mascoli (2003) 165. *Facetus*, 'eloquent', 'witty', 'facetious' (*TLL* 6.1, 41.83–2.41), is also attested in other epitaphs, for example *CE* 1307.10. Sidonius also uses the adjective to characterise people in *Ep.* 5.5.4 *vir facetissime* ('most facetious man'), 8.11.3 v. 35 *satis facetum* ('most eloquent') (in opposition to *rusticus*) and 8.13.1 *sine studio facetum* ('witty without effort').

vv. 12–15 General remarks
The epigram ends with four lines containing information about Filimatia's death (*descriptio mortis*). In contrast to the first eleven verses, Sidonius inserts new information not yet known from the prose letter; see the General remarks on *Ep.* 2.8.3 vv. 1–4. Filimatia died at the age of thirty, which Sidonius paraphrases with the expression *decimam ... trieteridem*.

vv. 12–13 Hinc est quod decimam tuae saluti | vix actam trieteridem dolemus: For *hinc ... quod*, see the commentary on *Ep.* 2.2.20 *daturus hinc veniam, quod....* Plin. *Ep.* 8.5.2 uses the same expression to describe the loss of Macrinus' wife: *sed hinc magis exacerbatur, quod amisit* ('but this is the reason why it is even more bitter that he lost her'). Sidonius addresses the late Filimatia in the second-person singular (*tuae*) and makes himself a part of the grieving crowd with the first plural of *dolemus*; Wolff (2014c) 209. The verb *dolere* frequently appears in funerary inscriptions (*TLL* 5.1, 1823.46–59); here it is construed with *quod ... actam (esse)*. The dative *tuae saluti* must be a dativus commodi, 'for your well-being, i.e. life'. Anderson's (1936) 449 translation does not take into account the dative case of this phrase: 'we grieve that you have hardly fulfilled three decades of existence', as does Loyen (1970a) 62. See also Köhler (2014) 55: 'Schmerzlich sehen wir, dass schon dein Leben endet, als zehnmal erst der Jahre drei vergangen'. Bonjour (1988) 49 n. 38, though, interprets *salus* as 'salvation' (*OLD* 1684, 6a) as it is also used in Sidon. *Ep.* 2.10.4 v. 30 and translates 'nous déplorons que tu aies à peine achevé la trentième année pour ton salut'; see Sanders (1965) 1038. *Trieteris*, 'a period of three years' (*OLD* 1974, 1), is attested several times in Martial, also in a funerary epitaph – see for example Mart. 10.53.3 *invida quem Lachesis raptum trietride nona* ('the envious Lachesis got me after nine lots of three years') – as well as in Statius' consolatory poem (*Silv.* 2.6.72) and in inscriptions, for example *CE* 539, *CE* 1355. With the poetic description of the thirty years of Filimatia's life, Sidonius refers back to the beginning of the letter, where he mentions only her early death (Sidon. *Ep.* 2.8.1 *immaturo exitu*). In his epitaphs, Ausonius also often uses elaborate paraphrases to indicate the age at which his relatives died, for example in Auson. *Parent.* 1.4 *undecies binas vixit Olympiadas* ('he lived eleven times each two Olympiads'), 6.9, 9.8, 9.25–6, 12.11.

vv. 14–15 atque in temporibus vigentis aevi | iniuste tibi iusta persoluta: In verse 14, Sidonius again emphasises the flourishing life from which Filimatia was torn. The poem ends with a figura etymologica: Sidonius connects the wrong of an early death (*iniuste*) with the right of honouring Filimatia (*iusta*); see similarly Ov. *Met.* 2.627 *iniustaque iusta peregit* ('and he did the right honours during a wrong action'). For Sidonius' fondness of puns, see the commentary on *Ep.* 2.1.1 *Seronati, inquam*....The idea of honouring the dead is also found in Sidon. *Ep.* 3.3.8 *iuste sic mortuis talia iusta solventes* ('rightly we honour the dead with their rights'), 3.12.6 *ut suo iusta solvisse didicerimus* ('we have heard that he performed funeral rites as for someone from his own family'), 7.17.3 *quae restant sepulto iusta persolvimus* ('I paid the remaining dues to the buried'); Mascoli (2003) 166. See also Auson. *Parent. Praef.* B v. 1 and *Parent.* 9.1 for the notion of a *funus iustum*, a 'just funeral'.

Placeat tibi carmen necne: tu propera civitatemque festinus invise: As an afterthought in prose, which follows the poem, Sidonius writes in a pose of modesty that the quality of the engraved poem is not important. The only important duty of a friend is to comfort the mourners. Sidonius thereby shows himself to be in full control of his own feelings. At the same time, he secures the survival of his poems by passing them on via two different media, stone and paper. Similarly, Pliny cites his own poems (Plin. *Ep.* 7.4.6, 7.9.11) or poems about him (Plin. *Ep.* 3.21.5, 4.27.4) in his letters and thus saves them, while his volumes of poetry are lost. For Sidonius' demonstrative modesty, see the commentary on *Ep.* 2.2.7 *Pauci tamen versiculi...* and on *Ep.* 2.9.10 *Dicerem et cenas ... nisi terminum nostrae loquacitati* .... For *festinus* in an adverbial sense as 'hurriedly', 'quickly' (*TLL* 6.1, 621.62–72), which mostly appears in Late Latin authors, see Sidon. *Ep.* 4.25.1, 5.16.3, 7.17.3; Amherdt (2001) 508.

Debes enim consolationis officium duorum civium domibus afflictis: *Officium* in combination with *debere* belongs to the vocabulary of social obligations; see Symm. *Ep.* 9.114; van Waarden (2010) 454. To console a friend with a letter or in person is one of those social duties; Hindermann (2014). After the death of his daughter-in-law, Ruricius (Ruric. *Ep.* 2.4.1) explicitly apologises to her parents for not having fulfilled this duty: *ab epistulari officio nimius dolor cordis retraxit* ('from the obligation to write, an all too great heartbreak kept me away'). For the duties of friendship, see Sidon. *Ep.* 2.9.2 on hospitality, and on the duty to read and comment on one's literary works see Plin. *Ep.* 8.9.2 *nulla enim studia tanti sunt, ut amicitiae officium deseratur, quod religiosissime custodiendum studia ipsa praecipiunt* ('no studies are important enough that one should neglect the duty of friendship, which the studies themselves teach to observer assiduously').

Quod ita solvas deum quaeso, ne umquam tibi redhibeatur. Vale: For similar pious interjections to assure God's help, see the commentary on *Ep.* 2.2.3 *Haec mihi cum meis praesule deo....* The verb *redhibere* means 'to give back', 'return' (*OLD*, 1590), and is also used in *Ep.* 3.1.3, 3.2.4, 5.16.2; Giannotti (2016) 117. For the letter's simple ending with *vale*, see the commentary on *Ep.* 2.1.4 *Vale*.

Epistula 9

Introduction

Summary

While in *Ep.* 2.2 Sidonius describes his own villa, in *Ep.* 2.9 he describes two adjoining villas: Prusianum, owned by Tonantius Ferreolus, and Vorocingus, owned by Apollinaris. Whereas in *Ep.* 2.2 Sidonius concentrated on the architecture of his villa and the surrounding landscape, here he focuses on the different activities in the countryside and the question of how to spend one's *otium* with friends. Like Pliny, Sidonius thus integrates various villa letters in his collection to highlight the different aspects of *otium* in the countryside. Sidonius frames his second villa letter in response to Donidius' question as to why it took him so long to travel to Nemausus, present-day Nîmes. The reason is that he had a pleasant stay at the estates of his uncles Tonantius Ferreolus and Apollinaris, who outbid each other to entertain him and to make him feel at home. Not only did they have messengers ambush him on the road to lead him to their homes, but they also arranged a contest every morning to see who could feed him. Sidonius describes a series of activities that fill his day: ball games, dice games, reading books, scholarly conversations and an excursion to the well stocked library at one of the villas. These activities are interrupted only by the cook, who calls for lunch, during which entertaining and educational stories are told. Lunch is followed by a siesta and then a bath together. As Tonantius Ferreolus and Apollinaris, unlike Sidonius, do not have functioning baths, Sidonius devotes two sections to the makeshift facilities in which he bathes with his hosts. At the end of the letter, as in his first long letter, 2.2, about his own villa, he apologises for the length of the letter and announces to Donidius that he will tell him about the dinners he enjoyed with Tonantius Ferreolus and Apollinaris at the meal he and Donidius will have together as soon as they finally meet.

Addressee

As Giannotti (2016) 37 shows, there are many parallels between Books 2 and 3, including the addressees of the letters; see the introductions to *Ep.* 2.1 and 2.3. The addressee of *Ep.* 2.9, Donidius, is also subject in *Ep.* 3.5.1 and mentioned as a *vir spectabilis* there (and as *venerabilis* in *Ep.* 6.5.1); on the honorary titles, see the commentary on *Ep.* 2.4.1 *Vir clarissimus Proiectus*.... Donidius is a contemporary of Sidonius, a Christian (see the commentary on *Ep.* 2.9.5 *Quos inter ... fidei nostrae...*) who also hails from the Auvergne (*Ep.* 3.5.3). Sidonius helped him to recover his estate, *praedium Eborolacense*, present-day Ebreuil near Gannat (*Ep.* 3.5.2), and recommended Donidius' client and his slaves to the bishop Theoplastus (*Ep.* 6.5.1); see *PLRE* 2, 376–7, *PCBE* 4, 594, Loyen (1970a) 219 n. 33, Kaufmann (1995) 297, Giannotti (2016) 164, Mathisen (2020a) 90–91.

Date

There is no evidence for the date of this letter; see the Introduction, '2. The date and order of letters in Book 2'.

Major themes and further reading

Structure and intertextuality

Formally, letter 2.9 is a letter of friendship; see the introduction to *Ep.* 2.3 and Lucht (2011) 81. He praises his uncles Tonantius Ferreolus and Apollinaris, on whose estates he is staying, and expresses his closeness to them; see the commentary on *Ep.* 2.9.1 *Reddo causas ... quia quae mihi dulcia sunt tibi quoque* and on 2.9.10 *Sed quia ... teque sub ope Christi actutum nobis invisere placet*.... The letter also contains elements of a letter of reporting (see Cain 2009, 212), as Sidonius gives Donidius a detailed account about his sojourn on the estates.

Letter 2.9, alongside *Ep.* 2.2. and 2.10, has attracted the most scholarly attention of the letters in the second book, including even a monograph devoted to it, by Lucht (2011). Structurally, it is closely related to the first villa letter: if the fourteen letters of Book 2 were to be divided in half, these two letters mirror each other's position, as the second letter of each half. *Ep.* 2.2 and 2.9 are intentionally juxtaposed and thus have to be interpreted together; see Hanaghan (2020) 217. Like *Ep.* 2.2, letter 2.9 describes a rural villa and deals with the question of how to spend one's leisure (*otium*) in a pleasant spot (*locus amoenus*); see the introduction to *Ep.* 2.2. Whereas Sidonius in *Ep.* 2.2 focuses on the architectural details of his villa and the landscape surrounding it, here the social aspects and the daily routine of the villas' inhabitants are prominent. Sidonius' description of staying with his uncles is autoptic and focalised through his perspective; see Hanaghan (2020) 128. Interestingly, the two estates intermingle in his representation and appear as one: Sidonius and his hosts move from one place to another, so that one does not know which activities take place in which villa and where the premises in question are located. Similarly, Pliny also includes two letters about his pastimes in the villa in chronological order (Plin. *Ep.* 9.36 and 9.40), and describes his buildings and gardens in two other letters (Plin. *Ep.* 2.17 and 5.6); Mielsch (1987) 128–33. Another intertext could be Plin. *Ep.* 3.19, about neighbouring estates. Pliny is considering whether he should buy an estate adjacent to his own. Then it would be pleasant, *voluptuosissimum* (see the commentary below on 2.9.1 *inter agros...*), to be able to visit both estates. While Pliny could go back and forth between his own estates, Sidonius visits the estates of others. The reference to Pliny's villa letters is certainly intentional, for Sidonius also begins *Ep.* 2.9, as he did in his first villa letter, 2.2, with linguistic allusions to Pliny; see the commentary on *Ep.* 2.9.1 *Quaeris, cur ... producam*.

There are also intratextual parallels to Sidon. *Ep.* 1.2, where Sidonius depicts the daily routine of king Theoderic II with his various activities, and to *Ep.* 2.13, where a luxurious feast at the court of the ruler Dionysius is described, while Sidonius and his relatives dine simply.

Leisure in the villa and a private library
Sidonius' leisure time as described in *Ep.* 2.9 is modelled on the classical Roman ideal of *otium*, with its typical pastimes such as ball and dice games, horse riding, discussions, philosophising, reading, eating and bathing; Woolf (1998) 164, Myers (2005) 108–10, 119–20, Wagner (2010) 93–5, Lucht (2011) 83–4. The letter is thus used as a source for pastimes and the life of Gallic aristocrats in the countryside in general; Stevens (1933) 68–75, Percival (1997) 284–6. Nicolas (1901) 7–11 focuses on its descriptions of lunch, sporting activities for digestion and the healing effect of the steam bath and interprets it from a medical perspective.

There are two important differences between Sidonius' villa and his uncles' estates: in one respect, Sidonius' villa surpasses those of his uncles; in another it is inferior to them. While Sidonius' villa has a splendid bath-house, described in *Ep.* 2.2.4–8, he does not mention a library in his villa. If the letters 2.2 and 2.9 are juxtaposed, their descriptions of baths form a clear contrast: the baths of Tonantius Ferreolus and Apollinaris are no longer in use, but one of the villas has a rich library, which Sidonius describes in *Ep.* 2.9.4–5. Augustine is found next to Varro, and Horace alongside Prudentius, and the library also has separate shelves with different literature for women and men; Bonjour (1988) 44–5, Rossiter (1991) 200–1, Clark (1993) 136–7, Näf (1995) 144, Eigler (2003) 104–6, André (2006) 78–9, Gemeinhardt (2007) 458, Henke (2008) 166, Mratschek (2008) 368, 377, Squillante (2009) 154–6, Egelhaaf-Gaiser (2010), Eigler (2013) 402–12. As Hanaghan (2020) shows, scholars have wondered why Sidonius' villa epistle does not mention a library, especially as he was clearly well educated and prided himself on his *paideia*; see also Hanaghan (2019) 28–37.

The closed-down baths of Tonantius Ferreolus and Apollinaris
In *Ep.* 2.2 Sidonius elaborates on the bath-house in his description of the villa, probably because it was no longer common to have one in his times; Harries (1994) 131–3. The description of his uncles' closed-down baths and the makeshift sauna is a major point of interest for historical and archaeological researchers, especially in connection with Sidonius' own functioning baths; see the introduction to *Ep.* 2.2 and the commentary on *Ep.* 2.9.8. As Hanaghan (2020) 127–8 notes, the baths at Avitacum are large, technologically advanced, well designed and well furnished, whereas his uncles' baths have a single room and use rudimentary technology. As Sidonius draws attention to the failure of his uncles' baths, Hanaghan (2019) 26–7, 56–7 and Hanaghan (2020) therefore suggest a competitive undertone in *Ep.* 2.9: Sidonius presenting himself as a better host than his relatives. To accommodate one's guest counted among the duties of an aristocratic host and was an important element of self-representation; see Rossiter (1991) 202 and the commentary on 2.9.2 *Quamquam de praediorum … cum restet hospitalitatis ordo*.

Commentary

Section 1

Sidonius Donidio suo salutem: For the simple greeting formula, see the commentary on *Ep.* 2.1.1 *Sidonius Ecdicio suo salutem*. For the addressee, Donidius, see the introduction to this letter.

Quaeris, cur ipse iam pridem Nemausum profectus vestra serum ob adventum desideria producam: Sidonius starts the letter with a fictive question and explains why he is late. For the *topos* of a letter as 'half of a dialogue', see the commentaries on *Ep.* 2.1.1 *'Quaenam?' inquis* and the beginning of the first villa letter, *Ep.* 2.2.1 *Ruri me esse causaris....* The combination of *quaeris* and *reddo* in the next sentence is also reminiscent of the *iubeo–pares* motif, that the letter writer's text complies with the addressee's request for a report; see the commentary on *Ep.* 2.10.2 *Dicto pareo....* In his first villa letter, Plin. *Ep.* 2.17.1, Pliny also starts with a question: *miraris, cur me Laurentinum vel, si ita mavis, Laurens meum tanto opere delectet* ('you wonder why my Laurentinum or, if you prefer, my Laurens gives me so much pleasure'). With the verbal analogy in the initial words of the letter Sidonius sets the overall tone of the letter and draws the attention to thematic parallels with Pliny, in this case the description of an estate; see Gualandri (2020) 307 and the introductions to Sidon. *Ep.* 2.2 and 2.9. Nemausum (n.) or Nemausus (f.) is a city in Gallia Narbonensis, present-day Nîmes, situated near the famous aquaeduct Pont du Gard. It became a *colonia* under the emperor Augustus in the year 27 AD. The city was the seat of a bishopric in Late Antiquity (first documented in 506) and was conquered by the Visigoths in 472. Its name derives from Nemausus, a Celtic deity of the spring nearby; Euskirchen (2000). It is also mentioned in Plin. *Nat.* 3.37, Auson. *Urb.* 161; see Green (1991) 583. *Desiderium*, 'desire', is a typical word to express the longing of one friend for another; see Sidon. *Ep.* 3.6.1, 3.11.1, 7.10.1, 7.14.2, Cic. *Fam.* 2.11.1 *vehementer exspecto et desidero* ('I expect and miss eagerly'); van Waarden (2010) 541, van Waarden (2016) 129. For the subject of missing a friend, see the commentary on *Ep.* 2.1.1 *'Quaenam?' inquis. praesentiam Seronati et absentiam tuam.* The verb *produco* here appears in the meaning of 'to lengthen', 'to prolong', 'to postpone' (*TLL* 10.2, 1638.60–9.7).

Reddo causas reditus tardioris nec moras meas prodere moror, quia quae mihi dulcia sunt tibi quoque: With a rhetorically stylised sentence Sidonius turns to the topic of the letter; see also *Ep.* 4.19; Lucht (2011) 32. It combines a chiasmus (*reddo–causas* and *moras–moror*) with puns and alliterations. Whereas *reddere* and *reditus* are not etymologically connected, *moras* and *moror* are a figura etymologica; see the commentary on *Ep.* 2.1.4 *Proinde moras tuas....* Sidonius explains why he still has not reached the addressee, Donidius. The reason for his delay is not explicitly mentioned but has to be guessed from his enthusiastic description of his uncles' estates, where he has spent his time. In *Ep.* 1.5.2 Sidonius also writes about a delay in his travel due to his friends and acquaintances who wanted to say goodbye: *vianti moram ... amicorum multitudo faciebat* ('the great number of friends delayed me on my journey'). The same reason is given in *Ep.* 4.8.1 *e tenaci caterva prosecutorum* ('from a tenacious crowd of companions'); Amherdt (2001) 229–30. For the subject of travelling and its different subtypes (official journey related to public life, pastoral journey, social trip, forced journey), see *Ep.* 1.5, 1.6, *Carm.* 24, Piacente (2005) on *Ep.* 1.5, Wolff (2016). At the end of the sentence, Sidonius assures his and his addressee's mutual feelings. Donidius thus appears to be the writer's alter ego according to the ancient ideal of friendship; Lucht (2011) 32, 81, Williams (2012) 15. For *dulcis*, 'sweet', 'agreeable', see the commentary on *Ep.* 2.8.3 vv. 5–11, on the epitaph for the deceased Filimatia.

Inter agros amoenissimos, humanissimos dominos, Ferreolum et Apollinarem, tempus voluptuosissimum exegi: Sidonius praises his agreeable visit in the countryside with three superlatives (*amoenissimos, humanissimos, voluptuosissimum*). The adjective *amoenus*, which refers to the notion of a villa being a *locus amoenus*, again appears in the last section of *Ep.* 2.9.10. Sidonius thus clearly frames his poetical description of the villa. The adjective *amoenus* is also used in *Ep.* 1.5.8 (about a fountain), 8.4.1 (another villa), 9.16.3 v. 53 (poetry) and the noun *amoenitas* appears in *Ep.* 4.3.8 (poetry) and 4.6.3 (peace). For the villa as *locus amoenus* in Late Antiquity, see Ruric. *Ep.* 1.11, Ennod. *Carm.* 2.128–9, Cassiod. *Var.* 8.32.1 and the introduction to *Ep.* 2.2. The adjective *humanissimus* refers to the education of Sidonius' relatives, Tonantius Ferreolus and Apollinaris; see also Cic. *Arch.* 19 *humanissimos homines* ('very learned men') as well as the description of the library in *Ep.* 2.9.4 and the introduction to *Ep.* 2.10, where the praise of education is an important subject. Sidonius calls his relatives reverentially *dominos*, a term he also uses in *Ep.* 4.12.2 and 7.4.4, about Simplicius and Apollinaris; van Waarden (2010) 238.

Tonantius Ferreolus, the addressee of *Ep.* 7.12, is also mentioned in *Carm.* 24.34, *Ep.* 1.7.4 and 9, where he appears as one of the three envoys sent to Rome to bring charges of treason against the Gallic prefect Arvandus in 468/9; see the introductions to *Ep.* 2.1, 2.3 and 2.5. He stems from a noble family (his maternal grandfather is usually identified as Flavius Afranius Syagrius, consul in 382; Mathisen 2020a, 122) and was *praefectus praetorio Galliarum* in 451–452/3; see below on *Ep.* 2.9.3. He is married to a relative of Papianilla, Sidonius' wife, and has a son called Tonantius, as well as other sons; see below on *Ep.* 2.9.7. His estate is called Prusianum (see *Ep.* 2.9.7) and he has another estate called Trevidos (*Carm.* 24.32–38). For Ferreolus' life, see *PLRE* 2, 465–6, *PCBE* 4, 762–4, Kaufmann (1995) 308–9, Köhler (1995) 239–40, Näf (1995) 137, Santelia (2002) 84–7, van Waarden (2016) 55–6, Hanghan (2019) 119, Mathisen (2020a) 95–6.

Apollinaris, the addressee of *Ep.* 4.6, 5.3, 5.6 and (together with his brother Simplicius) *Ep.* 4.4 and 4.12, is either held to be a paternal uncle of Sidonius according to Loyen (1970a) 219 n. 34, Kaufmann (1995) 278, *PLRE* 2, 113–14 n. 2, *PCBE* 4, 161–3, van Waarden (2010) 238 – or a paternal cousin according to Stevens (1933) 68, Gibson (2013b) 345, Mathisen (2020a) 58–9, 80–1. For his estate, Vorocingus, near Nîmes, see the commentary below on *Ep.* 2.9.7 and *Carm.* 24.52–3. After 469 he lived with his brother Simplicius at Vaison, in the Burgundian region, see *Ep.* 7.4.4.

The rarely used adjective *voluptuosus*, 'productive of pleasure' (*OLD* 2102, 1), is first attested in Plin. *Ep.* 3.19.2, which might be an intertext for the letter at hand; see the introduction to this letter. The adjective appears several times in Sidonius, in the superlative also in *Ep.* 4.11.2; Ernout (1949) 84, Köhler (1995) 187–8, Amherdt (2001) 133. In the comparative it occurs in Sidon. *Ep.* 2.10.4. For adjectives ending in *-osus* in general, see the commentary on *Ep.* 2.2.18 *Lacus ipse ... flexuosus nemorosusque*.... In another letter, Pliny also reports on a pleasant visit he spent with a friend: Plin. *Ep.* 3.1.1 *nescio, an ullum iucundius tempus exegerim, quam quo nuper apud Spurinnam fui* ('I do not know if I ever spent a more agreeable time than when I was recently at Spurinna's place').

Praediorum his iura contermina, domicilia vicina: Tonantius Ferreolus and Apollinaris are direct neighbours and their properties share a common border. Sidonius highlights this fact with legal terminology, *ius praediorum* for 'property' (*TLL* 7.2, 687.74–8.31), and *domicilium* for 'residence'; Lucht (2011) 35. For *praedium*, 'estate', see the commentary on *Ep.* 2.2.3 *nomen hoc praedio*.... For the adjective *conterminus*, 'adjacent', 'adjoining', 'neighbouring' in an absolute use like here, see *TLL* 4, 681.78–2.12. For *domicilium*, see the commentary on *Ep.* 2.2.3 *Sed donec domicilio competens*.... Sidonius praises good neighbourliness again at the very end of the second book, at *Ep.* 2.14.2 *vicinus aequalis*.

quibus interiecta gestatio peditem lassat neque sufficit equitaturo: Next, Sidonius describes a *gestatio*, 'promenade' (*TLL* 6.2, 1957.21–33), where one could ride, be carried in a sedan or go for a walk. Sidonius does not use this rare architectural term in his own villa letter, 2.2, but it frequently appears in Pliny's villa letters as part of the villa's surroundings; see Plin. *Ep.* 1.3.1, 2.17.13–15 and 18, 5.6.17, 9.7.4; Förtsch (1993) 74–5. Far more often, the term denotes 'a riding', 'a being carried' (*TLL* 6.2, 1956.49–7.20), for example in Sen. *Ep.* 55.1. Here it refers to the distance between the two properties. The distance is so long that a walk on foot is tiring, but too small to be worth saddling a horse. *Pedes* is originally a military term to denote a foot soldier. Here (and in Sidon. *Ep.* 2.10.4 v. 23) it is used for a walker or passerby (*TLL* 10.1, 968.8–21). With the future participle of *equito*, 'to ride a horse', used as a noun here, Sidonius refers to a pastime of the nobles; see Lucht (2011) 36 and the commentary below on 2.9.7. Pliny also mentions horse riding as an activity in the countryside, in *Ep.* 9.15.3. For the verb *equito*, see also Sidon. *Ep.* 9.16.3 v. 37 (in a figurative sense about a poem), *Carm.* 7.43, 9.46. For *interiectus*, 'lying in between', and thus denoting the distance between two places, see the commentary on *Ep.* 2.11.2 *raritatem colloquii de prolixa terrarum interiectione...* and *Ep.* 6.6.1 *interiecti itineris longitudine* ('by the long distance between us').

Colles aedibus superiores exercentur vinitori et olivitori: Sidonius describes how the land around the villa is cultivated. Both crops, grapes and olives, are sources of income in the Roman villa from the second century BC on and remained so in Late Antique Gaul; Mielsch (1987) 11–15, Fellmeth (2001) 28–32, 36–46, Gerlach (2001) 60–9, 102–6, Ruffing (2002), Lucht (2011) 37. In reference to the estate Octavianum, Sidonius, in *Ep.* 8.4.1, praises its vineyards and olive groves (*vinetis atque olivetis*), and he also writes about a rich wine harvest in *Ep.* 2.14.1. Compare also the description of the estate of Pastor in *Ep.* 5.20.4, which also has vineyards and olive groves. For the importance of drinking wine as part of the lifestyle in a villa, see the commentary on *Ep.* 2.9.8 *sed cum vel pauxillulum bibere....* Pliny also mentions his vineyards several times, see for example Plin. *Ep.* 3.19.5, 5.6.9 and 27–30, but never olive groves. The verb *exercere* is frequently linked to nouns like *ager* or *terra* to indicate the cultivating of the soil, see *TLL* 5.2, 1372.22–46, Plin. *Ep.* 1.20.16 *vineas ... arbusta ... campos curo et exerceo* ('I cultivate and crop vineyards ... orchards and fields'). The noun *vinitor* (*OLD* 2067) also appears for example in Cic. *Fin.* 5.40, Verg. *Ecl.* 10.36, *Georg.* 2.417, Apul. *Flor.* 15.2. For the profession of a vine dresser, a valuable slave, see Colum. 1.9.4–6, 3.3.8. The noun *olivitor*, an olive dresser, is post-classical for *olitor* and only attested in Sidonius (*TLL* 9.2, 567.73–5).

According to Kaufmann (1995) 240 n. 727, both tasks here are performed by slaves. In letter 2.9, other professions practised by slaves follow, such as *sphaerista, aleator, archimagirus, nuntius, assecula, famulus* – see below. For Sidonius' depiction of the slaves in his villas, see the introduction to *Ep.* 2.2.

Aracynthum et Nysam, celebrata poetarum carminibus iuga, censeas: The mountain called Aracynthus is located in Aetolia, on the border between Boeotia and Attica. The mountain is connected with the Boeotian singer Amphion; see Verg. *Ecl.* 2.24, Prop. 3.15.41–2. It is also mentioned in Sidon. *Carm.* 15.32; Anderson (1936) 226 n. 3. Nysa is a mythical mountain of uncertain location (probably India), named after the homonymous nurse who raised the god Dionysos there; see Verg. *Aen.* 6.804–5, Hom. *Il.* 6.132–3; Siegel (2000). Sidonius mentions the mountain also in *Carm.* 22.4 v. 233; Delhey (1993) 202. The praise of landscapes, mountains, rivers and cities is a frequent topic in ancient poetry and topography, for example Sidon. *Ep.* 1.5.1; Köhler (1995) 186–7, Lucht (2011) 38. Sidonius uses *iugum*, a poetic term for 'mountain' (*TLL* 7.2, 643.47–4.52).

uni domui in plana patentiaque, alteri in nemora prospectus, sed nihilominus dissimilis situs similiter oblectat: Both villas have spectacular views, one to the open plain and one to the forest. For the importance of the view (*prospectus*) in the construction of a villa, see the commentary on *Ep.* 2.2.10. The participle *patens*, 'to lie open', is used here in the neutral plural as a noun (*TLL* 10.1, 667.30–35). Together with the noun *planum*, 'a plain' in the plural, it forms a hendiadys. Sidonius ends section 2.9.1 with a wordplay (*paronomasia*) with three similar-sounding words (*dissimilis situs similiter*). For the opposition of *similis* and *dissimilis*, see Sidon. *Ep.* 7.6.9, 8.6.2; van Waarden (2010) 328 provides examples from other Late Antique writers. For Sidonius' predilection for adverbs ending in *-ter* like *similiter*, see the commentary on *Ep.* 2.1.1 *Duo nunc pariter mala sustinent*.

Section 2

Quamquam de praediorum quid nunc amplius positione, cum restet hospitalitatis ordo reserandus?: Sidonius explicitly announces in section 2 of this letter that he does not want to devote himself to architecture, as in letter 2.2, but to the daily routine and the various occupations. The order of the words in this first sentence of the section (notably the separation of the preposition *de* and the corresponding noun *positione* and the inserted rhetorical question *quid nunc amplius*) is striking. For *praedium*, 'estate', see the commentary on *Ep.* 2.2.3 *nomen hoc praedio....* For *amplius*, 'longer', see the commentary on *Ep.* 2.2.20 *Sed non amplius moror....* Sidonius announces the various elements of his sojourn (*hospitalitas*), which he will describe in temporal order (*ordo*). For *hospitalitas* in the meaning of 'stay', 'sojourn', as here, see *Ep.* 7.2.2; van Waarden (2010) 147–8. More frequently, Sidonius uses the term in the meaning of 'hospitality', that is, the reciprocal obligation to welcome friends, which was an important element in the ancient and Late Antique concept of friendship; see Sidon. *Ep.* 1.9.1, *Carm.* 23.3, 23.434, 24.83; see Wagner-Hasel (1998), Hutchings (2009), the introduction to this letter and the French research project on *hospitalitas* called HospitAm. In *Carm.* 23.436–506 Sidonius praises Consentius' hospitality and lifestyle at length; Consolino (2020) 345. For *hospitalitas* meaning 'the settlement of barbarians on rural estates', see the commentary on *Ep.* 2.1.3 *implet cotidie silvas fugientibus, villas hospitibus....* For the subject of friendship (*amicitia*) in Sidonius and ancient letters in general, see the introduction to *Ep.* 2.3. The poetic verb *resero* here is used in a transferred meaning, 'to make known', 'disclose', 'inform', 'tell' (*OLD* 1628, 4b) see also *Ep.* 1.5.11, 3.3.5, 3.13.10, 4.3.2, 6.9.1, 7.7.4, 7.14.9; Köhler (1995) 215, van Waarden (2010) 366. In its literal sense 'to open' it is used in *Ep.* 1.8.1, 2.2.8 (see the commentary on *Ep.* 2.2.8 *triplex medii parietis aditus per arcuata intervalla reseratur*) and 7.10.1.

Iam primum sagacissimis in hoc exploratoribus destinatis, qui reditus nostri iter aucuparentur: Sidonius humorously describes how his friends lie in wait for him to lead them to their home, using terms from war or hunting. The esteemed guest Sidonius is the prey that will eventually be caught by his hosts; Gualandri (1979) 132–3, Drinkwater (2001), Lucht (2011) 39–40. Hunting for animals is also a popular pastime during a stay in the countryside; see Sidon. *Ep.* 1.2.4–5, 3.3.2, 4.4.1, 4.9.3, 5.17.1, 8.6.10–11, *Carm.* 2.144–6, but not part of Sidonius' description in *Ep.* 2.9, where he mentions only riding a horse, in *Ep.* 2.9.7. As in his other villa letter, 2.2, Sidonius inserts humorous scenes with allusions to comedy and satire. For *explorator*, 'explorer', 'scout', as a military term, see *TLL* 5.2, 1742.67–3.38. Sidonius uses the term also in *Ep.* 9.3.2, but not in the poems. The adjective *sagax*, 'keen-scented, 'keen (in respect of any or all of the senses)' (*OLD* 1679, 1a–b), is often used of (hunting) dogs; see for example Plaut. *Curc.* 112, Cic. *Div.* 1.65, Ov. *Met.* 3.207. Similarly, the noun *sagacitas* is used in Sidon. *Ep.* 5.7.1. Here and in sections 3, 5, 6 and 7 of *Ep.* 2.9, the plural (*nostri*) indicates that Sidonius did not travel alone. Lucht (2011) 69 suggests that Sidonius includes other (nameless) guests by using the plural, but it is more probable that he thus denotes his own entourage. In *Ep.* 2.9.10 Sidonius uses the plural *modestiae*. For the complex play with 'you' and 'I' in Sidonius, see van Waarden (2010) 49–52, van Waarden (2016) 45–8, van Waarden (2020b). *Aucupor*, 'to chase', 'hunt', 'catch', is used in a metaphorical sense here and in *Ep.* 9.7.5; see *TLL* 2, 1239.21–40.34.

domus utraque non solum tramites aggerum publicorum verum etiam calles compendiis tortuosos atque pastoria diverticula insedit, ne quo casu dispositis officiorum insidiis elaberemur: Sidonius describes how the members of the families of Apollinaris and Tonantius Ferreolus (*domus* is here used in the meaning of *familia*) ambushed him on three different routes, which he enumerates from the most to the least important. First, 'the public road', *agger publicus*, a term from Roman law designating the property of the *populus Romanus*. Second, the smaller *calles*, 'footpaths for cattle', and finally the even narrower *pastoria diverticula*, 'the by-ways of shepherds'. Sidonius uses the term *agger* in the specific meaning of 'street' (*TLL* 1, 1309.17–57), which is attested from Vergil onwards and which appears frequently in Late Antique literature, several times in his letters as well as in the poems: see *Ep.* 1.5.3, 2.10.4 v. 22, 3.2.3, 4.15.3, 4.24.2, 5.13.1, 8.12.1, 9.3.2, 9.13.2 v. 5, 9.14.5, and for example *Carm.* 9.16, 24.5; Köhler (1995) 192, Amherdt (2001) 491, Lucht (2011) 40. Sidonius uses the term *callis*, 'footpath', 'mountain-path for cattle' (*TLL* 3, 173.57–4.20), here and in *Ep.* 1.5.2. For *compendium* in the meaning of 'shortcut', 'saving of time' (*TLL* 3, 2040.19–78), see Sidon. *Ep.* 9.9.8. In other instances (for example *Ep.* 1.6.4) it means 'profit', 'help', 'advantage'; see van Waarden (2010) 524 on *Ep.* 7.9.23. For *tortuosus*, 'winding', see the commentary on *Ep.* 2.2.6 *Absunt lubrici tortuosique pugilatu....* The rare adjective *pastorius*, 'of a shepherd' (*TLL* 10.1, 647.27–41), is attested from Ov. *Met.* 2.680 onwards. It is used similarly instead of a genitive attribute also in Sidon. *Ep.* 4.18.5; Amherdt (2001) 413. *Diverticulum* or *deverticulum*, 'by-road', 'by-path', 'sideway' (*TLL* 5.1, 853.75–4.23), in the concrete meaning of 'a street' is attested from Ter. *Eun.* 635 onwards. The term appears only here in Sidonius. With the description of the carefully disposed (*dispositis*) traps Sidonius continues the image of the chase and connects it with the duty (*officium*) of friendship, here hospitality; see the commentary on *Ep.* 2.8.3 *Debes enim consolationis officium....* The word *insidiae*, 'ambush', is also used in Verg. *Aen.* 7.478 and *Georg.* 1.271 to describe a hunt.

Quas incidimus, fateor, sed minime invite, iusque iurandum confestim praebere compulsi, ne, priusquam septem dies evolverentur, quicquam de itineris nostri continuatione meditaremur: Sidonius playfully admits that he is a willing prey to his hosts and that he has immediately assured them that he will stay at least a week. The interjection *fateor*, 'I admit', is colloquial and also used in Sidon. *Ep.* 8.11.4 and 9.13.1. It is also attested in comedy (for example Plaut. *Aul.* 88) and thus adds to the letter's colloquial tone. The juridical *terminus technicus ius iurandum*, 'oath' (*TLL* 7.2, 702.26–72), is associated with *iurare* or *dare* more often than with *praebere*. *Evolvere*, 'to pass', 'elapse' (of time) is Late Latin and mostly attested in Christian writers (*TLL* 5.2, 1067.66–68.20). The noun *continuatio*, 'continuation' (*TLL* 4, 721.68–2.21), is also used in connection with *iter* in Symm. *Ep.* 3.16, where it describes uninterrupted travel. The term again appears in Sidon. *Ep.* 4.22.5 (about historiography), 6.1.5 (about bad deeds) and 7.18.4 (about reading the Bible).

Section 3

Igitur mane cotidiano partibus super hospite prima et grata contentio: The daily competition to serve the guests starts in the morning (*mane cotidiano*). As in section 1 of this letter, Sidonius stresses that it is pleasant to be at the centre of the hosts' rivalry (*prima et grata contentio*). The adverb *mane* is used here as a noun, combined with the attribute *cotidianus*; see *TLL* 8, 279.27–80.7. We find similar expressions also in Sidon. *Ep.* 4.8.1 *mane primo* ('in the early morning'), *Ep.* 5.17.10 and *Carm.* 12.15 *mane novo* ('at dawn'); Amherdt (2001) 230. For *contentio*, 'contest', 'fight' (*TLL* 4, 675.32–83), see Sidon. *Ep.* 4.4.1, 7.14.2, 8.11.1, and for example Plin. *Ep.* 1.2.3, 2.11.4, 3.9.8, 7.9.4. In classical Latin, the object of the dispute is in the genitive or with *de* and ablative. The combination with *super* and ablative instead of *de* is frequent in Late Latin, see Lucht (2011) 42.

quaenam potissimum anterius edulibus nostris culina fumaret: The adverb *potissimum* refers to the rivalry for the guest, which begins with the decision on where to have breakfast (*ientaculum*). This was usually taken between the third and fifth hour of the day, that is, between eight and ten o'clock; Gutsfeld (1999). Because a Roman breakfast consisted of light and cold food (bread, cheese, olive oil, or *puls*, the Roman porridge), Lucht (2011) 42–3 wonders about the smoke in the kitchen mentioned by Sidonius and suspects that Sidonius' hosts ate warm food for breakfast. Of course, there is also the possibility that Sidonius and his hosts had warm drinks. Most probably *culina fumaret* is a metonym for 'preparing food' (see the commentaries rigt below on *culina* and *fumare*), even if there was no warm food for breakfast. With the rarely used adverb *anterius*, 'before' (*TLL* 2, 159.55–62), which always refers to the temporal aspect, Sidonius emphasises *prima* from the first part of the sentence. It is also used in Sidon. *Ep.* 2.13.4, 4.24.3, 9.11.3, *Carm.* 15.81. For *edulia*, 'eatables', 'food', 'eating', see the commentary on *Ep.* 2.2.13 *Edulibus terminatis....* The term *culina*, 'kitchen' (*TLL* 4, 1287.79–8.33), is frequently used in comedy and satire, and also in Sidon. *Ep.* 4.25.2, *Carm.* 12.19. In connection with smoke (*fumus* or *fumare*) the kitchen is again mentioned in Sidon. *Ep.* 8.11.3 v. 44 *fumificas ... culinas* ('the smoky kitchens'), and vv. 47–8 *aut nebulae vapore iuncto | fumant cum crepitantibus patellis* ('or where clouds of smoke mixed with steam of pots rise up amid the clattering of plates'), Sen. *Ep.* 64.1 *fumus fieret, non hic, qui erumpere ex lautorum culinis ... solet* ('there was smoke, not the kind which bursts from the kitchens of the rich'), 104.6 *illum odorem culinarum fumantium* ('and that smell of steaming kitchens'). In his epigrams Martial writes several times about a *nigra culina*, 'a black kitchen' (black from smoke), in Mart. 1.92.9, 3.2.3, 10.66.3; Montone (2017) 30.

nec sane poterat ex aequo divisioni lancem ponere vicissitudo: Sidonius immediately anticipates that alternating between the two houses is not a fair solution and explains the reasons for this. For *lancem*, see the commentary on *Ep.* 2.4.1 *et cum illi ... pari lance conquadrent. Ex aequo* means 'balanced', 'fair'; it also appears in *Ep.* 3.9.2, 7.6.1; van Waarden (2010) 280. *Vicissitudo* here means 'regular succession or alternation' (*OLD* 2057, 2), a term used several times by Cicero (for example Cic. *Off.* 1.134) and Apuleius in *Metamorphoses* (for example Apul. *Met.* 10.2.7). In the context of a mutual friendship, it also appears in Ruric. *Ep.* 2.9.3.

licet uni domui mecum, alteri cum meis vinculum foret propinquitatis, quia Ferreolo praefectorio viro praeter necessitudinem sibi debitam dabat aetas et dignitas primi invitatoris praerogativam: The different degrees of Sidonius' attachment to his hosts make it difficult to organise his visit. Tonantius Ferreolus is related to Sidonius' wife Papianilla, while Apollinaris is related to Sidonius. Sidonius emphasises this fact with the parallelism *uni domui–alteri/mecum–cum meis*. This could be read as a microcosm of Sidonius' own identity, as a Lyon native (his father's side) and adopted

Arvernus (his wife's). As a former prefect as well as being next of kin, Ferreolus had the prerogative of inviting Sidonius first. For the biographies of both men and the degree of kinship, see the commentary on *Ep.* 2.9.1 *Inter agros amoenissimos, humanissimos dominos, Ferreolum et Apollinarem...*; on the office of a prefect, see the commentary on *Ep.* 2.1.3 *exultans Gothis insultansque Romanis, inludens praefectis conludensque numerariis.* According to Lucht (2011) 44, Sidonius here contrasts the term *propinquitas*, which describes a friendship based on family relations, with the term *necessitudo*, the word for a close friendship based not only on family closeness or personal ties, but on the mutual fulfilment of the duties of friendship (*officia*). Although Sidonius is directly related to Apollinaris, Ferreolus is connected to him by the *necessitudo* and has the privilege of inviting him first. For the duties of a friendship, see also the commentary on *Ep.* 2.8.3 *Debes enim consolationis officium....* The term *necessitudo* prominently appears in *Ep.* 3.1.1, to Avitus, where it denotes a connection through kinship: *primum quia matribus nostris summa sanguinis iuncti necessitudo* ('first because our mothers were united by the closest tie of kindred blood'); Giannotti (2016) 111 and in book four and six, see *Ep.* 4.1.1, 4.3.1, 6.4.1, 6.7.1, see Amherdt (2001) 69–70, 116. For *propinquitas*, see *Ep.* 8.9.5 v. 53 *Phoebea tumeat propinquitate* ('he vaunts his kinship with Phoebus the Sun'), *Carm.* 23.253 *semideum propinquitates* ('his kinship with demigods'). *Aetas* and *dignitas* appear here personified as subjects and thus receive additional weight; Lucht (2011) 45. *Invitator*, 'one who invites', 'an inviter' (*TLL* 7.2, 226.77–7.41) is a rarely used noun; it is first attested in Martial and later mostly in Christian authors; see Mart. 9.91.2, where he claims to prefer an invitation to dinner from emperor Domitian to an invitation from Jupiter. Sidonius uses the term also in *Ep.* 9.13.4. For *praerogativa*, 'superiority', 'excellence', see the commentary on *Ep.* 2.7.2 *Igitur ignosce ad tam sanctae conscientiae praerogativam....*

Section 4

Ilicet a deliciis in delicias rapiebamur: In his letters Sidonius uses *ilicet* ten times as a transitory formula meaning 'immediately', 'instantly' (*TLL* 7.1, 329.59–75): here and in *Ep.* 1.5.1, 1.9.5, 1.9.8, 2.14.2, 4.8.4, 4.22.5, 5.21.1, 6.12.9, 8.5.1. The polyptoton *deliciis ... in delicias* announces the content of the next section, that is, the various entertainments, which fill the whole day, indicated by the iterative imperative *rapiebamur* ('we were rushed').

Vix quodcumque vestibulum intratum, et ecce huc sphaeristarum contrastantium paria inter rotatiles catastropharum gyros duplicabantur: As in *Ep.* 2.2.15 and *Carm.* 23.487–506 Sidonius mentions different forms of pastimes in the countryside, which start right in the entrance court of the house (*vestibulum*); see the commentary on *Ep.* 2.2.3 *Sed donec domicilio competens vestibuli campus aperitur*. Sidonius underlines his admiration for all the different forms of entertainment with a colloquial *et ecce* (*TLL* 5.2, 28.24–59), which refers instead to the unexpected; Köhler (1995) 170. It is also attested in *Ep.* 1.3.2 and in its inversed form *ecce et* in *Ep.* 2.9.6. It remains unclear exactly which game Sidonius' hosts are playing, but see the analysis of Lucht (2011) 47–9, who compares the passage to Sidon. *Ep.* 5.17.7, where a ball game is described in similar terms; see also Väterlein (1976) 91–4. The sentence is further complicated by the Greek technical terms and hapax legomena. In Sidonius' description, the verbs expressing movement predominate, giving a visual impression of the action and the entanglement of the players. This sentence and the next are conntected with *huc ... huc ... huc* in the meaning of *hic ... hic ... hic* ('here ... here ... and here'); see *TLL* 6.3, 3070.42–5. Although it is transmitted in all manuscripts (and is also used by Anderson (1936) 452 and Loyen (1970a) 64), Lütjohann (1887) 31 emends it to *hac ... hac ... hac*. The emendation is rightly rejected by Mohr (1895) XVII–XVIII and Lucht (2011) 46–7 with reference to similar passages with a double *huc* in Sidon. *Ep.* 8.6.14 and 8.13.3. The term *sphaerista*, 'ball player', derives from Greek and is a hapax; Gualandri (1979) 159 n. 53. Kaufmann (1995) 240 thinks that the two terms *sphaeristae* and *aleatores* in the next sentence refer to slaves who have to entertain the guests. One is reminded of the beginning of Petronius' *Cena Trimalchionis* 27.3, where the *dominus* plays ball with his slaves before the dinner starts. For the importance of ball games for Sidonius and the Romans in general and the term *sphaeristerium*, 'a place for playing ball', see the commentaries on *Ep.* 2.2.15 *pilae vacamus* and *Ep.* 2.2.15 *atque illic ... sphaeristerio faciat*. The adjective *rotatilis*, 'wheel-like', 'revolving', is very rarely used. It also appears in Prud. *Epil.* 8 to denote his verses: *sacramus et rotatiles trochaeos* ('we also dedicate tumbling trochees'); Lucht (2011) 50. *Catastropha*, also a Grecism, denotes 'turning', 'falling' (*TLL* 3, 598.50–54). Only Sidonius uses it in reference to the body – see *Ep.* 5.17.7 *per catastropham saepe pronatus aegre de ruinoso flexu se recolligeret* ('he would often bend low in a flying tackle and then scarcely manage to recover from his staggering swerve'); Schwitter (2015) 76. For the medieval gloss on this term, see Chronopoulos (2020) 647–8. For *gyrus*, 'the circular track a ship takes', see the commentary on

Ep. 2.2.19 *ubi supra molares ... trita gyris meta protuberant.* Here it denotes the circular movement of the player, that is, 'winding', 'turn' (*TLL* 6.2, 2387.56–7). *Duplico*, 'to bend' (*TLL* 5, 2277.27–57), but also refers to the bodies of the players. Sidonius uses the verb in the same meaning in *Carm.* 23.370 as well.

huc inter aleatoriarum vocum competitiones frequens crepitantium fritillorum tesserarumque strepitus audiebatur: For *huc*, see the commentary on *Ep.* 2.9.4 *Vix quodcumque vestibulum intratum, et ecce huc* .... Next, again as in *Ep.* 2.2.25 and in *Carm.* 34.490–1, Sidonius adds dice to ball games as a pastime. For the role of dice games in Sidonius and for the adjective *aleatorius*, see the commentary on *Ep.* 2.2.15 *atque illic aleatorium.... Competitio* in the meaning of a 'meeting together', 'agreement', is attested only in Sidonius (*TLL* 3, 2064.52–4). The noun *fritillus*, 'dice cup' (*TLL* 6.1, 1341.5–31), derives from the verb *fritinnio*, 'twitter', 'chirp'. Most often, it was made of ivory; Lucht (2011) 50. It also appears in Sidon. *Carm.* 23.491–92 in connection with the description of leisure activities with friends: *hic promens teretes pilas trochosque, | hic talos crepitantibus fritillis | nos ad verbera iactuum struentes* ('then you would bring out the shapely balls and hoops or the dice which with rattling box marshal us for the hurtling throw'). With this passage in the letter, Sidonius probably alludes to Mart. 4.14.8 *incertis sonat hinc et hinc fritillis* ('the dice cups are sounding here and there with an uncertain outcome'). Sidonius adds the term *tesserarum* to *fritillorum* and two more words indicating noise (*crepitantium, strepitus*) to *sonat*; Colton (1985b) 279. The term *fritillus*, 'dice cup', appears several times in Martial (5.84.3, 11.6.2, 13.1.7, 14.1.3) and also in Iuv. 14.5. A *tessera*, 'die' (*OLD* 1930, 1b), was marked on all six sides and mostly made of bone. It is mostly used in the plural, because two or three dice were thrown at the same time.

huc libri affatim in promptu (videre te crederes aut grammaticales pluteos aut Athenaei cuneos aut armaria extructa bybliopolarum): Whereas no library is mentioned as part of Sidonius' villa in *Ep.* 2.2 and reading is not listed as a pastime, here both are found in a lengthy *amplificatio*. This passage is much commented on; see the introduction to *Ep.* 2.9. It is not clear in whose house the library described is located – but it is probably that of Tonantius Ferreolus, whom Sidonius visited first, although Apollinaris may have had a similar one; Lucht (2011) 53. From the end of the republic on, private libraries were a standard item in the houses of members of the upper class (see for example Vitr. 1.2.7, 6.4.1, Sen. *Tranq.*

9.4, Cic. *Top.* 1.1) and also a status symbol (see Petron. 48.4, Page 2015, 286–93), of a significance similar to a private bath-house. The library in *Ep.* 2.9.4 also serves as a reception room for visitors and friends; Mratschek (2020b) 255. Sidonius often mentions other libraries in his friends' private houses and refers to these as *bybliotheca* or *bibliotheca*, a term he does not use here, however; see *Ep.* 3.7.1, 4.11.6 vv. 4–5 (Claudianus Mamertus), 7.9.1, 8.4.1 (Consentius), 8.11.2 (Lupus), 9.16.3 v. 28, *Carm.* 24.92 (Probus); Kaufmann (1995) 222, Mratschek (2008) 377, Squillante (2009) 151–6, van Waarden (2010) 415–16, Mratschek (2020b) 256. For Christian private libraries in Late Antiquity, see Wendel (1954) 251–3. Private as well as public libraries are also frequently mentioned in Pliny's letters: Plin. *Ep.* 1.8.2, 2.17.8, 3.7.8, 4.28.1, 8.28.1, 10.81.7; see also Mart. 7.17, about the library of Iulius Martialis. For reading as a pastime, see Sidon. *Ep.* 3.14.1, 5.17.6. For *huc*, see the commentary on *Ep.* 2.9.4 *Vix quodcumque vestibulum intratum, et ecce huc....* The term *liber*, 'what you (can) read', has various nuances in Sidonius; van Waarden (2016) 34. Here it denotes a book, independent of its subdivision.

Sidonius describes his uncle's library with three comparisons, that is, three different places (school, public library, bookshop) and technical terms (*pluteus, cuneus, armarium*), where books were stored or read; Eigler (2013) 405. First Sidonius compares his uncle's library with the bookshelves of a teacher. The adjective *grammaticales* here stands for the genitive *grammaticorum* and denotes a *grammaticus*, a 'grammarian', 'philologist', 'teacher of literature'. It is also used in Sidon. *Carm.* 23.212; Onorato (2016) 385. *Pluteus*, '(book)-shelf' (*TLL* 10.1, 2470.39–52), denotes a place to store books; see Iuv. 2.7. Next, Sidonius compares his uncle's library with the Athenaeum, the school of liberal arts founded by the emperor Hadrian (117–138) in Rome for public conferences and recitations; see *TLL* 2, 1031.16–33, Aur. Vict. *Caes.* 14.3, Hier. *Ep.* 66.9. Similar places were founded in smaller cities; Amherdt (2001) 248. Sidonius also mentions the Athenaeum in *Ep.* 4.8.5, 9.9.13 and 9.14.2 (cited on p. 263 in the commentary on *sic tamen quod...*) as a symbol of erudition; Mratschek (2020a) 234 n. 157. Like a theatre, the Athenaeum had tiers. The term *cuneus*, 'a wedge' (*TLL* 4, 1406.26–62), stands metonymically for 'the division of the rows of seats in a theatre'; see Vitr. 5.6.2, Verg. *Aen.* 5.664, Suet. *Aug.* 44.2, Iuv. 6.61. The term is also used in Sidon. *Carm.* 23.401 and in *Ep.* 3.3.7 for 'troops (drawn up for battle in the form of a wedge)'. In combination with the ranks of the Athenaeum, a very similar expression with the adjective *cuneatus*, 'in the form of a wedge', is found in Sidon. *Ep.* 9.14.2 *Athenaei subsellia cuneata* ('the wedge-shaped seats in the Athenaeum'). Thirdly, Sidonius compares the library with an *armarium*, a 'closet', 'chest' (*TLL* 2. 603.82–4.24), of a *bybliopola* (see the commentary immediately below on *sic tamen quod...*). The term *armarium* originally denoted a storage space for things like clothes, food or valuables. Pliny also uses it when he mentions a bookcase in his villa description in Plin. *Ep.* 2.17.8 *parieti eius in bibliothecae speciem armarium insertum est, quod ... libros ... capit* ('in its wall is a cupboard, a kind of bookcase, which contains books'); Santelia (2000) 219–20, Kleberg (1967) 42, 94 n. 62. *Extructa* is the participle of *exstruo* and means 'built high' (*TLL* 5.2, 1941.29–33). For the profession of a *bybliopola* in Sidonius' letters and the discussion of its meaning in Sidonius' time, see the commentary on *Ep.* 2.8.2 *mercennarius bybliopola suscipiet*. Santelia (2000) 219–20 thinks that the *bybliopolae* mentioned here are secretaries or clerks in a library, while Kleberg (1967) 55, 96 n. 123 and Kaufmann (1995) 222 n. 659 consider them to be professional booksellers and free merchants. I agree with the latter, since Sidonius uses related areas such as school, public library and finally a bookshop for comparison when describing the library of his hosts.

sic tamen quod, qui inter matronarum cathedras codices erant, stilus his religiosus inveniebatur: Interestingly, Sidonius makes a gender-related classification of the reading canon, but does not distinguish between Christian and pagan texts. Whereas Sidonius names four writers as examples of reading for men (see the commentary on *Ep.* 2.9.4 *nam similis scientiae viri ... hinc Augustinus hinc Varro, hinc Horatius hinc Prudentius...*), he does not specify the literature for women (*stilus religiosus*). Probably he means the Bible or saints' lives, that is, texts that can be read without further knowledge of rhetoric, grammar, philosophy, mythology or ancient history, which were the subjects, taught at school; Gualandri (1979) 11, Eigler (2003) 106, Egelhaaf-Gaiser (2010) 257, 260, Eigler (2013) 408–10, Montone (2017) 30. Hier. *Ep.* 29.1 similarly contrasts religious works (the Bible) with the classics (represented by Cicero and Demosthenes). See also Sidonius' praise of Claudianus Mamertus' learning in *Ep.* 4.11.6 vv. 4–5 *triplex bybliotheca quo magistro | Romana, Attica, Christiana, fulsit* ('under his teaching three literatures were illumined, Latin, Greek and Christian').

For the construction *sic tamen quod*, see Lucht (2011) 54, Köhler (1995) 160. *Quod* with indicative after *sic, tam, ita* instead of *ut consecutivum* is typical of Late Latin; see *Ep.* 1.2.9, 3.3.8. In *Ep.* 2.9.8, though, Sidonius combines *sic tamen, ut* with the conjunctive; see also *Ep.* 9.10.2. For *matrona*, the *terminus technicus* for a noble and honorable woman, see the commentary on

Ep. 2.8.1 Decessit nudius tertius non absque iustitio matrona Filimatia. Not only the texts, but also the seats (*cathedra* and *subsellia*) and the media (codex and scroll) are gendered. In classical Latin, *cathedra* is the term for 'a chair, esp. one furnished with cushions and supports for women' (*TLL* 3, 612.9–65); see for example Mart. 3.63.7, 12.38.1. Without referring to a chair for women the term also appears in Pliny's villa letter Plin. *Ep.* 2.17.21 as well as in Plin. *Ep.* 3.16.12 and 8.21.2. In the seventh and ninth book, Sidonius uses the term to refer to the episcopate, see Sidon. *Ep.* 7.6.9, 7.9.17 and 24, 9.11.5, 9.16.3 v. 66, and it also appears in 7.9.2 and 7.9.5 without reference to women. The codex (*TLL* 3, 1404.10–6.52), a type of book that resembles our modern book with superimposed leaves, was associated with Christian literature; Jochum (2007) 52–4, Eigler (2013) 406, Schipke (2013) 143–52. For the difference between codex and scrolls in use and distribution, see the commentary on *Ep.* 2.9.4 *licet quaepiam volumina....* *Stilus* here means 'mode of composition', 'style' (*OLD* 1820, 4b), and so *stilus religiosus* denotes 'religious literature'. With this term Sidonius often refers to the content of his writings – see *Ep.* 1.1.2, 3.3.2, 3.9.1, 3.14.1, 4.3.3, 4.22.1; Köhler (1995) 107. For *stilus* in the meaning of 'pen', see the commentary on *Ep.* 2.2.20 *Sed non amplius moror, ne, si longior stilo terminus.* For *religiosus*, see the commentary on *Ep.* 2.6.1 *opportunus elegans, ... parcus religiosus....* For adjectives ending in -*osus* in general, see the commentary on *Ep.* 2.2.18 *Lacus ipse ... flexuosus nemorosusque....*

qui vero per subsellia patrumfamilias, hi coturno Latiaris eloquii nobilitabantur: *Subsellium*, 'a low seat, bench' (*OLD* 1848, 1a), is a term used to denote the benches of the senators in their meeting room (*curia*) and the benches in court. The *subsellia* symbolise the male sphere, whereas the *cathedrae* refer to the place of women. Because *subsellia* were also used in school, shops and taverns, Lucht (2011) 55 suggests an opposition between the noble and elegant versus the low and common, but the gendered connotation of the seats seems more dominant. The term *cot(h)urnus*, 'a high Grecian shoe' (*TLL* 4, 1088.7–42), worn by the actors of Greek tragedy, is used in its transferred meaning for an 'elevated style' here (and in *Ep.* 8.11.5) and by several other authors, for example in Quint. 10.1.68, Apul. *Apol.* 37.3; Gualandri (1979) 82 n. 26. The term frequently appears in Ammianus, and Sidonius is probably inspired by him; see Amm. 20.1.2, 21.16.1, 27.11.2, 28.1.4, 28.4.27, 28.6.29. Sidonius uses the term *cot(h)urnus* also in the meaning of 'shoe', 'buskin', in *Ep.* 4.13.1, 8.11.3 v. 8, *Carm.* 2.401, 9.237, 23.125; Amherdt (2001) 330. He uses it for 'tragedy' in 9.13.5 v. 83. See also Sidon. *Carm.* 18.4 *cothurnato vertice* ('with its proud crest'). *Latiaris*, 'of Latium', 'Latin' (*OLD* 1006, 1a), originally was a cult title for Jupiter Latiaris, who was revered on Mons Albanus for unifying all cities in Latium. The adjective adds to the elevated tone. Sidonius also uses it in *Ep.* 2.10.1, 9.15.1 v. 30, *Carm.* 9.218, 14.2, 23.235; for the adjective referring to 'language', see the commentary immediately below, on *licet quaepiam volumina....* *Eloquium*, 'eloquence' (*TLL* 5.2, 412.9–17.81) is used thirteen times in Sidonius' letters and five times in the *Carmina*, for example *Ep.* 4.3.2 and *Carm.* 23.145. The prosaic synonym *eloquentia* (*TLL* 5.2, 412.44–13.59) is used only five times in the letters (e.g. *Ep.* 1.9.8, 4.22.3) and nowhere in the poems. The combination of *eloquium* with *Latiaris* is also found in Symm. *Ep.* 1.3.2 *unus aetate nostra monetam Latiaris eloquii Tulliana incude finxisti* ('you alone in our time coined money of Latin eloquence on the Ciceronian anvil') and Ennod. *Ep.* 7.26 *proinde valete, ostrum Latiaris eloquii* ('goodbye then, you purple of Latin eloquence'). *Latiaris* appears several times referring to language in Symmachus, who is an epistolary model for Sidonius (see Sidon. *Ep.* 1.1.1); see Symm. *Ep.* 1.15.2, 8.22, 8.69, 9.88; Bruggisser 2002. The verb *nobilito* means 'to raise in rank', 'ennoble' (*OLD* 1183, 3). Here not only the authors of the books are elevated by their education in rhetoric, but also their readers, the Gallo-Roman aristocrats (*nobiles*).

licet quaepiam volumina quorumpiam auctorum servarent in causis disparibus dicendi parilitatem: The noun *volumen* denotes 'a roll of papyrus forming a book or part of a book', 'a book in any form' (*OLD* 2100, 1a–b); see the commentary on *Ep.* 2.8.2 *Quam si non satis improbas, ceteris epigrammatum meorum voluminibus applicandam.* Around the end of the third or the beginning of the fourth century AD the scroll was mostly replaced by the codex; see Kleberg (1967) 69–86, Cavallo (1997a), Cavallo (1999) 125–33, Jochum (2007) 54, Schipke (2013) 143–52. In Sidonius' period the usual format for all content is the codex, but here it is only associated with the female sphere of religious texts. The medium of a scroll therefore anachronistically symbolises classical Latin literature and the conservatism of its readers; see Eigler (2013) 406, van Waarden (2016) 32–40 for the different types of books and the use of the different terms in Sidonius. Regardless of whether they are Christians or not and whether they write prose or poetry, all four authors Sidonius mentions in the next part of the sentence use the same sublime style of writing. Sidonius highlights this connection with the assonant wordplay *in causis disparibus dicendi parilitatem.*

For Sidonius' predilection of assonant wordplays, see the commentary on *Ep.* 2.2.13 *Edulibus terminatis ... aestuosum, maxime aestivum*. For *par/impar*, see also Sidon. *Ep.* 7.1.2, 7.14.7. The term *parilitas*, 'equality' (*TLL* 10.1, 397.10–39), is used here to denote the quality of the books; see Fascione (2019) 100–1 and the commentary on 2.2.4 *quae consequenti unguentariae spatii parilitate conquadrat....* The archaic indefinite pronoun *quispiam* is frequently used by Sidonius and Boethius, here conspicuously in a polyptoton (*quaepiam ... quorumpiam*); Lucht (2011) 56.

nam similis scientiae viri, hinc Augustinus hinc Varro, hinc Horatius hinc Prudentius lectitabantur: Next, Sidonius gives four examples of authors whose works are on the bookshelf for men; see the commentary on *Ep.* 2.9.4 *sic tamen quod, qui inter matronarum cathedras codices erant....* In chiastic order Augustine and Varro represent Christian and pagan prose, Horace and Prudentius pagan and Christian poetry. Sidonius here shows no fear of combining classical and Christian education; see also *Ep.* 4.3, 6.12.6–7; Bailey (2020) 266–7. These four authors are all connected by their *scientia*, which here means 'skills', 'artistic mastery' (see *Ep.* 2.10.6; for the meaning 'knowledge', see the commentary on *Ep.* 2.5.1 *et donec suarum ... vel vestra scientia...*). On a grammatical level they are connected with the adverb *hinc*; for the multiple use of *hinc*, see also the commentary on *Ep.* 2.10.4 v. 22 *Hinc agger sonat, hinc Arar resultat*).

The antiquarian Varro (116–27 BC) was more famous for his erudition than for his style; see Quint. 10.1.95 *plus scientiae conlaturus quam eloquentiae* ('he is more likely to enhance one's knowledge than one's style'), Aug. *Civ.* 6.2 *minus est suavis eloquio* ('even he is less agreeable in his eloquence'). Lucht (2011) 57–8 therefore wonders why Varro is mentioned as an example of eloquence and here compared to the church father Augustine (354–430). Anderson (1936) 454–5 n. 1 suggests that Sidonius compares the two authors because Augustine draws on Varro's historical research and mentions him often in his work *De Civitate Dei*. Augustine also followed Varro in his ambitious project of describing all of the *artes liberales*; Pollmann (1997) 295, Sallmann (2002). For the relation that Sidonius establishes between Augustine and Varro, see also Loyen (1970a) 219, Eigler (2013) 406–7. Sidonius mentions Varro again in *Ep.* 4.3.1, 8.6.18 (Sidonius sent Namatius a copy of Varro's *Libri logistorici*), *Carm.* 2.190 (in a catalogue of authors read by the emperor Anthemius); Piacente (1998), Onorato (2016) 46, Gualandri (2020) 285. Varro also appears in *Carm.* 23.150–1, in a catalogue of ancient writers who meet a certain standard of language

(*Carm.* 23.145 *quid vos eloquii canam Latini*, 'what should I sing to you of the Latin eloquence'); Amherdt (2001) 122–3, Santelia (2016b) 434–7.

Sidonius mentions the Roman poet Horace (65–8 BC) in fourteen different passages either in person or by the titles of his works, especially in the eighth and ninth book of his letters and in his *Carmina*; see Köhler (1995) 294–5 on *Ep.* 1.11.1, Flammini (2009), Egelhaaf-Gaiser (2010) 261–92, Bruzzone (2011), Stoehr-Monjou (2013) 138, Neger (2020), and my commentaries on *Ep.* 2.2, 2.8, 2.12.3 and 2.13, where Sidonius alludes to Horace's works several times. Here Sidonius argues that Horace is read for the quality of his style, but unlike Varro he does not figure among the authors that Sidonius suggests the emperor Anthemius reads (*Carm.* 2.182–92). Sidonius praises Horace's style also in *Ep.* 8.11.7. Horace is also an important figure for Sidonius' self-presentation as a poet, especially in his poetic epilogue in *Ep.* 9.16.3 and the prose section 4 – see Egelhaaf-Gaiser (2010) 261–92, Mratschek (2017) 316–22 – and also in Sidon. *Ep.* 1.5, which describes his journey to Rome referring to Hor. *Sat.* 1.5 – see Eigler (1997). See also the commentary on *Ep.* 2.10.1 *eam brevi … sermonum purpurae…*, where Sidonius alludes to Horace's *Ars poetica*.

The Christian poet Prudentius (348/9 till after 405) combines complicated lyric metres with Christian theology and is therefore called *Horatius Christianus*; see Kytzler (1998) 725, Pollmann (2001) 488, Richardson (2016) 26. He is an important reference for Sidonius regarding metrical technique; see Squillante (2009) 156 and Squillante (2010) on Sidonius and Prudentius' hymns. Together with Horace, Prudentius is also an important figure for Sidonius' self-portrayal as a letter-writer in the concluding letter 9.16; Egelhaaf-Gaiser (2010) 61–92. For the presence of Prudentius' *Peristephanon* in Sidonius' work, see Gualandri (1979) 5 n. 18. The importance of reading is finally reinforced by the intensive verb *lectito* and the iterative imperfect; Lucht (2011) 58. For the verb *lectito*, 'to read often, with eagerness, or with attention', see the commentary on *Ep.* 2.10.5 *quoque id facilius … opus est ut sine dissimulatione lectites, sine fine lecturias*.

Section 5

Quos inter Adamantius Origenes Turranio Rufino interpretatus sedulo fidei nostrae lectoribus inspiciebatur: Next, Sidonius describes a discussion among Christian laymen about the quality of a translation from Greek to Latin by Turranius/Tyrannius Rufinus (344/5–411). For Sidonius'

knowledge of Greek, see the commentary on *Ep.* 2.2.8 *si graecari mavis*....
Fom 397 to 407, Rufinus, who is famous for his Latin version and his
continuation of Eusebius' church history, also translated various works of
theology and exegesis of the controversial theologian Origen (185/6–252/4);
Humphries (2008), Robbe (2016), Hanaghan and Carlson (forthcoming).
Among them were five books of dialogues, *De recta fide in Deum*, also called
Adamantius, after its main speaker. This work was falsely attributed to Origen,
probably because he also had the same nickname ('the adamant'); see Hier.
Vir. ill. 54.1; Berschin (1980) 63–5, Pretty (1997) 9–16, Reutter (1997)
484, Ramelli (2020). Origen's work consisted of the allegorical exegesis
of the Bible, sermons and theological treatises. Unfortunately, most of his
numerous works (over 700 titles) are lost. Origen's theology was influenced
by Platonic dualism and highly controversial. Rufinus' support of Origen's
theology fuelled the First Origenist Controversy, which erupted in the 390s.
Parts of Origen's work were declared heretical by an edict of the emperor
Justinian the Great in 543 and at the Second (or fifth ecumenical) Council
of Constantinople, in 553; Anderson (1936) 455 n. 2, Clark (1992), Feichtinger
(1995) 52–64, Köhler (1995) 238 on *Ep.* 1.7.3, Habermehl (1997),
Markschies (2007) 6–13, Lucht (2011) 58–9. By inserting the discussion
about the value of translation, Sidonius alludes to Jerome (331/48–419/20),
who criticised Rufinus' translations. Rufinus and Jerome studied together
and were friends, but finally fell out. One reason was their argument about
Origen, whom Rufinus presented as an orthodox doctor of the church by
changing heretical passages in his translation of Origen's *De principiis*. For
other reasons of this public breach between Rufinus and Jerome, see Clark
(1992) 14–16. In his work *Apologia contra Rufinum* (402/3) Jerome accused
Rufinus of having obscured the real Origen in his translations. Sidonius
defends Rufinus against Jerome, whom he also mentions in *Ep.* 4.3.7 and
9.2.2 (as a translator of the Bible); Pricoco (1965), Loyen (1970a) 219–20,
Bonjour (1988) 41 n. 5, Prévot (1995) 220–21, Rebenich (1997) 318, Eigler
(1998) 550, Amherdt (2001) 149–52, Mathisen (2009) 200, Santelia (2012)
61. On Sidonius' and Jerome's shared interest in language and linguistic, see
Denecker (2015). See the commentary below on *Ep.* 2.9.5 *cur a quibusdam
... ad verbum sententiamque translatus*. The expression *fidei nostrae* proves
that the addressee, Donidius, was a Christian. For *fides* in the meaning of
'Christian faith', see *TLL* 6.1, 689.43–90.25. For Sidonius' knowledge and
use of the Bible in his letters in general see Styka (2008), Bailey (2020)
266–7. For the verb *inspicere*, see the commentary on *Ep.* 2.6.1 *Menstruanus
amicus tuus longo istic tempore inspectus*....

pariter et, prout singulis cordi, diversa censentes sermocinabamur: Sidonius here describes the atmosphere among his friends, in which controversial theological discussions take place, as relaxed and trusting. For *pariter*, 'in like manner, 'equally', see the commentary on *Ep.* 2.1.1 *Duo nunc pariter mala sustinent*. With *prout*, 'accordingly', 'in proportion', 'just as' (*TLL* 10.2, 2362.40–3.37) (see for example Cic. *Att.* 11.6.7), which also appears in Sidon. *Ep.* 2.9.6 and 2.9.9, Sidonius expresses that every guest can do what he wants. The verb *sermocinor*, 'to hold a conversation', 'chat' (*OLD* 1744), here refers to an informal conversation. The manuscripts NCT have *sermocinabantur*, LM have *sermocinabamur*, followed by Lütjohann (1887) 31, Anderson (1936) 454 and Loyen (1970a) 65. The first-person plural is more probable, since Sidonius in this way includes himself, see *Ep.* 2.9.6 *prandebamus ... hilararemur ... accipiebamur*, 2.9.7 *eramus ... referebamus ... eiciebamus ... equitabamus ... exacueremus*, 2.9.9 *ingerebamur ... solidabamur ...* . The verb *sermocinor* also appears in Sidon. *Ep.* 1.9.7, 4.3.1, 5.17.2, 7.2.2, 7.9.1, 9.11.9.

cur a quibusdam protomystarum tamquam scaevus cavendusque tractator improbaretur, quamquam sic esset ad verbum sententiamque translatus: Sidonius defends both Origen against teaching heretical doctrines and the quality of Rufinus' translation of Origen, comparing it to famous translations of ancient pagan texts by Apuleius and Cicero. The Grecism *protomysta* is a hapax, used here and in *Ep.* 4.17.3 (referring to the bishops Lupus of Troyes and Auspicius of Toul). It denotes someone who is initiated in religious matters and interprets theological texts; Gualandri (1979) 146 n. 14, Amherdt (2001) 394, Schwitter (2015) 196. For the medieval gloss on this term, see Chronopoulos (2020) 648. Sidonius thus probably refers to Jerome; see the commentary on *Ep.* 2.9.5 *Quos inter Adamantius Origenes Turranio Rufino interpretatus....* Sidonius uses the adjective *scaevus*, 'instinctively choosing what is wrong, perverse, contrary, misguided, etc.' (*OLD* 1698, 3) only once in his whole oeuvre. A *tractator* has the meaning of a 'masseur' (*OLD* 1955, 1, see Sen. *Ep.* 66.53) or an 'imperial official' (*OLD* 1955, 2). Here it denotes someone who deals with a literary text, an 'interpreter', 'exegete' (*Blaise* 821, s.v. 3). In this sense the word appears only at the end of the fourth century, in Hier. *Adv. Rufin.* 1.30, which probably inspired Sidonius; Amherdt (2001) 298, Lucht (2011) 60. Sidonius uses the term in a similar way also in *Ep.* 4.11.6 v. 9. Many Greek texts were translated into Latin in antiquity, usually only loosely based on the original text and oriented towards the target language. The two poles of a possible translation, literal (*ad verbum*) or sense-wise (*ad sensum*), have been discussed since antiquity. Jerome (Heir. *Ep.* 57.5–7, 84), for example, recommends word-for-word translation of the Bible, while pagan texts can be translated more freely; Fladerer (2002), Landfester (2003) 726. For Sidonius' and Jerome's shared interest in language and linguistics, see Denecker (2015). See the commentary above on *Ep.* 2.9.5 *Quos inter Adamantius Origenes....*

ut nec Apuleius Phaedonem sic Platonis neque Tullius Ctesiphontem sic Demosthenis in usum regulamque Romani sermonis exscripserint: To prove that Rufinus faithfully translated the writings of Origen from Greek into Latin (see the commentary on *Ep.* 2.9.5 *Quos inter Adamantius Origenes Turranio Rufino...*), Sidonius compares him with two famous pagan authors – Lucius Apuleius Madaurensis (124–70) and Marcus Tullius Cicero (106–43 BC) – who also translated authors – the famous philosopher Plato (28/427 or 424/423–348/347 BC) and the statesman and orator Demosthenes (384–322 BC) – from Greek into Latin. According to Sidonius, Apuleius translated Plato's dialogue *Phaedo* about Socrates' last hours and his discussion of the immortal soul, and Cicero translated Demosthenes' most famous speech *De corona oratio* in defence of the Athenian orator Ctesiphon (fourth century BC). Ctesiphon had proposed honours for Demosthenes' services for the city of Athens and was therefore accused by the statesman and orator Aischines (389–314 BC). Unfortunately, both texts are lost, so no comparison between original and translation is possible. We still have Cicero's *De optimo genere oratorum*, which he wrote as an introduction to his translations for and against Ctesiphon by Demosthenes (*De corona*) and Aischines (*In Ctesiphontem*); Anderson (1936) 455 n. 3. For the role of Plato's works in Sidonius, see Amherdt (2001) 82, 142–3. Apuleius is also mentioned in Sidon. *Ep.* 4.3.1 *ponderis Apuleiani fulmen* ('the thunderbolt of Apuleian weight') – see Amherdt (2001) 50–1, 56–8, 121–2 – in *Ep.* 2.10.5 together with his wife Pudentilla (see the commentary there). In *Ep.* 9.13.3 Apuleius (along with Pliny) is an essential model for Sidonius' language and style; Monni (1999) 31–2, Condorelli (2017), Wolff (2020) 400–1. Cicero is the author Sidonius mentions most often, sixteen times in total in the poems and the letters; see Köhler (1995) 107 on *Ep.* 1.1.2. In the second book, Sidonius alludes to Cicero in *Ep.* 2.1.1 – see the commentary on *Ep.* 2.1.1 *Rediit ipse Catilina ...* – and mentions him explicitly in *Ep.* 2.10.5 together with his wife Terentia – see the commentary there. Pliny also frequently mentions Cicero as well as Demosthenes in his letters, for example Plin. *Ep.* 1.2, 1.20 and 9.2.2. In Plin. *Ep.* 6.33.11 Pliny lets his friends compare his own speech for Attia Viriola with Demosthenes' *De corona oratio*. For *regula*, 'rule', 'standard', applied to rhetoric, see van Waarden (2010) 151. The expression *Romani sermonis* is used here instead of the more frequent *sermo Latinus* or *lingua Latina*. Sidonius chooses the word *sermo*, which is used only of spoken language, because *Phaedo* is a dialogue, *De corona oratio* an oration; Kramer (1998) 70, 76, Lucht (2011) 61. The verb *exscribere* is used here in the meaning of 'reproduce', 'translate' (*TLL* 5.2, 1831.1–16); see also Sidon. *Ep.* 8.3.1, 9.16.2.

Section 6

Studiis hisce dum nostrum singuli quique, prout libuerat, occupabantur, ecce et ab archimagiro adventans, qui tempus instare curandi corpora moneret: As in the last section, Sidonius again emphasises the relaxed atmosphere with the word *prout*, 'accordingly'; see the commentary on *Ep.* 2.9.5 *pariter et, prout singulis cordi....* Everyone could choose from the activities (*studiis hisce*) that he likes to do most. Sidonius finally interrupts his enumeration of the various activities with a colloquial exclamation (*ecce et*); see the commentary on *Ep.* 2.9.4 *Vix quodcumque vestibulum intratum, et ecce huc....* All persons in the house are finally reunited at the table. The *archimagirus*, 'chief cook' (*TLL* 2, 462.11–20), calls for lunch by sending his *nuntius*, probably the scullion, who also had to keep the clock running and announce lunch (*tempus instare curandi corpora*). The whole section shows the wealth of Sidonius' friends, who own many slaves. For Sidonius' depiction of the slaves in his villa, see the introduction to *Ep.* 2.2. The rarely used word *archimagirus* derives from Greek ἀρχιμάγειρος and appears in Latin literature first in Iuv. 9.109, where it is used in a list of members of the kitchen staff in a rich man's household. The term also appears in few other instances, for example Hier. *Quaest. hebr. gen.* 37.36 and *CIL* 6.8750; Gualandri (1979) 160–1, Colton (1982) 65, Kaufmann (1995) 240, Lucht (2011) 62–3. Wolff (2020) 405 shows that many hapax legomena and rare words in Sidonius' prose works come from Greek fields of knowledge like music, astrology or cooking; see also Sidon. *Ep.* 4.7.2 *chironomunta* ('carver'). They also abound in Sidonius' description of the architecture of his own villa in *Ep.* 2.2; see the commentary on *Ep.* 2.2.8 *si graecari mavis....*

quem quidem nuntium per spatia clepsydrae horarum incrementa servantem probabat competenter ingressum quinta digrediens: The fifth hour (around eleven in the morning) has begun and it is time to have an early lunch or late breakfast (see the commentary immediately below, on *Prandebamus breviter...*). The wording is strangely contorted, though, because *quinta*, the 'fifth hour', is the grammatical subject of the second part of the sentence. The hour confirms (*probabat*) the observations of the slave, who is the subject of the first part of the sentence (*adventans ... qui*). The sentence is reminiscent of Mart. 8.67.1–2 *horas quinque puer nondum tibi nuntiat et tu | iam conviva mihi, Caeciliane, venis* ('the slave has not yet announced the fifth hour and already you, Caecilianus, come as a guest to my house'). Hanaghan (2019) 75 points out that it is a slave who must watch over time while the aristocratic guests enjoy their timeless *otium*. The whole scene recalls Petronius' *Cena Trimalchionis*, where also many slaves are entrusted with the smallest tasks. Sidonius makes a typical shift of context; see the Introduction, '2. Book 2 as a response to Pliny the Younger's Letters and the question of intertextuality'. In Petronius one encounters bad taste and ostentation, while the lifestyle of Sidonius' guests shows a refinement accompanied by sobriety. On the role of the staff in a villa, see Mielsch (1987) 133–4. On the importance of the daily routine in a senator's life, see Sidon. *Ep.* 2.13.4, Mart. 8.67, Näf (1995) 141. The noun *clepsydra*, 'water clock' (*TLL* 3, 1138.16–51), is another Grecism (from κλεψύδρα). It also appears in Sidon. *Ep.* 2.13.4 and several times in Pliny's epistles referring to the time an orator speaks in court or in the Senate; see for example Plin. *Ep.* 2.11.14, 6.2.5–6, and Mart. 6.35.6 about a marathon speaker. Water clocks are known from archaeological excavations: there are various types, which all basically measure and display the time elapsed with the drained water; see Stutzinger (2001) 12–13, Dohrn-van Rossum (2002) 973–4, Lucht (2011) 63–5. A known Roman example which was used in private households consists of a hemispheric bronze bowl with a small hole at the bottom for the water to run through. On the inside of the bowl there are marks which indicate the hours of the day; see Stutzinger (2001) 5. *Incrementum*, 'growth', 'increase', 'augmentation' (*TLL* 7.1, 1043.70–7.83), is also used about the passing time in Manil. 3.287 *horarum diei* ('of the hours of the day'). The adverb *competenter*, 'suitably', 'properly' (*TLL* 3, 2069.78–70.81), is first attested in Apuleius, Apul. *Apol.* 65.8 *competentissime* ('very suitably'). It also appears in Sidon. *Ep.* 2.11.2, 5.5.2, 5.17.1, 6.1.5, 8.3.4, 9.15.1 v. 18, but not in the poems.

Prandebamus breviter copiose, senatorium ad morem: Sidonius insists that his hosts present their wealth in a decent and tasteful way. There is enough to eat at his hosts' table, but no excessive luxury as in the description of the dinner at Dionysius' court in *Ep.* 2.13. Egelhaaf-Gaiser (2018) shows that the setting of banquets in Sidonius' letters becomes central only in Books 8 and 9: *Ep.* 8.11, 8.12, 9.13. In *Ep.* 4.15.1 Sidonius asks Elaphius to organise a feast on the occasion of a baptistery donated by him: *epulum multiplex et capacissima lectisternia para* ('prepare a copious banquet and a huge spread of couches'). In his later letters, Sidonius, under the influence of the monastic movement, problematises both the frequency of banquets and the quantity of food eaten; see *Ep.* 7.13.3, 7.14.12; van Waarden (2016) 3, 93–4, 165–6, 194, Shanzer (2001) 220–1. On Sidonius' view regarding proper aristocratic diet, between fasting and luxurious banquets, see Raga (2009, 2019). In *Ep.* 4.24.3 Sidonius praises the modesty of eating at Maximus' house, an old friend and priest, who is a friendly host but usually offers more vegetables than meat. The *prandium* was 'a late breakfast' or 'luncheon', a light meal consisting of cold or warm dishes and taken around noon; Gutsfeld (1999). The adverb *copiose*, 'abundantly', 'plentifully' (*TLL* 4, 915.41–16.59), appears only here in Sidonius, but see also *percopiose* ('very abundantly') in *Ep.* 4.7.3. It is very frequently used by Cicero, for example *Att.* 13.52.2 of an opulent meal. For the superlative *copiosissimus*, see the commentary on *Ep.* 2.10.1 *Nam cum … copiosissimum fructum*…. See also the commentary below on *Ep.* 2.9.6 *Quid multa? Sancte pulchre abundanter accipiebamur*. *Senatorius*, 'senatorial', is a descriptive term for senators commonly used by Sidonius, for example in Sidon. *Ep.* 1.6.2, 9.14.3; Mathisen (2020a) 35.

quo insitum institutumque multas epulas paucis paropsidibus apponi: It is conspicuous that Sidonius does not attach any importance here to describing the various types of tableware or to valuable objects made of gold, silver or crystal, as is usual in other literary descriptions of banquets; see Petron. 31.9, Sen. *Ben.* 7.9.2–3, *Ep.* 123.7, Sidon. *Ep.* 9.13.5 vv. 54–67; Stein-Hölkeskamp (2005) 141–58. Sidonius uses the same topoi of modesty in *Carm.* 17.5–20, about an invitation to a birthday party in his house, and in *Ep.* 1.2.6–7, describing the eating habits of the Visigothic king Theoderic II; Raga (2019) 246–50, Shanzer (2001) 231–2. Instead, there is substantial conversation and finely cooked food. In the passage at hand, a great deal of tasty food is served but, as Sidonius emphasises, in only few bowls. Anderson (1936) 456 n. 1 explains the antithesis *multae epulae – paucae paropsides* with the rules against luxurious silverware issued by the censor C. Fabricius Luscinus (275 BC). A famous anecdote tells how he expelled Cornelius Rufinus, an ancestor of the dictator Sulla, from the Senate because he owned ten pounds of silver plate; see Val. Max. 2.9.4,

Gell. 4.8.7, Plin *Nat.* 33.142. This incident was still quoted by Tertullian as a criticism of luxury; see Tert. *Apol.* 6.2. This also would explain why Sidonius, with the wordplay *insitum institutumque*, stresses that the way the dinner is served is traditional. There is possibly also an allusion to *Ep.* 4.8, where Sidonius mentions the Goths' predilection for valuable silver vessels in his poem for queen Ragnahilda; see the commentary on *Ep.* 2.8.1 *morigera coniunx*.... The term *epulae* is here synonymous with *cibus*, 'food' (*TLL* 5.2, 701.26–71). It also appears in the description of the food served at the estate Octavianum; see Sidon. *Ep.* 8.4.1 *qui civitati fluvio mari proximus hospites epulis, te pascit hospitibus* ('it is very close to the city, the river and the sea, and feeds your guests with meals and you with guests'). For *epulae* in the meaning of 'banquet', see the commentary on *Ep.* 2.13.4 *Igitur ille, cuius anterius epulae mores*.... The term *paropsis* denotes a bowl to serve vegetables, but also other dishes, and is mentioned in a number of post-Augustan authors (*TLL* 10.1, 437.56–73), for example Mart. 11.31.18, Iuv. 3.142, Petron. 66. It is often mentioned together with the smaller but similar-looking *acetabulum*; Hilgers (1969) 33–4, Lucht (2011) 65–6. CT and Loyen (1970a) 65 have *parapsidius*; LVM and Anderson (1936) 456 *parabsidibus*. Even though all manuscripts have the form with 'a', Lütjohann (1887) 32 opts for the common form *paropsidibus*, which I think is the right choice, see Löfstedt (1985) 209.

quamvis convivium per edulia nunc assa, nunc iurulenta varietur: Although the food is presented modestly, it is varied. For *edulia*, see the commentary on *Ep.* 2.2.13 *Edulibus terminatis*.... The same opposition as here between *assus*, 'roasted', 'cooked dryly' of food (*TLL* 2, 939.57–40.1), and the rarely used adjective *iurulentus*, 'containing the juice', 'in a broth' (*TLL* 7.2, 678.51–65), is also found in Cels. 2.18.10 and Apul. *Apol.* 39.4. In addition, *iurulentus* is also used about food in Apul. *Met.* 2.7.2 and 4.22.3. More frequent is the combination of *assus*, 'roasted', 'cooked dryly', with *elixus*, 'thoroughly boiled'; see the examples in *TLL* 5.2, 394.20–61, which include Plaut. *Most.* 1115.

Inter bibendum narratiunculae, quarum cognitu hilararemur, institueremur: One shortens the time spent eating and drinking with stories that are both entertaining and instructive. For this topos, see famously Hor. *Ars* 333 *aut prodesse volunt aut delectare poetae* ('the poets either want to be of use or to please') and in the context of a meal Varro *Sat. Men.* 337–8, 340, Gell. 13.11.4, 13.11.5a, 13.11.5c. A noble restraint, with modest food and civilised entertainment instead of an opulent feast with decadent shows, is often described as ideal form of a dinner party; see for example Cic. *Cael.* 67, *Att.* 16.2.6, Nep. *Att.* 13.6–14.3, Sall. *Iug.* 85.39–43, Hor. *Sat.* 2.6.70–8, 2.8, Plin. *Paneg.* 49.7, *Ep.* 1.15, 9.17, 9.36.4, Sen. *Helv.* 10, *Ep.* 95.15–29, 110.12–20, 119.3–16, 122; Gualandri (1979) 71, Gerlach (2001) 70–8, Fellmeth (2001) 87–115, Stein-Hölkeskamp (2005) 220–52. For the custom of telling stories during a meal, see Sidon. *Ep.* 1.2.6 and 1.11.10–15; Loyen (1943) 56–94, Köhler (1995) 148, La Penna (1995) 16–17, Schwitter (2015) 192, van Waarden (2010) 135. See also Sidon. *Ep.* 9.13, where he inserts a poem that is recited during a banquet; Guipponi-Gineste (2017) 241–5. The expression *inter bibendum* is also found in Sidon. *Ep.* 1.4.2 and 9.13.2. The word *narratiuncula*, meaning 'little story' (*TLL* 9.1, 66.22–9), is attested only here, in Quint. 1.9.6 and in Aug. *Doctr. Christ.* 4.43. The word is also attested in Plin. *Ep.* 6.33.8 as an element of a juridical speech. The noun *cognitus*, 'a knowing' (*TLL* 3, 1489.7–9), is very rarely used, but see Apul. *Met.* 9.13.4. *Hilaro*, 'to make cheerful', 'cheer', of a person's mind (*TLL* 6.3, 2786.24–40), is a rarely used but classical verb, attested from Cicero and Catullus on, for example Cic. *Brut.* 44, Catull. 63.18. It also appears in the context of a meal in Sidon. *Ep.* 9.13.3 and in *Carm.* 22.5.

quia eas bifariam orditas laetitia peritiaque comitabantur: The conversation over lunch involves the telling of short stories which are entertaining and instructive at the same time. The adverb *bifariam* means 'on two sides', 'twofold', 'double' (*TLL* 2, 1978.49–86). The participle *orditus* (from *ordiri*, 'to begin', 'undertake') is attested from the fourth century AD onwards (*TLL* 9.2, 949.84–50.13). The situation Sidonius describes is comparable to *Ep.* 5.17.5 *audiebatur ambitiosissime; nec erat idcirco non distincta narratio, quia laetitia permixta. inter haec otio diu marcidis aliquid agere visum* ('People listened competitively and therefore each story was carefully designed to be mixed with entertainment. After a long period of inactivity had made us a little tired, we decided to do something').

Quid multa? Sancte pulchre abundanter accipiebamur: Sidonius ends his description of the meal with a question, which is typical of the oral literary style of writing; see the commentary on *Ep.* 2.1.1 *'Quaenam?' inquis*. The scene is reminiscent of Cic. *Att.* 13.52.2, about an opulent banquet Cicero hosted for Caesar: *Quid multa? Homines visi sumus*. ('In short, I believe we have passed with honour'). The expression *quid multa?*, 'what more?', which is already attested in Plautus, also appears in Sidon. *Ep.* 7.17.4, 8.6.8, 8.12.7, 9.9.8; van Waarden (2016) 250. Sidonius highlights his host's generosity with three adverbs in an asyndetic tricolon: *sancte*, 'with integrity', 'virtuously', 'innocently' (*OLD* 1686, 3), denotes the fulfilling of the rules of hospitality; *pulchre*, 'excellent of its kind', 'splendid' (*OLD* 1517, 2a), denotes the high standard of the entertainment; and *abundanter*, 'abundantly', 'copiously' (*TLL* 1, 236.82–7.44), the generosity of entertainment and food; Lucht (2011) 67. For generosity as a typical trait of Gallic invitations, see Sidon. *Ep.* 1.2.6 *abundantiam Gallicanam* ('Gallic abundance'); Köhler (1995) 151. See the commentary above on *Ep.* 2.9.6 *Prandebamus breviter copiose*....

Section 7

Inde surgentes, si Vorocingi eramus (hoc uni praedio nomen), ad sarcinas et deversorium pedem referebamus: After lunch (*prandium*) one held a short siesta between the sixth and seventh hour (*meridiatio*); see for example Mart. 4.8.4, Plin. *Ep.* 3.5.11, Sidon. *Ep.* 1.2.7; Stein-Hölkeskamp (2005) 112–16. Sidonius spends the siesta in different ways, depending on the estate on which he takes his lunch. Apollinaris' estate, Vorocingus, is situated near Nîmes at the River Gard – see *Carm.* 24.52; Santelia (2002) 101–2. Bernardy (1960) localises the estate to the north of Nîmes, in Dions. The manuscripts LNT[1] have *vorocingi*, MCT have *voroangi*, while in *Carm.* 24.52 the variants *veracingus* (F) and *voracingus* (PT) are attested. For an analysis of the variants in spelling and a critical take on the previous attempts to locate the estates, see Casado (2011). For *praedium*, 'estate', see the commentary on *Ep.* 2.2.3 *nomen hoc praedio*.... Sidonius had his *sarcina*, 'luggage', 'any movable goods', 'belongings', 'chattels' (*OLD* 1691, 2), stored at his lodging place (*deversorium*) and could walk there after a lunch in Apollinaris' house. For the different meanings of the term *deversorium* (also spelt *diversorium* or *devorsorium*, found five times in the letters), see the commentary on *Ep.* 2.2.13 *Edulibus terminatis excipiet te deversorium*. It is disputed whether Sidonius alternately stayed in the villa of his friends or whether he stayed outside their estates in a villa or an inn. It has been proposed that Sidonius lodged outside because there was no space in his friends' houses or that he chose a neutral place for his stay in order not to offend anyone; see the discussions by Anderson (1936) 456–9 n. 2, Percival (1997) 285–6, Hutchings (2009) 71, Lucht (2011) 67–9. The idea of Sidonius lodging in an inn is not convincing, however. It would completely undermine the aristocratic hospitality which the letter celebrates and boasts of. Carrié's (2010) 281–2 explanation that Vorocingus was equipped with a separate facility (an apartment for guests or guest house) to accommodate its noble visitors, while Prusianum lacked of a guestroom, seems the most plausible, in which case Sidonius and his entourage therefore always spent the night at Apollinaris' estate, Vorocingus, and switched back and forth between the two estates during the day. Since Sidonius mixes the activities in the two houses into a single day and one never knows where one is, it is logical that he does not state precisely whether he is staying with Tonantius Ferrolus or Apollinaris. The plural *referebamus* indicates that Apollinaris' *deversorium* was spacious enough for several guests. Anderson (1936) 456–7 n. 2 and Lucht (2001) 69 assume that there were other guests besides Sidonius, but it is more likely that the plural refers to Sidonius and his entourage.

si Prusiani (sic fundus alter nuncupabatur), Tonantium cum fratribus, lectissimos aequaevorum nobilium principes, stratis suis eiciebamus, quia nec facile crebro cubilium nostrorum instrumenta circumferebantur: Prusianum is one of the estates of Tonantius Ferreolus. It is named after the famous orator and philosopher Dion of Prusa (around 40–115) and is situated near Nîmes; Mratschek refers to Dio. Chrys. 46.7 (about the country estate at Prusa); Mratschek (2008) 375, Mratschek (2020b) 255. Bernardy (1960) localises the estate to the north of Nîmes, near Russan in the commune of Sainte-Anastasie. For an analysis of the variants in spelling and a critical take on the previous attempts to locate the estates, see Casado (2011). The term *fundus*, 'estate' (*TLL* 6.1, 1575.49–6.74), is used here and in *Ep.* 3.5.2 as a synonym for *praedium*; see the commentary on *Ep.* 2.2.3 *nomen hoc praedio....* The manuscripts LNT, Lütjohann (1887) 32, Anderson (1936) 458 and Loyen (1970a) 65 have *nuncupabatur*, MC have *nuncupatur*. In stemmatic terms the latter would be the likelier reading, but Sidonius does like the one-word cretic spondee clausulae, so I opt for *nuncupabatur*. If Sidonius and his attendants have their lunch at Prusianum, they spend the siesta in the rooms of the host's sons, who have to make way for them. Tonantius is the son of Tonantius Ferreolus – see *Carm.* 24.34, where he is described as *doctus* ('learned'). He is the addressee of *Ep.* 9.13 (dated around 479), described as *adhuc iuvenis* ('still a young man') in 9.13.3, who gets advice from Sidonius and who is also mentioned in *Ep.* 9.15.1; Loyen (1970a) 220 n. 38, Loyen (1970b) 162 n. 45, *PLRE* 2, 1123, *PCBE* 4, 1892, Kaufmann (1995) 352, Mathisen (2020a) 124. *Lectissimus*, the adjectival superlative of *lego*, in the sense of 'most honourable', 'excellent' (*TLL* 7.2, 1133.72–4.5), is used several times of persons in Cicero, for example *Inv.* 1.52; see also Sidon. *Ep.* 9.13.1. The adjective *aequaevus*, 'of equal age', 'of the same time' (*TLL* 1, 993.13–64), is attested from Vergil (for example *Aen.* 2.561) onwards, especially in poetry. It either refers to single persons, as here, or is used in a wider sense to denote contemporaneity; see Sidon. *Ep.* 3.8.1, 4.22.4, 7.2.4, 8.2.2, 8.4.2, 9.11.8; Giannotti (2016) 191. It is unclear what exactly Sidonius means by the expression *cubilium nostrorum instrumenta*. Anderson (1936) 459 translates it as 'sleeping-kit', Loyen (1970a) 66 as 'notre matériel de couchage'. Presumably it refers to the blankets and pillows. *Cubile* denotes a 'place of rest', 'bed' or 'bedroom' (*TLL* 4, 1269.59–73.23). In *Ep.* 2.1.3 Sidonius uses the term *cubiculum* to denote the 'bedroom' (see the commentary on *Ep.* 2.1.3 *in concilio iubet ... in cubiculo damnat...*) and in *Ep.* 2.2.10 he explicitly writes *dormitorium cubiculum*.

Excusso torpore meridiano paulisper equitabamus, quo facilius pectora marcida cibis cenatoriae fami exacueremus: Sidonius mentions sporting activities that support the digestion of the meal; Nicolas (1901) 8–11. The adjective *meridianus*, 'of mid-day' (*TLL* 8, 838.23–32), refers to the *meridiatio*, 'siesta'. It is used in connection with sleep as part of the daily routine also in Cels. 1.10.3, Plin. *Ep.* 9.40.2 and Sidon. *Ep.* 1.2.7 *dapibus expleto somnus meridianus saepe nullus, semper exiguuus* ('after eating he often does not nap, but when he does only shortly'). After the siesta, Sidonius and his hosts go horse riding (*equitabamus*), another leisure activity typical of a stay on the estate; see the commentary on *Ep.* 2.9.1 *quibus interiecta ... neque sufficit equitaturo*. The adjective *marcidus*, 'weak', 'feeble', 'exhausted', 'sluggish' (*TLL* 8, 375.76–6.26), is used of persons, animals or parts of the body. In Sidonius' letters it appears two more times in a similar context of spending one's leisure time (*otium*): Sidon. *Ep.* 1.6.3 *ad maiora se pingui otio marcidus et enervis animus attollat* ('and your mind, which is feeble and weak because of the deep rest, should rise to higher things') and 5.17.5 *inter haec otio diu marcidis aliquid agere visum* ('we decided to do something because we became weak during this long rest'). The adjective *cenatorius*, 'belonging to the cena' (*TLL* 3, 782.50–6), is rarely used, but see Apul. *Met.* 5.3.2. The verb *exacuo*, 'to incite', 'to stimulate' (*TLL* 5.2, 1139.3–32), is also used in connection with eating in Ov. *Pont.* 1.10.13.

Section 8

Balneas habebat in opere uterque hospes, in usu neuter: Bathing was part of the daily routine. One usually went to the bath after the siesta in the afternoon; see for example Plin. *Ep.* 3.1.8, where Spurinna bathes in winter during the ninth hour (around 3 p.m.), in summer during the eighth hour (around 2 p.m.); see also Mart. 10.48.1–4, 11.52.3–4; Stein-Hölkeskamp (2005) 112–16, Lucht (2011) 71. While Sidonius' own baths are functioning and the pride of his estate, his hosts have baths under construction; see the introduction to *Ep.* 2.9. With the two opposing expressions *in opere* and *in usu* Sidonius emphasises that they are not working. See also Sidon. *Carm.* 24.55, about construction work in Apollinaris' villa: *vestit frigore marmorum penates* ('he covers his house with the coolness of marble') and *Ep.* 1.8.2 *algent balnea* ('the baths are cold'), where cold baths are part of the world turned upside down. Because the baths in both villas no longer function, the hosts have built a makeshift bath for their guests; Pavlovskis (1973) 51, Percival (1997) 286–7, Hutchings (2009) 71, Lucht (2011) 71–2. In his description, Sidonius focuses on the funny and social aspects of spending time in a makeshift bath and does not complain about any inconvenience. Hanaghan highlights the competitive element in Sidonius' description of his uncles' baths, as he outdoes them as host; see Hanaghan (2019) 26–7, 56–7, Hanaghan (2020) and the introduction to *Ep.* 2.9. For the spelling of *balneum* (in the plural in all the manuscripts) versus *balineum*, see the commentary on *Ep.* 2.2.4 *Balneum ab Africo*.... For *hospes*, see the commentary on *Ep.* 2.1.3 *implet cotidie ... villas hospitibus*.... Pliny also mentions his baths (Plin. *Ep.* 2.17.11, 5.6.25–6) or bathing as part of the daily routine (Plin. *Ep.* 3.1.8, 3.5.14, 6.20.2), but not as extensively as other elements of the villa; see the introduction to *Ep.* 2.2.

sed cum vel pauxillulum bibere desisset assecularum meorum famulorumque turba conpotrix, quorum cerebris hospitales craterae nimium immersae dominabantur: While the slaves of the hosts and those of Sidonius prepare the bath, they drink together. The humorous tone of the scene is emphasised by archaic words from comedy (*pauxillulum*, *conpotrix*), similarly also in *Ep.* 7.2 and 9.6.1–2; Gualandri (1979) 168–9, Monni (1999) 36–7, van Waarden (2010) 143, 154–85, Gualandri (2020) 313. For Sidonius' depiction of the slaves in his villas, see the introduction to *Ep.* 2.2. Sidonius refers to the importance of wine for entertainment on an estate also in *Carm.* 22.2, 22.4 vv. 23–40, 219, 22.5, about Pontius Leontius' estate Burgus, where he playfully alludes to the presence of Bacchus. Unlike here, however, all buildings in Burgus are perfectly maintained. In *Carm.* 2.318–31 Oenotria (also a poetical name for Italy) appears allegorically as the goddess of wine. For vineyards as an important part of an estate, see the commentary on *Ep.* 2.9.1 *Colles aedibus superiores exercentur vinitori et olivitori.* The rarely used adverb *pauxillulum*, 'a little' (*TLL* 10.1, 861.72–2.7), is attested in comedy (for example Plaut. *Bacch.* 833, *Rud.* 729), in Hier. *Ep.* 66.10, and again in Sidon. *Ep.* 1.5.9 and 8.3.3; Köhler (1995) 209. The *famuli* mentioned here are the slaves of Apollinaris and Tonantius Ferreolus. Sidonius also uses the term to denote his own slaves – see the commentary on *Ep.* 2.2.5 *ita ut ministeriorum* ... and *Ep.* 7.14.11. Here, Sidonius' slaves are denoted by the term *assecula*, 'follower', 'attendant', 'servant' (*TLL* 2, 849.35–70). Kaufmann (1995) 241 and Lucht (2011) 72 interpret them also as slaves, that is, as part of the *familia* which accompanied Sidonius on his travels; see also *Ep.* 4.8.2. *Compotrix*, the female form of *compotor*, 'a drinking companion', is rare and only here attested as an adjective (*TLL* 3, 2144.21–6); see for example Ter. *And.* 232. The term *cratera* or *creterra* denotes a 'big vessel in which wine was mingled with water', 'large drinking cup' with handles, 'bowl'; Hilgers (1969) 52–3. The manuscripts LN, Anderson (1936) 458 and Loyen (1970a) 66 have *creterrae*, MCT and Lütjohann (1887) 32 have *craterae*, which is stemmatically preferable. The two variants are also attested in other writers (*TLL* 4, 1108.54–60).

vicina fonti aut fluvio raptim scrobis fodiebatur, in quam forte cum lapidum cumulus ambustus demitteretur: Sidonius inserts a detailed construction manual for a sweating room (*sudatio*) which is reminiscent of Vitruvius' professional description in Vitr. 5.10.5; Cam (2003) 145–6. Thébert (2003) 102 n. 79 interprets the passage as a description of a steam bath, which was not usually part of the Roman baths. It seems to be a combination of steam bath and hot bath in one pit (*scrobris* is in the singular; see the commentary, p. 281, on *antro in hemisphaerii*); see the commentary on *Ep.* 2.9.2 *quo, prout libuisset, effuso coctilibus aquis...*; Nicolas (1901) 9–11, Maréchal (2020) 52. Sidonius first reports how the slaves dig a hole and fill it with hot stones. In the second part of the clause he describes how they build a curved roof and cover it with blankets. He structures the individual phases of construction with clausulae ending with polysyllabic words (*raptim scrobris fodiebatur, ambustus demitteretur*; see also *inardescens operiebatur* and *excluso tenebrarentur* below); Lucht (2011) 73–4. In Sidonius' description of his own bathhouse, the sweating cure is left out, probably because the weather is already so hot; see the commentary on *Ep.* 2.2.4 *Balneum ab Africo....* The choice of places for the sauna (*vicina fonti aut fluvio*) seems strange and suggests that they dug a new hole every time they wanted to bathe. Possibly it denotes the different saunas on the two neighbouring estates or it is a gloss inserted into the text. Hanaghan (2020) 128 suggests that the imperfect tense refers to the repetition of the building process and that the adverb *forte* gives the impression of casual spontaneity (on *forte* see just below in this commentary). Hanaghan (2019) 26 argues that the verbs used in the passive highlight Ferreolus' and Apollinaris' inability to provide proper baths. Furthermore, Sidonius' frequent use of the conjunction *aut* in sections 8 and 9 of this letter repeatedly confuses the source of the water, a spring (*fons*) or a river (*fluvium*) which feeds the baths. There are also three different options for the cold-water supply; see the commentary on *Ep.* 2.9.9 *aut fontano deinceps frigore putealique aut fluviali copia solidabamur*. In any case, Sidonius' description of the bathing facilities is confusing and raises more questions than it answers. The term *scrobis* denotes 'a hole dug in the ground', 'pit' (*OLD* 1712, 1a). *Forte*, 'by chance', 'casually' (*TLL* 6.1, 1130.17–32.74), is an adverb Sidonius often uses in his *Carmina* to fill verses; see for example Sidon. *Carm.* 5.126, 7.17. *Ambustus*, the participle of *amburo*, means 'burnt around', 'scorched by a fire' (*TLL* 1, 1877.36–82); here, in an enallage, 'heated' is used to qualify *cumulus*, 'heap', 'pile', instead of the stones. It appears one more time in the letters, at *Ep.* 7.1.2; van Waarden (2010) 90.

antro in hemisphaerii formam corylis flexilibus intexto fossa inardescens operiebatur: A *hemisphaerium* is a 'half-globe', frequently used for heaven, the earth and the moon (*TLL* 6.3, 2604.75–5.46), here for the roof of the makeshift bath. The term also appears in Vitruvius' prescription of how to build a sweating room (Vitr. 5.10.5); see the commentary immediately above on *vicina fonti aut fluvio*. Hanaghan (2019) 26 suggests a connection to Sidonius' own bathhouse, whose roof is also domed; see the commentary on *Ep.* 2.2.5 *Primum tecti apice in conum cacuminato*. Sidonius also mentions his bathhouse's domed roof in *Carm.* 18.3–4. The roof here is made of *corylus*, 'branches of hazel or filbert' (*TLL* 4, 1080.59–82). Because the branches are flexible they can be bent to form a hemisphere. Most of the manuscripts, Anderson (1936) 458 and Loyen (1970a) 66 have *flexibilibus*, L has *flexibus*. R and Lütjohann (1887) have *flexilibus*, which I also think to be the right choice, because Sidonius uses the adjective *flexilis* several times; see the commentary on *Ep.* 2.2.4 *ubi et vis ... per parietem foraminatum flexilis....* The more common *flexibilis* instead is not found anywhere else in his oeuvre. The verb *inardesco*, 'to kindle', 'take fire', 'burn' (*TLL* 7.1, 832.70–3.73), is attested from Vergil onwards. Sidonius uses it one more time, in a transferred sense in *Ep.* 7.4.2; van Waarden (2010) 229.

sic tamen, ut superiectis Cilicum velis patentia intervalla virgarum lumine excluso tenebrarentur, vaporem repulsura salientem, qui undae ferventis aspergine flammatis silicibus excuditur: For the construction *sic tamen, ut*, see the commentary on *Ep.* 2.9.4 *sic tamen, quod*.... The Cilicians, the inhabitants of Cilicia, a province in the southern part of Asia Minor, present-day Turkey, produced a robust covering called *cilicium*, which was originally made of Cilician goat hair and used by soldiers and seamen; see Varro. *Rust.* 2.11.12. These plaids were also used to cover roofs (as here). Because the *Cilicum vela* are solid, they can hold back the steam and heat, which would otherwise escape through the gaps between the branches forming the roof. Sidonius mentions the *Cilicum vela* also in *Ep.* 4.24.3; Amherdt (2001) 493–4. The term *intervallum* ('interval') is used in the letter about Sidonius' own villa in an architectural context; see the commentary on *Ep.* 2.2.8 *triplex medii parietis aditus per reseratur arcuata intervalla reseratur*. Whereas usually the brightness of a bath is praised (see the commentary on *Ep.* 2.2.4 *Intra conclave ... abundantia lucis inclusae*), here a dark, intimate cave without light is built, where Sidonius and his hosts relax (see below). The verb *tenebro*, 'to make dark', 'to darken' (*OLD* 1918), is first attested in Apul. *Met.* 8.15.5, after which it is not uncommon, appearing for example in Amm. 19.8.5, Aug. *Eu. Io.* 13.16. The robust covering holds back the steam which rises from the hot stones over which water is poured. For this kind of improvised sauna, see <http://arqueotoponimia.blogspot.nl> with a reproduction of a beautiful twelfth-century miniature. For *aspergo*, 'a sprinkling', 'besprinkling', 'moisture', see the commentary on *Ep.* 2.2.16 *ita ut arborum ... superiectae asperginis....* Silex is a term applied to 'any hard rock or stone, flint, lava etc.' (*OLD* 1761, 1a). The verb *excudere* means 'shake out', 'bring out', 'send forth' (*TLL* 5.2, 1290.33–44). Together with *silex* it is also used to describe the lighting of a fire, for example in Verg. *Georg.* 1.135 *ut silicis venis abstrusum excuderet ignem* ('and thus brought out hidden fire from the veins of the flint'), *Aen.* 1.174 *ac primum silici scintillam excudit Achates* ('immediately Achates strikes a spark from the flint'); Gualandri (1979) 140. Elsewhere in Sidonius' letters *excudere* appears in a figurative sense; see *Ep.* 3.14.1, 6.3.2, 9.9.9, 9.11.4. The manuscripts LCP have *excluditur*, probably the archetypal reading, correctly emended to *excuditur*.

Section 9

Hic nobis trahebantur horae non absque sermonibus salsis iocularibusque: After describing how the temporary bath is built, Sidonius focuses on the social aspect of the bath and its health-promoting effects. The friends spend time in the bath engaging in entertaining conversation, which Sidonius describes with the adjectives *salsus*, 'salted with humour', 'witty', 'funny' (*OLD* 1682, 3), and *iocularis*, 'facetious', 'jocular' (*TLL* 7.2, 285.19–48); see also Hier. *Ep.* 31.2 *iocularis sermo* ('facetious conversation'). For the litotes *non absque*, 'without', see the commentary on *Ep.* 2.8.1 *Decessit nudius tertius non absque iustitio matrona Filimatia*.

quos inter halitu nebulae stridentis oppletis involutisque saluberrimus sudor eliciebatur: Sweating was part of the bathing routine and was deemed to have a positive effect on one's health; see Cels. 1.3.4, 2.17.1, Sidon. *Carm.* 19, Plin. *Nat.* 25.77; Lucht (2011) 76. In *Ep.* 5.14.1 Sidonius mentions the healing effects of the thermal baths of Baiae. For the benefits of alternating warm and cold baths see Gal. *Meth. Med.* 11.10; Busch (1999) 76–7. The onomatopoetic verb *stridere*, 'to hiss' (*OLD* 1827, 1d), here indicates the sound of water being poured over hot stones; in *Ep.* 2.10.4 v. 24 it is also used for the noise of a vehicle with the meaning of 'to creak', 'squeak', 'grate'. *Oppletis involutisque* ('we were covered completely') is an ablative absolute, and *nobis* has to be supplied from the previous clause. Sidonius uses the superlative *saluberrimus* ('very healthy') again in *Ep.* 7.8.1, 9.3.1, 9.13.3.

quo, prout libuisset, effuso coctilibus aquis ingerebamur harumque fotu cruditatem nostram tergente resoluti: For the third time (after 2.9.5 and 2.9.6), Sidonius adds a *prout*, 'accordingly', to express one's liberty to decide freely; see the commentary on *Ep.* 2.9.5 *pariter et, prout singulis cordi....* After the steam bath there follows the hot and then the cold bath, which both also are described in Sidonius' own villa letter. It is not clear whether there is another hot bath or whether sauna and hot bath are combined in one pit; see the commentary on *Ep.* 2.9.8 *vicina fonti aut fluvio raptim scrobis fodiebatur....* For a professional hot bath, see the commentary on *Ep.* 2.2.4 *Hinc aquarum surgit cella coctilium*. *Fotus*, a 'warming', 'fomenting' (*TLL* 6.1, 1215.80–16.9), is mostly used in the ablative; otherwise, it is rare, but see Auson. *Mos.* 343 also in the context of the bath, *mox amne refotos* ('straightway refreshed by the river'). *Cruditas*, 'an overloading of the stomach', 'indigestion', is frequently attested from Cicero (for example Cic. *Cat.* 44) and Varro (Varro *Rust.* 3.10.5) onwards; see *TLL* 4, 1233.3–67 for further references. The idea that warm water or warmth in general is good for digestive disorders is also found in other authors, for example Sen. *Ep.* 15.3, Cels. 2.17.1–10. *Tergeo* or *tergo* means 'to rub clean', 'wipe', 'polish' (*OLD*

1924–5, 1a), but here it means metaphorically 'to relieve the stomach'. The participle *resoluti*, 'relaxed', 'softened', derives from the verb *resolvere*, 'to untie', 'unfasten', which is used specifically of the human body, meaning 'to make less rigid or tense', 'relax' (most often because of sleep) (*OLD* 1630–31, 4a), and stands in opposition to *solidabamur*, 'make firm', 'consolidate'; see the commentary immediately below. In a transferred meaning, both verbs illustrate the effect of warmth and cold on the body.

aut fontano deinceps frigore putealique aut fluviali copia solidabamur: Just as confusing as Sidonius' description of the sauna/steam bath and hot bath is that of the cold bath; see the commentary on *Ep.* 2.9.8 *vicina fonti aut fluvio raptim scrobis fodiebatur....* Sidonius offers three possibilities for where the cold water can come from: a spring (*fons*), a well (*puteale*) or a river (*fluvium*). In any case, it is a natural bathing opportunity instead of the artfully built *frigidarium* on Sidonius' estate: *fontanus*, 'of a spring', 'from a fountain' (*TLL* 6.1, 1027.77–8.16), is a classic but not very frequently used adjective. The same goes for *putealis*, 'of or belonging to a well' (*TLL* 10.2, 2748.3–20), and *fluvialis*, 'of a river' (*TLL* 6.1, 977.42–69). The adjectives here are used instead of nouns in the genitive, as elsewhere in Sidonius; see the commentary on *Ep.* 2.2.9 *Hic si dominum seu domestica seu hospitalis turba circumstet*. The verb *solido*, 'to make firm', 'consolidate' (*OLD* 1782, 2a), is used figuratively of the relaxed body waking up in cold water. For the cold bath, see the commentary on *Ep.* 2.2.5 *Hinc frigidaria dilatatur....* The scene is reminiscent of Ausonius' *Mosella*, which describes how the guests refresh themselves in the cool river after sweating: see Auson. *Mos.* 341–4. Similar in content, but formulated in other words, in Plin. *Ep.* 5.6.25 one finds two different possibilities to cool down. One of them is also a well (*puteus*): *si natare latius aut tepidius velis, in area piscina est, in proximo puteus, ex quo possis rursus adstringi, si paeniteat teporis.* ('If one wants to swim more extensively or more warmly, there is a pool in the courtyard, and a well nearby, where one can cool down again when one has had enough of the tepid water').

siquidem domibus medius it Vardo fluvius, nisi cum deflua nive pastus inpalluit: Sidonius explains the third possibility, bathing in a river, in more detail. He starts with *siquidem* ('if only', 'if indeed'), which he frequently uses instead of *scilicet* ('namely', 'that is to say'), for example in *Ep.* 1.5.7, 3.3.5; Lucht (2011) 72. The River Vardo is called Gard today and famous because of the Roman aquaeduct Pont du Gard (near present-day Remoulin), which was built around AD 50 as part of the water supply for the city of

Nemausus (present-day Nîmes); Winkle (2002). According to Anderson (1936) 460 n. 1 and Lucht (2001) 77, this is the only passage where the ancient name of the river is mentioned. For the adjective *defluа*, 'flowing down', 'moving downstream', see the commentary on *Ep.* 2.2.16 *Lacus in Eurum defluus meat*.... See Stat. *Silv.* 1.3.1–3, where the villa of Vopiscus in Tibur is mentioned, through which the River Anio flows. The verb *impallesco*, 'to turn pale' (*TLL* 7.1, 516.32–9), is rarely used; it is first attested in Pers. 5.62 and only used here of a thing; Gualandri (1979) 141–2. It also appears in Sidon. *Ep.* 1.7.11; Köhler (1995) 251. The participle *pastus*, 'fed', 'nourished', is similarly used of a river in Sidon. *Ep.* 9.14.5; see also Stat. *Ach.* 2.144. For the whole image of a river being as clear as snow, see Plin. *Ep.* 8.8.4 *rigor aquae certaverit nivibus, nec color cedit* ('the coolness of the water competes with snow and its colour also is not inferior').

flavis ruber glareis et per alveum perspicuus quietus calculosusque neque ob hoc minus piscium ferax delicatorum: At the end of the section, Sidonius takes up again the theme of the beautiful place (*locus amoenus*) with which he began the letter. He inserts a detailed description of the River Vardo with five adjectives, the three middle ones arranged in an asyndeton; see the commentary on *Ep.* 2.9.1 *Inter agros amoenissimos*...; see Lucht (2011) 77. The river is reddish (*ruber*) because it is metalliferous (*flavis ... glareis*). For *glarea*, 'gravel', see the commentary on *Ep.* 2.2.1 *squalet glarea in vadis*.... *Alveus* denotes a 'channel' or 'river bed' (*TLL* 1, 1790.35–91.68); see Plin. *Ep.* 5.6.12, 8.17.1. The adjective *perspicuus*, 'transparent', 'clear' (*TLL* 10.1, 1748.12–25), appears in the context of water elsewhere; see Plin. *Ep.* 8.8.4 *perspicuus amnis* ('a clear river'), Ambr. *Ep.* 2.3 *sunt ergo et fluvii dulces atque perspicui* ('there are pleasant and clear rivers'). A similar context of clear water and savoury fish occurs in Sidon. *Carm.* 24.46–7 *limosum et solido sapore pressum* | *piscem perspicua gerens in unda* ('which carries in its translucent waters a fish that haunts the mud, loaded with solid savouriness'). For the clear water in Sidonius' lake, which is also illustrated by the visible pebbles, see the commentary on *Ep.* 2.2.18 *Aequor ab Africo ... sic aquas umbra perfundit*. The adjective *calculosus*, 'full of small stones' (*TLL* 3, 140.79–41.2), is attested from Vitruvius onwards (Vitr. 2.3.1). For adjectives ending in -*osus* in Sidonius in general, see the commentary on *Ep.* 2.2.18 *Lacus ipse ... flexuosus nemorosusque*.... Sidonius praises the fish in the river as *delicatus*, 'pleasing', 'delightful' (of food) (*TLL* 5.1, 443.16–29); see Mart. 4.30.16, who also writes about *pisces ... delicatos* ('delightful fish'). Unlike the fish mentioned in Sidonius, the fish Martial describes should not be caught and eaten, though, because they belong to the emperor. For *ferax*, 'fertile', 'abounding' (of things or animals) (*TLL* 6.1, 489.20–43), also in the context of water and fish, see Avien. *Ora.* 518–19 *piscium semper ferax | stagnum* ('a pond, always abounding in fish'). The adjective also appears in Sidon. *Ep.* 2.14.1 (about a vineyard), in *Carm.* 23.88 (his homeland) and 24.50 (a mountain).

Section 10

Dicerem et cenas et quidem unctissimas, nisi terminum nostrae loquacitati, quem verecundia non adhibet, charta posuisset: With a *praeteritio*, the announcement that he will not mention something, Sidonius omits the description of the most important and rich meal of the day, the *cena*, which took place around the ninth or tenth hour and consisted of several courses, depending of the wealth and status of the host; Gutsfeld (1997). An opulent dinner (*convivium*) is often described in Roman literature, for example Hor. *Sat.* 2.2, 2.4, 2.8, *Ep.* 1.5, Petron. 26.7–78.8, Iuv. 5, 11, Mart. 5.78, 10.48; Binder (1998) 803–6. This may be the reason why Sidonius omits it (*dicerem et cenas ... nisi*) and instead concentrates on the other meals (breakfast in 2.9.3 and lunch in 2.9.6) and elements of the daily routine.

The adjective *unctus*, 'covered, saturated, etc., with oil, oily, greasy (as typifying rich food)' (*OLD* 2090, 1b), combined with nouns which denote eating is also found in Mart. 5.44.7 *captus es unctiore mensa* ('you are attracted by a richer table', a complaint about a guest who prefers a richer table), Hor. *Ep.* 1.14.21 *uncta popina* ('a greasy kitchen', a positive thing from the viewpoint of the slave from the countryside) and Auson. *Parent.* 7.9 *et mensa commodus uncta* ('beneficial due to his delicious table', where Ausonius praises his uncle Julius Calippio on his epitaph). Stoehr-Monjou (2013) 159 thinks that with this superlative Sidonius wants to draw the attention of the addressee, Donidius, to the humorous intertext. The adjective also appears in Pers. 4.17 *uncta ... patella* ('of dainty dishes') and in connection with food again in Sidon. *Ep.* 4.24.3 *si quid in cibis unctius* ('if there was ever anything more dainty on the menu'); Amherdt (2001) 494. With the term *loquacitas*, 'talkativeness', 'loquacity' (*TLL* 7.2, 1652.28–3.35), Sidonius alludes to the topos of *brevitas*, which he also addresses at the end of his first villa letter; see the commentary on *Ep.* 2.2.20 *quod brevitatem sibi brevitatem sibi debitam paulo scrupulosior epistula excessit*. Both villa letters go far beyond the required ideal of brevity of a letter. The term *loquacitas* frequently appears in Sidonius: *Ep.* 1.7.11, 3.11.2, 4.10.2, 5.5.2 (about Cicero), 6.3.2, 9.15.1 v. 52, *Carm.* 14.4 v. 7 (in a positive sense in the meaning of *eloquentia*), 23.507; see also *Ep.* 1.9.7 *loquax ... charta* ('this garrulous sheet'); Amherdt (2001) 277. Sidonius very often complains about his so-called garrulity or his poor writing, a well known literary topos of modesty. Apart from the term *loquacitas*, Sidonius uses the following: *nugae* ('trifles') in *Ep.* 3.14.1, 4.8.5, 7.7.1, *Carm.* 9.9; *sermocinatio* ('chattiness') in *Ep.* 1.1.4; *garrire* ('to chatter'), *garrulitas* ('a chattering'), *garrulus* ('talkative') and *garritus* ('chatter') in *Ep.* 4.3.10, 5.3.1, 5.4.1, 7.2.10, 8.6.9, 8.6.13, 8.13.2, 9.1.3–4, 9.9.1, 9.11.9, 9.15.1, 9.15.1 v. 51; *neniae* ('trivialities', 'doggerel') in *Ep.* 1.9.7, 5.1.2, 7.18.4; *ineptiae* ('trifles, fooleries') in *Ep.* 8.9.4; Amherdt (2001) 277, Kaufmann (1995) 260. See also the commentary on *Ep.* 2.10.3 *Huius igitur ... tumultuarium carmen...* and, as an example of Sidonius' demonstrative modesty, *Ep.* 2.2.7 *Pauci tamen versiculi....* Sidonius' major epistolary models Pliny and Symmachus also use the term *loquacitas* about themselves: Plin. *Ep.* 5.20.8, Symm. *Ep.* 3.82.1, 5.78. For the adjective *loquax*, see the commentary on *Ep.* 2.2.10 *ubi publico ... loquacissimus chorus....* Sidonius uses the term *verecundia*, 'an attitude of restraint', 'modesty', several times to denote appropriate behaviour; see the commentary on *Ep.* 2.4.3 *benignitate responsi ... verecundiam munerare*. The term *charta* is used here in the meaning of 'material to write a letter on' (*TLL* 3, 1000.14–15), probably papyrus; Schipke (2013) 125–32. For Sidonius' various terms to denote his letters and letter volumes, see Gillett (2012) 833–5, van Waarden (2016) 32–40, 265. For *charta* in the meaning of 'paperwork', see the commentary on *Ep.* 2.5.1 *et donec suarum merita chartarum....*

quarum quoque replicatio fieret amoena narratu, nisi epistulae tergum madidis sordidare calamis erubesceremus: The reason Sidonius gives for not also describing the dinner, although it was remarkable, is that he does not want to write on the back of the letter; see Sidonius' descriptions of dinners in *Ep.* 1.11 and 9.13; Guipponi-Gineste (2017) 241. Usually, only the front side of a papyrus was written on, because the back was uneven. Writing on the back is attested for children practising their writing (Mart. 4.86.11), but also elsewhere: see Mart. 8.62, Plin. *Ep.* 3.5.17, Sidon. *Ep.* 8.16.1, Iuv. 1.6; Lucht (2011) 78. In classical Latin *replicatio* denotes a 'contrary rotation' or, as legal *terminus technicus*, an 'objection made by the plaintiff to the *exceptio* of a defendant' (*OLD* 1619). In later times *replicatio* is used as a rhetorical *terminus technicus* to translate the Greek term 'anadiplosis', that is, the repetition of the last word or words from the end of a verse or sentence at the beginning of the next (see Mart. Cap. 5.533), or 'a folding back', 'reflex movement'. Here it denotes a 'repetition of a thought or fact in general' (*Blaise* 713, s.v. 3), which Sidonius wants to avoid. The term also appears in Sidon. *Ep.* 1.5.1, see Köhler (1995) 187. The expression *amoena narratu* refers back to the idea of the pleasant spot (*locus amoenus*); see the commentary on *Ep.* 2.9.1 *Inter agros amoenissimos.... Tergum* is regularly used for 'the backside of a thing' (*OLD* 1925, 1d) – see for example Iuv. 1.6 about the back of a scroll – but I cannot find a single example of it being combined with *epistula* elsewhere. The adjective *madidus*, 'made wet', 'saturated', 'drenched', 'dripping' (*OLD* 1059, 1) and 'inebriated', 'drunk', 'tipsy' (*OLD* 1059, 6), refers to the ink as well as playfully to the wine Sidonius has been drinking during dinner; see also *Ep.* 8.11.3 v. 42 *maerens ad madidas eam tabernas* ('I should have to go sorrowfully to damp inns'). Similar texts are Mart. 4.14.12 *lascivis madidos iocis libellos* ('my books, which are saturated with playful jokes') and Plin. *Ep.* 8.15.2 *chartae ... si scabrae bibulaeve sint* ('the papyri ... if they are rough and absorbing moisture'). Ausonius warns Symmachus not to read the odd little poem unless he, too, has taken a drink, as he has written it while drinking: see Auson. *Griph*. The rarely used verb *sordido*, 'to dirty', 'to foul' (*Blaise* 767), appears only in Late Latin works; see also Sidon. *Ep.* 1.5.6, 7.9.9, *Carm.* 23.349. *Erubesco*, 'to redden', 'to blush with shame', is used here in the first-person plural, probably to denote Sidonius' modesty, and is constructed with the infinitive (*TLL* 5.2, 822.66–3.16). The verb appears several times in Sidon. *Ep.* 1.11.12 and 14, 3.9.1, 4.8.5, 4.10.1, 4.25.4, 5.10.2, 9.11.4, *Carm.* 7.434.

Sed quia et ipsi in procinctu sumus teque sub ope Christi actutum nobis invisere placet, expeditius tibi cenae amicorum in mea cena tuaque commemorabuntur: Sidonius returns to the starting point of the letter and announces that he will soon fulfil the addressee's wish to meet him in person and on that occasion will tell him about the dinners with Tonantius Ferreolus and Apollinaris. With a polyptoton (*cena–cenae*) and three pronouns (*tibi–mea–tua*) Sidonius announces his wish to tell Donidius during a dinner about these dinners. *Procinctus* was originally a military term meaning 'in readiness for battle', 'on active service'. Here, *in procinctu sumus* denotes 'we are ready to go' (*TLL* 10.2, 1531.33–7); see also Sev. Minor. 1.713. As in the previous clause (with *erubesceremus*), the first-person plural – *in procinctu sumus* and *nobis invisere placet* – is chosen to show modesty. The expression *sub ope Christi* is used in *Ep.* 4.4.2 as here to announce a visit. It also appears in Sidon. *Ep.* 1.9.8, 4.1.2, 4.4.2, 5.3.4, 5.11.3, 7.1.1,

7.6.3, 7.9.7; see also *sub ope ... dei* in *Ep.* 1.5.1. Outside of Sidonius the expression is not very common and it cannot help to date the letter as it is used by Sidonius before and after he became a bishop; van Waarden (2010) 88. Of all the exclamations made by Sidonius to express his gratitude for God's (or Christ's) help, it is the most frequent; see the commentaries on *Ep.* 2.2.3 *Haec mihi cum meis praesule deo...*, on 2.4.2 *quod Deo prosperante succedat* and on 2.12.3 *igitur ardori ... praevio Christo...*; Amherdt (2001) 79, Köhler (1995) 217. The adverb *actutum*, 'immediately', 'quickly', 'instantly' (*TLL* 1, 455.27–6.2), appears frequently in Plautus (for example Plaut. *Amph.* 354, 360, *Bacch.* 578, 748, but seldom in late republican and early imperial classical authors, although see Symm. *Ep.* 1.41, 2.64.2, 3.43.3. In Sidonius, the adverb appears frequently in the letters, but not in the poems: *Ep.* 1.1.4, 2.13.4, 3.3.9, 3.12.4, 3.13.4, 6.9.1, 7.2.4, 8.11.3 v. 33, 9.16.2. *Expeditus*, 'convenient', 'commodious' (*TLL* 5.2, 1618.45–66), is the participle of *expedio*, 'to set free', 'liberate', 'prepare', 'arrange'. Sidonius uses the adverb in the comparative *expeditius*, 'more conveniently', only here. For the positive form, see Sidon. *Ep.* 2.12.1 below.

modo nos quam primum hebdomadis exactae spatia completa votivae restituant esuritioni, quia disruptum ganea stomachum nulla sarcire res melius quam parsimonia solet. Vale: With *hebdomas*, 'seven days' (*TLL* 6.3, 2579.43–53), Sidonius refers back to *Ep.* 2.9.2, where he announced that he would stay at least that long with his friends. Here he writes that he needs another week for his overfilled stomach to recover through fasting and for him to be ready for his meals with Donidius. The term also appears in *Ep.* 1.7.12 and, in the form of the adjective *hebdomadalis*, 'of or belonging to a week', in *Ep.* 9.3.5. For the adjective *votivus*, 'granted in answer to one's prayers' (*OLD* 2103, 2), see Apul. *Met.* 5.20.6, 7.13.1, 8.30.5. *Esuritio*, 'hungering', 'hunger' (*TLL* 5.2, 867.72–8.11), is a classical but not frequently used noun; it is also attested for example in Mart. 1.99.10, 5.78.18. The noun *ganea* usually denotes a 'common eating-house'; here it is used in a figurative sense for 'gluttonous eating', 'gluttony' (*TLL* 6.2, 1689.54–76); see also Sidon. *Carm.* 5.340, Plin. *Paneg.* 49.6. The participle *disruptum*, 'burst', from the verb *di(s)rumpere*, 'to break', 'to burst', describes a stomach which is filled with too much food (*TLL* 5, 1265.35–57). For other instances of *parsimonia*, 'abstinence from eating or drinking', 'fasting' (*TLL* 10.1, 490.31–42), see Sidon. *Ep.* 8.14.2, Symm. *Ep.* 5.67. In the general sense of 'parsimony' it also appears in Sidon. *Ep.* 6.2.1, 7.2.3. For the letter's simple ending with *vale*, see the commentary on *Ep.* 2.1.4 *Vale*.

Epistula 10

Introduction

Summary

Sidonius starts the letter by praising Hesperius' education and achievements in his studies. His love for Hesperius is based on his friend's love of literature. Sidonius then goes on to express the pleasure he takes in young talents and his endeavours for the Latin language. Next, Sidonius declares that he will comply with Hesperius' request and send him verses as he wished, namely a poem for the new church of bishop Patiens in Lyon. Sidonius explains where his epigram will be set up in the church. Like the epitaph inserted in *Ep.* 2.8.3, this poem is also written in Phalaecian hendecasyllables and is placed in the apse together with the poems of two other authors, Constantius and Secundinus. In a show of modesty, Sidonius uses several comparisons to emphasise how much his poem falls short of the other two. The epigram, consisting of thirty verses, all of which Sidonius includes in section 4 of the letter, contains a praise of the visual aspect of the cathedral's interior, especially the various materials, colours and the effect of the wandering sunlight. Sidonius also describes how different people choose different paths to reach the cathedral of Lyon to pray there. In section 5 Sidonius changes the subject and asks Hesperius to continue his studies and also to send him samples of his literary activity, even though he is going to be married. Instead of describing his own experiences with the compatibility of marriage and studies, Sidonius adds two lists. He first discusses five married couples where the wife holds the candlestick for her husband during his nocturnal studies and then, in section 6, six other (married and unmarried) couples known from literature where the woman actively assists in writing literature. Having a wife therefore does not mean you cannot study anymore; on the contrary, a good wife is like a personal muse at home.

Addressee

The addressee of *Ep.* 2.10 is Hesperius, a young scholar and friend of Sidonius. In *Ep.* 4.22.1 Sidonius calls him a *vir magnificus, gemma amicorum litterarumque* ('an honourable man, a jewel of friends and letters') and praises him because of his literary interest. With the combination of gemstone and education, Sidonius takes up two themes that are formative for the present letter 2.10. Prévot (1999) 67 thinks that Hesperius taught at Clermont-Ferrand. He was the teacher of more than one of Ruricius' sons (probably Eparchius and Ommatius). Ruricius, the addressee of Sidon. *Ep.* 4.16, 5.15, 8.10, and *Carm.* 10, sends Hesperius three letters (Ruric. *Ep.* 1.3–5), in which he also addresses him with the honorific title *magnificus*; van Waarden (2020a) 15. On Hesperius, see Loyen (1970a) 220 n. 40, *PLRE* 2, 552 n. 2, Kaufmann (1995) 313–14, Mathisen (1999) 106–11, Müller (2013) 427–8, Mathisen (2020a) 55, 100. Coşkun (2002) 175 suggests that Hesperius may have been a descendant of Ausonius, whose elder son also was called Hesperius.

For the addressee of the embedded poem, bishop Patiens, see the commentary on *Ep.* 2.10.2 *Ecclesia nuper ... quae studio papae Patientis....* For the plurality of addressees in this letter (Hesperius, bishop Patiens, the reader of the letter and the visitors of the cathedral), see Egelhaaf-Gaiser (2014).

Date

The poem embedded in the letter pre-dates Sidonius' ordination. Kelly (2020a) 178 dates the poem to the 460s; see the Introduction, '2. The date and order of letters in Book 2'.

Major themes and further reading

Structure and intertextuality: lists and lucubratio

For the structure of the letter with its embedded poem, see Amherdt (2001) 224–6, who compares it to *Ep.* 4.8 and 4.18. *Ep.* 4.18, where Sidonius also writes a poem at the request of a bishop (Perpetuus), which is going to be inscribed in a church in Tours, is a particularly close parallel. For an intratextual comparison of these three letters see Fernández López (1994) 51–3. They all have in common that they pretend to be written at someone else's request (the *iubes–pareo* motif, see the commentary on *Ep.* 2.10.2 *Dicto pareo...*). In section 2 of *Ep.* 2.10 Hesperius is reported to have asked Sidonius to send him the last text he has written since their separation. Sidonius complies with this request, although he is older than Hesperius, and explains that he wrote his verses at the request of bishop Patiens for his new church in Lyon (see the commentary on *Ep.* 2.10.2 *Dicto pareo...* and 2.10.5 *Ecce parui tamquam iunior imperatis*). As Gibson (2013b) 347 shows, Sidon. *Ep.* 2.10 combines a response to a literary request (see also Plin. *Ep.* 2.5 and 2.19) with an exhortation to literary endeavour from the addressee, thus recalling Pliny's own letter Plin. *Ep.* 2.10.

The joy of literary activity and concern over the decline of the Latin language are leitmotifs in the letter, which structure the text. As proof that the Latin language is still flourishing, Sidonius inserts his own poem in the middle (section 4) and at the end (section 6) asks Hesperius to continue his studies now he has become a husband. Here, as in other letters and poems, Sidonius presents the writing and exchange of poems as a necessary duty of friendship; Köhler (1995) 102, Amherdt (2001) 398–400, 407–8, Guipponi-Gineste (2014) 248–50. See the commentary below on *Ep.* 2.10.1 *Amo in te quod litteras amas...* and *Ep.* 2.10.2 *Sed istinc alias: interea tu quod petis accipe*. On Sidonius' concern about the state of the Latin language, which must be defended against barbaric influences, see the commentary on *Ep.* 2.10.1 *Illud appone ... meram linguae Latiaris proprietatem....*

The theme of marriage and the enlightenment it can bring to the husband is another leitmotif and closely interwoven with the first one, the joy of literary activity. In section 4, before inserting his poem, Sidonius describes a radiant bride and her bridesmaid as a point of comparison. At the end of the letter, in sections 5 and 6, he then adds two lists of famous couples who produced literature together, to encourage Hesperius to continue his studies despite being married. With the two lists of poetic models, Sidonius creatively takes up a very popular form in ancient and especially late ancient literature; Rijser (2013), Elsner and Hernández Lobato (2017b) 17, Laemmle et al. (2021). In his work Sidonius uses the rhetorical device of the list in different ways; Gualandri (2017) 136–9, Hindermann (forthcoming a). Some lists demonstrate Sidonius' great erudition, for example *Carm.* 9.211–317 – Schindler (2018) 348–52, Gualandri (2020) 284–6, Consolino (2020) 348–52 – or *Carm.* 23 – Santelia (2016b) – or *Ep.* 4.3.5–7 – Amherdt (2001) 113–6, Gibson (2020) 382–3, Hindermann (forthcoming a). In his panegyrics there are epic enumerations to suggest enormous crowds of people or to accelerate the narrative tempo, for example in *Carm.* 5.470–83,

7.74–6, 79–82, 319–28; Gualandri (2017) 137–9, Stoehr-Monjou (2020) 332–3, 335–8. There are also lists with the main purpose of visual display (*enargeia*), as in *Carm.* 15.141–3, about Hercules' labours (also treated in *Carm.* 9.94–100, 13.1–20), and 11.17–28, about the description of Venus' palace in the *Epithalamium* for Ruricius and Hiberia; Gualandri (2017) 141–3. For Sidonius' catalogue of marbles, see the commentary on *Ep.* 2.2.7 *Iam, si marmora inquiras, non illic quidem*. Sidonius uses lists particularly often to describe people, for example Seronatus' behaviour in *Ep.* 2.1.2; Hindermann (forthcoming a). It is no coincidence that Sidonius includes his list of literary predecessors in the second book of letters, which is dedicated to the theme of aristocratic leisure; see the Introduction to this book and the commentary on *Ep.* 2.10.5 *quod olim Marcia Hortensio*….

Sections 5 and 6 of the letter have been studied for Sidonius' depiction of women and married couples. Gualandri (1979) 11–12 wonders whether women are part of the writing process of their partners and how this fits in with *Ep.* 2.9.4, where there are separate bookshelves for men and women. Bonjour (1988) 44 takes the sections as proof that Sidonius is positively minded towards women. Bonjour (1988) 48 refers to other lists of women in Sidonius (Sidon. *Carm.* 16, 24.37–42). Näf (1995) 144 and Santelia (2012) 63–4 n. 164 point to Sidonius' gendered approach to literary activities. Hindermann (2022a) analyses sections 5 and 6 with a focus on the motif of working by the light of the lamp (*lucubratio*). She analyses the meaning of the particular lamp (*candelabrum*) the women hold and shows that Sidonius alters the topos by joining a couple instead of a writer and his slave. At the same time, Hindermann (2022a) interprets the scene as an intertextual allusion to Pliny and to Ausonius; for Ausonius see McGill (2014). While Sidonius deals with Pliny's night work on a content level, he uses Ausonius' work for references to Hesperius' ancestors and his marriage. In Auson. *Ep.* 19a.24–30, a letter to his friend Paulinus, Ausonius boasts of how he writes verses in a short time at night and refers to his son Hesperius, probably an ancestor of Sidonius' friend Hesperius; see the introduction to this letter. Ausonius also completes another work, a wedding poem, his Vergilian *Cento Nuptialis*, in the night; see Auson. *Cento praef.* 21–4. Through the theme of night work, therefore, Sidonius links his two important literary role models, Pliny and Ausonius, and establishes a connection to the addressee of the letter.

With the theme of the happy marriage and the exemplary behaviour of women, Sidonius also makes an intratextual link to his letter 2.8, which, with the epitaph on Filimatia, contains the first poem of the second book; see Hindermann (2020b, 2022b) and the introduction to *Ep.* 2.8.

The poem for bishop Patiens (Carm. 27)

Sidonius' poem about the cathedral in Lyon, which he quotes in section 4, has aroused a great deal interest among scholars. The ekphrastic praise is reminiscent of Sidonius' description of Pontius Leontius' estate Burgus (*Carm.* 22.4 vv. 146–7) and abounds in allusions to other authors, especially Martial (see the introduction to *Ep.* 2.8 on the Late Antique forms of intertextuality, in which texts are transplanted from their original context into other forms), Statius, Prudentius and Paulinus of Nola. There are many detailed studies of and commentaries on the poem: Di Salvo (2005) 48, 138–42, Santelia (2007), Condorelli (2008) 196–8, Hernández Lobato (2010), van Waarden (2011) 102–3, Hernández Lobato (2012) 493–518, Hecquet-Noti (2013), Herbert de la Portbarré-Viard (2014), Wolff (2014c) 212–13, Egelhaaf-Gaiser (2014), Schwitter (2015) 157–60, Consolino (2020) 362–3, Onorato (2020a) 86–9.

In his poem, Sidonius emphasises the visual aspect of the cathedral's interior, especially the effect of the moving sunlight and the different shades of green and blue. The poem causes the reader to linger and marvel at the wonders around him. The divine light contrasts with Sidonius' 'shadowy' poem (*umbratiliter* in *Ep.* 2.10.4). The motif of light is central to Sidonius' poem and symbolises the power of God; Roberts (1989) 76, Harries (1994) 45–7, Santelia (2007) 314 ('un trionfo di luce e colori'), 316, Hernández Lobato (2010) 303, Hernández Lobato (2012) 504, Schwitter (2015) 158, Herbert de la Portbarré-Viard (2016) 291, Consolino (2020) 362. The motif that light stands for the power of God is also found in various Greek inscriptions in churches; see *Anth. Pal.* 1.10.49–64, 1.12, 1.15, 1.16, 26.1, 30.1, 112. See also Sidon. *Carm.* 2.422–3, where Sidonius praises the goddess Aurora's refulgence.

Like the poem in *Ep.* 2.8, the embedded poem is written in hendecasyllables; see the commentary on *Ep.* 2.8.2 *Post quae ... sed per hendecasyllabos*. For metrical patterns of *Carm.* 27, see Onorato (2016) 407, 411, 415, 417. As Onorato (2020a) 88 suggests, Sidonius chooses the Phaeleacian hendecasyllable because of his great familiarity with this metrical form and because it allows the poem to stand out among the other poems in the basilica, which are written in hexameters. The church of bishop Patiens is the setting for a series of letters, some of which also have poems inserted: *Ep.* 3.12, 4.25, 5.8, 6.12, 9.3.5; Neger (2019) 401–2. For the structure, content and intertextuality in detail, see the introduction to *Carm.* 27 and the commentaries to the verses below.

Commentary

Section 1

Sidonius Hesperio suo salutem: For the simple greeting formula, see the commentary on *Ep.* 2.1.1 *Sidonius Ecdicio suo salutem*. For the addressee Hesperius, see the introduction to this letter.

Amo in te quod litteras amas et usquequaque praeconiis cumulatissimis excolere contendo tantae diligentiae generositatem, per quam nobis non solum initia tua verum etiam studia nostra commendas: With a series of pronouns (*in te, nobis, tua, nostra* and, later, with the first-person plural *defleamus*) Sidonius underlines his and Hesperius' shared interest in literature and language; Denecker (2015) 411. He starts the letter with the polyptoton *amo–amas* to underline the similarity and closeness between him and Hesperius. They both love literature and everything connected with it; see Sidon. *Ep.* 1.1.3, where Sidonius expresses the same thought to the addressee, Constantius, whose poetry he also mentions in *Ep.* 2.10.3. There are also parallels with Letter 4.1, in which Sidonius praises his friendship with Probus and highlights their shared love of literature. Similarly, in *Carm.* 9 Sidonius inserts a list of poetic predecessors and connects them with the motif of a common attitude towards one's studies (with the addressee, Magnus Felix); Schlapbach (2020), Hindermann (forthcoming a). For the relationship between 'you' and 'I' in Sidonius' letters, see van Waarden (2010) 49–52, van Waarden (2016) 45–8, van Waarden (2020b) 433. Stressing the closeness between writer and addressee is a typical trait of letters of friendship. The subject of literary interest and the pose of the older friend guiding a younger writer in his endeavours is also found in several letters of Pliny the Younger to Caninius: Plin. *Ep.* 1.3, 2.8, 3.7, 6.21, 7.18, 8.4, 9.33; Ludolph (1997) 121, Hindermann (2011). The idea of encouraging a friend to write and praising his literary work is also found in other letters of Pliny, for example Plin. *Ep.* 4.20, 4.27 and 5.17.

With *amo–amas* Sidonius probably alludes to the basics of grammar at school, which he evokes a little later in the section; see the commentary immediately below on *Nam cum videmus in huiusmodi disciplinam iuniorum ingenia succrescere*.... It also gives an original twist to the trite *amo* or *amas*, which is frequently used in Cicero's and Pliny's letters: Plin. *Ep.* 9.25.1, in a similar context, *lusus et ineptias nostras legis, amas, flagitas* ('you read, love and ask for my playful little works'), 4.12.1, 5.6.41, 6.8.1, Cic. *Att.* 1.20.7

nunc, si me amas, si te a me amari scis ('now, if you love me, if you know that you are loved by me'), 3.15.4, 7.13.1, 10.11.3, 12.6.2, 13.1.3, *Fam.* 12.24.3, 14.2.2, 16.3.1. Cicero also starts a letter with an emphatic *amo*, in Cic. *Fam.* 9.22.1 *amo verecundiam vel potius libertatem loquendi* ('I love modesty or rather freedom of speech'), or puts it at the beginning of a sentence, in Cic. *Att.* 12.28.3, *Fam.* 7.24.1, 16.16.2. In Pliny's letters an emphatic *amo* is also found at the beginning of a sentence (Plin. *Ep.* 6.26.2 and 9.37.1) but not at the beginning of a letter. Instead of *amo*, Pliny uses *gaudeo* in Plin. *Ep.* 6.26.1 and 7.23.1 to start a letter; see also Plin. *Ep.* 4.13.1. Van Waarden (2020b) 433 shows the connection between the initial *amo* and the final *parui*, which is also in the first person.

To express modesty, Sidonius recites the inserted poem in the first-person plural; see the commentary on *Ep.* 2.10.4 *sic nostra... stipula vilescit*. Sidonius uses the local adverb *usquequaque* in its transferred meaning 'in every conceivable situation or circumstance' (*OLD* 2110, 2a) again in *Ep.* 9.3.7 and 9.15.1 v. 41; see also Plin. *Ep.* 1.7.5, 8.6.12. *Cumulatus*, the participle of *cumulo*, 'to accumulate', 'heap', is attested from Plautus onwards as an adjective (see *TLL* 4, 1384.15–17). In the superlative it appears from the third century on and only here in Sidonius. The manuscripts LMC, Lütjohann (1887) 33, Anderson (1936) 460 and Loyen (1970a) 68 have the verb *excolere*, 'to tend', 'cultivate' (*TLL* 5.2, 1277.18–9.41), also used in Sidon. *Ep.* 1.6.3, 1.9.1, 4.7.3, 4.14.4, 5.2.1, 6.12.9, 7.2.4, 7.10.1, 7.14.7, 7.17.1, 9.11.7; only T has the more common *extollere*, 'to praise' (*TLL* 5.2, 2031.50–9.33). *Generositas*, 'nobility', 'excellence', 'goodness', is used of human behaviour by Christian writers (see *TLL* 5.2, 1798.76–84), see for example Aug. *Ep.* 149.27. Sidonius uses the term as a code word to describe senatorial status, in *Ep.* 1.3.2 *calcata generositas* ('trampling on good birth') and *Carm.* 7.164 *generosa puerpera* ('his noble mother'); Mathisen (2020a) 35.

Nam cum videmus in huiusmodi disciplinam iuniorum ingenia succrescere, propter quam nos quoque subduximus ferulae manum, copiosissimum fructum nostri laboris adipiscimur: Sidonius focuses on his addressee's youth and his hopes for the next generation (*iuniorum ingenia*). Pliny likewise often writes about his hopes for the future and his efforts to find and support new talent; see for example Plin. *Ep.* 1.13, 2.18, 3.15, 4.3, 4.16, 5.17, 6.11, 6.23. For *disciplina*, see the commentary on *Ep.* 2.4.3 *Quocirca, quia dignus es, ut domus tuae celeberrimam disciplinam....* The verb *succresco*, 'to grow up as a replacement or successor' (*OLD* 1857, 1b), is classic, but rarely used; for examples see Cic. *De orat.* 3.230, Ov.

Met. 8.680. With the allusion to Iuv. 1.15 *et nos ergo manum ferulae subduximus* ('and I also pulled away my hand from the cane'), where Juvenal portrays himself receiving corporal punishment (the same as the bad poets he attacks in Iuv. 1.1–13), Sidonius evokes the context of schooling and youth. Juvenal's line was proverbial; see also Hier. *Adv. Rufin.* 1.17, *Ep.* 50.5, 57.12, Macrob. *Sat.* 3.10.2; Colton (1982) 65. There is an allusion to a similar beating in a classroom described in Mart. 10.62 in Sidon. *Ep.* 2.2.2; see the commentary on *Ep.* 2.2.2 *discipulis non aestu* .... The *ferula*, 'whip', 'rod' (*TLL* 6.1, 599.25–60), is also mentioned by other authors in connection with punishment; see Hor. *Sat.* 1.3.120, Iuv. 6.479, Mart. 14.80, 10.62.10, Mart. Cap. 3.224. Sidonius uses the term again in *Ep.* 5.5.2 (addressed to Syagrius) in the context of schooling: *post ferulas lectionis Maronianae* ('after the cane during the studies of Vergil'), and in *Ep.* 3.13.4 about the punishment of the parasite Gnatho. The superlative *copiosissimus*, from the very frequently used adjective *copiosus*, 'rich', 'copious', 'abundantly' (*TLL* 4, 912.48–16.59), appears in Sidon. *Ep.* 8.12.6, 9.7.1 and 9.14.7. The connection of *copiosus* with *fructus* is also attested in Herm. *Pal. sim.* 2.3 and Hil. *In Matth.* 10.2 according to *TLL* 4, 913.83–4. On the adverb *copiose*, see the commentary on *Ep.* 2.9.6 *Prandebamus breviter copiose*.... The combination of *fructus* and *laboris* or *laborum* is also attested elsewhere; see Cic. *Verr.* 1.11, *Cael.* 80. With the first-person plural *adipiscimur*, Sidonius includes Hesperius; see the commentary on *Ep.* 2.10.1 *Amo in te quod litteras amas*....

Illud appone, quod tantum increbruit multitudo desidiosorum, ut, nisi vel paucissimi quique meram linguae Latiaris proprietatem de trivialium barbarismorum robigine vindicaveritis: Here and elsewhere in his work, Sidonius is concerned about the survival of the correct Latin language and he repeatedly encourages his friends to stand up for it as vigorously as he does; see Sidon. *Ep.* 3.3.2, 3.14.2, 4.17.1–2, 5.5, 5.10.3–4, 7.14.10, 8.2.1–2, 9.7.2 and 4, 9.11.9; Gualandri (1979) 26–7, 81, Mathisen (1988) 46–7, Banniard (1992), Kaufmann (1995) 224–7, Amherdt (2001) 381, Gemeinhardt (2007) 224–30, Postel (2011) 176–7, Gerth (2013) 187–91, Denecker (2015) 410–18, Giannotti (2016) 138–41, Wolff (2020) 395–6. On Sidonius' and his contemporaries' fear of the loss of learning and knowledge in their time, see also Sidon. *Ep.* 8.6.3; Mathisen (1988) and Mathisen (1993) 105–10. Reading the classics, exchanging texts and discussing literature are a means of ensuring the social status of the educated elite. That school education was a common foundation of the Roman upper class in Gaul is also shown by Sidon. *Ep.* 5.9. In Sidonius' account, the knowledge of letters was the last remaining token of nobility and a field of activity to distinguish themselves from the 'barbarians' – see *Ep.* 8.2.2; Eigler (2003) 114–15, 126–7, Squillante (2009) 141, Schwitter (2015) 193, Hess (2019) 69–78, 107–8, Mratschek (2017) 314, Hanaghan (2019) 28–37, Mratschek (2020b) 242, Egetenmeyr (2021) 154–5. The educated form a party of good men – see the commentary on *Ep.* 2.4.3 *sicut decet bonarum partium viros*. According to Denecker (2015) 412, Sidonius presents standard Latin as a 'pure' or 'unmixed' form (*meram*), which follows its own 'proper nature' (*proprietatem*). *Merus* is often used of abstract things (see *TLL* 8, 846.82–7.77); in the context of speech or language the adjective *merus* is similarly used in Diom. *Gramm.* 1.299.2 *artem merae Latinitatis puraeque eloquentiae magistram* ('the art of genuine Latin and the teacher of pure eloquence'). For *Latiaris*, 'of Latium', 'Latin', see the commentary on *Ep.* 2.9.4 *qui vero ... hi coturno Latiaris eloquii nobilitabantur*. The term *proprietas*, 'property', 'peculiarity', is also used in Sidon. *Ep.* 3.14.2 *proprietas linguae Latinae* ('and propriety in the use of the Latin language'); Giannotti (2016) 266. It also appears in several Christian authors in discussions of language (*TLL* 10.2, 2088.74–9.13), for example Tert. *Adv. Marc.* 4.11.12 *si hominem alterius gentis probare voluisses, utique de proprietate loquelae probares* ('if you want to show us a different kind of man, then you would have to prove this with his peculiarity of speech'), Hier. *Ep.* 57.5. The standard for good Latin was set by the classical authors: they were learned at school and their style was adapted to Late Antique aesthetics; Schwitter (2015) 152–3. One reason for the decline, according to Sidonius, is the idleness and negligence of the upper class (*multitudo desidiosorum*); Denecker (2015) 412–13. Schwitter (2015) 231–3 refers to Claud. Mam. *Ep. Ad Sapaudum* ed. Engelbrecht, 204.22–4 for a similar thought: *video enim os Romanum non modo neglegentiae, sed pudori esse Romanis, grammaticam uti quondam barbaram barbarismi et soloecismi pugno et calce propelli* ('for I see that the Roman language is not only too cumbersome for the Romans, but even embarrassing, so that grammar is fought off like some barbarian with blows and kicks, i.e. with barbarism and solecism'). See John (2021b) for Claudianus Mamertus. The adjective *desidiosus* (used as a noun here and in Sen. *Tranq.* 9.9.7, *Ep.* 71.23) means 'very lazy' (*TLL* 5.1, 712.34–13.6) and is similarly used in Plin. *Ep.* 3.5.19, about Pliny's alleged laziness in comparison with his literarily extremely productive uncle. Another reason for the decline of the Latin language is the influence of the advancing Germanic language; Denecker (2015) 412–18, Mratschek (2020b) 238. Sidonius calls the widespread (*trivialis*) impropriety of speech *barbarismus*, a term he also uses in *Ep.* 4.17.1, 5.5.3, 9.3.3, 9.11.6. *Barbarismus* is a *terminus technicus* and denotes 'an impropriety of speech', 'barbarism' (*TLL* 2, 1734.58–5.9). It is primarily used by the ancient grammarians and rhetors (for example Quint. 1.5), but also by other authors, for example in Sen. *Ep.* 113.26, Mart. 6.17.2, Aug. *Doctr. Christ.* 2.19; Amherdt (2001) 386, Kaufmann (1995) 261–2, Condorelli (2008) 194 n. 37. Sidonius uses *barbarismus* not in a technical-grammatical sense, but in a cultural one: he fears that Latin is succumbing to the barbarians and that traditional Roman culture is lost in the process; Condorelli (2001). For Sidonius' attitude towards barbarians in general, see the commentary on *Ep.* 2.1.2 *indicit ut dominus ... calumniatur ut barbarus*. The noun *robigo*, 'rust', is used here in a figurative sense to describe incorrect language; Gualandri (1979) 129 n. 78. In Hier. *Ep.* 29.7, to his pupil Marcella, Jerome similarly apologises for his allegedly unsophisticated style and disapproves of the barbarian influence as being 'rust' (*rubiginem*) on his Latin speech; see also Hier. *Ep.* 1.1 *ingenii rubigo* ('a rust of my mind'), Hier. *Vita Malchi* 1; Denecker (2015) 406. Ruricius seems to be inspired by this Sidonian passage – see Ruric. *Ep.* 1.3.3; Neri (2009) 183–4. In Sidonius, *robigo* also appears in *Ep.* 6.6.1 (together with *affectus*) and in 8.6.18 (together with *loquendi*).

eam brevi abolitam defleamus interitamque; sic omnes nobilium sermonum purpurae per incuriam vulgi decolorabuntur: With the first-person plural *defleamus*, Sidonius underlines the general concern about the loss of the Latin language; see the commentary on *Ep.* 2.10.1 *Amo in te....* He describes the coming death of the Latin language with two participles: *abolitus*, from *aboleo*, 'to destroy', 'abolish', 'efface' (*TLL* 1, 116.34–19.9), and *interitus*, 'perished', 'destroyed' (*TLL* 7.1, 2188.74–83). *Abolitus* is also used in *Ep.* 4.17.2 in a very similar context about the Latin language: *quocirca sermonis pompa Romani, si qua adhuc uspiam est, Belgicis olim sive Rhenanis abolita terris in the resedit* ('thus the splendour of the Roman speech, if it still exists anywhere, has survived in you, though it has long been wiped out from the Belgian and Rhenic lands'); see also *Ep.* 8.6.7. While most of his peers do not care about the Latin language, Sidonius will be sad about its loss; Harries (1994) 2–3, Schwitter (2015) 233. The manuscripts L and M have *interim tamque*; MCTN[2] have *interitamque*. *Interemptamque*, the participle of *interimo*, 'take away', is a conjecture of Wouweren, followed by Lütjohann (1887) 33, Loyen (1970a) 68 and Anderson (1936) 462, which I do not think is necessary; see also the discussion in Mossberg (1934) 15. For the colour 'purple', *purpura*, which Sidonius also uses in the description of his villa in the sense of 'ornament', see the commentary on *Ep.* 2.2.8 *Nec pilae* ... *'aedificiorum purpuras' nuncupavere*. Sidonius uses a similar image when writing about the purple ornaments of aristocratic diction in *Carm.* 22.6 *multis isdemque purpureis locorum communium pannis* ('many purple patches of stock phrases'). This is a clear allusion to the beginning of Horace's influential *Ars poetica*, where the poet gives preference to poetic unity: Hor. *Ars* 14–16 *inceptis gravibus plerumque et magna professis | purpureus, late qui splendeat, unus et alter | adsuitur pannus* ... ('often a cloth of purple, which shines far away, is patched here and there to weighty beginnings and great promises'). The relationship between Sidonius' *Carm.* 22.6 and *Ep.* 9.16.4 and Horace's *Ars poetica* has often been commented upon. Unlike Horace, Sidonius opts for variety, but still cites Horace as an authority, that is, he reads Horace in the way that suits him best; Gualandri (1979) 82 n. 24, Delhey (1993) 209, Condorelli (2008) 159–60, Hernández Lobato (2012) 370, Newlands (2013) 74–5, Stoehr-Monjou (2013) 165–7, Pelttari (2016), Mratschek (2017) 316–19, Mratschek (2020b) 237–8. For Sidonius' relation to Horace, see the commentary on *Ep.* 2.9.4 *nam similis* ... *hinc Horatius*.... The allusion to Horace's purple is probably meant to distinguish the educated elite from the *vulgus*, 'common people'. Sidonius contrasts the aristocratic with the ordinary language also in *Ep.* 4.10.2. He uses the image of purple, which loses its colour, to symbolise the decline of the former noble style of writing. See also *Ep.* 3.14.2, where Sidonius uses the term *pompa*, 'grandeur', instead of *purpura*, to define his linguistic ideal; Denecker (2015) 412–13, Giannotti (2016) 266. The verb *decoloro*, 'to deprive of its natural colour', 'to discolour' (*TLL* 5.1, 200.34–77), thus appears here in a figurative sense; it is also used in *Ep.* 1.5.7, 8.14.3.

Section 2

Sed istinc alias: interea tu quod petis accipe: Sidonius interrupts his lament about the decline of the Latin language and, by announcing his own poem, shows that there is still hope. By mentioning that he is sending the poem at Hesperius' request, Sidonius connects him with bishop Patiens, who asked Sidonius to write a poem. The *iubeo–pares* motif is thus present twice in this letter and is made explicit by *tu* ... *petis* ... *petis* ... *pareo* ...; see Egelhaaf-Gaiser (2014) 389, van Waarden (2020b) 439, the introduction to this letter and the commentary below on *Ep.* 2.10.2 *Dicto pareo*.... Sidonius uses the adverb *istinc*, 'from there', which is attested several times in Plautus (see for example Plaut. *Ps.* 1164, *Rud.* 1077), but also used by Cicero (for example Cic. *Att.* 1.14.4) and Pliny (for example Plin. *Ep.* 2.12.7), here and in *Ep.* 3.4.2 in the secondary meaning of *de ista (hac) re*, 'thereof', 'of that thing' (*TLL* 7.2, 517.44–9). For the imperative *accipe*, see the commentary on *Ep.* 2.2.3 *Sane si placet ... situs accipe*.

Petis autem, ut si qui versiculi mihi fluxerint, postquam ab alterutro discessimus, hos tibi pro quadam morarum mercede pernumerem: With the image of flowing verses Sidonius refers to the beginning of his letter collection, *Ep.* 1.1.1 *si quae litterae paulo politiores varia occasione fluxerunt* ('if a bit more refined letters flowed on various occasions'); Amherdt (2001) 409, Köhler (1995) 103. He also alludes to Statius, who uses the verb *fluere* ('to flow') similarly in the introductory letter to the first book of his *Silvae*: Stat. *Silv.* 1 *praef.*: *libellos, qui mihi subito calore et quadam festinandi voluptate fluxerunt* ('these pieces which flowed to me in a sudden heat and a pleasurable rush'). For the diminutive *versiculi*, see the commentary on *Ep.* 2.2.7 *Pauci tamen versiculi....* Unlike other poets, Statius does not emphasise the laborious polishing of the poem, but is proud of his professional and quick virtuosity; Gauly (2006) 455, Condorelli (2008) 195, Squillante (2016). Ausonius, who is also an important model for Sidonius, emphasises several times how quickly he writes his poems, for example in the prefaces to the *Cento nuptialis*, the *Griphus* or in his letters to Petronius Probus (Auson. *Ep.* 9a) and Paulinus (Auson. *Ep.* 19a); McGill (2017) 252. Sidonius also presents himself as writing in creative flow, while nonetheless carefully editing his works; see Sidon. *Ep.* 4.8.4–5, 7.18.1, 9.13.4; Mratschek (2017) 314. The image of flowing verses or metre is also attested elsewhere (*TLL* 6.1, 973.12–25), for example Plin. *Ep.* 5.17.2 *elegis ... fluentibus* ('in flowing elegiac verses'). *Alteruter*, 'one of two', 'the one' or 'the other', is a classical but rarely used pronoun. In *Ep.* 2.8.2 Sidonius similarly emphasises how quickly he wrote the poem on the deceased Filimatia; see the commentary on *Ep.* 2.8.2 *marmori incisam planctu prope calente dictavi*. The verb *pernumero*, 'to count out', 'reckon up' (*TLL* 10.1, 1600.57–601.6), is also rarely used but does appear for example in Plaut. *Epid.* 632, Mart. 12.62.12 and also in Sidon. *Ep.* 3.3.5. The expression *mercede pernumerem* ('I can count as a payment') is attested only here.

Dicto pareo; nam praeditus es quamquam iuvenis hac animi maturitate, ut tibi etiam natu priores gerere morem concupiscamus: Sidonius explains why he obeys (*pareo*) the orders of Hesperius, even though he is younger than him. The motif is reinforced by the repetition in *Ep.* 2.10.5 of *parui* ('I have obeyed'). For further examples of *pareo* in response to a request for a poem or letter, see Sidon. *Ep.* 1.2.1, 8.9.2, 8.11.2, 9.2.1 (*non pareo*), 9.11.10, 9.13.2; for *parui*, see *Ep.* 1.1.3, 1.9.6, 2.10.5, 4.17.3 (*non parui*), 7.2.10; van Waarden (2020b) 439. The motif is used particularly impressively in *Ep.* 9.15.1 v. 1, where the inserted poem begins with *iubes* and ends with *parui* in verse 55. See also Sidon. *Ep.* 7.17.1 *iubes ... obsecundabo* ('you bid me ... and I obey'), 9.1.2, 9.9.2 *mitti paginam copiosam denuo iubes. parere properanti adsunt vota, causae absunt* ('you again order to send a comprehensive letter. I hasten to obey, but although the desire is there, subjects are missing'). For this prominent motif in Letters 9.12–16, see Stoehr-Monjou (forthcoming). Other epistles where Sidonius responds to the addressee's exhortations to send him his verses are Sidon. *Ep.* 4.18.3, 7.13.3, 7.17.1, 8.9.1, 9.13.2. The poems in *Ep.* 7.13.2, 8.9.5, 9.13.5, 9.15.1 are all included at the request of the recipient. For the writer's willingness to please, see *Ep.* 1.1.3, 2.10.5, 4.8.4, 7.13.3. The praise of the spirit of a young person which equals the virtues of an older one is also a subject in Pliny's letters, for example Plin. *Ep.* 2.7.4 and 4.15.6. Sidonius uses the term *maturitas* ('maturity') similarly about a person's style of writing or character in Sidon. *Ep.* 1.1.1, 4.3.4, 5.2.2, 9.16.3; see also 8.16.2 *maturo ... lectori* ('for an experienced reader'); Amherdt (2001) 131. By using the first-person plural *concupiscamus* ('we want') Sidonius suggests that others also think highly of Hesperius.

Ecclesia nuper exstructa Lugduni est, quae studio papae Patientis summum coepti operis accessit: Lugdunum, present-day Lyon, was founded as a Roman colony in 43 BC by the praetor of the province Gallia Transalpina, L. Munatius Plancus, and later became known as Colonia Copia Claudia Augusta Lugdunensis; Reynaud (1998) 18–19. It is where Sidonius was born and educated. Sidonius gives some hints as to the location of the cathedral (at the foot of a hill, near a river and a road), which he calls *ecclesia* here and *aedes* and *basilica* in *Ep.* 2.10.3. Sirmond (1614) 53 already argued for a church near the River Saône, which is the location of the cathedral of Saint-Jean-Baptiste-et-Saint-Étienne (built in the twelfth century, dedicated to Saint John the Baptist). The previous building, which is the one Sidonius writes about (and which is now lost), was probably built above the grave of Saint Justus, a former bishop of Lyon, who died around 390. With the adverb *iustius* in *Ep.* 2.10.4 Sidonius puns on the bishop's name; see the commentary there. For Saint Justus, see Sidon. *Ep.* 5.17.3 and the commentary on *Ep.* 2.8.1 *Decessit nudius tertius non absque iustitio matrona Filimatia*. There are different theories about the name of this older church (dating probably from the late fourth century), which bishop Patiens either renovated or built from scratch (*ecclesia nuper exstructa*) and to which Sidonius, Constantius and Secundinus contributed their poems, inscribed into the walls near the altar. There is some evidence of an episcopal complex of three buildings dedicated to different saints near the river, which Sidonius describes; Loyen (1970a) 220 n. 42, Harries (1994) 45–7, Reynaud (1998) 44–5, Santelia (2007) 320, van Waarden (2011) 102 n. 10, Hernández Lobato (2012) 495 with a reconstruction sketch of the architectural complex, Hecquet-Noti (2013) 220 n. 281, Egelhaaf-Gaiser (2014) 373 n. 2, Herbert de la Portbarré-Viard (2014) 381, 383. Unfortunately, there is no archaeological evidence for the three inscriptions mentioned by Sidonius, so we just have to rely on his account. Patiens was the bishop of Lyon from 449/50 onwards. He is also the addressee of *Ep.* 6.12. According to that letter he founded or renovated several churches (6.12.3–4) and generously helped several cities with his own resources during a famine (6.12.5). Sidonius also praises Patiens in *Ep.* 3.12.3 and 4.25.1. He died shortly after 480; Chadwick (1955) 288–92, Loyen (1970a) XXVIII–XXIX, *PCBE* 4, 1432–5, Kaufmann (1995) 330–1, Hanaghan (2019) 129–33, Bailey (2020) 265, 267–9, Mathisen (2020a) 112.

viri sancti strenui, severi misericordis, quique per uberem munificentiam in pauperes humanitatemque non minora bonae conscientiae culmina levet: The bishop's character is full of positive opposites ('a man pious but active, stern but compassionate'), recalling the description of Filimatia in *Ep.* 2.8.3 v. 6 *prudens, casta....* One of his virtues is his generosity (*munificentia*), a trait Sidonius praises him for in *Ep.* 6.12.5–7. The virtue of taking care of the poor is also mentioned in the description of other persons in Sidon. *Ep.* 4.7.2, 4.11.4, 6.2.1; Amherdt (2001) 17–21, 104, van Waarden (2016) 163. Another positive trait is his *humanitas*, here used like *munificentia* in the meaning of 'care', 'help', 'generosity'; see van Waarden (2010) 503 on *Ep.* 7.9.19. For *conscientia*, 'conscience', see the commentary on *Ep.* 2.7.2 *Igitur ignosce ... ad tam sanctae conscientiae....* Sidonius uses *culmina*, the plural of *culmen*, 'summit', several times in his letters and poems to denote a metaphorical 'top' (of a career, of the state), of high offices and dignitaries in *Ep.* 1.11.17, 2.13.1, 4.22.3 (in the singular), of a career in *Ep.* 1.4.1 (in the singular), 3.6.1, *Carm.* 2.89, 2.208. The term also denotes the 'top of a building' in *Ep.* 3.1.2, 3.2.4, 3.3.8, 4.15.1, 4.18.5 v. 20, 7.1.3, 7.6.8, 7.17.2 v. 22, and *Carm.* 18.3, 22.4 v. 149, 22.4 v. 191, 23.21, 23.444.

Similarly, Sidonius describes the former praetorian prefect Paulus in *Ep.* 1.9.1 as *illud tamen in eodem studiorum omnium culmen antevenit, quod habet huic eminenti scientiae conscientiam superiorem* ('And better still is the highest merit of all his studies, namely, that he has a conscience which surpasses his brilliant erudition').

Section 3

Huius igitur aedis extimis rogatu praefati antistitis tumultuarium carmen inscripsi trochaeis triplicibus adhuc mihi iamque tibi perfamiliaribus: Sidonius underlines that he wrote the inscription at the request of bishop Patiens and thus connects him to Hesperius; see the commentary on *Ep.* 2.10.2 *Sed istinc alias: interea tu quod petis accipe*. The expression *aedis extimis*, 'the most distant part of the building', here denotes the apse of the church, where Sidonius' poem will be displayed; Hernández Lobato (2012) 494. The participle *praefatus*, 'mentioned or stated before' (*TLL* 10.2, 651.59–61), is frequently used as an adjective or a noun in Sidonius (for example Sidon. *Ep.* 5.1.3, 7.5.3) and other Late Antique writers like Ennodius or Ruricius; see van Waarden (2010) 264. *Antistes* is used by Christian writers to denote a high church official, especially a bishop (*TLL* 2, 185.45–70). The term appears several times in Sidonius, for example in *Ep.* 4.6.1, 4.11.6 v. 18, and 4.17.3. There were three ranks of priests, the first, second and highest order (*primi/secundi/summi ordinis*); see *Ep.* 4.25.4; Amherdt (2001) 516, van Waarden (2010) 48–9, 569. For *tumultuarius*, 'hurried', 'hasty', as an attribute of poetry or written works in general, see Sidon. *Ep.* 1.9.6, 8.3.1, Gell. 11.7.3 *tumultuaria doctrina praeditus* ('with a haphazard kind of education'); Condorelli (2008) 62–3. The adjective is also used of plants; see the commentary on *Ep.* 2.2.18 *A Zephyro plebeius et tumultuarius frutex*. The idea of hurried writing in combination with the verb *fluere* (of a poem) also occurs in Statius' preface to the first book of the *Silvae*; see the commentary on *Ep.* 2.10.2 *Petis autem, ut si qui versiculi mihi fluxerint*.... In the context of his *Ep.* 3.12.4 and 4.11.7, Sidonius also stresses the haste with which he writes his poems; see the commentary on *Ep.* 2.8.2 *marmori incisam planctu prope calente dictavi*. See also Sidon. *Ep.* 7.9.4; Loyen (1943) 101–3, Paul. Nol. *Ep.* 32.4. The topos of rapid and spontaneous poetic composition in the context of aristocratic *otium* is found in Pliny too – see especially Plin. *Ep.* 4.14.2, where hendecasyllables and *otium* are explicitly linked: *accipies cum hac epistula hendecasyllabos nostros, quibus nos in vehiculo, in balineo, inter* *cenam oblectamus otium temporis* ('together with this letter you will receive my hendecasyllables, which I use to amuse myself during leisure hours in the carriage, in the bath, while eating'); Hindermann (2009). As he did early in section 2 with the expression *versiculi*, Sidonius also downplays his work in a gesture of modesty with the expression *tumultuarium carmen*; Bernt (1968) 91–2, Amherdt (2001) 408, Wolff (2014c) 212–13. However, this is only a pose, because Sidonius actually equates his poem with the basilica, which attracts both sunbeams and people passing by; Onorato (2020a) 87. With the verb *inscribere* ('to inscribe') Sidonius denotes the material reproduction of his poem on the wall of the church, as he does elsewhere with other verbs (*imprimere, incidere*) referring to his poems; see the commentaries on *Ep.* 2.2.7 *Quid plura? Nihil illis paginis impressum* … and on 2.8.2 *marmori incisam*…, as well as *Ep.* 3.12.5 *tabulae* … *celeriter indatur* ('it should be promptly cut on the slab'). Sidonius uses *inscribere* also in *Ep.* 7.17.1, about an epitaph for the late abbot Abraham: *neniam sepulchralem luctuosis carminibus inscribere* ('a sepulchral lament to be included among the mournful inscriptions'); van Waarden (2016) 215, Consolino (2020) 361–2. The poem for bishop Patiens is written in Phalaecian hendecasyllables (*trochaeis triplicibus*), like the epitaph inserted in *Ep.* 2.8.3. Sidonius uses the three trochees (_u) at the end of the hendecasyllable (_ _/_uu/_u/_u/_x) to stand as pars pro toto for the whole metre. For the hendecasyllable, see the commentary on *Ep.* 2.8.2 *Post quae* … *sed per hendecasyllabos*. The combination with the adjective *triplex* is also found in *Ep.* 5.8.1 *triplicibus trochaeis* ('in triple trochees') and in *Carm.* 23.25–7. For *triplex*, see the commentary on *Ep.* 2.2.8 *triplex medii parietis aditus*.… For *triplex* instead of *tres* with plural nouns, see van Waarden (2016) 63 on *Ep.* 7.12.1. With his choice of metre Sidonius sets himself apart from the hexameters of Constantius and Secundinus and follows the tradition of Martial and Catullus, the two most famous users of hendecasyllabic verse; see Egelhaaf-Gaiser (2014) 382 and the commentary below on *Ep.* 2.10.4 vv. 22–30: General remarks. With *adhuc mihi iamque tibi* Sidonius suggests that he is the only one who knows the poem, as it is not yet published, that is, inscribed in the church; Egelhaaf-Gaiser (2014) 386–8. Wolff (2014c) 212 n. 10 instead thinks (without considering the following *iamque tibi*, which refers to the addressee) that what Sidonius means is that he has begun his clerical career and will therefore no longer write light poetry. The adjective *perfamiliaris*, 'very familiar', 'very intimate' (*TLL* 10.1, 1349.39–42), is classical, but infrequently used. It appears several times of persons in Cicero and of things, as here, in Liv. 25.18.4 *perfamiliari hospitio iunctus* ('connected by a very familiar hospitality').

Namque ab hexametris eminentium poetarum Constantii et Secundini vicinantia altari basilicae latera clarescunt: Sidonius mentions two other poets whose verses are inscribed in the side walls of the apse. They are written in a different metre, in hexameters instead of hendecasyllables (see the commentary on *Ep.* 2.10.3 *Huius igitur ... carmen inscripsi trochaeis triplicibus*) and their poems are lost as Sidonius does not include them in his letter (see the commentary on *Ep.* 2.10.3 *quos in hanc paginam admitti nostra quam maxume verecundia vetat...*). The three poems offer a kind of textual enlightenment of the church space; see Schwitter (2015) 159–60 and the commentary on *Ep.* 2.10.4 *Quapropter illorum iustius epigrammata micant....* Sidonius introduces both authors with the particle *namque* as an aside; Kroon (1995) 147–8. Constantius, a priest in Lyon, is the addressee of the prestigious *Ep.* 1.1 and dedicatee of the first seven books of letters (as well as the addressee of *Ep.* 3.2, 7.18, 8.16), of noble birth (*Ep.* 3.2.3) and praised as an outstanding orator (*Ep.* 9.16.1) and patron interested in promoting writers and literature (*Ep.* 1.1.3). He is also the biographer of bishop Germanus of Auxerre (*Vita Germani Autissiodorensis*). He stands out as one of the few people who receive four letters; Mathisen (2020a) 41. For his life, see *PLRE* 2, 320 n. 10, *PCBE* 4. 521–2, Loyen (1970a) XXXI–XXXII, Kaufmann (1995) 294–5, Köhler (1995) 100–1, Giannotti (2016) 122–3, van Waarden (2016) 253–4, Mathisen (2020a) 89. Secundinus is the addressee of *Ep.* 5.8, where Sidonius praises his poetry and shows him living at the Burgundian court in Lyon; Schetter (1964), *PLRE* 2, 985 n. 3, *PCBE* 4, 1724, Kaufmann (1995) 146 n. 383, 346–7, Chronopoulos (2020) 662, Mathisen (2020a) 120. For the participle of the verb *vicinor*, 'to be neighbouring', 'near', see the commentary on *Ep.* 2.2.9 *cui continuatur vicinante textrino....* For *altarium*, 'altar', see the commentary on *Ep.* 2.1.3 *implet cotidie ... altaria reis....* Sidonius here calls the church a 'basilica'; see also *Ep.* 4.18.4, 5.17.3, 6.12.4; van Waarden (2010) 321. For *basilica* in the meaning of 'a hall in a private house' as part of a secular building, see the commentary on *Ep.* 2.8 *Huic basilicae appendix piscina forinsecus seu*. The verb *claresco*, 'to become or grow bright or clear', is often used in the sense of to 'appear' (see *TLL* 3, 1265.11). It is also used in Sidon. *Ep.* 1.8.3 and 3.8.2; *inclarescere*, which has the same meaning, appears in *Ep.* 4.3.2.

quos in hanc paginam admitti nostra quam maxume verecundia vetat, quam suas otiositates trepidanter edentem meliorum carminum comparatio premit: In his familiar pose of modesty Sidonius depreciates his own hendecasyllables in comparison with the hexameters of the other two poets. As their poems are lost, it is impossible to assess Sidonius' claim of the worth of his poetry relative to theirs. Whereas Sidonius depicts the two poets as serious and famous (*eminentium poetarum*) and their poems as better (*meliora*), he claims that his verses are a product of leisure (*otium*); see below on *otiositates*. While Sidonius' poem has been saved through its inclusion in the letter, the two others, excluded from the letter for being too good, are now paradoxically lost; Egelhaaf-Gaiser (2014) 374. Paper thus proves to be the more durable carrier of poetry than the supposedly eternal inscriptions in stone; Hindermann (2020b, 2022b). Pliny also cites verses (about him or his own) and thus saves them from being lost; see Plin. *Ep.* 3.21.5 (the poem of Martial about Pliny), 4.27.4 (the poem of Sentius Augurinus about Pliny), 7.4.6 and 7.9.11 (his own poems). For Sidonius' demonstrative modesty, see the commentaries on *Ep.* 2.2.7 *Pauci tamen versiculi...* and on *Ep.* 2.9.10 *Dicerem et cenas ... terminum nostrae loquacitati....* Sidonius does not only insert topical doubts about the value of his poetry into his letters. After becoming bishop he also presents himself as unworthy of his pastoral responsibilities in a number of letters, for example in *Ep.* 6.1.5; Bailey (2020) 269–75. This gesture of humility, however, is probably to be interpreted as being somewhat strategic: Sidonius was made bishop after holding secular office, and so he is aware of the need to express humility when writing to other, often more senior, church figures. For the various meanings of *pagina*, here denoting the 'letter' at hand, see the commentary on *Ep.* 2.2.7 *Quid plura? Nihil illis paginis....* Sidonius uses the term *verecundia*, 'an attitude of restraint', 'modesty', several times to denote appropriate behaviour; see the commentary on *Ep.* 2.4.3 *benignitate responsi ... verecundiam munerare*. Here it appears personified as the subject of the sentence. The adverb *trepidanter*, 'in a frightened manner' (*OLD* 1970), is rarely used but see for example Suet. *Nero* 49.3. The noun *otiositas*, 'leisure', 'idleness' (*TLL* 9.2, 1166.17–22), is Late Latin and rare. Its plural in the meaning of 'poem' is attested only here; see Ov. *Trist.* 2.224 *otia nostra* ('my leisure'); Wolff (2020) 403. As *otium* can have a negative ring there may be a further element of self-deprecation or modesty; Hindermann (2020a) 108–9. The same strategy is found in Ausonius, who insists that his poetry is worthless or trivial and a waste of his *otium*, for example in the prefaces to his *Technopaegnion*, *Bissula* and his *Eclogues*; Sowers (2016). Sidonius also reflects on the meaning of *otium* elsewhere and coins new expressions from the semantic field; see the introduction to *Ep.* 2.2 and the commentary on *Ep.* 2.14.2 *in otio fuliginoso....* The expression *comparatio premit* does not seem to be attested anywhere else (*TLL* 3, 2006.30–8.50).

Section 4

Nam sicuti novam nuptam nihil minus quam pulchrior pronuba decet, sicuti, si vestiatur albo, fuscus quisque fit nigrior: Sidonius adds two comparisons to illustrate how his poem suffers from the vicinity of better poems. The first comparison (a *pronuba* should not be prettier than the bride, the *nova nupta*) points to the subject of marriage and the link between wives and creativity, which is treated in sections 5 and 6 of the letter. The *pronuba*, a woman still married to her first husband, assisted the bride during the wedding in the *dextrarum iunctio* ('joining together the right hands of the couple') and their reciprocal declaration of *consensus* ('consent') (*TLL* 10.2, 1915.72–16.8); Oswald and Haase (1998) 651. Sidonius uses the term in *Ep.* 1.5.11 and in a transferred sense in *Carm.* 2.502; Köhler (1995) 213. The second comparison alludes to the widespread ancient notion of beauty, which valued fair skin over dark; see for example Ov. *Ars* 2.643–4, 3.270, *Fast.* 3.493, *Am.* 2.4.39–40, Mart. 4.42.5–6, Verg. *Ecl.* 2.15–8; Dilke (1980) 269, Gibson (2003) 171 with further references. In his *Ars amatoria*, Ovid gives his students of love the following styling advice: women with dark skin should wear white clothes (and women with white skin dark clothes); see Ov. *Ars* 3.189–92, and especially v. 191 *alba decent fuscas: albis, Cepheï, placebas* ('white fits dark skinned girls; clothed in white you looked pleasing, daughter of Cepheus' [i.e. the Ethiopian Andromeda]). *Fuscus*, 'dark', is regularly used of the colour of skin (*TLL* 6.1, 1654.7–35), for example in Verg. *Ecl.* 10.38, Prop. 2.25.42; André (1949) 123–5, Janka (1997) 457–8. Similar to the passage here is Ov. *Ars* 2.657–8 *fusca vocetur,* | *nigrior Illyrica cui pice sanguis erit* ('she shall be called dark-skinned, whose blood is blacker than Illyrian pitch'), *Rem.* 327 *si fusca est, 'nigra' vocetur* ('if she is dark-skinned, she shall be called black'). The poem for bishop Martin of Tours in Sidon. *Ep.* 4.18.5 (*Carm.* 31) is introduced with a similar comparison: *nisi forsitan inter omnia venusta sic epigrammatis istius foeditas placeat, ut niger naevus candido in corpore, qui quidem solet sic facere risu quod accipere suffragium* ('unless perhaps amid all that beauty the ugliness of this poem finds some favour like a black mole on a fair body which, though causing a smile, generally wins approval').

sic nostra, quantula est cumque, tubis circumfusa potioribus stipula vilescit: With the first person plural *nostra* and the following *effingimus* (at the end of the next sentence) the poet and sender of the poem withdraws into the background. Once the poem is delivered, Sidonius changes back to the first person (*parui* in *Ep.* 2.10.5); van Waarden (2020b) 433. On the tmesis *quantula est cumque* instead of *quantulacumque*, 'however small', 'how little soever' (*OLD* 1540), see Löfstedt (1985) 211. See Catull. 1.8–9 *quidquid hoc libelli | qualecumque* ('whatever and however this little book may be'). After the metaphors of the bride and the dark skin, Sidonius adds a third image, the comparison between pipe and trumpet, that is, instruments of different volume. He refers to his own poetry with the term *stipula*, 'stalk', 'stem', in the meaning of 'pipe' (*OLD* 1822, 1c). This usage is also attested in Verg. *Ecl.* 3.26–7 and thus evokes the idea of bucolic poetry: *solebas | stridenti miserum stipula disperdere carmen* ('you used to ruin a poor song on a squeaking stem'); see the commentary on *Ep.* 2.2.14 *Cui concentui licebit adiungas fistulae septiforis armentalem Camenam* and the commentary below on *culmus*, 'stalk', 'stem' (*Ep.* 2.10.4 *Sed quorsum ista? ... culmus immurmuret*). The poems of Constantius and Secundinus are referred to as *tuba*, 'trumpet', an instrument used for military purposes and other occasions, such as religious festivals, games and funerals. In opposition to the humble pipe, which symbolises 'minor' poetry in private use, it has an official purpose and stands symbolically for war, loud sound and for an elevated and grand style, especially in the epic; see Mart. 8.3.22, 8.55.4, 10.64.4, 11.3.8, Prud. *C. Symm.* 2.68; Amherdt (2001) 162–3, Schöffel (2001) 118–19, Armisen-Marchetti (2002), Santelia (2007) 307. Sidonius makes a similar comparison (*cicuta*, 'pipe', versus *tuba*) in *Carm.* 23.1–7. For the metaphor *tuba*, see also Sidon. *Ep.* 4.3.10, *Carm.* 9.315, Sen. *Ep.* 108.10, Macrob. *Sat.* 5.11.25, *Comm.* 2.8.4. The rarely used verb *vilesco*, 'to become cheap', 'to lose its value' (*Blaise* 848), is first found in the fourth century, for example in Hier. *Ep.* 66.7, 77.2, Aug. *Conf.* 3.4.7. Sidonius uses it on three other occasions in his correspondence: *Ep.* 4.6.2, 7.9.11 and 22; van Waarden (2010) 474.

quam mediam loco, infimam merito despicabiliorem pronuntiari non imperitia modo sed et arrogantia facit: Hidden under his pose of modesty, Sidonius cleverly repeats that his poem will be engraved in the most prominent place of the church (*mediam loco*). Still, he fears being accused of immodesty. For Sidonius' demonstrative modesty, see the commentaries on *Ep.* 2.2.7 *Pauci tamen versiculi...* and on *Ep.* 2.9.10 *Dicerem et cenas ... nisi terminum nostrae loquacitati....* The noun *meritum* in the *ablativus respectus* here has the meaning of 'weight', 'importance' (of things) (*TLL* 8, 820.78–21.14); see also Sidon. *Ep.* 1.2.8; and van Waarden (2016) 150 on 7.14.7 *cuius ad maximum culmen meritorum gradibus ascenditur* ('the highest peak of which is reached by the ladder of merits'). For *meritum* in the sense of 'worth', 'value', 'excellence', see the commentary on *Ep.* 2.5.1 *et donec suarum merita chartarum*.... The adjective *despicabilis*, 'contemptible', 'despicable' (of persons and things), appears only from the fourth century on (*TLL* 5.1, 742.49–3.4). In Sidonius, the adjective also occurs in *Ep.* 3.9.2, 4.7.3, 9.15.1 v. 50; Amherdt (2001) 220, Giannotti (2016) 198–9. For adjectives ending in *-bilis*, see the commentary on *Ep.* 2.2.16 *Is quidem ... vestigio inspectoris inadibilis*.

Quapropter illorum iustius epigrammata micant quam istaec, quae imaginarie tantum et quodammodo umbratiliter effingimus: The wording here suggests that Sidonius' inscription is marked lightly in charcoal before it is carved or painted. At the same time, this sentence can be read metaphorically, as the poems of the other poets shine in glory, while Sidonius' poem lies modestly in their shadow. This reading is suggested by the poet's play with the first-person plural (*effingimus*) – see the commentary on *Ep.* 2.10.4 *sic nostra*.... Hernández Lobato (2012) 498 interprets the poem as 'Gesamtkunstwerk' and emphasises the musical (see the commentary on *Ep.* 2.10.4 *Sed quorsum ista? ... cantilenae culmus immurmuret*) and visual aspects achieved with the terms *effingimus*, *imaginarie* and *umbratiliter*. The adverb *iustius* could be an allusion to Saint Justus, over whose grave the church is built; see *Ep.* 2.10.2 on *Ecclesia nuper exstructa Lugduni est...*; for the comparative see for example Hor. *Sat.* 2.4.86. For the use of the term *epigramma*, see the commentary on *Ep.* 2.8.2 *Quam si non satis improbas, ceteris epigrammatum meorum voluminibus applicandam*. The verb *mico*, 'to glitter', 'gleam', 'flash', is used here in a transferred sense in the meaning of 'to excel' (*TLL* 8, 931.75–2.8). Of poetry it is also used elsewhere, for example in Macrob. *Sat.* 5.14.7 and Maxim. *Eleg.* 1.30. Sidonius uses the verb here also in v. 8 of his inserted poem (see the commentary below). As with the verb *claresco* (used earlier in this letter), Sidonius hints at the predominance of light in the church to which the poems add; see the commentary on *Ep.* 2.10.3 *Namque ab hexametris ... clarescunt*. With the two adverbs *imaginarie* and *umbratiliter* Sidonius announces his poem, which he composed remembering the interplay of light and shadow in the church; see Herbert de la Portbarré-Viard (2014) 382. Hecquet-Noti (2013) 223 n. 294 suggests that the two adverbs gesture towards a symbolical and allegorical reading of the scene. *Imaginarie*, 'according to one's imagination', is rare and only used by Late Latin Christian authors, among them Augustine (for example Aug. *Conf.* 3.2.3; see also the adjective *imaginariam* in Aug. *C. Faust* 29.3); see *TLL* 7.1, 402.59–68, *Blaise* 405. The adjective *umbratilis*, 'remaining in the shade', 'private', is used of speech as part of the training in schools, opposed to public and political speech; see Cic. *De orat.* 1.157. *Umbratiliter* derives from the classical adjective *umbratilis*, 'spent, carried out, etc., in the shade or in retirement' (*OLD* 2088). In Aug. *Ep.* 149.25 it is opposed to *corporaliter*, 'bodily', and in Aug. *Ep.* 187.39 it has a spiritual connotation meaning 'symbolical'; see *Blaise* 856, Wolff (2020) 402. Lucarini (2002) 379 emends *effingimus* to *effinximus* as Sidonius had already written his poem and uses the perfect in similar passages: see Sidon. *Ep.* 2.10.3 *inscripsi* ('I have written'), 3.12.4 *feci* ('I made'), 4.11.6 *condidimus* ('I have composed').

Sed quorsum ista? Quin potius paupertinus flagitatae cantilenae culmus immurmuret: Like the following poem in the letter (*Carm.* 27), with *Sed quorsum ista?*, poems 29 and 31 inserted in *Ep.* 4.8.5 and 4.18.5 are introduced with rhetorical questions which imitate spoken language: respectively *sed ista vel similia quorsum?* ('but what is the point of all this sort of talk?') and *sed quid hinc amplius* ('but why say any more on the subject?'); Amherdt (2001) 225, 244, 413, Hanaghan (2019) 81–2 on narrative modes. For *quin potius*, '(but) rather', 'in fact', after a rhetorical question, see the commentary on *Ep.* 2.2.11 *Quin potius* .... The adjective *paupertinus*, 'poor', 'sorry' (*TLL* 10.1, 856.42–8), first occurs in Varro and then from Apuleius and Gellius on. Elsewhere it is also used of writing and style; see Symm. *Ep.* 1.14.1 *paupertini ingenii mei conscius* ('I am aware of my limited talent'). The term is also found in Sidon. *Ep.* 3.7.1, 7.17.2 v. 21; Gualandri (1979) 173 n. 98, Giannotti (2016) 183, van Waarden (2016) 239. *Cantilena*, 'a song' (*TLL* 3, 285.54–6.67), hints at the song of the sailors (*celeuma*) in v. 27 of the following poem. Sidonius uses the term again in *Ep.* 4.18.6, 5.17.11, 8.11.2; see also Symm. *Ep.* 1.1.2; Montone (2017) 41 n. 58. The adjective *cantilenosus*, 'pertaining to a song', is a Sidonian hapax; see Sidon. *Ep.* 3.14.1, 4.1.2. Again, as with *stipula* in the first sentence of the section, Sidonius evokes a bucolic image by calling his poem *culmus*, 'stalk', 'stem' (*TLL* 4, 1296.53–7); see also Serv. *Ecl.* 1.2. In Sidon. *Ep.* 7.17.2 v. 22 the term denotes the straw cover of a roof: *et casa, cui culmo culmina pressa forent* ('with a hut whose roof is thatched with straw'). The verb *immurmuro*, 'to murmur', is used of rivers and wind (see *TLL* 7.1, 509.18–25). Of a spell (*carmen*) it is also used in Ambr. *Hex.* 4.8.33. Egelhaaf-Gaiser (2014) 388 claims an allusion to Apul. *Met.* 1.1.1 *auresque tuas benivolas lepido susurro permulceam – modo si papyrum Aegyptiam argutia Nilotici calami inscriptam non spreveris inspicere* ('and caress your friendly ears with a pleasant murmur – if you do not spurn to take a look at the leaves from Egypt, which I have described with fine Nile reed'). Montone (2017) 35 refers to Verg. *Georg.* 4.261 *frigidus ... silvis inmurmurat Auster* ('the cold south wind whispers in the forests').

Carmen 27

This poem is the second of two epigrams which Sidonius inserts in his second book; see the Introduction to the commentary. For the extensive secondary literature on *Carm.* 27, see the Introduction on this letter, pp. xxi–xxiv, and the commentary below.

The poem is structured as follows:

vv. 1–4: Apostrophe to the reader and praise of bishop Patiens
vv. 5–21: Description of the church (exterior and interior appearance)
vv. 22–7: Descriptions of the surroundings of the church and of its visitors
vv. 28–30: Apostrophe to the reader and exhortation to come to the church

At thirty verses, the inscription is of considerable length, comparatively. Sidonius does not indicate how and where his poem has been placed on the wall of the apse, in a block of text or in several columns. It is also not clear whether it is painted or engraved (perhaps gilded) or placed as a mosaic. Harries (1994) 45–6 suggests that Sidonius' inscription was placed high up in the apse. Bernt (1968) 90–2 doubts that Sidonius' poems were actually intended as inscriptions and interprets them as literary fiction; for an overview of the older literature, which comes to the same conclusion, see Pietri (1988) 138–9. I doubt this thesis: contemporaries would find it strange for Sidonius simply to invent the honour of having his poem placed in the church. Egelhaaf-Gaiser (2014) 377–9 wonders who might have been able to read the poem in the church, as it would have been too far away for the lay members of the congregation. She suggests that Sidonius wrote it for the few educated (*literati*) among the clergy, who were able to appreciate all the elaborate allusions and to grasp the full meaning of the poem, and of course for the educated secondary readership of the letters. This, though, assumes that lay people needed to read it for themselves to understand it (when in all likelihood it was read to them).

There is some archaeological evidence from other (existing) churches, like the Archbishop's Chapel at Ravenna or the basilica at Nola. Paulinus of Nola describes Saint Felix's tomb and writes that the images in the church are explained by inscriptions; see Paul. Nol. *Carm.* 27.584–5 *quae super exprimitur titulis, ut littera monstret* | *quod manus explicuit* ... ('that is explained by inscriptions above, so that the script may make clear what the hand has expressed'). In Paul. Nol. *Ep.* 32.10, written in 401, Paulinus describes the paintings in the basilica at Nola. He also inserts examples of poems that were engraved on the wall to explain paintings or mosaics in the church; see Paul. Nol. *Ep.* 32.10. The apse is adorned by a vault of luminous mosaics, which depict the martyrium of Saint Felix; see Elsner (1998) 254–7 and the commentary below on vv. 11–15: General remarks. Wolff (2014c) investigates Sidonius' double publication of his poems as inscriptions and as parts of his letters, referring also to Paul. Nol. *Ep.* 32, Prud. *Perist.* 8, Ennod. *Carm.* 2.20, Auson. *Epic. praef.* 9. For the custom of poetic inscriptions in churches in Late Antiquity, see the first book of epigrams in the *Anthologia Palatina*; Steinmann (1892), Pietri (1988) 143, Zarini (2002), Hernández Lobato (2010) 298.

The poem reaches out to the senses: first the eyes, then hearing, both important for celebrating mass; Hernández Lobato (2012) 493–518. It thus creates the impression of an artificial place of leisure (*locus amoenus*). At the same time, the description of the church alludes to the garden of Eden and Heavenly Jerusalem in John's *Apocalypse*, for example *Apoc.* 21.21 *et platea civitatis aurum mundum, tamquam vitrum perlucidum* ('and the street of the city was of pure gold like translucent glass'); Hecquet-Noti (2013) 227–31, Onorato (2020a) 77–8.

vv. 1–2 Quisquis pontificis patrisque nostri | conlaudas Patientis hic laborem: The inscription begins with an indefinite pronoun (*quisquis*) and an address to the reader in the second-person singular (*conlaudas*), a widely attested form; see for example *CE* 429.1, 876.1, 1205.1, 1592.1; Delhey (1993) 63, Santelia (2007) 308, Hernández Lobato (2010) 301–2. The address to the reader is explicitly open and repeated with *omnibus* v. 29 and *omnes* v. 30. As stated by Egelhaaf-Gaiser (2014) 379, the basilica is a place for all believers, not just the wealthy. The verb *conlaudo*, 'to praise or commend very much', 'extol highly', is attested from Naevius onwards, appearing frequently in Plautus, Terence and Cicero. By Christian writers it is used to praise God (*TLL* 3, 1580.78–82.43). For the biography of Patiens, here paraphrased with an alliteration as *pater* and *pontifex*, see the commentary on *Ep.* 2.10.2 *Ecclesia nuper ... papae Patientis....* For Sidonius' phonological play with the consonants P–T–S, for Patiens' name, see Hernández Lobato (2010) 302, Hernández Lobato (2012) 502–3.

vv. 3–4 voti compote supplicatione | concessum experiare quod rogabis: The church is described as a place where the wishes of the faithful are fulfilled in exchange for their praise of bishop Patiens' church. The expression *compos voti*, 'having obtained or gratified one's wish', is also found in other inscriptions, for example *CE* 2035.4; Santelia (2007) 309. *Supplicatio*, 'the offering of propitiation to a deity' (*OLD* 1882), is used in classical texts of Roman gods, for example Liv. 10.23.1, and here transferred to the Christian God.

vv. 5–7 Aedes celsa nitet nec in sinistrum | aut dextrum trahitur, sed arce frontis | ortum prospicit aequinoctialem: With *aedes celsa nitet* Sidonius announces the major point of interest in his description of the cathedral: the abundance of light and its splendour (for possible intertexts, see the general remarks on vv. 11–15 and the introduction to the letter). As above section 2.10.3, the church is called an *aedes*, 'sanctuary', 'temple' (*TLL* 1, 911.51–13.81), in the spelling *aedes* in the manuscripts N²MCT and as *aedis* in LN¹; see also Sidon. *Ep.* 4.18.5 v. 12. With the adjective *celsus* (in v. 5 and in v. 17 *superbus*), Sidonius emphasises its height, as he similarly does in describing his own baths with their high conical roof (see *Ep.* 2.2.5) and the villa of Pontius Leontius in *Carm.* 22.4 vv. 115–19; Delhey (1993) 127. The adjective is also used in Mart. 4.64.9–10 to denote the height of Julius Martialis' villa, an important intertext for the whole poem: *puris leniter admoventur astris | celsae culmina delicata villae* ('rising gently to the clear stars are the delicate rooftops of a lofty villa'), see Onorato (2020a) 89 and the commentary below on vv. 22–30: General remarks. The verb *niteo*, 'to shine', 'look bright', 'glitter', 'glisten' (see the commentary on *Ep.* 2.2.11 *In hac stibadium et nitens abacus*), is also used of a building in Plaut. *Ps.* 161. See also Ennod. *Carm.* 2.10.2 *si niteant crustis aut domini merito* ('if they glitter because of their mosaics or the merit of their owner'). With the third-person singular *nitet* Sidonius personifies the church and its parts (*prospicit* v. 7, *erret* v. 10, *percurrit* v. 12, *flectit* v. 15, *vestit* v. 21), concealing at the same time human agency and use of the building; Hecquet-Noti (2013) 227, Schwitter (2015) 158. With *nitore* in v. 11 (see the commentary there) Sidonius repeats the importance of light and splendour. For the close connection in ancient literature between marble, light and radiance, see Herbert de la Portbarré-Viard (2016) 291, who refers to Sen. *Ben.* 4.6.2, Plin. *Nat.* 2.207. Sidonius highlights the church's perfect alignment, without any deviation to the left or right (*nec in sinistrum aut dextrum trahitur*); Reynaud (1998) 45, Santelia (2007) 309. Köhler (2014) 63 interprets the passage as meaning that the church has no transept. *Arx* is poetically used for 'height', 'summit', 'pinnacle' (of buildings or things in general) (*TLL* 1, 742.24–31). For a metaphorical use of the term, see the commentary on *Ep.* 2.4.1 *ita demum sibi ... ad arcem fastigatissimae felicitatis evectus....* As *arce frontis* can denote the east or west façade, it is not clear whether Patiens' church was oriented to the east or west; Coville (1928) 450 n. 1. It is possible that the pre-existing church was re-oriented when bishop Patiens had it renovated or rebuilt (i.e. after the renovation the entrance and front were at the west end and the apse and the altar at the east), a common practice from the fourth century onwards; Reynaud (1998) 45, Wallraff (2004) 118–19. This would explain Sidonius' focus on the east: *ortum aequinoctialem* is a technical expression denoting the point where the sun rises on only two days of the year, the equinoxes, and so the exact east (see Sen. *Nat.* 5.16.1). Here it stands for the east, in the Christian faith the part of the world towards which later churches were usually oriented, while the apses and altars of some of the earliest and most famous churches looked towards the west; see Paul. Nol. *Ep.* 32.13 *prospectus basilicae non, ut usitatior mos est, orientem spectat* ('the front of the church does not face the east, as is more common'), Ven. Fort. *Carm.* 2.10.13–16; Guericke (1817) 124, Voelkl (1949) 163–4, Podossinov (1991) 277–82, Wallraff (2004) 115–16, Di Salvo (2005) 139, Richter (2009) 12–16, Schwitter (2015) 158. For *prospicere* or *prospectare* in an architectural context, see the commentary on *Ep.* 2.2.10 *quae, quia nihil ipsa prospectat ...* and in combination with the orientation of a building Sidon. *Carm.* 22.4 v. 154–5, Stat. *Silv.* 2.2.45–6 *haec domus ortus | aspicit et Phoebi tenerum iubar* ('this house faces sunrise and the soft radiance of Phoebus'). The adjective *aequinoctialis* in combination with *(ex)ortus* also occurs elsewhere, for example in Sen. *Nat.* 5.16.3, Apul. *Mund.* 13, several times in Plin. *Nat.* (see *TLL* 1, 1009.53–69) and in reference to a building on an estate in Varro *Rust.* 1.12.1. In poetry, though, the adjective appears only here and in Catull. 46.2; Santelia (2007) 309, Hecquet-Noti (2013) 223, Onorato (2016) 386 n. 326.

vv. 8–9 Intus lux micat atque bratteatum | sol sic sollicitatur ad lacunar: For the important subject of light in the description of the church, see the general remarks on vv. 11–5 and the introduction to the letter. The expression *lux micat* is used from Sil. 17.477 onwards, both in literary texts and in Christian inscriptions (see for example *CE* 1448, *ILCV* 1784); Santelia (2007) 309–10. An important intertext is Prud. *Psych.* 851 *distincta micant* ('they sparkle conspicuously'); see the general remarks on vv. 11–15 and the commentary below on v. 11 and *distinctum*. For *mico*, see the commentary on *Ep.* 2.10.4 *Quapropter illorum iustius epigrammata micant*.... See also Santelia (2002) 77–8 on *Carm*. 24.19, where the late Saint Julian's influence is described with the words *vivens e tumulo micat potestas* ('his power shines alive out of his grave'). We find the same praise of light in a secular context, in Sidonius' description of his bathhouse; see the commentary on *Ep.* 2.2.4 *Intra conclave succensum* .... While Sidonius, in describing his bathhouse, emphasises its simplicity, here and in verses 11–15 he concentrates on the precious materials the church is made of. Sidonius uses *bratteatus*, 'covered with gold plate', 'gilt' (*TLL* 2, 2167.18–26), to describe the ceiling. This rarely used adjective (see Sen. *Ep.* 41.6, 115.9, Mart. Cap. 1.75) derives from *brattea* and is also found in Sidon. *Ep.* 8.8.3 (*gestatorias bratteatas*, 'gilded sedan chairs'). It probably refers to the vault over the apse, which regularly contained mosaic decorations; Anderson (1936) 465 n 3. Prudentius' description of the basilica di San Paolo fuori le Mura in Rome is an important intertext for Sidonius (see the commentaries on v. 10 and vv. 11–15), which also focuses on the gold plate and the light in the church, see especially Prud. *Perist.* 12.49–50 *bratteolas trabibus sublevit, ut omnis aurulenta | lux esset intus, ceu iubar sub ortu* ('he clothed the beams with gold leaf so as to make all the light within golden like the sun's radiance at its rising'); Di Salvo (2005) 139, Santelia (2007) 317. Herbert de la Portbarré-Viard (2014) 388 suggests that Sidonius had seen this church during his stay in Rome in the years 467/8 (see *Ep.* 1.5.9) and transferred his memories to the description of Patiens' church in Lyon, assuming it was really written after Sidonius' visit to Rome. The verb *sollicito*, 'stir', 'agitate', 'move', 'attract' (*OLD* 1785), with the triple alliteration and the repetition of *s-* (*sol sic sollicitatur*), implies the movement of the sunlight (see Hernández Lobato 2012, 505), which is also highlighted in similar descriptions of churches, for example in Prud. *Perist.* 12.42, Paul. Nol. *Carm.* 27.387–8, Ven. Fort. *Carm.* 2.10.13–6, 3.7.37–44. See also Paul. Nol. *Carm.* 28.28–30, where he praises the light in the basilica di San Felice and the commentary v. 10 on *erret*. Obviously, the sunrays reflected by the golden ceiling evoke the presence of God and prefigure Paradise; Roberts (1989) 72–3, Di Salvo (2005) 139, Santelia (2007) 316, Hernández Lobato (2010) 303–4, Hecquet-Noti (2013) 222–7, Herbert de la Portbarré-Viard (2016) 291–2. Hernández Lobato (2012) 504 refers to the doctrinal image of the Church of Christ as the seat and guardian of the one true *lux mundi* as described in Vulg. *Ioh.* 8.12. Onorato (2020a) 87 n. 53 suggests that Sidonius at the same time develops a topos of Late Antique ekphrasis of sacred buildings. While it is usually the eyes of the observer that are attracted by an architectural detail, here it is the sun that is fascinated by the magnificent ceiling. The term *lacunar* here probably refers to the semi-dome over the apse, which often was decorated with mosaics; Anderson (1936) 465 n. 3. For *lacunar*, 'the wainscoted ceiling', see the commentary on *Ep.* 2.2.5 *ut suspicientum visui fabrefactum lacunar aperiret.*

v. 10 fulvo ut concolor erret in metallo: The periphrasis *fulvo* ... *metallo* for 'gold' is attested from Sen. *Ag.* 857–8 onwards (see *TLL* 6.1, 1534.51–4) and also found in Sidon. *Carm.* 11.98, 22.4 v. 147, Claud. *Epith.* 10.57, Ennod. *Dict.* 10.13; Delhey (1993) 141, Di Salvo (2005) 139, Santelia (2007) 310. Prud. *Perist.* 12.51, an intertext for Sidonius' *Carm.* 27, also uses this adjective: *subdidit et Parias fulvis laquearibus columnas* ('he erected Parian columns to support the golden ceiling'). *Concolor*, 'of the same colour' (*TLL* 4, 81.5–6), here meaning 'golden', is a classical adjective, for example Verg. *Aen.* 8.82 and Ov. *Met.* 11.500, and frequently used later on. It also occurs in Sidon. *Ep.* 4.20.1, 7.7.3, 7.17.1, 8.9.5 v. 33, *Carm.* 2.334, 5.400, 10.6, 11.106, 22.4 v. 73, Stat. *Silv.* 1.2.149, 4.7.16, Auson. *Mos.* 74; Gualandri (1979) 42 n. 27, Delhey (1993) 102. For the preoccupation of Late Antique literary aesthetics with colour, see Roberts (1989) 66–79. Like the verb *sollicitatur* in v. 9, *erret* in v. 10 also hints at the motion of the sunlight. Despite the description of a static object, verbs of movement dominate the scene; Schwitter (2015) 159.

vv. 11–15: General remarks
In the description of his bathhouse Sidonius makes apologies for the use of precious marble, but here he describes it with unrestrained admiration. Herbert de la Portbarré-Viard (2016) analyses the importance of marble for Christian buildings and suggests that marble had both material and spiritual value. Herbert de la Portbarré-Viard (2016) 292–5 also looks into the Late Antique critique of luxurious material in Christian buildings and compares the passage here with Sidon. *Ep.* 4.18.5 vv. 15–16, where Sidonius writes about the interior of the church Saint Martin De Tours.

There are several intertextual references, which were probably recognised and appreciated by Hesperius, whose intellect and literary interests Sidonius praises at the beginning of the letter; see the commentary on *Ep.* 2.10.1 *Amo in te quod litteras amas*. The parallels to Prudentius here and in earlier poems are particularly striking (for example *Carm.* 11; see Onorato 2020), see Prud. *Perist.* 12.49–54, especially vv. 53–4, where the interior of the basilica San Paolo fuori le Mura in Rome is described with similar images (see the commentary above on vv. 8–9): *tum camiros hyalo insigni varie cucurrit arcus: | sic prata vernis floribus renident* ('then he covered the curves of the arches with splendid glass of different hues, like meadows that shine with spring flowers'). See also Prud. *Perist.* 3.198–200, on the basilica of Saint Eulalia (in present-day Mérida, Spain): *saxaque caesa solum variant | floribus ut rosulenta putes | prata rubescere multimodis* ('and cut stones vary the floor so that you think meadows abounding in roses are red with various flowers'). Onorato (2020a) 76, 86–9 highlights the parallels to Prudentius' ekphrasis of the temple of Sapientia, which is modelled on King Solomon's temple in Jerusalem; see Prud. *Psych.* 823–87, and especially the section on the gems (vv. 851–65). There are also parallels to Paul. Nol. *Ep.* 32.10, on the decoration of the apse in the new basilica for Saint Felix in Nola: *absidem solo et parietibus marmoratam camera musivo inlusa clarificat* ('the apse, which is covered with marble on the floor and on the walls, gets its light from a vault which is adorned with mosaics'; see the introduction to this letter), to Ennod. *Carm.* 2.10 (cited in the commentary on vv. 5–7, 13 and 14–15) and to Greg. Tur. *Hist. Franc.* 2.16 *parietes ad altarium opere sarsurio ex multa marmorum genera exornatos habet* ('the walls in the chancel are adorned with mosaics put together from various types of marble'). In Sidonius' description of bishop Patiens' church there are also parallels to poems describing paradise, with its green or multi-coloured meadows, such as Prud. *Cath.* 3.101–5, *Perist.* 12.53–4 (cited in the commentary above, on v. 10). For these intertextual references, see Roberts (1989), Di Salvo (2005) 140, Santelia (2007) 310, 316–17, Robert (2011) 388, Hernández Lobato (2012) 507–9, Hecquet-Noti (2013) 224–5, Herbert de la Portbarré-Viard (2014) 383, Herbert de la Portbarré-Viard (2016) 289 and the commentary above on vv. 8–9.

In *Carm.* 27 we find Christian and biblical references, but also echoes of classical pagan texts. A probable intertext is Stat. *Silv.* 2.2.90–1, about the villa of Pollius Felix, where Statius praises its various marbles: *hic et Amyclaei caesum de monte Lycurgi | quod viret et molles imitatur rupibus herbas* ('here too marble is quarried from Amyclean Lycurgus' mountain, which is green and with its rocks mimics soft grass'). See also Stat. *Silv.* 1.3.52–3, 1.5.34–50, 2.2.42–3, 4.2.30–31 for impressive buildings made of precious materials. For Statius' architectural descriptions, see Kreuz (2016). There are also parallels to the descriptions of the temple of Apollo Palatinus (see Prop. 2.31; Egelhaaf-Gaiser 2014, 385) and to the palace of Venus (see Claud. *Epith.* 85–96; Schwitter 2015, 161). Another important intertext is Martial's poem 4.64, about the Janiculum villa of his patron Julius Martialis; see the commentary below on vv. 22–30: General remarks. The magnificent decoration of the church is not only to show its wealth, but also to grant hospitality to the faithful; Onorato (2020a) 89.

To describe the church's precious interior, Sidonius uses Grecisms and rare or newly coined words, which adds to the elevated tone of the poem. His description of its location and its architecture is very vague, as he does not aim to give a precise description of its interior, but to depict the church's wealth while creating a spiritual atmosphere and praising God's power.

vv. 11–12 Distinctum vario nitore marmor | percurrit cameram solum fenestras: Sidonius begins verse 11 with the participle *distinctum*, thus recalling the intertext Prud. *Psych.* 851 *discincta micant* ('they sparkle conspicuously'); see the commentary on vv. 11–15: General remarks and the commentary above on v. 8 and *micat*. The expression is also reminiscent of Seneca's famous description of private baths in Sen. *Ep.* 86.6 *nisi Alexandrina marmora Numidicis crustis distincta sunt* ('unless marble from Alexandria is framed with marble from Numidia'). See also Stat. *Silv.* 1.5.40–1 in a similar context about marble: *viridis cum regula longo | Synnada distinctu variat* ('when a green streak [of Spartan marble] varies the Synnadian marble in an extended contrast'). Without restraint, but also without further detail, Sidonius describes the splendour of the marble used for the legitimate goal of praising God; see also Paul. Nol. *Ep.* 32.10 (cited above in the commentary on vv. 11–15: General remarks, p. 318); Bedon (2004) 375, Herbert de la Portbarré-Viard (2016) 290. On the use of marble in private buildings, see the commentary on *Ep.* 2.2.7 *Iam, si marmora inquiras, non illic quidem*. For *nitor*, 'brightness', 'splendor', 'lustre' of the marble, see Lucr. 5.783 *viridemque nitorem* ('and the green splendor') and the commentary above on v. 5 and *nitet*. The combination of *vario nitore ... percurrit* recalls Prud. *Psych.* 856 *nitor medius variabat* ('and the lustre between them varied') and *Perist.* 12.53, cited above in the commentary on vv. 11–15: General remarks. In his description of the church's ceiling, Sidonius combines *lacunar*, 'a wainscoted and gilded ceiling, panel-ceiling, ceiled roof' (see the commentary above on v. 9), and *camera*, 'vault', 'arched roof', 'arch'. The two terms are also combined in *Ep.* 2.2.5 in the description of Sidonius' bathhouse; see the commentary on *Ep.* 2.2.5 *ut suspicientum visui fabrefactum lacunar aperiret*. The dynamism of the scene (*percurrit*) is enhanced by the asyndeton *cameram solum fenestras*; Schwitter (2015) 159. For the description of a *solum*, 'floor', made of marble, see Auson. *Mos.* 48–9 *I nunc et Phrygiis sola levia consere crustis | tendens marmoreum laqueata per atria campum* ('go now and cover the light ground with Phrygian plates by extending a field of marble through the panelled halls'), Luc. 10.114–16 *nec summis crustata domus sectisque nitebat | marmoribus, stabatque sibi non segnis achates | purpureusque lapis, totaque effusus in aula | calcatur onyx* ('The building shone with varieties of marble that were cut into thin slabs; agate and porphyry were found there as ornaments. In the whole hall one stepped on laid out onyx plates').

v. 13 ac sub versicoloribus figuris: The adjective *versicolor*, 'having colours that change' (*OLD* 2039), either means that the marble changes its colours depending on the light in the church or that there are different colours in it. Probably both notions are evoked in connection here; see Plin. *Nat.* 36.44 and 46; André (1949) 231, Herbert de la Portbarré-Viard (2014) 385, Herbert de la Portbarré-Viard (2016) 290–1. The term *figura* here denotes the 'single figures, persons or patterns of the whole picture or mosaic' (*TLL* 6.1, 728.42–9.27); see Sidon. *Carm.* 22.4 v. 203; Delhey (1993) 181. It is used similarly of a woven representation in Claud. *Rapt.* 2.43. The combination of *versicolor* and *figura* is found elsewhere only in Lact. *Div. Inst.* 1.11.36 *sed ut figuris versicoloribus venustatem ac leporem carminibus suis addant* ('but to add charm and pleasure to their poems with the coloured figures'). Santelia (2007) 311 interprets the figures as biblical images and refers to contemporary texts about the educational value of pictures in churches (Paul. Nol. *Carm.* 27.580–86, Greg. Tur. *Hist. Franc.* 2.17). Di Salvo (2005) 140 interprets the expression as a possible reference to a zone above the mosaic (*crusta*, v. 14) with a series of paintings. See Herbert de la Portbarré-Viard (2014) 384–6 for a detailed analysis of the expression *sub versicoloribus figuris* and its various suggested translations. For the figurative programme of pictures in apses from the fourth to the eighth century, see Ihm (1992). See also Ennod. *Carm.* 2.10.5–6 (see the commentary on vv. 11–15: General remarks), who uses the term *figura* in the context of a mosaic: *fallat opus tamen arte, regat natura figuras, | viscera dum lapidum fingit imaginibus* ('let the work, however, deceive with its art and let nature guide the figures while imitating the inner parts with images of stones').

vv. 14–15 vernans herbida crusta sapphiratos | flectit per prasinum vitrum lapillos: Verses 14–15 abound in words indicating different shades of green and blue, closely associated through their assonances on *-i* and *-a*. The different elements are united in a *crusta*, 'mosaic work'; see the commentary on *Ep.* 2.2.7 *Paros, Carystos … rupium variatarum posuere crustas* and Plin. *Nat.* 35.2–3 on the use of various types of marble in a mosaic. Hernández Lobato (2010) 304–5 refers to the church of Sant' Apollinare in Classe in

Ravenna as an example of mosaic work with vividly coloured figures on a green background. Sidonius uses various rarely used terms for 'green', but not the most common, *viridis*. Based on the adjectives denoting the colours it is not possible to determine the kind of stones which are used to adorn the church. *Vernans* is the participle of *verno*, 'to carry on or undergo the process proper to spring' (*OLD* 2038). It usually refers to plants and here denotes a vernal, light green. It is also used of marble in Sidon. *Carm.* 22.4 v. 139 *et herbosis quae vernant marmora venis* ('and the marble that blooms with grass-green veins') – see Delhey (1993) 137 – and Prud. *Perist.* 12.54 *vernis floribus* (an important intertext for the whole passage, cited above in the commentary vv. 11–15: General remarks, p. 318). In Late Antiquity, *verno* is also a *terminus technicus* for rhetorical ornament and thus a reference on Sidonius' way of writing; Gualandri (1979) 77–8, Roberts (1989) 51, Schwitter (2015) 158. The adjective *herbidus* means 'green like grass', grass-colored' (*TLL* 6.3, 2625.16–23); André (1949) 189. A related adjective used by Sidonius is *herbosus*; see the commentary on *Ep.* 2.2.18 *Lacus ipse ... herbosus aequalis*. In connection with *lux*, the adjective *herbidus* also appears in Prud. *Psych.* 862–3, an important intertext of the whole passage: *smaragdina gramine verno* | *prata virent, volvitque vagos lux herbida fluctus* ('emerald meadows are green with their spring grass and the grass-coloured light spreads out in wandering waves'); see the general remarks on vv. 11–15. For the comparison of marble and herbs, see also the passages in Stat. *Silv.* 2.2.91 cited above in the commentary on vv. 11–15: General remarks, p. 318, an intertext for the whole passage, and Ennod. *Carm.* 2.10.3–4 (see the commentary on vv. 11–15: General remarks) *herbida pasturam simulantia saxa virentem* | *inliciant oculos nobiliore dolo* ('the grass-coloured stones imitate a blooming pasture and entice the eyes with a more noble fraud'). Sidonius uses the motif of grass-like marble in different works, such as Sidon. *Carm.* 5.38–9 *post caute Laconum* | *marmoris herbosi radians interviret ordo* ('after these there was green, radiant row inbetween with the Laconian grass-hued marble') and *Carm.* 22.4 v. 139 (cited above on *vernans*); Bedon (2004) 377. For *crusta*, 'mosaic work', see the commentary on *Ep.* 2.2.7 *Paros, Carystos ... rupium variatarum posuere crustas* and above on vv. 11–15: General remarks. *Sapphiratus*, 'adorned or set with sapphires', that is, a blue colour, is a Sidonian hapax, derived from *sapp(h)irus*, 'a blue gem, prob. lapis lazuli' (*OLD* 1691). It is coined in analogy to the Greek σαπφειρωτός; see Plin. *Nat.* 33.68, 36.198, 37.120, Prud. *Psych.* 855; Gualandri (1979) 159 n. 52, Di Salvo (2005) 140, Santelia (2007) 311, Onorato (2016) 300–1, Herbert de la Portbarré-Viard (2016) 286. The verb *flecto*, 'to bend', 'bow', 'curve'

(*TLL* 6.1, 891.64–8.23), here denotes the technique of creating a mosaic. It recalls the other verbs of movement in the poem; see the commentaries on *erret* (v. 10) and *percurrit* (v. 12). *Prasinus*, from Greek πράσινος, 'leek-green' (*TLL* 10.2, 1129.46–77), is attested from the first century AD onwards and attributed to various objects, including stones and jewels; see Plin. *Nat*. 37.181. *Prasinus* is also used three times in Petron. 27.2, 64.6, 70.13 to denote a piece of exotically coloured clothing (see Petron. 70.10 *prasinianus*, 'of the leek-green party of charioteers in the circus', and Petron. 28.8 *prasinatus*, 'wearing a leek-green garment'), and see also Mart. 3.82.11, 10.29.4. The term also appears in Tert. *De spect*. 9.5, where it indicates one of the colours worn by the charioteers in races. For the various meanings of the colour *prasinus*, see André (1949) 192, 233, Pociña (1985) 120–2. It is not certain whether *prasinum vitrum* refers to the windows of the church or to small pieces of glass which are part of the marble mosaic applied to the walls or to the floor. For the first interpretation, the prevailing one, see Loyen (1970a) 70 'sur toute la surface des vitraux verts', Anderson (1936) 467 'over the leek-green glass', Dalton (1915) 55 'through the ground of verdant glass'; Santelia (2007) 308 'su vetrate verdi', Schwitter (2015) 158 'in den lauchgrünen Fensterscheiben'. Dell'Acqua (2003) 29 also links the expression to the windows: 'delle finestre ornate con figure dai colori cangianti su fondo verde'. Köhler (2014) 63, 'grünend durch die glasierten Steinchen', and Onorato (2016) 301, 'tessere rivestite di paste vitree, che imitano gli zaffiri', interpret the expression as denoting a wall mosaic containing pieces of green glass. Herbert de la Portbarré-Viard (2014) 387, who refers to Sidon. *Carm*. 2.418–9 (cited above in the commentary on *Ep*. 2.2.7 *Paros, Carystos ... posuere crustas*) and analyses the expression at length, suggests two different interpretations: a veneer made of glass ('un placage qui pourrait être en pâte de verre') or a wall mosaic consisting of a glass background and inserted gemstones ('une mosaïque pariétale en pâte de verre, insérée à l'intérieur de l'*herbida crusta* ... dans laquelle seraient incrustés à leur tour les *lapillos sapphiratos*'). She ultimately translates the expression as 'à la surface du verre couleur poireau'.

vv. 16–19 Huic est porticus applicata triplex | fulmentis Aquitanicis superba, | ad cuius specimen remotiora | claudunt atria porticus secundae: After the interior of the church, Sidonius describes other buildings connected to it. He mentions two similar-looking porticos (*porticus*) and a forecourt/atrium (confusingly referred to with the plural *atria* – see below) which are attached to the church, but whose exact position remains unclear.

Coville (1928) 450 thinks that both porticos are in front of the main entrance at the west end of the cathedral, with a court in between ('À l'entrée était un porche à trois arcades en marbre d'Aquitaine; un second porche, dans la perspective du premier, précédait un *atrium* qui se développait en profondeur'). Hecquet-Noti (2013) 221 n. 285, however, interprets the portico described in v. 16 as a lateral attachment which leads to other clerical buildings, perhaps the episcopal palace or the baptistery. Köhler (2014) 63 thinks that a portico is built at both the east and west of the basilica as a three-sided extension in the form of a cloister, the fourth side being formed by the basilica. Anderson (1936) 466 n. 1 interprets the *porticus* as cloisters in front of the atrium. Paul. Nol. *Ep.* 32.10 also uses the term *porticus* to describe the arcade of the nave within the church; Elsner (1998) 255. In *Ep.* 5.17.3 Sidonius refers to the adjacent building of Patiens' church as *cryptoporticus*: *populus... quem capacissima basilica non caperet quamlibet cincta diffusis cryptoporticibus* ('a congregation too great for the very spacious church to contain, even with the expanse of covered porticoes which surrounded it'); see the commentary on *Ep.* 2.2.10 *quae ... saltim 'cryptoporticus'*.... For *porticus* as part of the Roman villa, see the commentary on *Ep.* 2.2.10 *Ab ortu lacum porticus intuetur*. The adjective *triplex*, 'triple', 'threefold' (*OLD* 1976), here denotes the three rows of columns the portico consists of; Anderson (1936) 466 n. 1. For *triplex*, see the commentary on *Ep.* 2.2.8 *triplex medii parietis aditus*.... With *fulmentis Aquitanicis* Sidonius refers to the columns made from Aquitanian marble (black with white veins), cut out of the mountains of the Pyrenees, probably in the quarries of Saint-Béat; Bedon (2004) 370, 372. The expression is also attested in the *Liber Pontificialis* (48.4), which describes the buildings of pope Hilarius (461–8): *nympheum et triporticum ante oratorium sanctae Crucis ... undique ornatum ex musibo et columnis aquitanicis et tripolitis et purphyreticis* ('a nymphaeum and threefold portico in front of the oratory of the Holy Cross ... it was adorned all around with mosaics and with columns from Aquitania and Tripolis and of porphyry'); Sirmond (1614) 54, Di Salvo (2005) 140, Santelia (2007) 311–12, Delbrueck (2007) XV. The term *fulmentum* denotes 'a prop', 'support' (*TLL* 6.1, 1530.84–31.25) in general (see Vitr. 5.1.9). To describe a basilica it is also used in Alc. Avit. *Hom.* 24, p. 142.30 *intercurrentibus ... fulmentis* ('with columns in between'). With the exception of Pliny the Elder (for example Plin. *Nat.* 31.4), the adjective *Aquitanicus*, 'Aquitanian' (*TLL* 2, 380.13–24), is used only by Late Antique authors, for example (as a noun) in Auson. *Mos.* 442, Symm. *Ep.* 9.44. For the use of different marbles and columns made of marble, see the commentary on *Ep.* 2.2.7 *Paros, Carystos ... posuere crustas* and Sidon. *Carm.*

22.4 vv. 135–6 *balnea ... fulta columnis* ('the baths, supported by columns'). The adjective *superbus* is used of buildings or their interior furnishings in the sense of 'grand', 'proud', 'sumptuous' (*OLD* 1874, 4a); see for example Catull. 64.85. It recalls the beginning of the poem; see the commentary on v. 5 and *celsa*. *Specimen*, a 'pattern', 'model', 'example' (*OLD* 1800, 2), is a favourite word with Cicero, for example Cic. *Tusc.* 5.55. Sidonius uses it to denote the second *porticus*, which is further away and closely resembles the first one. The manuscripts CN^2M^2, Lütjohann (1887) 34, Anderson (1936) 466, and Loyen (1970a) 70 have *remotiora*, LNM have *remotiores*. The verb *claudunt* here stands for *circumcludunt* (*simplex pro composito*); it is used in a military context also in Sidon. *Carm.* 22.4 v. 164; Delhey (1993) 154. *Atria*, 'hall', 'court', is here probably a poetic plural; see also Sidon. *Carm.* 22.4 v. 157, Claud. *Epith.* 10.85; Förtsch (1993) 30–41, Delhey (1993) 150, Picard (1998) 113 n. 20. As part of a church, the atrium (an architectural term) usually denotes the court in front of the main entrance, framed by porticos on at least three sides; Picard (1998) 107. See Paul. Nol. *Carm.* 27.378 and 485 on the *atrium* as part of the basilica of Saint Felix in Cimitile, and Paul. Nol. *Carm.* 28.9; Picard (1998) 112, 138, 140, 142, Santelia (2007) 312.

vv. 20–1 et campum medium procul locatas | vestit saxea silva per columnas: Only Sidonius (also in *Ep.* 2.2.3 – see the commentary on *Ep.* 2.2.3 *Sed donec domicilio competens vestibuli campus aperitur*) and Auson. *Mos.* 49 use the word *campus* to denote a part of a building or a place to build a house, that is, an artificially created space (*TLL* 3, 215.33–40); Green (1991) 470. The word adds to the whole picture of the church as *locus amoenus* of natural beauty and paradise on earth, as does the following *silva*; Hernández Lobato (2010) 305. *Campum medium* denotes the nave of the church; see the translations of Dalton (1915) 55 'and the mid-space is flanked afar by columns numerous as forest stems', Anderson (1936) 467 'a stone forest clothes the middle area (i.e. the nave)', Loyen (1970a) 70 'une forêt de pierre entoure la nef centrale', Köhler (2014) 63 'in der Mitte enspriesst ein Wald aus Steinen' (and in the footnote: 'Nach allgemeiner Auffassung ist damit das Kirchenschiff gemeint, das von den beiden Atrien eingeschlossen ist'). For *vestire*, 'to cover', 'clothe' (*OLD* 2049, 2c), see Sidon. *Ep.* 1.5.4, Cic. *Verr.* 2.4.55, Plin. *Ep.* 2.17.15, 8.8.4, Ov. *Fast.* 1.402, Claud. *Rapt.* 1.190, 3.231; Gualandri (1979) 53. *Saxeus*, 'made of stones', is used here in the literal sense; for its transferred meaning, see the commentary on *Ep.* 2.8.2 *si quid secus, sufficit saxo carmen saxeum contineri*. *Silva*, 'forest', is frequently used as a metaphor for a group of densely packed objects (*OLD*

1762, 4); Delhey (1993) 184. See for example the description of a dining room in Pontius Leontius' Burgus in Sidon. *Carm.* 22.4 v. 206 *saxea silva* ('a forest of stone'), Stat. *Theb.* 4.220–1 *ferrea ... silva* ('a forest of iron'), 5.533 *harundineam ... silvam* ('a forest of reeds'). Hecquet-Noti (2013) 226 also suggests a reference to the Temple of Solomon, *domus silvae Libani* ('the house of the Lebanon forest') in 1 Reg. 10.17 as well as to Psalm 131.6–8 *campis sylvae* ('in the fields of the forest').

vv. 22–30: General remarks
The following verses describe the position of the church between two traffic arteries: a street used by pedestrians and carriages, and the River Saône, navigable to tow boats and rowing boats. Having described the interior of the church and the buildings attached to it, Sidonius now describes its surroundings and the noisy visitors and passers-by. The transition from the static description of the church to its surroundings is marked by a change of focus, from the visual to the acoustic; Egelhaaf-Gaier (2014) 380–2. The church is not only a place for the educated elite, but for everybody on his or her way to heaven, accentuated with *omnibus* in v. 29 and *omnes* in v. 30; van Waarden (2011) 103. At the same time, several intertextual references aim at the exclusive circle of addressees, who, like Sidonius and Patiens, are committed to education; Egelhaaf-Gaiser (2014) 382. Verses 23–7 closely echo Mart. 4.64.18–22 with the rarely used words *essedum, helciarius* and *celeuma*; see the commentaries below for details. Sidonius transfers Martial's praise of the estate of his friend Julius Martialis into his poem to describe the hustle and bustle around the church. The very noises that are excluded from the estate of Julius Martialis on the Janiculum are part of the praise of God in Sidonius' poem; see Mart. 4.64.18–22 *illinc Flaminiae Salariaeque | gestator patet essedo tacente, | ne blando rota sit molesta somno, | quem nec rumpere nauticum celeuma | nec clamor valet helciariorum* ('from the other side on the via Flaminia and Salaria the traveller can be seen, but the vehicle is not heard and no wheel troubles the gentle slumber, which also cannot be disturbed by the song of the sailors nor by the cries of the men who draw the vessels upstream'). While Martial is content that external human sounds do not reach the villa of Julius Martialis, Sidonius shows how they echo within the church and blend with the hymns to God. Unlike Julius Martialis' villa, Patiens' church profits from its vicinity to the traffic in the street and on the river; Egelhaaf-Gaiser (2014) 383. The allusion to Martial in Sidonius' description of Patiens' church has been much commented on; see Colton (1976) 12–13, Gualandri (1979) 85–6, Baker (1996) 40–1, Fabbrini (2007)

26–7, Santelia (2007) 313, Hecquet-Noti (2013) 230–1, Wolff (2014a) 297, Wolff (2014c) 213, Consolino (2015) 74, Consolino (2020) 362, Onorato (2016) 176 n. 22, Onorato (2020a) 88–9. In *Carm.* 24.83 Sidonius alludes to the same epigram, Mart. 4.64.28; Consolino (2015) 74. For the seemingly inappropriate quotation of Martial in a serious context, see the Introduction to this volume, pp. xviii–xix, and the introduction to *Ep.* 2.8.

Another important intertext is Auson. *Mos.* 163–8, which also refers to the passers-by, the boatmen, the riverbanks and the echoes, and Hor. *Sat.* 1.5.14–17, which describes a trip to Brundisium; see the commentary on v. 28. Travelling by water instead of by road is mentioned elsewhere in Sidonius' letters: Sidon. *Ep.* 1.5.3 and 8.11.3 v. 31; Stevens (1933) 75 n. 1, Wolff (2016). With the quadruple anaphora *hinc*, by repeating syllables, with rhymes and with the parallel construction of vv. 22–5, Sidonius structures the various aspects of the church's surroundings and imitates the echoing sounds and voices; Hecquet-Noti (2013) 228. See also Plin. *Ep.* 9.39.5, about the temple of the goddess Ceres: *nam solum templi hinc flumine et abruptissimis ripis, hinc via cingitur* ('because the area of the temple is confined on the one side by the river and its very steep shore, on the other by the street'); Santelia (2007) 312. For the use of multiple *hinc*, see also Sidon. *Ep.* 2.9.4 *nam similis scientiae viri, hinc Augustinus hinc Varro, hinc Horatius hinc Prudentius lectitabantur* (for commentary and translation see there).

v. 22 Hinc agger sonat, hinc Arar resultat: For *agger*, 'the public road', see the commentary on *Ep.* 2.9.2 *Domus utraque non solum tramites aggerum publicorum*.... The River Arar, present-day Saône, is navigable from the point on where the River Dubis (Doubs) joins it and merges with the River Rhône in Lyon at this very point; Lafond (1996). The River Arar is mentioned in poetry before Sidonius, for example in Verg. *Ecl.* 1.62, Tib. 1.7.11. The lasting importance of Lyon for river transport and ship towing ('haleurs', 'batellerie halée') is noteworthy; see for example Rossiaud (1976) and the overview in <http://www.linflux.com/lyon-et-region/la-batellerie-sur-le-rhone-a-travers-les-siecles> (last accessed April 2022). Since his childhood, Sidonius could observe how ships were towed up the river and the sounds they made; see the commentary on v. 25 *curvorum hinc chorus helciariorum*. The two verbs *sonat* and *resultat* are more closely connected by the anaphora *hinc*, the alliteration on -*a* and the parallel structure of the two parts of the sentence. *Hinc* is repeated in the following v. 23; see Di Salvo (2005) 141 and the commentary on 2.9.4 *nam similis scientiae viri, hinc Augustinus hinc Varro, hinc Horatius hinc Prudentius lectitabantur*. Sidonius thus personifies nature, which also worships God. See also Stat. *Silv.* 4.3, where, on the one hand, the noise during the construction works on the Via Appia is described, and, on the other hand, the personified River Volturnus delivers a eulogy on Domitian. Combined with *resultat*, as here in v. 22, *sonat*, 'to sound', 'to make a noise', is also found in Verg. *Georg.* 4.50 and Stat. *Silv.* 1.2.223. The verb *resulto*, in a figurative sense of places or things which 'throw back a sound', 'give off an echo' (*OLD* 1639, 3b), is used more often of valleys, groves and hills than of bodies of water. The echo is also represented phonetically by echoing word pairs in the following verses (v. 25 *curvorum–helciariorum*, v. 26 *responsantibus–ripis*, v. 27 *levat–celeuma*).

v. 23 Hinc sese pedes atque eques reflectit: For *hinc* see the commentary above on v. 22. *Pedes* and *eques* are collective singulars and were originally used in a military context, for 'a foot-soldier' (*TLL* 10.1, 965.71–9.43) and a 'horse-soldier' (*TLL* 5.2, 708.32–17.54). For *pedes*, see the commentary on *Ep.* 2.9.1 *quibus interiecta gestatio peditem lassat....* Sidonius' uncommon reflexive use of the verb *reflectere*, 'to turn round' (*OLD* 1596, 2a), is translated in several ways. Sidonius describes the church's position at a bend in the street, and shows how the beauty of the church forces the passers-by on all different means of transport to turn their heads; see Dalton (1915) 55 'here turns', Anderson (1936) 467 'turn round', Loyen (1970a) 70 'qui prennent le tournant', Hernández Lobato (2010) 306 'al tomar la curva', Köhler (2014) 63 'hier verbeugt sich', Wolff (2014c) 213.

v. 24 stridentum et moderator essedorum: Verses 24 and 25 appear ponderous because of their four genitive plural forms. The noise is reproduced by the onomatopoetic verb *stridere*, 'to creak', 'squeak', 'grate' (*OLD* 1827, 1a), which is used elsewhere for vehicles, for example Ov. *Trist.* 3.10.59; see Hernández Lobato (2010) 307. Hernández Lobato (2010) 307 points out the predominance of the sounds s, t, d, r, y and m, which he interprets as an acoustic reflection of the squeaking of the carriages when taking the curve. For *stridere* in the meaning 'to hiss', see the commentary on *Ep.* 2.9.9 *quos inter halitu nebulae stridentis....* The term *moderator*, 'ruler', 'manager', 'director' (see *TLL* 8, 1209.84–10.8), is used in relation to animals and vehicles. The Celtic term *essedum* originally denoted the two-wheeled military chariot of the Celts (see Caes. *Bell. Gall.* 4.33); Hudson (2021) 181–207. It also generally stands for a 'vehicle for travel' (*TLL* 5.2, 862.9–41), for example in Cic. *Phil.* 2.58. For the notorious noisiness of the *essedum*, see Claud. *Carm. min.* 18.18 *esseda ... multisonora* ('loud-sounding vehicles'), which Sidonius probably had in mind, and Mart. 4.64.19 *essedo tacente* ('while the vehicle is silent'); see also Mart. 10.104.5–7, Sen. *Ep.* 56.4; Di Salvo (2005) 141. In the meaning of a 'vehicle of transport', the term also appears in Sidon. *Ep.* 4.18.1; Amherdt (2001) 404. See also Sidon. *Carm.* 5.229, 22.4 v. 23.

v. 25 curvorum hinc chorus helciariorum: Like v. 24, v. 25 is also framed by two forms in the genitive plural. A similar scene is described in Auson. *Mos.* 41–2 *et cum per ripas nusquam cessante remulco | intendunt collo malorum vincula nautae* ('and if on the banks – without the tow ropes getting slack – the boatsmen stretch with their necks the ropes tied to the masts of the ship'). On the noises associated with shipping, see v. 22 *Hinc agger sonat, hinc Arar resultat*. Sidonius refers to the bargemen with the adjective *curvus*, 'bent', which is also otherwise used for people who bend over their work, for example in Verg. *Ecl.* 3.42 (*arator*, 'farmer'), or more frequently because of age, for example Prop. 2.18.20 (*anus*, 'old woman') (*TLL* 4, 1549.57–50.4). Ovid also describes how the men sing as they laboriously pull their boat upstream in Ov. *Trist.* 4.1.5–8. The adjective *curvus* corresponds with *levat*, 'lift up', 'raise' (see v. 27): although the men are bent over physically, they are spiritually uplifted by the nearby church. For *hinc* see the commentary above on v. 22. The noun *helciarius*, 'one who draws small vessels up the stream' (*TLL* 6.3, 2592.34–38), appears only here and in Mart. 4.64.22, an important intertext for this poem – see vv. 22–30: General remarks. It derives from *helcium*, a 'yoke', 'horse collar'.

v. 26 responsantibus alleluia ripis: The riverbanks respond to the song of the boatmen with a hallelujah. The specific Christian response *alleluia* (*TLL* 1, 1672.63–3.18) picks up Martial's general noun *clamor*, which is used in the same verse as *helciarius* (Mart. 4.64.22); see the commentary above on v. 25. As here, the exclamatory term *alleluia* in Prud. *Cath.* 4.72 has a short -*e*-. It is attested in combination with *chorus* in Paul. Nol. *Ep.* 32.5 *hinc senior sociae congaudet turba catervae; | 'alleluia' novis balat ovile choris* ('there the older crowd rejoices with its fellow flock; in new choirs the sheepfold bleats alleluia'), and in combination with *celeuma*, 'song or chant of sailors' (see the commentary on v. 27 below) in Quodv. *Cant. Nov.* (*Serm.* 5) 2. Shores which resound from the cries of travellers and sailors are described in Auson. *Mos.* 163–8 (see especially *riparum subiecta*, 'the riverbed resound', in v. 166), one of the major intertexts of the passage. The text is cited in full below, p. 330, under v. 28 *Sic, sic psallite, nauta vel* *viator*. The combination of *responsare* and *ripae* is also found in Verg. *Aen.* 12.756–7; Di Salvo (2005) 141.

v. 27 ad Christum levat amnicum celeuma: Sidonius substitutes Martial's *nauticum celeuma* (Mart. 4.64.21, an important intertext for this poem – see vv. 22–30: General remarks) with *amnicum celeuma*. Both expressions are positioned at the end of the verse, while here the addressee, Christ, is at the beginning. The verb *levo*, 'to lift up', 'raise', 'elevate', is regularly used of voices and sounds (*TLL* 7.2, 1236.45–68). It contrasts the adjective *cursus*, 'bent', in v. 25 (see the commentary there). The adjective *amnicus*, 'of a river' (*TLL* 1, 1941.79–2.10), first appears in Plin. *Nat.* 3.148, 16.166. It does not occur very frequently, but features in some of the intertexts of this poem: see Prud. *Perist.* 7.81, Symm. *Ep.* 1.14.4, and especially Auson. *Mos.* 205. The adjective also appears in Sidon. *Ep.* 1.5.4 (*margines amnicos*, 'riverbank'). *Celeuma* is a 'boatswain's call or command to the other rowers', 'song or chant of sailors'. It is aimed at keeping them in rhythm. The term is also used in Mart. 3.67.4, 4.64.21 and (unlike the very rarely used *helciarius* in v. 25) also in other Late Antique writers, including Hier. *Ep.* 14.10, Paul. Nol. *Carm.* 17.109, Rut. Nam. 1.370, Ven. Fort. *Carm.* 8.19.6, Sulpic. *Vita Martini* 4.423, Quodv. *Cant. Nov.* (*Serm.* 5) 2; van Waarden (2011) 102–3. In *Ep.* 8.12.5 Sidonius uses *celeuma* of a song to be sung by rowers and helmsmen in praise of his friend Trygetius.

v. 28 Sic, sic psallite, nauta vel viator: *Sic, sic psallite* logically refers to the double subject *nauta* and *viator*. Phonetically it recalls v. 9 (*sol sic sol*); Hernández Lobato (2010) 307, Hernández Lobato (2012) 515. For the anaphora *sic, sic*, see Sen. *Med.* 90; Di Salvo (2005) 142. For examples of *psallere* in combination with *sic*, see *TLL* 10.2, 2397.53–6. In classical Latin, *psallere* means 'to play on the cithara' (*OLD* 1510), for example in Hor. *Carm.* 4.13.7. In ecclesiastical Latin it means 'to sing', especially 'to sing the Psalms of David' (*Blaise* 681, s.v. 3); see for example Hier. *Ep.* 107.10. Sidonius uses the term also in *Ep.* 9.16.3 v. 65 *e quibus primum mihi psallat hymnus* ('of these may he be the first theme of my hymn'), echoing Prud. *Perist.* 10.837–8; see also Sidon. *Ep.* 1.8.2, 5.14.3, *Carm.* 16.27; Squillante (2010) 253–4. Once again, in the collective singular (see v. 23), Sidonius addresses the two groups that pass the church on road and river path (see v. 22). Addressing a *nauta*, 'sailor', is an original Sidonian addition to the topos of addressing a traveller in an inscription and probably alludes to Hor. *Sat.* 1.5.15–17 ... *absentem cantat amicam | multa prolutus vappa nauta atque viator*

| *certatim* … ('and the sailor and the traveller who are wet from much vapid wine sing eagerly about their absent lover'), where a drunken sailor and traveller describe their lover; Egelhaaf-Gaiser (2014) 383–4. For Sidonius' habit of using classical texts in a new context, see the introduction to *Ep.* 2.8. The term *viator*, 'traveller', and the direct apostrophe are reminiscent of epigraphs, which frequently address their readers directly; see Sidon. *Ep.* 3.12.5 v. 3, 4.11.6 v. 22, *CE* 403.1, 1950.11, 2024.1; Santelia (2007) 313. The same combination of two ways of travelling, by foot and by ship, and the shouts of the travellers are also described in Auson. *Mos.* 163–8 *laeta operum plebes festinantesque coloni* | *vertice nunc summo properant, nunc deiuge dorso,* | *certantes stolidis clamoribus. Inde viator* | *riparum subiecta terens, hinc navita labens,* | *probra canunt seris cultoribus; adstrepit ollis* | *et rupes et silva tremens et concavus amnis* ('people, happy to work, and assiduous farmers hurry now on the highest mountain, now on the sloping ridge, and they argue with stupid cries. From here the traveller who walks on the shore below, from here the gliding sailor sing their reproach against slow farmers. For those the rock and the trembling woods and the riverbed resound').

Vv. 29–30 namque iste est locus omnibus petendus, | omnes quo via ducit ad salutem: After twenty-four verses about the architecture and topography of the church with its implicit metaphorical and spiritual meaning, Sidonius adds two verses to describe how the splendid sacred building unites all the believers (stressed with the polyptoton *omnibus–omnes*). The church is not a static place, but a doorway to heaven; see Paul. Nol. *Ep.* 32.12 *caelestes intrate vias per amoena virecta,* | *Christicolae; et laetis decet huc ingressus ab hortis,* | *unde sacrum meritis datur exitus in paradisum* ('enter the paths of heaven through these pleasant green groves, Christians: it is fitting to make an entrance from these joyous gardens to the place from where departure is granted to holy paradise to those who are worthy'); Santelia (2007) 313. Hecquet-Noti (2013) 230 refers to Catull. 46.9–11 as another intertext, where also various ways leading home are mentioned, and Hernández Lobato (2010) 308 refers to *Ps* 148 with the hallelujah and the motif of the natural elements which unify in praise of God. For *ducit*, see Tert. *Ad mart.* 2.9 *sed illam viam, quae ad Deum ducit* ('but this path which leads to God'), Sidon. *Carm.* 24.3; Santelia (2002) 65. For *salus*, 'salvation', see the commentary on *Ep.* 2.8.3 v. 12.

Section 5

Ecce parui tamquam iunior imperatis: With *ecce parui* Sidonius repeats the beginning of the letter where he introduced himself as a writer who obeys the orders of a friend (*iubes–pareo* motif), see the commentary on *Ep.* 2.10.2 *Dicto pareo...* and the introduction to this letter. While in section 2.10.4 Sidonius writes in the first-person plural (see the commentaries on *Ep.* 2.10.4 *sic nostra ... stipula vilescit* and 2.10.4 *Quapropter illorum iustius ... effingimus*), he changes back to the first person (*parui*) once the poem is delivered. He also points out that Hesperius is younger (*iunior*) and should thus obey him. For the combination with *ecce*, see Sidon. *Ep.* 7.2.10 *ecce parui* ('you see I obeyed'), 9.11.9 *ecce habes litteras* ('here you have a letter').

Tu modo fac memineris multiplicato me faenore remunerandum: Sidonius reminds Hesperius that he has to pay him back for the verses about the cathedral of Lyon by continuing his reading and writing; see for the same attitude (*do ut des*) after including a poem in a letter *Ep.* 4.18.6, 8.9.6, 9.15.1–2. Sidonius thus returns to the subject of education and learning, which he addressed in section 2.10.1 before the inserted poem. *Fac* with the subjunctive is frequently used in letters, especially in Cicero, but also in Pliny, for example Plin. *Ep.* 1.11.2; Cugusi (1983) 83. *Faenus*, 'the proceeds of capital lent out', 'interest' (*TLL* 6.1, 484.4–69), is used of various things, also in a transferred meaning. For this economical metaphor, see Sidon. *Carm.* 23.20–31 (v. 28 *blando faenore*, 'a flattering debt'), Plin. *Ep.* 9.28.5, Symm. *Ep.* 1.14.1 *qui nihil litterati faenoris credidisti* ('you who did not lend me anything of your learned capital').

quoque id facilius possis voluptuosiusque, opus est ut sine dissimulatione lectites, sine fine lecturias: For the adjective *voluptuosus*, see the commentary on *Ep.* 2.9.1 *Inter agros amoenissimos ... tempus voluptuosissimum exegi*. The comparative also occurs in Sidon. *Ep.* 1.9.7 and 7.13.4; Köhler (1995) 276. For adjectives ending in *-osus* in general, see the commentary on *Ep.* 2.2.18 *Lacus ipse ... flexuosus nemorosusque....* The term *dissimulatio* here means 'want of care', 'negligence', 'neglect', 'carelessness' (*TLL* 5.1, 1479.70–80.13). In Sidon. *Ep.* 1.7.6 the term is used with the meaning of 'concealing'; see also Plin. *Ep.* 6.27.3, 9.13.21. Sidonius emphasises his wish with the litotes *sine dissimulatione*, with the parallel structure, the variation of the verbs *lectito* and *lecturio*, and the rhyme *sine fine*. The combination *sine fine* is attested from Lucr. 2.92 onwards (*TLL* 6.1, 798.3–12) and also used in Sidon. *Ep.* 6.4.1, *Carm.* 2.186, 5.523, 9.268, 16.89. The verb *lectito*, 'to read often, with eagerness, or with attention' (*TLL* 7.2, 1089.61–90.43), is a frequently used and attested from Cicero on (it appears in Plin. *Ep.* 2.17.8, 3.5.1, 4.19.2, 4.23.1, 5.5.3, 5.16.3, 6.7.2, 7.17.4, Cic. *Fam.* 9.25.1, *Att.* 12.18.1, *Brut.* 121). It is also used in Sidon. *Ep.* 2.9.4, 4.9.3, 5.1.1, 5.8.1, 7.18.3, 8.6.1, 9.9.8, 9.11.6. The similar-sounding *lecturio*, 'to desire to read', 'be inclined to read' (*TLL* 7.2, 1096.17–25), is very rarely used. It also occurs in Sidon. *Ep.* 7.18.4, 9.7.1; Gualandri (1979) 180, van Waarden (2016) 271. Sidonius probably chooses it here for the double cretic clausula. Wolff (2020) 399 compares it to other verbs with a desiderative suffix used by Sidonius, such as *taciturire*, 'to want to be silent' (*Ep.* 8.16.3), and *scripturire*, 'to long to write' (*Ep.* 7.18.1, 8.11.8). For the importance of reading the classics to create an aristocratic identity, see Sidon. *Ep.* 4.17.2 *granditer laetor saltim in inlustri pectore tuo vanescentium litterarum remansisse vestigia, quae si frequenti lectione continuas, experiere per dies, quanto antecellunt beluis homines, tanto anteferri rusticis institutos* ('I rejoice greatly that at any rate in your illustrious breast there have remained traces of our vanishing culture. If you extend these by constant reading you will discover for yourself as each day passes that the educated are no less superior to the unlettered than men are to beasts'); Denecker (2015) 418, Mratschek (2017) 314–22, Mratschek (2020b) 242; see also the commentaries on *Ep.* 2.9.4 *nam similis scientiae viri, hinc Augustinus hinc Varro, hinc Horatius hinc Prudentius lectitabantur* and on *Ep.* 2.10.1 *Illud appone*....

neque patiaris, ut te ab hoc proposito propediem coniunx domum feliciter ducenda deflectat: Here we hear for the first time that Sidonius' friendship letter is actually a wedding present for his friend. There was a hint of this, though, in *Ep.* 2.10.4: see the commentary on *Ep.* 2.10.4 *Nam sicuti novam nuptam nihil minus quam pulchrior pronuba decet*. The jokes and mockery that follow are reminiscent of the Fescennine verses, the ancient wedding poems; see Sidon. *Ep.* 1.5.10, *Carm.* 12.2, 14.1; Egelhaaf-Gaiser (2014) 390. Sidonius also composed wedding poems (*epithalamia*); see *Carm.* 10, 11, 14, 15. For *coniunx*, see the commentary on *Ep.* 2.8.1 *morigera coniunx*....

sisque oppido meminens: *Oppido*, 'very', is an archaic adverb, frequently used in comedy; see Sidon. *Carm.* 22.1; Delhey (1993) 48. For Sidonius' predilection for archaisms, see Gualandri (1979) 172–3, Monni (1999). The verb *memini*, 'to remember', is regularly constructed with *quod* by Late Antique authors (*TLL* 8, 653.4–30). The participle *meminens*, 'remembering', 'aware', which is attested from the first century BC onwards, occurs five times in Sidonius (also in *Ep.* 4.3.10, 4.12.1, 6.3.1, 7.6.3); Amherdt (2001) 161–2.

quod olim Marcia Hortensio, Terentia Tullio, Calpurnia Plinio, Pudentilla Apuleio, Rusticiana Symmacho legentibus meditantibusque candelas et candelabra tenuerunt: To encourage Hesperius to continue his studies despite being married, Sidonius adds two lists of artistically productive couples. First, in section 5, we have a list of five married couples where the wife supports the husband; see the Introduction to this book, pp. xix–xx. The women hold a *candelabrum*, 'a candle holder', 'candelabra' (*TLL* 3, 233.1–75), while the men, five famous orators, study. Sidonius thus takes up the motif of light, which is central for his description of the interior of the church of Lyon; see the commentary on *Ep.* 2.10.4. As the sunlight in the church was his major point of interest, here the women throw light on their husbands. Pfäffgen (2008) 1205 defines the candelabra (Greek λύχνος, λυχνία; Latin *candelabrum*) as the device for carrying or holding various types of lighting, especially candles, torches or (oil-)lamps. The candelabra is used to support light sources and is either free-standing or fixed to the wall or ceiling. Candelabras are made of metal, usually bronze, but occasionally silver or gold, and rarely of marble, clay or wood. Unlike the common oil-lamp (*lampas, lanterna, lucerna*), which is usually associated with love or slavery, the *candelabrum* symbolises wealth or is used as a religious symbol, for example in Cic. *Verr.* 2.4.60, 2.4.64–5, 2.4.71, Ven. Fort. *Carm.* 5.5.7, 5.5.125, 9.2.118; Grawehr (2019), Hindermann (2022a). The term is also used in Mart. 14.43 and 14.44.2, about different kinds of lamps. While in other literary genres a scene with a lamp and a couple usually suggests an erotic atmosphere (for example Apul. *Met.* 2.11.3, Mart. 14.39, *Anth. Pal.* 5.4, 5.5), Sidonius creates a different context by alluding to the topos of *lucubratio*, 'working by lamp-light', which occurs in various Roman authors, for example Cic. *Fam.* 9.2.1, Sen. *Ep.* 8.1, Plin. *Nat. Praef.* 18, Gell. *Praef.* 4, Quint. 10.3.25–7; Ker (2004), Hindermann (2022c, 2022a). The motif can also be found in Late Antique literature, for example in the letters of Jerome, Hier. *Ep.* 64, 108.32 – Conring (2001) 111–18, Cain (2009) 175 – or in Ausonius, Auson. *Praef. Var.* 5 (Green) vv. 7–12, *Ep.* 19a.24–30, *Cento praef.* 21–4. For Sidonius' reference to Ausonius' *lucubratio*, see the introduction to this letter. In *Ep.* 8.10.3, Sidonius inserts a list of three orators (Cicero, Fronto, Pliny) who deliver their best speech when in peril.

Mixed with the motif of working by candlelight is the literary motif of the list; see the introduction to this letter. Although the five women belong to very different literary traditions and some are more famous than others, they are united in one single role through the object they are carrying. Sidonius enumerates the couples in their historical order; Hindermann (2022a). For Sidonius' examples from history in general, see Mathisen (2020a) 33, who notes that most of them date from the early second century and before. Wolff (2020b) 407 uses the enumeration of couples here and in the next section as an example of symmetry and parallelism, the dominant figures in Sidonius' writings. With *legentibus meditantibusque* and *candelas et candelabra* Sidonius combines parallel groups with the law of increasing members.

Marcia Hortensio. Marcia lived in the first century BC. She is usually mentioned as an example of the observance of Stoic ideals of friendship and rationality, because her first husband, the conservative senator Cato the Younger (95 to 46 BC), gave her away to marry the older rhetor and politician (consul in 69 BC) Quintus Hortensius Hortalus (114 to 50 BC), who wanted to have familial ties with his friend. After the death of Hortensius, Cato took Marcia back, who was now a wealthy widow; Tschiedel (1981) 96–105, Fehrle (1983) 201–4, Harich (1990). Early on the case was used as a subject of rhetorical exercises and to illustrate or defame Cato's character; see Quint. 3.5.11, 10.5.13, Tert. *Apol.* 39.12–13, Luc. 2.326–49. With the choice of Hortensius as Marcia's husband, Sidonius sets himself apart. He is not interested in the moral-philosophical discourse associated with the couple of Marcia and Cato, but in the opulent rhetorical style called *Asiatic* (see Cic. *Brut.* 301–4) for which Hortensius was known, although unfortunately none of Hortensius' speeches are extant. By letting Marcia hold the candelabra for Hortensius, Sidonius also changes her role. She is shown to take an interest in writing not mentioned anywhere else; Hindermann (2022a). Plin. *Ep.* 5.3.5 and probably also Ov. *Trist.* 2.441–2 mention Hortensius' immoral verses; Ingleheart (2010) 343.

Terentia Tullio. The next two writer-husbands are Cicero and Pliny, whom Sidonius explicitly mentions as his inspiration in his programmatic letter 1.1.1 (as well as the fifth example, Symmachus – see below). Cicero is the author whom Sidonius mentions most often by name in his letters. He alludes to him in various ways: see the commentaries on *Ep.* 2.1.1 *Rediit ipse Catilina...* and *Ep.* 2.9.5 *ut nec ... neque Tullius Ctesiphontem....* Cicero's wife Terentia (98 BC to 6 AD) is also well known; several ancient texts mention her (for example Cicero's *Ad familiares* and Plutarch's *Cicero*) and there are many modern studies, for example Claassen (1996), Ermete (2003), Grebe (2003), Treggiari (2007), Brennan (2012), Buonopane (2016). While Cicero praises

Terentia's practical and energetic nature in his letters from exile, in later letters he criticises her concern for her property and her excessive interest in money. Further ancient statements about Terentia are influenced by the attitude of the writers towards Cicero. In his biography of Cicero, for example, Plutarch mentions critically that Terentia was ambitious and more interested in Cicero's political career than in the household (Plut. *Cic.* 20.2; see Brennan 2012, 354–6). Her support of Cicero's literary activity is not mentioned in any other surviving ancient source, with the exception perhaps of Jerome, who, based on Seneca's lost writing *De matrimonio*, presents Terentia as a disciple of Cicero's philosophy (*sapientia*). See Hier. *Adv. Iovin.* 1.48, Sen. *Frg.* 13,61 (Haase) *illa interim coniux egregia et quae de fontibus Tullianis hauserat sapientiam* ('but she, an outstanding wife, who had drunk from the sources of Tullian wisdom'); Treggiari (2007) 149. The role of a supportive assistant in Cicero's impressively large literary production, on the other hand, is usually occupied by his secretary Tiro, although it is sometimes suggested that Terentia must also have been involved; see Gell. 6.3.8, Treggiari (2007) 153–4, 157, Brennan (2012) 365, Hindermann (2022a).

Calpurnia Plinio. The next writer mentioned by Sidonius is Pliny the Younger (61–113), his most important model for his letters, and especially prominent in Book 2; see the Introduction to this book and the introductions to *Ep.* 2.2, 2.8, 2.9. Sidonius mentions Pliny by name in Sidon. *Ep.* 1.1.1, 4.3.1, 4.22.2, 8.10.3, 9.1.1 and alludes to him in various ways in most of the letters of the second book. As he writes in his programmatic Letter 1.1, Sidonius explicitly wants the reader to compare him with Pliny; Amherdt (2001) 23–7, 123, Whitton (2013) 35. Pliny's wife Calpurnia is the only woman in the list whose literary interests are attested in sources other than Sidonius. In his letters, Pliny praises his wife for her support of his career and her interest in his studies by depicting her as an elegiac *puella docta* – see Plin. *Ep.* 4.19.2–5; Hindermann (2010). While Calpurnia remains hidden behind a curtain in Pliny's portrayal, Sidonius places her in the light, next to her husband. On Pliny's and Calpurnia's marriage see Gibson (2021), who also gives an overview of the older literature.

Pudentilla Apuleio. The next couple mentioned by Sidonius are Apuleius and his wife Pudentilla. Like Pliny, Lucius Apuleius Madaurensis (124–70) is an important style model for Sidonius. Both have a predilection for neologisms and archaisms, and Sidonius praises Apuleius' way of writing and translating in two other letters; see the commentary on *Ep.* 2.9.5 *ut nec Apuleius Phaedonem*.... Apuleius is the only author of the five examples who uses the word 'candelabrum' in his work, associating it with prophecy, in *Met.* 2.11.6 *cuncta caeli negotia et solem ipsum de specula candelabra contuetur* ('who surveys all the things in heaven and even the sun from the height of her candelabrum'). Also, the motif of light is essential to Apuleius' *Metamorphoses* – starting with the name of its protagonist, Lucius (from *lux*, 'light') and his lover Photis (from Greek φῶς, 'light'), followed by the role of lamps in the story of Amor and Psyche and the procession for the goddess Isis; De Smet (1987), Panayotakis (2001), Sabnis (2012). Aemilia Pudentilla is known from Apuleius' apology *De magia*, with which, in 158/9, he defended himself against the accusation of having won his wife by magic. The court case had been initiated by the family of Pudentilla, according to Apuleius out of greed for money on the part of the relatives. As with Marcia and Terentia, Pudentilla's interest in her husband's work is testified to by Sidonius alone. But Apuleius reports several times and with pride that his wife was able to read and write Latin and Greek, so well even that the uneducated accusers misunderstood their letters. See Apul. *Apol.* 30.11, 82.2, 83.1, 84.2, 87.5–6; Hemelrijk (1999) 200.

Rusticiana Symmacho. The last couple consists of Q. Aurelius Symmachus, consul in 391, whom Sidonius also mentions as a model in his programmatic letter 1.1.1 (he praises his *rotunditas*, 'well-roundedness', 'completeness' of style), and his wife Rusticiana; Matthews (1974) 65, *PLRE* 1, 786–7, 865–70, Bruggisser (1993) 78, Köhler (1995) 105–6, Mathisen (2020a) 122–3. Sidonius appreciates Symmachus as a stylistic model and he mentions him with admiration on two further occasions: *Ep.* 8.10.1, *Carm.* 9.304. Of all the wives Sidonius uses as examples, the least is known about Rusticiana, for whom the only source is her husband. In his letters, though, Symmachus never mentions his wife by name and does not give details about her activities or health or his feelings towards her; see Symm. *Ep.* 1.6.2, 1.11.1, 2.55.1, 9.150.3. Rusticiana's name appears only once in Symmachus' whole extensive work, at Symm. *Rel.* 34.12. Sidonius by contrast calls Rusticiana by her name and assigns her a role in her husband's studies; Salzman and Roberts (2011) 30–2. On Sidonius and Symmachus, see Bruggisser (1993) 78, Köhler (1995) 105–6, Gibson (2020) 389–91.

Section 6

Certe si praeter oratoriam contubernio feminarum poeticum ingenium: For *oratoria*, 'the oratorical art', 'oratory' (*TLL* 9.2, 902.28–42), see Quint. 2.14.1–2, Sidon. *Ep.* 5.2.1. The term *contubernium* usually denotes a 'concubinage, i.e. a union of a man with an unmarried woman' (*TLL* 4, 792.12–45), for example Colum. 12.1.2, Petron. 53.10, only very seldom a 'marriage' (*TLL* 4, 792.45–9). See the commentary on *Ep.* 2.2.2 *raptim subduceris ... contubernio nostro aventer insertus* for *contubernium* describing the reception of a friend into his family. The term *femina* originally was a term of honour, but gradually became a regular term for 'woman'; Axelson (1945) 53–7, Adams (1972), Santoro L'Hoir (1992). In Pliny's letters, the term *femina* is preferred over *mulier* and still has a reverential connotation; Hindermann (2013) 146–51. In *Ep.* 5.8.2, Sidonius also praises the poet Secundinus, mentioned in this same letter, in section 2.10.3, as the author of a poem, for his poetic talent: *ferventis fulmen ingenii* ('the lightning of your glowing genius').

et oris tui limam frequentium studiorum cotibus expolitam quereris obtundi: With *lima*, 'file', 'rasp', Sidonius uses a common metaphor for a polished and carefully revised literary composition (see *TLL* 7.2, 1400.55–82), for example Cic. *Brut.* 93, Ov. *Trist.* 1.7.30, *Pont.* 1.5.19, Quint. 10.4.4, Mart. 10.2.3. The topos also appears in important intertexts for Sidonius' letters, for example Plin. *Ep.* 1.8.3, 5.10.3, 8.4.7, Symm. *Ep.* 1.3.1; Gualandri (1979) 129, Amherdt (2001) 243–4. Sidonius takes up the idea several times, especially in his programmatic *Ep.* 1.1.3 (*limandas*), where he asks the addressee, Constantius, to revise his letters, and in *Ep.* 4.8.5 (*lima*), where he compares the work of a writer with the work of an artisan, a silver smith; Leatherbury (2017) 38. For the idea of refining one's work, see also *Ep.* 4.10.2, 8.6.18, 9.3.5, 9.15.1 v. 46, *Carm.* 2.187–8, 23.131 and 144. *Cos, cotis* denotes any 'hard stone' and in particular a 'whetstone', 'hone', 'grindstone' (*TLL* 4, 1083.10–25). Its use in a transferred meaning as *stimulus*, 'spur', 'incentive', is common. The term appears again in Sidon. *Ep.* 8.1.2; see Gualandri (1979) 129 n. 79 with further references. The metaphor of the file (*lima*) is connected with *expolitus*, 'polished', 'smooth', the participle of *expolio*, which also occurs in *Ep.* 3.12.4 and 4.8.5. Alternatively, Sidonius uses *politus* in *Ep.* 1.1.1, 9.3.3, 9.9.11, 9.15.1 v. 38; see also *Ep.* 4.18.3 (*impolitum*) and 4.10.2 (*poliri*), *Carm.* 2.187–8; Amherdt (2001) 276. See Catull's programmatic first poem (Catull. 1.1–2), where he describes his book as *lepidum novum libellum | arido modo pumice expolitum* ('the nice new little book, freshly smoothed with dry pumice stone'), and Mart. Cap. 3.226 *limam quandam artificialiter expolitam* ('a certain artificially smoothed file'). Sidonius argues against the idea that the poetic file could become duller – *obtundi*, 'to blunt', 'weaken', often used in a figurative sense about human qualities, talents and feelings (see *TLL* 9.2, 297.56–8.41) – because of living with a woman; see Sidon. *Ep.* 7.12.2 *fieret obtusior* ('to become numbly apathetic'); van Waarden (2016) 66.

reminiscere, quod saepe versum Corinna cum suo Nasone complevit, Lesbia cum Catullo, Cesennia cum Gaetulico, Argentaria cum Lucano, Cynthia cum Propertio, Delia cum Tibullo: As in section 5 (see the commentary on *Ep.* 2.10.5 *quod olim Marcia Hortensio…*), Sidonius again encourages Hesperius to remember couples of the past. In his second series of couples, in section 6, he lists six poets and their mistresses or wives, but reverses their roles. Now the women are writing, while their partners are sitting nearby; Hindermann (2022a). Sidonius thus again (as in his villa letters *Ep.* 2.2. and 2.9 – see the commentaries there) starts with a Plinian motif, but transforms it into something new. While in section 5 he displays the same attitude as Pliny concerning the role of wives in the literary process – the only difference being that Pliny discusses the subject by means of his own marriage, while Sidonius lists historical couples – in section 6 he presents an even longer list of couples, where women write together with their partners. The letter thus ends with a surprising twist: women here are not the object of poetry, but co-writers. Sidonius' list is also reminiscent of Apuleius' list of poets and their mistresses in his defence against the charges of using magic: *eadem igitur opera accusent C. Catullum, quod Lesbiam pro Clodia nominarit, et Ticidam similiter, quod quae Metella erat Perillam scripserit, et Propertium, qui Cunthiam dicat, Hostiam dissimulet, et Tibullum, quod ei sit Plania in animo, Delia in versu* (Apul. *Apol.* 10.2–3) ('they should also accuse C. Catullus, because he used the name Lesbia for Clodia, and likewise Ticidas, because he wrote Perilla for the woman who was Metella, and Propertius, because he says Cynthia and hides Hostia, and Tibullus, because he has Plania in his mind, but Delia in his verse'). While Apuleius' list is the first surviving attempt to identify the 'real' women behind the mistresses the poets praise in their poems, Sidonius sticks with their names known from the poems. Unlike in section 5, Sidonius here does not list them in chronological order. He starts and ends with two well-known couples representing the type *poeta–amator* and *puella* and belonging to the genre of Roman elegy or love epigram. For the elegiac motifs, see Lyne (1980), Holzberg (2001), Johnson (2012b), Miller (2012), Sharrock (2012), Wray (2012). On the importance of female learnedness as a poetic ideal, especially in Roman elegy, versus its reality, see Hemelrijk (1999) 92, James (2003) 71–152, 212–23. On the mistress as metaphor in Roman elegy, see Wyke (2002)

11–45. In between Sidonius places two married couples: Caesennia with Gaetulicus and Polla Argentaria with Lucan. All examples used here (Lucan, Gaetulicus, Tibullus, Propertius, Catullus and Ovid) are also mentioned together in another list, in Sidon. *Carm.* 9.239, 259, 260, 263, 266 and 270; Hindermann (forthcoming a). Formicola (2009) 86 refers to lists of poets in Propertius and Ovid as possible intertexts: see Prop. 2.34.85–94 (cited below in the commentary on *Cynthia cum Propertio*), Ov. *Am.* 3.9.61–6, *Trist.* 2.427–68. See also Ovid's list of contemporary writers in Ov. *Trist.* 4.16, *Am.* 1.15; Laemmle et al. (2021), Ingleheart (2010) 333–58.

Corinna cum suo Nasone: Corinna is the mistress in Ovid's *Amores*, a collection of elegies consisting of three books, where the lover/poet describes his joy and sorrow. Since Ovid (43–17/18 BC) treats the topic playfully and Corinna is mentioned only twelve times (starting with the famous siesta poem, Ov. *Am.* 1.5.9), there has been less research on the 'real' Corinna, especially since the name could also simply mean 'girl' in derivation from the Greek κόρη. Ovid does not write explicitly about Corinna's education, but with her name recalls the Greek lyric poet Korinna from Tanagra, who was famous for her beauty, the complexity of her poetry and her creative handling of the myths; Randall (1979) 34–5, Heath (2013). In his *Ars amatoria*, Ovid recommends that his female students should care about literature so that they are attractive to men; see Ov. *Ars* 3.329–48. For Ovid and Corinna, see also Sidon. *Carm.* 23.159–61, where Sidonius, unlike here, refers to Corinna's feigned name and recalls Ovid's exile because of alledgedly lascivious poems; Santelia (2016b) 432. Sidonius mentions Ovid among exiled poets also in *Carm.* 9.270 and he uses Ovid as a model when describing his own experience with barbarians in *Carm.* 12 and the danger of being a writer in *Ep.* 1.11; Montone (2014). Ovid's *Metamorphoses* are also an intertext for Sidonius' panegyric on Avitus, *Carm.* 6 and 7; Bruzzone (2014), Furbetta (2018a) 304–13. On Ovid and Sidonius, see also Montuschi (2001), Filosini (2014a) 42–6, Filosini (2014b), Onorato (2020b), Santelia (2020).

Lesbia cum Catullo. Gaius (or Quintus) Valerius Catullus was a Roman poet of the first century BC. Catullus' surviving work comprises 116 *carmina* in various metres. According to Apul. *Apol.* 10.2–3 (cited p. 338, at the beginning of this commentary on *reminiscere…*), the woman Catullus calls Lesbia in his poems (Catull. *Carm.* 5, 7, 8, 43, 51, 58, 72, 75, 79, 86, 87, 92, 107) is Claudia or Clodia, born around 90 BC, one of the three sisters of Publius Clodius Pulcher and Appius Claudius Pulcher, and married to Quintus Caecilius Metellus Celer. Catullus praises her quick-wittedness, cultivated manners and beauty (for example Catull. *Carm.* 51, 86). By comparing her to the Greek poet Sappho through the name Lesbia, he gives her personality a uniqueness that elevates her above her peers; Randall (1979) 28–30, Dyson (2007) 255, 264, 266, 272–3, Ingleheart (2010) 333–4, Skinner (2011) 126–44. Sidonius also mentions Catullus among other poets in *Carm.* 9.266. On Catullus and Sidonius, see Henke (2008) 164–5, Gualandri (2020) 284–8.

Cesennia cum Gaetulico. Cn. Cornelius Lentulus Gaetulicus, consul in 26 AD, is mentioned by two of Sidonius' major models, Martial and Pliny, as a writer of lascivious poems. See Mart. 1 *Praef.* 4 *lascivam verborum veritatem, id est epigrammaton linguam, excusarem, si meum esset exemplum: sic scribit Catullus, sic Marsus, sic Pedo, sic Gaetulicus* ('I would excuse myself for the naughty directness of my words, that is the language of epigrams, if I were the first example: but this is how Catullus, Marsus, Pedo and Gaetulicus write'); see Plin. *Ep.* 5.3.5; Howell (1980) 99–100, Courtney (2003) 345–6, Mindt (2013) 141–2. Sidonius also mentions Gaetulicus among other poets in *Carm.* 9.259; Hindermann (forthcoming a). Gualandri (2020) 285 wonders whether Sidonius actually knew the poets' work or just copied their names from Martial (see Mart. 1 *Praef.*), and she compares this passage to the list of Greek poets in Sidon. *Carm.* 9.211–16. Gaetulicus was married to Apronia Caesennia, daughter of L. Apronius (see Tac. *Ann.* 6.30); van Rohden (1895). Caesennia's interest in literature is not otherwise mentioned.

Argentaria cum Lucano. The Roman poet Marcus Annaeus Lucanus (39–65 AD) wrote the *Pharsalia*, an epic about the war between Caesar and Pompeius; Fantham (2011). That his wife, Argentaria Polla, was interested in literature is also mentioned in Mart. 10.64 and Stat. *Silv.* 2.7.83 *doctam atque ingenio tuo decoram* ('learned and matching your genius'); White (1975) 280–6, Damschen and Heil (2004) 239–40, Stevenson (2005) 48, Newlands (2011a) 243, Newlands (2011b), Santelia (2016a). In *Carm.* 23.166 Sidonius writes that after Lucan's death Argentaria married another poet; Anderson (1936) 295 n. 2, Fantham (2011) 20. In the older commentaries Statius was thought to have been her second husband, but according to modern research it was Statius' patron Pollius Felix; see van Waarden (2020c) 697 with an overview. See Furbetta (2016) on Lucan as a model for Sidon. *Carm.* 7 and *Ep.* 7.7; see also van Waarden (2010) 53–5, 69–70, 347, Gualandri (2020) 284–8, and the commentary below on *Ep.* 2.13.6–7. In *Carm.* 9.239–58 Sidonius recounts from Lucans' epic in length; Hinderman (forthcoming a).

Cynthia cum Propertio. The Roman poet Sextus Propertius (50/45 to 15 BC) composed four books of elegies. His work is dominated by a single woman, referred to sixty-two times, by the pseudonym Cynthia. According to Apul. *Apol.* 10.2–3 (cited p. 338, at the beginning of the commentary to this section) her real name was Hostia. Cynthia's name conjures up the god of the arts, Apollo, who was born on Mount Cynthus on the island of Delos, and his sister Diana; see Randall (1979) 31–3, Heath (2013) 157 with further literature. Propertius also frequently praises Cynthia as *docta puella* ('learned girl') – see Prop. 1.7.11, 2.11.6, 2.13.11, 2.24.21, 2.26.25–6 – and as a composer of poems – see 1.2.27–8; Wyke (1987) 54, 58, Wyke (2002) 46–77, Ingleheart (2010) 356–7, Johnson (2012b) 41–2. At the beginning of Book 2 (Prop. 2.1.3–4), he also states that she made him a poet. Sidonius also mentions Propertius among other poets in *Carm.* 9.263. On Propertius and Sidonius, see Formicola (2009). In Prop. 2.34.85–94, Propertius also inserts a list of poets and their lovers: *haec quoque perfecto ludebat Iasone Varro, | Varro Leucadiae maxima flamma suae; | haec quoque lascivi cantarunt scripta Catulli, | Lesbia quis ipsa notior est Helena; | haec etiam docti confessa est pagina Calvi, | cum caneret miserae funera Quintiliae. | et modo formosa quam multa Lycoride Gallus | mortuus inferna vulnera lavit aqua! | Cynthia quin etiam versu laudata Properti, | hos inter si me ponere Fama volet* ('Varro, for whom his Leucadia burned with the deepest love, also wrote such a poem after finishing his "Jason". This was also praised in his songs by the easy-going Catullus, who made Lesbia more famous than even Helen. This was also revealed in the poem of the learned Calvus, when he lamented the death of the pitiful Quintilia in song. And how many wounds, which only recently the beautiful Lycoris inflicted on him, did Gallus wet as a dead man with the waters of the Styx. Yes, Cynthia is also glorified by the poetry of Propertius, if public opinion is willing to admit me to the circle of those in the future').

Delia cum Tibullo. The Roman poet Tibullus (55 to 19/18 BC) wrote two books of poetry. The first comprises ten elegies, the second six; both were probably published during his lifetime. While Propertius' and Ovid's love poems are addressed to only one woman, in Tibullus' case, a young lover named Marathus appears in some of the poems in the first book. The first-person speaker breaks up with Delia at the end of the first book; in the second book a new lover named Nemesis appears. Delia's social status is not clear and Tibullus does not give any description of her as a dramatic character; instead, she primarily appears as an avaricious courtesan (*meretrix*); Miller (2012) 56, 68. Like Propertius' Cynthia, Delia's name also conjures up the god of the arts, Apollo, who was born on Mount Cynthus in Delos, and his sister Diana; Randall (1979) 33–4, Ingleheart (2010) 350–5, Heath (2013) 157 with further literature. Sidonius also mentions

Tibullus among other poets in *Carm.* 9.260. On Tibullus and Sidonius, see Gualandri (2020) 285.

Proinde liquido claret studentibus discendi per nuptias occasionem tribui, desidibus excusationem: For the expression *liquido claret*, 'it is obvious', see Sidon. *Carm.* 22.6 *istum liquido patet* ('it is perfectly clear'); Delhey (1993) 207. With the expression *per nuptias* Sidonius turns to the actual reason for writing the letter; see the commentary on *Ep.* 2.10.4 *Nam sicuti novam nuptam....* Sidonius advises Hesperius as an experienced husband and scholar. For Sidonius' marriage, see the commentary on *Ep.* 2.2.3 *nomen hoc praedio, quod, quia uxorium, patrio mihi dulcius.* In *Ep.* 5.7.7 Sidonius also mentions the good effect of a wife (Tanaquil) on her husband (Tarquinius Priscus/Chilperic).

Igitur incumbe, neque apud te litterariam curam turba depretiet imperitorum: At the end of his letter Sidonius repeats the theme that only a few insiders care about literary tradition. The adjective *litterarius*, 'belonging to reading and writing', occurs three times in Sidonius, here and in *Ep.* 7.11.1, 7.14.10; van Waarden (2010) 554, van Waarden (2016) 163. With the expression *turba ... imperitorum* Sidonius returns to the beginning of the letter, where he addresses the problem that in his time few people care about the Latin language and literature; see the commentary on *Ep.* 2.10.1 *Illud appone ... meram linguae Latiaris proprietatem....* Hanaghan (2019) 30 points to the dimension of social class in this discourse and cites *Ep.* 3.13.11 as a comparative text. For the wording, see also Sidon. *Ep.* 4.3.10 *turba numerosior illiteratissimis litteris vacant* ('most of them spend time with very unliterary letters') and *Ep.* 7.14.2 *imperitia civica* ('their ignorant fellow townsmen'); Squillante (2009) 142, van Waarden (2016) 129. Sidonius thus combines a congratulatory letter with an admonition to maintain traditional learning (*paideia*) also as a married man; Gerth (2013) 191. For *depretio*, 'to undervalue', 'depreciate', 'disregard' (*TLL* 5.1, 612.27–55), a rarely used verb and mostly by Late Antique writers, see Sidon. *Carm.* 22.4 v. 203, *Ep.* 1.7.8 possibly as a deponent (Köhler 1995) 246, Tert. *Apol.* 45.6, Paul. Nol. *Carm.* 25.56; Delhey (1993) 181.

quia natura comparatum est, ut in omnibus artibus hoc sit scientiae pretiosior pompa, quo rarior. Vale: In *Ep.* 3.14.2, a reply to critics of his literary work, Sidonius defines his own style by linking it with cultural ideals such as *scientia*, 'knowledge', and *pompa*; Denecker (2015) 412. For *pompa* in the meaning of 'grandeur', 'pomp', 'splendour', 'ostentation', see also *Ep.* 4.18.5, *Carm.* 22.4 v. 121; Delhey (1993) 83; compare Sidon. *Carm.* 2.376, 22.4 v. 41. For *scientia*, 'skills', see the commentary on *Ep.* 2.9.4 *nam similis scientiae viri...* and for the meaning 'knowledge', see the commentary on *Ep.* 2.5.1 *et donec suarum ... vel vestra scientia....* For Sidonius what is excellent is rare and therefore more valuable. For this notion, see also Sidon. *Ep.* 7.2.5; van Waarden (2010) 166. For the letter's simple ending with *vale*, see the commentary on *Ep.* 2.1.4 *Vale.*

Epistula 11

Introduction

Summary

In *Ep.* 2.11 Sidonius confirms his close friendship with Rusticus, which persists even though their homes are far apart.

Addressee

Rusticus is a friend of Sidonius and a neighbour of Pontius Leontius, who lives near Bordeaux; see *Ep.* 8.11.3 v. 36. Rusticus is described as *vir illustris* in *Ep.* 2.11.2. For Rusticus' life, see Loyen (1970a) 220 n. 47, Kaufmann (1995) 344, *PLRE* 2, 964 n. 4, *PCBE* 4, 1664, Mathisen (2020a) 119. He is also the addressee of Ruricius (Ruric. *Ep.* 2.20 and 2.54), bishop of Limoges, to whom Sidonius sends three letters (Sidon. *Ep.* 4.16, 5.15, 8.10, and *Carm.* 10); Mathisen (2020a) 54–5, van Waarden (2020a) 15.

Date

Loyen (1970a) 72, 247 n. 11 dates *Ep.* 2.11 after Sidonius' trip to Bordeaux (see *Ep.* 8.11.3). As Sidonius only talks about the long distance between him and Rusticus and not the attacks of the Visigoths (see the commentary on the date of *Ep.* 2.1), Loyen thinks that the letter was written in the Auvergne around 467 (or in Lyon around 469). Kelly (2020a) 173 points out that Sidonius might have made multiple trips to Bordeaux or Narbonne in the 460s. On the general difficulty of dating Sidonius' letters, see the Introduction, '2. The date and order of letters in Book 2'.

Major themes and further reading

Structure and intertextuality

The three long letters, 2.8–10, are followed by two short letters, 2.11 and 12, which both deal with a simple subject but offer an artful and elaborate description. Like Letters 2.3 and 2.6, Letter 2.11 belongs to the category of friendship letters with typical motifs; see the introduction to *Ep.* 2.3. There is also a connection between *Ep.* 2.11 and *Ep.* 2.14, because both address the subject of distance between friends. Fernández López (1994) 87–98 therefore treats them together as 'cartas de simple saludo, respuesta, y salutación familiar'. The main theme of the letter is the spatial separation between friends, which is expressed with several verbs and nouns; Montone (2017) 27–8. According to Whitton (2013) 35–6, 186–7, Sidonius' Letters 2.11 and 2.12 (addressed to Rusticus and Agricola, both meaning 'farmer') respond to a pair of letters of Pliny (Plin. *Ep.* 2.11 and 2.12) which are both addressed to Arrianus and the only two successive letters to the same addressee. This seems possible given Sidonius' penchant for playing with names and numbers. On this and other parallels in the second book of letters of Sidonius and Pliny, see Gibson (2013b) and Gibson (2020) 389–90. Complaining about the separation from a friend is also a theme in Pliny's *Ep.* 6.1. Fernández López (1994) 191–204 treats Sidon. *Ep.* 2.6 and 2.12 together under 'cartas descriptivas de lugares y personas: descripción breve'.

Commentary

Section 1

Sidonius Rustico suo salutem: For the simple greeting formula, see the commentary on *Ep.* 2.1.1 *Sidonius Ecdicio suo salutem*. For the addressee Rusticus, see the introduction to this letter.

Si nobis pro situ spatiisque regionum vicinaremur nec a se praesentia mutua vasti itineris longinquitate discriminaretur: Sidonius misses his friend Rusticus, who lives too far away for regular visits. While Sidonius lives on his estate, Avitacum, probably by lake Aydat (about 20 km from Clermont), Rusticus lives in Bordeaux, so a road journey of 364 km/226 miles lies between them. For the πόθος motif (missing a friend), a regular subject in letters of friendship, see the commentary on *Ep.* 2.1.1 *Praesentiam*

Seronati et absentiam tuam. Sidonius expresses his wish for a meeting with a conditional clause, as he does elsewhere in his letters, *Ep.* 4.2.1, 4.4.2, 7.8.1; van Waarden (2010) 384. With the expression *animorum coniunctioni* in the last sentence of *Ep.* 2.11.1, Sidonius repeats and stresses his longing; see the commentary there. For problems with travelling through unsafe regions, see *Ep.* 7.10.1; van Waarden (2010) 552. Van Waarden (2010) 57, 89 refers to similar expressions denoting the complex 'road' + 'region' + 'distance', as here (*pro situ spatiisque regionum*) in *Ep.* 7.1.1 *spatia tractumque regionum* ('the length and breadth of the country') and 9.4.1 *spatium viae regionumque* ('the stretch of the road and regions') to explain Sidonius' 'variation technique'. For *spatium* in the meaning of 'distance', 'journey' (*OLD* 1798, 6), see *Ep.* 7.8.2, 8.12.1, 9.4.1; van Waarden (2010) 390. For the verb *vicinor*, 'to be neighboring', 'near', see the commentary on *Ep.* 2.2.9 *cui continuatur vicinante textrino*.... For *praesentia*, 'presence', see the commentary on *Ep.* 2.1.1 *Praesentiam Seronati et absentiam tuam*. The term *longinquitas*, 'distance', 'remoteness' (*TLL* 7.2, 1623.49–4.82), is used of the length of a journey again in Sidon. *Ep.* 4.8.3. For the expression *longinquitas itineris*, see Tac. *Ann.* 3.5.2, Amm. 19.6.2; Montone (2017) 27. Sidonius repeats the subject of spatial separation with *prolixa terrarum* in the next section, 2.11.2; see there. For *discrimino*, 'to divide', 'part', 'separate', see the commentary on *Ep.* 2.2.9 *cui continuatur vicinante textrino cella penaria discriminata*....

nihil apicum raritati licere in coeptae familiaritatis officia permitterem neque iam semel missa fundamenta certantis amicitiae diversis honorum generibus exstruere cessarem: After the πόθος motif (missing a friend) in the previous clause, Sidonius adds another typical topos of the letter of friendship, the idea that a friendship is nourished by (frequently) exchanged letters; see also Sidon. *Ep.* 3.7.1, 4.10.1. The issue is often raised by Symmachus, for example in Symm. *Ep.* 5.8; Bruggisser (1993) 5–6, Amherdt (2001) 221. For *(nihil) licere alicui in aliquem/aliquid*, 'to have (no) power over someone/something else', see the commentary on *Ep.* 2.4.3 *et, qui ita ... ut nec superstiti Optantio in liberos suos decuerit licere*. *Apex* in the meaning of 'letter' (generally in the plural) is attested from the fourth century onwards and appears several times in Sidonius' letters, for example Sidon. *Ep.* 1.5.2, 4.5.1, 4.6.4, 4.7.1, 4.12.3; Amherdt (2001) 188–9. See also Neri (2009) 184 on Ruric. *Ep.* 1.4.1, 1.13.1, 2.40.1, 2.41.1. For other meanings of *apex* in Sidonius, see the commentary on *Ep.* 2.1.2 *epistulas, ne primis quidem apicibus sufficienter initiatus*.... *Raritas*, 'rarity of occurrence' (*OLD* 1574, 3a), is repeated in the next section, 2.11.2, where it is used about a conversation. Sidonius thus stresses the fact that he and his friend are not able to have a frequent exchange, neither by letter nor in person. *Fundamentum* is often used in a figurative sense about human relations (*TLL* 6.1, 1552.23–61). Giannotti (2016) 113–14 refers to *Ep.* 3.1.2 and especially 3.2.4, where Sidonius similarly uses architectural metaphors to praise a friendship: *et initiatae per te ubicumque gratiae longum tibi redhibeantur quam fundamenta tam culmina* ('and that not only the foundations but the completed edifice of that harmony which you have instituted everywhere for a long time bring you recompense'). With *amicitia* it is also used in Val. Cem. *Hom.* 6.1 *amicitiarum fundamenta destruere* ('to destroy the foundations of friendships') and is combined with *mittere*, 'to set', 'lay', in Sen. *Ep.* 52.5 and Lact. *Mort. Pers.* 2.4. For the expression *certantis amicitiae*, see Sidon. *Ep.* 1.5.2 *certantibus votis* ('surpassing each other with prayers'); Köhler (1995) 191. For the various duties (*officia*) of friendship, see the commentary on *Ep.* 2.8.3 *Debes enim consolationis officium*....

Sed animorum coniunctioni separata utrimque porrectioribus terminis obsistit habitatio, equidem semel devinctis parum nocitura pectoribus: For the importance of personal contact in a friendship, see the commentary on the first sentence of *Ep.* 2.11.1. The term *coniunctio*, 'connection by friendship', 'intimacy' (*TLL* 4, 328.51–9.43), is regularly used of close friendships. With the participle *separatus*, 'separated', Sidonius again evokes the πόθος motif (missing a friend) see also *Ep.* 7.11.1, 8.6.16, 8.12.1, 9.5.1; see van Waarden (2010) 553 and the commentary on *discretio*, 'separation', in *Ep.* 2.11.2. For the metaphorically used verb *devincere*, 'to bind together', 'to unite closely', see the commentary on *Ep.* 2.6.1 *Menstruanus amicus ... inter personas nobis quoque caras devinctasque censeri*. The participle *porrectus* derives from *porrigo*, 'to stretch or spread out'. It is used by other Late Antique authors to denote spatial distance, for example in Min. Fel. 17.10 (*TLL* 10.1, 2765.1–5).

Section 2

Sed tamen ex ipsa communium municipiorum discretione procedit quod, cum amicissimi simus: In the first sentence of the second section, Sidonius expresses the same idea in three ways, namely that the distance between him and his friend is the reason for their rare contact. *Communis* here means 'respective'; see van Waarden (2010) 280 on *Ep.* 7.6.1 *communem* *conscientiam* ('the character we share') and van Waarden (2016) 173. To refer to the cities of Bordeaux and Clermont, Sidonius chooses the term *municipium*, 'a free town' (*TLL* 8, 1648.45–9.83); see the commentary on *Ep.* 2.11.1 *Si nobis pro situ spatiisque regionum*.... *Discretio*, 'separation', appears here in the rare meaning of 'distance' (*TLL* 5.1, 1350.1–6), mostly used by Late Antique writers. It repeats *discriminaretur* and *separata* in *Ep.* 2.11.1. The superlative *amicissimus*, 'very amicable', 'the greatest friend' (*TLL* 1, 1910.25–40), is used by Cicero as well as by Pliny to denote a close friendship, for example Cic. *Fam.* 3.3.1, Plin. *Ep.* 3.21.6, 6.15.2, 8.5.3. In Sidonius' letters and poems, the superlative appears only here and therefore has special weight. For the subject of friendship (*amicitia*) in Sidonius and ancient letters in general, see the introduction to *Ep.* 2.3.

raritatem colloquii de prolixa terrarum interiectione venientem in reatum volumus transferre communem, cum de naturalium rerum difficultate nec culpa nos debeat manere nec venia: For *raritas*, 'small number', see the commentary on *Ep.* 2.7.1 *nihil apicum raritati licere*.... With *colloquium*, 'conversation' (*TLL* 3, 1650.15–44), Sidonius refers to his epistolary correspondence and thus alludes to the topos of a letter as 'half of a dialogue'; see the commentary on *Ep.* 2.1.1 '*Quaenam?*' *inquis*. The image is common; see Sidon. *Ep.* 4.10.2, 6.1.2, Cic. *Phil.* 2.7, Ov. *Pont.* 2.4.1. In Symmachus' letters, the term *colloquium* is used as a synonym for 'letter', for example in Symm. *Ep.* 1.34.1, 1.84; Bruggisser (1993) 156. Elsewhere (Sidon. *Ep.* 3.11.2, 4.7.3), Sidonius uses *alloquium* in a similar way; see Amherdt (2001) 221. In *Ep.* 8.14.8 he also uses *eloquium*. For *interiectio*, a 'placing between' (*TLL* 7.1, 2201.47–57), which is used only by Late Antique authors to express a distance, see the commentary on *Ep.* 2.9.1 *quibus interiecta gestatio peditem lassat*.... With *prolixa terrarum interiectione* Sidonius expresses for the second time (after *vasti itineris longinquitate* in *Ep.* 2.11.1) that he blames spatial distance for the rare contact between him and his friend. The expression *prolixa terrarum* also appears in Mart. Cap. 6.665. Sidonius uses the term *reatus* here in the meaning of 'accusation', 'charge' (*OLD* 1578, 2), but more often in the meaning of 'guilt'; see Sidon. *Ep.* 1.11.17, 4.9.4, 4.12.4, 6.1.1, 7.2.1, 7.6.3, 9.9.1, 9.11.7, *Carm.* 9.270; Amherdt (2001) 265. It is attested in the work of other Late Antique authors, for example Prud. *Cath.* 11.104 and Tert. *Apol.* 3.7; see also Apul. *Met.* 3.6.4, 7.9.2 where it is combined with the verb *sustinere*, 'bring forward'. Sidonius ends the sentence with a third assertion that natural circumstances are to blame for the separation of the friends (*de naturalium rerum difficultate*).

Domine inlustris, gerulos litterarum de disciplinae tuae institutione formatos et morum erilium verecundiam praeferentes opportune admisi, patienter audivi, competenter explicui. Vale: Sidonius ends the letter with a reverent address to Rusticus and also expresses his praise for Rusticus' messengers. For the expression *domine inlustris*, see the commentary on *Ep.* 2.3.1 *Gaudeo te, domine maior*.... For the title *illustris*, see the commentary on *Ep.* 2.4.1 *Vir clarissimus Proiectus*.... Mathisen (1984) 169 points out that even though Sidonius corresponded with most of the important Gallo-Roman aristocrats of his day, he only had two *viri illustres* among his correspondents in Visigothic territory prior to the occupation of Bourges (circa 470) and Clermont (475), Rusticus and Vettius in *Ep.* 4.9.1. Mathisen interprets this as proof of the decline of the Aquitanian aristocracy in comparison with the Gallo-Roman aristocracy in other parts of Gaul. For the role and importance of letter carriers in Sidonius' letters and in general, see the commentary on *Ep.* 2.3.1 *Sed id mihi ob hoc solum destinato tabellario nuntiatum*.... Most often, Sidonius uses the term *gerulus*, a 'bearer', 'carrier', in the special meaning of 'a private letter carrier' (*TLL* 6.2, 1952.70–84); see Sidon. *Ep.* 3.9.2, 4.5.1, 4.7.1, 6.5.1, 6.6.1, 6.10.1, 7.4.4, 8.13.3, 8.14.8, 9.3.2, 9.8.1; Amherdt (2001) 188. For *disciplina*, see the commentary on *Ep.* 2.4.3 *Quocirca ... celeberrimam disciplinam*.... For *institutio*, 'upbringing', 'education', see the commentary on *Ep.* 2.4.2 *Namque ipse, quantum ad institutionem spectat puellae*.... Sidonius uses the term *verecundia*, 'an attitude of restraint', 'modesty', several times to denote appropriate behaviour; see the commentary on *Ep.* 2.4.3 *benignitate responsi ... verecundiam munerare*. Sidonius ends the letter with a tricolon consisting of an adverb and verb in the first-person perfect. What kind of business Sidonius had with Rusticus' messengers remains obscure. The expression *opportune admisi* suggests that the messengers brought sensitive information, which could not be entrusted to paper but only delivered orally; see the commentary on *Ep.* 2.3.1 *Sed id mihi ob hoc solum destinato tabellario nuntiatum*.... The frequently used adverb *opportune*, 'suitably' (*TLL* 9.2, 779.30–80.77), is also used in Sidon. *Ep.* 7.16.2 and, like here, in combination with *competenter*, 'suitably', 'properly' in 8.3.4 *historiam flagitatam tunc recognosces opportune competenterque* ('you will study advantageously and adequately the tale you have requisitioned'). For the adverb *competenter*, see the commentary on *Ep.* 2.9.6 *quem quidem nuntium ... probabat competenter*.... The verb *explico* here means 'to send away' (*TLL* 5.2, 1738.61–3), a meaning which is unattested elsewhere; Mossberg (1934) 72. For *explico* in other meanings, see *Ep.* 2.1.4, 2.13.4.

Epistula 12

Introduction

Summary

Sidonius informs his brother-in-law, Agricola, that his daughter, Severiana, is very ill. He therefore cannot join him on a fishing trip and instead is leaving with his whole family for their suburban estate, hoping for an improvement in Severiana's condition. The letter ends with critical remarks about the incompetence of doctors. Despite fear for his daughter's life, Sidonius' scolding of the medical profession is witty and characterised by many literary allusions.

Addressee

Agricola, Sidonius' wife, Papianilla, and Ecdicius are siblings, children of emperor Avitus; see the introduction to *Ep.* 2.1. He was a *vir illustris* (for this title, see the commentary on *Ep.* 2.4.1 *Vir clarissimus Proiectus...*) and married to a daughter of Ruricius; see Ruric. *Ep.* 2.32, addressed to Agricola; Neri (2009) 340–1, 409, Mathisen (2020a) 55. He is also the addressee of Sidon. *Ep.* 1.2, which is Sidonius' portrait of the Visigothic king Theoderic II. On Agricola, see *PLRE* 2, 37 n. 2, *PCBE* 4, 106, Kaufmann (1995) 275, Mathisen (2020a) 77.

Date

It is clear from the letter that Sidonius' daughter is old enough to decide where she would like to be looked after, but beyond that the letter is not dateable. On the general difficulty of dating Sidonius' letters, see the Introduction, '2. The date and order of letters in Book 2'.

Major themes and further reading

Structure and intertextuality

Ep. 2.12 varies the subject of *Ep.* 2.2, a flight from the heat in the countryside to the sanitary rural estate. The connection is reinforced by the motif of fishing, which plays a role in both letters; see *Ep.* 2.2.12 and 17. It is not clear where the letter has been written and where the fishing trip should have taken place, as Sidonius only writes that it would have been on a river. For an overview of all the estates mentioned in Sidonius' letters, see Mratschek (2020b) 249 n. 90. The letter has been studied in connection with Sidonius' relation to his female family members (Mascoli 2010, 35–45, Mascoli 2014, 36) and Sidonius' attitude towards illness, medicine, and healing practices in Late Antiquity; Faure and Jacquemard (2014) 63–4, Clark (1993) 67–8, Hess (2021). The subject of health and medical cures is a frequent theme in the ancient epigram and letter. It often appears in Cicero's and Pliny's letters – see the Introduction (p. xvii) and the commentaries on 2.12.2 *Severiana ... lentae tussis impulsu febribus...* and 2.12.3 *simulque medicorum consilia....* Montone (2017) 31–3 shows that Sidonius inserts many literary allusions, mostly to Vergil and Martial. For the parallel construction of Sidon. *Ep.* 2.11–12 and Plin. *Ep.* 2.11–12 see the introduction to *Ep.* 2.11.

Commentary

Section 1

Sidonius Agricolae suo salutem: For the simple greeting formula, see the commentary on *Ep.* 2.1.1 *Sidonius Ecdicio suo salutem*. On the addressee, Agricola, see the introduction to this letter.

Misisti tu quidem lembum mobilem, solidum, lecti capacem iamque cum piscibus: Agricola sends Sidonius a boat with the request to accompany him on a fishing trip. Although the boat is easy to steer, it is big enough to offer space for a sofa next to the catch and thus is a comfortable place to spend one's leisure time. Hanaghan (2019) 80 thinks that Agricola sent Sidonius both fish and boat as a gift; see Williams (2014) 355–6, Shanzer (2001) on fish as a gift in Late Antiquity, and the translation of Loyen (1970a) 73. In my opinion the expression *iamque cum piscibus* is to be understood here as an indication of the size of the boat ('you have sent me a swift and solid boat, which has also room for a couch next to the catch of fishes'); see the translations of Anderson (1936) 471 and Köhler (2014) 65. It makes no sense for Sidonius to explain to Agricola why he cannot accompany him fishing when the latter would have already sent him a boat full of fish. For fishing as a pastime of the Gallo-Roman elite, see the commentary on *Ep.* 2.2.12 *Hinc iam spectabis ... piscator in pelagus*. The adjective *mobilis* (*TLL* 8, 1197.19–201.43) is not regularly used with vehicles, but with liquids; see the commentary on *Ep.* 2.2.16 *Attamen pelagi mobilis campus*.... For *lembus*, see the commentary on *Ep.* 2.2.18 *frequenterque lemborum superlabentum*.... The whole passage probably alludes to Verg. *Georg.* 1.201–3, describing the same type of ship which is rowed upstream: *non aliter quam qui adverso vix flumine lembum | remigiis subigit, si bracchia forte remisit, | atque illum in praeceps prono rapit alveus amni* ('not differently from someone who rows his ship with difficulty against the river and whom, if he would once let his arms rest, the ship would quickly rush downstream'). The term *lectus* denotes a 'couch', probably for dining (*TLL* 7.2, 1096.81–7.37); see *Ep.* 2.13.6 and the commentary on *Ep.* 2.2.5 *ita ut ministeriorum ... possit recipere sellas, quot solet sigma personas*. Sidonius frequently uses the adjective *capax*, 'spacious', 'roomy', here with an object, but the absolute use is much more frequent in his work; see the commentary on *Ep.* 2.2.4 *quae consequenti ... excepto solii capacis hemicyclio*.

tum praeterea gubernatorem longe peritum, remiges etiam robustos expeditosque, qui scilicet ea rapiditate praetervolant amnis adversi terga qua deflui: The ship is not only comfortable, but also safe and fast. Agricola's *gubernator*, 'steersman' (*TLL* 6.2, 2346.49–7.84), is experienced; see also Sidon. *Ep.* 8.10.2, 8.12.5, Plin. *Ep.* 9.26.4. For the combination with the adjective *peritus*, see Caes. *Bell. civ.* 1.58.3 *minus exercitatis remigibus minusque peritis gubernatoribus utebantur* ('they used less experienced rowers and less knowledgeable pilots'). The *remiges*, plural of *remex*, 'rower' (see Sidon. *Ep.* 8.12.5), are called *expeditus*, which means 'easy to move', 'quick', 'agile', of the body (*TLL* 5.2, 1619.70–83); see also Sidon. *Ep.* 4.24.3. For the comparative *expeditius*, see the commentary on *Ep.* 2.9.10 *Sed quia ... expeditius tibi cenae amicorum*.... The term *rapiditas*, 'swiftness', 'velocity', 'rapidity' (*OLD* 1573), probably refers to *rapit* in Verg. *Georg.* 1.201–3, the literary model for the whole passage (cited above in the commentary on the previous clause). The term is used elsewhere of a river in a military context – see Caes. *Bell. civ.* 1.62.2, *Bell. Gall.* 4.17.2, Frontin. *Strat.* 1.6.2. For the verb *praetervolo*, 'to fly by or past on a boat' (*TLL* 10.2, 1043.13–15), see a similar passage in Claud. *Bell. Get.* 26.321 *parva puppe lacum praetervolat* ('he hurried across the lake in a small boat'). *Adversus*, the participle of *adverto*, here means 'upstream'; see Verg. *Georg.* 1.201–3 (cited above, p. 352), Verg. *Aen.* 8.58, Liv. 45.35.3. See also Sidon. *Ep.* 1.5.4 *paulum per ostia adversa subvectus* ('I travelled a bit upstream from the point of confluence'). I have not found any parallel for going upstream as fast as downstream. Sidonius probably wrote this to emphasise the skill of the steersman. The passage is somewhat reminiscent of the description of the boat trip on the Clitumnus River in Plin. *Ep.* 8.8.3–4, but there the difference between the directions is explicitly mentioned. *Tergum* is frequently used in poetry to denote 'the outer covering or surface of anything (esp. of the ground, water, etc.)' (*OLD* 1925, 8); see Sidon. *Ep.* 9.14.6 *per turbulenti terga torrentis* ('over the surface of the agitated stream'). For *defluus*, 'flowing down', 'moving downstream', see the commentary on *Ep.* 2.2.16 *Lacus in Eurum defluus meat*....

Sed dabis veniam, quod invitanti tibi in piscationem comes venire dissimulo; namque me multo decumbentibus nostris validiora maeroris retia tenent, quae sunt amicis quoque et externis indolescenda: Sidonius plays with the image of fishing to explain that he is upset, which forbids him from joining Agricola on his fishing trip. For the second-person singular future *dabis*, see the commentary on *Ep.* 2.2.12 *videbis in calicibus repente perfusis*. *Piscatio*, 'the act of fishing' (*TLL* 10.1, 2198.33–51), is attested from Ulpian (second/third century AD) onwards; see also Ruric. *Ep.* 2.54.1; Neri (2009) 374. In Christian authors it is used more often and in a figurative, that is, spiritual sense; see for example Hier. *Ep.* 125.8. The verb *dissimulare*, 'to be reluctant to', 'to refuse' (*TLL* 5.1, 1483.32), appears several times in Sidonius' letters – *Ep.* 5.3.1, 7.9.14, 8.8.2, 9.9.6, 9.11.7; van Waarden (2010) 486. In *Ep.* 2.1.1 it appears in the meaning 'to conceal'. For *decumbo*, 'to lie ill', 'be confined by illness' (*TLL* 5.1, 221.62–22.2), see Sidon. *Ep.* 7.17.1, 9.14.1. *Rete*, 'net' (*OLD* 1640, 1e), appears here in a figurative sense. The image is used several times of love in ancient literature, for example Prop. 2.32.20, 3.8.37, Ov. *Ars* 1.263, Lucr. 4.1147–8, but nowhere else of grief (*maeroris retia*) besides Sidonius; Montone (2017) 32. See the similar Sidon. *Ep.* 4.12.3 *nubilo superducti maeroris* ('covered by a cloud of grief'); Amherdt (2001) 315–16. The manuscripts LV, Loyen (1970a) 73 and Anderson (1936) 470 have *quaeque*; MNTC and Lütjohann (1887) 36 have *quoque*, which is the archetypal reading according to Dolveck (2020). The verb *indolesco*, 'to feel pain', is used for both physical and emotional pain. For the construction with the accusative, see *TLL* 7.1, 1222.81–4.

Unde te quoque puto, si rite germano moveris affectu, quo temporis puncto paginam hanc sumpseris, de reditu potius cogitaturum: With the expression *germano ... affectu* ('with brotherly love') Sidonius appeals to Agricola to help him and his family as close relatives. Christian writers often use the adjective *germanus* figuratively in the sense of brotherhood because of faith or care for one another (*TLL* 6.2, 1918.74–19.7). The expression is also found in Aug. *Ep.* 149.34 *germano salutamus affectu* ('we greet with brotherly love'). The expression is reinforced by the commonly used adverb *rite*, 'in the manner required', 'properly', 'duly', 'correctly' (*OLD* 1656, 3), which is used only here in Sidonius' writings. For *pagina*, here used for the letter at hand, see the commentary on *Ep.* 2.2.7 *Quid plura? Nihil illis paginis....* For other instances of the use of *sumere*, 'to take up' (about a book or document with the intention to read it), see *Ep.* 7.9.4, 9.3.5, Symm. *Ep.* 1.95.1, 5.30, 5.94, 7.5, 7.6; van Waarden (2010) 430. It is similarly used in Sidon. *Ep.* 2.12.2 *litteras ... sumeremus*.

Section 2

Severiana, sollicitudo communis, inquietata primum lentae tussis impulsu febribus quoque iam fatigatur, hisque per noctes ingravescentibus: Sidonius had four children, a son Apollinaris, and three daughters, Severiana, Alcima and Roscia; Stevens (1933) 84 n. 8, Anderson (1936) 254 n. 1, Mascoli (2010) 42–3, Mascoli (2014) 37–8, MacDonald (2000) 65–8, van Waarden (2020a) 27. Severiana is mentioned only here by name; *PLRE* 2, 998, *PCBE* 4, 1739–40, Mathisen (2020a) 121. Sidonius mentions Roscia in *Ep.* 5.16.5 (cited just below); see *PLRE* 2, 950, *PCBE* 4, 1630, Günther (1997), Mathisen (2020a) 118. Alcima is mentioned only by Gregory of Tours (Greg Tur. *Hist. Franc.* 3.2, 3.12, *Glor. Mart.* 64); *PLRE* 2, 54, *PCBE* 4, 104, Mathisen (2020a) 128–9. Children in general rarely appear in Sidonius' work and he mentions only his own children by name; see Mathisen (2020a) 45 and the commentary on *Ep.* 2.8.1 *His additur, quod quinque liberum parens....* For the expression *sollicitudo communis*, 'our common cause of anxiety', see Sidon. *Ep.* 5.16.5, addressed to his wife, Papianilla, where Sidonius refers to their daughter Roscia similarly with *cura communis* ('our common anxiety'). One's own health or illness and that of relatives or friends is a frequent topic in ancient letters, for example in Cicero about his slave Tiro's illness (Cic. *Fam.* 16.8 and 16.13) or his daughter Tullia (*Att.* 11.6.4), and in Pliny's letters; see the Introduction (p. xvii) and Weilbach (2020). In Cic. *Fam.* 7. 26.1 Cicero writes that he flees to his Tusculum because of his stomach problems (*intestinis laborarem*); see Wöhrle (2010) on medicine in Cicero's writings. A possible intertext for Severiana's tenacious coughing (*lentae tussis impulsu*) and fever (*febribus*), which gets worse in the night, could, however, be an epigram, not a letter, namely Catull. 44.13–14 *hic me gravedo frigida et frequens tussis | quassavit* ('then a cold catarrh and a heavy cough shook me up'). In his *Carm.* 44 Catullus describes how he travelled to his estate in the countryside to recover from his fever and coughing; Montone (2017) 32–3. The adjective *lentus* here means 'lasting', 'tenacious', 'persistent' (of things) (*TLL* 7.2, 1162.17–42); it is also used of sickness in Celsus, for example Cels. 2.15.1, 2.17.4. The combination with *tussis* is not common; the adjective for 'chronic' cough in medical writers is *vetus*; Weilbach (2020) 191. *Febris*, 'fever' (*TLL* 6.1, 408.36–11.86), is combined with *nocturnus*, 'of the night', or *nox*, 'night', also in Plin. *Nat.* 29.64, Cels. 2.35 *si febris ... noctu increscit* ('if the fever increases at night'). Fever is a disease that is frequently mentioned both by the letter writers and in the medical literature; Weilbach (2020) 159–60. In *Ep.* 1.5.8, 5.3.3, Sidonius describes how he himself was stricken with a severe fever; see also *Ep.* 6.1.5. The verb *ingravesco*, 'to become heavier', 'to increase', is used elsewhere in a figurative sense of diseases getting worse (*TLL* 7.1, 1565.27–47), for example Cic. *Catil.* 1.31, *Div.* 2.16, Plin. *Ep.* 1.12.5, 2.20.5. To express that a disease is getting worse, medical authors use the phrase *increscit morbus* instead of *ingravescere*; Weilbach (2020) 118–19.

propter quod optat exire in suburbanum; litteras tuas denique cum sumeremus, egredi ad villulam iam parabamus: Severiana is old enough to decide which place is good for her health. For the idea that a stay in the country is healthy, see the commentary on *Ep.* 2.2.2 *quin tu mage, si quid tibi salubre cordi.* See the commentary immediately above on *Ep.* 2.12.2 *Severiana, sollicitudo communis* for Catull. 44 as a probable intertext for Sidonius' letter. Catullus also mentions his suburban villa as a place for recovery from illness and uses the term *suburbanum* to refer to his estate; see Catull. 44.6–7 *in tua suburbana | villa* ('in your suburban villa'). The term *suburbanum* denotes 'an estate, a suburban villa (usually near Rome)' (*OLD* 1855, 2). It also is used of estates near cities other than Rome, for example in Mart. 5.35.3, Suet. *Tib.* 11.1. Sidonius also uses the abstract *suburbanitas* in the same concrete sense in see *Ep.* 3.1.2, 7.2.7; van Waarden (2010) 178–9. For *literas ... sumere*, see the commentary on *Ep.* 2.12.1 *Unde te quoque puto ... paginam hanc sumpseris....*

The dimininutive *villula*, 'a small farmstead or country house' (*OLD* 2063), is used by classical authors, for example in Hor. *Sat.* 1.5.45, 2.3.10, Cic. *Att.* 8.13.2, 12.27.1, and also in Apul. *Met.* 3.29.5. Sidonius probably uses the term because Pliny ends his villa letter *Ep.* 2.17.29 with the loving description: *ut tot tantisque dotibus villulae nostrae maxima commendatio ex tuo contubernio accedat* ('so that all these beautiful gifts of my little villa would be given the greatest worth by being with you'). Like Sidonius, Pliny uses the term only once in his correspondence. Another intertext may be Ausonius' *De Herediolo*, which he begins by mentioning his little villa (*villulam*), the ideal place for composing light poetry; Sowers (2016) 518. Anderson (1936) 470, Loyen (1970a) 73 and Kaufmann (1995) 41 n. 9 situate the estate near Lyon, although it is not known that Sidonius also owned a country estate there. What would speak in favour of this theory is the mention of the river on which he and Agricola wanted to fish in 2.12.1; see the commentary on *Ep.* 2.12.1 *tum praeterea gubernatorem ... praetervolant amnis adversi terga, qua defluit*. It could be the River Arar, present-day Saône, which flows into the Rhone at Lyon. In *Ep.* 2.10.4 v. 22 and 25–8 Sidonius describes the work of the boatmen on the river. Hanaghan (2019) 80–1 n. 64 instead thinks that Sidonius is almost certainly referring to Avitacum, which is situated near Clermont. The diminutive force of *villula* is consistent with the language Sidonius employs in *Ep.* 2.2 and it would also be fitting that *Ep.* 2.12 might be seen as a negative counter-image to *Ep.* 2.2, where the flight from the city is described and evaluated in a positive light; see the introduction to *Ep.* 2.12. In addition, these letters have the motif of fishing in common.

Quocirca tu seu venias seu moreris, preces nostras orationibus iuva, ut ruris auram desideranti salubriter cedat ipsa vegetatio: Sidonius asks Agricola to pray for his daughter's health in any case, even if he cannot visit her. Sidonius uses the terms *preces*, 'prayer', and *oratio*, which actually means 'speech', but in ecclesiastical Latin is also used for 'prayer' (*TLL* 9.2, 888.8–17 and 890.68–92.15). After Sidonius became bishop, he often wrote about the power of prayer, for example *Ep.* 7.6.3 *orationum tuarum* ('of your prayers'), 9.3.4 *frequentissimis tuis illis et valentissimis orationum ... suffragiis* ('the gracious help of those unceasing and potent prayers of yours'); Bailey (2020) 272–3. The clean air in the countryside (*ruris auram*) is explicitly mentioned here as healing (*salubriter*); Sidonius thus probably alludes to the ancient notion of miasmata, poisonous vapours of the soil that are carried away with the air and thus contribute to the spread of diseases. Hippocrates of Kos (around 460–375 BC) is regarded as the founder of the miasmatic theory; Jouanna (2012). Sidonius thus anticipates the subject of medical art, which he will discuss in detail in section 3 of this letter. The adverb *salubriter*, 'with advantage to the health', 'profitably, to good effect' (*OLD* 1683, Blaise 734), also appears in *Ep.* 4.6.3. Here it is combined with *cedere*, 'turn out', 'to have some result' (*TLL* 3, 372.43–73), and the *dativus ethicus* referring to the sick daughter. For the adverbs ending in *-(i)ter* in general, see the commentary on *Ep.* 2.1.1 *Duo nunc pariter mala sustinent*. The noun *vegetatio*, 'the act of invigorating' (*OLD* 2019, Blaise 838, 2), first appears in Apul. *Met.* 1.2.3 and is very rare; Keulen (2007) 101. Here it is used in the meaning of 'quickening', 'excitement', 'movement'. For the notion that a stay in the countryside is good for one's health, see the commentary on *Ep.* 2.2.2 *quin tu mage, si quid tibi salubre cordi*.

certe ego vel tua soror inter spem metumque suspensi credidimus eius taedium augendum, si voluntati iacentis obstitissemus: Sidonius' wife Papianilla is Agricola's sister (*soror*); see the introduction to this letter. For Papianilla, see the commentary on *Ep.* 2.2.3 *nomen hoc praedio, quod, quia uxorium patrio mihi dulcius*. *Taedium* here denotes an 'indisposition', 'offensive condition', 'nuisance' (*OLD* 1900, 3b).

Section 3

Igitur ardori civitatis atque torpori tam nos quam domum totam praevio Christo pariter eximimus: Here and elsewhere (*Ep.* 1.8.1, 4.8.3, 5.17.4), Sidonius describes cities in negative terms, mentioning their heat and stuffy air which causes illness; Amherdt (2001) 236–7 and see the commentaries on *Ep.* 2.2.2 *Quin tu mage, si quid tibi salubre cordi* and *Ep.* 2.2.2 *raptim subduceris anhelantibus angustiis civitatis*.... Members of Sidonius' household are most often mentioned when he is travelling; see *Ep.* 4.8.1–2, 4.24.4. For other aristocrats travelling with their family, see Sidon. *Ep.* 4.18.2; Cloppet (1989), Piacente (2005), Hutchings (2009) 65–7, Mathisen (2020a) 64–5. The expression *praevio Christo* also appears in *Ep.* 4.10.2; the expression *praevio Deo* appears in *Ep.* 3.7.2 and *Deo praevio* in 4.15.3. The appeal to Christ is repeated again at the end of the section, framing Sidonius' account of the incompetent doctors. For similar formulaic interjections expressing faith in God, see the commentaries on *Ep.* 2.2.3 *Haec mihi cum meis praesule deo...*, 2.4.2 *quod Deo prosperante succedat* and 2.9.10 *sed quia et ipsi ... sub ope Christi ...*. For the adverb *pariter*, 'in like manner, 'equally', and adverbs ending in *-(i)ter*, see the commentary on *Ep.* 2.1.1 *Duo nunc pariter mala sustinent.* The verb *eximo*, 'to take away', 'remove', is often used to describe how to free oneself from adverse circumstances (*TLL* 5.2, 1499.51–500.41).

simulque medicorum consilia vitamus assidentum dissidentumque, qui parum docti et satis seduli languidos multos officiosissime occidunt: Sidonius turns to the role of the doctors (*medici*) in the healing process. The verb *assidere*, 'to attend upon', 'take care of', is often used about grieving or sick people (*TLL* 2, 877.35–8.51), for example Hor. *Sat.* 1.1.82, Ov. *Her.* 20.137, Plin. *Ep.* 7.19.1. The combination with *medicus* is attested elsewhere, for example Cels. 3.8 *ut aegri vires subinde adsidens medicus inspiciat* ('that the patient's strength should be continually under the eye of the attending practitioner'), Sen. *Ben.* 5.16.3, Pacian. *Paraen.* 9. It puns on *dissidere*, 'to disagree', 'to differ' about something (*TLL* 5.1, 1467.47–8.7); see also Sidon. *Carm.* 22.1; Delhey (1993) 48. Sidonius thus criticises the doctors, who are fighting with each other about the best cure, a well known topos in antiquity; see Plin. *Nat.* 23.32, 29.11; Savaron (1599) 158, Nicolas (1901) 6. Moreover, in a linguistically stylised sentence, he points to their poor knowledge, which is combined with an ominous zeal. See the construction of adverb–adjective: *parum/satis–docti/seduli*. To express his fear for his daughter and to generalise from his experience with doctors to their work in general, Sidonius alludes to Hor. *Ep.* 1.7.8–9, who writes in his letter to Maecenas: *officiosaque sedulitas et opella forensis | adducit febres et testamenta resignat* ('their officious eagerness and the little services in court bring fevers and open testaments'). Sidonius' adjective *seduli*, 'attentive', 'painstaking', 'sedulous' (see the commentary on 2.5.2 *Pro quo precem sedulam fundo...*), points to Horace's abstract noun *sedulitas*, 'assiduity', and Sidonius' superlative adverb *officiosissime*, 'very dutiful', 'attentive', to Horace's adjective *officiosa*. Sidonius also transforms Horace's allusion to death (*testamenta resignat*) into *occident* ('they kill'); see Colton (2000) 115–16. Sidonius combines Horace's warning about the dangers of the city with the topos of the doctor who kills his patient instead of curing him. Another intertext for the passage could therefore be Mart. 1.47, where it is also suggested that doctors kill their patients: *Nuper erat medicus, nunc est vispillo Diaulus: | quod vispillo facit, fecerat et medicus* ('until recently, Diaulus was a doctor, now he is an undertaker. What he does as an undertaker, he has also done as a doctor'); see also Mart. 6.53 and Mart. 5.9, about a doctor who makes him sick, where, similar to Sidonius (*languidos*, 'faint', 'weak'), Martial uses *languebam* to denote the illness: *languebam: sed tu comitatus protinus ad me | venisti centum, Symmache, discipulis. | Centum me* *tetigere manus aquilone gelatae:* | *non habui febrem, Symmache, nunc habeo* ('I was weak, but you immediately came to me, Symmachus, with a hundred students. A hundred hands, icy from the north wind, touched me. I did not have a fever, Symmachus, but now I do'); Hanaghan (2017a). See also Ruric. *Ep.* 1.1.3 *languori quoque meo* ('for my illness'), Neri (2009) 169. A general reluctance to depend on physicians and doubts about their knowledge are widespread in ancient literature and reflect an understandable fear of illness and death. Authors criticised the greed of doctors, who were considered of low social status: see for example Lucr. 6.1179, 5.9, Iuv. 10.219–21, Plin. *Nat.* 29.16–27, Phaedr. 1.14, Petron. 42.5, and several epigrams in the eleventh book of the *Anthologia Palatina*, such as *Anth. Pal.* 11.112, 11.113, 11.118. On the role and reputation of physicians in antiquity, see Kudlien (1986) 190–8, Matthäus (1987) 17–19, Achner (2009). For Sidonius' interest in health, physical features and medical cures, see *Ep.* 3.13, 4.13, 5.14, Nicolas (1901), Faure and Jacquemard (2014) 63–4.

sane contubernio nostro iure amicitiae Iustus adhibebitur: After his general statement about doctors, Sidonius talks about the doctor who treats his family and is also a friend. For *contubernium* in a similar context, see the commentary on *Ep.* 2.2.2 *raptim subduceris … contubernio nostro aventer insertus.* For the rights of friendship, which Sidonius highly esteems, see the introduction to *Ep.* 2.3. For the expression *iure amicitiae*, 'by right of friendship', see *Ep.* 4.1.5 *amicitiae iura*, 4.7.1 *amicitiarum iura*, 4.13.3 *iura amicitiae*, 6.2.3 *ius … amicitiae*, 7.6.1 *amicitiarum … iura*; Amherdt (2001) 90, 213. A synonymous collocation is *lege amicitiae*, 'according to the law of friendship'; see *Ep.* 7.17.1; van Waarden (2016) 212. Only Iustus, a doctor and family friend (*nostro*), is allowed to treat his family, although Sidonius doubts his abilities as a doctor. He is otherwise unattested; *PLRE* 2, 651 n. 2, *PCBE* 4, 1093, Mathisen (2020a) 65, 103. There might be a wordplay with *iure*, 'by right', and, *iustus*, 'just'. For Sidonius' fondness for puns with names, see the commentary on *Ep.* 2.1.1 *Seronati, inquam: de cuius ut primum etiam nomine loquar.*

quem, si iocari liberet in tristibus, facile convincerem Chironica magis institutum arte quam Machaonica: Despite his daughter's poor health Sidonius lightens up the mood with a pun and thus connects his remarks to *Ep.* 2.2, where the escape from the city to a country estate is described with a humorous touch. In other letters, Sidonius separates sad circumstances and humorous writing more strictly according to the rules of ancient epistolary topics; see *Ep.* 1.9.8, 7.7.1, 9.9.3, Cic. *Att.* 5.5.1, Symm. *Ep.* 1.101.2, 3.21; van Waarden (2010) 32 n. 71, 344–5. The centaur Chiron is distinguished for his knowledge of plants and medicine. He had many famous heroes as students, among them Achilles, Jason and Aesculapius, the father of Machaon, who became a successful doctor in the Greeks' long war against Troy; see Hom. *Il.* 2.732, 4.190–219, Verg. *Aen.* 2.263, Prop. 2.1.59, Mart. 2.16.5; Graf (1997), Dräger (1999). Sidonius mentions Chiron also in *Carm.* 1.17–20, 2.150–2, 9.135, 14.4 v. 27, 23.195. The joke is that Chiron, who is half man, half horse, is in charge of veterinary medicine, while Machaon is a doctor for humans. In addition, there is also a pun on the Greek term χείρων, 'worse'; Anderson (1936) 472 n. 1, Loyen (1970a) 74 n. 3, Köhler (2014) 66 n. 3. Sidonius suggests that his doctor has learned 'the art of making it worse', which fits with his low opinion of the medical profession expressed in the previous clause; see the commentary above on *Ep.* 2.12.3 *simulque medicorum consilia vitamus assidentum dissidentumque....* In their commentary from 1836, Grégoire and Collombet refer to Diogenes Laertius, *Lives* 6.2.51, who similarly plays with the meaning of Chiron's name; Furbetta (2020) 559. Less convincingly, Nicolas (1901) 7 explains the name as as genitive plural of Greek ἡ χείρ ('hand'). For the medieval gloss on this term, see Chronopoulos (2020) 649–50. There might also be a play with the similar-sounding *ars chirurgica*; see Hyg. *Fab.* 274. Both adjectives, *Chironica* and *Machaonica*, only appear here; Gualandri (1979) 176 n. 109, Onorato (2016) 424 n. 79. As Wolff (2020) 405 notes, many hapax legomena in Sidonius are adjectives derived from proper names. Ovid and Statius use the adjective *Machaonius* – see Ov. *Ars* 2.491, *Rem.* 546, Stat. *Silv.* 1.4.114. For the doctor Machaon, see Dräger (1999), Achner (2009) 9.

Quo diligentius postulandus est Christus obsecrandusque, ut valetudini, cuius curationem cura nostra non invenit, potentia superna medeatur. Vale. At the beginning of section 3 Sidonius refers to Christ (see the commentary on 2.12.3 *igitur ardori ... praevio Christo...*), and again at the end, where he asks him for help. Mixed in with the request for divine help is the metaphor of *Christus-medicus*, that is, the interpretation of redemption as a process of healing, a metaphor especially prominent in the fourth and fifth century in Ambrose, Jerome and Augustine (who was generally very interested in the subject of medicine), for example Ambr. *Ps.* 40.14, Hier. *Comm. Mich.* 2.7, Aug. *Serm.* 32.1, 155.10, 175.9, 176.4, 286.3, 302.3, 345.7; Honecker (1985), Hübner (1985), Gollwitzer-Voll (2007) 28–39, Weber (2013) with an overview of the older literature on the topos of

Christus-medicus in Augustine. For this topos in Ruricius' letters see Ruric. *Ep.* 1.1.3; Neri (2009) 168–9. Doctors appear elsewhere in Sidonius' letters, but not as named persons as here, but as representatives of their profession, in *Ep.* 1.7.7, 1.8.2, 8.10.2, 9.9.15. The term *valetudo* denotes 'health', 'health condition' or, as here, 'illness', 'indisposition' (*OLD* 2008, 3). It is frequently used in ancient letters and medical literature; Weilbach (2020) 63–4. The meaning 'illness' is predominantly found in Pliny, for example Plin. *Ep.* 1.22.1, 3.7.1, 5.16.3, 7.1.1, 7.19.1, 7.22.1, 7.30.1, 8.1.1. Sidonius ends the letter about his daughter's illness with a pun on *curatio* 'healing', 'medicine' (*TLL* 4, 1476.4–7.3), and *cura*, 'effort', 'concern', combined with the assonance on *cuius*. The word *curatio* is used a few times in letters with reference to medicine; see Cic. *Fam.* 16.4.1, Plin. *Ep.* 5.19.7. It frequently appears in medical literature, for example Cels. 5.26.24c, Plin. *Nat.* 23.74; Weilbach (2020) 268–9. The noun *potentia*, 'power', is combined with *superna*, 'that is above', 'celestial', and stands metonymically for God; see other examples in *TLL* 10.2, 298.80–9.10; see also Sidon. *Ep.* 2.13.4. For *mederi*, 'to heal', here constructed with the dative (*valetudini*), see van Waarden (2010) 281–2, Weilbach (2020) 286. The verb appears seven times in Sidonius: here and in *Ep.* 5.7.7, 7.5.3, 7.6.1, 7.7.4, 8.10.4, 9.14.4. While the subjects of the verb *mederi* in the medical literature are, above all, the remedies, in the letters it is usually people who (should) heal, and here God, for example Plin. *Nat.* 23.142, Plin. *Ep.* 5.16.11, Cic. *Att.* 10.10.3; Weilbach (2020) 286. For the letter's simple ending with *vale*, see the commentary on *Ep.* 2.1.4 *Vale*.

Epistula 13

Introduction

Summary

Sidonius writes to Serranus that Marcellinus has shown him Serranus' letter about the emperor, Petronius Maximus. Sidonius criticises Serranus' very positive portrayal of Petronius Maximus and doubts that he was happy. In a comparison with the Roman general Sulla, who also claimed for himself the epithet *felix*, Sidonius shows that the greatest power does not mean the greatest happiness. In sections 3–5 Sidonius reviews the career of Petronius Maximus, which came to an ominous end. In sections 6–8 Sidonius analyses the lives of great men in power using the historical example of Damocles, who lived at the court of Dionysius I, a ruler of Syracuse in the fourth century BC. Being an obsequious courtier, Damocles praised his ruler as the happiest man on earth. To show him the negative aspects of power, Dionysius forced his admirer to enjoy a luxurious meal while a sword was hanging above his head, held up only by a horsehair. Damocles, paralysed by fear, was unable to enjoy the luxury and greatly relieved to be released back into his ordinary life.

Addressee

The addressee, Serranus, is otherwise unknown; *PLRE* 2, 996, *PCBE* 4, 1736, Kaufmann (1995) 347–8, Mathisen (2020a) 121.

Date

The *terminus post quem* for *Ep.* 2.13 is the death of the emperor Majorian in 461; see the commentary on *Ep.* 2.13.3 *Hic si omittamus....* On the general difficulty of dating Sidonius' letters, see the Introduction, '2. The date and order of letters in Book 2'.

COMMENTARY, EPISTULA 13

Major themes and further reading

Structure

In the penultimate letter of his book on *otium*, Sidonius deals with the dangers of *negotium*. The letter, which Edward Gibbon praised for its elegant composition (van Waarden 2020c, 699), is a warning against the vicissitudes of politics and thus refers back to the closing letter of Book 1, *Ep.* 1.11, which shows Sidonius in the role of a politician. *Ep.* 2.13 belongs to the genre of reporting letters, since Sidonius gives a detailed account of the downfall of Petronius Maximus; Cain (2009) 212. Fernández López (1994) 170–7 treats *Ep.* 2.13 under 'suasoria y controversia'. Through the theme of human happiness treated here there is also a connection to *Ep.* 2.3, which is dedicated to Felix; see the introduction to *Ep.* 2.3. Together with *Ep.* 2.2, 2.9 and 2.10, *Ep.* 2.13 is one of the longer letters of the second book. The letter tells a short story about the cruel death of the emperor Petronius Maximus, and can therefore be read in connection with other narrative letters by Sidonius or Pliny, which also deal with political events or cruel death. See Sidon. *Ep.* 8.11 about the murder of the poet Lampridius, who had been strangled in his own home by the hands of his slaves, and Pliny's account of the murder of the ex-praetor Larcius Macedo (Plin. *Ep.* 3.14); Mratschek (2020c). For a narratological analysis of a similar passage in *Ep.* 7.2.3–8 about Amantius' conquests in Marseille, see van Waarden (2010) 154–6. For the narrating of a short story in Sidon. *Ep.* 3.12, see Henke (2012). The letter should also be interpreted in context with other passages describing (and renouncing) luxurious dinners, such as *Carm.* 17, *Ep.* 1.2 and 2, see Hindermann (forthcoming b).

Intertextuality and political context

In letter 2.13, Sidonius adapts the ancient idea of the misfortune and loneliness of tyrants to his own time by linking the story of Damocles to the downfall of Petronius Maximus. The letter stands out above all because of its detailed retelling of the well-known story of Damocles. The secondary literature therefore either focuses on an intertextual comparison of Sidonius' version with those of other authors or it examines which parallels can be found to persons and events from Sidonius' own time. For the example of Damocles in Late Antique literature, see Squillante (2007/2008), who shows that Sidonius merges various intertexts (Cicero, Horace, Lucan) in his account of the story; see the commentaries below on sections 7–8. Furthermore, she compares the versions of Sidonius, Ammianus Marcellinus 29.2.4,

Macrobius, *Comment. Somn. Scip.* 1.10.16 and Boeth. *Cons.* 3.5.6–11, who narrate the story with a different focus. Degl'Innocenti Pierini (2008) shows that Sidonius complements Cicero's description of luxury with texts by Horace, Juvenal and Lucretius. Catarinella (2000) refers to the parallels between *Ep.* 2.13.2 and the preface of Augustine's *De Civitate Dei*. She compares the negative and cautious tone of letter 2.13 with other letters that report positively on public offices and honours, especially in the first book; see Sidon. *Ep.* 1.3, 1.4, 1.6, 2.3, 3.6, 5.16, 8.8; Loyen (1970a) 248 n. 13. Gualandri highlights the verbal parallels between Sidonius' account of Damocles' story and the tenth book of Lucan; Gualandri (1979) 72–4 and Gualandri (2020) 310. See the commentaries below on sections 6–7. Köhler (1995) 234–5 on Sidon. *Ep.* 1.7.2 (*non esse felicem*, 'he is not happy') and 1.7.13 (*infelicius nihil est*, 'there is not anything unhappier') analyses the parallels to Arvandus' case, where Sidonius also reflects on human happiness. Van Waarden (2020a) 21 and 23 n. 72 interprets the letter about the demise of Petronius Maximus as a meditation on Avitus' tragic failure. Hanaghan (2019) 114, 187–8 reads Sidonius' account of Petronius Maximus' life as a justification for why he retired from his political career and a warning against the dangers of *negotium*. Fascione (2019) 85, 99 shows that Sidonius uses the story to contrast the emperor, who is confined to his palace, with the senators, who are engaged in working for the common good (see *Ep.* 3.8.1–2), thus criticising the system of rule.

Commentary

Section 1

Sidonius Serrano suo salutem: For the simple greeting formula, see the commentary on *Ep.* 2.1.1 *Sidonius Ecdicio suo salutem*. For the addressee, Serranus, see the introduction to this letter.

Epistulam tuam nobis Marcellinus togatus exhibuit, homo peritus virque amicorum: The beginning of the letter hints at the way books and letters were distributed in Sidonius' time. The author sends his writings to friends, who then have copies made and forward them to other acquaintances; see the commentary on *Ep.* 2.8.2 *mercennarius bybliopola suscipiet* and Sidon. *Carm.* 24. For letter carriers in general, see the commentary on *Ep.* 2.3.1 *Sed id mihi ob hoc solum destinato tabellario nuntiatum....* In *Ep.* 9.7.1 and

9.9.3 Sidonius also mentions writings that are not directly addressed to him but which he receives through other channels; Gerth (2013) 158 n. 385. Marcellinus was a lawyer in Narbonne – see Sidon. *Carm.* 23.464–74. He is attested only in Sidonius; *PLRE* 2, 708 n. 5, *PCBE* 4, 1239, Mathisen (2020a) 106–7. *Togatus*, 'wearing a toga' (*OLD* 1946, 1), refers to the formal dress of the law court; see for example Apul. *Met.* 10.33.1. The verb *exhibere*, 'to deliver', 'carry', 'bring' (*TLL* 5.2, 1418.29–40), is frequently used in relation to the transfer of letters, for example in Plin. *Ep.* 1.2.1, 2.5.1, 3.10.4, 4.27.5, 7.2.2, Symm. *Ep.* 1.27, 1.57, 1.87. For the qualitative genitive (*vir*) *amicorum* (*TLL* 1, 1907.44–51) without an attribute, see Sidon. *Ep.* 4.24.6 *vir caritatis* ('a man of charity'), Symm. *Ep.* 1.78.1 *ex summatibus litterarum viris* ('of the most noble men of letters'), Paul. Nol. *Ep.* 34.4 *viri divitiarum* ('a man of wealth'); Loyen (1970a) 220–21 n. 50, Amherdt (2001) 499.

Quae primoribus verbis salutatione libata reliquo sui tractu, qui quidem grandis est: Sidonius begins his critique of his friend's writing with praise. The adjective *primor*, 'the first', is attested elsewhere referring to the order within a speech or book (*TLL* 10.2, 1267.10–18), see for example Gell. 1.18.3. The verb *libo*, 'to pour', is used of words only by Late Antique authors (*TLL* 7.2, 1341.24–36), see for example Symm. *Ep.* 2.11. The noun *tractus* denotes 'the action of causing things to move in a particular course' and is also used in a transferred meaning of speech and style to denote a 'lengthening', 'protracting' (*OLD* 1955, 2a–b) in a narration, for example in Plin. *Ep.* 5.8.10 about the difference between *oratio* ('speech') and *historia* ('history'): *illa tractu et suavitate atque etiam dulcedine placet* ('it pleases with its drawing out and pleasantness and even sweetness'); see also Quint. 4.2.118, 5.8.2. Sidonius uses *grandis*, 'large', 'great', 'full', of a letter only here. Referring to style, the adjective means 'great', 'grand', 'lofty', 'sublime' (*TLL* 6.2, 2185.52–6.36). Sidonius probably alludes to the theory of three different levels of style (*genera dicendi*). The *genus grave* or *grande* is the 'sublime' style, while the other two are the 'middle' style (*genus mediocre*) and 'low' style (*genus humile*); Calboli (1998) 911. A parallel for the metaphorical usage 'important', 'weighty', is Sidon. *Ep.* 9.14.7 *quae materia tam grandis est* ('the subject is so colossal'), about Julius Caesar as the subject of a declamation; see also Sidon. *Carm.* 4.17–18. For the literal meaning 'long', 'big', see Cic. *Att.* 13.21.1 *ad Hirtium dederam epistulam sane grandem* ('I gave Hirtius a very long letter'), Iuv. 10.71 *verbosa et grandis epistula venit* ('a great and wordy letter came'), Paul. Nol. *Ep.* 50.14 *de resurrectionis forma non* *grandem sed plenam fidei instructione epistolam* ('your letter about the nature of resurrection was not copious, but full of instructions for faith').

patroni tui Petronii Maximi imperatoris laudes habebat: Sidonius relates to Serranus the content of the latter's letter of praise about Petronius Maximus. Petronius Maximus was born around 396 into the noble *gens Anicia* and became the western emperor (Augustus) in Rome from 17 March to 31 May 455 after his predecessor Valentinian III, who had reigned as western emperor for nearly thirty years, was murdered at his instigation. Petronius was killed after a short reign during the tumults caused by the Vandal attack on Rome; see Sidonius' account in *Ep.* 2.13.3 of his inglorious end, which is contrasted with his previous successful career, and the commentary on *Ep.* 2.13.3 *qui quamquam in arcem praefectoriam patriciam consularemque....* On Petronius Maximus, see *PLRE* 2, 749–51, Henning (1999) 20–32, Kulikowski (2020) 207, Mathisen (2020a) 108. Hanaghan (2019) 114 shows that Sidonius' portrait of Petronius also resonates with his other imperial portraits – of Valentinian III, Avitus, Majorian and Anthemius, who were all killed in office: Petronius is portrayed as a good senator, but not fit to be emperor. Sidonius mentions Petronius also in *Carm.* 7.360, 376, 464. In Sidon. *Ep.* 1.7.1 we find the same expression, *laudibus imperatoris* ('to the praise of the emperor'); Köhler (1995) 233.

quem tamen tu pertinacius aut amabilius quam rectius veriusque felicissimum appellas: Sidonius emphasises his argument that Serranus should not call Petronius Maximus happy, using four comparative adverbs (*pertinacius aut amabilius quam rectius veriusque*) in descending length (5–5–3–3 syllables). For *felicitas*, 'happiness', 'felicity', 'luckiness', 'success', to denote political success, see the commentary on *Ep.* 2.3.1 *et in lares ... felicitate remeaverit*.

propter hoc quippe, cur per amplissimos fascium titulos fuerit evectus usque ad imperium: Sidonius cites his own account of the life of Petronius Maximus to show that Petronius should not be called *felix* and thereby corrects Serranus' letter. Sidonius often uses *cur* with the subjunctive (instead of a causal *cum* or a factual *quod*) to refer to the opinion of another person; see *Ep.* 1.1.2, 1.11.12, 4.3.1, 7.9.15; Köhler (1995) 108–9. For the title *amplissimus*, 'the highest', see the commentary on *Ep.* 2.3.1 *Gaudeo te ... amplissimae dignitatis infulas consecutum*. *Fasces*, the technical term for the 'insignia of the highest Roman officials', that is, a bundle carried before the magistrates consisting of rods and an axe, is used here in a metonymical sense for 'office', 'magistracy' (*TLL* 6.1, 304.57–5.82); see also Sidon. *Ep.* 1.4.1, 2.13.4; Köhler (1995) 176. In addition, the genitive *fascium* is combined with *titulus*, 'the distinction, honour (arising from, consisting in)' (*OLD* 1945, 7b), that is, here the expression, an enallage, 'the highest honour deriving from the offices'; see Iuv. 5.110–11, which also combines the two terms: *namque et titulis et fascibus olim | maior habebatur donandi gloria* ('for in the days of old, the glory of giving was deemed grander than title or fasces').

Sed sententiae tali numquam ego assentior, ut fortunatos putem qui rei publicae praecipitibus ac lubricis culminibus insistunt: Here and in what follows Sidonius is critical of holding the highest power. In other letters, however, he is more positive about this career path; see the introduction to this letter. Note especially letter 2.3, the parallel letter to 2.13, where he praises the addressee for his professional success and plays with the name Felix and its meaning, 'luck'. The combination of *praeceps*, 'headlong', and *lubricus*, 'slippery', is also attested in Cic. *Phil.* 5.18.50, in a passage about the desire to rule (*cupiditas dominandi*); see also Cic. *Flacc.* 105, *Pis.* 68; Gualandri (1979) 133. Another intertext for the passage is Sen. *Thy.* 391–5 *stet quicumque uolet potens | aulae culmine lubrico. | me dulcis saturet quies | obscuro positus loco | leni perfruar otio* ('whoever wants to stand on the slippery summit of the royal honours, I may be satisfied with a sweet rest, placed in an unnoticed position, I enjoy a pleasant leisure time'), about the risky and strenuous life of mighty men; Degl'Innocenti Pierini (2008) 1326–7. For *lubricus*, see the commentary on *Ep.* 2.2.6 *Absunt lubrici tortuosique pugilatu* .... With the participle *fortunatus*, 'blessed', 'fortunate' (*TLL* 6.1, 1196.6–72), frequently used from Plautus and Terence onwards to describe a person, Sidonius varies the vocabulary of happiness. He anticipates the fate of Damocles; see Cic. *Tusc.* 5.62 *fortunatus sibi Damocles videbatur* ('Damocles felt fortunate'). See also the commentary on *Ep.* 2.13.5 *quod et exitus ... cruentavit Fortunae*.... For *culmina*, here referring to a 'high office', see the commentary on *Ep.* 2.10.2 *viri sancti strenui ... culmina levet*.

Section 2

Nam dici nequit, quantum per horas fert in hac vita miseriarum vita felicium istorum, si tamen sic sunt pronuntiandi qui sibi hoc nomen ut Sulla praesumunt: Sidonius artfully proves that the supposedly happy are not happy at all, but in fact miserable (*vita miseriarum vita felicium*). As an example, he takes the Roman politician and general P. Cornelius Sulla Felix (138–78 BC), consul in 88 BC. As a leading representative of the conservative aristocratic party (*Optimates*), Sulla marched on Rome in 88 and 83 BC to eliminate his popular opponents. After his victory in the civil war, he had himself appointed dictator in 82 BC. He carried out the first proscriptions in Roman history and had thousands of Roman nobles killed. His constitutional reforms aimed at a lasting restoration of senatorial rule and the weakening of democratic institutions such as the popular tribunate. In 79 BC Sulla resigned from the dictatorship and retired to private life. Sulla chose 'Felix' as his byname and openly expressed his trust in his luck, which he interpreted as a sign of the divine blessing of the personified goddess Felicitas; see Plut. *Sulla* 34.2–3, Plin. *Nat.* 7.137–8; Behr (1993) 19–20, 102, 111–13, 144–70, Eder (1997) 189–90. Sidonius, however, does not criticise Sulla, but other leaders who also want to be considered happy. Elsewhere (*Carm.* 2.458–60, 5.555–7, 7.79–82), Sidonius praises Sulla's military strength; see Montone (2017) 26, 40 n. 15 and Zecchini (1983) 102, who compare Sidonius' opinion with the evaluation of Sulla by other Late Antique authors. *Per horas*, 'every hour', 'hourly' (*TLL* 6.3, 2957.23–9), is also used in Sidon. *Ep.* 1.7.12, 3.13.7, 9.3.4.

nimirum qui supergressi ius fasque commune summam beatitudinem existimant summam potestatem: To satisfy their desire for domination, the ostensibly happy transgress the laws of men and gods. The expression *ius fasque* also appears in Sall. *Catil.* 15.1 and thus refers back to *Ep.* 2.1, where Seronatus appears as a new Catiline, the epitome of a bad ruler; Fascione (2019) 97. *Beatitudo*, 'happiness', 'felicity', 'blessedness' (*TLL* 2, 1794.60–1), is another term for happiness, frequently used by Christian authors, especially Augustine, for example Aug. *Civ.* 9.12, 11.11. It is also an honorary title for bishops and the pope; see Ruric. *Ep.* 1.15.3, 2.28.2; Neri (2009) 227. In his account of the story of Damocles, Cicero uses the term *beatus* several times: see Cic. *Tusc.* 5.61 *quamquam hic quidem tyrannus ipse iudicauit, quam esset beatus ... negaretque umquam beatiorem quemquam fuisse* ('although this tyrant showed himself how blessed he was ... and denied that there had ever been a more blissful man'), 5.62 *... ut impenderet illius beati cervicibus ... denique exoravit tyrannum ut abire liceret, quod iam beatus nollet esse. satisne videtur declarasse Dionysius nihil esse ei beatum cui semper aliqui terror impendeat?* ('... so that it hung directly over the top of that happy man's head.... Finally he begged the tyrant to let him leave because he no longer wanted to be happy. Does Dionysius seem to have told you clearly enough that nothing can be blissful for someone over whom some kind of terror is constantly hanging?'). Cicero discusses the philosophical meaning of the term *beatitudo* in Cic. *Nat.* 1.34.95; see Quint. 8.3.32 and Sidon. *Ep.* 1.6.3, 7.6.5. It is also used as a honorific address of bishops in Sidon. *Ep.* 6.6.2 and 7.1.6. Sidonius uses *potestas*, 'power', here and elsewhere to denote 'political power'; see Sidon. *Ep.* 1.7.3, 2.13.3, 4.25.4, 5.7.7, 5.18.1, *Carm.* 2.206, 24.19; Santelia (2002) 75–6. With the final adjective *beatus*, Sidonius again takes up Ciceronian terminology; see the commentary on *Ep.* 2.13.8 *quapropter ad statum huiusmodi ... tendere beatos....*

hoc ipso satis miseriores, quod parum intellegunt inquietissimo se subiacere famulatui: The adverb *satis*, 'fairly', 'pretty', 'quite' (*OLD* 1694, 9b), reinforces the comparative *miseriores*, 'more miserable', which echoes *miseriarum*, 'misery', from the beginning of the sentence. The superlative *inquietissimus*, 'most restless', is attested from Seneca onwards (*TLL* 7.1, 1804.51–3); see Sen. *Ben.* 7.26.5. *Famulatus*, 'servitude', 'slavery' (*TLL* 6.1, 260.32–47), is used here in a figurative sense to describe a person's devotion to a political career that is perceived as slavery; see the commentary on *Ep.* 2.2.5 *ita ut ministeriorum....*

Nam sicut hominibus reges, ita regibus dominandi desideria dominantur: Sidonius ends the second section with a stylistically elaborate sentence (alliteration on -d; polyptoton *reges–regibus* and *dominandi–dominantur*). The starting point is Cicero's expression *maiestatem dominatus* ('the glory of his reign') in Cic. *Tusc.* 5.61. There are two probable intertexts for the passage. On the one hand, Sidonius alludes to Sall. *Catil.* 2.2 *lubidinem dominandi* ('the desire to rule') and the entire context of Sallust's introduction; see the commentary on *Ep.* 2.1.1 *Rediit ipse Catilina....* Sidonius also refers to Sall. *Catil.* 1 in *Ep.* 7.14.4 – van Waarden (2016) 138–9 – to Sall. *Catil.* 20.4 in *Ep.* 5.3.2 and to Sall. *Catil.* 5.4 in *Ep.* 9.9.2. The second author Sidonius alludes to is Augustine, who also harshly criticises the desire to rule (*dominari*) in the preface to his *De Civitate Dei*: *unde etiam de terrena civitate, quae cum dominari adpetit, etsi populi serviant, ipsa ei dominandi libido dominatur, non est praetereundem silentio* ('that is the reason why I cannot be silent about the earthly city which seeks to reign and though its people are its slaves is governed by the desire to reign'). The Augustinian abstract *civitas*, 'city', is replaced here by *hominibus* and *reges*, but Sidonius maintains the polyptoton of *dominari*; Catarinella (2000). The collocation is repeated in Aug. *Civ.*

14.28 *illi in principibus eius vel in eis quas subiugat nationibus dominandi libido dominatur* ('the lust for power dominates him in his rulers or in the people he has subjugated'). Rousseau (2000) 257 compares the passage with *Ep.* 3.3.9, where Sidonius warns his brother-in-law Ecdicius against getting too close to the powerful.

Section 3

Hic si omittamus antecedentium principum casus vel subsecutorum, solus iste peculiaris tuus Maximus maximo nobis documento poterit esse: With his refusal (*recusatio*) to write about the demise of earlier and later rulers who also died violently, Sidonius concentrates on the case of Petronius Maximus to prove his theory about happiness and abstinence from a political career. Petronius Maximus' predecessors (*antecedentium principum casus*) were Flavius Honorius, the Western Roman emperor from 393 to 423, and Valentinian III. Sidonius in *Ep.* 5.9.2 mentions that his father served under Honorius as *tribunus* and *notarius*; Hanaghan (2019) 112–13, Kulikowski (2020) 199–202, Mathisen (2020a) 101, van Waarden (2020a) 19. Flavius Honorius was followed (after a brief interregnum) by Valentinian III, who reigned for thirty years, from 425 till 455, before he was murdered by Petronius Maximus. On Valentinian III, see *PLRE* 2, 1138–9, Henning (1999) 16–20, Mathisen (2020a) 125. He is mentioned in Sidon. *Carm.* 5.305–6, 7.359, 23.228, 23.310, 23.423, *Ep.* 5.9.2. Petronius Maximus was followed by the emperors Eparchius Avitus and Fl. Iulius Valerius Maiorianus, who were closely related to Sidonius. Avitus, Sidonius' father-in-law, reigned from 455 to 456/7 and is mostly known through Sidonius' panegyric, *Carm.* 7; see also *Carm.* 6, *Ep.* 1.3.1, 1.11.7. On Avitus, see *PLRE* 2, 196–8, Henning (1999) 32–6, Green (2016), Hanaghan (2017b), Mathisen (2020a) 84–5, Stoehr-Monjou (2020), van Waarden (2020a) 20–1, and the commentaries on *Ep.* 2.1.1 *Arverni tui* and *Ep.* 2.2.3 *nomen hoc praedio*.... Mathisen (1979) 169–70 and Hanaghan (2019) 104 show that, except in this passage, Sidonius alludes to his deceased father-in-law Avitus only in a covert way and suspect that it may have been too painful or too dangerous. Avitus was deprived of power and probably killed by Majorian and the *magister militum* Ricimer and died in 457 at the latest. Majorian succeeded Avitus as emperor after an interregnum from 457 and reigned till 461, when he was deposed and killed by Ricimer. He is praised by Sidonius in *Carm.* 5; see also *Carm.* 4, 13, *Ep.* 1.11.2–17, 9.13.4. On Majorian, see

PLRE 2, 702–3, Henning (1999) 36–40, Rousseau (2000), Santelia (2005), Montone (2014), Hanaghan (2019) 108–12, Mathisen (2020a) 106. This section is the only one that offers any firm evidence for the dating of the letter, as Sidonius writes about emperors (*casus vel subsecutorum*) who follow Petronius Maximus. Sidonius adds a pun on Maximus' name, that is, the polyptoton *Maximus/maximo*; Hanaghan (2019) 112 n. 101. For Sidonius' fondness for puns with names, see the commentary on *Ep.* 2.1.1 *Seronati, inquam: de cuius ut primum etiam nomine loquar*. This gives us a *terminus post quem*, the death of Majorian in 461. Manuscript C, Lütjohan (1887) 37 and Loyen (1970a) 75 have *subsecutorum*, NMT and Anderson (1936) 474 *secutorum* and L *sequitorum*. Anderson (1936) 474 and Loyen (1970a) 76 add *ad ista* after *tuus Maximus maximo nobis*, which is attested in M². LN have *ad isto*, omitted in manuscripts VCT and Lütjohann (1887) 37. Engelbrecht (1898) 296 suggests an emendation to *ad istoc*, the neuter singular of *istic*, 'this same', 'this', 'the very (person or thing)', an intensified form of the demonstrative pronoun *iste*. He interprets *ad istoc* as an explanation for the preceding *sicut hominibus reges, ita regibus dominandi desideria dominantur* (at the end of section 2).

qui quamquam in arcem praefectoriam patriciam consularemque intrepidus ascenderat eosque quos gesserat magistratus ceu recurrentibus orbitis inexpletus iteraverat: Next, Sidonius lists the various stages of Petronius' career. He was *praefectus urbi* in 420–1 and 439, *patricius* by 445 and consul in 433 and 443; see the commentary on *Ep.* 2.13.1 *patroni tui Petronii Maximi imperatoris....* Arx, 'top of', is used metaphorically here; see the commentary on *Ep.* 2.4.1 *ita demum sibi ... ad arcem fastigatissimae felicitatis evectus....* It is taken up by *apex*; see the commentary immediately below. For the office of a prefect (*praefectoriam*), see the commentary on *Ep.* 2.1.3 *exultans Gothis insultansque Romanis, inludens praefectis conludensque numerariis*. For the honorary title of *patricius*, see the commentary on *Ep.* 2.3.1 *et in lares Philagrianos patricius apex....* For *ascendere*, here in the figurative meaning of 'building a career' (as in Sidon. *Ep.* 3.6.1 and 7.14.7), see *Ep.* 2.2.11 *angustatisque gradibus ascenditur*. The term *orbita*, 'track', 'circuit' (*TLL* 9.2, 921.23–49), is used elsewhere of a predecessor's path; see Sidon. *Ep.* 9.1.1, *Carm.* 9.18, Verg. *Georg.* 3.293, Stat. *Silv.* 2.7.51. Petronius Maximus holds his honorary offices several times, which Sidonius criticises as a repetition. For the formulation, see Sidon. *Ep.* 4.10.2 *et nos vetustae loquacitatis orbitas recurremus* ('I will again run over the tracks of my old garrulousness'), *Ep.* 6.9.2, *Carm.* 9.16 *non nos currimus aggerem vetustum* ('I am not speeding over the old road'). The rarely used adjective *inexpletus*, 'insatiable' (*TLL* 7.1, 1327–70), is used of a person also in Verg. *Aen.* 8.559.

cum tamen venit omnibus viribus ad principalis apicis abruptum, quandam potestatis inmensae vertiginem sub corona patiebatur nec sustinebat dominus esse, qui non sustinuerat esse sub domino: After Petronius Maximus' rise to power, Sidonius describes his fall, which he explains psychologically. The crowning achievement of his career was the office of Western Roman emperor, which he held for two and a half months until he was killed on 31 May 455. To reach this highest peak of power, Petronius Maximus mobilised all his forces. Once at the top as emperor, he was seized by dizziness and his decline began. *Apicis* takes up *in arcem* and here means 'the highest ornament or honour'; see the commentary on *Ep.* 2.3.1 *et in lares Philagrianos patricius apex*.... For other meanings of *apex* in Sidonius, see the commentary on *Ep.* 2.1.2 *epistulas, ne primis quidem apicibus sufficienter initiatus*.... For *potestas*, see the commentary on *Ep.* 2.13.2 *nimirum qui supergressi ... summam potestatem. Vertigo* denotes 'a spinning sensation', 'dizziness' (*OLD* 2042). Liv. 44.6.8 uses the term to describe the feeling in front of an abyss: *ut despici vix sine vertigine quadam simul oculorum animique possit* ('you could not look down without a dizziness of eye and mind'). The term *corona*, 'garland', 'wreath', is used to denote an emblem of a prestigious office (*TLL* 4, 983.72–4.33), here the emperor's diadem. As in the previous section (see the commentary on *Ep.* 2.13.2 *Nam sicut hominibus reges, ita regibus dominandi desideria dominantur*), Sidonius ends the sentence with a double polyptoton (*sustinebat/sustinuerat* and *dominus/domino*) in a parallel construction. The expression is proverbial; see for example Sen. *De ira* 2.15.4 *nemo autem regere potest nisi qui et regi* ('no one can reign if they cannot also be ruled').

Section 4

Denique require in supradicto vitae prioris gratiam potentiam diuturnitatem eque diverso principatus paulo amplius quam bimenstris originem turbinem finem: In section 4, Sidonius contrasts Maximus Petronius' earlier, lengthy period of happiness with the very short and stressful time he experienced as emperor. The perfect passive participle *supradictus* means 'mentioned before', 'aforesaid' (*Blaise* 801); see for example Hier. *Ep.* 85.3. Alternatively, Sidonius uses *praefatus* – see the commentary on *Ep.* 2.10.3 *Huius igitur aedis extimis rogatu praefati antistitis tumultuarium carmen*; see also *Ep.* 5.14.3. The three qualities that characterise Petronius Maximus' earlier life (*gratiam potentiam diuturnitatem*) are contrasted by a similar tripartite asyndeton that characterises his death (*originem turbinem finem*). For asyndetic sequences in Sidonius, see van Waarden (2010) 58, 571–5. The attributes are connected with the expression *e diverso*, 'on the contrary', 'on the other hand', in use since the fourth century AD; see Sidon. *Ep.* 5.7.1, 7.5.5, 7.9.8, 9.14.7; van Waarden (2010) 270. For *potentia*, 'power', see the commentary on *Ep.* 2.12.3 *Quo diligentius postulandus ... potentia superna medeatur*. Here it refers to the power of the ruler. For *diuturnitas*, 'long duration', 'durability' (*TLL* 5.1, 1644.37–5.13) of a man's life, see with the genitive *humanarum vitarum* ('of human lives'), Aug. *Civ.* 15.9, and Plin. *Ep.* 5.8.2 *diuturnitatis amor et cupido* ('the love and desire for immortality'). The adjective *bime(n)stris*, 'for two months' (*TLL* 2, 1991.6–16), is classical (attested from Hor. *Carm.* 3.17.15 on), but rare. See Cic. *Fam.* 10.24.6 *consulatus bimestris* ('a consulate of two months'), Suet. *Claud.* 14, *Nero* 14, Ambr. *Ep.* 73.7 *bimenstres imperatores* ('emperors for two month'). *Turbo*, 'a circling course' (*OLD* 1992, 4b), is used in a figurative sense of time or fortune, meaning 'whirlwind' (*OLD* 1992, 2b), and refers to sudden violent disturbances of affairs (*OLD* 1992, 2b); see for example Cic. *Dom.* 137, Ov. *Met.* 7.614, Apul. *Met.* 8.31.4.

profecto invenies hominem beatiorem prius fuisse quam beatissimus nominaretur: Sidonius again inserts a pun with a polyptoton to emphasise Petronius' past happiness (*beatiorem*/*beatissimus*); see also Plin. *Ep.* 5.18.1 *homo felicior ante quam felicissimus fieret* ('a quite happy man before he became very happy') and Auson. *Grat.* 8.38 *aut verius Sulla Felix, qui felicior ante quam vocaretur* ('or truly Sulla Felix, who was happier before he was so named'). *Beatissimus* becomes an epithet for emperors in the fourth century AD in the post-Constantinian period; see Ruric. *Ep.* 1.1.1; Neri (2009) 162. In Christian writers, the term is also used for church dignitaries, especially the pope; see Sidon. *Ep.* 6.12.1, 8.13.1, Hier. *Ep.* 141.1.

igitur ille, cuius anterius epulae mores, pecuniae pompae, litterae fasces, patrimonia patrocinia florebant: In another typical series of asyndeta, Sidonius lists the daily routine of Petronius Maximus, consisting of senatorial duties and occupations; see also Sidon. *Ep.* 2.9.6, where the *clepsydra*, 'water clock', measures the senatorial activities; Näf (1995) 140–1. On *anterius*, 'before', see the commentary on *Ep.* 2.9.3 *quaenam potissimum* *anterius edulibus nostris culina fumaret*. *Epulae* here means 'banquet', 'feast', 'sumptuous meal', as part of the emperor's entertainment; see also Sidon. *Ep.* 1.11.10 *postridie Augustus iussit ut epulo suo circensibus ludis interessemus* ('the next day Augustus ordered me to take part in his banquet on the occasion of the circus games'), 4.15.1 *epulum multiplex* ('a copious banquet'), 7.12.4 *cum epulum festivitas publica facit* ('when a public celebration provides a banquet'); Amherdt (2001) 359–60, Dunbabin (2003) 78, 82, van Waarden (2016) 78–9. In *Ep.* 2.9.6 *epulae* means 'food'; see the commentary there. For the plural *fasces*, metonymically for a 'high office', see the commentary on *Ep.* 2.13.1 *propter hoc quippe, cur per amplissimos fascium titulus...*. The similar-sounding words *patrimonium*, 'inheritance', 'patrimony', (see the commentary on *Ep.* 2.4.1 *et cum illi ... patrimonii facultas...*) and *patrocinium*, 'patronage' (*TLL* 10.1, 774.42–5.43), describe two tasks of an aristocrat, namely to preserve his paternal inheritance and to provide protection for clients as a patron. The idea is similarly found in Sidon. *Ep.* 7.1.7 *pars patrocinii ... pars patroni* ('a share in your patronage ... a fragment of our patron saint'); van Waarden (2010) 125. For the combination of the two terms, see also *Ep.* 3.1.4. In *Ep.* 1.5.9 the term is applied to God: *post quae caelestis experimenta patrocinii* ('after which proof of heavenly protection').

cuius ipsa sic denique spatia vitae custodiebantur, ut per horarum disposita clepsydras explicarentur: Sidonius again emphasises Petronius Maximus' orderly life before he became emperor, which is equated with happiness. The verb *disponere*, 'to arrange', 'set in order' (*TLL* 5.1, 1425.25–55), is regularly used to denote the order of time and actions. Referring to an orderly life of leisure, it is also used in Sen. *De brev. vit.* 10.16, Plin. *Ep.* 4.23.1, Mart. 5.20.3. The manuscripts LNT[1], Lütjohan (1887) 37, Anderson (1936) 476 and Loyen (1970a) 76 have *disposita*, MCT[2] have *dispositas*. For *clepsydra*, 'water clock', see the commentary on *Ep.* 2.9.6 *quem quidem nuntium per spatia clepsydrae horarum incrementa...*. The verb *explico*, 'to unfold', 'spread out', is used in a figurative sense about the development of things in a certain sequence (*TLL* 5.2, 1728.1–20). It is used of time also in Boeth. *Cons.* 4.6.10 *haec temporalis ordinis explicatio* ('the unfolding of this order of time'). For *explico* in other meanings, see *Ep.* 2.1.4 *moras tuas citius explica* and 2.11.2 *competenter explicui*.

is nuncupatus Augustus ac sub hac specie Palatinis liminibus inclusus ante crepusculum ingemuit, quod ad vota pervenerat: Petronius Maximus is a *princeps clausus* in his palace; that is, Sidonius presents him as locked up in his palace, unlike the Visigothic king Theoderic II; see Sidon. *Ep.* 1.2.4. Sidonius inverts the panegyric topos that a ruler should live openly and be approachable by describing Petronius Maximus as a prisoner of his status and his possessions; see Köhler (1995) 138 and Apul. *Mund.* 26. *Palatinus* means 'belonging to the Palatine', one of the seven hills of Rome. The Roman emperors from Augustus on had their residence on the Palatine hill (*mons Palatinus*), hence *palatium* denotes 'a palace'; Nielsen (2000) 168, 180. For *crepusculum*, 'twilight', 'dusk', see the commentary on *Ep.* 2.2.14 *ranas crepusculo incumbente blaterantes*. Sidonius implies that Petronius Maximus is already depressed after the first day of his reign.

Cumque mole curarum pristinae quietis tenere dimensum prohiberetur, veteris actutum regulae legibus renuntiavit atque perspexit pariter ire non posse negotium principis et otium senatoris: With this sentence Sidonius explains the difference between leisure (*otium*) and *negotium* (business). This topic has a longstanding tradition and is discussed by Sidonius' models Cicero and Pliny, among others; André (2006). For the importance of leisure (*otium*) in Sidonius' letters, see the introduction to this commentary and that to *Ep.* 2.1; for *negotium*, 'business', which Sidonius describes in negative terms here, see the commentary on *Ep.* 2.5.1 *Iohannes familiaris meus inextricabilem labyrinthum negotii multiplicis incurrit*. The combination of *moles*, 'weight', 'mass', and *cura*, 'trouble', 'concern', is attested elsewhere: Tac. *Ann.* 12.66.1, Amm. 14.11.9 and see especially Plin. *Paneg.* 44.4, about the burden of the emperor Trajan: *quis enim curae tuae molem sponte subeat?* ('Who would voluntarily take on the burden of your responsibility?'). The noun *dimensum* (*TLL* 5.1, 1195.51–65) is derived from the perfect passive participle of *dimetior*, 'to measure', and used here in the meaning of *dimensio*, 'extent'; see also Symm. *Ep.* 1.1.1. For the adverb *actutum* 'immediately', see the commentary on *Ep.* 2.9.10 *sed quia et ipsi ... sub ope Christi actutum nobis invisere placet.... Regula* here means 'rule', 'standard', 'principle' (*OLD* 1602, 2), that is, the rhythm of Petronius Maximus' former life; see also Sidon. *Ep.* 7.17.3; van Waarden (2016) 245. Pliny writes similarly about Spurinna's way of life: Plin. *Ep.* 3.1.2–3 *senibus placida omnia et ordinata conveniunt ... hanc regulam Spurinna constantissime servat* ('for old people everything calm and orderly is fitting ... Spurinna observed this rule constantly'), Plin. *Ep.* 9.26.8. For the adverb *pariter*, 'in like manner', 'equally', and adverbs ending in *-(i)ter*, see the commentary on *Ep.* 2.1.1 *Duo nunc pariter mala sustinent*. For the expression *pariter ire*, 'to go in the same way as', see Quint. 1.1.14.

Section 5

Nec fefellerunt futura maerentem; namque cum ceteros aulicos honores tranquillissime percurrisset, ipsam aulam turbulentissime rexit inter tumultus militum popularium foederatorum: Petronius Maximus' premonitions on the first day of his new office are confirmed: after an unhappy short reign he suffers a cruel death. Once again, Sidonius uses linguistic devices to underline the difference between Petronius Maximus' earlier life and his unhappy imperial rule (*aulicos* is contrasted with *aulam*, and *tranquillissime* with *turbulentissime*). For *maerere*, 'to mourn', 'to be sad', used of situations of political tension, see Sidon. *Ep.* 7.7.6; van Waarden (2010) 375–6. Sidonius uses *aulicus*, 'of or belonging to a prince's court', 'princely' (*TLL* 2, 1462.15–70), as an adjective also in *Ep.* 1.2.10, 8.3.4, *Carm.* 23.312, and as a noun in *Ep.* 1.2.9, 1.5.10. It is also attested in Suetonius (for example Suet. *Nero* 45.1), but mostly in Late Antique authors, for example Symm. *Ep.* 3.3.1, 8.48. It is repeated by *aula*, 'palace', 'royal court' (*TLL* 2, 1456.15–67), which stands for Petronius Maximus' imperial rule. The adjectives *tranquillus*, 'calm' (*OLD* 1960, 2), and *turbulentus*, 'unruly', 'riotous', 'turbulent' (*OLD* 1993, 3), are both regularly used to characterise people; the latter is especially frequent in Cicero, for example Cic. *De orat.* 2.48, *Brut.* 108, *Cluent.* 94. Sidonius uses the adjective also to describe persons in *Ep.* 1.7.12 *carnificis* ('executioner'), 7.1.7 *persecutori* ('persecutor'). Köhler (1995) 256 and van Waarden (2010) 124 translate *turbulentus* in these instances as 'self-willed', 'high-handed', which does not fit here, where *turbulentissime* ('in circumstances of great turbulence') stands as the opposite of *tranquillissime* ('in great calm'). The adverb *tranquille*, 'quietly', 'calmly' (*OLD* 1960), is attested from Plautus onwards, for example Plaut. *Cist.* 110. For the superlative, see Suet. *Aug.* 2.2. The adverb *turbulente*, 'with violent disorderliness in behaviour' (*OLD* 1993, Blaise 833), is also used by Cicero, for example Cic. *Dom.* 139, *Tusc.* 4.60. For the superlative *turbulentissime*, see Schol. Bob. 119, Stangl *post annum tribunatus sui quem turbulentissime gesserat* ('after the year of his tribunate, which he held high-handedly'). *Foederatus* is the Roman term for a '(barbarian) military ally' (*TLL* 6.1, 995.34–64) who lives within or close to the border of the Roman Empire. Sidonius thus alludes to the Visigoths, who were (probably with the treaty of 382) allowed by the Roman emperor Theodosius I to settle as *foederati* between the River Danube and the Balkan Mountains. Groups of them left the allocated land and, after wandering through Italy, settled in Gaul in 418. Further treaties were made in the years 439, 453 and 458; see the commentary on Sidon.

Ep. 2.1.3 *leges Theodosianas calcans Theodoricianasque proponens*.... In 466, Euric killed his older brother Theoderic II and succeeded to the throne. Euric finally dissolved the *foedus* with the Romans and instead enlarged the power of the Visigoths, which led to an independent Visigothic kingdom in 475 AD; see the introduction to *Ep.* 2.1. Sidonius shows the same dismissive attitude towards the *foederati* in *Ep.* 1.8.2, 3.8.2; see Anderson (1965) 34–5 n. 1, Heider (1998), Köhler (1995) 263. For Sidonius' attitude towards barbarians, see the commentary on *Ep.* 2.1.2 *indicit ut dominus ... calumniatur ut barbarus.*

quod et exitus prodidit novus celer acerbus, quem cruentavit Fortunae diu lenocinantis perfidus finis, quae virum ut scorpius ultima sui parte percussit: Petronius Maximus was violently killed on 31 May 455, probably by an angry mob. On 2 June 455, three days later, the Vandals under king Geiseric invaded and plundered Rome; see the commentary on *Ep.* 2.13.1 *patroni tui Petronii Maximi imperatoris laudes habebat*. For Sidonius, Petronius Maximus' cruel end is proof of his theory that great power leads to misfortune (*exitus prodidit*). Similar expressions are found in Pliny: Plin. *Paneg.* 72.4 *et sane priorum principum exitus docuit* ('and of course the death of former leaders proved'), 5.4 *ut docuit eventus* ('as the outcome showed'), Plin. *Ep.* 3.14.6 *ut exitus docuit* ('as the end showed'). *Acerbus*, 'harsh', 'bitter', 'grievous' (*TLL* 1, 368.17–36), is often used of a premature death (*mors acerba*); see Plin. *Ep.* 5.5.4, Ruric. *Ep.* 2.4.1 *acerbissimum casum* ('the very grievous death'); Neri (2009) 246. For the combination with *exitus*, see Val. Max. 6.6. ext. 1 *tam acerbo exitu damnatum* ('condemned to such a cruel death'). Sidonius uses the adjective *acerbus* also in *Ep.* 4.14.4, 9.3.1. The verb *cruentare*, 'to make bloody', 'to splatter with blood', is used in a figurative sense 'to stain', 'defile', 'disgrace' (*TLL* 4, 1237.63–74), but because of Petronius Maximus' cruel death, the literal sense also resonates. Sidonius uses the verb also in *Ep.* 4.9.2 in the meaning 'to injure', 'offend'. The starting point is Cicero's expression *et fortunam experiri meam ... fortunatus sibi Damocles videbatur* ('and to experience my fate ... Damocles felt fortunate') in Cic. *Tusc.* 5.61–2, which Sidonius elaborates; see the commentary on *Ep.* 2.13.1 *Sed sententiae ... ut fortunatos putem*.... With his reflection on destiny Sidonius personifies Fortuna, as he does in *Ep.* 1.7.12 and 2.1.1, *Carm.* 2.96 and 214, 7.126, 11.114; Köhler (1995) 254. With his negative description he follows the literary tradition (for example Plin. *Nat.* 2.22) of Fortuna/Tyche as a cruel and unreliable force; Kajanto (1972) 187–8, 192–3, Graf (1998) 601. Sidonius also recalls the typical Roman notion that a military leader was expected to be lucky, that is, to be supported by Fortuna; see for example Cic. *Manil.* 28, *Arch.* 24; Kajanto (1972) 184–5. For *lenocinor*, 'to pander', 'flatter', see the commentary on *Ep.* 2.2.14 *Quae tamen varia ... confovendo sopori tuo lenocinabuntur*. Manuscript L, Anderson (1936) 476 and Loyen (1970a) 77 have *scorpios*, NMCT and Lütjohann (1887) 37 have *scorpius*. Both spellings, *scorpios* or *scorpius*, are derived from Greek σκορπίος and attested in other authors (*OLD* 1708, 1a). The scorpion was feared in antiquity because of the poisonous sting of its tail. There are several theories about its origin; see for example Ov. *Met.* 15.371. It is also used as a metaphor for a malicious person, here for the personified Fortuna; Hünemörder (2001d) 828.

Dicere solebat vir litteratus atque ob ingenii merita quaestorius, partium certe bonarum pars magna, Fulgentius ore se ex eius frequenter audisse: Quite unexpectedly, Sidonius inserts a quotation from the learned Fulgentius (*vir litteratus*) to support his theory. Fulgentius held the office of a *Quaestor Sacri Palatii*, one of the four ministers of the court. He is only mentioned in Sidonius and otherwise unknown; Loyen (1970a) 221 n. 53, *PLRE* 2, 487 n. 1, *PCBE* 4, 845, Mathisen (2020a) 97. The word order *Fulgentius ore* is conscpicuos. Sidonius thus hints at the adjective *fulgens* or *fulgidus*, 'flashing', 'shining', 'illustrious', which could be an allusion to Fulgentius' eloquence. Interestingly, Cicero in his version of the story describes the sword of Damocles as *fulgentem gladium* ('a glittering sword'), in Cic. *Tusc.* 5.62. Fulgentius combines two of the qualities that Sidonius repeatedly praises in the second book: education and belonging to the circle of good men. For the expression *ob ingenii merita*, 'because of the merits of his mind', see the commentary on *Ep.* 2.5.1 *et donec suarum merita chartarum....* For *partium certe bonarum pars magna*, 'an important part of the party of good men', see the commentary on *Ep.* 2.4.3 *sicut decet bonarum partium viros*.

cum perosus pondus imperii veterem securitatem desideraret: 'felicem te, Damocles, qui non uno longius prandio regni necessitatem toleravisti.' Fulgentius is Sidonius' source for Petronius Maximus feeling reminded of Damocles, whose story Sidonius details in sections 6–8. *Perosus*, the perfect participle of *perodi*, here has the active meaning of 'detesting', 'hating greatly' (*TLL* 10.1, 1607.63–8.28), and is combined with the accusative object *pondus*; see also Sidon. *Ep.* 1.9.7. For adjectives ending in -*osus*, see the commentary on 2.2.18 *Lacus ipse ... flexuosus nemorosusque....* For the expression *pondus imperii* 'the burden of command', see Val. Max. 2.2.2.

For *felicitas*, 'happiness', 'felicity', 'luckiness', 'success', to denote political success, see the commentary on *Ep.* 2.3.1 *et in lares ... felicitate remeaverit*. While Cicero in his version of the story (see Cic. *Tusc.* 5.61–2) focuses on the happiness of Dionysius, Sidonius targets the unhappiness of Damocles; Squillante (2007/2008) 254–5. For *necessitas*, 'necessity', 'constraint' (*OLD* 1165, 2a), see Sidon. *Ep.* 7.5.2, 9.12.3; van Waarden (2010) 260. For the famous story about the sword of Damocles in Sidonius and his literary predecessors, see the commentary on *Ep.* 2.13.6 below.

Section 6

Iste enim, ut legimus, Damocles provincia Siculus, urbe Syracusanus, familiaris tyranno Dionysio fuit: In section 6, Sidonius narrates the anecdote of Damocles, an obsequious courtier, and tyrant Dionysius I of Syracuse (ca. 430–367 BC), which is mainly known through Cic. *Tusc.* 5.61–2; Meister (1997) 628. Cicero and Sidonius are the only Latin writers who mention the courtier by his name Damocles; Degl'Innocenti Pierini (2008) 1326–7. They both call him a courtier, but only Cicero describes him as one of Dionysius' supporters (Cic. *Tusc.* 5.61 *quidam ex eius adsentatoribus*, 'one of his flatterers'). Sidonius indicates his origin by calling him *Siculus*, 'of or belonging to Sicily', and *Syracusanus*, 'of or belonging to Syracuse'. In Sidonius' account, there are also several verbal parallels to Vergil's *Georgica*; see the commentary on section 8 of this letter. *Provincia*, of course is an anachronistic form of reference, as Sicily became a Roman province only in 241 BC, after the First Punic War, long after the story happened. Sidonius therefore thinks and writes in Roman terminology. The Romanisation of the scene continues with the depiction of Dionysius and Damocles as patron and client (see the commentary immediately below).

Qui cum nimiis laudibus bona patroni ut cetera scilicet inexpertus efferret: 'vis', inquit Dionysius, 'hodie saltim in hac mensa bonis meis pariter ac malis uti?' – 'libenter', inquit: Both Cicero and Sidonius present the episode vividly in direct speech; see Cic. *Tusc.* 5.61 *'visne igitur', inquit, 'o Damocle, quoniam te haec vita delectat, ipse eam degustare et fortunam experiri meam?'* ("'Do you, Damocles, want to taste this life, since it delights you so much, and experience my fate?'"). For dialogues in Sidonius' letters and the you–I structure in general, see Hanaghan (2019) 139–69, van Waarden (2020b) 434–5. Sidonius also recalls the very beginning of Book 2, where he starts *Ep.* 2.1 with *Duo nunc pariter mala sustinent*. In Sidonius' account, Damocles appears anachronistically as a flattering client (*cliens*) who praises the wealth of his patron (*patronus*) Dionysius; see the commentary immediately above. With the contrast of *bona* (used twice) and *mala*, two philosophical terms, Sidonius underlines his message that great power also brings equally great misfortune; Degl'Innocenti Pierini (2008) 1327. For the adverb *pariter*, 'in like manner,' 'equally', and adverbs ending in *-(i)ter*, see the commentary there on *Ep.* 2.1.1 *Duo nunc pariter mala sustinent*. The manuscripts MT, Lütjohann (1887) 37, Anderson (1936) 478 and Loyen (1970a) 77 have *libenter inquit* (in the spelling *inquid* CN²), while the manuscripts LN¹ have *inquam*; see the discussion in Mossberg (1934) 16–18.

Tunc ille confestim laetum clientem quamquam et attonitum plebeio tegmine erepto muricis Tyrii seu Tarentini conchyliato ditat indutu: After Damocles has expressed how he envies Dionysius' luxurious life, the tyrant orders that the latter's clothes (*plebeio tegmine*) be taken away (*erepto*) and instead covers him with precious purple garments – the colour of royalty and of Roman magistrates; see Plin. *Nat.* 9.127; Schneider (2001) 605. The adjective *plebeius*, 'plebeian', 'of or belonging to the common people', is regularly used of clothes (*TLL* 10.1, 2375.50–58) and often, like here, as an opposite to purple clothes; see Lucr. 2.36, Luc. 2.18 and Sidon. *Carm.* 7.594 *plebeium ... amictum* ('common ... cloak'). For *plebeius* (of plants), 'widespread', 'wild', see the commentary on *Ep.* 2.2.18 *A Zephyro plebeius et tumultuarius frutex*. Sidonius adds the source of the colour purple, *murex*, 'the purple fish', in the genitive; see also Tib. 2.4.28, Hor. *Carm.* 2.16.35–7; Schneider (2001). Sidonius mentions two places where the purple comes from, the Phoenician city of Tyre, which was the centre of ancient purple dye production (see for example Plin. *Nat.* 9.127, Tib. 2.3.62, Ov. *Ars* 3.170, *Met.* 11.166), and the southern Italian city of Tarentum (see Plin. *Nat.* 9.137). See also *Carm.* 7.17.6, where Sidonius indicates another place of production of purple dyes: *Assyrius murex* ('Assyrian purple'). For *murex*, see also *Carm.* 2.96, 2.481, 7.542, 15.128. For the adjective *conchyliatus*, 'of a purple colour' (*TLL* 4, 30.5–13), which is derived from the noun *conchylium*, 'purple colour', 'purple', see Sidon. *Ep.* 1.2.6 (cited at the end of the next commentary, p. 382), Cic. *Phil.* 2.67, Plin. *Nat.* 9.138, Petron. 38.5, 54.4, Suet. *Iul.* 43, Sen. *Ep.* 62.3 (used as a noun); Köhler (1995) 150. For *conchylium*, see the commentary on *Ep.* 2.2.7 *abrupta purpurea genuino fucata conchylio*. For *dito*, 'to enrich someone with a thing' (*TLL* 5.1, 1556.27–33), see Stat. *Theb.* 6.920 *atque ambos aurata casside ditat* ('and he enriches both with a golden helmet'). *Indutus*, 'a putting on', 'garment' (*TLL* 7.1, 1280.44–62), is a rarely used word, attested from Varro *Ling.* 5.131 on; see Sidon. *Ep.* 8.3.5, Apul. *Apol.* 56.2, *Flor.* 9.18, Amm. 24.2.5, 30.7.4, Symm. *Ep.* 3.10.

et renidentem gemmis margaritisque aureo lecto sericatoque toreumati imponit: In addition to the purple clothing, Dionysius has Damocles adorned with jewels (*gemmis*) and pearls (*margaritis*) and laid on a golden bed with silk blankets. For *lectus*, 'couch', see the commentary on *Ep.* 2.12.1 *Misisti tu quidem ... lecti capacem....* Cicero uses the same term in his account of the story, Cic. *Tusc.* 5.61 *aureo lecto* ('on a golden bed'), but chooses other terms for the spreading: *pulcherrimo textili stragulo, magnificis operibus picto* ('covered with a magnificently woven and sumptuously embroidered carpet'). To describe the luxury of Dionysius' household, Sidonius alludes to various other ancient authors. Gualandri refers to Lucan as an intertext for this scene, where Luc. 10.122–4 describes the opulent dinner of queen Cleopatra in similar terms: *fulget gemma toris et iaspide fulva supellex | strata micant, Tyrio quorum pars maxima fuco | cocta* ('gems were glittering on the cushions, the dishes were tawny from jasper, and the rugs were gleaming, most of them boiled in Tyrian purple'); Gualandri (1979) 73 and Gualandri (2020). See also Claud. *Ruf.* 1.204–16. Sidonius repeats the topos of barbarian opulence and uses the passage about Cleopatra's luxury again to describe the court of Sigismer in *Ep.* 4.20.1; Fascione (2018) 39–43, Fascione (2019) 26. For *renidere*, 'to shine', 'to gleam', 'to reflect' (*OLD* 1614), see Lucr. 2.27 *nec domus argento fulget auroque renidet* ('the house does not shine with silver and glimmer with gold'), Hor. *Carm.* 2.18.1–2 *non ebur neque aureum | mea renidet in domo lacunar* ('not of ivory nor of gold shines the ceiling in my house'); Degl'Innocenti Pierini (2008) 1327 n. 17. *Sericatus* usually means 'clothed in silks' (*OLD* 1743); see for example Suet. *Cal.* 52. Here it rather means 'made of silk'; Gualandri (1979) 157 n. 47. See also Sidon. *Ep.* 1.7.8, 4.20.1, *Carm.* 15.128, 22.4 v. 197, 23.424. *Toreuma*, from Greek τόρευμα, denotes 'an article decorated by engraving in relief', 'embossed work' (*OLD* 1949–50), and is elsewhere used of cups and vases, for example in Cic. *Verr.* 2.2.52, 2.4.18, Mart. 4.46.16, 10.87.16, 14.94.1, 14.102.2, Apul. *Flor.* 7.8. In Sidonius' letters, the term is applied to cloth, in Sidon. *Ep.* 1.2.6, 9.13.5 v. 14. Anderson (1936) 340 n. 1 (following Sirmond *ad loc.* 1.2.6) refers to Prud. *Psych.* 370 and Salv. *Eccl.* 4.33, where *toreuma* can be translated as *torus*, 'a bolster', 'palliasse' (*OLD* 1952, 4a), that is, a 'couch' or 'matress of a couch'. Gualandri (1979) 156–8 argues in favour of 'drappi', that is, 'cloths', as the most probable translation. Condorelli (2013b) 124 n. 43 translates *toreuma* here as 'draperies to set the table', but in connection with the verb *imponere aliquem*, 'to put someone (on to something)', it must refer to the couch Damocles is lying on. Köhler (1995) 149 refers to Petronius, Petron. 38.5 *nulla non aut conchyliatum aut coccineum tomentum habet* ('there is no cushion that is not stuffed with purple or scarlet'), as a possible source for Sidonius here. This is convincing because of the rarely used adjective *conchyliatus*, 'of a purple colour' (see the commentary on the previous clause, p. 380), which is used by both authors. Moreover, Trimalchio, who is inclined towards luxury and rules his house despotically, is a fitting Roman parallel for Dionysius. Sidonius combines *toreuma* and *conchyliatus* also in his description of the luxurious dinner of king Theoderic II in *Ep.* 1.2.6 *toreumatum peripetasmatumque modo conchyliata profertur supellex, modo byssina* ('The couches, with their spreading draperies, show an array sometimes of scarlet cloth, sometimes of fine linen').

Section 7

Cumque pransuro Sardanapallicum in morem panis daretur e Leontina segete confectus, insuper dapes cultae ferculis cultioribus apponerentur: In section 7, Sidonius expands Cicero's relatively short description of Dionysius' table luxuries, which contains all the relevant keywords, with intertextual references to other authors – see Cic. *Tusc.* 5.62 *aderant unguenta, coronae, incendebantur odores, mensae conquisitissimis epulis extruebantur* ('there were perfumes and wreaths, incense was burnt and platters of the most exquisite dishes were served'). Conspicuously, Sidonius omits Cicero's two mentions of the attractive young slaves, in *Tusc.* 5.61–2 *tum ad mensam eximia forma pueros delectos iussit consistere eosque nutum illius intuentis diligenter ministrare. ... itaque nec pulchros illos ministratores aspiciebat* ('he had boys of exquisite beauty brought up to serve at table, with orders to wait on them carefully at every hint. ... so he no longer looked at the beautiful slaves'). Sidonius inserts yet another historical example to describe the luxurious way in which Damocles ate. Sardanapallus, a legendary king of Assyria from the seventh century BC, was held to be a decadent and violent ruler and because of his wealth a symbol of a luxurious lifestyle; see Hdt. 2.150; Renger (2001). Sicily was one of the granaries of the Roman Empire and Leontini is an ancient Greek town on the eastern side of Sicily, present-day Lentini, also mentioned in Cicero, not in the *Tusculanae disputationes*, the model for Sidonius' story about Damocles, but several times in his *In Verrem*, Cic. *Verr.* 2.2.66, 2.3.18, 2.3.44, 2.3.46; see Spina (1999) and Sidon. *Carm.* 22.4 v. 173. Squillante (2007/2008) 255 also claims Horace to be a model for this scene as both refer to Sicily and contain the term *daps*; see Hor. *Carm.* 3.1.17–21, where Horace compares the stressful pursuit of honours and wealth with the pleasures of simple life: *destrictus ensis cui super inpia | cervice pendet, non Siculae dapes | dulcem elaborabunt saporem, | non avium citharaeque cantus | somnum reducent* ('over whose impious neck hangs the drawn sword, to him the Sicilian meal will not taste sweet, nor will the song of the birds and the kithara bring back sleep'). See also Iuv. 10.362; Degl'Innocenti Pierini (2008) 1327 n. 17. *Daps*, 'meal', 'feast' (*TLL* 5.1, 36.9–8.54), is used here and in Sidon. *Ep.* 1.2.7, 3.13.6, 8.12.8, *Ep.* 9.13.5 v. 12; Köhler (1995) 152. With the polyptoton *cultae–cultioribus* Sidonius shows that the sumptuous food goes with the precious platters on which it is brought in. *Ferculum* here denotes 'plate' (*TLL* 6.1, 490.9–23); see also Sidon. *Ep.* 1.2.6, *Carm.* 17.11.

spumarent Falerno gemmae capaces inque crystallis calerent unguenta glacialibus: As in *Ep.* 2.2.12, Sidonius describes the drink the guest consumes from a precious cup. The wine is a Falernian one, known to be one of the most sought-after wines in antiquity; see Sidon. *Carm.* 17.15, Plin. *Nat.* 9.62–3; Gutsfeld (2002). Sidonius writes about the grape harvest and the enjoyment of wine elsewhere in his work; see the commentaries on *Ep.* 2.9.1 *Colles aedibus superiores exercentur vinitori et olivitori* and *Ep.* 2.9.8 *sed cum vel pauxillulum bibere....* An intertext for the passage at hand is Luc. 10.159–63, which describes another unlucky ruler, the Egyptian queen Cleopatra, whose wealth Lucan criticises. Both passages contain the keywords *gemmae, capax, crystallus, spumare* and *Falernum*; see Gualandri (1979) 73–4 and Gualandri (2020) 310: *manibusque ministrat | Niliacas crystallos aquas, gemmaeque capaces | excepere merum, sed non Mareotidos uvae, | nobile sed paucis senium cui contulit annis | indomitum Meroe cogens spumare Falernum* ('for the hands a crystal vase served water from the River Nile and the large cups made of gems contained pure wine, but not from Mareotic grapes, instead the noble Falernian wine, which Meroe, forcing the untamed liquid to ferment, makes old in a few years'). Arweiler (1999) 323–7 refers to Sidonius' younger relative Avitus of Vienne (bishop from 490 to 518), who combines the Sidonian and the Lucanian passage in his critique of luxury in Alc. Avit. *Hist.* 3.221–32. Sidonius also might allude to Iuv. 6.303–4, as both passages contain *unguenta* and *spumare* accompanied by the ablative

Falerno and *gemmae capaces*. Juvenal writes: *cum perfusa mero spumant unguenta Falerno, | cum bibitur concha* ('when unguents foam, poured into the unmixed Falernian wine, when one drinks from shell-shaped vessels'). In addition, Squillante (2007/2008) 255 refers to Hor. *Carm.* 3.1.41–4 as a parallel for Sidonius' description of Dionysius' wealth. In his poem, Horace describes the plights of a rich man: *quodsi dolentem nec Phrygius lapis | nec purpurarum sidere clarior | delenit usus nec Falerna | vitis Achaemeniumque costum* ('when neither the Phrygian stone can soothe the sufferer, nor the use of purple more brilliant than the stars, nor the Falernian vine, nor Persian nard'). Formicola (2009) 100 refers to Prop. 2.33b.39–40 *largius effuso madeat tibi mensa Falerno, | spumet et aurato mollius in calice* ('may your table overflow even more abundantly with spilled Falernian wine and may it foam even more temptingly in the gilded chalice'). The combination of *spumare* and wine is also found in the negative description of the parasite Gnatho in *Ep.* 3.13.4 *spumans vinum* ('he foams with wine'). *Gemma*, 'jewel', 'gem', here stands for 'cup' (*TLL* 6.2, 1756.61–72); see Verg. *Georg.* 2.506 (for the Vergilian allusions in this passage, see the commentary on *Ep.* 2.13.8 *et satis cavens ne beatum ultra diceret duceretque qui saeptus armis...*), Mart. 12.74.4, 14.94.2, Apul. *Met.* 2.19.3, Paul. Nol. *Ep.* 49.12. For *capax*, 'spacious', 'roomy', see the commentary on *Ep.* 2.2.4 *quae consequenti ... excepto solii capacis hemicyclio*. For the combination of *gemma* and *capax*, see Luc. 10.159 (cited just above, on p. 383), Sen. *Ben.* 7.9.3 *capacibus gemmis* ('in wide cups'). In addition, the same Senecan passage also contains the word crystal: *video istic crystallina* ('I see there objects of crystal'). Whereas in Sidon. *Ep.* 2.2.12 the cups are iced by the cold drink, here they look like ice, but contain hot unguents which give off pleasant odours. On the antithesis between *calerent* and *glacialibus* (hot–cold) and *crystallis* ('a cup made of crystal' or 'ice-crystal'), see Gualandri (1979) 158–9. It was customary to pour out *unguentum*, 'fragrant ointment' (*OLD* 2092–3, 1a), during dinner; see for example Petron. 47.1, Suet. *Nero* 31.2. *Glacialis*, 'icy', 'frozen', 'full of ice', is used here in a transferred meaning of 'looking like ice' (*TLL* 6.2, 2001.1–13).

hinc suffita cinnamo ac ture cenatio spargeret peregrinos naribus odores: Sidonius specifies the fragrant ointments that are poured out, namely cinnamon and incense. The aromatic bark of the cinnamon tree (*cinnamum*) was used in antiquity to aromatise burnt offerings, as an ingredient of unguents or perfumes and to spice wine; see Ov. *Fast.* 3.731, Plin. *Nat.* 14.107; Hünemörder (2002c). See also Sidon. *Carm.* 9.325.

Incense (*tus*), a resin, was also burnt on various festive occasions because of its fragrance; see Plin. *Nat.* 12.62–5; Hünemörder (2002a). The manuscripts LN[1], Loyen (1970a) 77 and Anderson (1936) 478 have *huc* ('to this place', 'hither'), MCTN[2] and Lütjohann (1887) 37 *hinc* ('from this place', 'from this side', 'here'). *Suffio*, 'to subject to aromatic fumes, fumigate', is used mostly in poetry and in post-Augustan prose (*OLD* 1861, 1a), in connection with *odor*, 'scent', also in Colum. 12.18.3 *cella quoque vinaria ... bonis odoribus suffienda* ('and one should fumigate the wine cellar with good scents'). *Cenatio*, 'dining room' (*TLL* 3, 782.14–43), appears in post-Augustan prose; it is used several times in Pliny's description of his estates: *Ep.* 2.17.10, 2.17.12, 2.17.15, 5.6.21. See also Sidon. *Carm.* 22.4 v. 207, Suet. *Nero* 31.2, Sen. *Ep.* 90.9, 90.15.

et madescentes nardo capillos circumfusa florum serta siccarent: To crown participants with wreaths and anoint their heads was a regular part of a symposium; Hurschmann (1999). The Ciceronian detail of the crowns slipping off Damocles' head seems to have inspired Sidonius' image of the crowns 'drying out' because of the hair impregnated with ointments; see Cic. *Tusc.* 5.62 *aderant unguenta, coronae ... iam ipsae defluebant coronae* ('there were perfumes and wreaths ... the wreaths fell to the ground'); Degl'Innocenti Pierini (2008) 1327 n. 17. There are other passages where Sidonius mentions the custom of anointing one's hair, such as *Carm.* 5.226–7, about a barbarian wedding, *fercula captivasque dapes cirroque madente | ferre coronatos redolentia serta lebetas* ('and servants crowned with perfumed garlands carrying wine-bowls on their oily top-knots'), *Carm.* 11.106, and *Ep.* 9.13.5 vv. 42–5. *Madesco*, 'to become moist or wet' (*TLL* 8, 35.12–51), or more often *madeo*, is used to describe hair which is moist from oil, but also to describe drunkenness, that is, 'to be moist from wine'. In *Ep.* 9.9.8 Sidonius uses the verb in connection with tears. The combination of *nardus*, 'nard', which in a symposiastic or erotic context metonymically denotes 'nard oil' (*TLL* 9.1, 55.44–69), and *madere/madidus* is attested elsewhere: Mart. 3.65.8 *quod madidas nardo passa corona comas* ('like a wreath that touched the hair wet with nard oil'), Sen. *Herc. Fur.* 468–9 *cuius horrentes comae | maduere nardo* ('whose ruffled hair was soaked in nard'). For *nardus* in a symposiastic context, see also Hor. *Carm.* 2.11.13–17 *cur non sub alta vel platano vel hac | pinu iacentes sic temere et rosa | canos odorati capillos, | dum licet, Assyriaque nardo | potamus uncti?* ('why do we not casually lie down under the tall plane tree or this pine tree and drink, as long as it is possible, our grey hair fragrant from roses and anointed with Assyrian nard'); see also Ov. *Ars* 3.443.

coepit supra tergum sic recumbentis repente vibrari mucro destrictus e lacunaribus, qui videbatur in iugulum purpurati iam iamque ruiturus: After describing the luxury of the table, Sidonius switches to the danger posed to Damocles by the sword hanging over him. The danger of being decapitated by a sword is addressed by Sidonius in his description of another dinner attended by the emperor Majorian in *Ep.* 1.11.15. For *coepit* with infinitive as an alternative for the perfect tense in later Latin (especially in Petronius), see Köhler (1995) 326 on *Ep.* 1.11.14 *coepit consulere* ('he asked'), van Waarden (2010) 93–4 on *Ep.* 7.1.2 *coepit initiari* ('has been initiated'). Sidonius alludes to the motif of the sword hanging menacingly also in *Ep.* 1.7.13; Köhler (1995) 256. For *recumbo*, 'to lie down', 'to recline', see the commentary on *Ep.* 2.2.11 *Quo loci recumbens....* For *mucro*, 'sword', see the commentary immediately below on *Ep.* 2.13.7 *nam filo ... et ita pondere minax....* For *lacunar*, 'the wainscoted ceiling', see the commentary on *Ep.* 2.2.5 *ut suspicientum visui fabrefactum lacunar aperiret*. With the description of Damocles as *purpuratus*, 'clad in purple' (*TLL* 10.2, 2706.17–7.31), Sidonius recalls the tension of a ruler's life between pleasure and danger. The adjective is also used in Sidon. *Ep.* 1.9.2, 1.11.15, 7.9.19, 8.3.5. For *purpur*, 'purple', see the commentary on *Ep.* 2.2.8 *Nec pilae ... 'aedificiorum purpuras' nuncupavere.*

nam filo equinae saetae ligatus et ita pondere minax ut acumine gulam formidolosi Tantaleo frenabat exemplo, ne cibi ingressi per ora per vulnera exirent: With his description of the hanging sword, Sidonius follows Cicero, Cic. *Tusc.* 5.62 *fulgentem gladium e lacunari saeta equina aptum demitti iussit* ('he ordered a glittering sword to be hung from the ceiling fixed with a horsehair'); see also Amm. 29.2.4 *ex summis domorum laqueariis, in quibus discumbebant, saetis nexos equinis et occipitiis incumbentes gladios perhorrebant* ('they saw in fear that from the top of the ceiling of the house, where they lay down for dinner, swords were hanging fixed with horse hair and threatening their heads'). See also the version of Hor. *Carm.* 3.1.17–18 cited on p. 383, at the beginning of the commentary on *Cumque pransuro Sardanapallicum in morem panis daretur.* The adjective *equinus*, 'of or belonging to horses' (*TLL* 5.2, 725.12–78), is used instead of the genitive of *equus*. It also occurs in Sidon. *Carm.* 7.457, 16.2. For *minax*, 'overhanging', 'threatening', 'menacing' (*TLL* 8, 996.74–82), used of weapons or other things, see Firm. *Math.* 1.7.3, who, like Sidonius, applies the adjective to *mucro*, 'sword' (*TLL* 8, 1555.55–6.82), *minacem mucronis aciem* ('the threatening sharpness of the sword'). Squillante (2007/2008) 257 refers to Verg. *Aen.* 8.668–9 also as a parallel text: ... *et te, Catilina, minaci | pendentem scopulo* ('and you, Catiline, hanging from a threatening cliff'). *Acumen*, 'a point to prick or sting with', is used of instruments made of different materials; see *TLL* 1, 459.8–25 on instruments made of iron. In combination with a sword (*gladii*), *acumen* also appears in Hil. *In Psalm.* 63.7, Amm. 16.12.54. *Gula*, 'throat', here metonymically means 'appetite', 'gluttony', 'greediness', 'voracity' (*TLL* 6.2, 2356.5–7.11). For the expression *gulam frenare*, 'to rein in one's greed', see Tert. *Ieiun.* 1, p. 274.14 *gulae frenos imbuentem* ('to teach limits to greed'), *Adv. Marc.* 2.18.2 *et frenos impositos illi gulae agnosce* ('and acknowledge the reins applied to this greed'). The adjective *formidulosus* (or *formidolosus*) is not frequently used with a passive meaning, 'experiencing fear', 'afraid', 'timid', 'frightened' (*TLL* 6.1, 1100.81–101.19), but see for example Ter. *Eun.* 756, Apul. *Met.* 9.16.1, Sen. *Clem.* 1.16.4. Cicero (for example Cic. *Verr.* 2.5.6) uses it only in its active meaning, 'producing fear', 'terrible'; see also Plin. *Ep.* 6.20.3. Sidonius, in his version of the story, adds a comparison of Damocles with Tantalus, one of the famous sinners of the underworld. He was a king of Phrygia, son of Zeus and father of Pelops and Niobe. Hom. *Od.* 11.582–92 describes how he had to suffer hunger and thirst even though he was standing in a lake with fruit hanging over his head. However, both receded as soon as he tried to reach for them. There are various explanations for why Tantalus was punished so severely; see Stenger (2002). The point of comparison is that both Damocles and Tantalus cannot eat, although food and drink are within reach. There is also a version of the story in which Tantalus' torment is intensified by a weight that threatens to fall on him; Squillante (2007/2008) 257. Degl'Innocenti Pierini (2008) shows the connection between the story of Damocles and the myth of Tantalus. With his additions, Sidonius thus fleshes out Cicero's narrative and makes it more vivid. See Cic. *Tusc.* 5.62 *nec manum porrigebat in mensam* ('and he no longer reached out for the table').

Section 8

Unde post mixtas fletibus preces atque multimoda suspiria vix absolutus emicatimque prosiliens: In the concluding section 8, the punch line of the story follows. Damocles asks to be freed from the luxury and dangers of his ruler. Again, Sidonius embellishes Cicero's relatively short and sober narrative, Cic. *Tusc.* 5.62 *denique exoravit tyrannum* ... cited above, p. 368, in the commentary on *Ep.* 2.13.2 *nimirum qui supergressi....* The adjective *multimodus*, 'manifold', 'various' (*TLL* 8, 1589.54–90.14), is attested from Tertullian onwards; see Tert. *Anim.* 52.3, Paul. Nol. *Carm.* 21.85, 23.101, Prud. *Perist.* 3.200 (cited in *Ep.* 2.10.4 vv. 11–15: General remarks, p. 318). The adverb *emicatim*, 'springing forth', 'in a flash' (*TLL* 5.2, 483.22–4), is derived from *emicare*, 'to spring out', 'spring forth' (see Verg. *Aen.* 6.5, 12.327) and is a Sidonian hapax. Gualandri (1979) 176 also refers to *superemicare*, another hapax of the same verbal family used in *Ep.* 9.9.7 and *Carm.* 15.75.

illa refugit celeritate divitias deliciasque regales, qua solent appeti, reductus ad desideria mediocrium timore summorum: After his experience, Damocles flees from royal privileges and gladly returns to his prior life. Sidonius refers to the ancient ideal of the *aurea mediocritas*, the golden middle, which is preferable to the height of power. For this notion, see especially Horace, who coined the expression and counts among Sidonius' models for the story of Damocles: Hor. *Carm.* 2.10.5 *auream ... mediocritatem* ('the golden middle'); Squillante (2007/2008) 254–6. *Deliciae* here denotes 'delicacies', 'delicious food' (*TLL* 5.1, 448.58–80) see also Sidon. *Carm.* 22.4 v. 219, Colum. 8.16.5, Tert. *Adv. Marc.* 4.28.11, Hier. *Ep.* 43.3; Delhey (1993) 193.

et satis cavens, ne beatum ultra diceret duceretque qui saeptus armis ac satellitibus et per hoc raptis incubans opibus ferro pressus premeret aurum: After his experience, Damocles changes his attitude about what the attributes of happiness are. A *satelles* is a 'bodyguard or escort to a prince or despot' (*OLD* 1692, 1); here, attendants (of the tyrant Dionysius) are meant; see also Sidon. *Ep.* 1.2.4, Plin. *Paneg.* 23.3, Liv. 24.5.3 *satellites armatos* ('armed bodyguards'), 32.39.8, 34.27.5, Cic. *Phil.* 2.112; Köhler (1995) 139, Squillante (2007/2008) 256–7. In this pointed sentence at the end of the letter there are many verbal parallels to Verg. *Georg.* 2.507 *condit opes alius defossoque incubat auro* ('another hides treasures and sits on buried gold'), where Vergil describes greedy people and contrasts their lifestyle with the quiet life of peasants. *Opibus* ('riches', 'wealth') echoes Vergil's *opes*, *incubans* Vergil's *incubat*, and *aurum* Vergil's *auro*; Colton (2000) 40. In addition, *gemma*, 'jewel', 'gem', stands for 'cup' in both texts; see the commentary on *Ep.* 2.13.7 *spumarent Falerno gemmae capaces....* Fascione (2019) 58 refers to Mart. 12.53.3–5 as a parallel. For the verb *incubare* meaning 'to sit on', 'rest on', 'to be attached to', see also Verg. *Aen.* 6.610, Sidon. *Ep.* 8.7.2 *sic vitiis ut divitiis incubantes* ('they are attached to their vices as they are to their wealth'). In the polyptoton and chiasmus *ferro pressus–premeret aurum* Sidonius contrasts iron and gold and uses the verb *premere* in two different meanings, that is, 'to press down', 'burden', 'weigh down' (*TLL* 10.2, 1176.60–8.48; see for example Plin. *Ep.* 2.11.13) and 'to sit', 'to lie on' (*TLL* 10.2, 1168.54–9.8). The latter appears frequently in Ovid, for example Ov. *Am.* 1.4.15, *Her.* 12.30, *Met.* 5.317; see also Petron. 131.9 *premebat illa ... aureum torum* ('she lay on a golden bed').

Quapropter ad statum huiusmodi, domine frater, nescio an constet tendere beatos, patet certe miseros pervenire. Vale: The conclusion and the return to the initial situation of the letter is limited to a single short sentence. For *dominus* in the vocative as an honorific address, see the commentary on *Ep.* 2.3.1 *Gaudeo te, domine maior*.... The collocation *domine frater*, a formula of respect for equals, occurs only in Sidonius (here and in *Ep.* 4.8.4, 7.17.1); van Waarden (2016) 211. Loyen (1970a) 78 n. 56 instead suggests that *domine frater* should be understood not in a honorific, but in a religious sense as 'frère par la religion' (see Sidon. *Ep.* 4.4.3, 7.17.1). In other instances in Sidonius' letters (*Ep.* 4.8.4, 4.18.2, 5.17.6), *frater* clearly means 'friend'; Amherdt (2001) 240. For the different meanings of *frater* as a marker of familial relationship, of status in the patronage system and in the Christian idiom, see van Waarden (2016) 43–5, 211–12 with further references. With the final adjective *beatus*, Sidonius again takes up Ciceronian terminology; see the commentary on *Ep.* 2.13.2 *nimirum qui supergressi ... summam beatitudinem*.... The opposition of *beati* and *miseri* is reminiscent of Aug. *Civ.* 9.13, where Augustine discusses the subject of happiness. See also Aug. *De libero arbitrio* 2.9.26; Squillante (2007/2008) 257. For the letter's simple ending with *vale*, see the commentary on *Ep.* 2.1.4 *Vale*.

Epistula 14

Introduction

Summary

The second book ends with a letter about *otium* in the countryside. Sidonius congratulates his friend Maurusius on a rich harvest and hopes to see him soon. If Maurusius prefers to enjoy the peace and quiet of the countryside, Sidonius will travel to join him on his estate as friendship is the thing that he values the most.

Addressee

The addressee, Maurusius, is unattested elsewhere; *PLRE* 2, 738, Kaufmann (1995) 324, Mathisen (2020a) 107. As we know from the letter at hand, he owns an estate in the Auvergne in the Pagus Vialoscensis (probably present-day Marsat or Volvic near Clermont-Ferrand), is of the same age as Sidonius and is playfully addressed in section 2 as *magnus dominus*, which hints at his senatorial rank.

Date

There is no evidence for the date of this letter; see the Introduction, '2. The date and order of letters in Book 2'.

Major themes and further reading

Structure

The last letter of the second book is again a letter of friendship (see the introduction to *Ep.* 2.3) and, like a kind of summary, takes up again all the important themes of the second book. Like *Ep.* 2.2 and 2.9 it addresses the life in the villa and the subject of leisure (*otium*). The second book follows the course of the seasons: it was still high summer in letter 2.2, but now, at the end of the second book, we are in winter; see the introduction to *Ep.* 2.2, and André (2006), Hanaghan (2019) 73–4, 170–1, Hindermann (2020a) 109–11. There are also intratextual connections between the closing letter, 2.14, and other letters of the second book. As in *Ep.* 2.11, Sidonius addresses the subject of separation and remoteness of friends; see the introduction to *Ep.* 2.11. Another parallel is *Ep.* 2.13, about the dangers of *negotium*, where Sidonius praises the safety and joy of a life in the golden middle. Sidonius repeats this thought at the end of *Ep.* 2.14 by claiming that he prefers a good neighbour over profit.

Intertextuality
In the last letter of the second book, the theme of the harvest is dominant, which of course can also be read as a poetological metaphor for putting together a collection of poems or letters; see for example *Anth. Pal.* 4.2, and the commentary on *Ep.* 2.14.1 *Audio industriae ... respondere vindemiam*. Sidonius again alludes to Pliny, who links the theme of seasons and villas in his letters and ends his letter collection by writing about darkness and dimming of light; see Plin. *Ep.* 9.36 and 9.40, Gibson (2015) 189–90, and *Ep.* 7.2 and Gibson and Morello (2012) 188–9. The harvest is also mentioned in Pliny's letter of friendship Plin. *Ep.* 9.16.

Pliny and Martial also play an important role in the final letter as references for life in the villa. The major intertext is Plin. *Ep.* 7.3, where Pliny criticises his friend Praesens for staying on his own estates and not joining him in the city. In both letters, the subject of dress code is addressed, symbolising appropriate behaviour in leisure; see the commentaries on *Ep.* 2.2.2 *Et nunc, ...* and 2.14.2 *in otio fuliginoso ... sive tunicata quiete*. For another parallel see Plin. *Ep.* 5.6.45, where one finds the same combination of *otium* and clothing. In contrast to Pliny, Sidonius writes that he will meet Maurusius in the countryside, because he values friendship above *negotium*. Sidonius here again addresses the contrast between city and country and between *otium* and *negotium* (as in *Ep.* 2.2 – see the introduction there). With his allusions to Martial, Sidonius also underlines the connection between his first villa letter, *Ep.* 2.2, and the closing letter, 2.14; see the commentaries on *Ep.* 2.2.6 *Absunt ridiculi vestitu...*, on *Ep.* 2.14.1 *Unde et in pago Vialoscensi, qui Martialis aetate...* and on 2.14.2 *illic usque ad adventum hirundineum vel ciconinum....* Sidonius and Pliny combine several villa letters for their self-portrayal. Both describe other people who behave differently as a counter-image or complement to their exemplary behaviour; see Hanaghan (2020) and Amherdt (2004) 383–4 on Sidon. *Ep.* 1.6, where Sidonius castigates Eutropius for spending too much time on his farm.

Commentary

Section 1

Sidonius Maurusio suo salutem: For the simple greeting formula, see the commentary on *Ep.* 2.1.1 *Sidonius Ecdicio suo salutem*. For the addressee, Maurusius, see the introduction to this letter.

Audio industriae tuae votisque communibus uberiore proventu, quam minabatur sterilis annus, respondere vindemiam: By starting with the first-person singular *audio*, 'I hear', Sidonius again creates the illusion of the letter as one half of a conversation, as he has done in other letters of the second book – see the commentaries on *Ep.* 2.1.1 *'Quaenam?' inquis* and the beginning of the first villa letter *Ep.* 2.2.1 *Ruri me esse causaris....* For the beginning of the letter with *audio*, see Sidon. *Ep.* 5.1.1, Plin. *Ep.* 3.21.1, 9.34.1. Sidonius begins the first section with the topic of the harvest, which will run through the whole letter. Several times in the second book Sidonius writes about the grape harvest and the enjoyment of wine: see the commentaries on *Ep.* 2.9.1 *Colles aedibus superiores exercentur vinitori et olivitori*, *Ep.* 2.9.8 *sed cum vel pauxillulum bibere...*, and 2.13.7 *spumarent Falerno gemmae capaces.... Proventus* means 'growth', 'increase' of fruits and crops (*TLL* 10.2, 2313.76–14.46); of wine it is also used in Colum. 4.18.2, Suet. *Claud.* 16.4 *uberi vinearum proventu* ('when the harvest of wine was abundant'), Mart. 9.98.1–2 *vindemiarum non ubique proventus | cessavit* ('the wine harvest did not decline everywhere'). For *sterilis*, 'fruitless', 'barren', in combination with a season, see Cic. *Ad Q. fr.* 2.12.2 *Februarium sterilem futurum* ('February will be a sterile month', where Cicero figuratively refers to his meagre literary production). *Vindemia*, 'grapes', 'wine', 'vintage' (*OLD* 2066), is personified here and fulfils (*respondere*) the wishes of Sidonius and his addressee, Maurusius. For the combination *sterilis annus* ('dry year'), see Sen. *Nat.* 4.2.2.

Unde et in pago Vialoscensi, qui Martialis aetate citeriore vocitatus est propter hiberna legionum Iulianarum, suspicor diuturnius te moraturum:

Sidonius starts with a paraphrase of Maurusius' place of residence, the meaning of which is not clear. First he uses the term *pagus*, which is ambiguous and varies according to time and place. In the later Western Roman Empire a *pagus* denotes the 'smallest administrative district of a province'; Heumann and Seckel (1907) 401, Tarpin (2002). According to Sidonius, the district is called Vialoscensis in the Gallic language and Martialis ('of the god Mars', 'martial') in Latin. It is part of the Auvergne, and is identified with present-day Marsat or Volvic, which are, respectively, 15 and 20 km north-west of Clermont;Anderson (1936) 480 n. 1, Dupieux (1956) 286, Loyen (1970a) 221 n. 57, Köhler (2014) 70 n. 1, Mathisen (2020a) 165. In connection with the name of a god, *pagus* appears elsewhere (*TLL* 10.1, 95.49–62), in combination with *Martialis* also in *CIL* 9.1455. Perhaps Sidonius also uses the paraphrase *pagus Martialis* because he alludes to the poet Martial in the next section; see the commentary on *Ep.* 2.14.2 *illic usque ad adventum hirundineum vel ciconinum....* It might be a reference to Mart. 3.1 (sent from *Gallia togata*) and thus an announcement of Sidonius' third book of letters (thanks to Margot Neger for this idea). For *pagus*, see also Sidon. *Carm.* 17.17. For the expression *aetate citeriore*, 'more recently' (*TLL* 1, 1136.12–18), see Sidon. *Ep.* 8.1.2 *quorum anterior orator Demaden, citerior Antonium toleravere derogatores* ('the earlier orator [i.e. Demosthenes] had to tolerate Demades as a detractor, the more recent [i.e. Cicero], Antonius'). What is meant by the *legiones Iulianae* is also not clear; Loyen (1970a) 79 translates it as 'les légions de César', Köhler (2014) 70 n. 1 'Truppen Caesars'. For the rare use of the comparative of the adverb *diuturnius*, 'longer' (*TLL* 5.1, 1647.6–15), see Sidon. *Ep.* 8.3.1, 9.9.9, Aug. *Mor. Manich.* 2.16.43.

quo loci tibi cum ferax vinea est, tum praeter ipsam praedium magno non minus domino: Maurusius owns a vineyard and an estate nearby. On vineyards as part of an estate, see the commentary on *Ep.* 2.9.1 *Colles aedibus superiores exercentur vinitori et olivitori*. For *ferax*, 'fruitful', 'fertile', see the commentary on *Ep.* 2.9.9 *flavis ruber glareis ... ob hoc minus piscium ferax delicatorum*. For *praedium*, 'estate', see the commentary on *Ep.* 2.2.3 *nomen hoc praedio....* With the pun *magno non minus domino*, 'not inferior to its important master', Sidonius praises the owner of the villa and at the same time, as in his other villa letters, plays with the motif that an estate depicts its owner and vice versa; see the introduction to *Ep.* 2.2.

quod te tuosque plurifaria frugum mansionumque dote remoretur: The adjective *plurifarius*, 'in many parts or places' (*TLL* 10.1, 2466.37–47), is rarely used, but not a hapax, as Gualandri (1979) 180 suggests; see also Tert. *Adv. Marc.* 1.4.4. It is also used in Sidon. *Ep.* 6.11.2. The adverb *plurifariam*, 'in many parts or places', appears several times in Suetonius, see for example Suet. *Aug.* 46, *Ner.* 24.2. *Mansio* here translates as 'a dwelling', 'habitation' (*TLL* 8, 324.82–5.14); the term appears again in *Ep.* 3.2.3. The term *dos*, 'dowry', is used here in a figurative sense for the pleasure, that is, 'delight', 'gift', 'virtue', 'merit' (*TLL* 5.1, 2047.42–76), that the estate offers its residents. Sidonius uses the term several times to describe the character of a person; see the commentary on *Ep.* 2.6.1 *opportunus elegans ... et his morum dotibus praeditus*. The term is used in a similar context about the values of one's estate in Plin. *Ep.* 1.24.4 *si praediolum istud, quod commendatur his dotibus* ('if he buys this little estate, which recommends itself with such gifts') and Plin. *Ep.* 2.17.29 *tot tantisque dotibus villulae nostrae* ('to the many great endowments of my little villa'). See also Sidon. *Ep.* 1.8.3, Symm. *Ep.* 6.11.2.

Section 2

Ilicet si horreis apothecisque seu penu impleta destinas: For *ilicet*, 'immediately', 'instantly', see the commentary on *Ep.* 2.9.4 *Ilicet a deliciis in delicias rapiebamur*. Sidonius uses it here to refer to Maurusius' spontaneous decision to stay in the villa, in the countryside, instead of returning to the city. Sidonius enumerates three different types of store rooms (granaries, wine cellars and the larder) to illustrate Maurusius' abundance of supplies. First is the *horreum*, 'a storehouse esp. for preserving grain', 'a barn', 'a granary' (*TLL* 6.3, 2985.9–9.14), a term used in widely different contexts (rural transactions, military, commercial dealings, metaphorical uses) to denote buildings where anything could be stored, for example Cic. *Verr.* 2.3.8, Verg. *Georg.* 1.49, Hor. *Carm.* 1.1.9; see Rickman (1971) 1. Sidonius uses the term also in *Ep.* 6.12.5, *Carm.* 22.4 v. 169, 187, 23.42. Next is *apotheca*, 'a repository', 'storehouse', 'magazine' (*TLL* 2, 255.23–60), especially for wine; see Hor. *Sat.* 2.5.7, Phaedr. 4.5.25, Tert. *Adv. Marc.* 4.28.11, Plin. *Nat.* 14.56, 14.93. The third term, *penus*, usually denotes 'provisions', 'food', but here and in Sidon. *Ep.* 8.4.1, 8.12.6 it is used metonymically for 'a place to store food', 'pantry', 'larder' (*TLL* 10.1, 1125.19–33); see also Paul. Nol. *Carm.* 19.577, Claud. *Eutr.* 1.194. For the combination of different types of storage facilities, see the description of Pontius Leontius' villa in Sidon. *Carm.* 22.4 v. 219 *deliciis redolent iunctis apotheca penusque* ('and the wine store and the pantry are fragrant from the delicacies within'), Plin.

Ep. 2.17.13 *lata post apotheca et horreum* ('behind a spacious storeroom for wine and a granary'); Delhey (1993) 193.

illic usque ad adventum hirundineum vel ciconinum Iani Numaeque ninguidos menses: While Sidonius' first villa letter is set in summer, in this villa letter it is winter; see the Introduction to this book, p. xiv. The beginning of spring is announced by two kinds of birds, *hirundo*, 'swallow', and *ciconia*, 'stork'. Both birds are migratory and the first to head back north after wintering in Africa. Instead of the genitive of the nouns, Sidonius coins the very rarely used adjectives *hirundineus*, 'of a swallow' (*TLL* 6.2, 2827.79–83), and *ciconinus*, 'of a stork' (*TLL* 3, 1051.73–6). Wolff (2020) 398 classifies *hirundineus* as a doublet of the classical *hirundininus*, which has the same meaning and appears for example in Plaut. *Rud.* 598, Mart. 11.18.20. Wolff (2020) 399 also shows that hapax legomena often appear in pairs in Sidonius. The expression *ad adventum hirundineum vel ciconinum* probably is inspired by the Bible: Vulg. Ier. 8.7 *milvus in caelo cognovit tempus suum; turtur et hirundo et ciconia custodierunt tempus adventus sui; populus autem meus non cognovit iudicium Domini* ('a stork in the sky knows its time, a turtle-dove, a crane and a swallow know their time to return, but my people do not want to know the right of God'). The idea that the seasons influence the behaviour of both animals and people is also found in Claud. Mam. *Anim.* 1.21 (Engelbrecht p. 71, l. 13) *nam et nidos ciconiae atque hirundines post annum revisunt* ('because the storks and swallows seek out their nests again after a year'), Isid. *Orig.* 12.7.1 *aliae adventiciae, quae propriis temporibus revertuntur, ut ciconiae, hirundines* ('others are migratory birds that return at certain times, like storks and swallows'). The same collocation of swallow and stork is found in Varro *Rust.* 2.1.27 *neque enim hirundines et ciconiae, quae in Italia pariunt, in omnibus terris pariunt* ('indeed, swallows and storks, which have offspring in Italy, do not have offspring in all countries'), 3.5.6 *non ut advenae volucres pullos faciunt, in agro ciconiae, in tecto hirundines* ('thrushes do not make their young like migratory birds, storks in the fields, swallows in the roofs'). For the swallow and stork as a symbols of spring, see Ov. *Fast.* 2.853 *fallimur, an veris praenuntia venit hirundo?* ('am I mistaken or does the swallow come as a messenger of spring?') and Petron. 55.6 *ciconia etiam, grata peregrina hospita ... avis exul hiemis, titulus tepidi temporis* ('the stork, the dear guest from a foreign land, in exile in winter, herald of the mild season'). With his comments on the birds Sidonius refers back to *Ep.* 2.2.14, which is dedicated to the sound of the birds one can hear in his villa. January was the month of Ianus, the Roman god of beginnings, gates, and transitions. *Numa* refers to the legendary king Numa Pompilius, who supposedly reigned 715–672 BC and added January and February to the original ten Roman months of the year; see Censor. *De die natali* 20, Sidon. *Ep.* 9.16.2; Haase (2000). Sidonius calls them *ninguidos menses*, 'snowy months'. The adjective *ninguidus*, 'full of snow', 'snowy' (*Blaise* 555) appears first in Ausonius, who uses it several times in different contexts, most often of the Pyrenees; see Auson. *Urb.* 102, *Ep.* 27.69 [24.61], 29.51 [21.51], *Prof.* 21.21, Prud. *Perist.* 2.540, Paul. Nol. *Carm.* 10.203; Colton (2000) 200. In Sidonius' works, *ninguidus* also appears in *Carm.* 5.546 and *Ep.* 3.7.4.

in otio fuliginoso sive tunicata quiete transmittere: Sidonius uses the term *otium* frequently and in all semantical nuances; see the introduction to *Ep.* 2.2 for the importance of leisure in his letters. *Otium* denotes 'retirement', 'leisure', in *Ep.* 1.11.1, 3.14.1, 5.7.3, 8.3.4; it denotes 'quiet', 'calmness', 'recreation' in *Ep.* 3.3.5, 4.24.5, 5.17.9 and *Carm.* 5.577; it denotes 'idleness', 'abstinence', in *Ep.* 3.6.2, 3.7.1, 5.7.2, 5.17.5 and *Carm.* 2.198; Hindermann (2020a) 96–9. Sidonius' intensive preoccupation with leisure is also reflected in his creation of new expressions in the semantic field. In *Ep.* 4.18.3 (and *Ep.* 8.9.6) he creates the new term *otiabundus*, 'having *otium*' (*TLL* 9.2, 1164.10–13), only attested in Sidonius; Amherdt (2001) 406, Hindermann (2020a) 111. See also the commentary on *Ep.* 2.10.3 *quos in hanc paginam ... suas otiositates....* The combination of *otium* with the very rarely used adjective *fuliginosus*, 'full of soot', 'sooty' (*TLL* 6.1, 1522.78–81), here used in the figurative meaning of 'domestic', 'at home', shows his awareness of the problematic aspects of self-concealment in the countryside instead of an active life. The only two other instances are Prud. *Perist.* 10.261 and *Querol.* p. 21.18–9 (ed. Peiper, *Teubner*). For adjectives ending in *-osus*, see the commentary on *Ep.* 2.2.18 *Lacus ipse ... flexuosus nemorosusque....* With the greasy smoke of the oven clouding his *otium*, Sidonius also alludes to Pliny's expression *pingue otium* ('deep leisure) in Plin. *Ep.* 9.3.1, which Sidonius also uses in *Ep.* 1.6.3. In its basic sense *pinguis* means 'fat', or 'oily', but it is also used symbolically for leisure. Plin. *Ep.* 5.6.45, where one finds the same combination of *otium* (plus adjective *pinguis*) and clothing, is a particularly close parallel: *altius ibi otium et pinguius eoque securius; nulla necessitas togae* ('there is a deeper and more comfortable and thus uninterrupted quiet and therefore no need for the toga'). See also Plin. *Ep.* 1.3.3, 7.26.3; Hindermann (2016) 117, Hindermann (2020a) 110. The expression *tunicata quies*, which Sidonius combines with his own expression, is a citation of Mart. 10.51.6 (*o soles, o tunicata quies!*, 'oh sunny days, oh leisure in the tunic!'). Martial describes the comfortable, leisurely life led by Faustinus in his villa at Anxur; Colton (1985b) 279. In a pun on the toponym of the same name, Sidonius explicitly mentions 'Martial' in the previous section and thus probably marks the intertextual reference explicitly – see the commentary on *Ep.* 2.14.1 *Unde et in pago Vialoscensi, qui Martialis aetate...*; Wolff (2014a) 297–8. *Tunicatus* is the participle of *tunico*, 'to clothe with a tunic'; see Cic. *Cael.* 11. With the allusion to the clothing worn during leisure time, Sidonius refers back to letter 2.2 and the sweating Domitius – see the commentary on *Ep.* 2.2.2 *Et nunc, dum in carbaso sudat unus...* and the introduction to *Ep.* 2.14. The tunic was worn with a belt in public, but unbelted at home; Hurschmann (2002a). While in the city of Rome in Martial's time one had to wear the formal *toga* (for doing business), in the countryside the *tunica* was allowed. To get rid of one's toga was used in a transferred meaning to denote the relaxed lifestyle in the country; see Plin. *Ep.* 7.3.2 *toga feriata* ('the toga went on holiday'), Mart. 10.96.11–12 *quattuor hic aestate togae pluresve teruntur | autumnis ibi me quattuor una tegit* ('here you use up four or more *togae* in one summer, there one covers me during four summers'), Mart. 12.18.17–18 *ignota est toga, sed datur petenti | rupta proxima vestis a cathedra* ('The toga is unknown here, but when I ask for it, I am handed the next best piece of clothing from a broken chair'), Sidon. *Ep.* 5.7.3 *hi sunt, qui invident tunicatis otia* ('these men envy retired men for their leisure'); Ackerman (1990) 35, Goette (2013). The opposition of toga to tunic was archaic in Sidonius' day since the toga was no longer worn, and so the reference is all the more literary; see Verg. *Aen.* 1.282, Mart. 14.124, Pausch (2003) 31; von Rummel (2007) 83–96, Hindermann (2020a) 110–11. Sidonius is very aware of the importance and symbolic value of clothing and appearance, as can be seen in his predominantly negative depictions of barbarians, who differ from the Romans by wearing fur clothing – see Sidon. *Carm.* 5.563, 7.219, *Ep.* 1.2.4, 7.9.19; von Rummel (2007) 166–81. For preferring a quiet life dedicated to one's studies, see Plin. *Ep.* 9.6.1 *omne hoc tempus ... iucundissima quiete transmisi* ('I have spent all this time in very agreeable quiet').

nobis quoque parum in oppido fructuosae protinus amputabuntur causae morarum: The classical (first appearance in Cicero) and very common adjective *fructuosus*, 'fruitful', 'productive', also appears in Sidon. *Ep.* 3.5.3, 4.21.5, 8.6.12; Amherdt (2001) 446–7, Ernout (1949) 74, 84. For adjectives ending in -*osus*, see the commentary on *Ep.* 2.2.18 *Lacus ipse ... flexuosus nemorosusque....* The verb *amputo* means 'to remove', 'to efface', 'abolish' (*TLL* 1, 2022.14–3.67). As a participle it is also used in Sidon. *Ep.* 9.9.12. The syntagma *amputare* and *causa* is also attested in Hier. *Ep.* 60.17 *nec amputamus causas morbi* ('and we do not remove the reasons of the illness'); Montone (2017) 28. With *mora*, 'delay', Sidonius refers back to the end of the first letter of the second book – see the commentary on *Ep.* 2.1.4 *Proinde moras tuas…..*

ut, dum ipse nimirum frueris rure, nos te fruamur, quibus, ut recognoscis, non magis cordi est aut voluptati ager cum reditibus amplis, quam vicinus aequalis cum bonis moribus. Vale: Sidonius ends his second book of letters by claiming that he prefers a good neighbour to a great deal of revenue. He thus gives more weight to the *otium* than to the *negotium*. This passage also concludes his thoughts on *otium* in the second book – he will return to the subject in the following books – and shows once again the great importance that he gives to friendship and the social aspect of *otium*. See the commentary on *Ep.* 2.14.2 *in otio fuliginoso….* With the polyptoton and chiasmus *frueris–fruamur* Sidonius repeats the adjective *fructuosus* from the first part of the clause. At the same time, he draws a parallel between friendship and the use of a country estate. Pliny similarly enumerates the pleasures in the countryside that his addressee enjoys: Plin. *Ep.* 5.18.1 *frueris mari, fontibus, viridibus, agro, villa amoenissima* ('you enjoy the sea, the fountains, the trees, the field and your very pleasant villa'). *Reditus*, 'a return', 'revenue', 'output' (in money or kind) (*OLD* 1592, 3), is also used in Plin. *Ep.* 4.6.1 and 6.3.1 about the revenue of an estate. The adjective *amplus*, 'great', 'large', is frequently used with nouns denoting wealth (*TLL* 1, 2007.18–39). Montone (2017) 28 refers to Hor. *Sat.* 1.1.49–53, where Horace compares his own small granaries with those of a wealthier neighbour. As in *Ep.* 2.13, the letter about the dangers of *negotium*, Sidonius praises the safety of the golden middle (*aurea mediocritas*), an ideal also influenced by Horace; see Hor. *Carm.* 2.10.5 and the commentary on *Ep.* 2.13.8 *illa refugit celeritate divitias deliciasque regales….* For the ideal of good neighbourliness, see the commentary on *Ep.* 2.9.1 *Praediorum his iura contermina, domicilia vicina.* For *aequalis*, see the commentary on *Ep.* 2.8.1 *cui debuerit domi forisque … aequalis affectum.* For the letter's simple ending with *vale*, see the commentary on *Ep.* 2.1.4 *Vale*.

Bibliography

The abbreviations of journal titles in this bibliography are those of *L'Année philologique*

Achner, H. (2009) *Ärzte in der Antike*, Mainz a. R.
Ackerman, J. S. (1990) *The Villa: Form and Ideology of Country Houses*, Princeton.
Adams, J. N. (1972) 'Latin words for "Woman" and "Wife"', *Glotta* 50: 234–55.
Adams, J. N. (2007) *The Regional Diversification of Latin, 200 BC–AD 600*, Cambridge.
Aiello, O. (2005) '*Varia vocum cantuumque modulamina*: Sidonio Apollinare, *ep.* 2.2.14 ed il "Carmen de Philomela" (*Anth. Lat.* 762 Riese)', *Sileno* 31: 1–11.
Amherdt, D. (2001) *Sidoine Apollinaire: Le quatrième livre de la correspondance: Introduction et commentaire*, Bern.
Amherdt, D. (2004) '*Rusticus politicus*: Esprit de caste? L'agriculture et la politique chez Sidoine Apollinaire: Réalité et lieux communs', *Hermes* 132: 373–87.
Amory, P. (1993) *People and Identity in Ostrogothic Italy 489–554*, Cambridge.
Anderson, W. B. (1936) *Sidonius: Poems and Letters. Vol. 1, Poems and Letters, Books 1–2*, London.
Anderson, W. B. (1965) *Sidonius: Poems and Letters. Vol. 2, Letters, Books 3–9* (finished by W. H. Semple and E. H. Warmington), London.
André, J. (1949) *Étude sur les termes de couleur dans la langue latine*, Paris.
André, J.-M. (1962) *Recherches sur l'otium Romain*, Paris.
André, J.-M. (2006) 'La survie de l'*otium litteratum* chez Sidoine Apollinaire: Culture et lyrisme', in L. Castagna (ed.), *Quesiti, temi, testi di poesia tardolatina*, Frankfurt a. M., 63–86.
André, J.-M. (2009) 'Le culte des Muses dans l'esthétique de Sidoine Apollinaire', *Aevum* 83: 209–20.
Arjava, A. (1996) *Women and Law in Late Antiquity*, Oxford.
Armisen-Marchetti, M. (2002) 'La *poetica tuba*: sens et devenir d'une image dans la littérature latine', *Pallas* 59: 271–80.
Arweiler, A. (1999) *Die Imitation antiker und spätantiker Literatur in der Dichtung* De spiritalis historiae gestis *des Alcimus Avitus*, Berlin.
Asso, P. (ed.) (2011) *Brill's Companion to Lucan*, Leiden.
Axelson, B. (1945) *Unpoetische Wörter: Ein Beitrag zur Kenntnis der lateinischen Dichtersprache*, Lund.
Badian, E. (1996) 'Amicitia', *DNP* 1: 590–91.
Bailey, L. K. (2020) 'Sidonius and Religion', in Kelly and van Waarden (2020a), 261–75.
Baker, R. J. (1996) 'Martial "Sells" a Villa: IV, 64', *PP* 51: 33–45.
Balmelle, C. (2001) *Les demeures aristocratiques d'Aquitaine: Société et culture de l'Antiquité tardive dans le sud-ouest de la Gaule* (*Aquitania*, suppl. 10), Paris.
Banniard, M. (1992) 'La rouille et la lime: Sidoine Apollinaire et la langue classique en Gaule au Ve siècle', in L. Holz and J.-C. Fredouille (eds), *De Tertullien aux Mozarabes*, vol. 1, *Antiquité tardive et Christianisme ancien (IIIe–VIe siècles): Mélanges offerts à Jacques Fontaine*, Paris, 413–27.

Barnish, S. J. B. (1986) 'Taxation, Land and Barbarian Settlement in the Western Empire', *PBSR* 54: 170–95.

Barnwell, P. S. (1992) *Emperor, Prefects and Kings: The Roman West, 395–565*, London.

Becht-Jördens, G. (2017) 'Ein Silberbecken mit Versinschrift des Sidonius als Danaergeschenk für die Gotenkönigin Ragnahild. Zur Bedeutung von Materialität, Handwerks- und Dichtkunst im Diskurs der Ohnmächtigen (Sidon. epist. IV 8)', *A&A* 63: 125–53.

Bedon, R. (2004) '*Stabunt et Parii lapides, spirantia signa*. Les roches décoratives chez les poètes latins', in P. Chardron-Picault et al. (eds), *Les roches décoratives dans l'architecture antique et du Haut Moyen Âge*, Paris, 369–86.

Behr, H. (1993) *Die Selbstdarstellung Sullas. Ein aristokratischer Politiker zwischen persönlichem Führungsanspruch und Standessolidarität*, Frankfurt a. M.

Benz, L. (2000) 'Mimos. II Römisch', *DNP* 8: 205–7.

Bergmann, B. (2016) 'Visualizing Pliny's Villas', in R. Gibson and Ch. Whitton (eds), *The Epistles of Pliny*, Oxford, 201–24.

Bergmann, M. (2000) 'La villa di Chiragan', in S. Ensoli and E. La Rocca (eds), *Aurea Roma. Dalla città pagana alla città cristiana*, Rome, 168–71.

Bernardy, A. (1960) *À la recherche de la villa de Tonance Ferréol: La villa galloromaine de Marignargues à Saint-Maurice-de-Cazevieille*, Uzès.

Bernert, E. (1949–50) 'Otium', *WJA* 4: 89–99.

Bernstein, N. W. (2008) 'Each Man's Father Served as His Teacher: Constructing Relatedness in Pliny's *Letters*', *ClAnt* 27: 203–30.

Bernt, G. (1968) *Das lateinische Epigramm im Übergang von der Spätantike zum frühen Mittelalter*, Munich.

Berry, D. H. (2020) *Cicero's Catilinarians*, Oxford.

Berschin, W. (1980) *Griechisch-lateinisches Mittelalter. Von Hieroymus zu Nikolaus von Kues*, Bern.

Binder, G. (1998) 'Gastmahl. II Rom', *DNP* 4: 803–6.

Blänsdorf, J. (1993) 'Apollinaris Sidonius und die Verwandlung der römischen Satire in der Spätantike', *Philologus* 137: 122–31.

Bonjour, M. (1980) 'La *patria* de Sidoine Apollinaire', in *Mélanges de littérature et d'épigraphie latines, d'histoire ancienne et d'archéologie. Hommage à la mémoire de Pierre Wuilleumier*, Paris, 25–37.

Bonjour, M. (1988) 'Discrétion mondaine ou réserve chrétienne? Les femmes chez Sidoine Apollinaire', in D. Porte and J.-P. Néraudau (eds), Res sacrae: *Hommages à Henri Le Bonniec, Collection Latomus* 201, Brussels, 40–52.

Bonner, S. (1977) *Education in Ancient Rome: From the Elder Cato to the Younger Pliny*, London.

Borghini, G. (ed.) (2004) *Marmi antichi*, Rome.

Bouet, A. (1997–1998) 'Les thermes de la *villa* de Montmaurin (Haute-Garonne) et la pratique balnéaire et sportive dans l'Antiquité tardive', *Aquitania* 15: 213–44.

Bouet, A. (2003) *Thermae Gallicae. Les thermes de Barzan (Charente-Maritime) et les thermes des provinces gauloises*, Bordeaux.

Brennan, T. C. (2012) 'Perceptions of Women's Power in the Late Republic: Terentia, Fulvia, and the Generation of 63 BCE', in James and Dillon (2012), 354–66.

Brödner, E. (1983) *Die römischen Thermen und das antike Badewesen: Eine kulturhistorische Betrachtung*, Darmstadt.

Brolli, T. (2013) 'Writing Commentary on Sidonius' Panegyrics', in van Waarden and Kelly (2013), 93–109.

Bruggisser, P. (1993) *Symmaque ou le rituel épistolaire de l'amitié littéraire: Recherches sur le premier livre de la correspondance*, Fribourg.

BIBLIOGRAPHY

Bruggisser, P. (2002) 'Clin d'œil latin. *Latiaris* avant, chez et après Symmaque', in J.-M. Carrié and R. Lizzi Testa (eds), *Humana sapit. Étu- des d'antiquité tardive offertes à Lellia Cracco Ruggini*, Bibliothèque de l'antiquité tardive 3, Turnhout, 97–110.
Bruzzone, A. (2011) 'Riprese oraziane nella Gigantomachia del carme 6 di Sidonio Apollinare', *InvLuc* 33: 13–21.
Bruzzone, A. (2013) 'Mito e politica nei *Panegyrici* di Sidonio Apollinare', in Diefenbach and Müller (2013), 355–78.
Bruzzone, A. (2014) 'Ovidio (e altri) in Sidonio Apollinare, carme 6', in Poignault and Stoehr-Monjou (2014), 305–32.
Buonopane, A. (2016) 'Terenzia, una matrona *in domo et in re publica agens*', in F. Cenerini and F. Rohr Vio (eds) *Matronae in domo et in re publica agentes – spazi e occasioni dell'azione femminile nel mondo romano tra tarda repubblica e primo impero*, Trieste, 51–64.
Busch, S. (1999) *VERSVS BALNEARVM: Die antike Dichtung über Bäder und Baden im römischen Reich*, Stuttgart.
Cain, A. (2008) '*Liber Manet*: Pliny, *Ep.* 9.27.2 and Jerome, *Ep.* 130.19.5', *CQ* 58: 708–10.
Cain, A. (2009) *The Letters of Jerome: Asceticism, Biblical Exegesis, and the Construction of Christian Authority in Late Antiquity*, Oxford.
Cain, A. (2013a) *Jerome's Epitaph on Paula: A Commentary on the Epitaphium Sanctae Paulae with an Introduction, Text, and Translation*, Oxford.
Cain, A. (2013b) 'Terence in Late Antiquity', in A. Augoustakis and A. Traill (eds) *A Companion to Terence*, Oxford, 380–96.
Calboli, G. (1998) 'Genera dicendi', *DNP* 4: 911–3.
Cam, M.-T. (2003) 'Sidoine Apollinaire, lecteur de Vitruve', *Latomus* 62: 139–55.
Cameron, A. (1965) 'The Fate of Pliny's *Letters* in the Late Empire', *CQ* 15: 289–98.
Cameron, A. (1967) 'Pliny's *Letters* in the Later Empire: An Addendum', *CQ* 17: 421–2.
Cameron, A. (2011) *The Last Pagans of Rome*, Oxford 2011.
Canobbio, A. (2013) 'Una supplica tra serio e faceto: Marziale nel carme 13 di Sidonio Apollinare', *Lexis* 31: 366–90.
Carlon, J. M. (2009) *Pliny's Women. Constructing Virtue and Creating Identity in the Roman World*, Cambridge.
Carrié, J.-P. (2010) 'Le *deversorium* dans les *villae* occidentales tardives: éléments pour une identification archéologique', *AntTard* 18: 277–96.
Carter, J. M. (1990) 'Games Early Medieval People Played: Sidonius Apollinaris and Gallo-Roman-German Sports', *Nikephoros* 3: 225–31.
Casado, P. (2011) 'Réflexions onomastiques à propos de *Vorocingus* et *Prusianum*, deux noms de lieux chez Sidoine Apollinaire', *Cahiers de la Société Française d'Onomastique* 3, 63–73.
Castagna, L. (2004) 'Sidonio e la *palliata*', *Aevum(ant)* n.s. 4: 349–56 (repr. in G. Aricò and M. Rivoltella (eds) *La riflessione sul teatro nella cultura romana*, Milan, 2008, 349–56).
Catarinella, F. M. (2000) 'Una ripresa agostiniana in Sidonio Apollinare (*ep.* II,13,2)', *VetChr* 37, 413–8.
Cavallo, G. (1997a) 'B. Rolle und Codex', *DNP* 2: 811–2.
Cavallo, G. (1997b) 'C. Buchproduktion und Buchverbreitung (Buchhandel)', *DNP* 2: 812–4.
Cavallo, G. (1999) 'Vom Volumen zum Codex. Lesen in der römischen Welt', in R. Chartier and G. Cavallo (eds) *Die Welt der Lesens. Von der Schriftrolle zum Bildschirm*, Frankfurt a. M, 97–133.
Ceccarelli, P., L. Doering, T. Fögen and I. Gildenhard (eds) (2018) *Letters and Communities. Studies in the Socio-political Dimensions of Ancient Epistolography*, Oxford.
Chadwick, N. K. (1955) *Poetry and Letters in Early Christian Gaul*, London.

Christian, T. (2015) *Gebildete Steine. Zur Rezeption literarischer Techniken in den Versinschriften seit dem Hellenismus*, Göttingen.
Chronopoulos, T. (2020) 'Glossing Sidonius in the Middle Ages', in Kelly and van Waarden (2020a), 643–64.
Claassen, J.-M. (1996) 'Documents of a Crumbling Marriage: The Case of Cicero and Terentia', *Phoenix* 50: 208–32.
Clark, E. A. (1992) *The Origenist Controversy: The Cultural Construction of an Early Christian Debate*, Princeton.
Clark, G. (1993) *Women in Late Antiquity: Pagan and Christian Life-styles*, Oxford.
Clausen, W. (1994) *A Commentary on Virgil, Eclogues*, Oxford.
Cloppet, C. (1989) 'À propos d'un voyage de Sidoine Apollinaire entre Lyon et Clermont-Ferrand', *Latomus* 48: 857–68.
Coleman, R. (ed.) (1977) *Vergil, Eclogues*, Cambridge.
Collins, R. J. H (1998) 'Law and Ethnic Identity in the Western Kingdom in the Fifth and Sixth Centuries', in A. P. Smith (ed.) *Medieval Europeans: Studies in Ethnic Identity and National Perspectives in Medieval Europe*, London, 1–23.
Colombi, E. (1996) '*Rusticitas* e *vita in villa* nella Gallia tardoantica: tra realtà e letteratura', *Athenaeum* 84: 405–31.
Colton, R. E. (1976) 'Traces of Martial's Vocabulary in Sidonius Apollinaris', *CB* 53: 12–6.
Colton, R. E. (1982) 'Echoes of Juvenal in Sidonius Apollinaris', *RPL* 5: 59–74.
Colton, R. E. (1985a) 'Some Echoes of Martial in the Poems of Sidonius Apollinaris', *RPL* 8, 21–33.
Colton, R. E. (1985b) 'Some Echoes of Martial in the Letters of Sidonius Apollinaris', *AC* 54, 277–84.
Colton, R. E. (2000) *Some Literary Influences on Sidonius Apollinaris*, Amsterdam.
Condorelli, S. (2001) 'Una particolare accezioni di *barbarismus* in Sidonio Apollinare', in U. Criscuolo (ed.) Mnemosynon*: Studi di letteratura e di umanità in memoria di D. Gagliardi*, Naples, 323–38.
Condorelli, S. (2008) *Il poeta doctus nel V secolo d.C. Aspetti della poetica di Sidonio Apollinare*, Naples 2008.
Condorelli, S. (2013a) 'Gli epigrammi funerari di Sidonio Apollinare', in Guipponi-Gineste and Urlacher-Becht (2013), 261–79.
Condorelli, S. (2013b) 'Improvisation and Poetical Programme in Sidonius, *Ep.* 9.13', in van Waarden and Kelly (2013), 111–32.
Condorelli, S. (2017) 'Una memoria apuleiana in Sidonio Apollinare: tra stile epistolare e modelli retorici', in G. Matino, F. Ficca, and R. Grisolia (eds) *La lingua e la società: Forme della comunicazione letteraria fra antichità ed età moderna*, Naples, 51–73.
Condorelli, S. (2020) 'Metrics in Sidonius', in Kelly and van Waarden (2020a), 440–61.
Conring, B. (2001) *Hieronymus als Briefschreiber. Ein Beitrag zur spätantiken Epistolographie*, Tübingen.
Consolino, F. E. (2013) 'Sidonio e le *Silvae*', in P. Galand and S. Laigneau-Fontaine (eds) *La silve. Histoire d'une écriture libérée en Europe, de l'Antiquité aux XVIIIe siècle*, Latinitates 5, Turnhout, 213–36.
Consolino, F. E. (2015) 'Le mot et les choses: *epigramma* chez Sidoine Apollinaire', in P. F. Moretti, R. Ricci, and Ch. Torre (eds), *Culture and Literature in Latin Late Antiquity. Continuities and Discontinuities*, Turnhout, 69–98.
Consolino, F. E. (2020) 'Sidonius' Shorter Poems', in Kelly and van Waarden (2020a), 341–72.
Coşkun, A. (2002) *Die Gens Ausoniana an der Macht. Untersuchungen zu Decimius Magnus Ausonius und seiner Familie*, Oxford 2002.

Cotton, H. M. (1985) '*Mirificum genus commendationis*: Cicero and the Latin letter of recommendation', *AJP* 106: 328–34.
Courtney, E. (ed.) (2003) *The Fragmentary Latin Poets*, Oxford.
Coville, A. (1928) *Recherches sur l'histoire de Lyon du Vme siècle au IXme siècle (450–800)*, Paris 1928.
Cugusi, P. (1983) *Evoluzione e forme dell' epistolografia latina nella tarda repubblica e nei primi due secoli dell' Impero con cenni sull' epistolografia preciceroniana*, Rome.
Curtius, E. R. (1948) *Europäische Literatur und Lateinisches Mittelalter*, Bern.
Dalton, O. M. (1915) *The Letters of Sidonius*, translated, with introduction and notes, two volumes, Oxford.
Damschen, G. and A. Heil (eds) (2004) *Marcus Valerius Martialis, Epigrammaton liber decimus, Das zehnte Epigrammbuch. Text, Übersetzung, Interpretationen*, Frankfurt a. M.
Dark, K. (2005) 'The Archaeological Implications of Fourth- and Fifth-Century Descriptions of Villas in the Northwest Provinces of the Roman Empire', *Historia* 54: 331–42.
Degl'Innocenti Pierini, R. (2008) 'La spada di Damocle: Cicerone e il banchetto col tiranno (*Tusc.* 5.61–62)', in L. Castagna and C. Riboldi (eds) *Amicitiae templa serena. Studi in onore di G. Aricò*, Milan, 1323–44.
Delaplace, C. (2014) 'Le témoignage de Sidoine Apollinaire: Une source historique toujours fiable? À propos de la "conquête de l'Auvergne" par les Wisigoths', in Poignault and Stoehr-Monjou (2014), 19–32.
Delaplace, C. (2015) *La fin de l'Empire romain d'Occident. Rome et les Wisigoths de 382 à 531*, Rennes.
Delbrueck, R. (2007) *Antike Porphyrwerke*, Rome (originally Berlin 1932).
Delhey, N. (1991) 'Porphyr bei Apollinaris Sidonius: Zu Apollinaris Sidonius Epist. 2,2,7', *Hermes* 119: 126–7.
Delhey, N. (1993) *Apollinaris Sidonius, Carm. 22: Burgus Pontii Leontii, Einleitung, Text und Kommentar*, Berlin.
Dell'Acqua, F. (2003) *'Illuminando colorat'. La vetrata tra l'età tardo imperiale e l'alto medioevo: le fonti, l'archeologia*, Spoleto.
Dell'Anno, L. (2020) 'Sidonius' Carm. 22: An *Ecphrasis* of *Otium*', *JLA* 13, 137–48.
Denecker, T. (2015) 'Language Attitudes and Social Connotations in Jerome and Sidonius Apollinaris', *VChr* 69: 393–421.
De Smet, R. (1987) 'La notion de lumière et ses fonctions dans les Métamorphoses d'Apulée', in C. Saerens, R. De Smet and H. Melaerts (eds), *Studia Varia Bruxellensia ad orbem Graeco-Latinum pertinentia*, Leuven, 29–41.
Dewar, M. (2014) *Leisured Resistance: Villas, Literature and Politics in the Roman World*, London.
Diefenbach, S. and G. M. Müller (eds) (2013) *Gallien in Spätantike und Frühmittelalter. Kulturgeschichte einer Region*, Berlin.
Dilke, O. A. W. (1980) 'Heliodorus and the Colour Problem', *PP* 35, 264–71.
Di Salvo, L. (2005) *Felicis munera mali. Momenti di vita quotidiana nella poesia di età romano-barbarica*, Rome.
Di Stefano, A. and M. Onorato (eds) (2020) *Lo specchio del modello. Orizzonti intertestuali e Fortleben di Sidonio Apollinare*, Naples.
Dodge, H. and B. Ward-Perkins (eds) (1992) *Marble in Antiquity: Collected Papers of J. B. Ward-Perkins*, London.
Dohrn-van Rossum, G. (2002) 'Uhr II. Klassische Antike', *DNP* 12.1: 971–6.
Dolveck, F. (2020) 'The Manuscript Tradition of Sidonius', in Kelly and van Waarden (2020a), 479–542.
Doob, P. R. (1990) *The Idea of the Labyrinth from Classical Antiquity through the Middle Ages*, Ithaca.

Dräger, P. (1999) 'Machaon', *DNP* 7: 622.
Dräger, P. (2012) *Decimus Magnus Ausonius. Sämtliche Werke. Band 1 (Auto-)biographische Werke. Herausgegeben, übersetzt und kommentiert*, Trier.
Drerup, H. (1959) 'Bildraum und Realraum in der römischen Architektur', *Mitteilungen des deutschen Archäologischen Instituts, Römische Abteilung* 66: 147–74.
Drerup, H. (1981) *Zum Ausstattungsluxus in der römischen Architektur* (2nd revised edition), Münster.
Drerup, H. (1990) 'Die römische Villa', in F. Reutti (ed.), *Die römische Villa*, Darmstadt, 116–49. [Nachdruck aus Marburger Winckelmann-Programm, Marburg, 1959, 1–24.]
Drinkwater, J. F. (2001) 'Women and Horses and Power and War', in T. S. Burns and J. W. Eadie (eds), *Urban Centers and Rural Contexts in Late Antiquity*, East Lansing, 135–46.
Drinkwater, J. F. (2013) 'Un-becoming Roman. The End of Provincial Civilisation in Gaul', in Diefenbach and Müller (2013), 59–77.
Drinkwater, J. F. and H. Elton (eds) (1992) *Fifth-Century Gaul: A Crisis of Identity?*, Cambridge.
Dunbabin, K. M. D. (1989) '*Baiarum Grata Voluptas*: Pleasures and Dangers of the Baths', *PBSR* 57: 6–46.
Dunbabin, K. M. D. (1991) 'Triclinium and Stibadium', in Slater (1991), 121–48.
Dunbabin, K. M. D. (2003) *The Roman Banquet: Images of Conviviality*, Cambridge.
Dupieux, P. (1956) 'Les noms de lieux de la vallée de l'Allier', *Revue Internationale d'Onomastique* 4: 283–7.
Du Prey, P. de la Ruffinière (1994) *The Villas of Pliny from Antiquity to Posterity*, Chicago.
Dyson, J. T. (2007) 'The Lesbia Poems', in M. B. Skinner (ed.), *A Companion to Catullus*, Malden, 254–75.
Eastman, D. L. (2015) *The Ancient Martyrdom: Accounts of Peter and Paul. Translated with an Introduction and Notes*, Atlanta.
Ebbeler, J. (2007) 'Mixed Messages. The Play of Epistolary Codes in Two Late Antique Latin Correspondences', in Morello and Morrison (2007), 301–23.
Ebbeler, J. (2009) 'Tradition, Innovation, and Epistolary Mores', in Rousseau (2009), 270–84.
Eck, W. (1998) '[2] Germanicus', *DNP* 4: 963–6.
Eck, W. (2002) '[1] Imp. T. Caesar Augustus', *DNP* 12.1: 532–5.
Eder, W. (1997) '[I 90] C. Sulla Felix, L.', *DNP* 3: 186–90.
Egelhaaf-Gaiser, U. (2010) 'Bleibende Klänge: Das hymnische Briefsiegel des Bischofs Sidonius (*epist.* 9,16)', *Millennium* 7: 257–92.
Egelhaaf-Gaiser, U. (2014) 'Who Reads What? Intended Plurality of Addressees in the Epistolary Votive of Bishop Sidonius (*Epist.* 2,10)', in J.-C. Julhe (ed.), *Pratiques latines de la dédicace: Permanences et mutations, de l'Antiquité à la Renaissance*, Paris, 369–93.
Egelhaaf-Gaiser, U. (2018) 'Vom Epulonenschmaus zum Fest der Worte. Konviviale Gelegenheiten im Briefcorpus des Sidonius', in G. M. Müller (ed.), *Zwischen Alltagskommunikation und literarischer Identitätsbildung. Studien zur lateinischen Epistolographie in Spätantike und Frühmittelalter*, Stuttgart, 255–85.
Egetenmeyr, V. (2021) 'Sidonius Apollinaris' Use of the Term *Barbarus*: An Introduction', in M. Friedrich and J. M. Harland (eds), *Interrogating the 'Germanic': A Category and Its Use in Late Antiquity and the Early Middle Ages*, Berlin, 145–65.
Eickhoff, F. C. (ed.) (2016) *Muße und Rekursivität in der antiken Briefliteratur: Mit einem Ausblick in andere Gattungen*, Tübingen.
Eickhoff, F. C., W. Kofler and B. Zimmermann (2016) 'Muße, Rekursivität und antike Briefe. Eine Einleitung', in Eickhoff (2016), 1–11.
Eigler, U. (1997) 'Zwei Reisen nach Rom', *JbAC* 40, 168–77.

Eigler, U. (1998) '[8] Hieronymus', *DNP* 5: 548–51.
Eigler, U. (2003) *Lectiones Vetustatis: Römische Literatur und Geschichte in der lateinischen Literatur der Spätantike*, Munich.
Eigler, U. (2013) 'Gallien als Literaturlandschaft. Zur Dezentralisierung und Differenzierung lateinischer Literatur im 5. Und 6. Jahrhundert', in Diefenbach and Müller (2013), 399–419.
Ellis, S. P. (1995) 'Classical Reception Rooms in Romano-British Houses', *Britannia* 26: 163–78.
Elsner, J. (1998) *Imperial Rome and Christian Triumph*, Oxford.
Elsner, J. and J. Hernández Lobato (eds) (2017a) *The Poetics of Late Latin Literature*, Oxford.
Elsner, J. and J. Hernández Lobato (2017b) 'Notes Towards a Poetics of Late Antique Literature', in Elsner and Hernández Lobato (2017a), 1–22.
Elvers, K.-L. (1998) '[I 28] F. Maximus Rullianus, Q.', *DNP* 4: 371–2.
Engelbrecht, A. (1898) 'Beiträge zum lateinischen Lexikon aus Sidonius', *WS* 20: 293–308.
Epp, V. (1999) *Amicitia. Zur Geschichte personaler, sozialer und geistlicher Beziehungen im frühen Mittelalter*, Stuttgart.
Ermete, K. (2003) *Terentia und Tullia: Frauen der senatorischen Oberschicht*, Frankfurt a. M.
Ernout, A. (1949) *Les adjectifs latins en -osus et en -ulentus*, Paris.
Euskirchen, M. (2000) 'Nemausus 1', *DNP* 8: 811.
Everschor, B. (2007) *Die Beziehungen zwischen Römern und Barbaren auf der Grundlage der Briefliteratur des 4. Und 5. Jahrhunderts*, Bonn.
Fabbrini, D. (2007) *Il migliore dei mondi possibili. Gli epigrammi ecfrastici di Marziale per amici e protettori*, Florence.
Fagan, G. F. (1999) *Bathing in Public in the Roman World*, Ann Arbor.
Fages, B. (2015) 'Le devenir des *villae* aristocratiques aquitaines de la fin du IVe au VIe siècle à travers l'exemple de Séviac (Montréal-du-Gers, Gers)', *Villae and Domain at the End of Antiquity and the Beginning of Middle Age: Studies on the Rural World in the Roman Period* 8, 141–60.
Fantham, E. (2011) 'A Controversial Life', in Asso (2011), 3–20.
Faral, E. (1946) 'Sidoine Apollinaire et la technique littéraire du moyen âge', in *Miscellanea Giovanni Mercati*, vol. 2, *Letteratura medioevale*, Vatican City, 567–80.
Fascione, S. (2016) 'Seronato, Catilina e la *moritura libertas* della Gallia', *Koinonia* 40: 453–62.
Fascione, S. (2018) 'Retorica e realtà: i barbari di Sidonio Apollinare', *InvLuc* 40: 35–44.
Fascione, S. (2019) *Gli 'altri' al potere: Romani e barbari nella Gallia di Sidonio Apollinare*, Bari.
Faure, É. and N. Jacquemard (2014) 'L'émergence du paludisme en Gaule: Analyse comparée des écrits de Sidoine Apollinaire et Grégoire de Tours', in Poignault and Stoehr-Monjou (2014), 55–70.
Fehrle, R. (1983) *Cato Uticensis*, Darmstadt.
Feichtinger, B. (1995) *Apostolae apostolorum. Frauenaskese als Befreiung und Zwang bei Hieronymus*, Frankfurt a. M.
Fellmeth, U. (2001) *Brot und Politik. Ernährung, Tafelluxus und Hunger im antiken Rom*, Stuttgart.
Fernández López, M. C. (1994) 'Sidonio Apolinar, humanista de la antigüedad tardía: Su correspondencia', *Antigüedad y Cristianismo* 11: 11–291.
Filosini, S. (2014a) *Sidonio Apollinare: Epitalamio per Ruricio ed Iberia*, Turnhout.
Filosini, S. (2014b) 'Ovidio nell'Epitalamio per Ruricio ed Iberia (Sidon. *Carm.* 11)', in Poignault and Stoehr-Monjou (2014), 349–76.
Fladerer, L. (2002) 'Übersetzung. III Lateinischer Bereich', *DNP* 12.2: 1186–90.
Flammini, G. (2009) 'La presenza di Orazio negli scritti di Caio Sollio Sidonio Apollinare: La *cultura* di un *auctor* cristiano nella Gallia del secolo V', *GIF* 61: 221–56.

Fögen, T. (2018) 'Ancient Approaches to Letter-Writing and the Configuration of Communities through Epistles', in Ceccarelli et al. (2018), 43–79.

Fögen, T. (2020) 'Vom Epigramm zur Ekphrasis: Zum Topos der *brevitas* in den Briefen des Jüngeren Plinius', in G. M. Müller, S. Retsch and J. Schenk (eds), *Adressat und Adressant in antiken Briefen. Rollenkonfigurationen und kommunikative Strategien in griechischer und römischer Epistolographie*, Berlin, 207–31.

Fontaine, J. (1977) 'Unité et diversité du mélange des genres et des tons chez quelques écrivains latins de la fin du Ive siècle: Ausone, Ambroise, Ammien', in M. Fuhrmann (ed.), *Christianisme et formes littéraires de l'antiquité tardive en occident*, Geneva, 425–82.

Formicola, C. (2009) 'Poetica dell'*imitatio* e funzione del modello: Properzio nei versi di Sidonio Apollinare', *Voces* 20: 81–101.

Förtsch, R. (1993) *Archäologischer Kommentar zu den Villenbriefen des Jüngeren Plinius*, Mainz.

Fowden, G. (2004) *Quṣayr 'Amra. Art and the Umayyad Elite in Late Antique Syria*, Berkeley.

Franzoi, A. (2008) 'Memoria di Marziale in Sidonio Apollinare (carm. 3 e 4)', *Incontri Triestini di Filologia Classica* 7: 321–7.

Frass, M. (2008) 'Intervention und Protektion in den Briefen Plinius des Jüngeren. Empfehlungsschreiben für Voconius Romanus', in Ch. Antenhofer and M. Müller (eds), *Briefe in politischer Kommunikation vom Alten Orient bis ins 20. Jahrhundert*, Göttingen, 67–82.

Frye, D. (1994) 'The Meaning of Sidonius, *Ep.* 2.1.4', *Eranos* 92: 60–1.

Frye, D. (2003) 'Aristocratic Responses to Late Roman Urban Change: The Examples of Ausonius and Sidonius in Gaul', *CW* 96: 185–96.

Fuhrmann, M. (1979) 'Persona, ein römischer Rollenbegriff', in O. Marquard and K. Stierle (eds), *Identität*, Munich, 83–106.

Furbetta, L. (2013) 'Les objets et les lieux: Quelques réflexions sur les épigrammes de Sidoine Apollinaire', in Guipponi-Gineste and Urlacher-Becht (2013), 243–59.

Furbetta, L. (2014/2015) 'Tracce di Ausonio nelle lettere di Sidonio Apollinare (appunti di lettura)', *IfilolClass* 14: 107–33.

Furbetta, L. (2015a) 'La lettre de recommandation en Gaule (Vᵉ–VIIᵉ siècles) entre tradition littéraire et innovation', in A. Bérenger and O. Dard (eds), *Gouverner par les lettres, de l'Antiquité à l'époque contemporaine*, Metz, 347–68.

Furbetta, L. (2015b) 'L'epitaffio di Sidonio Apollinare in un nuovo testimone manoscritto', *Euphrosyne* n.s. 43, 243–54.

Furbetta, L. (2016) 'La mémoire de Lucain dans l'oeuvre de Sidoine Apollinaire: l'exemple du *carm*. VII', in F. Galtier and R. Poignault (eds), *Présence de Lucain, Caesarodunum* 48–9 bis, Clermont-Ferrand, 397–428.

Furbetta, L. (2017) 'La rhétorique du "petit" dans les épigrammes de Sidoine Apollinaire: Stratégies littéraires et enjeux politiques', in Meyer and Urlacher-Becht (2017), 251–66.

Furbetta, L. (2018a) 'Presence of, References to and Echoes of Ovid in the Works of Rutilius Namatianus, Sidonius Apollinaris and Avitus of Vienne', in F. E. Consolino (ed.), *Ovid in Late Antiquity*, Turnhout, 293–323.

Furbetta, L. (2018b) 'Présence d'Ausone dans les panégyriques de Sidoine Apollinaire', in Wolff (2018), 349–66.

Furbetta, L. (2020) 'Sidonius Scholarship: Fifteenth to Nineteenth Centuries', in Kelly and van Waarden (2020a), 543–63.

Galsterer, H. (1998) 'Grabinschriften', *DNP* 4: 1186.

Garton, C. (1982) 'A Revised Register of Augustan Actors', *ANRW II* 30.1: 580–609.

Gauly, B. M. (2006) 'Das Glück des Pollius Felix. Römische Macht und privater Luxus in Statius' Villengedicht *silv.* 2,2', *Hermes* 134: 455–70.

Geisler, E. (1887) 'Loci similes auctorum Sidonio anteriorum', in Lütjohann (1887), 351–416.

Gemeinhardt, P. (2007) *Das lateinische Christentum und die antike pagane Bildung*, Tübingen.
Gerbrandy, P. (2013) 'The Failure of Sidonius' Poetry', in van Waarden and Kelly (2013), 63–76.
Gerlach, G. (2001) *Zu Tisch bei den alten Römern. Eine Kulturgeschichte des Essens und Trinkens*, Stuttgart.
Germerodt, F. (2015) *Amicitia in den Briefen des jüngeren Plinius*, Speyer.
Gerth, M. (2013) *Bildungsvorstellungen im 5. Jahrhundert n. Chr.: Macrobius, Martianus Capella und Sidonius Apollinaris*, Berlin.
Giannotti, F. (2001a) 'Criteri organizzativi nell'Epistolario di Sidonio Apollinare: Il caso del terzo libri', *AFLS* 22: 27–38.
Giannotti, F. (2001b) 'Appunti sul quarto libro dell'epistolario sidoniano', *InvLuc* 23: 103–10.
Giannotti, F. (2002) 'L'epistola III 3 di Sidonio Apollinare fra encomio di Ecdicio e misobarbarismo', *Romanobarbarica* 17: 161–82.
Giannotti, F. (2016) Sperare meliora*: Il terzo libro delle* Epistulae *di Sidonio Apollinare: Introduzione, traduzione e commento*, Pisa.
Gibson, B. J. and R. D. Rees (eds) (2013a) *Pliny in Late Antiquity*, Arethusa 46.
Gibson, B. J. and R. D. Rees (2013b) Introduction: *Pliny the Younger in Late Antiquity*, Arethusa 46: 141–65.
Gibson, R. (2003) *Ovid: Ars amatoria Book 3*, Cambridge.
Gibson, R. (2011) '<*Clarus*> Confirmed? Pliny, *Epistles* 1.1 and Sidonius Apollinaris', *CQ* 61: 655–9.
Gibson, R. (2012) 'On the Nature of Ancient Letter Collections', *JRS* 102: 56–78.
Gibson, R. (2013a) 'Reading the Letters of Sidonius by the Book', in van Waarden and Kelly (2013), 195–219.
Gibson, R. (2013b) 'Pliny and the Letters of Sidonius: From Constantius and Clarus to Firminus and Fuscus', in Gibson and Rees (2013a), 333–55.
Gibson, R. (2015) 'Not Dark Yet: Reading to the End of Pliny's Nine-Book Collection', in I. Marchesi (ed.), *Pliny the Book-Maker, Betting on Posterity in the* Epistles, Oxford, 185–222.
Gibson, R. (2020) 'Sidonius' Correspondence', in Kelly and van Waarden (2020a), 373–92.
Gibson, R. (2021) 'Calpurnia of Comum and the Ghost of Umbria: Marriage and Regional Identity in the *Epistulae* of Pliny', in L. Galli Milic and A. Stoehr-Monjou (eds), Au-delà de l'épithalame. Le marriage dans la literature latine (IIIe s. av. – VIe s. ap. J.-C.), Turnhout, 245–66.
Gibson, R. and R. Morello (2012) *Reading the Letters of Pliny the Younger: An Introduction*, Cambridge.
Gillett, A. (1999) 'The Accession of Euric', *Francia* 26: 1–40.
Gillett, A. (2009) 'The Mirror of Jordanes: Concepts of the Barbarian, Then and Now', in Rousseau (2009), 392–408.
Gillett, A. (2012) 'Communication in Late Antiquity: Use and Reuse', in Johnson (2012a), 815–46.
Gizewski, C. (1997a) 'Censores', *DNP* 2: 1056–7.
Gizewski, C. (1997b) 'Decemviri', *DNP* 3: 342–3.
Gizewski, C. (1998) '*Illustris vir*', *DNP* 5: 930–40.
Gizewski, C. (2000) '*Numerarius*', *DNP* 8: 1052–3.
Gnilka, Ch. (1973) 'Trauer und Trost in Plinius' Briefen', *SO* 49: 105–25.
Gnoli, R., M. C. Marchei and A. Sironi (2004) 'Repertorio', in Borghini (2004), 131–95.
Goette, H. R. (2013) 'Die römische "Staatstracht": *Toga, Tunica* und *Calcei*', in M. Tellenbach, R. Schulz and A. Wieczorek (eds), *Die Macht der Toga: Dresscode im Römischen Weltreich*, Regensburg, 39–52.

Goffart, W. (2013) 'Administrative Methods of Barbarian Settlement in the Fifth Century: The Definitive Account', in Diefenbach and Müller (2013), 45–56.

Gold, B. K. (ed.) (2012) *A Companion to Roman Love Elegy*, Malden, MA.

Goldlust, B. (2013) 'L' héritage de Stace: Nature et culture dans l'écriture silvaine de la latinité tardive (Symmaque, Macrobe, Sidoine Apollinaire)', in P. Galand and S. Laigneau (eds), *La silve, histoire d'une écriture libérée en Europe de l'Antiquité au XVIIIe siècle*, Turnhout, 183–211.

Gollwitzer-Voll, W. (2007) *Christus Medicus – Heilung als Mysterium. Interpretationen eines alten Christusnamens und dessen Bedeutung in der Praktischen Theologie*, Paderborn.

Gordon, R. (2001) 'Pontifex, Pontifices', *DNP* 10: 135–8.

Graf, F. (1997) 'Chiron', *DNP* 2: 1127–8.

Graf, F. (1998) 'Fortuna', *DNP* 4: 598–602.

Grawehr, M. (2019) 'Of Toddlers and Donkeys. Roman Lamps with Slaves and Self-Representations of Slaves', in A. Binsfeld and M. Ghetta (eds) *Ubi servi erant? Die Ikonographie von Sklaven und Freigelassenen in der römischen Kunst*, Stuttgart, 91–118.

Grebe, S. (2003) 'Marriage and Exile: Cicero's Letters to Terentia', *Helios* 30: 127–46.

Green, R. (1991) *The Works of Ausonius. Edited with Introduction and Commentary*, Oxford.

Green, R. (2016) 'The Sadness of Eparchius Avitus (Sidonius, *Carm.* 7.519–21)', *CQ* 66: 821–5.

Green, R. (2020) 'Translating Sidonius', in Kelly and van Waarden (2020a), 618–27.

Greenhalgh, M. (2009) *Marble Past, Monumental Present. Building with Antiquities in the Mediaeval Mediterranean*, Leiden.

Grégoire, J. F. and F.-Z. Collombet (eds) (1836) *Oeuvres de C. Sollius Apollinaris Sidonius, traduites en français avec le texte en regard et des notes*, 3 vols, Lyon.

Grewing, F. (1997) *Martial, Buch VI. Ein Kommentar*, Göttingen.

Grey, C. (2008) 'Two Young Lovers: An Abduction Marriage and Its Consequences in Fifth-Century Gaul', *CQ* 58: 286–302.

Griffin, M. (2003) '*De Beneficiis* and Roman Society', *JRS* 93: 92–113.

Griffin, M. and B. Inwood (eds) (2011) *Seneca. On Benefits*, Chicago.

Groß-Albenhausen, K. (2001) '*Spectabilis*', *DNP* 11: 799–800.

Groß-Albenhausen, K. (2002) '*Vir clarissimus*', *DNP* 12.2: 241.

Gruber, J. (2013) *D. Magnus Ausonius, Mosella. Kritische Ausgabe, Übersetzung, Kommentar*, Berlin.

Gualandri, I. (1979) *Furtiva lectio. Studi su Sidonio Apollinare*, Milan.

Gualandri, I. (1993) '*Elegi acuti*: Il distico elegiaco in Sidonio Apollinare', in G. Catanzaro and F. Santucci (eds), *La poesia cristiana Latina in distici elegiaci. Atti del convegno internazionale Assisi 20–22 marzo 1992*, Assisi, 191–216.

Gualandri, I. (2000) 'Figure di barbari in Sidonio Apollinare', in G. Lanata (ed.), *Il tardoantico alle soglie del duemila: Diritto, religione, società. Atti del Quinto Convegno Nazionale dell'Associazione di Studi Tardoantichi*, Pisa, 105–29.

Gualandri, I. (2017) 'Words Pregnant with Meaning: The Power of Single Words in Late Latin Literature', in Elsner and Hernández Lobato (2017a), 125–46.

Gualandri, I. (2020) 'Sidonius' Intertextuality', in Kelly and van Waarden (2020a), 279–316.

Guericke, H. E. F. (1817) *Lehrbuch der christlichen Archäologie*, Berlin.

Guérin-Beauvois, M. (1997) '*Montes suspensi testudinibus marmoreis*: à propos de la représentation d'une coupole de Baïes', *MEFRA* 109, 691–740.

Guipponi-Gineste, M.-F. (2014) 'Poème-bijou et objet précieux: la merveille entre esthétique, épidictique et politique dans la correspondance de Sidoine Apollinaire (*epist.* IV, 8)', in Poignault and Stoehr-Monjou (2014), 245–57.

Guipponi-Gineste, M.-F. (2017) 'Le *lusus* poétique à la lumière du *convivium* et autres formes d'*otium* dans les poèmes de la correspondance de Sidoine Apollinaire', in Meyer and Urlacher-Becht (2017), 235–50.
Guipponi-Gineste, M. F. and C. Urlacher-Becht (eds) (2013) *La renaissance de l'épigramme dans la latinité tardive*, Paris.
Günther, R. (1982) 'Apollinaris Sidonius. Eine Untersuchung seiner drei Kaiserpanegyriken', in G. Wirth (ed.), *Romanitas-Christianitas. Untersuchungen zur Geschichte und Literatur der römischen Kaiserzeit. Iohannes Straub zum 70. Geburtstag am 18. Oktober 1982 gewidmet*, Berlin, 654–60.
Günther, L.-M. (1997) 'Roscia: Aristokratentochter und Bischofskind im spätantiken Gallien (zu Sid. Ap. *Ep.* 5, 16, 3)', *Laverna* 8: 48–58.
Gutsfeld, A. (1997) 'Cena', *DNP* 2: 1054.
Gutsfeld, A. (1999) 'Mahlzeiten', *DNP* 7: 705–7.
Gutsfeld, A. (2001a) 'Praefectus praetorio', *DNP* 10: 249–52.
Gutsfeld, A. (2001b) 'Praefectus urbi', *DNP* 10: 252.
Gutsfeld, A. (2002) 'D. Weinsorten und -Qualitäten', *DNP* 12.2: 434–5.
Haase, M. (2000) 'Numa Pompilius', *DNP* 8: 1045–6.
Habermehl, P. (1997) 'Origenes', in O. Schütze (ed.), *Metzler Lexikon Antiker Autoren*, Stuttgart, 484–5.
Häger, H.-J. (2019) *Plinius über die Ehe und den idealen Ehemann. Zur literarischen Inszenierung von Männlichkeiten und Emotionen in Ehe und Familie der römischen Kaiserzeit*, Heidelberg.
Halsall, G. (2007) *Barbarian Migrations and the Roman West, 376–568*, Cambridge.
Hanaghan, M. P. (2017a) 'All in a Word or Two; Micro Allusions in Sidonius' Programmatic Epistles', *International Journal of the Classical Tradition* 24: 249–61.
Hanaghan, M. P. (2017b) 'Avitus' Characterisation in Sidonius' *Carm.* 7', *Mnemosyne* 70: 262–80.
Hanaghan, M. P. (2017c) 'Latent Criticism of Anthemius and Ricimer in Sidonius Apollinaris' *Epistulae* 1.5', *CQ* 67: 631–49.
Hanaghan, M. P. (2018) 'Sidonius Apollinaris and the Making of an Exile Persona', in D. Rohmann, J. Ulrich, and M. V. Girvés (eds), *Mobility and Exile at the End of Antiquity*, Frankfurt, 259–72.
Hanaghan, M. P. (2019) *Reading Sidonius' Epistles*, Cambridge.
Hanaghan, M. P. (2020) 'Competing at *Otium*? A Juxtaposed Reading of Sidonius' Baths', *JLA* 13: 117–36.
Hanaghan, M. P. and S. Carlson (forthcoming) 'Rufinus's Version of Eusebius's *Origen* and the Politics of Martyrdom', *Journal of Early Christian Studies* 31.2.
Handley, M. A. (2003) *Death, Society and Culture: Inscriptions and Epitaphs in Gaul and Spain, AD 300–750*, Oxford.
Harich, H. (1990) 'Catonis Marcia. Stoisches Kolorit eines Frauenportraits bei Lucan (II 326–350)', *Gymnasium* 97: 212–23.
Harich-Schwarzbauer, H. and J. Hindermann (2020) 'Leisure and the Muses in Sidonius Apollinaris', *JLA* 13: 2–9.
Harries, J. D. (1992) 'Sidonius Apollinaris, Rome and the Barbarians: A Climate of Treason', in Drinkwater and Elton (1992), 298–308.
Harries, J. D. (1994) *Sidonius Apollinaris and the Fall of Rome AD 407–485*, Oxford.
Harries, J. D. (forthcoming) 'East versus West: Sidonius, Anthemius and the Empire of Dawn', in N. Kıvılcım Yavuz, R. Broome and T. Barnwell (eds), *Festschrift for Ian Wood*.
Harter, B. (2016) '*De otio* – oder: die vielen Töchter der Muße. Ein semantischer Streifzug als literarische Spurensuche durch die römische Briefliteratur', in Eickhoff (2016), 21–42.

Hasebrink, B. and P. P. Riedl (2014) *Muße im kulturellen Wandel. Semantisierungen, Ähnlichkeiten, Umbesetzungen*, Berlin.
Hausmann, M. (2009) *Die Leserlenkung durch Tacitus in den Tiberius- und Claudiusbüchern der Annalen*, Berlin.
Heath, J. (2013) 'Why Corinna?', *Hermes* 141: 155–70.
Heather, P. (1992) 'The Emergence of the Visigothic Kingdom', in Drinkwater and Elton (1992), 84–96.
Heather, P. (1999) 'The Barbarian in Late Antiquity: Image, Reality, and Transformation', in R. Miles (ed.), *Constructing Identities in Late Antiquity*, London, 234–58.
Hecquet-Noti, N. (2013) 'Le temple de Dieu ou la nature symbolisée: La dédicace de la cathédrale de Lyon par Sidoine Apollinaire (*Epist.* 2,10)', in F. Garambois-Vasquez and D. Vallat (eds), *Le lierre et la statue: La nature et son espace littéraire dans l'épigramme gréco-latine tardive*, Saint-Étienne, 217–31.
Heider, U. (1998) 'Foederati', *DNP* 4: 579–80.
Hemelrijk, E. A. (1999) *Matrona Docta: Educated Women in the Roman Elite from Cornelia to Julia Domna*, London.
Henke, R. (2008) 'Eskapismus, poetische Aphasie und satirische Offensive. Das Selbstverständnis des spätantiken Dichters Sidonius Apollinaris', in A. Arweiler and M. Möller (eds), *Vom Selbst-Verständnis in Antike und Neuzeit/Notions of the Self in Antiquity and Beyond*, Berlin, 155–73.
Henke, R. (2012) 'Der Brief 3,12 des Sidonius Apollinaris an Secundus: Eine Novelle in einer Epistel?', *Hermes* 2012: 121–5.
Henning, D. (1999) *Periclitans res publica: Kaisertum und Eliten in der Krise des Weströmischen Reiches 454/5–493 n. Chr.*, Stuttgart.
Henriksén, C. (2012) *A Commentary on Martial, Epigrams Book 9*, Oxford.
Herbert de la Portbarré-Viard, G. (2014) 'Les descriptions et évocations d'édifices religieux chrétiens dans l'oeuvre de Sidoine Apollinaire', in Poignault and Stoehr-Monjou (2014), 379–406.
Herbert de la Portbarré-Viard, G. (2016) 'Dire le marbre des édifices chrétiens dans les textes latins tardifs (IVe–VIe siècles)', in G. Herbert de la Portbarré-Viard and A. Stoehr-Monjou (eds) *Studium in libris: Mélanges en l'honneur de Jean-Louis Charlet*, Paris, 279–96.
Hernández Lobato, J. (2010) 'La écfrasis de la Catedral de Lyon como híbrido intersistémico. Sidonio Apolinar y el *Gesamtkunstwerk* tardoantiguo', *AntTard* 18: 297–308.
Hernández Lobato, J. (2012) *Vel Apolline muto: Estética y poética de la Antigüedad tardía*, Bern.
Hernández Lobato, J. (2015) *Sidonio Apolinar: Poemas*, Madrid.
Hernández Lobato, J. (2017) 'To Speak or Not to Speak: The Birth of a "Poetics of Silence" in Late Antique Literature', in Elsner and Hernández Lobato (2017a), 278–310.
Herrero de Jáuregui, M. (2017) 'Etniquetas del derecho gótico en Sidonio y Procopio', *Seminarios Complutenses de Derecho Romano* 30: 137–50.
Hess, H. (2019) *Das Selbstverständnis der gallo-römischen Oberschicht. Übergang, Hybridität und Latenz im historischen Diskursraum von Sidonius Apollinaris bis Gregor von Tours*, Berlin.
Hess, H. (2021) 'Gallien zwischen *imperium* und *regna*. Kontingenzdarstellung und -bewältigung in den Briefsammlungen des Sidonius Apollinaris, des Ruricius von Limoges und des Avitus von Vienne', in M. Becher and H. Hess (eds), *Kontingenzerfahrungen und ihre Bewältigung zwischen imperium und regna Beispiele aus Gallien und angrenzenden Gebieten vom 5. Bis zum 8. Jahrhundert*, Bonn, 155–99.
Heumann, H. G. and E. Seckel (1907) *Heumanns Handlexikon zu den Quellen des römischen Rechts* (9th edition), Jena.
Hilgers, W. (1969) *Lateinische Gefäßnamen. Bezeichnung, Funktion und Form römischer Gefäße nach den antiken Schriftquellen*, Düsseldorf.

Hindermann, J. (2009) 'Orte der Inspiration in Plinius' *Epistulae*', *MH* 66: 223–31.
Hindermann, J. (2010) '*Similis excluso a vacuo limine recedo:* Plinius' Inszenierung seiner Ehe als elegisches Liebesverhältnis', in M. Formisano and T. Fuhrer (eds), *Gender-Studies in den Altertumswissenschaften: Gender-Inszenierungen in der antiken Literatur, Iphis* 5, Trier, 45–63.
Hindermann, J. (2011) 'Verliebte Delphine, schwimmende Inseln und versiegende Quellen beim älteren und jüngeren Plinius: *mirabilia* und ihre Erzählpotenz (epp. 4,30; 8,20; 9,33)', *Gymnasium* 118: 1–10.
Hindermann, J. (2013) 'Mulier, femina, uxor, coniunx: die begriffliche Kategorisierung von Frauen in den Briefen von Cicero und Plinius dem Jüngeren', *Eugesta* 3: 143–61.
Hindermann, J. (2014) 'Beispielhafte männliche Trauer in Plinius' *Epistulae*. Zum Normdiskurs römischer Konsolation', in S. Plotke and A. Ziem (eds), *Sprache der Trauer. Verbalisierung einer Emotion in historisches Perspektive*, Heidelberg, 285–303.
Hindermann, J. (2016) '*Locus amoenus* und *locus horribilis* – zur Ortsgebundenheit von *otium* in den *Epistulae* von Plinius dem Jüngeren und Seneca', in Eickhoff (2016), 113–31.
Hindermann, J. (2020a) 'At Leisure with Pliny the Younger: Sidonius' Second Book of the *Epistulae* as a Book of *Otium*', *JLA* 13: 94–116.
Hindermann, J. (2020b) 'La lettre comme lieu de publication des épigrammes: Les épigrammes dans les épîtres de Sidoine Apollinaire et leur modèle Pline le Jeune', in L. Furbetta and C. Urlacher-Becht (eds), *Les 'lieux' de l'épigramme latine tardive: vers un élargissement du genre, Revue des études tardo-antiques RET*, Supplément 8: 75–95.
Hindermann, J. (2021) 'Der *locus amoenus* als Ort der Muße in der antiken Literatur', in F. C. Eickhoff (ed.), *Mußeräume der Antike und der frühen Neuzeit*, Tübingen, 65–95.
Hindermann, J. (2022a) '*Lucubratio* (Night Work) and the Candelabra as a Symbol of Marriage and Inspiration in Sidonius Apollinaris (*ep.* 2,10,5)', in H. Harich-Schwarzbauer and C. Scheidegger Lämmle (eds), *Women and Objects in Antiquity*, Iphis 12, Trier, 205–22.
Hindermann, J. (2022b) 'Grabepigramm und Trauerbrief: Plinius der Jüngere, Martial, Ausonius, Hieronymus und Sidonius Apollinaris', in T. Fögen and N. Mindt (eds), *Brief und Epigramm: Bezüge und Wechselwirkungen zwischen zwei Textsorten in Antike und Mittelalter*, Berlin (in press).
Hindermann, J. (2022c) 'The Elder Pliny as Source of Inspiration: Pliny the Younger's Reception of the *Naturalis Historia* and His Uncle's Writing by the Light of a Lamp (*lucubratio*)', in M. Neger and S. Tzounakas (eds), *Absorbing Genres in Letters: Intertextual Studies in Pliny's Epistles*, Cambridge (in press).
Hindermann, J. (forthcoming a) 'Lists as a Means of Education: The Inclusion of Literary Authorities in Sidonius Apollinaris' Letters and Poems', in V. Egetenmeyr and T. Meurer (eds), *Gallia docta? Learning and Its Limitations in Late Antique Gaul*, Tübingen.
Hindermann, J. (forthcoming b) 'A New Splendour: The *recusatio* of Precious Materials in Sidonius Apollinaris' Letters and Poems', in M. Guggisberg and A. Kaufmann-Heinimann (eds), *Licht und Glanz: Edelmetall im Verwendungskontext der Spätantike*, Basel.
Hobert, E. (1967) *Die französische Frauensatire, 1600–1800 unter Berücksichtigung der antiken Tradition*, Marburg.
Höcker, C. (1999) 'Lacunar', *DNP* 6: 1046–7.
Höcker, C. (2001) 'Säule. II Griechisch-Römische Antike', *DNP* 10: 1214–25.
Hoffer, S. E. (1999) *The Anxieties of Pliny the Younger*, Atlanta.
Holzberg, N. (2001) *Die römische Liebeselegie. Eine Einführung.* 2, völlig überarbeitete Auflage, Darmstadt.
Honecker, M. (1985) 'Christus Medicus', *KuD* 31: 307–23.
Horváth, A. T. (2000) 'The Education of Sidonius Apollinaris in the Light of His Citations', *ACD* 36: 151–62.

HospitAm <https://hospitam.hypotheses.org>.
Housman, A. E. (1900) 'On Apollinaris Sidonius', *CR* 14: 54.
Howell, P. (1980) *A Commentary on Book One of the Epigrams of Martial*, London.
Hübner, J. (1985) 'Christus Medicus. Ein Symbol der Erlösungsgeschehens und ein Modell ärztlichen Handelns', *KuD* 31: 324–35.
Hudson, J. (2021) *The Rhetoric of Roman Transportation: Vvehicles in Latin Literature*, Cambridge.
Humphries, M. (2008) 'Rufinus's Eusebius: Translation, Continuation, and Edition in the Latin *Ecclesiastical History*', *JECS* 16: 143–64.
Hünemörder, C. (1998a) 'Frosch', *DNP* 4: 680–2.
Hünemörder, C. (1998b) 'Gans', *DNP* 4: 778–80.
Hünemörder, C. (1998c) 'Huhn (Hahn)', *DNP* 5: 749–51.
Hünemörder, C. (1999) 'Lachs', *DNP* 6: 1042.
Hünemörder, C. (2000) 'Nachtigall', *DNP* 8: 6072–3.
Hünemörder, C. (2001a) 'Rabe', *DNP* 10: 743–4.
Hünemörder, C. (2001b) 'Schwalbe', *DNP* 11: 270–2.
Hünemörder, C. (2001c) 'Schwan', *DNP* 11: 272–4.
Hünemörder, C. (2001d) 'Spinnentiere', *DNP* 11: 827–9.
Hünemörder, C. (2002a) 'Weihrauch', *DNP* 12.2: 418.
Hünemörder, C. (2002b) 'Zikade', *DNP* 12.2: 805–6.
Hünemörder, C. (2002c) 'Zimt', *DNP* 12.2: 807.
Hurschmann, R. (1997) 'Ballspiele', *DNP* 2: 426–7.
Hurschmann, R. (1999) 'Kranz', *DNP* 6: 805–7.
Hurschmann, R. (2002a) 'Tunica', *DNP* 12.1: 920–1.
Hurschmann, R. (2002b) 'Würfelspiel(e)', *DNP* 12.2: 577–8.
Hutchings, L. (2009) 'Travel and Hospitality in the Time of Sidonius Apollinaris', *Journal of the Australian Early Medieval Association* 5: 65–74.
Ihm, M. (1900) 'Comata Gallia', *RE* 4.1: 604–5.
Ihm, C. (1992) *Die Programme der christlichen Apsismalerei: Vom 4. Jahrhundert bis zur Mitte des 8. Jahrhundert, 2, durchgesehene und durch Zusätze erweiterte Auflage*, Stuttgart.
Ingleheart, J. (2010) *A Commentary on Ovid, Tristia, Book 2*, Oxford.
James, S. L. (2003) *Learned Girls and Male Persuasion. Gender and Reading in Roman Love Elegy*, Berkeley.
James, S. L. and S. Dillon (eds) (2012) *A Companion to Women in the Ancient World*, Chichester.
Janka, M. (1997) *Ovid, Ars Amatoria: Buch 2. Kommentar*, Heidelberg.
Jochum, U. (2007) *Kleine Bibliotheksgeschichte* (3rd revised edition), Stuttgart.
John, A. (2021a) 'Learning Greek in Late Antique Gaul', *CQ* 70: 846–64.
John, A. (2021b) '(Mis)Identifying Teachers in Late Antique Gaul: Sidonius' *Ep.* 4.11, Mamertus Claudianus and Classical vs. Christian Education', *Mnemoysne*: 1–25.
Johnson, S. F. (ed.) (2012a) *The Oxford Handbook of Late Antiquity*, Oxford.
Johnson, W. R. (2012b) 'Propertius', in Gold (2012), 39–52.
Jouanna, J. (2012) 'Air, Miasma and Contagion in the time of Hippocrates and the Survival of Miasmas in Post-Hippocratic Medicine (Rufus of Ephesus, Galen and Palladius)', in Ph. Van der Eijk (ed.), *Greek Medicine from Hippocrates to Galen*, Leiden, 119–36.
Kajanto, I. (1972) 'Fortuna', *RAC* 8: 182–97.
Kaster, R. A. (1988) *Guardians of Language. The Grammarian and Society in Late Antiquity*, Berkeley.
Kaufmann, F.-M. (1995) *Studien zu Sidonius Apollinaris*, Frankfurt.
Kaufmann, H. (2015) '*Papinius noster*: Statius in Roman Late Antiquity', in W. J. Dominik, C. E. Newlands and K. Gervais (eds), *Brill's Companion to Statius*, Leiden, 481–96.

Kaufmann, H. (2017) 'Intertextuality in Late Latin Poetry', in Elsner and Hernández Lobato (2017a), 149–75.
Kelly, G. (2008) *Ammianus Marcellinus, the Allusive Historian*, Cambridge.
Kelly, G. (2020a) 'Dating the Works of Sidonius', in Kelly and van Waarden (2020a), 166–94.
Kelly, G. (2020b) 'Sidonius as a Reader of Rutilius Namatianus', *InvLuc* 42: 151–61.
Kelly, G. (2021) 'A Textual and Onomastic Problem in Sidonius' <http://ausonius.blogspot.com/2021/10/a-textual-and-onomastic-problem-in.html>.
Kelly, G. and J. A. van Waarden (eds) (2020a) *The Edinburgh Companion to Sidonius Apollinaris*, Edinburgh.
Kelly, G. and J. A. van Waarden (2020b) 'Introduction', in Kelly and van Waarden (2020a), 1–9.
Ker, J. (2004) 'Nocturnal Writers in Imperial Rome: The Culture of *Lucubratio*', *CP* 99: 209–42.
Keulen, W. H. (2007) *Apuleius Madaurensis Metamorphoses, Book I, Text, Introduction and Commentary*, Groningen.
Kierdorf, W. (1980) *Laudatio funebris. Interpretationen und Untersuchungen zur Entwicklung der römischen Leichenrede*, Meisenheim am Glan.
Kierdorf, W. (2000) 'Nenia', *DNP* 8: 821–2.
Kleberg, T. (1967) *Buchhandel und Verlagswesen in der Antike*, Darmstadt.
Klodt, C. (2012) '*Patrem mira similitudine exscripserat*. Plinius' Nachruf auf eine perfekte Tochter (epist. 5,16)', *Gymnasium* 119: 23–61.
Klodt, C. (2015) 'Das Grabmal des Verginius Rufus (Plinius, epist. 2,1, 6,10 und 9,19)', *Gymnasium* 122: 339–87.
Knox, P. E. (1986) 'Adjectives in *-osus* and Latin Poetic Diction', *Glotta* 64: 90–101.
Köhler, H. (1995) *C. Sollius Apollinaris Sidonius Briefe Buch 1: Einleitung, Text, Übersetzung, Kommentar*, Heidelberg.
Köhler, H. (2014) *C. Sollius Apollinaris Sidonius, Die Briefe: Eingeleitet, übersetzt und erläutert*, Stuttgart.
Kolb, A. and J. Fugmann (2008) *Tod in Rom. Grabinschriften als Spiegel römischen Lebens*, Mainz a. R.
Konstan, D. (1997) *Friendship in the Classical World*, Cambridge.
Kramer, J. (1998) *Die Sprachbezeichnungen Latinus und Romanus im Lateinischen und Romanischen*, Berlin.
Krause, J.-U. (1991) 'Familien- und Haushaltsstrukturen im spätantiken Gallien', *Klio* 73: 537–62.
Krause, J.-U. (1995) *Witwen und Waisen im Römischen Reich. Rechtliche und soziale Stellung von Waisen*, vol. 3, Stuttgart.
Krause, J.-U. (2002) 'Waisen', *DNP* 12.2: 378–80.
Kreuz, G. (2016) *Besonderer Ort, poetischer Blick: Untersuchungen zu Räumen und Bildern in Statius' Silvae*, Hypomnemata 201, Göttingen.
Krieger, R. A. (1991) *Untersuchungen und Hypothesen zur Ansiedlung der Westgoten, Burgunder und Ostgoten*, Bern.
Kroon, C. (1995) *Discourse Particles in Latin: A Study of nam, enim, autem, vero and at*, Amsterdam.
Kudlien, F. (1986) *Die Stellung des Arztes in der römischen Gesellschaft. Freigeborene Römer, Eingebürgerte, Peregrine, Sklaven, Freigelassene als Ärzte*, Stuttgart.
Kulikowski, M. (2020) 'Sidonius' Political World', in Kelly and van Waarden (2020a), 197–213.
Küppers, J. (2005) 'Autobiographisches in den Briefen des Apollinaris Sidonius', in M. Reichel (ed.), *Antike Autobiographien. Werke–Epochen–Gattungen*, Cologne, 251–77.

Kuhn, C. (1998) 'Fischerei, Fischereigewerbe', *DNP* 4: 527–9.
Kytzler, B. (1998) '[7] H. Flaccus, Q. der Dichter Horaz, 65–8 v. Chr.', *DNP* 5: 720–7.
Laemmle, R., C. Scheidegger Laemmle and K. Wesselmann (eds) (2021) *Lists and Catalogues in Ancient Literature and Beyond: Towards a Poetics of Enumeration*, Berlin.
Lafond, Y. (1996) 'Arar', *DNP* 1: 954–5.
Landfester, M. (2003) 'Übersetzung. B. Entwicklung. 1. Antike und Mittelalter', *DNP* 15.3: 726–7.
La Penna, A. (1995) 'Gli svaghi letterari della nobiltà gallica nella tarda antichità. Il caso di Sidonio Apollinare', *Maia* 47: 3–34.
Lattimore, R. (1962) *Themes in Greek and Latin Epitaphs*, Urbana.
Lausberg, M. (1982) *Das Einzeldistichon. Studien zum antiken Epigramm*, Munich.
Leatherbury, S. V. (2017) 'Writing (and Reading) Silver with Sidonius: The Material Contexts of Late Antique Texts', *Word and Image* 33: 35–56.
Levick, B. (2015) *Catiline*, London.
Liebeschütz, W. (2006) 'Cities, Taxes, and the Accommodation of the Barbarians. The Theories of Durliat and Goffart', in T. F. X. Noble (ed.), *From Roman Provinces to Medieval Kingdoms*, London, 309–23.
Liebs, D. (1987) *Die Jurisprudenz im spätantiken Italien (260–640 n. Chr.)*, Berlin.
Liebs, D. (2002) *Römische Jurisprudenz in Gallien (2. Bis 8. Jahrhundert)*, Berlin.
Lintott, A. W. (2000) 'C. Patronat im Gerichtswesen', *DNP* 9: 422–3.
Littlewood, A. R. (1987) 'Ancient Literary Evidence for the Pleasure Gardens of Roman Country Villas', in E. B. MacDougall (ed.), *Ancient Roman Villa Gardens*, Washington, DC, 7–30.
Löfstedt, B. (1985) 'Sprachliches und Textkritisches zu Sidonius' Briefen', *ALMA* 44–5: 207–11.
Löhken, H. (1982) *Ordines dignitatum. Untersuchungen zur formalen Konstitutierung der spätantiken Führungsschicht*, Cologne.
Lolli, M. (1997) *D. M. Ausonius, Parentalia, Introduzione, testo, traduzione e commento*, Brussels.
Lot, F. (1928) 'Du régime de l'hospitalité', *RBPh* 7: 975–1011.
Loyen, A. (1943) *Sidoine Apollinaire et l'esprit précieux en Gaule aux derniers jours de l'empire*, Paris.
Loyen, A. (1960) *Sidoine Apollinaire, Tome I. Poèmes*, Paris.
Loyen, A. (1970a) *Sidoine Apollinaire, Tome II. Lettres (Livres I–V)*, Paris.
Loyen, A. (1970b) *Sidoine Apollinaire, Tome III. Lettres (Livres VI–IX)*, Paris.
Lucarini, C. M. (2002) 'Congetture a Sidonio Apollinare e al Carmen adv. Marcionitas', *SCO* 48: 377–92.
Lucht, B. (2011) *Gastfreundschaft und Landleben bei Sidonius Apollinaris am Beispiel von* epist. *2,9 (an Donidius). Text, Übersetzung, Kommentar und Interpretation*, Münster.
Ludolph, M. (1997) *Epistolographie und Selbstdarstellung. Untersuchungen zu den 'Paradebriefen' Plinius des Jüngeren*, Tübingen.
Lütjohann, Ch. (ed.) (1887) *Gai Solii Apollinaris Sidonii epistulae et carmina*, Berlin.
Luiselli, B. (1992) *Storia culturale dei rapporti tra mondo romano ed mondo germanico*, Rome.
Lyne, R. O. A. M. (1980) *The Latin Love Poets. From Catullus to Horace*, Oxford.
Maas, M. (2012) 'Barbarians, Problems and Approaches', in Johnson (2012a), 60–91.
MacDonald, E. (2000) *Representations of Women in Sidonius Apollinaris and Gregory of Tours: Coniuges et reginae*, Ottawa.
Maier, G. (2005) *Amtsträger und Herrscher in der Romania Gothica. Vergleichende Untersuchungen zu den Institutionen der ostgermanischen Völkerwanderungsreiche*, Stuttgart.
Malherbe, A. J. (1988) *Ancient Epistolary Theorists*, Atlanta.

Marchesi, I. (2008) *The Art of Pliny's Letters: A Poetics of Allusion in the Private Correspondence*, Cambridge.

Maréchal, S. (2020) *Public Baths and Bathing Habits in Late Antiquity: A Study of the Evidence from Italy, North Africa and Palestine A.D. 285–700*, Leiden.

Markschies, C. (2007) *Origenes und sein Erbe. Gesammelte Studien*, Berlin.

Marolla, G. (2021) *Sidonius Apollinaris, Letters Book 5.1–10. Text, Translation, and Commentary*, PhD dissertation, San Marino.

Mascoli, P. (2000) 'Personaggi femminili in Sidonio Apollinare', *InvLuc* 22: 89–107.

Mascoli, P. (2003) 'L'elogio funebre di Filomazia (Sidon. *Epist.* 2,8). Saggio di commento', *InvLuc* 25: 153–67.

Mascoli, P. (2010) *Gli Apollinari: Per la storia di una famiglia tardoantica*, Bari.

Mascoli, P. (2014) '*Multum est quod debemus et matribus*: le donne della famiglia degli Apollinari', in Poignault and Stoehr-Monjou (2014), 33–9.

Mastrorosa, I. (2002) 'Tipologia edilizia e diletti bucolici in Sidonio Apollinare (*Ep.* II 2): Il dono di Enoch d'Ascoli all' Alberti', *Albertiana* 5: 191–236.

Mathisen, R. W. (1979) 'Sidonius on the Reign of Avitus: A Study in Political Prudence', *TAPA* 109: 165–71.

Mathisen, R. W. (1981) 'Epistolography, Literary Circles and Family Ties in Late Roman Gaul', *TAPA* 111: 95–109.

Mathisen, R. W. (1984) 'Emigrants, Exiles, and Survivors: Aristocratic Options in Visigothic Aquitania', *Phoenix* 38: 159–70.

Mathisen, R. W. (1988) 'The Theme of Literary Decline in Late Roman Gaul', *CP* 83: 45–52.

Mathisen, R. W. (1989) *Ecclesiastical Factionalism and Religious Controversy in Fifth-century Gaul*, Washington, DC.

Mathisen, R. W. (1991) *Studies in the History, Literature, and Society of Late Antiquity*, Amsterdam.

Mathisen, R. W. (1993) *Roman Aristocrats in Barbarian Gaul: Strategies for Survival in an Age of Transition*, Austin.

Mathisen, R. W. (1998) 'Anthemius (12 April 467–11 July 472 A.D.)' <https://www.roman-emperors.org/anthemiu.htm>.

Mathisen, R. W. (1999) *Ruricius of Limoges and Friends: A Collection of Letters from Visigothic Gaul*, Liverpool.

Mathisen, R. W. (2003/2004) 'Les plaisirs de la vie à la campagne chez les écrivains de la fin du Ve s. et du VIe s. ap. J.-C.', *Caesarodunum* 37–8: 343–58.

Mathisen, R. W. (2009) 'The Use and Misuse of Jerome in Gaul during Late Antiquity', in A. Cain and J. Lössl (eds), *Jerome of Stridon: His Life, Writings and Legacy*, Aldershot, 191–208.

Mathisen, R. W. (2013) 'Dating the Letters of Sidonius', in van Waarden and Kelly (2013), 221–48.

Mathisen, R. W. (2020a) 'Sidonius' People. A Prosopography of Sidonius. Persons Mentioned in the Works of Sidonius (Fourth and Fifth Centuries)', in Kelly and van Waarden (2020a), 29–154.

Mathisen, R. W. (2020b) 'Sidonius' Earliest Reception and Distribution', in Kelly and van Waarden (2020a), 631–42.

Matthäus, H. (1987) *Der Arzt in römischer Zeit. Literarische Nachrichten–archäologische Denkmäler. 1. Teil*, Stuttgart.

Matthews, J. F. (1974) 'The Letters of Symmachus', in J. W. Binns (ed.), *Latin Literature of the Fourth Century*, London, 58–99.

Maugan-Chemin, V. (2006) 'Les couleurs du marbre chez Pline l'Ancien, Martial et Stace', in A. Rouveret, S. Dubel and V. Naas (eds) *Couleurs et matières dans l'Antiquité. Textes, techniques et pratiques*, Paris, 103–25.

Mayer, J. W. (2005) *Imus ad villam. Studien zur Villeggiatur im stadtrömischen Suburbium in der späten Republik und frühen Kaiserzeit*, Stuttgart.

McGill, S. (2014) 'Ausonius at Night', *AJP* 135: 123–48.

McGill, S. (2017) 'Rewriting Ausonius', in Elsner and Hernández Lobato (2017a), 252–77.

McGuire, M. (1960) 'Letters and Letter Carriers in Christian Antiquity', *CW* 53: 148–53.

Meister, K. (1997) 'Dionysios I', *DNP* 3: 625–9.

Mendner, S. (1956) *Das Ballspiel im Leben der Völker*, Münster.

Meyer, D. and C. Urlacher-Becht (eds) (2017) *La rhétorique du "petit" dans l'épigramme grecque et latine: Actes du colloque de Strasbourg (26–27 mai 2015). Études d'archéologie et d'histoire ancienne*, Paris.

Mielsch, H. (1987) *Die römische Villa. Architektur und Lebensform*, Munich.

Mielsch, H. (2001) *Römische Wandmalerei*, Darmstadt.

Miles, R. (2005) 'The *Anthologia Latina* and the Creation of Secular Space in Vandal Carthage', *AntTard* 13: 305–20.

Miller, P. A. (2012) 'Tibullus', in Gold (2012), 53–69.

Mindt, N. (2013) *Martials 'epigrammatischer Kanon'*, Munich.

Mohr, P. (ed.) (1895) *C. Sollius Apollinaris Sidonius*, Leipzig.

Mohrmann, C. (1935/36) 'Das Wortspiel in den Augustinischen *Sermones*', *Mnemosyne* 3: 33–61.

Momigliano, A. (1973) 'La caduta senza rumore di un impero nel 476 D.C.', *ASNP* 3: 397–418.

Mondin, L. (2008) 'La misura epigrammatica nella tarda latinità', in A. M. Morelli (ed.), *Epigramma longum. Da Marziale alla tarda antichità. From Martial to Late Antiquity*, Cassino, 397–494.

Monni, A. (1999) 'L'arcaismo in Sidonio Apollinare e nel suo milieu culturale', *AFLS* 20: 23–39.

Montebelli, C. R. (2009) *Halieutica. Pescatori nel mondo antico*, Pesaro.

Montone, F. (2014) 'I rapporti di Sidonio Apollinare con l'imperatore Maioriano, con i barbari *foederati* … e con Ovidio', *Salternum* 18: 29–37.

Montone, F. (2017) 'Vita e svaghi di un aristocratico del V secolo. Il secondo libro dell' epistolario di Sidonio Apollinare', *Salternum* 21: 23–45.

Montuschi, C. (2001) 'Sidonio Apollinare e Ovidio: Esempi di riprese non solo verbali (Sidon. *Carm.* 2, 405–435; 22, 47–49)', *InvLuc* 23: 161–81.

Morello, R. and A. D. Morrison (eds) (2007) *Ancient Letters: Classical and Late Antique Epistolography*, Oxford.

Morvillez, E. (2017) '"Avec vue sur jardin": vivre entre nature et paysage dans l'architecture domestique, de Cicéron à Sidoine Apollinaire', *Mondes Anciens* 9: 1–35.

Mossberg, K.-Å. (1934) *Studia Sidoniania critica et semasiologica*, Uppsala.

Mratschek, S. (2002) *Der Briefwechsel des Paulinus von Nola. Kommunikation und soziale Kontakte zwischen christlichen Intellektuellen*, Göttingen.

Mratschek, S. (2008) 'Identitätsstiftung aus der Vergangenheit: Zum Diskurs über die trajanische Bildungskultur im Kreis des Sidonius Apollinaris', in T. Fuhrer (ed.), *Die christlich-philosophischen Diskurse der Spätantike: Texte, Personen, Institutionen*, Stuttgart, 363–80.

Mratschek, S. (2013) 'Creating Identity from the Past: The Construction of History in the Letters of Sidonius', in van Waarden and Kelly (2013), 249–71.

Mratschek, S. (2017) 'The Letter Collection of Sidonius Apollinaris', in C. Sogno, B. K. Storin and E. J. Watts (eds), *Late Antique Letter Collections: A Critical Introduction and Reference Guide*, Oakland, 309–36.

Mratschek, S. (2020a) 'Sidonius' Social World', in Kelly and van Waarden (2020a), 214–36.

Mratschek, S. (2020b) 'Creating Culture and Presenting the Self in Sidonius', in Kelly and van Waarden (2020a), 237–60.

Mratschek, S. (2020c) 'The Silence of the Muses in Sidonius Apollinaris (*Carm.* 12–13, *Ep.* 8.11): Aphasia and the Timelessness of Poetic Inspiration', *JLA* 13: 10–43.

Müller, C. (2000) '[I 15] P. Cursor, L.', *DNP* 9: 291–2.

Müller, G.M. (2013) 'Freundschaften wider den Verfall. Gemeinschaftsbildung und kulturelle Selbstverortung im Briefwechsel des Ruricius von Limoges', in Diefenbach and Müller (2013), 421–54.

Muth, S. (2005) 'Im Angesicht des Todes. Zum Wertediskurs in der römischen Grabkultur', in A. Haltenhoff, A. Heil and F.-H. Mutschler (eds), *Römische Werte als Gegenstand der Altertumswissenschaft*, Munich, 259–86.

Myers, K. S. (2005) '*Docta otia*: Garden Ownership and Configurations of Leisure in Statius and Pliny', *Arethusa* 38: 103–29.

Näf, B. (1995) *Senatorisches Standesbewusstsein in spätrömischer Zeit*, Freiburg.

Nathan, G. S. (2000) *The Family in Late Antiquity: The Rise of Christianity and the Endurance of Tradition*, London.

Neger, M. (2018) '*Quid nobis cum epistula*? Zur Kombination von Brief und Epigramm bei lateinischen Autoren', *Diomedes* NF 8: 43–61.

Neger, M. (2019) 'Epigramme im narrativen Kontext. Das Handtuch des Philomatius bei Sidonius, Epist. 5,17', *RhM* 162: 392–422.

Neger, M. (2020) 'Brief, Satire und Epigramm. Literarische Traditionen und narrative Strategien in Epist. 1,11 des Sidonius Apollinaris', *Gymnasium* 127: 361–88.

Neger, M. (2021) *Epistolare Narrationen. Studien zur Erzähltechnik des jüngeren Plinius*, Tübingen.

Neger, M. (2022) 'Epigrams and Letters: The Reception of Martial's Prose-Epistles', in É. Wolff (ed.), *Influence et réception du poète Martial, de sa mort à nos jours*, Scripta Antiqua 150, Bordeaux, 33–47.

Neri, M. (ed.) (2009) *Lettere. Ruricio di Limoges*, Pisa.

Newlands, C. E. (ed.) (2011a) *Statius: Silvae Book II*, Cambridge.

Newlands, C. E. (2011b) 'The First Biography of Lucan: Statius' Silvae 2.7', in Asso (2011), 435–51.

Newlands, C. E. (2013) 'Architectural Ecphrasis in Roman Poetry', in T. D. Papanghelis, S. J. Harrison and S. Frangoulidis (eds), *Generic Interfaces in Latin Literature: Encounters, Interactions and Transformations*, Berlin, 55–78.

Nicolas, J. (1901) 'La médecine dans les oeuvres de Sidoine Apollinaire (430–489)', *La revue médicale du Mont-Dore*: 3–12.

Nielsen, I. (1990) *Thermae et Balnea: The Architecture and Cultural History of Roman Public Baths*, Aarhus.

Nielsen, I. (2000) 'Palast', *DNP* 9: 168–85.

Nikitinski, O. (2001) 'Die (mündliche) Rolle von Briefboten bei Cicero', in L. Benz (ed.), *Script Oralia Romana. Die römische Literatur zwischen Mündlichkeit und Schriftlichkeit*, Tübingen, 229–47.

Odahl, C. M. (2010) *Cicero and the Catilinarian Conspiracy*, New York.

Oliver, G. J. (2000) *The Epigraphy of Death: Studies in the History and Society of Greece and Rome*, Liverpool.

Onorato, M. (2016) *Il castone e la gemma. Sulla tecnica poetica di Sidonio Apollinare*, Naples.

Onorato, M. (2020a) 'The Poet and the Light: Modulation and Transposition of a Prudentian Ekphrasis in Two Poems by Sidonius Apollinaris', in F. Hadjittofi and A. Lefteratou (eds), *The Genres of Late Antique Christian Poetry: Between Modulations and Transpositions*, Berlin, 75–92.

Onorato, M. (2020b) 'La parola e il silenzio. Echi dell'ultimo Ovidio in un dittico paratestuale sidoniano', in R. Poignault and H. Vial (eds), *Présences ovidiennes, Caesarodunum*: 52–53 bis, Clermont-Ferrand, 221–45.

Oswald, R. and M. Haase (1998) 'Hochzeitsbräuche- und ritual', *DNP* 5: 649–56.

Overwien, O. (2009a) 'Kampf um Gallien: Die Briefe des Sidonius Apollinaris zwischen Literatur und Politik', *Hermes* 137: 93–117.

Overwien, O. (2009b) 'Ironie in den Briefen des Sidonius Apollinaris', in R. F. Glei (ed.), *Ironie. Griechische und lateinische Fallstudien*, Trier, 247–64.

Page, S. (2015) *Der ideale Aristokrat. Plinius der Jüngere und das Sozialprofil der Senatoren in der Kaiserzeit*, Heidelberg.

Panayotakis, C. (2001) 'Vision and Light in Apuleius' Tale of Psyche and Her Mysterious Husband', *CQ* 51: 576–83.

Panayotakis, C. (2010) *Decimus Laberius. The Fragments, Edited with Introduction, Translation, and Commentary*, Cambridge.

Pausch, M. (2003) *Die römische Tunika: Ein Beitrag zur Peregrinisierung der antiken Kleidung*, Augsburg.

Pausch, D. (2004) *Biographie und Bildungskultur, Personendarstellungen bei Plinius dem Jüngeren, Gellius und Sueton*, Berlin.

Pavlovskis, Z. (1973) *Man in an Artificial Landscape: The Marvels of Civilization in Imperial Roman Literature*, Leiden.

Peachin, M. (2001) *Aspects of Friendship in the Graeco-Roman World*, Portsmouth.

Pelttari, A. (2014) *The Space that Remains: Reading Latin Poetry in Late Antiquity*, Ithaca.

Pelttari, A. (2016) 'Sidonius Apollinaris and Horace, *Ars poetica* 14–23', *Philologus* 160: 322–36.

Pensabene, P. (2004) 'Amministrazione dei marmi e sistema distributivo nel mondo romano', in Borghini (2004), 43–54.

Percival, J. (1992) 'The Fifth-Century Villa: New Life or Death Postponed?', in Drinkwater and Elton (1992), 156–64.

Percival, J. (1997) 'Desperately Seeking Sidonius: The Realities of Life in Fifth-Century Gaul', *Latomus* 56: 279–92.

Piacente, L. (1998) 'Sopravvivenze dei classici: I *Logistorici* di Varrone', *InvLuc* 20: 191–9.

Piacente, L. (2005) 'In viaggio con Sidonio Apollinare', in A. Gargano and M. Squillante (eds), *Il viaggio nella letteratura occidentale tra mito e simbolo*, Naples, 95–106.

Picard, J.-Ch. (1998) 'L'atrium dans les églises paléochrétiennes d'Occident', in J.-Ch. Picard (ed.), *Évêques, saints et cités en Italie et en Gaule. Études d'archéologie et d'histoire*, Rome, 107–55.

Pietri, L. (1988) 'Pagina in pariete reserata: épigraphie et architecture religieuse', in A. Donati (ed.), *La terza età dell'epigrafia*, Faenza, 137–57.

Pfäffgen, B. (2008) 'Leuchter', *RAC* 22: 1205–18.

Pociña, A. (1985) 'Πράσινος, prasinus. Historia de un adjetivo', in M. Jiménez and J. Luis (eds), *Symbolae Ludovico Mitxelena septuagenario oblatae, Vol. 1*, Bilbao, 119–24.

Podossinov, A. (1991) 'Himmelsrichtung (kultische)', *RAC* 15: 233–86.

Poignault, R. and A. Stoehr-Monjou (eds) (2014) *Présence de Sidoine Apollinaire*, Clermont-Ferrand.

Pollmann, K. (1997) 'Augustinus, Aurelius', *DNP* 2: 293–300.
Pollmann, K. (2001) 'Prudentius', *DNP* 10: 488–9.
Postel, V. (2011) '*Libertas und Litterae*: Leitbegriffe der Selbstdarstellung geistlicher und weltlicher Eliten im frühmittelalterlichen Gallien und Italien', in F. Bougard, H.-W. Goetz and R. Le Jan (eds), *Théorie et pratiques des élites au Haut Moye Âge. Conception, perception et réalisation sociale / Theorie und Praxis frühmittelalterlicher Eliten. Konzepte, Wahrnehmung und soziale Umsetzung*, Turnhout, 169–86.
Poster, C. (2007) 'A Conversation Halved: Epistolary Theory in Greco-Roman Antiquity', in C. Poster and L. C. Mitchell (eds), *Letter-Writing Manuals and Instruction from Antiquity to the Present*, Columbia, 21–51.
Prescendi, F. (1999) 'Libitina', *DNP* 7: 146.
Pretty, R. A. (1997) *Adamantius. Dialogue on the True Faith in God. De recta in Deum fide*, Leuven.
Prévot, F. (1993) 'Deux fragments de l'épitaphe de Sidoine Apollinaire découverts à Clermont-Ferrand', *AnTard* 1: 223–9.
Prévot, F. (1995) 'Origène, Lactance, Jérôme et les autres: La culture chrétienne de Sidoine Apollinaire', *BSAF*: 215–28.
Prévot, F. (1999) 'Sidoine Apollinaire et l'Auvergne', in B. Fizelier-Sauget (ed.), *L'Auvergne de Sidoine Apollinaire à Grégoire de Tours. Histoire et Archéologie. Actes des XIIIèmes Journées Internationales d'Archéologie Mérovingienne, Clermont-Ferrand (3–6 octobre 1991)*, Clermont-Ferrand, 63–80.
Prévot, F. (2013) 'La construction de son image par Sidoine Apollinaire à travers la publication de sa correspondence', in S. Benoist and C. Hoët-van Cauwenberghe (eds), *La vie des autres. Histoire, prosopographie, biographie dans l'Empire romain*, Villeneuve d'Ascq, 231–48.
Pricoco, S. (1965) 'Sidonio Apollinare, Girolamo e Rufino', *Nuovo Didaskaleion* 15, 141–50.
Pullen, H. W. (2015) *Manuale dei marmi romani antichi, tradotto, curato, illustrato e aggiornato da Francesco Crocenzi*, Rome.
Raff, T. (1994) *Die Sprache der Materialien. Anleitung zu einer Ikonologie der Werkstoffe*, Munich.
Raga, E. (2009) 'Bon mangeur, mauvais mangeur. Pratiques alimentaires et critique sociale dans l'œuvre de Sidoine Apollinaire et ses contemporains', *RBPh* 87: 165–96.
Raga, E. (2019) 'Romans and Barbarians at the Table: Banquets and Food as Tools of Distinction According to Sidonius Apollinaris (Fifth-Century Gaul)', in Y. Fox and E. Buchberger (eds), *Inclusion and Exclusion in Mediterranean Christianities, 400–800*, Turnhout, 239–58.
Rakoczy, T. (1996) *Böser Blick, Macht des Auges und Neid der Götter. Eine Untersuchung zur Kraft des Blickes in der griechischen Literatur*, Tübingen.
Ramelli, I. (2020) '*De recta in Deum fide*', in D. G. Hunter, P. J. J. van Geest and B. J. L. Peerbolte (eds), *Brill Encyclopedia of Early Christianity Online* <http://dx.doi.org/10.1163/2589-7993_EECO_SIM_036558>.
Randall, J. G. (1979) 'Mistresses' Pseudonyms in Latin Elegy', *LCM* 4: 27–35.
Rebenich, S. (1997) 'Hieronymus', in O. Schütze (ed.), *Metzler Lexikon Antiker Autoren*, Stuttgart, 315–18.
Rees, R. (2007) 'Letters of Recommendation and the Rhetoric of Praise', in Morello and Morrison (2007), 149–68.
Renger, J. (2001) 'Sardanapal', *DNP* 11: 54.
Reutter, U. (1997) 'Rufin', in O. Schütze (ed.), *Metzler Lexikon Antiker Autoren*, Stuttgart, 613–14.
Reynaud, J.-F. (1998) *Lugdunum christianum. Lyon du IVe au VIIIe s.: topographie, nécropoles et édifices religieux*, Paris.

Richardson, N. (2016) *Prudentius' Hymns for Hours and Seasons. Liber Cathemerinon*, London.
Richter, D. (2009) *Der Süden. Geschichte eines Himmelsrichtung*, Berlin.
Rickman, G. (1971) *Roman Granaries and Store Buildings*, Cambridge.
Riess, W. (2012) '*Rari exempli femina*: Female Virtues on Roman Funerary Inscriptions', in James and Dillon (2012), 491–501.
Riggsby, A. M. (1997) ' "Public" and "Private" in Roman Culture: The Case of the *cubiculum*', *JRA* 10: 36–56.
Riggsby, A. M. (2003) 'Pliny in Space (and Time)', *Arethusa* 36: 167–86.
Rijser, D. (2013) 'The Poetics of Inclusion in Servius and Sidonius', in van Waarden and Kelly (2013), 77–92.
Robbe, S. A. (2016) *Ecclesiasticam historiam in latinum vertere: Rufino traduttore di Eusebio di Caesarea: persecuzioni e martiri*, Supplementi Adamantius 5, Brescia.
Robert, R. (2011) 'La description du *Burgus* de Pontius Leontius: entre réalité et objet de mémoire littéraire (Sidoine Apollinaire, *carm.* 22)', in C. Balmelle, H. Eristov and F. Monier (eds), *Décor et architecture en Gaule entre l'Antiquité et le haut Moyen Âge*, Bordeaux, 377–90.
Roberts, M. (1984) 'The *Mosella* of Ausonius: An Interpretation', *TAPA* 114: 343–53.
Roberts, M. (1989) *The Jeweled Style: Poetry and Poetics in Late Antiquity*, Ithaca.
Rodenwaldt, G. (1923) 'Sigma', *RE* II A.2: 2323–4.
Ronning, Ch. (2011) 'Von Frauen erzählen … Männlichkeit und Weiblichkeit in den römischen Grabinschriften', in U. Egelhaaf-Gaiser, D. Pausch and M. Rühl (eds), *Kultur der Antike. Transdisziplinäres Arbeiten in den Altertumswissenschaften*, Berlin, 83–111.
Rossiaud, M. (1976) 'Les haleurs du Rhône au XVe siècle', *Actes des congrès de la Société des historiens médiévistes de l'enseignement supérieur public* 7: 283–304.
Rossiter, J. (1991) 'Convivium and Villa in Late Anqituity', in Slater (1991), 199–214.
Rousseau, P. (2000) 'Sidonius and Majorian: The Censure in *Carmen* V', *Historia* 49: 251–7.
Rousseau, P. (ed.) (2009) *A Companion to Late Antiquity*, Malden MA.
Rüpke, J. and A. Glock (2005) *Fasti sacerdotum. Die Mitglieder der Priesterschaften und das sakrale Funktionspersonal römischer, griechischer, orientalischer und jüdisch-christlicher Kulte in der Stadt Rom von 300 v. Chr. bis 499 n. Chr., Teil 2, Biographien*, Stuttgart.
Ruffing, K. (2002) 'A Weinbau', *DNP* 12.2: 424–32.
Sabnis, S. (2012) 'Invisible Slaves, Visible Lamps: A Metaphor in Apuleius', *Arethusa* 45: 79–108.
Sallmann, K. (2002) '[2] V. Terentius, M. (Reatinus) römischer Universalschriftsteller, 116–27 v. Chr.', *DNP* 12.1: 1130–44.
Salzman, M. R. and M. Roberts (2011) *The Letters of Symmachus, Book 1*, Atlanta.
Samson, R. (1992) 'Slavery, the Roman legacy', in Drinkwater and Elton (1992), 218–27.
Sanders, G. (1965) *Licht en duisternis in de christelijke grafschriften*, Brussels.
Santelia, S. (2000) 'Sidonio Apollinare ed i *bybliopolae*', *InvLuc* 22: 217–39.
Santelia, S. (2002) *Sidonio Apollinare. Carme 24*: Propempticon ad libellum. *Introduzione, traduzione e commento*, Bari.
Santelia, S. (2005) 'Maioriano-Ercole e Sidonio *supplex famulus* (Sidon. *carm.* 13)', *AFLB* 48: 189–208.
Santelia, S. (2007) 'Sidonio Apollinare autore di una epigrafe per l'ecclesia di Lione: *epist.* 2,10,4 (= Le Blant *ICG* 54)', *VetChr* 44: 305–21.
Santelia, S. (2012) *Sidonio Apollinare. Carme 16:* Eucharisticon ad Faustum episcopum. *Introduzione, traduzione e commento*, Bari.
Santelia, S. (2016a) 'Polla Argentaria, *patrona* di poeti: forse poetessa *univira*', *Vichiana* 53: 75–84.

Santelia, S. (2016b) 'Sidonio Apollinare, *carm*. 23.101–66: una "proposta paideutica"?', *Lexis* 34: 425–44.

Santelia, S. (2020) 'Non solo Ovidio: giochi di intertestualità in Sidonio Apollinare *carm*. 12', in Di Stefano and Onorato (2020), 173–90.

Santoro L'Hoir, F. (1992) *The Rhetoric of Gender Terms: 'Man', 'Woman', and the Portrayal of Character in Latin Prose*, Leiden.

Savaron, J. (1599) *Caii Sollii Apollinaris Sidonii Arvernorum episcopi opera Io. Savaro ... multo quam antea castigatius quam antea recognovit et librum commentarium adiecit*, Paris.

Scheibelreiter-Gail, V. (2012) 'Inscriptions in the Late Antique Private House: Some Thoughts About Their Function and Distribution', in S. Birk and B. Poulsen (eds), *Patrons and Viewers in Late Antiquity*, Aarhus, 135–65.

Scheidegger Laemmle, C. (2021) 'Cataloguing Contemporaries: Ovid *Ex Ponto* 4.16 in Context', in Laemmle et al. (2021), 361–400.

Schetter, W. (1964) 'Der gallische Dichter Secundinus', *Philologus* 108: 153–6.

Schiemann, G. (2002) '*Tutela*', *DNP* 12.1: 932–5.

Schindler, C., E. Moormann, and J. Deckers (2013) 'Musen', *RAC* 25: 184–220.

Schindler, C. (2018) 'Macht und Übermacht der Tradition. Dichterkataloge in der lateinischen Literatur von Ovid bis Sidonius', in S. Finkmann, A. Behrendt and A. Walter (eds), *Antike Erzähl- und Deutungsmuster. Zwischen Exemplarität und Transformation. Festschrift für Christiane Reitz zum 65. Geburtstag*, Berlin, 335–57.

Schipke, R. (2013) *Das Buch in der Spätantike. Herstellung, Form, Ausstattung und Verbreitung in der westlichen Reichsthälfte des Imperium Romanum*, Wiesbaden.

Schlapbach, K. (2013) 'Muße', *RAC* 24: 357–69.

Schlapbach, K. (2014) 'The Temporality of the Muses: A Reading of the Sister Goddesses in Late Antique Latin Literature', in K. W. Christian, C. E. L. Guest and C. Wedepohl (eds), *The Muses and Their Afterlife in Post-Classical Europe*, London, 33–58.

Schlapbach, K. (2020) '*Veriora Nomina Camenarum*: Erudition, Uncertainty, and Cognitive Displacement as Poetic Strategies in Sidonius Apollinaris', *JLA* 13: 44–61.

Schlinkert, D. (1996) *Ordo senatorius und nobilitas. Die Konstitution des Senatsadels in der Spätantike*, Stuttgart.

Schmitzer, U. (2015) 'Sidonius Apollinaris: Unfruchtbare Muse oder Erneuerung der Poesie im Zeichen des Mythos?', in H. Leppin (ed.), *Antike Mythologie in christlichen Kontexten der Spätantike*, Berlin, 71–92.

Schneider, H. (2001) 'Purpur', *DNP* 10: 604–5.

Schneider, K. (1995) *Villa und Natur. Eine Studie zur römischen Oberschichtkultur im letzten vor- und ersten nachchristlichen Jahrhundert*, Munich.

Schöffel, C. (2001) *Martial, Buch 8. Einleitung, Text, Übersetzung, Kommentar*, Stuttgart.

Schönbeck, G. (1962) *Der locus amoenus von Homer bis Horaz*, Diss. Heidelberg.

Schröder, B.-J. (2007) *Bildung und Briefe im 6. Jahrhundert*, Berlin.

Schröder, B.-J. (2018) 'Couriers and Conventions in Cicero's Epistolary Network', in Ceccarelli et al. (2018), 81–100.

Schulzki, H.-J. (1998) 'Iugerum', *DNP* 5: 1211–2.

Schwerdtner, K. (2015) *Plinius und seine Klassiker. Studien zur literarischen Zitation in den Pliniusbriefen*, Berlin.

Schwitter, R. (2015) *Umbrosa lux: Obscuritas in der lateinischen Epistolographie der Spätantike*, Stuttgart.

Schwitter, R. (2020) 'Rival Friends: Sidonius Apollinaris and Literary Competitiveness in Late Antique Gaul', *JLA* 13: 73–93.

Shanzer, D. (2001) 'Bishops, Letters, Fast, Food, and Feast in Later Roman Gaul', in R. W.

Mathisen and D. Shanzer (eds), *Culture and Society in Later Roman Gaul: Revisiting the Sources*, Ashgate, 217–36.

Shanzer, D. and I. Wood (eds) (2002) *Avitus of Vienne. Letters and Selected Prose*, Liverpool.

Sharrock, A. (2012) 'Ovid', in Gold (2012), 70–85.

Sherwin-White, A. N. (1966) *The Letters of Pliny: A Historical and Social Commentary*, Oxford.

Siegel, D. (2000) 'Nysa 2', *DNP* 8:1074–5.

Sirmond, J. (1614) *C. Sollii Apollinaris Sidonii Avernorum episcopi opera, Iac. Sirmondi Soc. Iesu Presb. cura et studio recognita, notisque illustrata*, Paris.

Sivan, H. S. (1989) 'Sidonius Apollinaris, Theodoric II, and Gothic-Roman Politics from Avitus to Anthemius', *Hermes* 117: 85–94.

Sivan, H. S. (1993) *Ausonius of Bordeaux. Genesis of a Gallic Aristocracy*, London.

Sivonen, P. (2006) *Being a Roman Magistrate. Office-holding and Roman Identity in Late Antique Gaul*, Helsinki.

Skinner, M. B. (2011) *Clodia Metelli. The Tribune's Sister*, Oxford.

Slater, W. J. (ed.) (1991) *Dining in a Classical Context*, Ann Arbor.

Sowers, B. P. (2016) '*Amicitia* and Late Antique *Nugae*: Reading Ausonius' Reading Community', *AJP* 137: 511–40.

Spina, S. D. (1999) 'Leontinoi', *DNP* 7: 62–4.

Squillante, M. (2007/2008) 'La felicità e il potere: l'*exemplum* di Damocle nella rielaborazione tardoantica', *IFilolClass* 7: 249–60.

Squillante, M. (2009) 'La biblioteca di Sidonio Apollinare', *Voces* 20: 139–59.

Squillante, M. (2010) '... *de hymno tuo si percontere quid sentiam*: l'inno secondo Sidonio Apollinare', *Paideia* 65: 449–63.

Squillante, M. (2014) 'Giocchi d'acqua tra invenzione e citazione', in Poignault and Stoehr-Monjou (2014), 215–25.

Squillante, M. (2016) 'Le *silvulae* di Stazio per Sidonio Apollinare', in A. Setaioli (ed.), *Apis Matina. Studi in onore di Carlo Santini*, Trieste, 669–78.

Squillante, M. (2018) 'Dalla *poetandi ineptia* di Ausonio alle *nugae poetarum cantilenosae* di Sidonio Apollinare', in Wolff (2018), 367–76.

Starr, R. J. (1987) 'The Circulation of Literary Texts in the Roman World', *CQ* 37: 213–23.

Stein-Hölkeskamp, E. (2005) *Das römische Gastmahl. Eine Kulturgeschichte*, Munich.

Steinmann, E. (1892) *Die Tituli und die kirchliche Wandmalerei im Abendlande vom V. bis bis zum XI. Jahrhundert*, Leipzig.

Stenger, J. (2002) 'Tantalos', *DNP* 12.1: 11.

Stevens, C. E. (1933) *Sidonius Apollinaris and His Age*, Oxford.

Stevenson, J. (2005) *Women Latin Poets: Language, Gender, and Authority from Antiquity to the Eighteenth Century*, Oxford.

Stirling, L. (2012) 'Patrons, Viewers, and Statues in Late Antique Baths', in S. Birk and B. Poulsen (eds), *Patrons and Viewers in Late Antiquity*, Aarhus, 67–81.

Stoehr-Monjou, A. (2013) 'Sidonius and Horace: The Art of Memory', in van Waarden and Kelly (2013), 133–69.

Stoehr-Monjou, A. (2018) 'Le rôle du poète dans la Gaule du Ve siècle: Sidoine Apollinaire et son public', *InvLuc* 40: 135–67.

Stoehr-Monjou, A. (2020) 'Sidonius' Panegyrics', in Kelly and van Waarden (2020a), 317–40.

Stoehr-Monjou, A. (forthcoming) 'How to Conclude? A Poetics of Contrast and Paradox in Book 9 and Especially in Epist. 9,13–16 by Sidonius Apollinaris', International conference and workshop, *The Stumbling Texts (and Stumbling Readers) of Late Latin Poetry (Lector, quas patieris hic salebras!)*, organised by Markus Kersten, Ann-Kathrin Stähle and Christian Guerra, September 2021, Basel, Switzerland.

Stoffel, E. (1999) 'Libertas', *DNP* 7: 144–5.
Stutzinger, D. (2001) *Eine römische Wasserauslaufuhr. Museum für Vor- und Frühgeschichte*, Frankfurt a. M.
Styka, J. (2008) 'Römische Schule der Spätantike im Lichte der Briefe von Sidonius Apollinaris', *Classica Cracoviensia* 12: 157–76.
Tarpin, M. (2002) *Vici et pagi dans l'Occident romain*, Rome.
Teitler, H. C. (1992) 'Un-Roman Activities in Late Antique Gaul: The Cases of Arvandus and Seronatus', in Drinkwater and Elton (1992), 309–17.
Thébert, Y. (2003) *Thermes Romains D'Afrique du Nord et Leur Contexte Méditerranéen*, Rome.
Thraede, K. (1970) *Grundzüge griechisch-römischer Brieftopik*, Munich.
Thompson, E. A. (1963) 'The Visigoths from Fritigern to Euric', *Historia* 12: 105–26.
Traulsen, Ch. (2004) *Das sakrale Asyl in der Alten Welt. Zur Schutzfunktion des Heiligen von König Salomo bis zum Codex Theodosianus*, Tübingen.
Treggiari, S. (1997) 'Ehe; III Rom', *DNP* 3: 896–9.
Treggiari, S. (2007) *Terentia, Tullia and Publilia. The Women of Cicero's Family*, London.
Tschiedel, H. J. (1981) *Caesars Anticato. Eine Untersuchung der Testimonien und Fragmente*, Darmstadt.
Tzounakas, S. (2011) 'Seneca's presence in Pliny's epistle 1.12', *Philologus* 155: 346–60.
van der Laan, A. and F. Akkerman (eds) (2002) *Rudolph Agricola, Letters*, Assen.
Väterlein, J. (1976) *Roma ludens. Kinder und Erwachsene beim Spiel im antiken Rom*, Amsterdam.
van Rohden, P. (1895) '11. Apronia', *RE* 2.1: 275.
van Waarden, J. A. (2010) *Writing to Survive: A Commentary on Sidonius Apollinaris, Letters Book 7. Vol. 1, The Episcopal Letters 1–11*, Leuven.
van Waarden, J. (2011) 'Sidonio Apollinare, poeta e vescovo', *VetChr* 48: 99–113.
van Waarden, J. A. (2016) *Writing to Survive: A Commentary on Sidonius Apollinaris, Letters Book 7. Vol. 2, The Ascetic Letters 12–18*, Leuven.
van Waarden, J. (2020a) 'Sidonius' Biography in Photo Negative', in Kelly and van Waarden (2020a), 13–28.
van Waarden, J. (2020b) '"You" and "I" in Sidonius' Correspondence', in Kelly and van Waarden (2020a), 418–39.
van Waarden, J. (2020c) 'Sidonius Reception: Sixteenth to Nineteenth Centuries', in Kelly and van Waarden (2020a), 686–704.
van Waarden, J. (2020d) '*Amicitia, Otium*, and the Chronotope of Sidonius' Correspondence', *JLA* 13: 149–72.
van Waarden, J. (2021) 'Leafing through Pliny with Sidonius: Sidon. *Ep.* 1.1, Plin. *Ep.* 1.1, 1.2, and 1.5, and Satire', *Mnemosyne*: 1–23.
van Waarden, J. and G. Kelly (eds) (2013) *New Approaches to Sidonius Apollinaris*, Leuven.
van Waarden, J. and G. Kelly (2020) 'Prose Rhythm in Sidonius', in Kelly and van Waarden (2020a), 462–75.
Veremans, J. (1991) 'La présence de Virgile dans l'œuvre de Sidoine Apollinaire, évêque de Clermond-Ferrand', in M. Van Uytfanghe and R. Demeulenaere (eds), Aevum inter utrumque. *Mélanges offerts à Gabriel Sanders*, Steenbrugge, 491–502.
Vidman, L. (1971) '*Inferiae* und *iustitium*', *Klio* 53: 209–12.
Visser, J. (2014) 'Sidonius Apollinaris, *Ep.* II.2: The Man and His Villa', *JLARC* 8: 26–45.
Voelkl, L. (1949) 'Orientierung im Weltbild der ersten christlichen Jahrhunderte', *RAC* 25: 155–70.
von Hesberg-Tonn, B. (1983) *Coniunx carissima. Untersuchungen zum Normcharakter im Erscheinungsbild der römischen Frau*, Stuttgart.
von Rummel, Ph. (2007) *Habitus barbarus: Kleidung und Repräsentation spätantiker Eliten im 4. und 5. Jahrhundert*, Berlin.

Wagner, Y. (2010) '*Otium* und *negotium* in den *Epistulae* Plinius' des Jüngeren. Zwischen Tradition und Wertewandel', *Diomedes* NF 5: 89–100.
Wagner-Hasel, B. (1998) 'Gastfreundschaft. III. Griechenland und Rom', *DNP* 4: 794–7.
Walde, C. (2000) 'Musen', *DNP* 8: 511–4.
Waldner, K. (2001a) 'Prokne', *DNP* 10: 388–9.
Waldner, K. (2001b) '2. Syrinx', *DNP* 11: 1181–2.
Wallace-Hadrill, A. (ed.) (1989) *Patronage in Ancient Society*, London.
Wallraff, M. (2004) 'Gerichtetes Gebet. Wie und warum richten Juden und Christen in der Spätantike ihre Sakralbauten aus?', in A. Gerhards and H. H. Henrix (eds), *Dialog oder Monolog? Zur liturgischen Beziehung zwischen Judentum und Christentum*, Freiburg i. Br., 110–27.
Ward-Perkins, B. (2005) *The Fall of Rome and the End of Civilization*, Oxford.
Watson, P. (1983) '*Puella* and *Virgo*', *Glotta* 61: 119–43.
Watson, L. (1998) 'Representing the Past, Redefining the Future: Sidonius Apollinaris' Panegyrics of Avitus and Anthemius', in M. Whitby (ed.), *The Propaganda of Power: The Role of Panegyric in Late Antiquity*, Leiden, 177–98.
Watson, L. and P. Watson (eds) (2014) *Juvenal, Satire 6*, Cambridge.
Weber, D. (2013) '*Medicorum pueri* – Zu einer Metapher bei Augustinus', *ZAC* 17: 125–42.
Weeber, K.-W. (2015) *Luxus im alten Rom. Die Schwelgerei, das süße Gift...* (3rd revised edition; 1st edition 2003), Darmstadt.
Weilbach, C. (2020) *Wie Laien und Fachleute über Medizinisches sprechen. Ein Vergleich medizinischer Äusserungen in Briefen und Fachtexten aus der Zeit der späten römischen Republik bis in die frühe Kaiserzeit*, Heidelberg.
Wendel, C. (1954) 'Bibliothek', *RAC* 2: 231–74.
White, P. (1975) 'The Friends of Martial, Statius, and Pliny, and the Dispersal of Patronage', *HSCP* 79: 265–300.
Whitton, C. (ed.) (2013) *Pliny the Younger, Epistles Book II*, Cambridge.
Wiegandt, D. (2020) *Otium: Historisch-semantische Studie eines aristokratischen Konzepts in Später Republik und Frühem Prinzipat*, Berlin.
Will, W. (2001) '[I 3] P. Magnus, Cn. Der Gegner Caesars', *DNP* 10: 99–107.
Williams, C. A. (2012) *Reading Roman Friendship*, Cambridge.
Williams, J. (2014) 'Letter Writing, Materiality, and Gifts in Late Antiquity: Some Perspectives on Material Culture', *JLA* 7: 351–9.
Winkle, Ch. (2002) 'Vardo', *DNP* 12.1: 1125–6.
Wöhrle, G. (2010) 'Cicero über Gesundheit, Krankheit, Ärzte', *Göttinger Forum für Altertumswissenschaften* 13: 159–88.
Wolff, É. (2000) *La poésie funéraire épigraphique à Rome*, Rennes.
Wolff, É. (2014a) 'Sidoine Apollinaire lecteur de Martial', in Poignault and Stoehr-Monjou (2014), 295–303.
Wolff, É. (2014b) 'Martial dans l'Antiquité tardive (IVe–VIe siècles)', in L. Cristante and T. Mazzoli (eds), *Il calamo della memoria VI. Riuso di testi e mestiere letterario nella tarda antichità*, Trieste, 81–100.
Wolff, É. (2014c) 'Sidoine Apollinaire et la poésie épigraphique', in A. Pistellato (ed.), *Memoria poetica e poesia della memoria. La versificazione epigrafica dall'antichità all'umanesimo*, Venice, 207–18.
Wolff, É. (2016) 'Sidoine Apollinaire voyageur', *AntTard* 24: 193–201.
Wolff, É. (ed.) (2018) *Ausone en 2015: Bilan et nouvelles perspectives*, Paris.
Wolff, É. (2020) 'Sidonius' Vocabulary, Syntax, and Style', in Kelly and van Waarden (2020a), 395–417.

Wood, I. N. (2000) 'The North-Western Provinces', in A. Cameron, B. Ward-Perkins and M. Whitby (eds), *Cambridge Ancient History XIV: Late Antiquity: Empire and Successors, A.D. 425–600*, Cambridge, 497–524.

Woolf, G. (1998) *Becoming Roman: The Origins of Provincial Civilization in Gaul*, Cambridge.

Wray, D. (2012) 'Catullus the Roman Love Elegist?', in Gold (2012), 25–38.

Wyke, M. (1987) 'Written Women: Propertius' *Scripta Puella*', *JRS* 77: 47–61.

Wyke, M. (2002) *The Roman Mistress: Ancient and Modern Representations*, Oxford.

Wyslucha, K. (2018) '*Tibia multifora, multiforatilis, multiforabilis* … Depictions of a "Many-Holed" Tibia in Written Sources', in A. Garcia-Ventura, C. Tavolieri and L. Verderame (eds), *The Study of Musical Performance in Antiquity: Archaeology and Written Sources*, Cambridge, 227–46.

Yegül, F. (1992) *Baths and Bathing in Classical Antiquity*, Cambridge.

Zanker, P. (1979) 'Die Villa als Vorbild des späten pompejanischen Wohngeschmacks', *JDAI* 94: 460–523.

Zarini, V. (2002) 'À la plus grande gloire de Martin? Deux *epigrammata* de la basilique de Tours au Vème siècle', in J. Dion (ed.), *L'épigramme de l'Antiquité au XVIIe siècle ou Du ciseau à la pointe*, Nancy, 247–62.

Zarmakoupi, M. (2011) '*Porticus* and *cryptoporticus* in Luxury Villa Architecture', in E. Poehler, M. Flohr and K. Cole (eds), *Pompeii: Art, Industry and Infrastructure*, Oxford, 50–61.

Zecchini, G. (1983) 'Momenti della fortuna tardoantica di Silla', in G. Zecchini (ed.), *Ricerche di storiografia Latina tardoantica*, Rome, 93–102.

Zeller, J. (1905) 'Das concilium der Septem Provinciae in Arleate', *Westdeutsche Zeitschrift* 24: 1–19.

Zelzer, M. (1994/1995) 'Der Brief in der Spätantike. Überlegungen zu einem literarischen Genos am Beispiel der Briefsammlung des Sidonius Apollinaris', *WS* 107/108: 541–51.

Zelzer, K. and M. Zelzer (2002) '"Retractationes" zu Brief und Briefgenos bei Plinius, Ambrosius und Sidonius Apollinaris', in W. Blümer, R. Henke and M. Mülke (eds), *Alvarium. Festschrift für Christian Gnilka*, Münster, 393–405.

Index Locorum

ACHILLES TATIUS
Leucippe and Clitophon
   1.15.8, 149

AELIAN
De natura animalium
   1.5, 144
   3.31, 150

AESCHYLUS
Choephori
   506–7, 144

ALC. AVIT. *see* AVITUS, ALCIMUS ECDICIUS

AMBROSE OF MILAN
Epistulae
   2.3, 285
   73.7, 373
Hexaemeron
   4.8.33, 311
Hymni
   1.7.26–8, 151
In Psalmos
   40.14, 360

AMMIANUS MARCELLINUS
Res gestae
   14.11.9, 375
   16.12.54, 387
   17.13.33, 183
   18.1.2, 110
   18.5.6, 97
   19.6.2, 346
   19.8.5, 282
   19.9.7, 97
   20.1.2, 264
   20.8.1, 89
   21.16.1, 264
   24.2.5, 381
   27.11.2, 264
   28.1.4, 264
   28.1.15, 110, 223
   28.4.27, 264
   28.6.29, 264
   29.2.4, 363, 386
   29.2.10, 97
   29.2.15, 223
   30.4.16, 110
   30.7.4, 381

ANTHOLOGIA LATINA
   236.5, 91
   762, 148, 149

ANTHOLOGIA PALATINA
   1, 313
   1.10.49–64, 294
   1.12, 294
   1.15, 294
   1.16, 294
   4.2, 391
   5.4, 333
   5.5, 333
   7.224.1–2, 238
   7.331.5, 238
   9.92, 150
   9.606, 112
   9.619, 112
   9.633, 112
   11.112, 359
   11.113, 359
   11.118, 359
   26.1, 294
   30.1, 294
   112, 294

APENDIX VERGILIANA, CULEX
   153, 149

APULEIUS
Apologia pro se de magia
   10.2–3, 338, 339, 341
   30.11, 336
   37.3, 264
   39.4, 274
   56.2, 381
   65.8, 272
   82.2, 336
   83.1, 336
   84.2, 336
   87.5–6, 336

De deo Socratis
   16, 184
De Mundo
   13, 315
   23, 160
   26, 375
Florida
   3.1, 153
   7.8, 381
   9.18, 381
   13, 148
   15.2, 253
   17.17, 150
   19.8, 230
Metamorphoses
   1.1.1, 311
   1.2.3, 357
   2.7.2, 274
   2.11.3, 140, 333
   2.11.6, 336
   2.15.6, 140
   2.19.1, 140
   2.19.3, 384
   2.24.5, 140
   3.6.4, 348
   3.29.5, 356
   4.7.4, 140
   4.22.3, 274
   5.3.2, 278
   5.20.6, 289
   6.1.3, 105
   7.9.2, 348
   7.13.1, 289
   8.11.3, 140
   8.15.5, 282
   8.30.5, 289
   8.31.4, 373
   9.9.1, 160
   9.13.4, 275
   9.16.1, 387
   9.22.6, 113
   10.2.7, 258
   10.32.2, 153
   10.33.1, 365
   11.3.1, 203

ARISTOPHANES
Ranae
   226–69, 149

ATHENAEUS
Deipnosophistae
   7.302d–f, 166
   9.399c–d, 166

AUGUSTINE
Confessiones
   3.2.3, 310
   3.4.7, 309
Contra epistulam Parmeniani
   2.10.20, 104
Contra Faustum Manichaeum
   29.3, 310
De civitate dei
   Praef., 369
   5.10, 63
   6.2, 266
   8.23, 63
   9.12, 368
   9.13, 389
   11.11, 368
   12.12, 160
   14.28, 369–70
   15.9
   15.27, 68
De dialectica
   6, 64
De doctrina christiana
   2.19, 299
   4.43, 275
De libero arbitrio
   2.9.26, 389
De moribus Manichaeorum
   2.16.43, 393
Epistulae
   36.22, 216
   149.25, 311
   149.27, 296
   149.34, 354
   187.39, 311
Expositio in Evangelium Iohannis
   13.16, 282
Sermones
   32.1, 360
   155.10, 360
   175.9, 360
   176.4, 360
   286.3, 360
   302.3, 360
   345.7, 360

AURELIUS VICTOR *see* VICTOR, AURELIUS

AUSONIUS, DECIMIUS MAGNUS
Cento nuptialis
   praef., 301
   praef. 21–4, 293
Commemoratio professorum Burdigalensium
   1.33, 138
   21.21, 396

INDEX LOCORUM

De Herediolo
    87, 356
Epicedion in patrem
    praef. 9, 313
Epistulae
    9a, 301
    13.56–7, 165
    15.42–3, 161
    19a, 301
    19a.24–30, 293, 333
    27.69 [24.61], 396
    29.51 [21.51], 396
Gratiarum actio
    8.38, 373
    14.64, 113
Griphus
    288, 301
Mosella
    41–2, 328
    48, 119
    48–9, 319
    48–52, 117
    49, 324
    67, 92
    74, 317
    75–149, 144
    85, 167
    88, 144
    104, 144
    104–5, 165–6
    105, 166
    109, 133
    129, 144
    163–8, 326, 328, 330
    192–3, 167
    205, 329
    217–18, 171–2
    244, 145
    245–6, 143
    250, 145
    338–40, 105
    341–4, 284
    342, 107
    343, 283
    442, 323
Ordo nobilium urbium
    102, 396
    161, 250
Parentalia
    Praef. A, 116
    Praef. B v. 1, 244
    Praef. B v. 5, 232
    1–8, 228
    1.4, 244
    2, 237
    2.3, 225
    2.5, 240
    2.6, 242
    6.9, 244
    7.9, 286
    7.11, 243
    9–30, 228
    9.1, 244
    9.2, 232
    9.4, 238
    9.8, 244
    9.23, 243
    9.25–6, 244
    12.11, 244
    15.2, 232
    16.4, 225
    17.2, 232
    19.3, 239
    24.11–12, 133
    28.7, 232
Praefationes variae
    5 vv. 7–12, xx n. 56, 333

AVIENIUS
De ora maritima
    518–19, 286
Phaenomena (Aratus)
    1486, 165

AVITUS, ALCIMUS ECDICIUS (of Vienne)
De spiritalis historiae gesti
    1.83, 153
    3.221–32, 383
Epistulae
    50, 106
    78.18–19, 106
Homiliae
    1, 137.16, 135
    6, 112.8, 155
    24, 142.30, 323
    29, 150.11–13, 106

BELLUM HISPANIENSE
    29.2, 160

BIBLE see *VULGATA*

BOETHIUS
De consolatione philosophiae
    3.5.6–11, 364
    4.6.10, 374

CAESAR
De bello civili
    1.58.3, 352
    1.62.2, 352
De bello Gallico
    1.31, 61
    1.45, 61
    4.17.2, 352

4.33, 327
7.7, 61
7.47, 134
7.69.2, 103

CALPURNIUS SICULUS
Carmina Priapea
15.5, 152
Eclogae
1.29, 153
6.85, 152

CASSIODORUS
Historia ecclesiastica tripartita
11.18.7, 160
Variae (epistulae)
8.32.1, 251

CASSIUS FELIX
De medicina
4, 146

CATO
De agri cultura
1.7, 103
14.1, 125
128, 163

CATULLUS
1.1–2, 337
1.8–9, 309
5, 339
5.5–6, 238
7, 339
8, 339
43, 339
44, 96, 355
44.6–7, 355
44.13–14, 355
46.2, 315
46.9–11, 330
50.4, 116
51, 339
58, 339
63.18, 275
63.21, 155
64.85, 324
66.33, 241
67.1, 241–2
72, 339
75, 339
79, 339
86, 339
87, 339
92, 339
107, 339

CELSUS
1.3.4, 283
1.10.3, 278
2.15.1, 355
2.17.1, 283
2.17.1–10, 283
2.17.4, 355
2.18.10, 274
2.35, 355
3.8, 358
5.26.24c, 361

CENSORINUS
20, 396
24, 148

CICERO
Brutus
44, 275
93, 337
108, 376
121, 332
213, 176
301–4, 334
Cato maior de senectute
44, 283
56, 129
De divinatione
1.65, 255
2.16, 355
2.120, 116
De domo sua
137, 373
139, 376
De finibus bonorum et malorum
1.65–70, 209
2.66, 241
5.40, 253
5.64, 241
5.67, 242
De haruspicum responso
55, 223
De inventione
1.34, 63
1.52, 277
1.67, 202
De lege agraria
2.49, 181
De legibus
2.3, 96
2.55, 231
De natura deorum
1.34.95, 369
3.85, 213
De officiis
1.128, 114
1.134, 258

De oratore
  1.157, 311
  2.48, 376
  2.163, 204
  2.107, 204
  3.153, 227
  3.230, 296
De re publica
  1.1, 96
  2.63, 241
Epistulae ad Atticum
  1.14.4, 301
  1.16.10, 204
  1.20.2, 186
  1.20.7, 295–6
  2.1.6, 186
  2.4.7, 158
  2.16.4, 71
  3.15.4, 296
  5.1.3, 116
  5.5.1, 360
  5.14.1, 146
  7.13.1, 296
  8.13.2, 356
  10.10.3, 361
  10.11.3, 296
  11.6.4, 354
  11.6.7, 269
  12.6.2, 296
  12.18.1, 332
  12.27.1, 356
  12.28.3, 296
  13.1.3, 296
  13.21.1, 365
  13.52.2, 273, 275
  16.2.6, 275
Epistulae ad Brutum
  1.14.1, 116
Epistulae ad familiares
  2.11.1, 250
  3.3.1, 348
  5.8.2, 191
  5.14.3, 212
  7.18.2, 203
  7.24.1, 296
  7.26.1, 355
  9.2.1, xx n. 56, 333
  9.15.1, 181
  9.22.1, 296
  9.25.1, 332
  10.24.6, 373
  10.31.4, 181
  12.24.3, 296
  13, 190
  14.2.2, 296
  16.3.1, 296
  16.4.1, 361
  16.8, 354
  16.13, 354
  16.16.2, 296
Epistulae ad Quintum fratrem
  1.1.45, 62
  2.12.2, 392
  3.1.1, 90, 130
  3.1.2, 133, 146
In Catilinam
  1.1, 67
  1.31, 355
In L. Pisonem
  8, 238
  18, 238
  24, 110
  29, 233
  68, 367
  71, 110
In M. Antonium orationes Philippicae
  1.8, 150
  2.7, 348
  2.58, 228, 327
  2.67, 158, 380
  2.112, 388
  5.18.50, 367
  8.27, 81
  8.29, 73, 110
  14.1, 192
In Verrem actio prima, secunda
  1.11, 297
  2.1.41, 194
  2.2.2, 129
  2.2.52, 381
  2.2.53, 73
  2.2.66, 383
  2.3.8, 394
  2.3.15, 68
  2.3.18, 383
  2.3.23, 73
  2.3.34, 73
  2.3.44, 383
  2.3.46, 383
  2.3.87, 191
  2.4.16, 137
  2.4.18, 191, 381
  2.4.25, 137–8
  2.4.26, 120
  2.4.42, 114
  2.4.47, 176
  2.4.55, 324
  2.4.60, 333
  2.4.64–5, 333
  2.4.71, 333
  2.5.6, 387
  2.5.11, 73
  2.5.37, 162
Laelius de amicitia
  1.2, 105
  50, 209

62, 209
65–6, 209
Orator
  14, 176
  154, 114
Pro A. Cluentio
  23, 191
  94, 376
  123, 185
Pro Archia poeta
  19, 251
  24, 378
Pro Cn. Plancio
  100, 110
Pro L. Murena
  76, 118
Pro L. Valerio Flacco
  28, 118
  105, 367
Pro lege Manilia
  28, 378
Pro M. Caelio
  11, 397
  67, 275
  77, 197
  80, 297
Pro Sex. Roscio Amerino
  15, 94
Pro T. Annio Milone
  23.61, 213
Topica
  1.1, 262
  35, 63
Tusculanae disputationes
  1.44, 212
  4.60, 376
  5.5, 192
  5.26.74, 90
  5.55, 324
  5.61, 138, 368, 369, 377, 379, 381, 382
  5.62, 367, 368, 377, 378, 379, 382, 385, 386, 387

CIL see CORPUS INSCRIPTIONUM LATINARUM

CLAUDIAN
Bellum Geticum
  26.321, 353
Carmina minora
  18.18, 327
  26.46, 143
  35.1, 91
De consulatu Stilichonis
  3.28, 186
De raptu Proserpinae
  1.190, 324
  3.231, 324
  2.43, 320
  2.176, 91
Epithalamium dictum Honorio Augusto et Mariae
  10.57, 317
  10.85, 324
  85–96, 318
In Eutropium
  1.194, 394
In Rufinum
  1.204–16, 381

CLAUDIANUS, MAMERTUS
De statu animae
  Praef., 176
  1.21, 395
Epistula ad Sapaudum
  204.22–4, 298

CODEX EURICANUS
  227, 76

CODEX THEODOSIANUS
  3.17.4, 196
  6.28.7, 183
  9.19.4 pr., 213
  9.34.1–10, xxi

COLUMELLA
  1.9.4–6, 253
  2.2.3, 242
  3.3.1, 103
  3.3.8, 253
  8.3.7, 104
  8.16.5, 388
  8.17.3, 105
  12.1.2, 337
  12.18.3, 385
  4.18.2, 392

CORNELIUS NEPOS see NEPOS, CORNELIUS

CARMINA LATINA EPIGRAPHICA (CE/CLE)
  52, 236, 240
  237, 239
  403.1, 330
  429.1, 313
  492, 240
  539, 244
  656, 241
  675.1, 231
  843, 241
  876.1, 313
  959 B, 240
  1136, 239

1140, 241
1205.1, 313
1307, 241
1307.10, 243
1311, 240
1355, 244
1431, 240
1448, 315
1551 D, 241
1592.1, 313
1950.11, 330
2024.1, 330
2035.4, 314

CORPUS INSCRIPTIONUM LATINARUM (CIL)
2.3596, 101
5.2095, 242
6.8012, 114
6.8750, 271
8.8854, 242
8.11294, 225
8.12952, 226
9.1455, 393
10.1483, 225
10.1804, 231
11.298, 239
12.2660, 214
13.2104.7, 237

CURTIUS RUFUS
3.4.8, 92
4.7.22, 92

DAMASUS
Carmina
12.1, 143

DIOGENES LAERTIOS
De clarorum philosophorum vitis
6.2.51, 360

DIOMEDES GRAMMATICUS
Ars grammatica
1.299.2, 298

DONATUS
Ars maior
3.6, 64

ENNODIUS
Carmina
2.1, 237
2.2, 237
2.5, 237
2.6, 237
2.10, 318

2.10.2, 120, 314
2.10.3–4, 321
2.10.5–6, 320
2.20, 313
2.128–9, 251
Dictiones
10.13, 317
Epistulae
2.26.3, 214
7.26, 265

EURIPIDES
Bacchae 96

EUSTATHIUS
In Hexameron Basilii
6.8.5, 89

EUTROPIUS
2.8, 185

FAUSTUS OF RIEZ
Epistulae ad Ruricium aliosque
265.9, 1, 216

FIRMICUS MATERNUS
Mathesis
1.7.3, 386
3.6.9, 225
3.6.12, 225

FRONTINUS
Strategmata
1.6.2, 352

FRONTO
Ad M. Antoninum de eloquentia liber
2.4, 70
Epistulae
1.3, 190
1.9, 190

GALEN
De methodo medendi
11.10, 283

GELLIUS, AULUS
Atticae noctes
Praef. 4, xx n. 56, 333
Praef. 13, 175
1.18.3, 365
4.8.7, 273
6.3.8, 335
11.1.1, 155
11.7.3, 304
12.1.8, 112

13.11.4, 274
13.11.5a, 274
13.11.5c, 274
13.14.16, 230
13.21.16, 155
14.5.4, 202
16.5.3, 102
16.12.4, 101
18.13.6, 158
19.12.9, 163

GREGORY OF TOURS
Gloria martyrum
   64, 354
Histories
   2.16, 318
   2.17, 320
   2.24, 58
   3.2, 354
   3.12, 354
   4.12, 71
   6.30, 223

HERODOTUS
   1.212, 66
   1.214, 66
   2.150, 382
   3.80, 60

HERMAS (PASTOR HERMAE)
Similitudines
   2.3, 297

HESIOD
Theogonia
   758–9, 231

HIERONYMUS see JEROME

HILARY OF POITIERS
In Evangelium Matthaei commentarius
   10.2, 297
Tractatus super Psalmos
   63.7, 387

HISTORIA AUGUSTA
Geta
   5.4–5, 148
   5.5, 152

HOMER
Iliad
   2.732, 360
   4.190–219, 360
   6.132–3, 254
   16.672, 231

Odyssey
   1.64, 127
   11.582–92, 387

HORACE
Ars poetica
   14–16, 300
   333, 274
Carmina/Odes
   1.1.9, 394
   1.1.20, 106
   1.2.11, 163
   1.3.16, 162
   1.17, 84
   1.17.17–18, 97
   1.19.5–6, 118
   1.24, 220
   2.10.5, 388, 398
   2.11.13–17, 385
   2.16.35–7, 380
   2.17, 220
   2.18.1–2, 381
   2.18.2, 111
   2.18.8, 133
   2.18.17, 117
   2.20.23–4, 229
   3.1.17–18, 386
   3.1.17–21, 383
   3.1.20–2, 155
   3.1.41, 119
   3.1.41–4, 384
   3.4.21, 153
   3.16, 84
   3.17.15, 373
   3.27.11–12, 151
   3.29.17–24, 90
   3.30.1, 237
   4.8.13, 166
   4.13.7, 329
Epistulae
   1.5, 96, 286
   1.7.8–9, 358
   1.10.13–17, 90
   1.10.20, 105
   1.14.21, 286
   1.18.8, 127
   1.20.1–8, 175
   2.2.180–2, 117
Epodi
   17.53, 203
Saturae
   1.1.49–53, 398
   1.1.82, 358
   1.3.120, 297
   1.5, 267
   1.5.14–15, 149
   1.5.14–17, 326

INDEX LOCORUM

1.5.15–17, 329
1.5.45, 356
2.1, xxi n. 61
2.2, 286
2.2.4, 138
2.2.11, 123
2.3.10, 356
2.3.84, 233
2.4, 286
2.4.42, 169
2.4.86, 310
2.5.7, 394
2.6.16–19, 96
2.6.70–8, 275
2.8, xxi n. 61, 275, 286

HYGINUS
Fabulae
  40.3, 201
  45, 151
  274, 360

INSCRIPTIONES LATINAE CHRISTIANAE VETERES (ILCV)
  1784, 315

ISIDORE OF SEVILLE
Origines
  12.2.25, 148
  12.7.1, 395
  20.1.2, 137

IUVENALIS see JUVENAL

JEROME
Adversus Iovinianum
  1.48, 353
Apologia adversus libros Rufini
  1.17, 297
  1.30, 269
Commentarius in Ezechielem prophetam
  28.45, 216
  40.44, 132
  42.12, 132
Commentarius in librum Iob
  41.23, 132
Commentarius in Michaeam
  2.7, 360
Contra Vigilantium
  1.6, 63
De viris illustribus
  54.1, 268
Epistulae
  1.1, 299
  1.2, 165
  14.10, 329
  14.11, 78

29.1, 263
29.7, 299
31.2, 283
43.3, 388
50.5, 297
57.5, 298
57.5–7, 270
57.12, 297
60.12, 163
60.17, 398
64, xx n. 56, 333
66.7, 309
66.9, 262
66.10, 280
77.2, 309
78.35, 64
84, 270
85.3, 372
107.10, 329
108.32, xx n. 56, 233, 333
108.33, 233
108.33 v. 2, 227
108.34, 231
117.4, 229
125.8, 353
130.14, 120
141.1, 373
Quaestiones hebraicae in genesim
  37.36, 271
Vita Malchi
  1, 299

JORDANES
Getica
  240–1, 57

IULIANUS
Digesta
  2.1.5, 187

IULIUS VICTOR
Ars rhetorica
  27, 74

JUSTINIAN
Institutiones
  3.23.1, 71

JUVENAL
Satires
  1.1–13, 297
  1.6, 287, 288
  1.15, 297
  1.57, 140
  2.7, 262
  3.82, 139
  3.103, 93

434

3.142, 274
3.191, 103
5, 286
5.50, 86, 140
5.110–11, 367
6.61, 262
6.190, 134
6.211, 240
6.246, 93
6.259–60, 86, 93
6.263, 94
6.303–4, 383–4
6.432, 240
6.438–40, 134
6.479, 297
7.182, 119
8.175, 230
8.252, 230
9.69, 149
9.75.8, 119
9.109, 271
10.71, 365
10.219–21, 359
10.362, 383
11, 286
11.175, 117, 119
14.5, 261
14.306–7, 119

LABERIUS, DECIMUS
Mimus
38, 131

LACTANTIUS
De mortibus persecutorum
2.4, 347

Divinae institutiones
1.11.36, 320

LIVY
Ab urbe condita
1.57.6–58.7, 241
3.27.2, 223
3.44–8, 241
4.14.2, 185
8.30.1–35.9, 185
8.30.11, 185
9.16.11–19, 185
9.40.1–14, 185
10.23.1, 314
24.5.3, 388
25.18.4, 305
25.18.7, 127
27.49.2, 238
32.39.8, 388
34.27.5, 388

34.39.13, 134
39.36.12, 214–15
44.6.8, 372
45.35.3, 353

LUCAN
Epigrammata
10, 206
Pharsalia/De bello civili
1.427–8, 172
1.186–7, 239
2.18, 380
2.326–49, 334
5.219–20, 156
5.232, 118
6.690, 152
8.812, 159
9.185, 155
10.110–22, 117
10.111–17, 117
10.114–15, 120
10.114–16, 320
10.115–16, 125
10.122–4, 381
10.159, 384
10.159–63, 383
10.247, 160

LUCIAN
Hippias
5–8, 117

LUCRETIUS
De rerum natura
2.27, 381
2.36, 380
2.92, 331
2.376, 161
4.1147–8, 353
5.9, 359
5.783, 319
5.1216, 92
6.428, 162
6.1179, 359

MACROBIUS AMBROSIUS
  THEODOSIUS
Comment. Somn. Scip.
1.10.16, 364
2.8.4, 309
Saturnalia
1.3.12–15, 148
1.5.11, 158
3.10.2, 297
5.11.25, 309
5.14.7, 310
7.5.2, 201

INDEX LOCORUM

MAMERTUS CLAUDIANUS see
    CLAUDIANUS, MAMERTUS

MANILIUS
Astronomica
    3.287, 272
    3.314, 89
    4.153, 155

MARCELLUS EMPIRICUS
De medicamentis
    36.57, 124

MARTIAL
Epigrams
    1 *Praef.*, 237, 340
    1 *Praef.* 4, 340
    1.3, 175
    1.30.1–2, 230
    1.43, 96
    1.47, 358
    1.47.1–2, 230
    1.49.27, 104
    1.49.35–6, 155
    1.55.5, 119, 121
    1.55.5–8, 117
    1.71.1, 141
    1.88.2–3, 118
    1.92.9, 258
    1.99.10, 289
    2.1.10, 140
    2.16.5, 360
    2.41.15, 112
    2.47, 240
    2.61.3, 230
    3.1, 393
    3.2.3, 258
    3.9.1, 116
    3.44.13, 107
    3.58, 84, 86, 113
    3.58.25, 113
    3.60, 96
    3.63.7, 264
    3.65.8, 385
    3.67.4, 329
    3.82.11, 322
    4.8.4, 276
    4.14.8, 261
    4.14.12, 288
    4.19, 93
    4.19.6–7, 157
    4.25.1, 107
    4.30.8, 171
    4.30.16, 285
    4.42.5–6, 308
    4.43.6, 140
    4.46.16, 381
    4.64, 84, 318
    4.64.9–10, 314
    4.64.18–22, 325
    4.64.19, 328
    4.64.21, 329
    4.64.22, 328
    4.64.28, 326
    4.72.2, 235
    4.85.2, 140
    4.86.11, 287
    5.9, 358–9
    5.18.8, 145
    5.20.3, 374
    5.34, 230
    5.35.3, 355
    5.44.7, 286
    5.64.2, 140
    5.78, 286
    5.78.18, 289
    5.84.3, 261
    6.13.3, 118
    6.17.2, 299
    6.25.1, 227
    6.28, 230
    6.35.6, 272
    6.38.7, 227
    6.42, 86, 119
    6.42.8–10, 106
    6.42.11, 119
    6.42.11–15, 117
    6.42.12–13, 119
    6.42.21, 118
    6.52, 230
    6.53, 358
    6.62.4, 230
    6.86, 140
    7.17, 262
    7.24.3–4, 180
    7.32.7, 157
    7.32.7–8, 158
    7.71, 240
    7.96, 230
    8.3.22, 309
    8.53.8, 119
    8.55.4, 309
    8.61.6, 146
    8.62, 287
    8.67, 272
    8.67.1–2, 272
    8.75.14, 230
    9.2.12, 230
    9.22.8, 140
    9.29, 134
    9.56.11, 113
    9.75.7, 118
    9.75.7–9, 117
    9.75.8, 119
    9.75.9, 119

9.87.1, 140
9.91.2, 259
9.98.1–2, 392
10.2.3, 337
10.12, 96
10.20.7–8, 122
10.29.4, 322
10.30, 84
10.30.16–18, 143
10.48, 286
10.48.1–4, 279
10.48.6, 110
10.51.6, 396–7
10.53, 230
10.53.3, 244
10.58.3, 149
10.61, 230
10.62, 86, 89, 297
10.62.6–7, 92
10.62.6–12, 95
10.62.10, 297
10.63, 230, 237
10.63.5–8, 238
10.64, 340
10.64.4, 309
10.66.3, 258
10.79.3–4, 108
10.87.16, 381
10.96.11–12, 397
10.97.1, 231
10.104.5–7, 328
11.3.8, 309
11.6.2, 261
11.13, 230
11.13.5, 239, 240
11.13.7, 239
11.18.20, 395
11.31.18, 274
11.52.3–4, 279
11.69, 230
11.91.1, 230
12.17.6, 140
12.18.5, 93
12.18.17–18, 397
12.18.19–20, 104
12.38.1, 264
12.50.4, 117
12.50.5, 132
12.53.3–5, 388
12.60.12, 121
12.62.12, 301
12.74.4, 384
12.82.1–6, 158
13.1.7, 261
13.3.4, 235
13.34, 220
14.1.3, 261
14.39, 333

14.43, 333
14.44.2, 333
14.45–8, 157
14.75.1–2, 151
14.80, 297
14.87, 110, 137
14.94.1, 381
14.94.2, 384
14.102.2, 381
14.109, 140
14.116, 86 140
14.117–18, 140
14.118.1, 140
14.124, 397
14.126, 93
14.163, 158
14.194.2, 236

MARTIANUS CAPELLA
1.75, 316
3.224, 297
3.226, 337
5.533, 288
6.608, 129
6.665, 348

MAXIMIANUS
Elegiae
   1.30, 310
   2.49, 151

MINUCIUS FELIX
17.10, 347

NEPOS, CORNELIUS
Atticus
   13.6–14.3, 275
   15.1, 243

OPPIAN
Halieutica
   3.72–8, 144
   3.79–84, 144
   4.47–64, 165

OROSIUS
Historiae adversus paganos
   6.3.1, 65
   6.6.5–7, 65
   7.43.6, 76–7

OVID
Amores
   1.4.15, 389
   1.5.9, 339
   1.15, 339
   2.4.39–40, 308

3.6.91, 128
3.9.61–6, 339
Ars amatoria
  1.263, 353
  1.271, 149
  2.491, 360
  2.112, 207
  2.643–4, 308
  2.657–8, 308
  3.170, 380
  3.189–92, 308
  3.270, 308
  3.329–48, 339
  3.443, 385
Epistulae ex Ponto (Pont.)
  1.5.19, 337
  1.10.13, 278
  2.4.1, 348
  4.8.31–2, 118
  4.14.56, 185
Fasti
  1.317–34, 63
  1.402, 324
  2.775, 92
  2.853, 395
  3.394, 206
  3.493, 308
  3.731, 384
Heroides
  2.128, 161
  7.2, 150
  12.30, 389
  20.137, 358
Ibis
  396, 238
  613, 226
Metamorphoses
  1.570, 164
  1.572–3, 163
  1.689–712, 153
  2.338–9, 121
  2.627, 244
  2.680, 256
  2.689, 167
  3.59, 171
  3.144, 157
  3.195, 108
  3.207, 255
  3.586–7, 145
  4.589, 152
  5.317, 389
  5.461, 144
  6.426–674, 151
  6.668–9, 152
  7.465, 118
  7.614, 373
  8.611–724, 156
  8.680, 296
  9.282, 77
  10.659, 77
  11.166, 380
  11.500, 317
  12.158, 153
  15.371, 378
  15.548, 103
  15.574, 167
Remedia amoris
  196, 163
  327, 308
  546, 360
Tristia
  1.1, 175
  1.2.25, 162
  1.7.30, 337
  2.224, 307
  2.309, 241
  2.427–68, 339
  2.441–2, 334
  3.1, 175
  3.4.11–12, 143
  3.10.24, 141
  3.10.59, 327
  4.1.5–8, 328
  4.16, 339

PACIANUS
Paraenesis sive exhortatorius libellus ad paenitentiam
  9, 358

PALLADIUS
  6.11.3, 114

PANEGYRICI LATINI
  2(12).1.3, 204
  3(11).3.2, 213
  4(9).20.2, 177

PASSIO CORONAE
  4, 130

PASSIO PAULI
  13, 77

PAULINUS OF NOLA
Carmina
  4.17, 225
  6.68, 142
  10.203, 396
  17.109, 329
  19.577, 394
  21.85, 388
  21.588, 114
  23.101, 388
  25.56, 342

27.2, 238
27.378, 324
27.387–8, 316
27.485, 324
27.580–86, 320
27.584–5, 313
28.9, 324
28.28–30, 316
Epistulae
22.2, 142
32, 313
32.4, 304
32.5, 328
32.10, 313, 318, 319, 323
32.12, 330
32.13, 315
32.17 v. 22, 119
34.4, 365
49.12, 384
50.14, 365–6

PAULINUS PELLAEUS (of Pella)
Eucharisticus deo sub ephemeridis meae textu
205–6, 128
207, 138

PAULUS, JULIUS
Digesta
28.6.43, 187

PERSIUS
Satirae
4.17, 286
5.62, 285

PETRONIUS
Satyrica
26.7–78.8, 286
27.2, 322
27.3, 260
28.8, 322
31.9, 273
34.5, 110
38.5, 380, 382
42.5, 359
47.1, 384
48.4, 262
53.10, 337
54.4, 380
55.6, 395
64.6, 322
66, 274
70.10, 322
70.13, 322
79.4, 125
100.4, 78
131.9, 389

PHAEDRUS
Fabulae
1.11.4, 169
1.14, 359
2.7.5, 154
4.5.25, 394

PLATON
Phaedrus
230c, 149

PLAUTUS
Amphitruo
354, 289
360, 289
Aulularia
88, 257
357, 152
465, 150
Bacchides
279, 169
431, 132
578, 289
748, 289
833, 280
1205, 214
Captivi
849, 150
Cistellaria
110, 376
549, 132
Curculio
112, 255
Epidicus
632, 301
Menaechmi
359, 182
Mercator
193, 169
Miles gloriosus
277, 148
618–23, 204
729, 165
789, 133
1182, 143
Mostellaria
153, 148
956, 222
1115, 274
Persa
772, 141
Poenulus
75, 127
274, 141
Pseudolus
161, 314
427, 122

432, 165
453, 122
1128, 165
1164, 301
Rudens
  112, 173
  598, 395
  604, 151
  729, 280
  1077, 301
Stichus
  309, 77
Truculentus
  95, 122
  400, 122

PLINY THE YOUNGER
Epistulae
  1.1, 63
  1.1.1, xvi n. 42
  1.2, 270
  1.2.1, 71, 365
  1.2.3, 257
  1.2.6, 236
  1.3, xvii, xx n. 54, 295
  1.3.1, 106, 253
  1.3.3, 396
  1.5, xiv, xvii, 83
  1.5.8, 60
  1.5.9, 197
  1.5.10, 79
  1.5.16, 79
  1.6, 83
  1.6.1, 62, 174
  1.7.5, 296
  1.8.2, 262
  1.8.3, 337
  1.8.5, 174
  1.8.6, 155
  1.8.13, 71
  1.9, xvii, 85
  1.10, xvii
  1.10.2, 207
  1.11.2, 331
  1.12, xvii
  1.12.5, 355
  1.12.9, 216
  1.12.12, 233
  1.13, xvii, 296
  1.14, xvii, 190, 192
  1.14.1, 240
  1.14.5–6, 191
  1.14.8, 195, 241
  1.15, 96, 275
  1.16, xvii
  1.16.6, 196
  1.19.4, 208
  1.20, xiv, xvii, 270

  1.20.16, 253
  1.22, xvii
  1.22.1, 361
  1.24.4, 394
  2.1, 60
  2.1.10, 192, 228
  2.3.7, 236
  2.5, 292
  2.5.1, 365
  2.5.10, 71
  2.5.13, 175
  2.7, xvii, 219
  2.7.4, 302
  2.8, xx n. 54, 295
  2.8.1, 142
  2.9, xvii, 190
  2.10, 219
  2.11, 345, 351
  2.11.4, 257
  2.11.13, 389
  2.11.14, 272
  2.12, 345, 351
  2.12.6, 181
  2.12.7, 301
  2.13, xvii, 190
  2.13.1, 192, 208
  2.13.8, 192
  2.15.2, 99
  2.16, xvii
  2.17, xvi n. 44, xvii, 85, 87, 98, 146, 159, 248
  2.17.1, 88, 250
  2.17.3, 89
  2.17.4, 122
  2.17.4–5, 130
  2.17.5, 128, 131, 137
  2.17.6, 130
  2.17.7, 106, 128, 135
  2.17.8, 147–8, 262, 263, 332
  2.17.9, 105, 133, 134
  2.17.10, 135, 136, 385
  2.17.11, 86, 104, 107, 122, 123, 279
  2.17.12, 135, 136, 158, 385
  2.17.13, 128, 130, 163, 394–5
  2.17.13–15, 253
  2.17.14, 163
  2.17.15, 130, 136, 324, 385
  2.17.16, 107
  2.17.16–20, 132
  2.17.17, 121
  2.17.18, 253
  2.17.20, 130, 131, 136
  2.17.21, 264
  2.17.22, 134, 147
  2.17.23, 105
  2.17.24, 134, 136
  2.17.25, 127
  2.17.28, 142

INDEX LOCORUM

2.17.29, 356, 394
2.18, 95, 296
2.19, 219
2.19.7, 155
2.20, xiv, xvii
2.20.2, 240
2.20.5, 355
3.1, xvii
3.1.1, 252
3.1.2–3, 375
3.1.8, 158, 279
3.1.11, 134, 192
3.2, xvii, 190
3.2.4, 139, 197
3.3, xvii, 190
3.3.1, 191
3.3.3, 114
3.3.6, 115
3.4, xvii
3.4.6, 208
3.5.1, 332
3.5.7, 175
3.5.11, 276
3.5.14, 279
3.5.17, 287
3.5.19, 298
3.5.20, 175
3.7, xx n. 54, 295
3.7.1, 361
3.7.8, 262
3.8, xvii
3.9, xvii
3.9.8, 257
3.9.27, 176
3.10.4, 365
3.13.5, 135
3.14, 363
3.14.6, 230, 377
3.15, 296
3.15.1, 234
3.16.12, 264
3.18.6, 195
3.18.10, 174
3.19, 248
3.19.2, 252
3.19.5, 253
3.20, xvii
3.21, xvii, xxii n. 69, 219
3.21.1, 392
3.21.2–5, 116
3.21.5, 244, 307
3.21.6, 348
4.2, xiv, xvii
4.2.5, 67
4.3, xvii, 296
4.4, xvii
4.4.3, 208
4.6.1, 398

4.7, xiv, xvii
4.8, xvii, 180
4.9, xvii
4.10, xvii
4.12, xvii
4.12.1, 295
4.13, 95
4.13.1, 296
4.14, 234
4.14.2, 232, 304–5
4.14.8–9, 232
4.15, xvii
4.15.3, 228
4.15.6, 302
4.16, 296
4.17, xvii
4.19, xvii
4.19.2, 241, 332
4.19.2–5, 335
4.19.5, 99
4.20, xx n. 54, 295
4.20.2, 177
4.21, xvii
4.21.2, 195, 228
4.22, xvii
4.23, xvii
4.23.1, 332, 374
4.24, xvii
4.25.4, 174
4.27, xx n. 54, 295
4.27.4, xxii n. 69, 244, 307
4.27.5, 365
4.28.1, 262
4.29, xvii
4.30, xvii, 85
4.30.2, 136, 159, 164
4.30.9, 166
5.1, xvii
5.3, 234
5.3.1, 235
5.3.5, 334, 340
5.4, xvii
5.5.3, 332
5.6, xvi n. 44, xvii, 83, 85, 87, 89, 98, 146, 159, 248
5.6.1–2, 96
5.6.3, 98
5.6.3–6, 90
5.6.4, 97, 175
5.6.7, 156
5.6.8, 101, 104
5.6.9, 253
5.6.12, 285
5.6.15, 131, 133
5.6.15–23, 130
5.6.17, 253
5.6.19, 128, 131, 132, 156
5.6.20, 117, 163, 170

5.6.20–1, 136
5.6.21, 134, 385
5.6.22, 117, 148
5.6.23, 127, 128, 130, 131
5.6.24, 117, 135, 164
5.6.24–5, 105
5.6.25, 107, 123, 284
5.6.25–6, 86, 107, 279
5.6.26, 104
5.6.27, 158
5.6.27–8, 136
5.6.27–30, 253
5.6.27–31, 132
5.6.28, 130, 132
5.6.29, 135
5.6.29–31, 128
5.6.30, 121
5.6.31, 135, 136
5.6.32, 147
5.6.32–3, 132
5.6.33, 105
5.6.35, 91, 99
5.6.36, 117, 118, 137, 167, 169, 176
5.6.37, 148
5.6.38, 117
5.6.39, 156
5.6.40, 117, 132, 175
5.6.41, 175, 295
5.6.44, 175, 176
5.6.45, 96, 391, 396
5.7, xvii
5.8.2, 373
5.8.10, 365
5.9, xvii
5.10.1–2, 232
5.10.3, 337
5.12.2, 71
5.13, xvii
5.14, xvii, 180
5.14.8, 202
5.16, xvi, xvii, 219, 226
5.16.1, 195, 222
5.16.2, 128, 224
5.16.3, 216, 332, 361
5.16.9, 226
5.16.11, 361
5.17, xvii, xx n. 54, 295, 296
5.17.2, 301
5.18.1, 373, 398
5.19, xvii
5.19.7, 96
5.20.8, 287
5.21, xvii
6.1, xvii, 345
6.2, xiv, xvii
6.2.5–6, 272
6.3.1, 398
6.4, xvii

6.4.1, 96
6.4.4, 62
6.5, xvii
6.5.7, 213
6.6, xvii
6.6.9, 78
6.7.1, 62
6.7.2, 332
6.8, xvii
6.8.1, 295
6.8.9, 135
6.9, xvii
6.10, xvii
6.10.4, 219
6.11, xvii, 296
6.13, xvii
6.15.2, 348
6.16.14, 136
6.16.20, 231
6.18, xvii
6.19, xvii
6.19.4, 192
6.20.2, 279
6.20.3, 387
6.21, xvii, xx n. 54, 295, 296
6.22, xvii
6.23, xvii, 296
6.23.1, 62, 214
6.24.2, 62
6.26.1, 191, 192, 225
6.26.2, 296
6.27.3, 331
6.29, xvii
6.31, xvii
6.32.2, 195
6.33, xvii
6.33.8, 275
6.33.11, 270
7.1, xvii
7.1.1, 198, 361
7.1.7, 216
7.2.2, 365
7.3, xvii, 87, 391
7.3.1, 62
7.3.2, 397
7.4.1, 232
7.4.3, 232
7.4.6, xxii n. 69, 244, 307
7.4.8, 232
7.5.1, 99, 136
7.6, xvii
7.8, xvii
7.9.4, 257
7.9.7, 174
7.9.11, xxii n. 69, 244, 307
7.9.16, 175
7.10, xvii
7.11.5, 99

7.12.6, 235
7.14.1, 214
7.16, xvii
7.17.2, 71
7.17.4, 332
7.17.7, 71
7.18, xx n. 54, 295
7.19, xvii
7.19.1, 358, 361
7.19.4, 241, 242
7.19.7, 242, 361
7.20.3, 234
7.21.2, 132
7.22, xvii
7.22.1, 361
7.23.1, 296
7.24.1, 128
7.26, xvii
7.26.3, 396
7.27.5, 177
7.27.9, 148
7.28, xvii
7.29.2, 219
7.30, xvii
7.30.1, 361
7.31, xvii
8.1, xvii
8.1.1, 96, 361
8.1.3, 96
8.3.1, 181
8.4, xx n. 54, 295
8.4.7, 337
8.5, xvii, 219
8.5.1, 224–5
8.5.2, 243
8.5.3, 348
8.6.12, 296
8.6.13–15, 219
8.6.14, 233
8.8, xvii, 85
8.8.2, 103
8.8.3–4, 353
8.8.4, 167, 285, 324
8.8.7, 125
8.9.2, 245
8.10, xvii
8.10.2, 228
8.11, xvii
8.14, xvii
8.15.2, 288
8.16.5, 192
8.17.1, 285
8.20, xvi n. 44, xvii, 85, 159
8.20.3, 94
8.20.4, 167
8.20.7, 161
8.21, 234
8.21.2, 264

8.22.1, 69
8.23, xvii
8.23.7, 196
8.24.2, 126–7
8.28.1, 262
9.2.2, 270
9.3.1, 396
9.6.1, 62, 397
9.7.2, xvii, 85
9.7.4, 142, 177, 253
9.9, xvii
9.9.2, 219, 243
9.11.2, 236
9.13, xxi n. 61
9.13.1, 214
9.13.21, 60, 331
9.13.26, 175
9.15.3, 253
9.16, xvii, 391
9.16.2, 116
9.17, 275
9.19, xvii
9.19.1, 219
9.23.4, 139
9.25.1, 295
9.25.3, 192
9.26.4, 352
9.26.8, 209, 375
9.28.5, 331
9.30, xvii
9.30.2, 143
9.33, xx n. 54, 295
9.34.1, 392
9.36, xvii, 89, 98, 248, 391
9.36.3, 132
9.36.4, 275
9.37.1, 296
9.39.4, 125
9.39.5, 326
9.40, xvii, 63, 89, 98, 248, 391
9.40.2, 278
9.48, 166
10.5.1, 208
10.6.3, 208
10.26.1, 208
10.37.2, 124
10.81.7, 262
Panegyricus
2.7, 216
5.4, 377
23.3, 388
25.1, 176
30.2, 92
44.4, 375
49.6, 289
49.7, 275
51.5, 74
58.3, 139

443

61.2, 139
72.4, 377
82.8, 216
83.1, 74

PLINY THE ELDER
Naturalis historia
  Praef. 18, xx n. 56, 333
  1.36.3, 121–2
  2.22, 377
  2.123, 162
  2.207, 314
  3.37, 250
  3.148, 329
  4.30, 103
  4.64, 118
  4.67, 118
  4.105, 81
  5.151, 118
  7.137–8, 368
  7.153, 151
  7.188–90, 229
  7.206, 169
  9.62–3, 383
  9.127, 120, 380
  9.137, 380
  9.138, 380
  10.46, 150
  11.107, 149
  11.283, 166
  12.13, 156
  12.42, 169
  12.62–5, 385
  13.48, 169
  13.68–76, 170
  14.30, 107
  14.56, 394
  14.93, 394
  14.107, 384
  16.4, 169
  16.166, 329
  16.177, 94
  16.178, 169
  16.225, 114
  16.236, 227
  17.11, 162
  17.141, 104
  18.363, 150
  21.114, 165
  22.115, 142
  23.32, 358
  23.74, 361
  23.88, 123–4
  23.142, 361
  25.77, 283
  26.36, 169
  27.25, 169
  29.11, 358

29.16–27, 359
29.64, 355
30.52, 134
31.4, 323
31.40, 140
32.95, 161
33.68, 321
33.142, 273
34.93, 227
35.2–3, 320
35.154, 120
36.7, 122
36.14, 118
36.44, 320
36.46, 320
36.48, 118
36.55, 119
36.57, 121
36.63, 120
36.91, 201
36.95, 160
36.157, 120
36.198, 321
37.45, 231
37.120, 321
37.181, 322

PLUTARCH
Cicero
  20.2, 335
Sulla
  34.2–3, 368

POLEMIUS SILVIUS
  p. 544.18, 144

PROBUS
In Vergilium commentarius
4.371, 167

PROPERTIUS
Elegies
  1.2.27–8, 341
  1.3.6, 167
  1.7.11, 341
  1.11.23, 100
  2.1.3–4, 341
  2.1.59, 360
  2.11.6, 341
  2.13.11, 341
  2.18.20, 328
  2.24.21, 341
  2.25.42, 308
  2.26.25–6, 341
  2.31, 318
  2.32.20, 353
  2.33.40, 140

2.33b.39–40, 384
2.34.83–4, 150
2.34.85–94, 339, 341
3.8.37, 353
3.15.41–2, 254
4.7.28, 233
4.9.3, 173

PRUDENTIUS
Cathemerinon
   3.101–5, 318
   4.72, 328
   9.103, 238
   11.104, 348
Contra Symmachum
   2.68, 309
Epilogus
   8, 260
Peristephanon
   2.540, 396
   3.198–200, 318
   3.200, 388
   5.556, 231
   7.81, 329
   8, 313, 316
   10.261, 396
   10.837–8, 329
   12.42, 316
   12.49–50, 316, 317
   12.51, 118, 317
   12.53, 319
   12.53–4, 318
   12.54, 321
Psychomachia
   370, 381
   823–87, 318
   851, 315, 319
   855, 321
   856, 319
   862–3, 321

PS.-DEMETRIUS
De elocutione
   223, 62
   228, 174

QUEROLUS SIVE AULULARIA
   p. 21.18–19, 396

QUINTILIAN
Institutio oratoria
   1.1.14, 375
   1.5, 299
   1.9.6, 275
   2.14.1–2, 336
   2.17.40, 203
   3.5.11, 334
   3.5.15, 235
   4.2.22, 64
   4.2.118, 365
   5.8.2, 365
   6.3.44, 99
   8.3.32, 369
   10.1.68, 264
   10.1.95, 266
   10.2.27, 204
   10.3.25–7, xx, 333
   10.4.4, 337
   10.5.13, 334

QUODVULTDEUS
De cantico novo
   (*Serm.* 5) 2, 328, 329

RURICIUS
Epistulae
   1.1.1, 204, 373
   1.1.3, 216, 359, 361
   1.3–5, 291
   1.3.2, 70, 116
   1.3.3, 299
   1.4.1, 346
   1.5.2, 105
   1.10.2, 180
   1.11, 251
   1.11.1, 156
   1.11.2, 90, 148
   1.13.1, 346
   1.15.3, 368
   1.17.2, 160
   2.4.1, 245, 377
   2.4.2, 240
   2.9.3, 258
   2.20, 344
   2.28.2, 368
   2.32, 350
   2.40.1, 346
   2.41.1, 346
   2.54, 344
   2.54.1, 353

RUTILIUS NAMATIANUS
De reditu suo
   1.269–70, 115, 116
   1.309–12, 63
   1.370, 329
   1.616–17, 162

SALLUST
De bello Iugurthino
   18.8, 122
   85.39–43, 275
   95.3, 184

De coniuratione Catilinae
  1, 369
  2.2, 369
  3.1, 69
  5, 65
  5.4, 67, 69, 70, 71, 369
  15.1, 368
  20.4, 369
  22.1, 66
  24.2, 67
In M. Tullium invectiva (PS.-SALLUST)
  3, 73

SALVIANUS
Ad ecclesiam
  4.33, 381

SENECA THE YOUNGER
Ad Helviam
  10, 275
Agamemnon
  130, 206
  348, 153
  857–8, 317
Apocolocyntosis
  9.1, 122
De beneficiis
  1.9.3, 160
  1.9.4, 227
  4.6.2, 120, 314
  4.12.3, 96
  5.16.3, 358
  7.9.2–3, 273
  7.9.3, 384
  7.26.5, 369
De brevitate vitae
  10.16, 374
De clementia
  1.16.4, 387
De ira
  2.15.4, 372
  2.28.7–8, 60
  2.28.8, 69
De tranquillitate animi
  9.4, 261–2
  9.9.7, 298
Epistulae morales
  3, 209
  6, 209
  8.1, xx, 333
  8.3, 145
  15.3, 273
  17.1, 78
  41.6, 316
  43.5, 213
  47.7, 73
  52.5, 347
  55.1, 253
  56.1, 158
  56.2, 107
  56.4, 328
  62.3, 380
  64.1, 258
  66.53, 269
  71.23, 298
  73.9, 208
  84.11, 197
  86.4–12, 106
  86.6, 117, 119, 319
  87.7, 131
  90.9, 385
  90.15, 385
  90.42, 169
  95.15–29, 275
  95.43, 230
  104.1, 96
  104.6, 96, 258
  104.33, 157
  108.10, 309
  110.12–20, 275
  113.26, 299
  115.9, 316
  119.3–16, 275
  122, 275
  123.7, 273
Fragmenta
  13,61 (Haase), 335
Hercules furens
  468–9, 385
  483, 127
  540, 161
Medea
  90, 329
Naturales quaestiones
  4.2.2, 392
  5.16.1, 315
  5.16.3, 315
  6.20.6, 125
Thyestes
  391–5, 367
Troades
  836, 118

SERVIUS
Commentarius in Vergilii Aeneida
  1.698, 137
Commentarius in Vergilii eclogas
  1.2, 311
Commentarius in Vergilii georgica
  2.437, 159

SIDONIUS
Carmina
Carm. 1: Preface to the Panegyric of Anthemius
  1.9, 153, 155
  1.16, 153
  1.17–20, 360
Carm. 2: Panegyric of Anthemius
  2, x, 79
  2.25–6, 198
  2.89, 303
  2.90, 183
  2.96, 377, 380
  2.144–6, 255
  2.146, 163
  2.150–2, 360
  2.173, 193
  2.182–92, 267
  2.186, 332
  2.187–8, 337
  2.190, 266
  2.198, 396
  2.206, 369
  2.207, 183
  2.208, 303
  2.214, 377
  2.287, 154
  2.294, 154
  2.318–31, 279
  2.334, 317
  2.336, 163
  2.337, 70
  2.343, 151
  2.365, 230
  2.376, 343
  2.400, 94
  2.401, 264
  2.402, 101
  2.418–19, 120, 322
  2.422–3, 294
  2.427–8, 157
  2.458–60, 368
  2.481, 380
  2.502, 308
  2.513, 230
  2.515, 225
  2.529, 146
  2.537, 93
Carm. 3: *Editio ad libellum*
  3.10, 212
Carm. 4: Preface to the Panegyric of Majorian
  4, 370
  4.1, 154
  4.6, 153
  4.17–18, 365
Carm. 5: Panegyric of Majorian
  5, x, 370
  5.14, 104
  5.27, 170
  5.28, 225
  5.34–6, 120
  5.34–9, 117
  5.35–6, 119
  5.37, 119
  5.37–8, 121
  5.38–9, 119, 321
  5.39, 167
  5.50–1, 120
  5.57, 183
  5.91, 108
  5.126, 225, 281
  5.201, 74
  5.210, 141
  5.226–7, 385
  5.229, 328
  5.273, 229
  5.287–9, 180
  5.303, 135
  5.305–6, 370
  5.340, 289
  5.373, 153
  5.400, 317
  5.408, 163
  5.453, 146
  5.470–83, 292
  5.495, 155
  5.523, 332
  5.535, 168
  5.546, 396
  5.555–7, 368
  5.563, 74, 397
  5.568, 153
  5.577, 396
  5.591, 122
  5.592, 163
Carm. 6: Preface to the Panegyric of Avitus
  6, 339, 370
  6.26, 168
  6.30–1, 153
  6.36, 153
Carm. 7: Panegyric of Avitus
  7, ix, 339, 340, 370
  7.14, 153, 229
  7.17, 281
  7.17.6, 380
  7.27, 170
  7.43, 253
  7.74–6, 293
  7.79–82, 293, 368
  7.80, 186
  7.126, 377
  7.219, 397
  7.139–40, 172
  7.139–52, 61

7.156, 178, 182
7.157, 183
7.164, 296
7.174, 153
7.277, 104
7.319–28, 293
7.325–6, 142
7.331, 229
7.359, 370
7.360, 366
7.371, 169, 170
7.376, 366
7.383, 225
7.407–10, 92
7.412, 108
7.434, 288
7.457, 386
7.464, 366
7.495–6, 76
7.520, 222
7.542, 380
7.571, 163
7.579, 222
7.586, 163
7.594, 380
Carm. 8: Editio libelli
  8.3, 234
  8.5, 212
  8.7–10, x n. 13
  8.10, 155
Carm. 9: Excusatoria ad v.c. Felicem
  9, 60, 178, 183, 232, 295
  9.5, 183
  9.9, 287
  9.16, 256, 371–2
  9.18, 153, 371
  9.21, 151
  9.46, 253
  9.94–100, 293
  9.110, 222
  9.130, 153
  9.135, 360
  9.187, 113
  9.211–16, 340
  9.211–317, 292
  9.215, 153
  9.218, 265
  9.233, 229
  9.237, 264
  9.239, 339
  9.239–58, 340
  9.259, 339, 340
  9.260, 339, 342
  9.261, 153
  9.263, 339, 341
  9.266, 339, 340
  9.268, 332
  9.270, 339, 348

9.276, 153
9.300, 186
9.304, 336
9.305, 116
9.313, 153
9.315, 309
9.318, 153
9.325, 384
9.330, 178
9.341, 153
Carm. 10: Preface to the Epithalamium for Ruricius and Hiberia
  10, 291, 332, 344
  10.3, 113, 138
  10.6, 317
  10.17, 153
Carm. 11: Epithalamium for Ruricius and Hiberia
  11, xix n. 50, 317, 332
  11.17, 119
  11.17–18, 119
  11.17–19, 120
  11.17–26, 117
  11.17–28, 293
  11.18, 119
  11.53, 183
  11.66, 201
  11.87, 113
  11.96, 120
  11.98, 317
  11.106, 317, 385
  11.114, 377
Carm. 12: Epigramma ad v.c. Ommatium
  12, 68, 232, 339
  12.2, 332
  12.10, 153
  12.11, 153
  12.12–13, 183
  12.15, 70, 257
  12.19, 258
  12.20, 153
  12.22, xxi n. 61
Carm. 13: Epigram to Majorian
  13, 370
  13.1–20, 293
  13.21–40, 232
  13.25–6, 63
  13.35, 134, 153
  13.36, 96
Carm. 14: Preface to the Epithalamium for Polemius and Araneola
  14, 232, 332
  14.1, 234, 332
  14.2, 265
  14.4 v. 6, 153
  14.4 v. 7, 287
  14.4 v. 11, 197

14.4 v. 21, 241
14.4 v. 27, 360
Carm. 15: Epithalamium for Polemius and Araneola
15, 332
15.24, 230
15.32, 254
15.37, 201
15.70, 124
15.75, 388
15.81, 258
15.126, 129
15.127–8, 120
15.128, 380, 381
15.129, 120
15.136, 229
15.141–3, 293
Carm. 16: Eucharisticon ad Faustum episcopum
16, 293
16.1–6, 153
16.2, 386
16.18, 64, 173
16.27, 329
16.35, 64
16.40, 64
16.45, 220
16.46, 230
16.47, 64
16.64, 64
16.79–80, 91
16.80, 105
16.82, 91
16.89, 332
16.107, 141
16.123, 230
16.127–8, 63
Carm. 17: Birthday invitation to Ommatius
17, 363
17.5–20, 273
17.6, 110
17.7–8, 138
17.10, 120
17.11, 383
17.15, 383
17.17, 393
17.19–20, 80
Carm. 18: The baths of his villa
18, 84, 86, 88, 115–16
18.1, 98, 99
18.3, 107, 303
18.3–4, 108, 281
18.4, 265
18.5, 128
18.5–6, 126
18.7–8, 168
18.7–10, 144
18.8, 159
18.9–10, 166

Carm. 19: On the swimming pool
19, 84, 86, 88, 115–16, 283
19.1, 103
19.1–2, 124
Carm. 20: To Ecdicius
20.3, 225
Carm. 21: On fish caught at night
21, 43
Carm. 22: Burgus Pontii Leontii
22, x n. 15, 84, 86–7, 117
22.1, 332, 358
22.2, 279
22.3, 99, 150, 212, 222
22.4 v. 8, 93
22.4 v. 12, 153
22.4 v. 10, 207
22.4 v. 20, 153
22.4 v. 23, 328
22.4 vv. 23–40, 279
22.4 v. 41, 343
22.4 v. 47, 225
22.4 v. 49, 151
22.4 v. 73, 317
22.4 v. 98, 225
22.4 v. 110, 159
22.4 vv. 115–19, 314
22.4 v. 117, 212
22.4 v. 121, 343
22.4 vv. 132–3, 163
22.4 vv. 133–4, 171
22.4 vv. 134–41, 86
22.4 v. 135, 103
22.4 vv. 135–6, 323–4
22.4 vv. 136–41, 117
22.4 v. 138, 119
22.4 v. 139, 167, 321
22.4 v. 140, 118
22.4 v. 141, 125
22.4 v. 142, 110
22.4 v. 146, 120
22.4 vv. 146–7, 294
22.4 v. 147, 317
22.4 v. 149, 303
22.4 v. 154–5, 315
22.4 v. 157, 324
22.4 v. 164, 324
22.4 v. 169, 394
22.4 v. 170, 138
22.4 v. 173, 383
22.4 v. 179, 131, 146
22.4 vv. 179–82, 147
22.4 vv. 179–83, 126
22.4 vv. 179–86, 86
22.4 vv. 184–6, 126
22.4 v. 185, 126
22.4 v. 187, 394
22.4 v. 189, 155
22.4 vv. 189–90, 135

22.4 v. 190, 105
22.4 v. 191, 303
22.4 vv. 192–3, 129
22.4 v. 194, 225
22.4 v. 197, 381
22.4 vv. 197–9, 129
22.4 v. 203, 320, 342
22.4 v. 206, 325
22.4 v. 207, 385
22.4 v. 212, 110, 135
22.4 v. 214, 153
22.4 v. 219, 279, 388, 394
22.4 v. 233, 254
22.5, 73, 104, 198, 275, 279
22.6, 103, 174, 235, 300, 342
Carm. 23: *Ad Consentium civem Narbonensem*
23, x n. 15, 232, 292
23.1–7, 309
23.3, 255
23.8, 153
23.20–31, 331
23.21, 303
23.25–7, 305
23.28, 331
23.42, 394
23.69–74, 76
23.88, 286
23.124, 153
23.125, 264
23.131, 337
23.141, 186
23.142, 193
23.144, 337
23.145, 265, 267
23.147, 96
23.150–1, 266
23.156, 176
23.159–61, 339
23.166, 340
23.195, 360
23.205, 153
23.208, 134
23.212, 262
23.223, 129
23.228, 370
23.235, 265
23.253, 70, 259
23.266, 153
23.287, 141
23.306, 153
23.310, 370
23.312, 376
23.327, 105
23.349, 288
23.370, 261
23.376, 163
23.400, 186

23.401, 262
23.411, 124
23.416, 163
23.420, 155
23.421–2, 160
23.423, 370
23.424, 381
23.430, 99
23.434, 255
23.435, 153
23.436–506, 255
23.439, 73
23.444, 303
23.461, 176
23.464–74, 364
23.487–506, 260
23.490–2, 261
23.490–4, 158
23.495, 103
23.495–9, 86, 108
23.498–9, 106
23.500–6, 118
23.501, 153
23.507, 287
23.512, 74
Carm. 24: *Propempticon libelli*
24, 232, 251, 364
24.3, 330
24.5, 256
24.10, 82, 84
24.10–15, 82
24.19, 316, 369
24.26–30, 180
24.32–8, 252
24.34, 251, 277
24.37, 225
24.37–42, 293
24.37–43, 224
24.46, 92
24.46–7, 285
24.50, 286
24.52, 276
24.52–3, 252
24.55, 121, 279
24.67, 132
24.82, 207
24.83, 326, 255
24.91, 178
24.92, 262
24.93, 182
24.96–8, 241
Carm. 27 (in *Ep*. 2.10.4)
27, 294, 311, 312, 317, 318
Carm. 29 (in *Ep*. 4.8.5)
29, 116, 311
Carm. 31 (in *Ep*. 4.18.5)
31, 308, 311

Carm. 33 (in *Ep.* 7.17.2)
  33, 232
Carm. 34 (in *Ep.* 8.9.5)
  34.490–1, 261

Epistulae
Liber 1
  1.1, xi, xvi, 58, 63, 306, 335
  1.1–10, xv
  1.1.1, xvi, xvi n. 42, 130, 181, 265, 301, 302, 334–7
  1.1.2, 107, 213, 264, 366
  1.1.3, xix n. 53, 295, 302, 306, 337
  1.1.4, 287, 289
  1.2, xi, 59, 76, 248, 350, 363
  1.2.1, 133, 174, 176, 183, 207, 302
  1.2.2, 70
  1.2.3, 129, 198
  1.2.4, 139, 195, 207, 375, 388, 397
  1.2.4–5, 255
  1.2.5, 169
  1.2.6, 73, 166, 275, 276, 380, 381, 382, 383
  1.2.6–7, 273
  1.2.7, 72, 158, 207, 276, 278, 383
  1.2.8, 171, 201, 309
  1.2.9, 150, 166, 263, 376
  1.2.10, 174, 208, 376
  1.3, 179, 217–18, 223, 364
  1.3.1, 191, 197, 370
  1.3.2, 95, 183, 223, 260, 296
  1.3.3, 73, 213
  1.4, 179, 364
  1.4.1, 100, 107, 181, 183, 193, 195, 207, 303, 367
  1.4.2, 275
  1.5, xii, 58, 80, 251, 267
  1.5.1, 196, 254, 259, 288, 289
  1.5.2, 77, 102, 251, 256, 346, 347
  1.5.3, 138, 256, 326
  1.5.4, 152, 161, 170, 324, 329, 353
  1.5.5, 154, 209
  1.5.6, 105, 171, 288
  1.5.7, 92, 230, 284, 300
  1.5.8, 251, 355
  1.5.9, 146, 280, 316, 374
  1.5.10, 89, 183, 201, 332, 376
  1.5.11, 255, 308
  1.6, 179, 251, 364, 392
  1.6.2, 68–9, 78, 89, 102, 193, 273
  1.6.3, xiii, 84–5, 89, 122, 278, 296, 369, 396
  1.6.4, 73, 256
  1.7, xii, 59, 80
  1.7.1, 366
  1.7.3, 72, 107, 116, 186, 369
  1.7.4, 189, 199, 251
  1.7.4–5, 199
  1.7.5, 198, 236
  1.7.6, 68, 331
  1.7.7, 201, 202, 361
  1.7.8, 175, 207, 342, 381
  1.7.9, 71, 202, 215, 251
  1.7.11, 167, 214, 285, 287
  1.7.12, 112, 289, 368, 376, 377
  1.7.13, 61, 106, 386
  1.8.1, 89, 255, 357
  1.8.2, 68, 70, 75, 91, 102, 103, 134, 279, 329, 361, 377
  1.8.3, 306, 394
  1.9, xii
  1.9.1, 80, 183, 213, 255, 296, 304
  1.9.2, 181, 193, 213, 386
  1.9.3, 127, 183, 212
  1.9.5, 181, 259
  1.9.5–6, 79
  1.9.6, 302, 304
  1.9.6–7, 153
  1.9.7, 134, 163, 211, 232, 269, 287, 331, 378
  1.9.8, 71, 96, 173, 259, 265, 288, 360
  1.10, xii
  1.10.1, 212
  1.10.2, 148, 163
  1.11, xiii, xiii n. 31, xv, xxi n. 61, xxii n. 66, xxiii, 174, 287, 339, 363
  1.11.1, xiii, xiii n. 32, 396
  1.11.2, 174
  1.11.2–17, 370
  1.11.3, 70
  1.11.5, 96
  1.11.6, 76, 139, 211
  1.11.7, 66, 125, 197, 370
  1.11.9, 68, 230
  1.11.10, 139, 374
  1.11.10–15, 275
  1.11.11, 145, 163
  1.11.12, 184, 288, 366
  1.11.13, 225
  1.11.14, xxi n. 61, 110, 288, 386
  1.11.15, 71, 163, 194, 386
  1.11.16, 60
  1.11.17, 181, 303, 348
Liber 2
  2.1, xi n. 22, xiii, xv, xvii, 57–81, 83, 89, 179–80, 368, 380
  2.1.1, xi n. 22, 88, 270, 353, 377
  2.1.2, 293, 61
  2.1.3, 278
  2.1.4, 349
  2.2, xiii, xiv, xv, xvi, xvi n. 42, xvii, xviii, 82–177, 246–9, 254–5, 261, 271, 338, 351, 356, 363, 391, 397
  2.2.2, 89, 297

INDEX LOCORUM

2.2.3, 242, 324
2.2.4, 123
2.2.4–8, 249
2.2.5, 70, 85, 314, 319
2.2.6, 117, 123
2.2.7, 287
2.2.8, 105, 123, 255
2.2.10, 73, 85, 123, 125, 278
2.2.10–11, 123
2.2.11, 123, 371
2.2.12, 61, 113, 124, 168, 351, 383, 384
2.2.13, 74, 85
2.2.14, 148, 395
2.2.15, xiii, 57, 101, 123, 139, 260
2.2.16, 92, 102, 141
2.2.17, 102, 159, 351
2.2.18, 92, 103, 113, 143, 152
2.2.19, 61
2.2.20, 112, 114, 117, 140
2.2.25, 261
2.3, xi n. 22, xvii, xiv n. 39, 57, 59, 80, 178–88, 199, 205, 345, 363, 364, 367
2.3–7, xv, 218
2.3.2, 107, 173, 189
2.4, xvii, xiv n. 39, 189–98, 200, 210
2.4.1, 104, 183, 207, 240
2.5, xvii, xiv n. 39, 59, 190, 199–204
2.5.1, 203, 216
2.5.2, 216
2.6, xvii, xiv n. 39, 59, 205–209, 345
2.6.1, 61, 110, 173, 187, 191, 192
2.6.1–2, 197
2.6.2, xi n. 22, 61, 124
2.7, xvii, xiv n. 39, 200, 210–16
2.7.1, 110, 176, 187, 192, 216
2.7.2, 61, 201, 204
2.8, xiv, xv, xvi n. 42, xvii, xxi, xxiii, 194, 217–245, 293–4
2.8–10, 345
2.8.1, 101, 110, 207, 238, 239, 244
2.8.1–2, 237
2.8.2, 115, 166, 195, 301
2.8.2–3, xix
2.8.3, xxi, 101, 218, 224, 234, 290, 305
2.8.3 v. 5, 192
2.8.3 vv. 5–6, 207
2.8.3 v. 6, 303
2.8.3 v. 11, 78
2.8.3 v. 13, 175
2.9, xi n. 22, xiv, xv, xvi, xvii, 57, 84, 85, 122, 123, 158, 174, 246–89, 338, 363, 391
2.9.1, 61, 102
2.9.1–2, 99
2.9.2, 124, 173, 289
2.9.3, 99, 145, 193, 213, 255
2.9.4, xix, 104, 128, 157, 158, 202, 223, 236, 251, 293, 326, 332

2.9.4–5, 249
2.9.5, 61, 255
2.9.6, 61, 73, 85, 123, 145, 255, 260, 269, 373, 374
2.9.7, 99, 134, 145, 146, 152, 255, 255, 269
2.9.8, 85, 103, 105, 124, 263
2.9.8–9, 86
2.9.9, 92, 114, 159, 167, 222, 269
2.9.10, 198, 202, 251, 256
2.10, xiv, xv, xvi n. 42, xvii, xviii, xix, xxi, xxiii, 218, 221, 247, 290–343, 363
2.10.1, 95, 196, 265
2.10.2, 98, 116, 242
2.10.3, xvi, xix n. 53, 75, 114, 115, 122, 124, 129, 153, 169, 198, 302, 311, 314, 337
2.10.4, xix, xxi, 61, 135, 232, 234, 235, 252, 294, 302, 331, 332
2.10.4 v. 7, 131
2.10.4 v. 8, 106
2.10.4 v. 9, 111
2.10.4 v. 11–12, 118
2.10.4 v. 12, 110
2.10.4 v. 14, 120
2.10.4 v. 16, 124
2.10.4 v. 21, 236
2.10.4 v. 22, 256, 356
2.10.4 v. 23, 253
2.10.4 v. 24, 283
2.10.4 vv. 25–8, 356
2.10.4 v. 30, 243
2.10.5, xvi n. 42, 61, 225, 270, 302, 308, 338
2.10.5–6, xviii, xx
2.10.6, 97, 202, 266
2.11, xv, xvii, xiv n. 39, 205, 344–49, 351, 391
2.11.1, 129, 198, 207
2.11.2, 181, 182, 195, 196, 198, 272, 344, 346
2.12, xiv, xv, xvi, xvii, 84, 97, 142, 194, 205, 345, 350–61
2.12.1, 104, 114, 140, 159, 169, 289, 356
2.12.1–2, 99
2.12.2, 61, 96
2.12.3, 61, 97
2.13, xiv, xv, xvii, 59, 248, 273, 362–89, 391, 398
2.13.1, 113, 181, 183, 303
2.13.2, 183
2.13.3, 139, 183, 193, 369
2.13.4, 61, 88, 149, 173, 192, 201, 258, 272, 289, 349, 361, 367
2.13.5, 155, 197, 201
2.13.6, 61, 169, 352, 366
2.13.7, 104, 111, 139, 141
2.14, xiv, xv, xvii, 84, 345, 390–98

452

INDEX LOCORUM

2.14.1, 99, 253, 286
2.14.2, xvi, 226, 252, 259
Liber 3
  3.1, xii, 59, 84
  3.1–14, xv
  3.1.1, 98, 104, 226, 259
  3.1.2, 99, 303, 347, 355
  3.1.3, 245
  3.1.4, 374
  3.1.5, 100
  3.2, 84, 306
  3.2.1, 61, 102, 212
  3.2.3, 113, 256, 306, 394
  3.2.4, 197, 245, 303, 347
  3.3, xi n. 22, 57, 59, 84
  3.3.1, xi n. 22, 61
  3.3.2, 158, 255, 264, 297
  3.3.3, 69, 187
  3.3.4, 154
  3.3.5, 84, 104, 105, 255, 284, 301, 396
  3.3.6, 103
  3.3.7, 57, 154, 230, 262
  3.3.8, 102, 124, 169, 244, 263, 303
  3.3.9, 66, 134, 216, 289, 370
  3.4, 178
  3.4.1, 142, 181, 186, 203
  3.4.2, 301
  3.5, xi n. 22, 194
  3.5.1, 191, 247
  3.5.2, 69, 99, 183, 198, 247, 277
  3.5.3, 196, 247, 397
  3.6, 179, 364
  3.6.1, 139, 182, 250, 303, 371
  3.6.2, 197, 396
  3.6.3, 104, 181, 187, 193
  3.7, xi n. 22, 178, 187
  3.7.1, 262, 311, 346, 396
  3.7.2, 173, 357
  3.7.3, 212
  3.7.3–4, 69
  3.7.4, 104, 134, 213, 396
  3.8.1, 278
  3.8.1–2, 364
  3.8.2, 142, 306, 377
  3.9, 190
  3.9.1, 198, 207, 264, 288
  3.9.2, 97, 215, 258, 310, 349
  3.10, 190
  3.10.1, 191, 201, 204, 209, 235
  3.10.2, 216
  3.11.1, 109, 197, 250
  3.11.2, 71, 209, 287, 348
  3.12, 100, 363, 294
  3.12.1, 230, 232
  3.12.3, 303
  3.12.4, 114, 233–4, 289, 311, 337
  3.12.5, xxi, 305
  3.12.5, 218, 232, 233, 238, 304 v. 3, 330
  3.12.5 v. 8, 239
  3.12.5 v. 17, 240
  3.12.6, 171, 244
  3.13, xi, 59, 359
  3.13.1, 96, 97, 142, 241
  3.13.2, 134
  3.13.2–4, 67
  3.13.3, 69, 75
  3.13.4, 209, 212, 289, 297, 384
  3.13.5, 230
  3.13.6, 138, 147, 153, 171, 383
  3.13.7, 141, 164, 368
  3.13.9, 101, 166
  3.13.10, 184, 255
  3.13.11, 114, 134, 342
  3.14, xi
  3.14.1, xiii n. 31, 234, 262, 264, 282, 287, 311, 396
  3.14.2, 66, 202, 297, 298, 300, 342
Liber 4
  4.1, 295
  4.1.1, 225, 259
  4.1.2, 288, 311
  4.1.3, 112, 216
  4.1.4, 231
  4.1.5, 195, 359
  4.2.1, 346
  4.2.3, 175
  4.3, 266
  4.3.1, xvi n. 42, 63, 88, 173, 181, 182, 195, 211, 213, 259, 266, 269, 270, 335, 366
  4.3.2, 143, 255, 265, 306
  4.3.3, 264
  4.3.4, 302
  4.3.5, 107, 112
  4.3.5–7, 292
  4.3.6, 160
  4.3.6–7, 68
  4.3.7, 268
  4.3.8, 188, 251
  4.3.9, 153, 176
  4.3.10, 139, 186, 226, 287, 309, 333, 342
  4.3.17, 71
  4.4, 252
  4.4.1, 104, 158, 191, 255, 257
  4.4.2, 192, 288, 346
  4.4.3, 389
  4.5, 178
  4.5.1, 181, 198, 346, 349
  4.5.2, 197
  4.6, 210, 252
  4.6.1, 97, 160, 207, 304
  4.6.2, 102, 103, 128, 224, 309
  4.6.3, 251, 357
  4.6.4, 120, 195, 346
  4.7, 182
  4.7.1, 346, 349, 359

INDEX LOCORUM

4.7.2, 70, 102, 271, 303
4.7.3, 273, 296, 310, 348
4.8, 274, 291
4.8.1, 77, 182, 251, 257
4.8.1–2, 357
4.8.2, 103, 151, 280
4.8.3, 346, 357
4.8.4, 104, 171, 235, 259, 302, 389
4.8.4–5, 301
4.8.5, xxi, 218, 262, 287, 288, 311, 337
4.8.5 vv. 7–8, 224, 240
4.9.1, 84, 85, 101, 225, 226, 349
4.9.2, 377
4.9.3, 69, 255, 332
4.9.3–5, 227
4.9.4, 225, 227, 229, 348
4.9.5, 216
4.10, 178, 187
4.10.1, 178, 181, 288, 346
4.10.2, xiii n. 30, 178, 211, 287, 300, 337, 348, 357, 371
4.11, 83, 194, 239
4.11.1, 209
4.11.2, 201, 252
4.11.3, 64, 175
4.11.4, 75, 102, 165, 303
4.11.5, 99, 196
4.11.6, xxi, 218, 220, 232, 238, 311
4.11.6, v. 1, 239
4.11.6 v. 4, 124
4.11.6 vv. 4–5, 262, 263
4.11.6 v. 9, 269
4.11.6 v. 14, 75
4.11.6 v. 18, 304
4.11.6 v. 22, 330
4.11.7, 233, 237, 304
4.12, 252
4.12.1, 171, 333
4.12.1–2, 96
4.12.2, 251
4.12.3, 64, 162, 346, 353
4.12.4, 124, 181, 348
4.13, 359
4.13.1, 191, 264
4.13.3, 359
4.14.2, 181, 184
4.14.3, 216
4.14.4, 296, 377
4.15, 84
4.15.1, 97, 104, 133, 197, 273, 303, 374
4.15.2, 75
4.15.3, 91, 138, 139, 163, 256, 357
4.16, 291, 344
4.16.1, 222
4.16.2, 122
4.17, 68
4.17.1, 69, 70, 173, 181, 204, 299
4.17.1–2, 297

4.17.2, 77, 299, 332
4.17.3, 196, 201, 269, 302, 304
4.18, 291
4.18.1, 66, 122, 328
4.18.1–2, 99
4.18.2, 128, 224, 357, 389
4.18.3, 84, 88, 302, 337, 396
4.18.4, 104, 122, 306
4.18.4–5, 235
4.18.5, xxi, 152–3, 256, 308, 311, 343
4.18.5 v. 12, 110, 314
4.18.5 vv. 15–16, 317
4.18.5 v. 20, 63, 231, 303
4.18.6, 311, 331
4.19, 250
4.20.1, 207, 317, 381
4.21.1, 226
4.21.3, 61, 80
4.21.6, 84, 97, 191, 197
4.22.1, xiii n. 31, 264, 291
4.22.2, xvi n. 42, 335
4.22.3, 201, 265, 303
4.22.4, 278
4.22.5, xxi n. 61, 257, 259, 397
4.23, 210
4.24, 211
4.24.1, 63, 99
4.24.2, 78, 149, 256
4.24.3, 80, 258, 273, 282, 286, 352
4.24.4, 357
4.24.5, 175, 396
4.24.6, 365
4.24.8, 194
4.25, 294
4.25.1, 73, 196, 215, 244, 303
4.25.2, 70, 99, 163, 207, 258
4.25.4, 75, 288, 304, 369
4.25.5, 75, 139
Liber 5
5.1, 199
5.1.1, 332, 392
5.1.2, 232, 287
5.1.3, 201, 202, 304
5.2.1, 125, 153, 296, 336
5.2.2, 175, 302
5.3, 252
5.3.1, 198, 287, 353
5.3.2, 369
5.3.3, 355
5.3.4, 166, 288
5.4.1, 287
5.4.2, 116, 175
5.5, 189, 297
5.5.2, 95, 272, 287, 297
5.5.3, 69, 176, 299
5.5.4, 243
5.6, 252
5.6.1, 89, 222, 227

5.6.2, 114
5.7.1, 69, 255, 373
5.7.2, 176, 396
5.7.3, 76, 99, 396, 397
5.7.4, 69, 72, 73
5.7.7, 342, 361, 369
5.8, 294, 306
5.8.1, 124, 232, 305, 332
5.8.2, 78, 103, 337
5.8.3, xxi n. 61
5.9, 298
5.9.1, 104, 182
5.9.2, 89, 97, 100, 370
5.10.2, 183, 288
5.10.3–4, 297
5.10.4, 112, 175
5.11.1, 62, 207
5.11.2, 72, 109
5.11.3, 288
5.12.1–2, 114
5.12.2, 78
5.13.1, 128, 160, 162, 166, 256
5.13.1–3, 59
5.13.2, 167
5.13.4, 216
5.14, 359
5.14.1, 70, 85–6, 88, 139, 164, 201, 283
5.14.2, 95
5.14.3, 85, 97, 329, 373
5.15, 291, 344
5.15.1, 236
5.16, 100, 179, 364
5.16.1, 57, 183, 193
5.16.2, 212, 245
5.16.3, 225, 244
5.16.4, 101, 183
5.16.5, 354
5.17, xxii n. 66, 87, 217, 218, 223
5.17.1, 84, 153, 255, 272
5.17.2, 97, 134, 226, 269
5.17.3, 104, 122, 132, 228, 302, 306, 323
5.17.3–7, 223
5.17.4, 189, 357
5.17.5, 275, 278, 396
5.17.6, 157, 158, 202, 211, 262, 389
5.17.6–7, 158
5.17.7, 223, 260
5.17.8, 164
5.17.9, 153, 176, 204, 222, 396
5.17.10, xxi, 218, 235, 236, 257
5.17.10 v. 1, 103
5.17.10 v. 4, 161
5.17.11, 311
5.18, 179
5.18.1, 369
5.19, 133
5.19.2, 71
5.20.1, 73

5.20.2, 186
5.20.3, 71
5.20.4, 207, 253
5.21.1, 153, 259
Liber 6
6.1, 59
6.1.1, 348
6.1.2, 122, 348
6.1.3, 97, 140
6.1.4, 134
6.1.5, 141, 257, 272, 307, 355
6.2, 194, 211, 218
6.2–5, 190
6.2.1, 69, 195, 289, 303
6.2.1–4, 224
6.2.3, 359
6.2.4, 215
6.3.1, 193, 333
6.3.2, 282, 287
6.4.1, 222, 229, 259, 332
6.4.3, 216
6.5.1, 89, 247, 349
6.6.1, 182, 253, 299, 349
6.6.2, 212, 216, 369
6.7.1, 91, 259
6.8.1, 235
6.8.2, 204
6.9.1, 114, 129, 255, 289
6.9.2, 94, 121, 371
6.10, 190
6.10.1, 212, 349
6.10.2, 127
6.11, 190
6.11.1, 66
6.11.2, 203, 394
6.12, 294, 303
6.12.1, 62, 196, 207, 373
6.12.2, 196
6.12.3, 69, 141, 160, 165
6.12.3–4, 303
6.12.4, 69, 122, 141, 306
6.12.5, 303, 394
6.12.5–7, 303
6.12.6, 231
6.12.6–7, 266
6.12.7, 172
6.12.8, 66
6.12.9, 259, 296
Liber 7
7.1.1, 80, 288, 346
7.1.2, 61, 111, 266, 281, 386
7.1.3, 109, 128, 303
7.1.4, 157, 222
7.1.6, 369
7.1.7, 90, 374, 376
7.2, 182, 279, 391
7.2.1, 348
7.2.2, 114, 176, 182, 255, 269

455

INDEX LOCORUM

7.2.3, 142, 289
7.2.3–8, 363
7.2.4, 226, 278, 289, 296
7.2.5, 195, 343
7.2.6, 129, 146
7.2.7, 192, 207, 355
7.2.7–9, 195
7.2.8, 175
7.2.9, 66, 174
7.2.10, 134, 287, 302, 331
7.3.1, 71, 233
7.3.2, 211
7.4.2, 184, 192, 215, 281
7.4.3, 107, 196
7.4.4, 251, 252, 349
7.5.1, 71, 120, 141
7.5.2, 97, 379
7.5.3, 304, 361
7.5.4, 195, 213
7.5.5, 196, 373
7.6.1, 179, 258, 347, 359, 361
7.6.2, 227–8
7.6.3, 74, 75, 198, 289, 333, 348, 356
7.6.4, 122
7.6.5, 369
7.6.6, 193, 202, 209
7.6.8, 75, 122, 152, 155, 167, 303
7.6.9, 207, 254, 264
7.7, 340
7.7.1, 61, 287, 360
7.7.2, 59, 65, 66, 69, 74, 154, 172
7.7.3, 317
7.7.4, 73, 255, 361
7.7.4–5, 73
7.7.5, 65, 78
7.7.6, 78, 89, 135, 203, 376
7.8.1, 71, 122, 165, 204, 283, 346
7.8.2, 191, 201, 346
7.8.3, 67, 109, 134, 186, 209
7.8.4, 135, 236
7.9, xiii, xiv n. 35, 174
7.9.1, 262, 269
7.9.2, 264
7.9.4, 304, 354
7.9.5, 264
7.9.7, 289
7.9.8, 112, 197, 373
7.9.9, 288
7.9.10, 141
7.9.11, 197, 309
7.9.12, 65
7.9.14, 353
7.9.15, 102, 182, 366
7.9.16, 141
7.9.19, 96, 206, 209, 264, 386, 397
7.9.21, 229
7.9.22, 72, 97, 183, 186, 212, 309
7.9.24, 224, 264

7.10.1, 250, 255, 296, 346
7.10.2, 159, 175
7.11.1, 207, 342, 347
7.12, 251
7.12.1, 99, 124, 181, 183, 189
7.12.2, 108, 338
7.12.3, 216
7.12.4, 222, 374
7.13.1, 206
7.13.2, 72, 302
7.13.3, 69, 71, 145, 273, 302
7.13.4, 73, 198, 331
7.13.5, 191, 207, 216
7.14, 182
7.14.1, 91, 129, 196, 209
7.14.2, 68, 89, 250, 257, 342
7.14.3, 166
7.14.4, 369
7.14.7, 75, 139, 213, 266, 296, 309, 371, 373
7.14.8, 112, 202
7.14.9, 94, 207, 255
7.14.10, 68, 97, 297, 342
7.14.11, 68, 101, 226, 280
7.14.12, 273
7.15, 85
7.16, 68
7.16.1, 61, 78
7.16.2, 93, 349
7.17.1, 179, 181, 196, 232, 296, 302, 305, 317, 353, 359, 389
7.17.2, xxi, 115, 218, 220, 232, 233
7.17.2 v. 15, 163
7.17.2 v. 21, 311
7.17.2 v. 22, 303, 311
7.17.3, 244, 375
7.17.4, 275
7.18, 306
7.18.1, 138, 301, 332
7.18.2, 233
7.18.3, 202, 332
7.18.4, xxiii, 175, 232, 257, 287, 332

Liber 8
8.1, 65, 199
8.1.1, 155, 199
8.1.2, 112, 337, 393
8.2.1, 83, 171
8.2.1–2, 297
8.2.2, 278, 298
8.2.3, 102
8.3.1, 271, 304, 393
8.3.2, 68, 129, 134, 146, 161, 229
8.3.3, 76, 127, 140, 163, 280
8.3.4, 89, 139, 272, 349, 376, 396
8.3.5, 141, 212, 381, 386
8.3.6, 165, 226
8.4.1, 74, 86, 101, 102, 113, 124, 125, 130, 140, 150, 181, 253, 262, 274, 394

8.4.1–2, 84, 251
8.4.2, 130, 209, 232, 278
8.4.3, 139
8.5.1, 114, 259
8.5.2, 64, 73, 203
8.6.1, 129, 193, 332
8.6.2, 191, 198, 254
8.6.3, 71, 297
8.6.5, 100
8.6.6, 198
8.6.7, 215, 299
8.6.8, 275
8.6.9, 66, 134, 212, 287
8.6.10, 107, 125
8.6.10–11, 255
8.6.11, 187
8.6.12, 397
8.6.13, 287
8.6.14, 171, 260
8.6.15, 172
8.6.16, 198, 209, 347
8.6.17, 89
8.6.18, 266, 299, 337
8.7, 179
8.7.2, 113, 388
8.7.4, 160
8.8, 65, 84, 179, 189, 364
8.8.1, 65, 158, 183
8.8.2, 186, 353
8.8.3, 146, 212, 316
8.9, 85
8.9.1, 153, 182, 302
8.9.2, 144, 302
8.9.3, 182, 235
8.9.4, 114, 150, 287
8.9.5, 232, 302
8.9.5 v. 1, 153
8.9.5 v. 12, 154
8.9.5 v. 14, 150
8.9.5 v. 19, 139
8.9.5. v. 31, 170
8.9.5 v. 33, 161, 171, 317
8.9.5 v. 34, 153
8.9.5 v. 50, 222
8.9.5 v. 53, 259
8.9.5 v. 56, 154
8.9.6, 331, 396
8.10, 291, 344
8.10.1, 235, 336
8.10.2, 352, 361
8.10.3, xvi n. 42, 138, 333, 335
8.10.4, 122, 361
8.11, 219, 273, 363
8.11.1, 192, 257
8.11.2, 59, 262, 302, 311
8.11.3, xxi, 69, 114, 218, 232, 344
8.11.3 v. 2, 153
8.11.3 v. 8, 264

8.11.3 vv. 12–14, 94
8.11.3 v. 13, 94
8.11.3 v. 31, 326
8.11.3 v. 33, 289
8.11.3 v. 35, 243
8.11.3 v. 36, 344
8.11.3 v. 42, 288
8.11.3 v. 44, 258
8.11.3 vv. 47–8, 258
8.11.4, 73, 257
8.11.5, 112, 113, 232, 264, 329
8.11.6, xxi n. 61, 160
8.11.7, 167, 235, 267
8.11.8, 158, 332
8.11.11, 151, 230
8.11.12, 101, 171
8.11.13, 175
8.11.14, 114
8.12, 87, 273
8.12.1, 171, 256, 346, 347
8.12.2, 89
8.12.5, 97, 158, 352
8.12.6, 171, 297, 394
8.12.7, 75, 113, 144, 275
8.12.8, 73, 383
8.13.1, 71, 172, 186, 243, 373
8.13.2, 193, 275, 287
8.13.3, 260, 349
8.14.2, 102, 289
8.14.3, 300
8.14.4, 114
8.14.5, 160, 209
8.14.7, 114
8.14.8, 348–9
8.15.2, 212, 222
8.16, 306
8.16.1, 199, 207, 287
8.16.2, 153, 302
8.16.3, 175, 199, 332
8.16.5, 211

Liber 9
9.1.1, xvi n. 42, 335, 371
9.1.2, 124, 176, 302
9.1.3, 114
9.1.3–4, 287
9.2.1, 66, 302
9.2.2, 150, 268
9.2.3, 112, 198
9.3.1, 283, 377
9.3.2, 61, 182, 255, 256, 349
9.3.3, 159, 299, 337
9.3.4, 89, 122, 356, 368
9.3.5, 289, 294, 337, 354
9.3.6, 114
9.3.7, 66, 176, 215, 296
9.4.1, 129, 179, 182, 346, 346
9.4.2, 73
9.5.1, 347

9.6.1, 97, 176
9.6.1–2, 279
9.6.2, 171, 192, 227
9.6.4, 100, 203
9.7.1, 165, 236, 297, 332, 364
9.7.2, 297
9.7.3, 113, 120, 130
9.7.4, 297
9.7.5, 256
9.8.1, 349
9.9.1, 287, 348
9.9.2, 70, 114, 302, 369
9.9.3, 75, 360, 365
9.9.5, 100
9.9.6, 162, 182, 353
9.9.7, 388
9.9.8, 236, 256, 275, 332, 385
9.9.9, 98, 282, 393
9.9.10, 202
9.9.11, 337
9.9.12, 112, 207, 398
9.9.13, 262
9.9.14, 71
9.9.15, 122, 361
9.9.16, 226
9.10.1, 198
9.10.2, 263
9.11.3, 212, 258
9.11.4, 212, 282, 288
9.11.5, 114, 134, 264
9.11.6, 222, 229, 299, 332
9.11.7, 296, 348, 353
9.11.8, 227, 278
9.11.9, 112, 134, 161, 269, 287, 297, 331
9.11.10, 184, 302
9.12–16, 302
9.12.1, xxiii, xxiii n. 74, 114
9.12.2, 112, 198
9.12.3, 234, 235, 379
9.13, 87, 273, 275, 277, 287
9.13.1, 257, 277
9.13.2, xxiii, 302
9.13.2 v. 1, 232
9.13.2 v. 5, 256
9.13.2 v. 16, 235
9.13.3, 139, 270, 275, 277, 283
9.13.4, 73, 259, 301, 370
9.13.5, xxiii, 198, 212, 235, 302
9.13.5 v. 12, 383
9.13.5 v. 14, 381
9.13.5 v. 17, 120
9.13.5 v. 19, 161
9.13.5 v. 39, 104
9.13.5 v. 41, 138
9.13.5 vv. 42–5, 385
9.13.5 v. 49, 110
9.13.5 vv. 54–67, 273

9.13.5 v. 76, 153
9.13.5 v. 83, 265
9.13.5 vv. 88–91, 201
9.13.5 v. 99, 153
9.13.5 v. 110, 163
9.13.5 v. 118, 159
9.13.5 v. 119, 147
9.13.6, 234
9.14.1, 353
9.14.2, 66, 212, 262–3
9.14.3, 97, 104, 198, 273
9.14.4, 361
9.14.5, 123, 256, 285
9.14.6, xxii n. 68, xxiii, 234, 235, 353
9.14.7, 297, 365
9.14.8, 163
9.15.1, xxiii, 114, 232, 277, 287, 302
9.15.1–2, 331
9.15.1 v. 1, 302
9.15.1 v. 18, 272
9.15.1 v. 30, 222, 265
9.15.1 vv. 32–4, 150
9.15.1 v. 38, 337
9.15.1 v. 41, 296
9.15.1 v. 45, 148
9.15.1 v. 46, 337
9.15.1 v. 50, 310
9.15.1 v. 51, 287
9.15.1 v. 52, 71, 287
9.16, xxi, 63, 83, 267
9.16.1, 207, 306
9.16.2, 114, 271, 289, 396
9.16.3, xxiii, xxiii n. 72, 176, 302
9.16.3–4, 267
9.16.3 v. 3, 202
9.16.3 v. 25–8, x n. 13
9.16.3 v. 28, 262
9.16.3 v. 37, 253
9.16.3 vv. 37–8, 232
9.16.3 v. 53, 251
9.16.3 v. 57, 235
9.16.3 v. 65, 329
9.16.3 v. 66, 264
9.16.3 v. 74, 230
9.16.4, 300

SILIUS ITALICUS
Punica
   3.129, 143
   11.51–4, 66
   14.591, 91
   17.477, 315

SOLINUS
De mirabilibus mundi
   29.4, 91

STATIUS, PUBLIUS PAPINIUS
Achilleid
  2.144, 285
Silvae
  1 *praef.*, 301
  1 *praef.* 29–31, 84
  1.2, 86
  1.2.148, 119
  1.2.148–53, 117
  1.2.149, 317
  1.2.149–50, 118
  1.2.150–51, 210
  1.2.223, 327
  1.3, 130
  1.3.1–3, 285
  1.3.18–19, 168
  1.3.52–3, 318
  1.3.54, 159
  1.3.67, 105
  1.4.114, 360
  1.5, 84, 86, 112
  1.5.34, 118
  1.5.34–41, 117
  1.5.34–50, 318
  1.5.36, 119
  1.5.36–8, 119
  1.5.37–8, 119
  1.5.37–41, 119
  1.5.39, 119
  1.5.40, 119
  1.5.40–1, 319
  1.5.54, 171
  1.5.57–9, 105, 158
  2.1, 220
  2.2, 86
  2.2.23, 183
  2.2.30, 130
  2.2.42–3, 318
  2.2.45–6, 315
  2.2.73–4, 137
  2.2.73–85, 130
  2.2.83, 136
  2.2.83–96, 136
  2.2.85–93, 117
  2.2.87–9, 119
  2.2.90–1, 119, 318
  2.2.91, 321
  2.2.92, 119
  2.2.107, 183
  2.2.122, 183
  2.2.151, 183
  2.6, 220
  2.6.72, 244
  2.7.51, 371
  2.7.68, 242
  2.7.69, 186
  2.7.83, 340
  3.3, 220
  3.5.26, 99
  4.2.26–9, 117
  4.2.27, 119
  4.2.28, 118
  4.2.30–1, 318
  4.3, 327
  4.7.16, 317
  4.7.37, 230
  5.1, 220
  5.1.36, 164
  5.1.43–4, 99
  5.3, 220
  5.3.207, 165
  5.5, 220
Thebaid
  1.473–7, 180
  2.379, 159
  3.719, 206
  4.45, 173
  4.220–1, 325
  4.708, 91
  5.52, 168
  5.150, 164
  5.533, 325
  6.920, 380–81
  7.370, 118
  8.332, 195
  9.325, 159
  10.47, 164
  10.229, 173
  10.317, 238
  10.704, 206

SUETONIUS
Caligula
  37.1, 118
  52, 381
Divus Augustus
  2.2, 376
  6, 129
  44.2, 262
  46, 394
  67, 225
  83, 157
Divus Claudius
  14, 373
  14.1–15.4, 73
  16.4, 392
Divus Iulius
  22, 81
  43, 380
Divus Tiberius
  11.1, 355
  52.1, 223
Divus Vespasianus
  1.3, 192
  20.1, 158

Domitianus
  17.3, 230
Nero
  14, 373
  24.2, 394
  31.2, 384, 385
  45.1, 376
  48, 140
  49.3, 307

SULPICIUS SEVERUS
Chronica
  2.1.5, 193
  2.46–51, 65
Dialogi
  1.8.3, 207
Vita Sancti Martini
  4.423, 329

SYMMACHUS, Q. AURELIUS
Epistulae
  1.1, 84, 99
  1.1.1, 375
  1.1.2, 146, 311
  1.1.4, 150
  1.3.1, 337
  1.3.2, 265
  1.6.2, 336
  1.11.1, 336
  1.12.1, 119
  1.13.4, 101
  1.14, 144
  1.14.1, 311, 331
  1.14.4, 329
  1.15.1, 233
  1.15.2, 265
  1.27, 365
  1.34.1, 348
  1.39.2, 165
  1.41, 289
  1.57, 365
  1.78.1, 365
  1.79, 112
  1.84, 348
  1.87, 365
  1.94, 112
  1.95.1, 354
  1.101.2, 360
  2.6.2, 89
  2.11, 365
  2.22.1, 96
  2.55.1, 336
  2.64.1, 182
  2.64.2, 289
  2.68, 183
  3.3.1, 376
  3.10, 381
  3.16, 257
  3.21, 360
  3.25.2, 101
  3.43.3, 289
  3.50, 90, 96
  3.82.1, 287
  3.86.2, 101
  4.28.1, 165, 182
  5.8, 346
  5.30, 354
  5.67, 289
  5.76.1, 212
  5.78, 287
  5.94, 354
  6.11.2, 394
  6.17, 153
  7.5, 354
  7.6, 354
  8.1, 184
  8.18, 89
  8.22, 265
  8.48, 376
  8.69, 265
  8.74, 193
  9.44, 323
  9.84, 197
  9.88, 265
  9.108, 198
  9.112.1, 197
  9.114, 245
  9.150.3, 336
Orationes
  1.8, 223
  2.23, 159
Relationes
  12.4, 198
  19.10, 215
  26.2, 212
  34.12, 336

TACITUS, CORNELIUS
Annales
  2.26.5, 187
  2.71.1–2, 187
  2.75, 228
  3.5.2, 346
  3.44.4, 184
  6.30, 340
  12.66.1, 375
  13.31.3, 202

TERENCE (PUBLIUS TERENTIUS AFER)
Andria
  232, 280
Eunuchus
  107, 96
  635, 256
  756, 387

INDEX LOCORUM

Phormio
   610, 148

TERTULLIANUS
Ad martyras
   2.9, 330
Adversus Marcionem
   1.4.4, 394
   2.18.2, 387
   4.11.12, 298
   4.28.11, 388, 394
Apologeticum
   3.7, 348
   6.2, 274
   16.6, 112
   39.12–13, 334
   45.6, 342
De anima
   52.3, 388
De ieiunio adversus psychicos
   1, p. 274.14, 387
De pallio
   4.4, 93–4
De spectaculis
   9.5, 322

THEOCRITUS
Idylls
   1.148, 149

TIBULLUS
   1.7.11, 326
   2.3.62, 380
   2.4.28, 380
   2.5.77, 233
   2.5.98, 140
   3.3.13, 119
   3.3.14, 118, 119

ULPIAN
Digesta
   36.1.17 pr., 192

VALERIANUS CEMELIENSIS
Homilia
   6.1, 347

VALERIUS FLACCUS
   1.538, 159
   2.11, 164

VALERIUS MAXIMUS
   2.2.2, 378
   2.7.8, 185
   2.9.4, 273
   3.2.9, 185
   4.7, 180
   5.8.5, 65
   6.6. ext. 1, 377
   8.7. ext. 9, 174

VARRO
De lingua Latina
   5.131, 381
Res Rusticae
   1.7.9, 103
   1.8.4, 116
   1.12.1, 315
   1.13.7, 135
   2 *praef.* 2, 123
   2.1.27, 395
   2.11.12, 282
   3.5.2, 128
   3.5.6, 395
   3.10.1, 123
   3.10.5, 283
Saturae Menippeae
   96, 104
   337–8, 274
   340, 274

VELLEIUS PATERCULUS
   2.92.4, 185

VENANTIUS FORTUNATUS
Carmina
   1.15.55–8, 106
   1.18, 115
   1.20, 115
   2.10.13–16, 315, 316
   3.5.5, 240
   3.7.37–44, 316
   4.1–4.28, 237
   5.5.7, 333
   5.5.125, 333
   7.4.13, 167
   8.19.6, 329
   9.2.118, 333

VERGIL
Aeneid
   1.154, 168
   1.174, 282
   1.267–8, 63
   1.282, 397
   1.593, 118
   2.53, 148
   2.263, 360
   2.270, 222
   2.432, 238
   2.561, 278
   3.270, 103
   3.534, 163

3.555, 168
3.587, 150
4.242, 114
4.534, 197
4.569, 77
5.124–286, 172
5.129, 171
5.159, 171
5.171, 171
5.664, 262
5.870, 168
6.5, 388
6.27, 200–201
6.55, 203
6.278, 231
6.297, 160
6.328, 231
6.471, 118
6.610, 388
6.804–5, 254
6.885–6, 229
7.27–8, 162
7.478, 256
7.515, 148
8.58, 353
8.82, 317
8.250, 171
8.559, 372
8.668–9, 65, 386–7
11.52, 229
11.571, 153
11.625–6, 163
11.793, 183
12.77, 151
12.327, 388
12.524, 164
12.756–7, 329

Eclogues
1.1, 154
1.53–5, 154–5
1.62, 326
1.68, 122
1.78, 170
1.79, 154
2.13, 149
2.15–18, 308
2.24, 254
2.32, 153
2.36–7, 152
3.7, 204
3.20, 154
3.26–7, 309
3.42, 328
3.59, 153
3.96, 154
3.327–8, 149
5.5, 159

5.12, 154
6.4, 154
7.2, 154
7.16, 154
8.55, 154
9.23–4, 154
9.35–6, 150
10.36, 253
10.38, 308

Georgics
1.49, 394
1.108–10, 125–6
1.116, 92
1.135, 282
1.141–2, 144
1.173, 156
1.201–3, 352, 353
1.265, 94
1.271, 256
1.342, 154
1.378, 149
1.422–3, 152
2.13, 170
2.188, 92
2.199, 167
2.293, 162
2.353, 91
2.417, 253
2.449, 156
2.506, 384
2.507, 388
3.34, 118
3.223, 155
3.293, 371
3.340, 122
3.431, 149
3.479, 91
4.50, 327
4.176, 176
4.181–2, 170
4.183, 156
4.261, 312
4.427–8, 92
4.514–15, 152
4.566, 154

VICTOR, AURELIUS
Liber de Caesaribus
14.3, 262

VITRUVIUS
De architectura
1.2.2–4, 109
1.2.7, 103, 261
1.2.8, 121
1.6.5, 103
2.3.1, 285

3.1.4, 109
4.1.12, 109
4.5.2, 131
5.1.8, 105
5.1.9, 323
5.3.6, 131
5.6.2, 262
5.10, 103
5.10.1, 103, 104, 107
5.10.2, 105
5.10.4, 104
5.10.5, 280, 281
5.11.2, 107, 133
6.1.2, 102
6.4.1, 103, 261
6.4.2, 146, 147
6.5.1, 146
6.5.1–2, 102
6.5.2, 122–3
6.7.4, 146
7.2, 111
7.3.4, 146
8.2.4, 104
8.3.7, 160
8.3.22, 236
8.6.5, 131
8.6.10, 105

VULGATA
Apocalypsis
   21.21, 313
Gospel of John
   5.2, 126
   8.12, 316
   9.7, 126
Gospel of Matthew
   7.26, 159
   22.1, 138
Jeremiah
   8.7, 395
Psalms
   131.6–8, 325
   148, 330
Reges/Kings
   1.10.17, 325

Index of Personal Names (Antiquity)

Only the most relevant passages in which the ancient persons are mentioned in the text are index here. Polyonymous individuals are identified by the most familiar name (e.g. Marcus Aurelius under M), but otherwise, as individuals from the late Roman period are normally identified, in accordance with onomastic norms, by the last of their names (e.g. Julius Caesar under C). Short descriptors (e.g. major offices held) are given selectively, as are dates. For further information on individuals marked with an asterisk (*) see also the Index locorum.

Abraham, abbot of Clermont, 115, 218, 220, 232, 305
Achilles, mythological figure, 360
Aemilia Aeonia, mother of Ausonius, 237, 242–3
Aeneas, mythological figure, 201, 203, 222
Aesculapius, god, 360
Agricola, brother-in-law of Sidonius, 44–5, 350–7
Alaric II, king of the Visigoths (r. 484–507), 76
Alcima, daughter of Sidonius, 354
Alethius, client of Sidonius, *decurio*, 24–5, 212, 214
Alexander the Great, 185–6
Alypia, daughter of Anthemius, 80
Amantius, *lector*, letter-bearer of Sidonius, 363
*Ambrosius, bishop of Milan (374–97), 360
Amphion, mythological figure, 254
Anthemius, emperor (r. 467–72), x, xii, 2, 5, 58, 79–80, 178–80, 185, 187, 266–7, 366
Apollinaris, grandfather of Sidonius, 100, 218, 232–3, 238–9, 240
Apollinaris, son of Sidonius, 354
Apollinaris, uncle of Sidonius, 30–1, 84–6, 110, 246–9, 251–2, 258–9, 261, 277, 280
Apollo (Phoebus), god, 149–51, 201, 203, 218, 318, 341
*Apuleius, poet, 32–3, 40–1, 269–70, 335–6
Arbogastes, *comes civitatis*, 181
Argentaria Polla, 40–1, 338–40
Arrianus, correspondent of Pliny, 345
Arvandus, *Praefectus praetorio Galliarum* (464–8), 59, 72, 179, 199, 200, 364

Arvernians, xi n. 22, 2–3, 22–3, 61, 79, 172, 209
Athaulf, king of the Visigoths (411–15), 76
Attusia, wife of Ausonius, 238
*Augustine, bishop of Hippo (395–430), xix, 32–3, 60, 63, 266
Augustus (Octavian), emperor (r. 27 BC–14 AD), 157, 186–7, 250, 375
Aurora, personification, 12, 120, 151, 294
*Ausonius (cos. 379), poet, xviii, xxii, 86, 142–5, 159, 219–20, 228, 232, 234, 243–4, 291, 293, 301, 307
*Auspicius, bishop of Toul, 269
*Avitus, bishop of Vienne, 383
Avitus, cousin? of Sidonius, 259
Avitus, Eparchius, emperor (r. 455–6), Sidonius's father-in-law, ix–x, 61, 98–100, 125, 127, 178, 339, 350, 364, 366, 370

Bacchus, god, 95–6, 279, 254

*Caesar, Julius, Roman general and statesman (100–44 BC), 81, 186, 275, 340, 365, 393
Caesennia, wife of Lentulus Gaetulicus, 40–1, 339–40
Calpurnia, wife of Pliny the Younger, xviii, 40–1, 99, 335
Camena, muse, 12–13, 152–3
Caninius, friend of Pliny the Younger, xx, 295
Catiline, L. Sergius, Roman politician, 2–3, 57, 60, 64–7, 69–71, 73, 368, 387
*Cato, the Younger, viii, 157, 242, 334
Catullinus, senator, 183
*Catullus, poet, 40–1, 305, 338–41
Chiron, centaur, 44–5, 359–60

464

INDEX OF PERSONAL NAMES (ANTIQUITY)

Christus, 34–5, 38–9, 44–5, 126, 216, 288–9, 329, 357, 360–1
*Cicero, Marcus Tullius, orator (cos. 63 BC), 2, viii, 32–3, 40–41, 64–5, 67, 69, 73, 263, 269–70, 287, 333–5, 354–5, 363–4, 375
Citonatus, deacon under bishop Symmachus of Rome in 499, 63
*Claudian (Claudius Claudianus), poet, 60
*Claudianus Mamertus, 68, 181, 218, 220, 232–3, 238–9, 262–3, 298
Claudius, emperor (r. 41–54), 73
Claudius Etruscus, 119
Cleopatra, Egyptian queen, 381, 383
Clodia, wife of Quintus Caecilius Metellus Celer, 339–40
Consentius, *cura palatii*, 74, 106, 108, 181, 255, 262
Constantius, priest, dedicatee of the correspondence, xix n. 53, 36–7, 63, 290, 295, 303, 305–6, 309, 337
Corinna, mistress, 40–1, 338–9
Crassus, Marcus Licinius, politician, 186
Cynthia, mistress, 40–1, 338–41

Damocles, 48–9, 362–4, 367–8, 377–81
Delia, mistress, 40–1, 338–9
Demosthenes, orator, 32–3, 263, 270
Desideratus, correspondent, 26–7, 217
Diana, goddess, 341
Diaulus, a dubious doctor/undertaker, 230
Dion of Prusa, orator and philosopher, 277
Dionysius I, a ruler of Syracuse, 4th century BC, 48–9, 248, 273, 362, 379–82, 384, 388
Dionysos *see* Bacchus
Domitian, emperor (r. 81–96), 259, 327
Domitius, *grammaticus*, xiv, 6–7, 82–4, 93–6, 141
Donidius, correspondent, xi n. 22, 30–1, 57, 246–7, 251, 268, 286

Ecdicius, brother-in-law of Sidonius, xi n. 22, xiii, 2–3, 12–13, 57–9, 61, 77, 79–80, 156–8, 350, 370
Elaphius, correspondent, 273
*Ennodius, bishop of Pavia, xxii
Eparchius, son of Ruricius, 291
Eparchius Avitus *see* Avitus, Eparchius, emperor
Eriphius, husband of Filimatia, 218, 223, 228–9
Eulalia, cousin of Sidonius, 241
Euric, king of the Visigoths (466/7–84), x, xiii, 57, 59, 76, 79, 232, 377,

Eusebius, bishop of Caesarea, 268
Eutropia, widow, 69, 218
Eutropius, Praefectus praetorio Galliarum (470), xiii, 89, 181, 392
Explicius, correspondent, 24–5, 210–16

Fabius Maximus Rullianus, Quintus, 16–17, 180, 185
Fabricius Luscinus, Gaius, republican role model, 273
Fannia, friend of Pliny the Younger, 241–2
Fates (Parcae), goddesses, 2–3, 63–4
Faustinus, wealthy friend of the poet Martial, 397
*Faustus, bishop of Riez, 81, 91, 216
Felix, Magnus, *praefectus praetorio Galliarum* (469), xi n. 22, 16–17, 57, 178–88, 199, 295
Felix, Pollius, addressee of Statius, 130, 183, 318, 340
Felix, saint, bishop (Nantes, 6th century), 240
Felix, saint, martyr (Nola, 3rd century), 312–13, 318, 324
Ferreolus, Tonantius, *Praefectus praetorio Galliarum* (451/3), 30–31, 84–6, 108, 110, 246–9, 251–2, 258–9, 261, 277, 280
Filimatia, friend of Sidonius, xix, 26–7, 101, 217–30, 237–40
Filimatius, father of Filimatia, 217–19, 223, 227
Firminus, correspondent of Pliny, 63
Fortuna, personification, 2–3, 48–9, 63, 377–8
Fulgentius, *quaestor sacri palatii*, 48–9, 378

Gaetulicus, early imperial poet, 40–1, 339–40
Geiseric, king of the Vandals, 377
Germanicus Caesar, (d. 19), *exemplum*, 16–17, 180, 186–7
Gnatho, epitome of vices, xi, 59, 67, 69, 134, 141, 153, 166, 230, 297, 384
Gozolas, *cliens*, 181

Hadrian, emperor (r. 117–38), 262
Hector, mythological figure, 222
Hercules, mythological figure, 293
Hermes, god, *see* Mercury
Hesperius, rhetor, xviii–xx, 36–7, 290–97, 300–4, 331, 333, 338, 342
Hiberia, wife of Ruricius, 293
*Hieronymus (Jerome) of Stridon (d. c. 420), 60, 63, 268–70, 335, 360
Himerius, priest, 69

INDEX OF PERSONAL NAMES (ANTIQUITY)

Hippocrates of Kos (around 460–375 BC), 356–7
Honorius, emperor (r. 393–423), 370
*Horace, poet, viii, xix, 32–3, 154, 266–7, 300, 363–4, 383
Hortensius, rhetor, 40–1, 334
Hostia, mistress, 338, 341

Ianus, god, 52–3, 395–6
Iohannes, defendant, 20–1, 199–202
Iohannes, *grammaticus*, 83
Iustus, bishop of Lyon, 302, 310
Iustus, physician, 44–5, 359

Jason, mythological figure, 360
Jupiter, god, 151, 259, 265
Justinian the Great, emperor (r. 527–65), 268
*Juvenal, satirist, xviii, 86, 93, 230, 364

Lampridius, rhetor and poet, 59, 218, 232, 363
Larcius Macedo, senator, 363
Leontius, Pontius, owner of Burgus, 84, 86–8, 117, 126, 129, 135, 147, 279, 294, 314, 325, 344, 394
Lesbia, mistress, 40–1, 338–41
*Livy (T. Livius), historian, 180, 224
*Lucan, poet, xviii, 40–1, 117, 338–40, 363
Lucretia, legendary heroine, 224, 241
*Lucretius, poet, 364
Lupus, bishop of Troyes, 269
Lupus, rhetor, 262,

Machaon, mythological figure, 44–5, 359–60
Maiorianus (Majorian), emperor (r. 457–61), x, xii, xxi, 127, 154, 225, 362, 366, 370–1, 386
Mamertus Claudianus *see* Claudianus Mamertus
Marcellinus, *advocatus*, 46–7, 364–5
Marcia, 40–1, 334
*Martial, poet, xviii, xix, 86, 93, 112, 117, 219–20, 230, 232, 294, 305, 325–6, 391
Martialis, Julius, 262, 314, 318, 325
Maurusius, correspondent, xiv, 52–3, 84, 390–4
Maximus, Petronius, emperor (r. 455), xiv, 46–7, 362–6, 370–8
Menstruanus, friend of Sidonius, 22–3, 59, 205–9
Mercury (Hermes), god, 114
Messala, Valerius Corvinus, Roman general, author, 116
Minerva, goddess (also Pallas), 129

Minicia Marcella, 219, 222, 224, 226
Minicius Fundanus, 219
Minotaur, mythological monster, 201
Montius, correspondent, 181
Muses, goddesses, 82, 118, 149, 153, 155

Namia Pudentilla, Ausonius' sister-in-law, 239
Nepos, Iulius, emperor (r. 474–5), 57, 79
Nero, emperor (r. 54–68), 140
Numa Pompilius, legendary Roman king, 52–3, 395–6
Numidians, 8–9, 119
Nymphidius, correspondent, 175

Octavian *see* Augustus
Oenotria, personification of Italy, 279
Ommatius, son of Ruricius, 291
Optantius, *vir clarissimus*, 18–19, 189, 193–6
Orestes, mythological figure, 180
Origenes, Adamantius, theologian writer, 32–3, 267–70
*Ovid, Naso, poet, 40, 41, 339

Pallas, freedman (d. 62), 219
Papianilla, wife of Sidonius, ix, xviii, 57, 99–101, 251, 258, 350, 354
Papianilla, wife of Tonantius Ferreolus, 224
Papirius Cursor, 16–17, 180, 185
Parcae *see* Fates
Paris, pantomimus, 239–40
Pastor, correspondent, 253
Patiens, bishop of Lyon, xix, xxi, 36–9, 69, 116, 290–4, 300, 303–5, 312–18, 323, 325
Paula, friend of Jerome, 233
Paulinus of Nola, xxii, 293–4, 301, 312–13
Paulus, client of Sidonius, *decurio*, 24–5, 212, 214
Pegasius, correspondent, 22–3, 205–6, 208
Perpetuus, bishop of Tours, 291
*Petronius, author, 272
Petronius, correspondent, 20–1, 199–204
Petrus, *magister epistularum*, xxiii n. 72, 201
Philagrius, correspondent, 101, 225–6
Philagrius, *patricius*, 16–17, 182
Philistio, mime, 8–9, 112
Philomela, mythological figure, 12–13, 151–2
Phoebus *see* Apollo
Phrygians, 8–9, 119
Pirithous, mythological figure, 180
Placidus Valentinianus *see* Valentinianus III
Plato, philosopher, 32–3, 216, 268, 270–1
*Pliny the Elder, 117, 159, 231, 234

INDEX OF PERSONAL NAMES (ANTIQUITY)

*Pliny the Younger, viii, ix, xi–xxiv, 40–1, 60, 81, 88, 333, 335–6
Polemius, *Praefectus praetorio Galliarum* (?471–2), 181
Pompeius Magnus, Gnaeus, politician, 16–17, 185–6, 340
Pompeius Quintianus, friend of Plny, 243
Pontius Leontius *see* Leontius
Potentinus, correspondent, 72
Praesens, friend of Pliny, 391
Probus, Petronius (cos. 371), 301
Probus, son of Magnus and schoolmate of Sidonius, 262, 295
Procne, mythological figure, 12–13, 151–2
Proiectus, suitor, 18–19, 189–95
*Propertius, poet, 40–1, 338–42
*Prudentius, poet, xix, 32–3, 266–7, 294
Pudentilla, wife of Apuleius, 40–1, 335–6
Pylades, mythological figure, 180

*Quintilian, rhetor, 114

Ragnahilda, wife of Euric, 218, 224, 240
Regulus, enemy of Pliny the Younger, xiii, xiv n. 33, xvii, 67
Ricimer, *patricius*, *Magister utriusque militiae* (456–72), x, 80, 370
Roscia, daughter of Sidonius, 354
Rufinus, Cornelius, ancestor of Sulla, 273
Rufinus, Tyrannius, writer, translator, 32–3, 267–70
*Ruricius, bishop of Limoges, 81, 216, 245, 291, 293, 299, 350
Rusticiana, wife of Symmachus, 40–41, 336
Rusticus, neighbour of Pontius Leontius, 42–3, 344–5, 349

Sagittarius, tutor, 18–19, 189–98
*Sallust, historian, viii, 65–7, 69–71, 369
Sappho, poet, 340
Sardanapallus, a legendary king of Assyria, seventh century BC, 48–9, 382
Secundinus, correspondent, poet, 36–7, 290, 303, 305–6, 309, 337
*Seneca the Younger, viii, xii, 60, 335
Seronatus, *vicarius VII provinciarum*, xiii, xiv, 2–3, 59–75, 79, 205
Serranus, correspondent, 46–7, 362, 366
Severiana, daughter of Sidonius, 44–5, 84, 97, 350, 354–5
Sibyl, 201, 203
*Sidonius Apollinaris, *passim*
Sigismer, Burgundian (?) prince, 381

Simplicius, uncle of Sidonius, 251–2
Solomon, ruler of the united kingdom of Israel (10th century BC), 318, 325
Spartans, 8–9, 119
Spurinna, Vestricius, friend and role model of Pliny, 252, 279, 375
*Statius, poet, xviii, 86, 117, 129–30, 294, 340
Sulla Felix, P. Cornelius, Roman politician and general, 46–7, 273, 362, 368, 373
Syagrius, *advocatus*, 297
Syagrius, Fl. Afranius (cos. 382), 251
Syagrius *see* Sagittarius
*Symmachus, Q. Aurelius (cos. 391), letter-writer, xxii, 40–1, 60, 81, 88, 179, 183, 190, 288, 336

*Tacitus, P. Cornelius, historian, 180, 187
Tantalus, mythological figure, 50–1, 386–7
*Terence, poet, 93–4, 96
Terentia, wife of Cicero, 40–1, 334–6
Thalia, muse, 218
Thaumastus, cousin of Sidonius, 72
Thaumastus, uncle of Sidonius, 199
Theoderic, king of the Ostrogoths, 76
Theoderic I, king of the Visigoths (418–52), 76
Theoderic II, king of the Visigoths (453–66), xi, 2–3, 59, 72, 76, 183, 248, 273, 350, 375, 377, 382
Theodosius I, emperor of the Eastern Roman Empire (r. 379–395), 376
Theodosius II, emperor of the Eastern Roman Empire (r. 408–450), xxi, 2–3, 76
Theoplastus, bishop, 247
Theseus, mythological figure, 180
Tiberius, emperor (r. 14–37), 16–17, 180, 186–7
*Tibullus, poet, 40–1, 338–9, 341–2
Tiro, freedman of Cicero, 335, 354
Tityrus, shepherd, 12–13, 154
Tonantius, son of Tonantius Ferreolus, 32–3, 251–2, 277
Trajan, emperor (r. 98–117), xviii, 73, 208, 375
Trimalchio, novel character, 382
Troiani, 14–15, 172
Trygetius, correspondent, 97, 329
Tryphon, bookseller, 235
Tullia, daughter of Cicero, 354
Tyndaris, mistress, 97

Valentinian III, emperor (r. 425–55), 366, 370
Vandals, 115, 366, 377

*Varro, antiquarian, xix, 32–3, 123, 266–7
Venus, goddess, 117, 150, 224, 293, 318
Vercingetorix, Arvernian king (d. 46 BC), 61
*Vergil, poet, xviii, 86, 90, 144, 149, 152, 154, 159, 162, 172, 379
Verginia, legendary heroine, 241
Verginius Rufus, politician, role model of Pliny the Younger, 60, 219
Verres, governor of Sicily, 69, 73
Vettius, correspondent, 69, 84–5, 101, 227, 229, 349
Visigoths, xi, 2–3, 58–9, 74–6, 79, 250, 344, 376–7
*Vitruvius, architect, xviii, 86, 102, 107, 109, 111

EU representative:
Easy Access System Europe
Mustamäe tee 50, 10621 Tallinn, Estonia
Gpsr.requests@easproject.com

www.ingramcontent.com/pod-product-compliance
Lightning Source LLC
Chambersburg PA
CBHW061702300426
44115CB00014B/2532